D0844298

THE OFFICIAL RULES

5,427 Laws, Principles, and Axioms
to Help You Cope with Crises,
Deadlines, Bad Luck,
Rude Behavior, Red Tape,
and Attacks by Inanimate Objects

PAUL DICKSON

DOVER PUBLICATIONS, INC.
Mineola, New York

To the fellows of the Murphy Center, and especially Martha Moutray for first seeing the possibilities of serving humanity with its own set of rules and to Jack Limpert for keeping the idea alive for a decade in the pages of *The Washingtonian Magazine.*

Copyright

Bibliographical Note

The Official Rules: 5,427 Laws, Principles, and Axioms to Help You Cope with Crises, Deadlines, Bad Luck, Rude Behavior, Red Tape, and Attacks by Inanimate Objects is a new work, first published by Dover Publications, Inc., in 2013.

Library of Congress Cataloging-in-Publication Data

Dickson, Paul.
The official rules : 5,427 laws, principles, and axioms to help you cope with crises, deadlines, bad luck, rude behavior, red tape, and attacks by inanimate objects / Paul Dickson.
pages cm.
Summary: "According to Murphy's Law, "If anything can go wrong, it will." This humorous hardcover compilation offers a wealth of variations on the well-known adage, including maxims related to business matters, excuses, efficiency, and legal jargon. It also features a "Bureaucratic Survival Kit," "Old Saws Resharpened," "How to Tell the Difference Between Democrats and Republicans," and other comic truths"—Provided by publisher.
ISBN-13: 978-0-486-48210-1 (hardback)
ISBN-10: 0-486-48210-3
1. American wit and humor. I. Title.
PN6162.D4885 2013
818'.540208—dc23
2013008655

Manufactured in the United States by Courier Corporation
48210301 2013
www.doverpublications.com

Contents

All things are subject to fixed laws.

—Marcus Manilius, *Astronomica,* I, c. 40 B.C.

Natural laws have no pity.

—Long's 22nd Note, from Robert A. Heinlein's *Time Enough for Love*

If you know a good story, tell it from time to time.

—McCabe's Law

Turn off the TV and computer and exercise your mind with a good book.

—Fortune cookie message obtained in Duxbury, Massachusetts, on August 19, 2009.

Arms of the Murphy Center

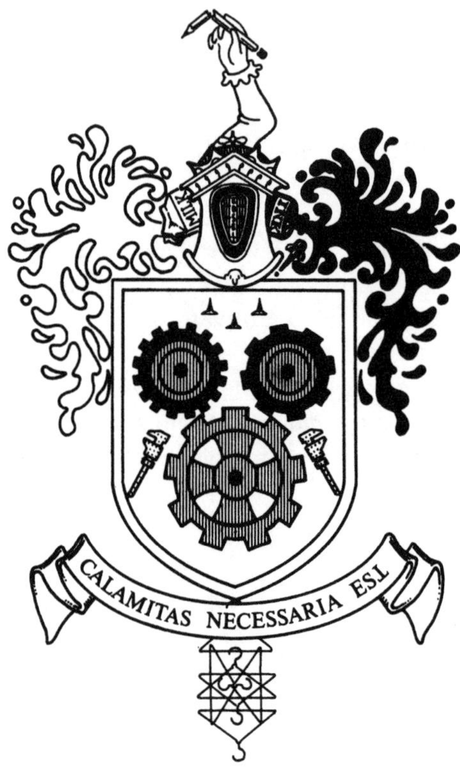

Arms: Gules three mismatched cogwheels, or two monkey wrenches salient, or three tack caltrops rampant.

Crest: An arm dressed, holding a broken pencil proper; spilt milk and India ink mantling.

Motto: *Calamitas Necessaria Est* (Disaster Is Inevitable).

Preface

For centuries mathematics and the pure sciences held a seemingly unbreakable monopoly on natural laws, principles, and named effects. At the gradual pace of a law at a time, researchers and scholars worked to show us that some element of the universe was working in perfect accord with an immutable rule that, in its purest form, could be stated without taking a breath.

The *Second Law of Thermodynamics,* for instance, told us that in every energy transaction some of the original energy is changed into heat energy, while Boyle's Law informed us that at a constant temperature the volume of a given quantity of gas is inversely proportional to the pressure on the gas. Hundreds and hundreds of laws were created, with most of the great names in science in possessive possession of at least one solid law (e.g., Newton's, Ohm's, Darwin's, Mendel's, Archimedes', Einstein's, and so forth). To get through four years of college (let alone four years of Sunday crossword puzzles) one is forced into contact with a few score such laws, which are liable to range from the *Law of Action and Reaction* to the *Laws of Vibrating Strings.*[1]

Yet as new laws were discovered, posted, and accepted by the textbook publishers, people outside the hard sciences increasingly felt that a whopping injustice was in force. Not only were the soft sciences, humanities, and workaday pursuits excluded from the business of lawmaking but—even more to the point—there was a deep and demonstrable prejudice at work as all these big-name scientists were busy describing a perfect Universe when, as everyone else (including the not-so-big scientists) was fully aware, it is not all that perfect.

Over the years, there were a few exceptions. Economists were able to gain acceptance for such items as the *Law of Supply and Demand*: "As demand increases the price goes up which attracts new suppliers who increase the supply bringing

[1] The *Law of Action and Reaction* is the one that says for every action there is an equal and opposite reaction. *The Laws of Vibrating Strings* go like this: (1) The frequency of vibration of a wire is inversely proportional to its length. The shorter the string, the higher the pitch. (2) The frequency of vibration varies directly as the square root of tension. (3) The frequency of a vibrating string varies inversely with the square root of its weight per unit of length. Thick, heavy strings vibrate more slowly and hence give tones of lower pitch.

the price back to normal," and *Say's Law:* "Supply creates its own demand." But these were exceptions to the rule. Then in the years after World War II, more and more people began hearing series of laws—more often said than written—attached to such names as Murphy, Finagle, and Sod, which had an uncanny ability to describe things as they could be and often were—screwed up, dysfunctional. Murphy looked right into our lives and concluded, "If anything can go wrong, it will," and Finagle was able to perceive via his Fourth Law: "No matter what occurs, there is always someone who believes it happened according to his pet theory." It cannot be proven, but it has been suggested that Murphy, Finagle, and their disciples (all to be discussed in the pages ahead) have helped more people get through crises, deadlines, bad days, the final phases of projects, and attacks by inanimate objects than either pep talks, uplifting epigrams, or the invocation of traditional rules. It is true that if your paperboy throws your paper in the bushes for five straight days, it can be explained by *Newton's Law of Gravity.* But it takes Murphy to explain why it is happening to *you.*

As these explanations of the perversity of nature grew in popularity and importance, other laws and principles came along to explain how other things worked. In 1955 an obscure historian named C. Northcote Parkinson wrote an article called "Parkinson's Law," in which he showed that "Work expands so as to fill the time available for its completion." Parkinson became famous, and his law has become a permanent tenet of organizational life. Parkinson begat more laws as others brought out their own discoveries. Some were highly successful, such as Dr. Laurence J. Peter and his famous *Peter Principle* (1969), while others created laws that only those in a specific circle could fully appreciate, like the great body of laws created by and for computer programmers. By the early 1970s laws were coming in from all over and showing up everywhere: newspaper columns, books, laboratory and lavatory walls. What more and more people were discovering in their own lives and jobs are those universal truths which have been begging to be stated scientifically and shared with the rest of the world. In most cases these laws are being discovered by average, not famous men and women—although nothing prevents senators, scientists, press pundits, and other VIPs from getting into the act. Yet, regardless of whether a law is discovered by a Nobel Laureate or an insurance company clerk, a good law is a good law and able to move around the country with remarkable speed. Unfortunately, a law often moves so quickly that it is soon separated from the person who discovered and named it.

As a result an important new law like *Anthony's Law of Force* which says, "Don't force it, get a larger hammer," is known far and wide to people who have no idea who Anthony is.

Often a group of a dozen or so new laws are collected and typed out on a sheet of paper. These sheets are drawn to copying machines like metal filings to a magnet, and once copied are posted on bulletin boards, passed out at water coolers, dropped into inter-office mail systems, and swapped at conventions. Whether by jet, teletype, or mail, a list compiled and copied in Boston on a Monday is liable to show up in Santa Monica by the end of the week. The creation and distribution of laws has become a full-fledged cultural phenomenon: a computer-age folk idiom.

Thusly... on a fateful night in late 1976 yours truly picked up a cardboard shoebox and a set of alphabetical dividers and began filing slips of paper on which he had been collecting "odd mock-scientific rules and laws that helped to describe our flawed universe." The box was given the imposing title of the Murphy Center for the Codification of Human and Organizational Law. I appointed myself its first director, and have been, since 1989, its self-appointed "Director for Life." It originally amounted to nothing more than a shoebox into which rules and laws were filed. The Center was created in an effort to collect, test, and make a few bucks from revealed truth that is often the by-product of what the center likes to think of fondly as Other Folks' Foibles, Misfortunes and General Confusion (O.F.F.M. & G.C.). It was mainly inspired by Murphy's Law and influenced by the fact that we had put men on the moon but still seemed unable to create shoelaces that didn't break at inopportune moments. The Center also subscribed to the belief that inanimate objects and substances were possessed of an innate perversity, as in the updraft over wastebaskets or the ability of wire coat hangers to multiply in dark places.

In those early days of the Center, I received help from a number of collectors and codifiers who freely contributed their efforts to the work of the Center. Six collections were especially important, and they deserve mention. These were the collections belonging to writer Fred Dyer, who was instrumental in getting the Center started; *Wall Street Journal* columnist Alan Otten, who has done so much to popularize the idiom through his excellent articles on the subject; Jack Womeldorf of the Library of Congress; Robert Specht of the RAND Corp.; and two computerized files: the John Erhman file at Stanford University, and the seminally important University of Arizona Computing Center collection, which was begun in January 1974, by Conrad Schneiker and maintained by Gregg Townsend, Ed Logg, and others.

The central principle of the Center was and is that the more one understood the imperfectability of things, the more one can get out of life. Anyone unwilling to understand that there will be days during which Murphy's Law is in effect is bound to be unhappy. Lest there be any question, these laws, rules, observations, and maxims are meant to make life easier. I have one taped to the visor of my car that simply reminds me "You're Not Late Until You Get There." Another helpful maxim that comes into play when, say, you are late because of a flat tire is *Burnham's Tenth Law:* "If there's no alternative, there's no problem."

There is no household contingency for which I do not have a rule to help me cope. Whenever I work around the house, for example, I always take comfort in The Poorman Flaw, "In any home-improvement project, there will be one mistake so gross that the only solution is to incorporate it into the design."

Creative, happy, well-adjusted people see the humor in adversity and use it for fuel. More than a quarter of a century back, Tom Gill, one of the Center's longtime contributors, sent me a rule he had spotted on the wall of the Home Plate Diner in Lubbock, Texas:

Caudill's Law on Losing. "Even Betty Crocker burns a cake now and then." (Bill Caudill, Oakland A's)

I now have this hung above my desk, not because I intend to lose, but when I do I want to give the event some wry perspective. This ability to turn adversity into a one-line lesson is why the now-esteemed and verging-on-venerable Murphy Center is still alive and well and enjoying its perverse nature. This means that it thrives on a little turmoil, human error, and the widespread awareness that the universe is flawed. The Center soon spread out into a dozen shoeboxes and two file drawers.

In 1978, the Center published its first research report in book form, titled *The Official Rules.* The title was appropriated from the back of a box of breakfast cereal where a contest was announced and the rules were posted.

It was arranged alphabetically, and contained special sections (cleverly called Special Sections) on areas of special importance, followed by a subject index. To the extent possible each law is accompanied by the identity of the person who discovered it and, when applicable, the person who first collected it. Laws that could not be connected to their discoverers are noted with a *U,* which means "unknown to this collector." There were a number of *U*s, but this is to be expected because the nature of lawgiving is such that a good law is often separated from its owner. More confusing, words taken from the utterings of famous people have been stated as laws and named in their honor. (Conversely, famous people have been known to make up laws and affix bogus names to them. John Kenneth Galbraith has done this on several occasions. See, for instance, *Crump's Law.*) As a result of this, one is liable to come up with a law like *Parker's Law of Parliamentary Procedure,* "A motion to adjourn is always in order," and have no way of knowing if the Parker in question was (a) Dorothy Parker, (b) Charlie Parker, (c) a claims adjuster named Parker who created it at a claim adjusters' convention, or (d) John Kenneth Galbraith.

The book brought the work of the Center to the attention of many who were then in touch with its director to share their own universal discoveries. Within a matter of months the book attracted thousands of letters—more than 5,000 actually—containing rules, laws, principles, maxims, and "whatevers," with more coming in each day. Two annexes were added to the original site (a pair of cardboard file boxes), and the Center's existence was noted by the national news media. An edition was published in the UK and the book was translated into Japanese, German, and Danish.

Meanwhile the names of hundreds of dedicated contributors were added to the roll of the Official Fellows of the Center. This title is bestowed on people who contribute to the work of the Center in accord with *The Compensation Corollary,* which states, "In a society where credentials are important, the cheapest form of payment is a fancy title." This is closely associated with *The Résumé Rule:* "With few exceptions (Jack the Ripper, Attila the Hun, etc.) just about anyone can be made to look good on a piece of paper."

The material was good enough to inspire a sequel published in 1980 entitled *The Official Explanations* which contained the following comment by the Director: "If the submissions coming into the Center are a barometer for our collective state of mind at this point in history, it would seem that we are doing pretty well despite OPEC, Congress, rampant automation, inflation, the energy crisis, and the many other ducks that collectively threaten to peck us to death. Specifically, the material is comfortably cynical, puckish, unswayed by large institutions, and possessed of a widespread quasi-religious faith in gremlins, institutional tomfoolery, human imperfectability, and the perversity of inanimate objects."

This book led to even more publicity and a small cottage industry of "Official Rules" products—posters, wall plaques, pencils, greeting cards, cocktail napkins, note pads, rubber stamps and stickers—and a 2nd British edition (this time with many rules from the UK) and a 2nd Japanese translation. The contributions just kept coming in and the Center began turning its compilations of new rules into magazine articles including ten for the *Washingtonian* magazine (1978–1996) and eventually *The New Official Rules* in 1989.

In the mid-1990s, the number of letters received by the Center began to dwindle as the number of e-mails increased. At the end of 1999, the center geared up for what was billed as the greatest manifestation of Murphy's Law ever—the coming Y2K debacle when all things electronic would shut down as microcircuits told them that the year 1900 had arrived. It was feared that computers would crash, power grids would go black, air traffic control systems would cease to operate, and chaos would be the order of the day for the new millennium. But what really happened was that Y2K proved one of the extended corollaries to Murphy's Law, which is that you cannot depend on Murphy's Law; hence, Murphy's Law obeys Murphy's Law.

Today this 20th-century institution is ready and willing to again become a vital force in the second decade of the 21st century. As the Great Recession comes to an end the world needs the guidance of the Murphy Center and the cumulative wisdom of its far-flung network of fellows.

As a public service the center offers herewith a set of laws that would seem to have a classic and steady relevance in the 21st century. The rules that follow appear in the exact language of the person who discovered the phenomenon or universal truth, including his or her name for that discovery. Similarly, I have tried whenever possible to credit other collections from which laws have been collected. To save space, these sources have been abbreviated, and the key to these abbreviations starts on page xiii.

Finally, one must thank all the people—dozens of them—who have helped with this effort. For their contributions, they have been made Fellows of the Murphy

Center, a more than honorary title that might come in handy in a number of situations. For instance, should any of them ever need not to have to explain a nonproductive period in their life, they can simply say they are on a research fellowship from the Murphy Center. A list of the Senior Fellows appears on page 399.

Books by Paul Dickson Which Attempt to Bring Order to a Disorderly Universe:
The Official Rules (1979)
The Official Explanations (1980)
The New Official Rules (1989)
The Official Rules at Home (1996)
The Official Rules at Work (1996)
The Official Rules for Lawyers, Politicians and All They Torment (1996)
The Official Rules for Golfers (1997)
The Official Rules and Explanations (1999)
The Official Rules of Life (2000)
The Unwritten Rules of Baseball (2009)

Source Codes

AIC. Advanced Instruments' "Compilation of Very Important but Little Known Scientific Principles." A brochure, numbered SNAFU 8695, put out by this Newton Highlands, Massachusetts company about 1970.

AO. Alan Otten of *The Wall Street Journal.*

ASF. *Astounding Science Fiction.* From that magazine's long-running series of letters on laws. (See *The Finagle File* for a full description.)

Co. A notation indicating "common"—i.e., difficult to pin to any collection because it appears in so many.

DRW. Donald R. Woods, Stanford, California.

EV. Elaine Viets, from her columns on laws in the *St. Louis Post-Dispatch.*

FD. Fred Dyer.

FL. Farber's Laws. From an article of that title in *The New York Times Magazine* for March 17, 1968.

FSP. Frank S. Preston, Charlotte, North Carolina.

GT. Gregg Townsend, who is now in charge of the collection of laws that was begun by Conrad Schneiker and developed by Ed Logg and others. The seminal laws collection. Tucson, Arizona.

HE. Hans Einstein, the RAND Corp.

HW. *Harper's* "Wraparound." Laws solicited from readers for the section of "Wraparound" items in the August 1974 issue.

JCG. Joseph C. Goulden, Washington, D.C.

JE. John Erhman computerized collection housed at the Stanford Linear Accelerator Center.

JIR. *The Journal of Irreproducible Results.*

JMcC. John McClaughry, Concord, Vermont.

JS. John Shelton, Dallas, Texas.

JW. Jack Womeldorf, Washington, D.C.

LSP. *Life's Simple Philosophies.* A collection of laws that I have been unable to attribute to any person or publication. Several copies were sent to me by people who found copies circulating around their offices.

MB. *Malice in Blunderland,* Thomas Martin's important book (McGraw-Hill, 1971).

MBC. Mark B. Cohen, Pennsylvania House of Representatives.

ME. M. Mack Earle, Baltimore, Maryland.

MLS. Marshall L. Smith, Washington, D.C.

NDB. N. D. Butcher.

POR. "Principles of Operations Research." From the series of articles by Robert Machol from *Interfaces.*

PQ. *Peter's Quotations.* Dr. Lawrence J. Peter's invaluable reference.

RA. Ryan Anthony, Tucson, Arizona.

Ra. Radio. These are rules and laws that were called in to radio talk shows on which the author appeared to talk about the Murphy Center. Many of these are marked with *U* for unknown, as their authors typically did not have time or chance to give their full names.

RM. Robert Matz.

RS. Robert Specht, the RAND Corp.

Scientific Collections. Designation for several one-page collections of "Scientific Laws" found floating through or tacked up in such places as the National Institutes of Health and the National Bureau Of Standards.

S.T.L. University of Arizona Computing Center collection, which was begun in January, 1974, by Conrad Schneiker and maintained by Gregg Townsend, Ed Logg, and others.

TCA. Theodore C. Achilles, Washington, D.C.

TG. Tom Gill.

TJR. Timothy J. Rolfe.

T'OB. Tom O'Brien, the Department of Labor.

U. Unknown to this collector.

The Rules A to Z

A

Abbott's Admonitions. (1) If you have to ask, you're not entitled to know. (2) If you don't like the answer, you shouldn't have asked the question. (Charles C. Abbott, former Dean of the Graduate School of Business Administration, University of Virginia; *AO.)*

Abercrombie's Theory of Parallel Universes. There exists a parallel universe into which all our lost objects are sucked, never to be seen again. (Denis Abercrombie; from Larry Groebe.)

Abley's Explanation. Marriage is the only union that cannot be organized. Both sides think they are management. (William J. Abley, Kamloops, British Columbia.)

Abourezk's First Eight Laws of Politics. (1) Anybody who really would change things for the better in this country could never be elected president anyway. (2) Don't worry about your enemies; it's your allies who will do you in. (3) In politics people will do whatever is necessary to get their way. (4) The bigger the appropriations bill, the shorter the debate. (5) If a politician has a choice between listening and talking, guess which one he will choose. (6) When voting on the confirmation of a presidential appointment, it's always safer to vote against the son of a bitch, because if he is confirmed, it won't be long before he proves how wise you were. (7) If you want to curry favor with a politician, give him credit for something that someone else did. (8) Don't blame me, I voted for McGovern. (Senator James Abourezk, from his article "Life Inside the Congressional Cookie Jar," *Playboy,* March 1979. When elected in 1973, he became the first Arab-American to serve in the United States Senate.)

Abramson's Law of Bachelorhood. Always have plenty of underwear. (Joe Abramson; from Dallas Brozik, Huntington, West Virginia.)

Abrams's Advice. When eating an elephant, take one bite at a time. (General Creighton W. Abrams; *HE.*)

Abrey's Law. The motive for motiveless crimes is that the wrongdoers wish to demonstrate their own rottenness. (John Abrey, Cleveland, England.)

Accounting, The Four Laws of. (1) Trial balances don't. (2) Working capital doesn't. (3) Liquidity tends to run out. (4) Return on investments never will. (Anonymous.)

Accuracy, Rule of. When working toward the solution of a problem, it always helps if you know the answer. *Advanced Corollary:* Provided, of course, you know there is a problem. (Also known by other titles, such as the Ultimate Law of Accuracy; *AIC.*)

Acheson's Comment on Experts. An expert is like a eunuch in a harem—someone who knows all about it but can't do anything about it. (Former Secretary of State Dean Acheson; recalled by Harold P. Smith for *AO.*)

Acheson's Rule of the Bureaucracy. A memorandum is written not to inform the reader but to protect the writer. (Dean Acheson, as Secretary of State; recalled by Harold P. Smith for *AO.*)

Achilles' Biological Findings. (1) If a child looks like his father, that's heredity. If he looks like a neighbor, that's environment. (2) A lot of time has been wasted arguing over who came first—the chicken or the egg. It was undoubtedly the rooster. (The late Ambassador Theodore C. Achilles, Washington, D.C.)

Ackley's Axiom. The degree of technical competence is inversely proportional to the level of management. (Bob Ackley, T. Sgt., USAF, Plattsmouth, Nebraska. He adds, "Originally defined—in 1967—as, 'The level of intelligence is inversely proportional to the number of stripes,' then I had to modify it as I accrued more stripes.")

Ackley's Lastest Business Findings. (1) A man who'll steal for you, will steal from you. (2) If you are a big enough company, your mistakes become standards. (Bob Ackley, Plattsmouth, Nebraska, who dedicated his second business finding to IBM.)

Ackley's Law. Every recovery is hailed by an incumbent president as the result of his own wise policies, while every recession is condemned by him as the result of the mistaken policies of his predecessor. (Gardner Ackley, chairman of the Council of Economic Advisors under President Lyndon B. Johnson, who revealed his law upon his retirement as professor of economics at the University of Michigan; from Neal Wilgus, Albuquerque, New Mexico.)

Ackley's Second Axiom. Familiarity breeds attempt. (See *Ackley's Lastest Business Findings.*)

Ackley's Third Law of Roller Skating. Everyone spends at least *some* time on the floor—or sidewalk. (See *Ackley's Lastest Business Findings.*)

Acton's Law. Power tends to corrupt, absolute power corrupts absolutely. (Lord Acton; *Co.* This is, perhaps, the most oft-quoted of all political tenets. There are many variations on Acton's Law. Here is one from the "Vent" column in the *Atlanta Journal-Constitution,* January 25, 2004, "Power corrupts, but absolute power is kind of neat." Then there is the variation which appeared in one of John Leo's collections of top axioms—this one for the year 1995, "All vodka corrupts; Absolut Vodka corrupts absolutely," which he attributed to author Steve Kanfer—*Washington Times,* December 23, 1995.)

ACW's Theorems of Practical Physics. (1) When reading a magazine story, it is always continued on an unnumbered page—usually in the middle of the special advertising section. (2) The value of an object is inversely proportional to the security of its packaging (compare a 25¢ package of faucet washers with the velvet-lined box containing a $6,000 diamond ring). (3) The volume times the frequency of the neighboring dog's bark is inversely proportional to the intelligence of its owner. (Ashley C. Worsley, Baton Rouge, Louisiana.)

Adams's Axiom. It doesn't matter what you say, as long as you keep talking. (Harold "Buck" Adams, Capt., USAF, c. 1974; from Bob Ackley, Plattsmouth, Nebraska.)

Adams's Law. (1) Women don't know what they want; they don't like what they have got. (2) Men know very well what they want; having got it, they begin to lose interest. (A. W. Adams, Magdalen College, Oxford, England.)

Adam's Law of Gossip. Ninety-two percent of the stuff told you in confidence you couldn't get anyone else to listen to. (Journalist, poet, and humorist Franklin Pierce Adams.)

Adams's Political Discovery. Practical politics consist of ignoring facts. (Historian Henry Adams.)

Adams's Reality. Far out in the uncharted backwaters of the unfashionable end of the Western Spiral arm of the Galaxy lies a small unregarded yellow sun. Orbiting this at a distance of roughly ninety-eight million miles is an utterly insignificant little blue-green planet whose ape-descended life forms are so amazingly primitive that they still think digital watches are a pretty neat idea. (Douglas Adams, *The Hitchhiker's Guide to the Galaxy.*)

Addis's Admonitions. (1) If it don't fit in a pigeonhole, maybe it ain't a pigeon. (2) Never play cat-and-mouse games if you're a mouse. (3) Ambiguity is the first refuge of the wrong. (4) The shadow of your goalpost is better than no shade at all. (5) There's no cure for the common scold. (6) The weak shall inhibit the earth. (7) You will never see a cat obedience school. (Don Addis, St. Petersburg, Florida, cartoonist and columnist for the *St. Petersburg Times,* whose first rule of humor is "If you're going to joke—be funny.")

Addis's Collected Wisdom. (1) A lawmaker's work is never done. He sees to that. (2) What mindless drivel goes unsaid, when teenagers say "like, ya know" instead. (3) No paper bag can hold all the garbage produced by the groceries that came into the house in it. (4) Relativity: It only seems like an eternity between the time a glass is empty and the time the kid stops going "guuuurk" with the straw. (5) No human on earth can refold a road map, but some excellent origami and paper airplanes have resulted from the effort. (6) If there were only one wrong way to wire your VCR to the TV, you would find it on the first try. (7) I drink—therefore rye am. (8) Nobody will leave you alone—until you want company. (9) A magazine that travels thousands of miles in the care of the Postal Service will wait until you bring it in the house to drop its loose subscription cards on the floor. (10) If the instructions on the child-proof cap say to push down hard while twisting, the contents are arthritis medicine. If it can only be opened by tearing at it with your teeth, it's denture cream. (11) If wishes were horses, you could horse upon a star. (12) The chief advantage of homo sapiens getting up on two feet was that they then could distinguish their dogs from their children. (13) Infinity is nature's way of putting things off. (14) OK, so what's the speed of dark? (15) The only time you'll know what people really think of your beard is after you've shaved it off. (16) The problem with the genetic pool is that there is no lifeguard. (17) Life is not too short; it's too narrow. (18) There's nothing that can happen on a football field that can't be described with a cliché. (19) After you have submitted to toilet training, every act of rebellion is anticlimactic. (20) Western man is the only creature that shows its appreciation for the beauties of nature by encasing them in plastic. (21) A barking dog never bites, but he may stop barking at any moment. (22) There is no substitute for Honorable Mention. (23) He who takes comfort in the overwhelming odds against being hit by lightning will be convinced the same odds cannot prevent him from winning the lottery. (24) Beat a better door mouse and the path will build a trap to your world. (25) Any given company policy, rules or procedure will outlast everybody's memory of why it was instituted. (26) If at first you don't succeed, redefine success. (27) Everyone has a photographic memory. Some just don't have film. (28) Shin: a device for finding furniture in the dark. (29) Eagles may soar, but weasels don't get sucked into jet engines. (Don Addis, St. Petersburg, Florida.)

Addis's Remark on the Current State of Affairs. Our main social activities are whining and dining. (Don Addis, St. Petersburg, Florida.)

Adenauer's Advice. An infallible method of conciliating a tiger is to allow oneself to be devoured. (Dr. Conrad Adenauer.)

Ade's Law. Anybody can win—unless there happens to be a second entry. (American humorist George Ade; *PQ*.)

Ade's Reminder. A bird in the hand may be worth two in the bush, but remember also that a bird in the hand is a positive embarrassment to one not in the poultry business. (American humorist George Ade.)

Adkin's Rule of Milk and Other Precious Commodities. The less you have, the more you spill. (Betsy Adkins, Gardiner, Maine.)

Adlai's Axiom. He who slings mud generally loses ground. (Adlai Stevenson, 1954; *MLS.*)

Adler's Distinction. Language is all that separates us from the lower animals, and from the bureaucrats. (Jerry Adler, *Newsweek,* December 15, 1980; *RS.*)

Adler's Explanation. Life intrudes. (Pet expression of acting teacher Stella Adler, widely quoted.)

Advertising Admonition. In writing a patent medicine advertisement, first convince the reader that he has the disease he is reading about, secondly, that it is curable. (R. F. Fenno, 1908.)

Advertising Agency Song, The. When your client's hopping mad, put his picture in the ad. If he still should prove refractory, add a picture of his factory. (Anonymous, from *Pith and Vinegar,* edited by William Cole, Simon & Schuster, 1969.)

Advice to Officers of the British Army. (1) Ignorance of your profession is best concealed by solemnity and silence, which pass for profound knowledge upon the generality of mankind. A proper attention to these, together with extreme severity, particularly in trifles, will soon procure you the character of a good officer. (2) As you probably did not rise to your present distinguished rank by your own merit, it cannot reasonably be expected that you should promote others on that score. (3) Be sure to give out a number of orders.... The more trifling they are, the more it shews (sic) your attention to the service; and should your orders contradict one another, it will give you an opportunity of altering them, and find subject for fresh regulations. (Discovered by Stuart G. Vogt of Clarkesville, Tennessee, who has a copy of the sixth edition of *Advice to the Officers of the British Army,* published in 1783.)

Agel's Law of Tennis Doubles in which a Husband and Wife are on the Same Side. Whenever the husband poaches on his wife's side of the court and shouts, "I've got it, I've got it," you can safely bet that he doesn't. (Jerome Agel, *The New York Times,* July 30, 1980.)

Agnes Allen's Law. Almost anything is easier to get into than out of. (Agnes Allen was the wife of the famous historian Frederick Lewis Allen. When her husband was teaching at Yale, he encountered an ambitious student named Louis Zahner, who wanted to create and be remembered for a law of his own. Zahner worked on it and finally hit upon one that states: "If you play with anything long enough it will break." Inspired by his student, Allen then went to work on his own and came up with *Allen's Law:* "Everything is more complicated than it looks to most people." Agnes Allen then got into the act and proceeded to outdistance

Zahner and her husband by creating the law that to this day carries her full name. Frederick Allen later wrote of his wife's law: "... at one stroke human wisdom had been advanced to an unprecedented degree." All of this was revealed in a column by Jack Smith in the *Los Angeles Times* after he had researched the question of who Murphy and Agnes Allen were. Needless to say, he proved Ms. Allen's law in the process. Personal Note from the Director: Over time this law has proven to have great personal value as "anything" applies to everything from arguments, to debt, to installment plans, to committees. It is most useful as a caution. I still serve on the occasional committee and attend an occasional meeting, but I have chosen not to serve on others thanks to this law. It seems like it was created to keep me questioning new levels of involvement which may be superfluous, costly and/or a bona fide waste of time.)[2]

Agrait's Law. A rumor will travel fastest to the place where it will cause the greatest harm. (Gustavo N. Agrait, Rio Piedras, Puerto Rico.)

AIR (Annals of Improbable Research) Dining Principle #1. If you go to a restaurant that's called "So-and-so's X House," or "House of X," or "X Grill," you should order the X. Example: If you go to a restaurant called "Frank's Steak House," order the steak. Explanation: Go to a restaurant called "Frank's Steak House" and order the veal scaloppini. You will immediately see why you should have ordered the steak. (*Mini-Annals of Improbable Research* ("mini-AIR") Issue # 2001–02.)

Air Force Inertia Axiom. Consistency is always easier to defend than correctness. (Anonymous; from Russell Fillers, Bethel, Connecticut.)

Air Force Law. Two percent don't get the word. (*U/LSP.*)

Airline Food Facts. Believe it or not, there are only two things wrong with airline food—One, the food. Two, the way it's prepared. (In an ad for Midway Metrolink, *The New York Times,* June 7, 1983; *JCG.*)

Airplane Law. When the plane you are on is late, the plane you want to transfer to is on time. (*U/S.T.L.*)

Akre's Axiom. Do not readily ascribe to malice what can be more easily ascribed to incompetence. *Akre's Corollary:* Beware of malicious incompetent! (James Akre, Confignon, Switzerland.)

Albert's Law of the Sea. The more they are in a fog, the more boats (and people) toot their horns. (Bernard L. Albert, M.D., Scarsdale, New York.)

Albinak's Algorithm. When graphing a function, the width of the line should

[2] Phillip Jenks has noted: Foreshadowing Agnes Allen by some twenty-five hundred years was Aesop, whose fable of "The Lion, the Fox and the Beasts" concluded with the moral, "While I see many hoof marks going in I see none coming out. It is easier to get into the enemy's toils than out again."

be inversely proportional to the precision of the data. (Marvin J. Albinak, Professor of Chemistry, Essex Community College, Baltimore, Maryland.)

Albrecht's Analogy. I have a vacuum-tube mind in a solid-state world. (George Albrecht, Bethesda, Maryland.)

Albrecht's Epistolary Effort. Troublesome correspondence that is postponed long enough will eventually become irrelevant. (Mark Albrecht; from Brooks Alexander, Berkeley, California. Belden Menkus of Hillsboro, Tennessee has pointed out that this "appears to be a reworking of an anecdote that I first heard some 40 years ago. In that account, it was Napoleon Bonaparte's practice when in the field to simply stack incoming correspondence in a pile on the desk that was set up in his tent; upon being asked why he did this, he gave the response cited by Albrecht.")

Alcoholic Axiom. The effort and energy an intoxicated person spends trying to prove he is sober is directly proportionate to how intoxicated he is. (Randall L. Koch, Kenosha, Wisconsin.)

Alden's Laws. (1) Giving away baby clothes and furniture is a major cause of pregnancy. (2) Always be backlit. (3) Sit down whenever possible. (Nancy Alden, Drexel Hill, Pennsylvania.)

Alderson's Theorem. If at first you don't succeed, you are running about average. (M. H. Alderson; from the *Lawrence County Record,* Missouri.)

Alexander's Rules. (1) If a wife is happy about the toilet seat, the husband should spend more time at home. (2) Help a man who is in trouble and that man will remember you when he is in trouble again. (Paul Alexander, Venice, California.)

Alex's Iron Axiom. Life is the ultimate I.Q. test. (Alex Fraser, Washington, D.C.)

Alfalfa's Observation. Another day, another zero! (From T. A. Moore III, M.D., New Orleans, Louisiana, who recalls it from "a memorable scene in the *Our Gang* comedies when Spanky, Buckwheat, and Alfalfa are descending the steps of their school after another day of intellectual disaster." Moore adds, "This is certainly a universal sentiment and could not be more succinct.")

Algren's Precepts. Never eat at a place called Mom's. Never play cards with a man named Doc. And never lie down with a woman who's got more troubles than you. (Nelson Algren, *What Every Young Man Should Know,* Random House, 1977.)

Alicat Shop Generalization. The more gushing they do, the less they buy. (Florenz Baron, Yonkers, New York. Named for the Alicat Bookshop run by Florenz and her late husband, Oscar.)

Alice's Conclusion. A genius is never housebroken, and if a writer, he is always too much in the house, with his overflowing books and papers that must not be touched, and his odd visitors, and his superhuman need of quiet—or of immediate comforting companionship. (Jacques Barzun, on Alice Gibbens's understanding of Henry James, in *A Stroll with William James; FD.*)

Alice's Law. The purpose of Presidential office is not power, or leadership of the Western World, but reminiscence, best-selling reminiscence. (Roger Jellinek, *The New York Times Book Review,* March 10, 1968.)

Alice's Law of Compensatory Cash Flow. Any money not spent on a luxury one considered even briefly is the equivalent of windfall income and should be spent accordingly. (Alice Trillin, quoted by her husband, Calvin, in *Alice, Let's Eat;* Random House, 1978; from John R. Labadie, Seattle, Washington.)

Alicia's Discovery. When you move something to a more logical place, you only can remember where it used to be and your decision to move it. (Alicia K. Dustira, New Haven, Connecticut.)

Alida's Rule. The larger the house, the more likely the addition. (Alida Kane, Washington, D.C.)

Alinsky's Sword. Favors granted always become defined as rights. (Saul Alinsky, 1960s community organizer; from Stu Goldstein, M.D., who adds, "Cuts both ways: to the 'ins,' as a warning, to the 'outs' as a device. Can't we just this once, as a special favor, have a variance from the code; stay up late; etc.?")

Alkula's Observation. A library will be most busy on Thursday. Everyone remembers Thursday that they have something due on Friday, hence the rush. Corporate/R&D/technical libraries will be the most busy 11–2 Thursdays because everyone decides to "do a little research on my lunch hour." (Joan C. Alkula, Fort Jackson, South Carolina.)

Allan's Theorem. In any group of eagles, you will find some turkeys. (Allan B. Guerrina, Woodbridge, Virginia.)

Allcock's Law of Communication. The time that passes before you hear about an event is in direct proportion to the extent to which it affects you. (John Allcock, University of Bradford, West Yorkshire, England.)

Allen's Axiom. When all else fails, read the instructions. (*U; Scientific Collections.* Sometimes called *Cahn's Law.*)

Allen's Circus Axiom. If a circus is half as good as it smells, it's a great show. (Radio with Fred Allen.)

Allen's Distinction. The lion and the calf shall lie down together, but the calf won't get much sleep. (Woody Allen, from *Without Feathers,* Random House, 1977.)

Allen's Formula. If you want to be a success in life, just show up 80 percent of the time. (Writer/actor/director Woody Allen; quoted in Chuck Conconi's column, *Washington Post,* November 30, 1984.)

Allen's Lament. Everybody wants to be waited on. (Mary Allen, McLean, Virginia.)

Allen's Law of Civilization. It is better for civilization to be going down the drain than to be coming up it. (Henry Allen, *Washington Post.*)

Allen's Law of Popularity. The more popular something is, the more likely it is that a religious personage will object to it. (Stephen Allen, Essex Junction, Vermont.)

Allen's Motto. I'd rather have a free bottle in front of me than a prefrontal lobotomy. (Fred Allen; *DRW.*)

Allen's Reassurance. He's got more talent in his whole body than you've got in your little finger. (Gracie Allen, heard on the rebroadcast of an old radio show, WAMU-FM, Washington, D.C.)

Allen's Rule of Universal Constancy. The only thing constant in the Navy is the varying rate of change. (From Daniel K. Snyder, Pearl City, Hawaii, who attributes it to Bob Allen and adds, "Codified at the Fleet Ballistic Missile Training Center in Charleston, South Carolina, in early 1977, but since that time found to be applicable not only to the Navy, but to the world in general." Belden Menkus of Hillsboro, Tennessee has much wider application than he suggests and appears to be a restatement of Jonathan Swift's 1710 observation that there is nothing in this world constant, but inconstancy.)

Allen's Tenet. The strength of one's opinion on any matter in controversy is inversely proportional to the amount of knowledge that the person has on that subject. (Patrick J. Allen, Chicago, Illinois.)

Alley's Axiom. Justice always prevails... three times out of seven! (*U.* The law itself comes from Michael J. Wagner of Miami, Florida.)

Allison's Advice. It doesn't do any good to put the brakes on when you're upside down. (NASCAR driver Bobby Allison after a crash; from Jim Murrison, Port Orange, Florida.)

Allison's Precept. The best simple-minded test of expertise in a particular area is an ability to win money in a series of bets on future occurrences in that area. (Graham Allison, the John F. Kennedy School of Government; *AO.*)

Almeida's Law of Book Reviews. No book is as good or as bad as its reviewer says. *Corollary:* If the reviewer says it's neither, it definitely is not that either. *Almeida's Law of Name Forgetting:* The chances of forgetting a person's name will be directly proportional to the importance of the person and the need you have to introduce her, times the number of people present. (Onesimo T. Almeida, Brown University.)

Alsop's Law of Political Oratory. The important thing is to be able to say,

"Most oranges are round" and sound as if you mean it. (John Alsop, who believed that Adlai Stevenson lost the 1952 election because of his inability to fulfill Alsop's Law.)

Alt's Axiom. A parent will always worry about the wrong child. *Scholl's Corollary:* A child will always worry about the wrong parent. (Don Alt and Marilyn Alt Scholl, Deerfield, Illinois; from the latter.)

Aman's Discovery. Management is always trying to fine-tune the solution before it defines the problem. (Wayne Aman, Burnsville, Minnesota.)

Ambrose's Axiom. When asking street directions, the first three people questioned will be: (1) foreign (2) stupid (3) dead wrong. (Jack Hauler, Malvern, Pennsylvania.)

Ames's Working Hypothesis. The self-employed person is uniquely in a position to define success however he pleases. (Mary E. Ames, *Washington Post,* March 6, 1983.)

Amis's Collected Wisdom. *Amis's Admonition:* You can't believe anyone but yourself, and don't trust yourself too completely. *Amis's Advice:* Go ahead and be different—if you think you can stand the beating you'll get. *Amis's Calculation:* Any fool can line up two fence posts. It's when you add the third that it gets tough. *Amis's Discovery:* There are a lot more cowboy boots than there are cowboys. *Amis's Famous Saying:* Obesity looks best on fat people. *Amis's Reminder:* Humor is the reminder that no matter how high the throne one sits on, one sits on one's bottom. (Jim Amis, Springfield, Missouri.)

Amos's Law. All my ideas are good: it's only the people who put them into practice that aren't. (The character Amos Brearly, British *Emmerdale Farm* television series; from Peter Scott, Portsmouth, England.)

Amundsen's Discovery. Victory awaits those who have everything in order. People call this luck. (Polar explorer Roald Amundsen; *MLS.*)

Ancient Volkswagen Proverb. Anything adjustable will sooner or later need adjustment. (Newspaper ad, *California Aggie,* November 23, 1983.)

Andersen's Answer. It's all the same. (Lance Andersen, Anchorage, Alaska; submitted with this notation: "Five or six years ago, after twenty-one years of fruitlessly searching for my own personal ticket to immortality, I was approaching a state of abject despair. On my twenty-second birthday, in what might be loosely described as a beatific visitation, I was provided with *Andersen's Answer.*... Anyway, I was afraid that I might lose track of this indispensable truth, so I went and had it tattooed onto my right arm." A photo of the tattoo was enclosed.)

Andersen's Discovery. It matters not so much whether you do something well or badly, but how you get out of doing it honestly. (Kurt Andersen, *The Real Thing.*)

Anderson's Distinction. My grandfather believed there are two kinds of people—those who know how the world fits together and those who think they know. The former work in hardware stores, the latter in politics. (Josef Anderson, *Los Angeles Times,* October 5, 1980; *RS.*)

Anderson's Law. I have yet to see any problem, however complicated, which, when you look at it in the right way, did not become still more complicated. (Writer Poul Anderson; *JW.*)

Anderson's Maxims. (1) Colleges and universities are immune to their own knowledge. (2) You can't outthink a person who isn't thinking. (Phil Anderson, Assistant Professor, College of St. Thomas, St. Paul, Minnesota.)

Anderson's Observation. Institutions tend to treat their employees as they do their clients. Schools, prisons, uptight corporations, etc., structure time for their clients and employees as well. Laid-back free clinics, certain mental health units, universities, etc., do not structure time for their clients; thus they do not structure time for their employees. (E. Frederick Anderson, Assistant Dean, San Diego State University.)

Andrea's Admonition. Never bestow profanity upon a driver who has wronged you in some way. If you think his window is closed and he can't hear you, it isn't and he can. (Margo-Rita Andrea Kissell, Toledo, Ohio.)

Andrea's Law of Diminishing Returns. The time it takes to return from someplace is always shorter than the time it took to get there. This is because you've been there already. (Andrea L. Miller, Downey, California.)

Andrews's Canoeing Postulate. No matter which direction you start, it's always against the wind coming back. (Alfred Andrews; *JE.*)

Anjard's Teen Theorem. Their mouths grow disproportionate to their height. (Dr. Ron Anjard, Kokomo, Indiana.)

Ann's Law of Inevitability. You never meet that terrific person until the day before your vacation ends. (Ann L. Moore, Exeter, New Hampshire.)

Anon's Congressional Razor. A complicated truth never stands a chance against a simple falsehood. (Anonymous Congressional staffer during a briefing on nuclear waste, November 1991; from Steven Woodbury, Springfield, Virginia.)

Anon's Contribution to the National Security Debate. The difference between the military and the Boy Scouts of America is the Boy Scouts are allowed to carry knives and they have adult leadership. (Found by Lt. Col. N. E. Kass, Fort Walton Beach, Florida.)

Anon's Dietary Law. The fat you eat is the fat you wear. (Bob Norris, Palma de Majorca, Spain.)

Anon's Reminder to Mind the Real Objective. Why worry about low tire pressure when you're out of gas? (Anonymous, Santa Ana, California.)

Anonymity, Superior Credibility of. People are more likely to believe a quote if it is anonymous. (Steve Stine, Skokie, Illinois, who adds, "I have noted that people believe a quote 'author unknown' so much better that sometimes known attributions are deleted." See following example.)

Anonymous's Bodily Discovery. Whatever doesn't stick out is hanging down. (Name withheld by request.)

Anthony's Law of Force. Don't force it, get a larger hammer. (*U/S.T.L*)

Anthony's Law of the Workshop. Any tool, when dropped, will roll into the least accessible corner of the workshop. *Corollary:* On the way to the corner, any dropped tool will first always strike your toes. (*U/S.T.L.*)

Apartment Dweller's Law. One person's floor is another person's ceiling. (*U/Ra.*)

Apotheosis Assumption, The. The boss already has the right answers. (Sidney I. Riskin, Tarrytown, New York.)

Approval Seeker's Law. Those whose approval you seek the most give you the least. (This is one of a number of laws created by Washington, D.C. writer Rozanne Weissman. She is a natural-law writer whose style is characterized by restraint. Note that all of her laws bear situational titles.)

Aquinas Axiom, The. What the gods get away with, the cows don't. (*DRW.*)

Arden's Rules. (1) A new driver's license means you will move. (2) Transferring the stuff from your old dilapidated address book into a neat, legible, new address book means all your friends will move. (3) If you lose your wallet, it will have more money in it than it has for the past five years. (Lynne Arden, Oakland, California.)

Armey's Axioms. (A selection): (1) The politics of greed always come wrapped in the language of love. (2) If you want the government to get off your back, you've got to get your hands out of its pocket. (3) You can't put your finger on a problem when you've got it to the wind. (4) It's easier (and more fun) to pass new laws than to enforce existing ones. (Former House Majority Leader Richard Armey from his 1995 book *The Freedom Revolution;* and quoted in *The Hill,* July 26, 1995).

Armitage's Finding. Anything put off this morning will reach critical mass during lunch break. (R. Armitage, Scunthorpe, England.)

Armor's Axiom of Morality. Virtue is the failure to achieve vice. (John C. Armor, Baltimore, Maryland.)

Armstrong's Collection Law. If the check is truly in the mail, it is surely made out to someone else. (James S. Armstrong, San Francisco, California.)

Army Axiom. An order that can be misunderstood will be misunderstood.

Army Law. If it moves, salute it; if it doesn't move, pick it up; and if you can't pick it up, paint it. (Both Army entries have been around at least since World War II, if not longer.)

Arnold's Square Wheel Theory. A prevalent form of decision-making holds that if three out of four schools, firms, or whatever, are using square wheels, then the fourth will follow. (Richard Arnold, Keezletown, Virginia.)

Aronfy's Law of the Post Office. The likelihood of a letter getting lost in the mail is directly proportional to its importance. (Andrew G. Aronfy, M.D., Seabrook, Maryland. *Aronfy's proof:* "I sent the IRS a substantial check for estate taxes. A month and a half later they sent us a bill for an additional $207.00 for interest and penalties. Needless to say, they never got the original.")

Aronfy's Observation on Fast-Food Restaurants. The waiting period in fast-food restaurants is always twenty minutes. (Andrew G. Aronfy, M.D., Seabrook, Maryland, explains: "During lunch hour there are twenty people waiting. There are four efficient servers behind the counter. The line goes fast, and one is served in twenty minutes. During off hours there is one person waiting in line. He/she is ordering for seven unruly kids who keep changing their minds about what they want. Behind the counter stands one surly, stupid, rude, and uncaring server who gets the orders all mixed up. Waiting time is twenty minutes.")

Aronfy's Rule. All earaches start Saturday night. (Andrew G. Aronfy, M.D., Seabrook, Maryland.)

Asa's Law. Every author hopes that at least one of his epigrams will grow up to be a cliché. (Asa Wilgus, *Sparks from the Scissor Grinder,* Profile Press, 1950; from distant relative Neal Wilgus.)

Ashley-Perry Statistical Axioms. (1) Numbers are tools, not rules. (2) Numbers are symbols for things; the number and the thing are not the same. (3) Skill in manipulating numbers is a talent, not evidence of divine guidance. (4) Like other occult techniques of divination, the statistical method has a private jargon deliberately contrived to obscure its methods from nonpractitioners. (5) The product of an arithmetical computation is the answer to an equation; it is not the solution to a problem. (6) Arithmetical proofs of theorems that do not have arithmetical bases prove nothing. (Drawn from Colonel G. O. Ashley's "A Declaration of Independence from the Statistical Method," *Air University Review,* March/April 1964, interpreted by R. L. Perry of the RAND Corp.; *RS.*)

Ash's Axiom. Any request prefaced by the word, "just" will be unjust; e.g., this will take just a second, this will hurt just for a moment, etc. (Bill Ash, Miami Lakes, Florida.)

Asimov's Corollary (to *Clarke's First Law*). When the lay public rallies 'round an idea that is denounced by distinguished but elderly scientists, and supports that idea with great fervor and emotion—the distinguished but elderly scientists are then, after all, right. (Isaac Asimov in his article "Asimov's Law" in the February 1977, *Fantasy and Science Fiction Magazine.* See *Clarke's Laws and Bartz's Law of Hokey Horsepuckery*, and *Robotics, The Three Laws of.*)

Astor's Economic Discovery. A man who has a million dollars is as well off as if he was rich. (John Jacob Astor.)

Astrology Law. It's always the wrong time of the month. (Rozanne Weissman.)

Atwood's Fourteenth Corollary. No books are lost by lending except those you particularly wanted to keep. (Alan Atwood, a programmer at the University Computing Center, University of Arizona; *S.T.L.*)

Augustine's Laws. I: The best way to make a silk purse from a sow's ear is to begin with a silk sow. The same is true of money. II: If today were half as good as tomorrow is supposed to be, it would probably be twice as good as yesterday was. III: There are no lazy veteran lion hunters. IV: If you can afford to advertise, you don't need to. V: One-tenth of the participants produce over one-third of the output. Increasing the number of participants merely reduces the average output. VI: A hungry dog hunts best. A hungrier dog hunts even better. VII: Decreased business base increases overhead. So does increased business base. VIII: The most unsuccessful four years in the *education* of a cost-estimator is fifth grade arithmetic. IX: Acronyms and abbreviations should be used to the maximum extent possible to make trivial ideas profound...Q.E.D. X: Bulls do not win bullfights; people do. People do not win people fights; lawyers do. XI: If the earth could be made to rotate twice as fast, managers would get twice as much done. If the earth could be made to rotate twenty times as fast, everyone else would get twice as much done since all the managers would fly off. XII: It costs a lot to build bad products. XIII: There are many highly successful businesses in the United States. There are also many highly paid executives. The policy is not to intermingle the two. XIV: After the year 2015, there will be no airplane crashes. There will be no takeoffs either, because electronics will occupy 100 percent of every airplane's weight. XV: The last 10 percent of performance generates one-third of the cost and two-thirds of the problems. XVI: In the year 2054, the entire defense budget will purchase just one aircraft. This aircraft will have to be shared by the Air Force and Navy 3½ days each per week except for leap year, when it will be made available to the Marines for the extra day. XVII: Software is like entropy. It is difficult to grasp, weighs nothing, and obeys the *Second Law of Thermodynamics;* i.e., it always increases. XVIII: It is very expensive to achieve high unreliability. It is not uncommon to increase the cost of an item by a factor of ten for each factor of ten degradation accomplished. XIX: Although most products will soon be too costly to purchase, there will be a thriving market in the sale of books on how to fix them. XX: In any given year, Congress will appropriate the amount of funding approved the prior year plus three-fourths of whatever change the administration requests, minus 4-percent tax. XXI: It's easy to get a loan unless you need it. XXII: If stock market experts were so expert, they would be buying stock, not selling advice. XXIII: Any task can be completed in only one-third more time than is currently estimated. XXIV: The only thing more costly than stretching the *schedule* of an established project is accelerating it, which is itself the most costly action known to man. XXV: A revised schedule is to business what a new season is to an athlete or a new canvas to an artist. XXVI: If a sufficient number of management layers are superimposed on each other, it can be assured that disaster is not left to chance. XXVII: Rank does not intimidate hardware. Neither does the lack of rank. XXVIII: It is better to be the reorganizer than the reorganizee. XXIX: Executives who do not produce successful results hold on to their jobs only about five years. Those who produce effective results hang on about half a decade. XXX: By the time the people asking the questions are ready for the answers, the people doing the work have lost track of the questions. XXXI: The optimum committee has no members. XXXII: Hiring consultants to conduct studies can be an excellent means of turning problems into gold, your problems into their gold. XXXIII: Fools rush in where incumbents fear to tread. XXXIV: The process of competitively selecting contractors to perform work is based on a system of rewards and penalties, all distributed randomly. XXXV: The weaker the data available upon which to base one's conclusion, the greater the precision which should be quoted in order to give the data authenticity. XXXVI: The thickness of the proposal required to win a multimillion dollar contract is about one millimeter per million dollars. If all the proposals conforming to this standard were piled on top of each other at the bottom of the Grand Canyon it would probably be a good idea. XXXVII: Ninety percent of the time things will turn out worse than you expect. The other 10 percent of the time you had no right to expect so much. XXXVIII: The early bird gets the worm. The early worm... gets eaten. XXXIX: Never promise to complete any project within six months of the end of the year, in either direction. XL: Most projects start out slowly, and then sort of taper off. XLI: The more one produces, the less one gets. XLII: Simple systems are not feasible because they require infinite testing. XLIII: Hardware works best when it matters the least. XLIV: Aircraft flight in the 21st century will always be in a westerly direction, preferably supersonic, crossing time zones to provide the additional hours needed to fix the broken electronics. XLV: One should expect that the expected can be prevented, but the unexpected should have been expected. XLVI: A billion saved is a billion earned. XLVII: Two-thirds of the earth's surface is covered with water. The other third is covered with auditors from headquarters. XLVIII: The more time you spend talking about what you have been doing, the less time you have to spend doing what you have been talking about. Eventually, you spend more and more time talking about less and less until finally you spend all your time talking about nothing. XLIX: Regulations grow at the same rate as weeds. L: The average regulation has a life span one-fifth as long as a chimpanzee's and one-tenth as long as a human's, but four times as long as the officials who created it. LI: By the time of the United States Tricentennial, there will be more government workers than there are workers. LII: People working in the private sector should try to save money. There remains the possibility that it may someday be valuable again. (Norman R. Augustine, president and chief operating officer of Martin Marietta, has written a book (available in paperback) called *Augustine's Laws* in which he succinctly sums up the pitfalls that confront business managers today.)

Augustine's Plea. Give me chastity and self-restraint, but do not give it yet. (Saint Augustine.)

Aunt Emmie's Laws. (1) A cigarette placed in an ashtray will go out if you stay in the room; if you leave the room, the cigarette will topple to the table, burn through, and drop to the floor, where it will smolder until it descends to ignite the drapes in the room below. (2) A clever remark is one you don't make at the appropriate moment but compose immediately after. (3) A pair of scissors should be a true pair; the second pair is to be used in place of the pair that is never where it is always supposed to be. (Owen Elliott, Ridgefield, Connecticut. Aunt Emmie was the youngest of his mother's eight sisters.)

Austen's Rule of Hospitality. One cannot have too large a party. (Jane Austen in *Emma*.)

Austin's Law. If there is no legitimate objection to progress, an illegitimate one will be found. (E. H. Austin; from James Honig, Cocoa, Florida.)

Automatic. (Defined). If something is automatic, that simply means that you can't repair it yourself. (*U;* radio call-in, KDKA, Pittsburgh, Pennsylvania.)

Avery, Sayings of. (1) No ball game is ever much good unless the people involved hate each other. (2) On Monday mornings I am dedicated to the proposition that all men are created jerks. (3) Some performers on television appear to be horrible people, but when you finally get to know them in person, they turn out to be even worse. (4) There's such a thing as too much point on a pencil. (5) When there are two conflicting versions of a story, the wise course is to believe the one in which people appear at their worst. (These are from the late H. Allen Smith's *Let the Crabgrass Grow,* Bernard Geis Associates, 1960. Avery is Smith's [presumably] fictional neighbor who is also responsible for the next four items. The second Avery item has shown up on various lists and may or may not have come from Smith's Avery.)

Avery's Law of Lubrication. Everything needs a little oil now and then. (This as Smith finds Avery, a destructive do-it-yourselfer, pouring oil into the tiny hinges by which the bows of his glasses are attached to their frames.) *Avery's Observation:* It does not matter if you fall down as long as you pick up something from the floor while you get up. *Avery's Razor:* Show me a man that doesn't like Cadillacs and I'll show you a man of violent opinions. All of them wrong. *Avery's Rule of Three:* Trouble strikes in series of threes, but when working around the house, the next job after a series of three is not the fourth job—it's the start of a brand new series of three. (The late H. Allen Smith, from his fictional neighbor, Avery.)

B

Babbitt's Evolutionary Discovery. Evan Mecham proves that Darwin was wrong. (Senator Bruce Babbitt, former governor of Arizona, on the then-governor; quoted in *Newsweek,* November 16, 1987.)

Baber's Rule. Anything worth doing is worth doing in excess. (Susan Baber, St. Louis. Missouri.)

Bacchanalian Conclusion. One can get just as drunk on water... as one can on land! (Eldred O. Schwab, Ojibwa, Wisconsin.)

Backhouse's Law. Salary is inversely proportional to the amount of time spent serving the public. (Roger Backhouse, Ilford, Essex, England.)

Backlund's Automotive Constant. The sun always shines *between* the visors. (Peggy-Lynn Backlund, Walla-Walla, Washington.)

Backus's Law. All water is one inch over your boot tops. (Named for Dr. Richard Backus of Woods Hole, Massachusetts; reported by Ken S. Norris, Professor of Natural History, Santa Cruz, California. Norris, who says, "No law I know is more completely immutable," adds that he and Backus have sighted a rock south of Cape Horn that offers a silhouette close to that of Backus with water sloshing over his boots.)

Badger's Indiana State Police Rule. Few motorists have a clean enough conscience to pass a police car on the highway even when it is traveling below the speed limit. (Joseph E. Badger, Santa Claus, Indiana.)

Baer's Quartet. What's good politics is bad economics; what's bad politics is good economics; what's good economics is bad politics; what's bad economics is good politics. (Eugene W. Baer of Middletown, Rhode Island; *AO.* Baer also allows that it can all be stated somewhat more compactly as "What's good politics is bad economics and vice versa, vice versa.")

Bagdikian's Law of Editor's Speeches. The splendor of an editor's speech and the splendor of his newspaper are inversely related to the distance between the city in which he makes his speech and the city in which he publishes his paper. (Ben Bagdikian, writer and press critic, Berkeley, California.)

Bagdikian's Observation. Trying to be a first-rate reporter on the average American newspaper is like trying to play Bach's *Saint Matthew's Passion* on a ukulele.... (Ben Bagdikian, *The Effete Conspiracy;* Harper and Row, 1972; *RS.*)

Bailey's Law of the Disappearing Signature. An ink pen will run dry in the middle of a flourishing signature on a very important letter that has just been retyped for the fifth time. (Kent Bailey, Vienna, Virginia.)

Bailey's Law of the Kinked Helix. A telephone cord hangs freely with no kinks only in television shows. (Kent Bailey, Vienna, Virginia.)

Bailey's Laws of Memory. (1) The people with the worst memories think they have the best: they cannot remember the last time they forgot something. *Extension:* Ignorant people are, by definition, unaware they are ignorant—they don't know about the rest of the stuff they are ignorant of. (2) When you have a good idea write it down *immediately.* Otherwise you will only remember that you had a good idea, not what the idea was. (3) I neglected to write this down, but remember I *had* thought of it—hence Law 2. (Jeff Bailey, Thame, Oxon, UK.)

Bailey's Revised Conclusion. We certainly got the evil of two lessers. (Lansing Bailey, letter to *Newsweek,* December 1, 1980. He was alluding to the recent presidential election: "How can we convince the major parties they must never again send us two proven incompetents—a failed president and a grade-B movie actor?" *RS.*)

Baird's Law. Sex, like money, is an inexhaustible commodity. The problem is getting others to part with it. *Corollary 1:* Getting others to part with it is exhausting. *Corollary 2:* The other person will become exhausted second. (J. Stacey Baird, Hanover Park, Illinois.)

Bair's Rule of Lighting. Fuses never blow during daylight hours. *Corollary:* Only after the fuses blow do you discover the flashlight batteries are dead and you're out of candles, or matches, or both. (Penny Bair, Austin, Texas.)

Bakalar's Three Laws of Publishing. (1) Whenever you show an author the cover of his book before publication, he hates it. (2) Whenever an author cites a specific clause of his contract, he cites it incorrectly and the error is in his favor. (3) Whenever anyone in the world of publishing—author, editor, publisher, anyone—says, "It's not the money, it's the principle," it's... well, you know what it is. (Nicholas Bakalar, New York, New York.)

Baker's Byroad. When you are over the hill, you pick up speed. (Unknown origin from Donald R. Woods, Stanford, California.)

Baker's First Law of Federal Geometry. A block grant is a solid mass of money surrounded on all sides by governors. (Ross K. Baker, *American Demographics,* January 1982.)

Baker's Law. Misery no longer loves company. Nowadays it insists on it. (Columnist Russell Baker.)

Baker's Law of Economics. You do not want the one you can afford. (Scott R. Baker, Cleveland, Ohio.)

Baker's Secrets of Losing Politics. (1) Address yourself to the issues. (2) Identify as closely as possible with politicians. (3) Be a loyal party person. (4) Invoke the memories of your party. (5) If you are squeamish about your partisanship, at least have the good grace to refer to the accomplishments of your party's major officeholders. (6) Take the high road. (7) Never criticize your opponent's absenteeism on votes if you are seeking his congressional seat. (8) Never criticize your opponent for spending too much time in the district. (9) Avoid squandering huge amounts of money in media markets where only a fraction of the television audience is made up of your potential voters. (10) Forget about the endorsements of Hollywood celebrities and sports figures. (Ross K. Baker, Professor of Political Science, Rutgers University. First revealed in *The New York Times,* December 5, 1978.)

Baldwin's Cinematic Razor. When reading a script always ask yourself what would it be like to watch this film. Then you ask yourself the second question, "What would it be like to *shoot* this film?" (Alec Baldwin, *Washington Post,* January 10, 2010. He is quoted "You know the script always reads one way when you're tucked into bed with the Manhattan skyline glittering in the distance, you have a nice beverage, everything nice and cozy, you read it and you laugh and you forget the rule.")

Baldy's Law. Some of it plus the rest of it is all of it. (*U;* From the collection of laws assembled by Charles Wolf, Jr., of the RAND Corp.)

Balliew's Laws for Switchboard Operators. (1) The phone rings least when you have nothing else to do. (2) When a person asks to be put on hold, he will not be there when you get back to him, no matter how fast you do it. (3) People who are away from the office get the most calls. (4) Callers give very long messages only when at least two other calls are coming. (5) Employees change extension numbers only if you have just revised the list of extension numbers. (6) Callers who address you by name always call you by the name of the person who worked there before you. (7) Callers give their area code only when it's the same as yours. (8) Callers are least likely to believe someone is out of the office when the person is out of the office. (9) The most persistent callers are the ones with the least important business. .(10) The phone will not ring for the first fifteen minutes of the day unless you're late. If you're late, it will ring continuously until you arrive. (11) Personal calls always come when you are away from your desk or very busy.

(12) Callers will ask for extension numbers instead of names only when the person they want is away from his usual extension. (13) The most important calls always have the worst connections. (14) The call you make the greatest effort to answer will be a wrong number. (William Luther Balliew IV, San Francisco, California.)

Ballweg's Discovery. Whenever there is a flat surface, someone will find something to put on it. (Col. Lawrence H. Ballweg, USAF [retired], Albuquerque, New Mexico.)

Balzer's Law. Life is what happens to you while you are making other plans. (Robert Balzer.)

Banacek's Eighteenth and Nineteenth Polish Proverbs. (18) The hippo has no sting, but the wise man would rather be sat upon by the bee. (19) If the butterfly had the teeth of the tiger, it would never make it out of the hangar. (Television show *Banacek;* from Leslie Nelson, Santa Ana, California.)

Banacek's Law. When the owl shows up at the mouse picnic, he's not there to enter the sack race. (Television character Banacek [George Peppard]; *MLS.*)

Bang!'s Laws. (1) The ability to concentrate on what's being said varies inversely with its importance. (2) Church sermons have an unsettling habit of relating to your questionable behavior of the previous week. (3) The people who cheat at games are the ones who complain the loudest when a clever player exploits an unusual (but perfectly legitimate) strategy to win. (Television critic Derrick Bang! [who added the exclamation point to his name]; *TG.*)

Bank's Law of Misplaced Objects. You always find something in the last place you look for it. (Jim Banks, Bozeman, Montana.)

Bank's Law of Misplaced Objects, Anon's Proof Positive to. Of course. Because once you find it, you stop looking. (Andrew G. Arnofy)

Banks's Revision. If at first you do succeed—try to hide your astonishment. (Harry F. Banks.)

Barach's Rule. An alcoholic is a person who drinks more than his own physician. (originally quoted in Dr. Robert Matz's article, "Principles of Medicine," which appeared in the January 1977 issue of the *New York State Journal of Medicine. U*)

Barbara's Fashion Observation. Permanent press isn't. *Barbara's Law of Exploitation:* You can't be treated like a doormat if you don't lie down. *Barbara's Rules of Bitter Experience:* (1) When you empty a drawer for his clothes and a shelf for his toiletries, the relationship ends. (2) When you finally buy pretty stationery to continue the correspondence, he stops writing. (Barbara K. Mehlman, Great Neck, New York.)

Barber's Laws of Backpacking. (1) The integral of the gravitational potential taken around any loop trail you choose to hike always comes out positive. (2) Any stone in your boot always migrates against the pressure gradient to exactly the point of most pressure. (3) The weight of your pack increases in direct proportion to the amount of food you consume from it. If you run out of food, the pack weight goes on increasing anyway. (4) The number of stones in your boot is directly proportional to the number of hours you have been on the trail. (5) The difficulty of finding any given trail marker is directly proportional to the importance of the consequences of failing to find it. (6) The size of each of the stones in your boot is directly proportional to the number of hours you have been on the trail. (7) The remaining distance to your chosen campsite remains constant as twilight approaches. (8) The net weight of your boots is proportional to the cube of the number of hours you have been on the trail. (9) When you arrive at your campsite, it is full. (10) If you take your boots off, you'll never get them back on again. (11) The local density of mosquitoes is inversely proportional to your remaining repellant. (Milt Barber, formerly a consultant at the Control Data Corp.; *S.T.L.*)

Barber's Rule of Uniformity. If it sticks out, cut it off. (Linda Marsh, barber, Portland, Oregon; from Gary M. Knowlton.)

Barbour's Law of Television. In TV, you have six weeks to make history or be history. (John Barbour, host of the television show *That's Incredible;* from Steve Stine.)

Baribeau's Debunking Proof. People believe in what they want regardless of the facts. (From Mike Baribeau. "I made this one up all by myself so named as such. It was inspired by this live ESP and magic special on TV several years ago. A self-proclaimed psychic claimed that he was stretching out with his powers over the TV broadcast waves into every watching home. He instructed that everyone then look around the room for something out of the ordinary as proof of his powers. Many viewers called in saying their clocks had stopped, etc. He then admitted that he was a retired magician that debunks ESP and that they were attributing the supernatural to ordinary events. Another 'psychic' on the show then claimed that this was only proof that the magician must be psychic and just didn't know it. A few years later on another show the debunker gave a lecture on astrology and handed out to students a description of traits of their astrological signs. Most were *amazed* at the accuracy until he told them he had changed all the signs so that they were actually reading descriptions to the wrong signs. Even with this knowledge many of them were not deterred in their belief in astrology.")

Barilleaux's Observations on Eating Out. (1) The price of the meal varies directly with the accent of the waiter. (2) If you need help to translate the menu, you can't afford the meal. (3) If a salad is served with the meal, the portions will be smaller. (4) If soup is also served with the meal, the portions will be even smaller. (Ryan J. Barilleaux, Lafayette, Louisiana.)

Barker's Law. The future will always surprise you, but you needn't be dumbfounded. (Business futurist Joel Barker, interviewed by Ian Punnett on "Coast to Coast AM," January 16, 2010; *TG*.)

Barker's Proof. Proofreading is more effective *after* publication. (Phil Barker, Selly Park, Birmingham, England.)

Barnes's Industrial Admonition. Dueling with forklifts will be discontinued immediately. (E. E. Barnes, *Design News,* May, 5, 1975.)

Barnes's Law of Probability. There's a 50 percent chance of anything—either it happens or it doesn't. (Michael R. Barnes, Dallas, Texas; *JS*.)

Barnum's Dictum. Every crowd has a silver lining. (P. T. Barnum.)

Baron's Law. The world is divided between victims and predators, and you have to defend yourself against both. (Florenz Baron, Yonkers, New York.)

Barrett's Laws of Driving. (1) You can get *anywhere* in ten minutes if you go fast enough. (2) Speed bumps are of negligible effect when the vehicle exceeds triple the desired restraining speed. (3) The vehicle in front of you is traveling slower than you are. (4) This lane ends in 500 feet. (*U;* from John L. Shelton, President, Sigma Beta Communications, Inc., Dallas, Texas.)

Barr's Comment on Domestic Tranquility. On a beautiful day like this it's hard to believe anyone can be unhappy—but we'll work on it. (Donald Barr, Highland Park, Illinois; *AO*.)

Barrymore's Conclusion. The thing that takes up the most amount of time and causes the most amount of trouble is sex. (John Barrymore.)

Barry's Version of Newton's Law of Gravity. A dropped object will fall with an acceleration of 32 feet per second per second. And if it is your wallet, it will make every effort to land in a public toilet. (Dave Barry in his column of March 16, 1997.)

Bars, Rules for. (1) Never try to pick up a woman who is wearing a Super Bowl ring. (2) Never order a drink where you get to keep the glass. (The first by comedian Garry Shandling, the second by columnist Roger Simon; from Steve Stine.)

Bartel's Law. When someone is kicking your ass, at least you know that you are out in front. (Donald E. Bartel, Palo Alto, California.)

Bartender's Rule. Never drink anything that's still on fire. (Uttered to Roger

Welsch by the bartender of the Golden Nugget Tavern of Cody, Wyoming; "Life Au Naturel," by Roger Welsch, in the March 1992 issue of *Natural History*.)

Barth's Distinction. (See *Benchley's Distinctions*.)

Bartlesville Argument for the Abolition of Foreign Language Classes, The. If English was good enough for Jesus, it's good enough for us. (From Joshua M. Bear of Ankara, Turkey, who points out that this argument was used by a group in Bartlesville, Oklahoma, opposing the teaching of foreign languages in the schools.)

Bartlett's Observation of Input/Output. The problem with pulling names out of a hat is that it is possible that you'll end up with a size. (H. A. Bartlett, East Norwalk, Connecticut.)

Bartol's Observations. (1) If the bottom falls out, you can rest assured that the sides will tumble down on top of you. (2) Whatever kind of sandwich you order, the guy next to you will have one that is bigger and juicier and smells better. (Karen Marie Bartol, Silver Spring, Maryland.)

Bartz's Law of Hokey Horsepuckery. The more ridiculous a belief system, the higher the probability of its success. (Wayne R. Bartz in his article "Keys to Success," *Human Behavior,* May, 1975.)

Baruch's Rule for Determining Old Age. Old age is always fifteen years older than I am. (Bernard M. Baruch.)

Barzun's Laws of Learning. (1) The simple but difficult arts of paying attention, copying accurately, following an argument, detecting an ambiguity or a false inference, testing guesses by summoning up contrary instances, organizing one's time and one's thought for study—all these arts . . . cannot be taught in the air but only through the difficulties of a defined subject; they cannot be taught in one course or one year, but must be acquired gradually in dozens of connections. (2) The analogy to athletics must be pressed until all recognize that in the exercise of intellect, those who lack the muscles, coordination, and will power can claim no place at the training table let alone on the playing field. (Jacques Barzun, from *The House of Intellect,* Harper & Row, 1959. Appeared in Martin's *MB* and a number of subsequent lists, including *S.T.L.,* where it appears in conjunction with *Forthoffer's Cynical Summary of Barzun's Laws*: (1) That which has not yet been taught directly can never be taught directly. (2) If at first you don't succeed, you will never succeed.)

Basham's Law of Debugging Recursive Programs. It's always harder than you expect to debug a recursive program, even after taking *Basham's Law* into account. (*Open Apple* newsletter, February 1986; from Shel Kagan.)

Bastl's Laws. (1) If there are two parts to anything, you will always miss the first part. (2) Through many years of diligence, perseverance, and hard work, one can successfully maintain one's position at the bottom of one's profession. (James F. Bastl, Westchester, Illinois; originally published in the *Chicago Tribune,* November 20, 1983.)

Battista's Explanation. The fellow who says he'll meet you halfway usually thinks he's standing on the dividing line. (O. A. Battista, *Philadelphia Bulletin.*)

Battleson's Blatherskite. Caveats are always* forgotten. **Caveat:* except in rare instances (Kirk Battleson, Oakton, Virginia who amplified in a 2004 letter: "Battleson's Blatherskite may also be applied in the political realm by replacing 'Every technology huckster knows and uses' with 'Every Spin Meister knows and uses.' Either phrase has significant application in the Washington environment.")

Batt's Laws. (1) The piece you pick out of a mixed box of chocolates will always be the kind you can't eat. (2) Once you overcome your fear of public speaking, you'll never be asked to speak again. (3) The long-winded person will always answer your long distance calls. (Al Batt, Hartland, Minnesota.)

Bax's Rule. You should make a point of trying every experience once—except incest and folk dancing. (Arnold Bax; quoted by Nigel Rees in *Quote, Unquote,* George Allen and Unwin, 1978.)

Baxter's First Law. Government intervention in the free market always leads to a lower national standard of living. *Baxter's Second Law:* The adoption of fractional gold reserves in a currency system always leads to depreciation, devaluation, demonetization and, ultimately, to complete destruction of that currency. *Baxter's Third Law:* In a free market good money always drives bad money out of circulation. (Sources unknown to the Murphy Center.)

BB's Group Dynamics Dictum. In a group, the unknowing will try to teach the lesser skilled or knowing; for example, a poor bridge player will coach a new player in bidding even though some of the advice will be wrong. *BB's Poker Theorems.* (1) Poker and sleep do not mix. (2) A poker player always will feel that he/she will get even on the very next hand—two at the most. (Bruce "BB" Brown, Mar Vista, California.)

Beals's Preparedness Principle. Nothing happens unless you're unprepared for it. (Ellen Wade Beals in her *Chicago Tribune* column of August 6, 1982. For example "The boss always wants to see you on the morning you're late," or, "On Saturday night you either have no date at all or you've managed to make two conflicting ones.")

Beardsley's Warning to Lawyers. Beware of and eschew pompous prolixity. (Charles A. Beardsley, the late president of the American Bar Association.)

Bear's Observation on Belaborers of the Obvious. Some people seem to think that the expression is "to make a short story long." (Joshua M. Bear, Ankara, Turkey.)

Beauregard's Law. When you're up to your nose, keep your mouth shut. (Uttered by Henry Fonda in the role of Jack Beauregard in the film *My Name Is Nobody; MLS.*)

Becker's Law. It is much harder to find a job than to keep one. (Jules Becker of Becker and Company, San Francisco, California; *AO.* Becker, who claims that his law permeates industry as well as government, goes on to explain, ". . . once a person has been hired, inertia sets in, and the employer would rather settle for the current employee's incompetence and idiosyncrasies than look for a new employee.")

Beckmann's Lemma. Where there is no patrol car, there is no speed limit. (Petr Beckmann; from Richard Stone, Stanford, California.)

Beck's Political Laws. (1) A politician's gestures increase in direct proportion to the number of his media consultants. (2) Campaign expenses always rise to exceed contributions. (3) In politics, an ounce of image is worth a pound of good ideas. *Corollary:* A good slogan beats a good solution. (4) Flubs get more news coverage than facts. (Joan Beck, *Chicago Tribune,* January 23, 1984; from Steve Stine.)

Bedard's Laws of Fossil Fuel. (1) The last gas station for 50 miles will be closed when you get there. (2) At the moment of any departure, the level of gas in your tank depends entirely on how late you are. (3) You only run out of gas after your wife tells you to stop for gas before you run out. (Patrick Bedard, *Car and Driver* magazine.)

Beebe's Law for Teachers and Preachers. Heads should be weighed, not counted. (Rev. Richard K. Beebe, Litchfield, Connecticut.)

Beichman's Law. Whenever an intellectual says "we" or "our"—as, for example, "we are overfed" or "our guilt,"—and the subsequent sentences are highly derogatory to the pronominal antecedent, the intellectual absolves himself and his immediate audience from any of the psychopathological symptoms he is describing, and, consequently, from any responsibility for what is happening or is about to happen. (Arnold Beichman, *Nine Lies About America,* The Library Press, 1972; from Joseph C. Goulden.)

Beifeld's Principle. The probability of a young man meeting a desirable and receptive young female increases by pyramidical progression when he is already in the company of (1) a date, (2) his wife, (3) a better looking and richer male friend. (Ronald H. Beifeld, Philadelphia attorney; submitted to *AO* with alternative title, *The Law of Inverse Proportion of Social Intercourse.*)

Beiser's Brass Tack. Facts without theory are trivia. Theory without facts is bullshit. (*U/RA.*)

Belcher's Law. Traffic increases to fill the road space available. (J. R. Belcher, London, England.)

Belknap's Fat Flow Formula. Fat is lost last where it is wanted the least. *Corollary 1:* Fat is lost first from areas of high desirability. *Corollary 2:* With time fat flows from areas of high to low desirability. (Hal R. Belknap, M.D., Norman, Oklahoma.)

Belle's Constant. The ratio of time involved in work to time available for work is usually about 0.6. (From a 1977 *JIR* article of the same title by Daniel Mclvor and Oslen Belle, in which it is observed that knowledge of this constant is most useful in planning long-range projects. It is based on such things as an analysis of an eight-hour workday in which only 4.8 hours are actually spent working (or 0.6 of the time available), with the rest being spent on coffee breaks, bathroom visits, resting, walking, fiddling around, and trying to determine what to do next.)

Bell's Law of Frustration. When responding to an urgent message requesting an immediate return call, you will get: (1) a wrong number, (2) a busy signal, or (3) no answer. (Named for Ma and Alexander Graham Bell by Joseph P. Sullivan, Indianapolis, Indiana.)

Bell's Rules. (1) The average time between throwing something away and needing it badly is two weeks. This time can be reduced to one week by retaining the thing for a long time first. (2) Linear objects (such as wire, string, etc.), when left to their own devices, occupy time by twisting themselves into tangles and weaving knots. (3) Tiny objects, when dropped, run and hide. (4) There is an updraft over wastebaskets. (Norman R. Bell, Associate Professor of Engineering, North Carolina State University.)

Benchley's Discovery. It took me fifteen years to discover I had no talent for writing, but I couldn't give it up because by that time I was too famous. *Benchley's Lesson:* A dog teaches a boy fidelity, perseverance, and to turn around three times before lying down. *Benchley's Therapy:* Tell us your phobias and we will tell you what you are afraid of. (Robert Benchley.)

Benchley's Distinctions. (1) There may be said to be two classes of people in the world; those who constantly divide the people of the world into two classes and those who do not. (2) In America there are two classes of travel—first class, and with children. (Robert Benchley. The first is often listed as *Barth's Distinction* [*S.T.L.*, *JE*, etc.], but the Benchley quote is clearly much older.)

Benchley's Law. Anyone can do any amount of work, provided it isn't the work he is supposed to be doing at that moment. (Robert Benchley, from his essay, "How to get things done"; from Charles H. Stats, Oak Park, Illinois.)

Bender's Laws. (1) No two office machines are compatible. (2) In word processing, the worst typos remain invisible until the printout. If the typo also creates an error in fact, it will remain invisible until the letter is in the mail. (Georgia Bender, Kittanning, Pennsylvania.)

Bendiner's Election Rule. No matter how frighteningly the campaigners warn you that the salvation of the world depends on their winning, remember that on November 9, after the election, half of them will be wiring congratulations to the other half on their great victory and promising to co-operate fully in the predicted disaster. (Robert Bendiner, from his article "How To Listen To Campaign Oratory If You Have To," *Look,* October 11, 1960.)

Bennett's Accidental Discoveries. (1) Most auto accidents are caused by people with driver's licenses, so I tore up my license. (2) According to the latest statistics, most auto accidents happen within 8 miles of your own home, so I moved. (William S. Bennett, San Mateo, California.)

Bennett's Beatitudes. (1) Blessed is he who has reached the point of no return and knows it, for he shall enjoy living. (2) Blessed is he who expects no gratitude, for he shall not be disappointed. (W. C. Bennett, Trinity Avenue Presbyterian Church, Durham, North Carolina.)

Bennett's Laws of Horticulture. (1) Houses are for people to live in. (2) Gardens are for plants to live in. (3) There is no such thing as a houseplant. *Bennett's Law of the Do-It-Yourself Movement:* Every job you tackle turns out to be seven times more bloody awkward than it ought to be. (H. Bennett, West Midlands, England.)

Ben's Highway Rule. If you see one Army truck, you'll see a hundred more. (Six-year-old Ben Brown, Chicago, Illinois.)

Bentov's Law. One's level of ignorance increases exponentially with accumulated knowledge. For example, when one acquires a bit of new information, there are many new questions that are generated by it, and each new piece of information breeds five or ten new questions. These questions pile up at a much faster rate than does the accumulated information. The more one knows, therefore, the greater his level of ignorance. (Itsahak Bentov, *Stalking the Wild Pendulum,* E.P. Dutton, 1977; from Neal Wilgus.)

Berger's Economics for the Masses. The more there are of anything, the less they cost. Exclusivity has its price. (Martin Berger, Mount Vernon, New York.)

Berg's Constant. Every time you learn a new word, you hear it five times the next day. (Stephanie Berg, *Johns Hopkins Magazine,* May 1978.)

Berkeley Beatitude. The real world is just a special case of the theoretical. (Don Smith, MBA, University of California, Berkeley.)

Berkeley's Laws. (1) The world is more complicated than most of our theories make it out to be. (2) Ignorance is no excuse. (3) Never decide to buy something while listening to the salesman. (4) Most problems have either many answers or no answer. Only a few problems have a single answer. (5) Most general statements are false, including this one. (6) An exception TESTS a rule; it never PROVES it. (7) The moment you have worked out an answer, start checking it—it probably isn't right. (8) If there is an opportunity to make a mistake, sooner or later the mistake will be made. (9) Check the answer you have worked out once more—before you tell it to anybody. (Edmund C. Berkeley, "common sense" researcher and former editor of *Computers and Automation.* This is a mere sampling of Berkeley's to-the-point statements. They come from his article "Right Answers—A Short Guide for Obtaining Them," which appeared in the September 1969 issue of *Computers and Automation.*)

Berla's Version. If you file it, you'll never need it. If you need it, you never file it. (Michael Berla, Columbia, Maryland.)

Berliner's Law of Mineral Propagation. Wire coat hangers multiply in dark closets. (The late Josephine Mitchell Berliner, Washington, D.C.; from her daughter Joie Vargas, Reno, Nevada.)

Bernstein's Book Principles. *Set I. Acquisition by Purchase:* (1) If you buy a hardcover edition of a book, the paperback edition will appear next week, at a much lower price. (2) If you buy a paperback edition of a book, the hardcover will be remaindered next week, at a much lower price. (3) If you buy a paperback edition, or a hardcover edition, or a remaindered copy of a book, the next week you will find that a copy in excellent condition will be available in a used-book shop—at a much lower price than any of the other three. (4) If you buy a used hardcover copy of a book, a new edition that will make all previous editions obsolete will appear in hardcover next week. (5) A publisher will allow a book to go out of print just in time for you to begin looking for it.... *Set II. Borrowing from a Library:* (1) If you go to the library for a book, the library will probably not have it in its collection. (2) If it does have the book in its collection, it will be checked out, or overdue, or lost, or stolen. (3) If it does have the book at hand, the pages you need to consult will be torn out. (4) If the book is available, at hand, and undamaged, it will probably be outdated and therefore useless. (5) If the book is available, at hand, undamaged, and current, it will probably be too useful to be used effectively in the library away from your other materials, and it will not be in the circulating collection.... (Richard B. Bernstein, *Harvard Law Record,* Cambridge, Massachusetts; from his larger collection of Book Principles.)

Bernstein's Law. A falling body always rolls to the most inaccessible spot. (Theodore M. Bernstein; from *The Careful Writer,* Atheneum, 1965. See *Anthony's Law of the Workshop.*)

Bernstein's Law of Declining Progress. One begins to lose interest in any given task and slacks off just as one is beginning to get somewhere in accomplishing that task. (Richard B. Bernstein.)

Bernstein's Laws for Presenting Science to a Lay Audience. (1) Do not try to make things more visual than they are. (2) Do not speak more clearly than you think. (3) Don't overplay your hand. (Jeremy Bernstein, in commenting on Public Broadcasting Service TV science shows in *Natural History,* February 1986; from Steve Stine.)

Bernstein's Principle of Homogeneity. Behavior and personality traits are relatively constant even in very different situations and relationships. *Corollary 1:* You can't be one kind of person and another kind of president. *Corollary 2:* You can't be a wonderful friend and an abusive parent. *Corollary 3:* Someone who treats a relative fairly will do the same with a stranger. (Barbara Bernstein, Bowie, Maryland.)

Berra's Law. You can observe a lot just by watching. (Yogi Berra; *RS.*)

Berra's Rule of Attendance. If people don't want to come out to the park, nobody's going to stop them. (Yogi Berra; from Steven D. Mirsky, Ithaca, New York.)

Berton's Party Laws. *Children's Birthday Parties:* (1) Any birthday party of more than seven male children under the age of eleven will inevitably end in a fight. (2) Any child's birthday party in which the number of guests exceeds the number of the actual age of the child for whom the party is being given will end in disaster. *Adults at Parties:* (1) If a party is scheduled to run from 4 to 7 p.m., then that party will run from 5:30 to 10 p.m. (2) If twenty-two people are invited to a party commencing at 9 p.m., one person will invariably turn up at 9 p.m. (3) At any party lasting more than three hours and twenty-two minutes, at least one woman will be crying. (4) At any party catering to more than ten people, at least two glasses will be broken. (5) At any party catering to more than seventeen people, at least four glasses will be broken. (6) At any afternoon party in which the guests stay until after midnight, all glasses will be broken. (7) A wife who has had two drinks on being offered a third will decline it. She will then drink half of her husband's drink. She will then change her mind and say that she would like a third drink. Her husband will drink this drink. (8) Exactly fourteen minutes and seventeen seconds after the host announces that there is nothing more to drink, all guests will leave, no matter what the hour is. (Pierre Berton; from his book *My War With the 20th Century,* Doubleday, 1965.)

Berson's Corollary of Inverse Distances. The farther away from the entrance of the market (theater, or any other given location) that you have to park, the closer the space vacated by the car that pulls away as you walk up to the door. (Judith deMille Berson, Silver Spring, Maryland.)

Beshere's Formula for Failure. There are only two kinds of people who fail: those who listen to nobody, and...those who listen to everybody. (Thomas M. Beshere, Jr., Charleston, South Carolina.)

Beste's Law Librarian's Rules. (1) Lawyers don't read law books, they stack them. Once the stack is full enough, the research memo is written. (2) You will receive at least ten advertisements from any publisher for a book you would never, ever need to buy. (3) The attorneys most likely to bombard you with handwritten notes to buy a particular book or reporting service are partners who haven't set foot in the firm library in ten years. (4) The attorney who calls to ask you to find a "vitally important" article will never remember the title, author or date it was published, but that he needs it by 5:00 p.m. today. (5) If you can't find a book, look for it by the copy machine. (6) The attorney who raises hell about a missing book will have at least six in his office he didn't bother checking out. (7) The books on contracts, small claims court, and do-it-yourself divorce are always missing. (Ian R. Beste, Montrose, California.)

Beste's "Rose by Any Other Name" Principle. The more the name of a product promises, the less it delivers. For example, cheap stereo equipment often has the word "super" in its name, while the best equipment is usually named like a consulting firm. (Ian Beste, Berkeley, California.)

Bethell's Iron Law of Washington. The laws of supply and demand do not apply to Washington—they are turned inside out. Problems elsewhere in the country merely contribute to the wealth of Washington. (Tom Bethell in *Harper's* magazine.)

Beton's Discovery. Expressways aren't. (John A. Beton, Chicago, Illinois.)

Bettman's Revision. History does not repeat itself; historians simply repeat each other. (Otto Bettman, *The New York Times,* October 18, 1981; from Shel Kagan.)

Beville's Rule of Secrecy in Business. Secrecy is the enemy of efficiency, but don't let anyone know it. (Richard Beville, London, England.)

Bialac's Conclusion. Statistics are no substitute for common sense. (Richard N. Bialac, Cincinnati, Ohio.)

Bianculli's Fourth, Seventh, and Tenth Laws of TV. *Fourth:* All TV heroes can find parking spaces whenever and wherever they need them. *Seventh:* Any motor-driven vehicle that becomes temporarily airborne is required to fly, and land, in slow motion. *Tenth:* Few people on TV have TV sets in their living rooms, and almost no one on TV watches TV. (David Bianculli, Knight-Ridder Newspaper television column, January 3, 1986.)

Bicycle Law. All bicycles weigh 50 pounds: A 30-pound bicycle needs a 20-pound lock and chain. A 40-pound bicycle needs a 10-pound lock and chain. A 50-pound bicycle needs no lock and chain. (*S.T.L.*)

Bicycling, First Law of. No matter which way you ride, it's uphill and against the wind. (*S.T.L.*)

Biczynski's Quantification of Parental Fatigue. The amount of the work is the square of the number of children. (Patricia Biczynski, Dallas, Texas. She explained in a 1988 letter to the Murphy Center: "This law came to me, as through a Socratic leap of understanding, in the midst of a Connecticut snow storm, as my four little children [16 times the work] rotated in and out of the house, while I, like a perpetual motion machine, was engaged in putting on and pulling off four sets of boots, mittens, hats, snowsuits, while simultaneously running them into and out of the bathroom and mopping up the muddy puddles of melted snow. It has comforted me with understanding in the ensuing years.)"

Bierman's Law of Contracts. (1) In any given document, you can't cover all the "what ifs." (2) Lawyers stay in business resolving all the unresolved "what ifs." (3) Every resolved "what if" creates two unresolved "what ifs." (Melvin Bierman, APO, Miami, Florida.)

Big Mac Principle, The. The whole is equal to more than the sum of its parts. The whole is equal to less than the sum of its parts. (Robert J. Samuelson, *The National Journal,* August 12, 1978. This apparently contradictory principle bears some explanation. In Samuelson's own words, "Anyone can understand the relationship of these truths to the real-life Big Mac. A Big Mac, of course, is 'two all-beef patties, special sauce, lettuce, cheese, pickles, onion on a sesame seed bun.' Depending on your taste, these few ingredients produce one of the magnificent gastronomical delights of American civilization [*the whole is equal to more than the sum of its parts*] or an insult to the sensitive stomach [*the whole is equal to less than the sum of its parts*]." He says that the principle explains a lot about what is going on in Washington as things fall on one side or the other of the more-than/less-than scale. It explains, for instance, why as Congress becomes harder working and better educated, it falls in public esteem and contributes to the general creakiness of government. Congress then is equal to less than the sum of its parts.)

Bilbo's Proverb. Never laugh at live dragons. (The character Bilbo Baggins in J. R. R. Tolkien's *The Hobbit.*)

Bill Babcock's Law. If it can be borrowed and it can be broken, you will borrow it and you will break it. (W. W. Chandler, Lyons, Kansas; *AO.*)

Billings Phenomenon. The conclusions of most good operations research studies are obvious. (Robert E. Machol, from "Principles of Operations Research"; *POR.* The name refers to a well-known Billings story in which a farmer becomes concerned that his black horses are eating a lot more than his white horses. He does a detailed study of the situation and finds that he has more black horses than white horses. Machol points out that the obvious conclusions are not likely to be obvious *a priori* but obvious after the results are in. In other words, good research does not have to yield dramatic findings.)

Billings's Advice (a smattering). (1) Don't ever prophesy; for if you prophesy wrong, nobody will forget it; and if you prophesy right, nobody will remember it. (2) Never work before breakfast; if you have to work before breakfast, get your breakfast first. (3) There are two things in this life for which we are never fully prepared and that is—twins. (4) I don't care how much a man talks, if he only says it in a few words. *Billings's Law.* Live within your income, even if you have to borrow to do so. *Billings's Realization.* Life consists not in holding good cards, but in playing those we do hold well. (19th-century American humorist Josh Billings.)

Bill's Briefing on Annoying Events. One time is an accident. Two times is a coincidence. Three times is an enemy action. (Anonymous; from Aden Wilson, San Francisco, California.)

Bing's Rule of Oblique Logic. Don't try to stem the tide; move the beach. (Wallace Bing, Mill Valley, California.)

Bishop's Basketball Rule. If the player isn't sure of making a free throw, do not have him make the sign of the cross. (*U;* from a Frank Deford article in *Sports Illustrated* from Mel Loftus.)

Bishop's Definition. Tact is the art of telling someone to lose thirty pounds without ever using the word "fat." (Betty Bishop, Chester, California.)

Bishop's Law. The less you know about an opportunity, the more attractive it is. (*U;* from Sidney Gross, Seattle, Washington.)

Bishop's Query. If "sense" is so common, how come we don't see more of it around? (C. B. "Cleve" Bishop, Littleton, Colorado.)

Bishop's Theorem. When you have accumulated sufficient knowledge to get by, you're too old to remember it. (Columnist Jim Bishop.)

Bismarck's Laws. (1) The less people know about how sausages and laws are made, the better they'll sleep at night. (2) When you say that you agree to a thing in principle, you mean that you have not the slightest intention of carrying it out in practice. (Otto von Bismarck.)

Bixby's Law of Theater Seating. In any given row, the people with seats on the aisle always arrive first. *Corollary:* The probability that someone in the middle of the row will leave during the performance is directly proportional to the number of persons to be climbed over in reaching the aisle. (Sandra W. Bixby, Chicago, Illinois.)

Blaauw's Law. Established technology tends to persist in the face of new technology. (Gerrit A. Blaauw, one of the designers of IBM's System/360; *JE.*)

Black's Discovery. He who laughs first, laughs last... if nobody laughs in the middle. (Barney C. Black, Alexandria, Virginia, who discovered this on a bathroom wall in 1966.)

Blackstock's Observation in Counterpoint to The David by Michelan-

gelo. In most circumstances, the human body is sufficiently imperfect in design and function that, after age 10, it should not be disclosed naked, except after having firmly established a strong personal relationship with the observer. (James F. Blackstock, Brentwood, Tennessee.)

Blackwell's Impossibilities. (1) You cannot tighten one shoelace without tightening the other one. (2) A true gardener cannot pull just one weed. (Alexander W. Blackwell, Pebble Beach, California.)

Blake's Lament. If I'd known I was gonna live this long, I'd have taken better care of myself. (Jazzman Eubie Blake on his 100th birthday, February 1983.)

Blake's Law. Anything that can change, is changing. (Kathleen Blake, Dallas, Texas; from F. D. McSpiritt.)

Blanchard's Newspaper Obituary Law. If you want your name spelled wrong, die. (Al Blanchard, Washington bureau chief for the *Detroit News; AO.*)

Blattenberger's Marital Principle. Marriages are like union contracts in that six weeks after the fact, both parties feel that they could have done better if they had held out a little longer. (Larry A. Blattenberger, Martinsburg, Pennsylvania.)

Blay's Discovery. Long-playing recordings scratch, pop, click, wobble, and warp in direct proportion to the value placed on them by their owner. Hated recordings have built-in damage inhibitors that only self-destruct when the record is passed on to a loving recipient. (Robert E. Blay, Rutland, Vermont.)

Blewett's Rules for Dealing with Difficult Personalities. (1) Identify the bears. (2) Tree the bears. (3) Stroke the bears. (4) Never forget how many bears you've treed. (5) Never let on to the bears who the other bears are. For that matter, never let any of the other creatures in the forest know who the bears are. (Lt. Col. John H. Blewett, U.S. Army.)

Blick's Rule of Life. You have two chances, slim and none. (*U;* from J. Patricia Reilly, New York, New York.)

Bloom's Law of Chocoholism. Anything tastes better if it's made with chocolate. (Judith Ilene Bloom, Los Angeles, California.)

Bloom's Law of the Profitable Inertia of Gold. Certain things shouldn't be moved. (Writer Murray Teigh Bloom, who first reported his discovery in his first book, *Money of Their Own,* Scribners, 1957. As he explained in a recent letter, "Once the Philadelphia Mint experimented and found $5.00 was lost by abrasion every time a million dollars worth of gold coin was handled. Just lifting the bags—each filled with $5,000 worth of gold coin—to the truck resulted in a $5.00 loss; transferring them back to the mint caused another $5.00 loss. Letting the stuff rest quietly at Fort Knox instead of moving it around nervously to Sub-Treasuries makes us richer.")

Bloom's Seventh Law of Litigation. The judge's jokes are always funny. *Bloom's Theorem of Reduced Expectations.* Less is less. (Judith Ilene Bloom.)

Blount's Law of Bluffing. You can never appear to be cleverer than you are if you never fake anything. (Roy Blount, Jr., quoted in the *Atlantic Monthly,* September 1984; from Steve Stine.)

Blumenthal's Observation on Government. The difference between business and government is that the government has no bottom line. (Secretary of the Treasury W. Michael Blumenthal; *TCA.*)

Blutarsky's Axiom. Nothing is impossible for the man who will not listen to reason. (The character Blutarsky, played by John Belushi in the 1978 movie *Animal House.*)

Boatman's Law. Common sense is exceeded only by the ability to recognize it. (Earl Boatman, Rockford, Tennessee.)

Bobbitt's Law of TV. Television network trouble never occurs except during the most exciting part of your favorite TV show. (Larry D. Bobbitt, Amarillo, Texas.)

Bob's Rule of Grammar. Double negatives are a *no-no.* (Bob Johnston, Richmond Hill, Ontario, Canada.)

Bodine's Law. In self-service stores, one usually has a fool for a clerk. (Walt Bodine, "The Walt Bodine Show," November 9, 1979.)

Boehm's Entropic Addendum. Matter cannot be created or destroyed, nor can it be returned without a receipt. (John Michael Boehm, *The New York Times.*)

Boettcher's Attribution. If you have a bunch of clowns, you're going to have a circus. (R. J. Boettcher, Bridgewater, New Jersey, Letters to the Editor, *Time,* March 19, 1979. Boettcher attributes the maxim to the late W. L. Gilman.)

Bogart's Rule. When a dog bites a man, that is not news. But if a man bites a dog...that is news. (John B. Bogart, city editor of the *New York Sun,* attributed to him in Frank M. O'Brien's *The Story of the Sun,* George H. Doran, 1918. The original quote contains the words "because it happens so often" after dog bites man.)

Bok's Law. If you think education is expensive, try ignorance. (Derek Bok, president, Harvard University; quoted by Ann Landers in her column for March 26, 1978.)

Bokum's Advice. You can't be happy with a woman who pronounces both d's in Wednesday. ("Dog" Bokum, from Bob Specht's *Expectation of Days,* 1982. Bokum is a character in Peter De Vries's *Sauce for the Goose,* Little, Brown, 1981.)

Boling's Postulate. If you're feeling good, don't worry. You'll get over it. (Source unknown to the Murphy Center.)

Boliska's Realization. Do you realize that if it weren't for Edison, we'd be watching TV by candlelight? (Ed Boliska, quoted in Jack Smith's column, *Los Angeles Times,* February 11, 1981; *RS.*)

Boller's Law of Compression of Matter. If you shove hard enough, it WILL fit. (Diana Johnston Chandler, Arizona.)

Bolten's Law of Ascending Budgets. Under current practices, both expenditures and revenues rise to meet each other, no matter which one may be in excess. (Joe Bolten, Fellow of the RAND Graduate Institute; *RS.*)

Bombeck's Law. The more absurd the item, the more likely you are to need it the day after you throw it away. (Erma Bombeck, *Chicago Sun-Times,* January 7, 1987; from Steve Stine.)

Bombeck's Principles. (1) Any college that would take your son, he should be too proud to go to. (2) Know that a happy dieter has other problems. (3) A man who checks out of the express lane with seven items is the same man who will wear Supp-Hose and park in the Reserved for Handicapped spaces. (4) An old car that has served you so well will continue to serve you until you have just put four new tires under it and then will fall apart. (5) A pregnancy will never occur when you have a low-paying job which you hate. (6) An ugly carpet will last forever. (Erma Bombeck, from her column of January 10, 1978.)

Bombeck's Rule of Medicine. Never go to a doctor whose office plants have died. (Erma Bombeck.)

Bonafede's Revelation. The conventional wisdom is that power is an aphrodisiac. In truth, it's exhausting. (Dom Bonafede in a February 1977, article in the *Washingtonian* entitled "Surviving in Washington.")

Bone's Labor Discovery. Unlimited manpower can solve any problem except what to do with the manpower; e.g. if a man can dig a hole in a minute, why can't sixty men dig a hole in one second? (Jonathan Bone, Chicago, Illinois.)

Bonham's Educational Proposal. Deans of education schools should insist that no doctoral candidate be allowed to get by without presenting a dissertation that can be read and understood by the first ten intelligent passersby at the school's front door. (George W. Bonham, *Change,* April 1978; *RS.*)

Booker's Law. An ounce of application is worth a ton of abstraction. (*U/S.T.L.*)

Boorstin's Observation. Two centuries ago, when a great man appeared, people looked for God's purpose in him; today we look for his press agent. (Daniel J. Boorstin; from *The Image; Or, What Happened to the American Dream,* Athenaeum, 1962)

Boozer's Revision. A bird in the hand is dead. (Rhonda Boozer, an elementary school pupil from Baltimore, Maryland. This was produced when a teacher gave fourth and fifth graders the first half of an old adage and asked them to supply the second half. Other results of the adage improvement project according to an Associated Press report: "Don't put all your eggs in your pocket." [Celestine Clark.] "Don't bite the hand that has your allowance in it." [Lisa Tidier.] "If at first you don't succeed, blame it on the teacher." [Stacey Bass.])

Boquist's Exception. If for every rule there is an exception, then we have established that there is an exception to every rule. If we accept "For every rule there is an exception" as a rule, then we must concede that there may not be an exception after all, since the rule states that there is always the possibility of exception, and if we follow it to its logical end, we must agree that there can be an exception to the rule that for every rule there is an exception. (Bill Boquist, San Francisco, California; *HW.*)

Boren's Law. Nothing is impossible until it is sent to a committee. *Boren's Laws of the Bureaucracy.* (1) When in doubt, mumble. (2) When in trouble, delegate. (3) When in charge, ponder. (James H. Boren, founder, president, and chairperson of the board of the International Association of Professional Bureaucrats [INATAPROBU]. *Boren's Law* is from *The Bureaucratic Zoo*, APM, 1976.)

Boren's Presidential Motto. I've got what it takes to take what you've got. (Humorist James Boren's 1984 presidential platform.)

Borklund's Law. Communications is equal to the square root of the mistakes times confusion times contradictions. (C. W. Borklund; from a November 1966 editorial in *Armed Forces Management* magazine.)

Borkon's Rule. The farther a seat is from the aisle in a theater or concert hall, the later the patron arrives. (Bernard B. Borkon, D.M.D., San Francisco, California.)

Borkowski's Law. You can't guard against the arbitrary. (*U/JC.*)

Born Loser's Sixty-seventh Law. Ask some people what time it is, and they'll tell you how to make a watch. (*Born Loser* comic strip, December 15, 1985; *TG.*)

Boroson's Conclusion. There is always a professor of astronomy at a major Ivy League university who believes that the world is flat. (Warren Boroson.)

Borstelmann's Rule. If everything seems to be coming your way, you're probably in the wrong lane. (*U/DRW.*)

Boston's Discovery. Cash flow is an oxymoron. (Bruce O. Boston, Fairfax, Virginia.)

Boston's Irreversible Law of Clutter. In any household, junk accumulates to fill the space available for its storage. (Bruce O. Boston, Fairfax, Virginia.)

Boswell's MPG Rule. Nothing gives a used car more miles per gallon than the salesman. (Billy Boswell of Gaithersburg, Maryland; quoted in Bob Levey's column, *Washington Post,* November 7, 1985.)

Boucher's Corollary to Murphy's Law. Murphy's Law holds no more than 80 percent of the time; unfortunately, it is impossible to predict when. (Wayne Boucher; from his article "A Practical Guide for Perplexed Managers," *MBA Magazine,* August/September 1978.)

Boucher's Observations. (1) He who blows his own horn always plays the music several octaves higher than originally written. (2) You can't have the ocean except at sea level. (Sharon Boucher, Placerville, California.)

Boultbee's Criterion. If the converse of a statement is absurd, the original statement is an insult to the intelligence and should never have been said. (Arthur H. Boultbee, Greenwich, Connecticut; *AO.* The author adds, "It is best applied to statements of politicians and TV pundits.")

Bowers's Law. Hubris always boomerangs. (Dr. John Bowers; from Jo Rozanski, Normal, Illinois.)

Bowie's Theorem. If an experiment works, you must be using the wrong equipment. (*U/RS.*)

Boxmeyll's First Law of Nicknames. If it fits, it sticks. (Don Boxmeyll, *Washington Post,* January 3, 1980.)

Boyd's Criteria for Good County Fairs. (1) A really good fair must have enormous traffic jams and lousy parking. (2) Good carnivals must have plenty of overpriced junk food. (3) Good fairs must have nauseating rides. (4) Top-drawer fairs must have ridiculous come-ons. (5) Good country fairs must have a "serious" side to them. (6) A four-star carnival must have plenty of "toughs" around. (7) An excellent fair must separate you from your money faster than OPEC and the IRS combined. (Ronald Wray Boyd, in his review of the Pinellas County Fair for the *St. Petersburg Times,* March 14, 1979. This article also contains Boyd's tips on fair etiquette, offering such timeless bits of advice as, "Don't ask for four cheese dogs, six large Pepsis, three caramel apples and then try to charge it on your Carte Blanche card," and "Don't feel as though you should tip 'The Slime Man.' ")

Boyd's Managerial Survival Law #1. When faced with a crisis, take the inevitable and turn it around to make it look like a conscious decision. (Richard D. Boyd, Ukiah, California.)

Boyle's Laws. (1) The first pull on the cord will always send the drapes the wrong way. (2) Your career will unfold as a series of miscalculations, not all yours. (3) There are people you cannot trust with your money; so with your emotions. (4) Your future will depend on having the courage of your miscalculations. (5) If they discover your standards, they will use them against you. (6) If you gain the doctorate, you will lose your first name. (7) Today's disaster is tomorrow's archaeology. (8) It is possible to make the right mistake. (9) Anything sore will be bumped more often. (10) No one will grow who is not stretched. (11) Every life is a solo flight. (12) The ears have walls. (13) Fate will do all possible to put you into publicly embarrassing situations. (14) The success of any venture will be helped by prayer, even in the wrong denomination. (15) When things are going well, someone will inevitably experiment detrimentally. (16) The deficiency will never show itself during the dry runs. (17) Information travels more surely to those with a lesser need to know. (18) An original idea can never emerge from committee in the original. (19) When the product is destined to fail, the delivery system will perform perfectly. (20) The crucial memorandum will be snared in the out-basket by the paper clip of the overlying correspondence and go to file. (21a) Success can be insured only by devising a defense against failure of the contingency plan. (21b) Success in a skill will be interpreted as management ability, causing disastrous promotions. (22) Performance is directly affected by the perversity of inanimate objects. (23) If not controlled, work will flow to the competent man until he submerges. (24) The lagging activity in a project will invariably be found in the area where the highest overtime rates lie waiting. (25) Talent in staff work or sales will recurringly be interpreted as managerial ability. (26) The "think positive" leader tends to listen to his subordinates' premonitions only during the postmortems. (27) Clearly stated instructions will consistently produce multiple interpretations. (28) On successive charts of the same organization, the number of boxes will never decrease. (29) A child being dressed will insert the opposite limb. (30) Intent and result seldom match. (31) Handwriting refutes the rule of practice makes perfect. (32) Almost every flat surface will become a shelf. (33) The past is prologue, if it's not too far past. (34) A not-knotted rope not watched will knot. (35) Progress will lag in areas where the highest overtime rates lie waiting. (36) Even a bad example can be a good example. (37) Along most dotted lines, perforations will prove stronger than the paper. (38) In the dictionary or the phone book you will repeatedly straddle the needed page. (39) A trailing line will always snag. (Charles P. Boyle, Annapolis, Maryland, Goddard Space Flight Center, NASA.)

Brabender's Law. The most inactive player during the World Series will be the most active during the clubhouse follies. (Named for Gene Brabender of the Baltimore Orioles, who first demonstrated the law in the 1966 World Series; by George Vecsey of *The New York Times,* who noted that Brabender never got off the bullpen bench during the four game sweep of the Los Angeles Dodgers but "went nuts" spraying fellow players, writers, and innocent bystanders with champagne. Vecsey discussed the law in his column October 18, 1983.)

Bracken's First Law of Thermodynamics. The more thermal the weather gets, the less dynamic you feel. (Peg Bracken in *Family Circle.*)

Bradford's Law. Remembering to remember is a constant reminder to not forget. (Darlene B. Martinez, R.N.)

Bradley's Reminder. Everything comes to him who waits—among other things, death. (English writer Francis H. Bradley; *ME.*)

Brady's First Law of Problem Solving. When confronted by a seemingly difficult problem, it is more easily solved by reducing it to the question, "How would the Lone Ranger have handled this?" (Karyn Brady, Phoenix, Arizona.)

Brady's Law of Reporting. Sources always return phone calls as you're leaving the office for home. (The late Dave Brady, sportswriter for the *Washington Post;* quoted shortly after his death by Ken Denlinger, April 12, 1988; *JCG.*)

Branch's First Law of Crisis. The spirit of public service will rise, and the bureaucracy will multiply itself much faster, in time of grave national concern. (Taylor Branch, from his March 1974 article in *Harper's* entitled "The Sunny Side of the Energy Crisis.")

Brandstadt's Dilemma. It's very difficult to cope if you haven't anything to cope with. (Wayne Brandstadt, Chicago, Illinois.)

Brattman's Rules. *Unpleasant Physical Work:* When coworkers want to prove that they are macho, let them. It's better than doing the work yourself. *Used Textbooks:* Only use the underlinings of an A student. *Elementary School Fights:* The one who tells the teacher first is generally believed. Be first. *Periodicals:* Magazines always come in faster than you can read them. *Hobby Spending:* After you have purchased the most expensive piece of equipment your hobby requires, you will soon tire of the whole thing. (Steven Ronald Brattman, Los Angeles, California.)

Brauer's Warning. He who tries to pick all the flowers is sure to get some poison ivy. (David F. Brauer, Orlando, Florida.)

Brecht's Hierarchy of Needs. Grub first, then ethics. (Bertolt Brecht; *RS.*)

Brecht's Reminder. As a grown man you should know better than to go around advising people. (Bertolt Brecht; from Bernard L. Albert.)

Breider's Rules. (1) Inertia has its own momentum. (2) Bodies age, emotions don't. (3) Bad weather lasts; good weather doesn't. (4) An idea that doesn't work is not creative. (Alice Breider, Madison, Wisconsin.)

Bremner's Qualification. You must have a dirty mind to be a successful copy editor. (Journalism professor John B. Bremner; quoted in the *Wall Street Journal,* along with some examples of headlines that passed clean-minded copy editors: "Textron Inc. Makes Offer to Screw Co. Stockholders" and "Uranus Rings Gaseous.")

Brennan's Laws. (1) *Pay Expectancy:* Everyone wants to be paid exactly what they are worth, as long as it is more than they are making. (2) *2nd Law of Consulting:*

When management concludes that someone from the outside is always smarter than an employee, they are telling their employees that no one with any brains could be expected to work here. (E. James Brennan, Chesterfield, Missouri.)

Brenner's Location Is Everything Rule. If you want to run with the big dogs, you've got to go potty in the tall grass. (Television sports anchor Glenn Brenner, Washington, D.C., quoted in the *Washington Post,* March 15, 1986.)

Brenne's Laws of Life. (1) You never get it where you want it. (2) If you think it's tough now, just wait. (From Carol Pike, Mesa, Arizona, who heard them from her father at least once a week during her formative years. She says, "These laws can be applied to anything.")

Breslin's Rule. Don't trust a brilliant idea unless it survives the hangover. (Jimmy Breslin, on the television show *Saturday Night Live,* May 18, 1986.)

Bressler's Law. There is no crisis to which academics will not respond with a seminar. (Professor Marvin Bressler of Princeton University; from Arnold Brown, New York, New York.)

Brewster's Exception. Every rule has its exceptions except this one: A man must always be present when he is being shaved. (Eugene V. Brewster, from his 1925 work *The Wisdom of the Ages.*)

Brewster's Observation on Chicken. No other meat looks so much like what it used to. (Christopher R. Brewster, Alexandria, Virginia.)

Brian's Law. The longer you wait to write a thank-you note, the longer it must be. (*U;* from Jean Pike, Modesto, California.)

Bribery, Mathematical Formula for. OG = PLR [[times]] AEB: The opportunity for graft equals the plethora of legal requirements multiplied by the number of architects, engineers, and builders. (Harold Birns, New York Buildings Commissioner, on the confusion of housing and building laws, *The New York Times,* October 2, 1963.)

Bridge, First Law of. It's always the partner's fault. (*S.T.L.*)

Brien's First Law. At some time in the life cycle of virtually every organization, its ability to succeed in spite of itself runs out. (Richard H. Brien, "The Managerialization of Higher Education," from *Educational Record,* Summer 1970. Appears in *MB, S.T.L.,* etc.)

Briggs's Physics. A spilled drink flows in the direction of the most expensive object. *Briggs's Inevitabilities.* (1) There is no such thing as a flattering snapshot of oneself. (2) A pimple will attract more attention at a party than a facelift. (3) If the alarm really doesn't go off, it is still a fake-sounding excuse for being late to work. (4) If it's not on the shelf, then there is none in the back of the store either. (5) If the doctor (or dentist) says the procedure will produce "a little discomfort," it will hurt like medieval torture. (Judye Briggs, Dallas, Texas.)

Briggs's Restaurant Rule. The seafood is always fresh, even in Arizona. (Thomas E. Briggs, Jacksonville, Florida.)

Broadersen's Never, Never Land. (1) Never shake hands with a man holding a chainsaw. (2) Never try to put on a pullover while eating a caramel apple. (3) Never kiss the hand of a lady after she's been to the self-service gas station. (4) Never try to adjust your clothing in a crowded elevator. (5) Never use a felt-tipped marker to clean your ears. (6) Never ask the highway commissioner if he plays bridge. (7) Never wave to your friends at an auction. (William E. Broadersen, Northfield, Minnesota.)

Brock's Advice. Always wear well-made, good-fitting, expensive shoes and keep them clean, no matter how poor you are. (D. R. Brock, Dayton, Ohio.)

Broder's Law. Anybody that wants the presidency so much that he'll spend two years organizing and campaigning for it is not to be trusted with the office. (David S. Broder in *Washington Post,* July 19, 1973; *JW.*) *Broder's Warning.* When "everybody" in the nation's capital agrees on something, it is prudent to be skeptical. (David S. Broder, in his *Washington Post* column, May 22, 1988.)

Brodie's Law of the Consumption of Canapés. As many as are served will be eaten...if left long enough. (Robert N. Brodie, New York, New York, who points out, "This law applies equally to social and business affairs but operates with special force at new office openings and functions where it is understood that the food costs no individual money.")

Brogan's Constant. People tend to congregate in the back of the church and the front of the bus. (John C. Brogan, Merion, Pennsylvania.)

Brogan's Rules. (1) When in doubt, blame the schools. (2) Also blame the press. (Patrick Brogan, Washington correspondent of the *Times* [London] in a January 14, 1979, article for the *Washington Post.*)

Broken Mirror Law. Everyone breaks more than the seven-year-bad-luck allotment to cover rotten luck throughout an entire lifetime. (Rozanne Weissman.)

Bronfman's Rule. To turn $100 into $110 is work. To turn $100 million into $110 million is inevitable. (Edgar Bronfman, chairman, Seagram Company, quoted in *Newsweek,* December 2, 1985.)

Brontosaurus Principle. Organizations can grow faster than their brains can manage them in relation to their environment and to their own physiology: when this occurs, they are an endangered species. (Thomas K. Connellan, from his 1976 book *The Brontosaurus Principle: A Manual for Corporate Survival,* Prentice-Hall, 1976.)

Bronx Law of Dominance. No matter what year it is or how many teams are in the league, the odds are 1:2 that the Yankees will win the pennant. (You could look it up.) (Steven D. Mirsky, Ithaca, New York.)

Brooks's Catch-22 of Conservation and Renewable Energy. (1) If savings from a proposed conservation measure are small, the measure is not considered worth the government's time; however, if savings are large, the measure is said to be too disruptive of the economy. (2) If the measure depends on voluntary compliance, the objection is that it will not work; however, if it depends on mandatory compliance, it cannot be countenanced by the government. (3) If the measure is cost-effective, it is asked why the government should give people money to do something they should do by themselves anyway; if it is not cost-effective, it is asked why the government should give people money to do something that will not pay off. (4) And finally, the measure can be quashed completely by declaring the matter a provincial responsibility. (David Brooks, former director, Office of Energy Conservation, Canada; from Steven Woodbury.)

Brooks's Law. Adding manpower to a late software project makes it later. (Frederick P. Brooks, Jr., from *The Mythical Man-Month: Essays on Software Engineering,* Addison-Wesley, 1975; *S.T.L.*)

Brooks's Observation. If it's not the same thing, it's the same thing. (Wally Brooks; from E. C. Pesterfield, Summit, New Jersey.)

Broome's Discovery. A good-looking (wo)man will get your attention. A bright (wo)man will hold your attention. *Broome's Domestic Discoveries. Kitchen equation:* Neatness counts; sloppiness multiplies. *Practice:* Everything gets easier with practice—except getting up in the morning. (David Broome, Phoenix, Arizona.)

Broome's Revision. Cast your bread upon the waters and you will be accused of polluting the environment. (Jon Broome, Vienna, Virginia.)

Brother Roy Smith's Observation. At banquets the microphone is always too short for tall people and too tall for short people. Also, the microphone whistles and hums louder the closer it is to the time for the main speaker to address the audience. (Brother Roy Smith, C.S.C., Notre Dame, Indiana.)

Brothers's Distinction. The biggest difference between men and boys is the cost of their toys. (Dr. Joyce Brothers; quoted in Bennett Cerf's *The Sound of Laughter,* Doubleday, 1970.)

Brotman's Discoveries. (1) The reason that there are more obnoxious New Yorkers and Texans is because there are more New Yorkers and Texans. (2) College is a fountain of knowledge where students have come to drink. (Sol G. Brotman, Baltimore, Maryland. Number 2 is more a statement than a law.)

Brown's Law of Business Success. Our customer's paperwork is profit. Our own paperwork is loss. (Tony Brown, programmer at the Control Data Corp.; *S.T.L.*)

Brown's Law. Too often I find that the volume of paper expands to fill the available briefcases. (quoted in *State Government News,* March 1973; *AO.*) *Brown's Law of Issues:* Issues are the last refuge of scoundrels. (Governor Jerry Brown; *MBC.*)

Brown's Law. Never offend people with style when you can offend them with substance. (Sam Brown, from the *Washington Post,* January 26, 1977; *JW.*)

Brown's Laws. (1) Any sentence with more than three punctuation marks should be rewritten. (2) If a speaker takes a physical breath because a sentence is too long, the audience will take a mental pause that will break concentration—Whew! (3) Anything written to another person is sure to (a) end up in someone else's hands; (b) be misunderstood, and (c) be photocopied. (4) Middle age begins when you start thinking about it, but stop talking about it. (5) You are old when you cite a historical event—and you were there. (6) A memo longer than one page no longer is a memo. (7) Your self-imagined importance is in direct proportion to the illegibility of your signature. (8) I give ulcers, I don't get them. (9) Any newspaper ad for a movie that takes up a full page means it is a loser. (David H. Brown, Rockville, Maryland.)

Brown's Point. One of the virtues of propaganda is that it is easy to understand. *Brown's Postulate:* No matter how low your own self-esteem, there are probably others who think less of you. *Brown's Revision:* Man does not breed by love alone. *Brown's Third Aphorism:* Nothing worth learning is learned quickly, except parachuting. (Professor David S. Brown, Washington, D.C.)

Brozik's Law. Never ask a question you *really* don't want to know the answer to. *Brozik's Laws About Hitting People.* (1) Never hit anybody bigger than you are because (a) it is not a nice thing to do, and (b) you will get the snot beat out of you. (2) Never hit anybody the same size as you are because (a) it is not a nice thing to do, and (b) regardless of the outcome you will experience some degree of pain and suffering. (3) Never hit anybody smaller than you are because (a) it is not a nice thing to do, and (b) when you turn around to walk away, the victim will rise up and nail you from behind. *Brozik's Second Law:* In any organization, it is more important to pick your enemies than it is to pick your friends. *Brozik's Third Law:* Never buy anything expensive from somebody who dresses better than you do. One of you is playing in the wrong league. (Dallas Brozik, Huntington, West Virginia.)

Bruce-Briggs's Law of Traffic. At any level of traffic, any delay is intolerable. (Barry Bruce-Briggs of the Hudson Institute, from his article "Mass Transportation and Minority Transportation," in *The Public Interest.* In explaining his law he adds, "It is amusing for someone accustomed to the traffic in New York to hear residents of places like Houston and Atlanta complain about congestion on the highways. Imagine, in rush hour they have to slow down to 35 miles an hour!")

Brumfit's Law. The critical mass of any do-it-yourself explosive is never less than half a bucketful. (*ASF* letter from Eric Frank Russell, who explained that the law was first demonstrated by Emmanuel Brumfit. Beginning with a half-ounce of homemade gunpowder, Brumfit attempted to see what would happen if he lit it. When nothing happened he went on mixing and adding until, on his fifty-fourth match, he reached exactly half a bucketful and "went out the window without bothering to open it.")

Bryan's Laws. (1) *Animal Behavior:* The owner of a dog or cat that bites a veterinarian during a visit to a clinic will invariably state, "Gee, Doc, he's never done that before." *Corollary:* The more serious the injury to the doctor, the more the owner will claim it was the doctor's fault. (2) *Human Intelligence:* Basic statistics indicate that half the population of the nation is above average intelligence. However, the odds of finding a member of the average group is inversely proportional to the importance of the question you are trying to get help on. (Douglas Bryan, D.V.M., Springfield, Missouri.)

Bryant's Law. The toughest stitch on a pair of trousers is that which affixes the price tag. *Bryant's Rule.* When a stranger identifies you from a friend's description, it's just as well you didn't hear the description. (Larry W. Bryant, Alexandria, Virginia; quoted in the Spring 1995 *Phoenix Newsletter.*)

Buchwald's Law. As the economy gets better, everything else gets worse. (Art Buchwald, *Time,* January 1972; *JW.*)

Buchwald's Rule. The first two times you use a joke, give your source credit. From then on, to hell with it. (Art Buchwald, quoted from Mo Udall's *Too Funny to be President.*)

Buchwald's Sans Souci Rules. (1) Any rumor which survives forty-eight hours is most likely true. (2) When any cabinet officer comes to dine, everyone's lunch is tax deductible. (Art Buchwald, who formulated them over soft-shell crabs at the Sans Souci Restaurant. They were quoted by Hugh Sidey in his column in the *Washington Star,* February 11, 1979.)

Buchwald's Theorem. Tax reform is when you take the taxes off things that have been taxed in the past and put taxes on things that haven't been taxed before. (Art Buchwald; quoted in *Forbes,* April 26, 1982.)

Bucy's Law. Nothing is ever accomplished by a reasonable man. (Fred Bucy, Texas Instruments, Inc.) *Simpson's Corollary to Bucy's Law:* Therefore, if I am being unreasonable, I am trying to accomplish something. (Don Simpson, Texas Instruments, Inc., Houston, Texas.)

Budget Analyst's Rule. Distribute dissatisfaction uniformly. (A. A. Lidberg, Tempe, Arizona.)

Budri's Generalizations. (1) People always find time to do the things they want to do. (2) People always find the money to get the things they want to get. (Vincent Budri, Longmeadow, Massachusetts.)

Buechner's Principle. The simplest explanation is that it doesn't make sense. (Professor William Buechner; from Richard Stone, Stanford, California.)

Buffett's Poker Principle. If you've been in the game thirty minutes and you don't know who the patsy is, *you're* the patsy. (Warren E. Buffett, Chairman, Berkshire Hathaway, Inc.; quoted in *The New York Times,* April 5, 1988; from Joseph C. Goulden.)

Buffett's Razor. Only when the tide goes out do you discover who's been swimming naked. (Warren Buffett quoted in Ann Landers's column of December 10, 1996.)

Bugs Baer's Perception. You can always judge a man by what he eats, and therefore a country in which there is no free lunch is no longer a free country. (Arthur "Bugs" Baer; *ME.*)

Bulen's Advice. Don't put off until tomorrow what you can put off until the day after tomorrow. (E. H. Bulen, Los Angeles, California.)

Bunch's Commandment. Thou shall not tattle, whine or point. (Lonnie Bunch, founding director of the National Museum of African American History and Culture; sighted on his desk, 2009.)

Bullfrog's Laws of Survival. (1) If it's bigger than you, run from it. (2) If it's smaller than you, eat it. (3) If it's the same size, mate it.(Tony Vecchio, director of the Roger Williams Park Zoo; from Barry Nordin, Warwick, Rhode Island.)

Bunker's Conclusion. You cannot buy beer, you can only rent it. (The character Archie Bunker, on the television show *All in the Family.*)

Bunn's Discoveries. (1) A drunk will never spill a drink on another drunk. (2) Half the world doesn't know how the other half lives. (3) If a person is stubborn and wins, he's got guts. If he's stubborn and loses, he's dumb. (4) No matter what one is going to use it for, the extension cord is always a foot too short. (5). No matter how large your vegetables grow, your neighbor's will be larger. (Dean Bunn, Brooklyn Center, Minnesota.)

Bunuel's Law. Overdoing things is harmful in all cases, even when it comes to efficiency. (*U/DRW.*)

Burdg's Philosophy. It's not the time you put in, but what you put in the time. (Henry B. Burdg, Auburn, Alabama.)

Bureau Termination, Law of. When a government bureau is scheduled to be phased out, the number of employees in that bureau will double within twelve months after that decision is made. (James A. Cassidy, Philadelphia, Pennsylvania.)

Bureaucracy, The Second Order Rule of. The more directives you issue to solve a problem, the worse it gets. (Jack Robertson, *Electronic News;* quoted in *New Engineer,* November 1976.)

Bureaucratic Cop-Out #1. You should have seen it when *I* got it. (Marshall L. Smith, WMAL, Washington, D.C.)

Bureaucratic Survival Kit—Essential Items

1. Credo of a Bureaucrat.

You start by saying no to requests. Then if you have to go to yes, okay. But if you start with yes, you can't go to no. (Mildred Perlman revealed this secret when she retired in 1975 as Director of Classification for New York City's Civil Service Commission.)

2. The Bureaucrat's Ten Commandments.

I. Don't discuss domestic politics on issues involving war and peace.
II. Say what will convince, not what you believe.
III. Support the consensus.
IV. Veto other options.
V. Predict dire consequences.
VI. Argue timing, not substance.
VII. Leak what you don't like.
VIII. Ignore orders you don't like.
IX. Don't tell likely opponents about a good thing.
X. Don't fight the consensus and don't resign over policy. (Widely quoted set of instructions by Leslie H. Gelb and Morton M. Halperin.)

3. Ode to Bureaucratic Immortality.

When Senator Lawton Chiles of Florida discovered that among the 4,987 forms used by the federal government was one that would be sent to city officials after a nuclear attack asking how many citizens survived, he was moved to comment, "The implication is that even if nothing else survives a nuclear blast, the bureaucracy will rise from the ashes."

4. Useful Motto.

Do not fix the mistake—fix the *blame.* (George Barbarow, Bakersfield, California.)

5. Confessions of an IRS Agent.

(*McCoy's Laws.*) (1) If all line sections of government ceased to function, the administrative staff sections would function for three years before they discovered the other sections were gone. (2) Bureaucracy goes beyond the *Peter Principle:* When someone reaches his highest level of incompetence in a bureaucracy, the only way to get rid of him is to promote him. This continues until he retires or reaches the top of the ladder. (Michael P. McCoy, Special Agent, Internal Revenue Service, Criminal Investigation Division, Spring, Texas.)

6. Bureaucrat's Lament.

I had a little document,
As pure as driven snow,
Yet everywhere that paper went,
It wandered to and fro.
I thought that people gladly
And swiftly would concur,
But while I waited sadly,
They'd cavil and demur.
Some thought the paper much too short;
Others much too long.
Some thought the language much too weak;
Others much too strong.
So by the time that document
Came dawdling back my way
It made no difference where it went—
The issue was passé!

(Found in a file at the National Aeronautics and Space Administration. *U.*)

7. Deliverance.

God told Moses he had good news and bad news.

"The good news first," said Moses.

"I'm planning to part the Red Sea to allow you and your people to walk right through and escape from Egypt," said God, adding,

"And when the Egyptian soldiers pursue, I'll send the water back on top of them."

"Wonderful," Moses responded, "but what's the bad news?"

"You write the environmental-impact statement."

(Oft-told Washington parable, c. 1977.)

8. Brownian Motion Rule of Bureaucracies.

It is impossible to distinguish, from a distance, whether the bureaucrats associated with your project are simply sitting on their hands or frantically trying to cover their asses. (*U;* Submitted by Paul Martin to *DRW.*)

Burgess's Law of Best Sellers. A book will sell best if it is very long and very unreadable, since then the buyer feels he is buying a durable commodity. If he races through the book he buys in a single sleepless night, he will feel cheated. (Anthony Burgess, in *Washington Post Book World,* April 8, 1979.)

Burgy's Definition of Statistics. A bunch of numbers running around looking for an argument. (George Burgy, Rockville, Maryland; quoted by Bob Levey in his column, *Washington Post,* November 16, 1984.)

Burke's Correlation. The increasing scale and grandeur of *Burke's Peerage* counterbalances the decline in the power and prestige of the peerage. (John Martin Robinson from "The Last of a Noble Line." *The Spectator,* 22 May 2004. The new, 107th edition of *Burke's Peerage* comes in three massive volumes. It is likely to be the last in printed book format. The previous, 106th edition from 1999 was in two volumes, and all the editions before that were single volumes back to No. 1 in 1826.)

Burma Shave Certainty. Within this vale...of toil...and sin...your head grows bald...but not your chin. (Set of sequential signs advertising Burma Shave, c. 1946. This is more of a quip than a law.)

Burnham's Discovery. There are two types of drivers: Those who slow down to merge and those who speed up to merge. The latter will always be behind the former. (Sharon Burnham, Pearl City, Hawaii.)

Burnham's Tenth Law. If there's no alternative, there's no problem. (James Burnham, quoted in the *National Review* of June 24, 1988.)

Burns's Autobiographical Explanation. I got paid. If they give me some more money, I may even read it. (Comedian George Burns on his new book, *USA Today,* October 17, 1984.)

Burns's Balance. If the assumptions are wrong, the conclusions aren't likely to be very good. (Robert E. Machol, from "Principles of Operations Research." The principle refers to the late radio comedian Robert Burns and his method for weighing hogs. Burns got a perfectly symmetrical plank and balanced it across a sawhorse. He would then put the hog on one end of the plank and began piling rocks on the other end until the plank was again perfectly balanced across the sawhorse. At this point he would carefully guess the weight of the rocks.)

Burns's Estimating Formula. Things cost about a dollar a pound. (From Martin Berger, Mount Vernon, New York, who explained in late 1970, "Burns was a college professor from whom I first heard this law. He was also the inventor of the ferrous wheel pictured at right. It has been my observation that this law was surprisingly true over a very long period of time. However, inflation

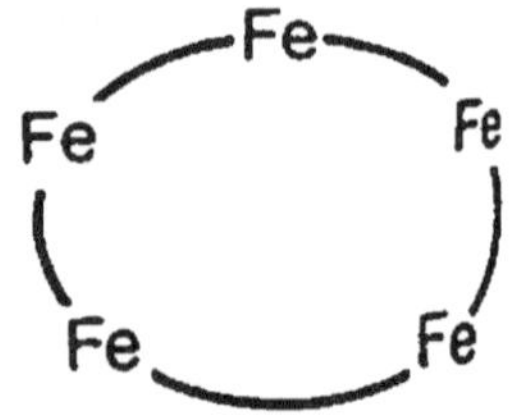

Fe Fe Fe Fe Fe Fe

has finally caught up with it; in today's world, two dollars a pound seems closer to the mark." Today the figure is closer to $4.00 a pound based on the cost of a pound of Brussell sprouts in the spring of 2011. The ferrous wheel went onto new fame when it was depicted on the television show *The Big Bang Theory*.)

Burns's Flaws. (1) You always discover you're out of toothpaste the morning of your dental appointment. (2) Your sons will remember to put the toilet seat lid down only in public restrooms. (3) Children acquire an ear for good music only after they have suffered a hearing loss at rock concerts. (4) A child will forget to change his socks only when you take him shopping for new shoes. (5) A teenager will only return your car with a full tank of gas when he's had a fender bender. (Catherine Burns, Winslow, Maine.)

Burns's Lament. Too bad that all the people who know how to run the country are busy driving taxicabs and cutting hair. (Comedian George Burns.)

Busch's Law of the Forty-Hour Week. The closer a day is to a weekend, holiday, or vacation, the greater the probability of an employee calling in sick. *Corollary:* No one gets sick on Wednesdays. (Walter Busch, St. Louis, Missouri; *EV.*)

Bush's Revision. You can fool some of the people some of the time, and those are the folks you should concentrate on. (George W. Bush at the March, 2001 gridiron dinner in Washington D.C. where he described this as a key piece of political advice.)

Business Maxims

Signs, real and imagined, that belong on the walls of the nation's offices (credits follow the maxims).

1. Never Try to Teach a Pig to Sing; It Wastes Your Time and It Annoys the Pig.
2. Sometimes the Crowd Is Right.
3. Customers Want ¼″ Holes—Not ¼″ Drills.
4. Dollars Become What You Label Them.
5. The Real World Is Only a Special Case, Albeit an Important One.
6. The Easiest Way to Make Money Is to Stop Losing it.
7. Auditors Are the People Who Go in After the War Is Lost and Bayonet the Wounded.
8. Criticize Behavior, Not People.
9. Give More Than They Ask for. More Is Less, but It Looks Like More.
10. If You Don't Measure It, It Won't Happen.

11. There Is More Than One Way to Skin a Cat; but Be Sure the Boss Likes Cat.
12. If You Can't Get Your Day's Work Done in Twenty-four Hours—Work Nights.
13. Whom You Badmouth Today Will Be Your Boss Tomorrow.
14. Remember, the Key to Success Opens Many Doors.
15. To Err Is Human—To Forgive Is Not Company Policy.
16. No Matter How Long the Day May Be, You Cannot Shingle a Roof with Prunes.
17. Fish Die by Their Mouth.
18. The Best Way to Get Credit Is to Try to Give It Away.
19. It Takes Two, but Give Me the Credit.
20. Even Monkeys Fall from Trees.

Many of these maxims were inspired by a collection of business maxims that appeared in *MBA Magazine.* The first four maxims originally appeared in *MBA.* The sources of the other maxims are: (5) Barry Keating, Assistant Professor of Business Economics, Notre Dame University; (6–8) Paul Rubin, Toledo; (9) Sal Rosa, New York City; (10) Boake A. Sells, Chagrin Falls, Ohio; (11) B. J. Carroll, Lake Forest, Ill.; (12) Alfred deQuoy, McLean, Va.; (13) S. M. Oddo, San Diego; (14) Seth Frankel, Chicago; (15) E. H. Bulen, Los Angeles; (16) Andrew Weissman, New York City; (17) Ron Wilsie, Solana Beach, Cal.; (18) business leader Charles Hendrickson Brower, quoted in *Reader's Digest,* March 1971; (19) T. Camille Flowers, Cincinnati; (20) Arthur E. Klauser, Washington, D.C.

Bustlin' Billy's Bogus Beliefs. (1) The organization of any program reflects the organization of the people who develop it. (2) There is no such thing as a "dirty capitalist," only a capitalist. (3) Anything is possible, but nothing is easy. (4) Capitalism can exist in one of only two states—welfare or warfare. (5) I'd rather go whoring than warring. (6) History proves nothing. (7) There is nothing so unbecoming on the beach as a wet kilt. (8) A little humility is arrogance. (9) A lot of what appears to be progress is just so much technological rococo. (Bill Gray, formerly of the Control Data Corp., friend of compilers of *S.T.L.*)

Butler's Conclusion. A hen is only an egg's way of making another egg. *Butler's Law of Progress:* All progress is based on a universal innate desire on the part of every organism to live beyond its income. *Butler's Marketing Principle:* Any fool can paint a picture, but it takes a wise man to be able to sell it. (Samuel Butler, *RS.*)

Butler's Expert Testimony. The function of the expert is not to be more right than other people, but to be wrong for more sophisticated reasons. (David Butler, *The Observer,* London, England.)

Buxbaum's Law. Anytime you back out of your driveway or parking lot, day or night, there will always be a car coming, or a pedestrian walking by. (*U/JW.*)

Buxbaum's Rule. Nothing stimulates interest in foreign affairs like having a son of military age. (Martin Buxbaum, quoted in Bill Gold's column, *Washington Post,* May 6, 1981.)

Byars's Bylaws. (1) Never work for a boss who opens the company mail. (2) The customer is always right... and ignored. (Betty Joe Byars, High Point, North Carolina.)

Bye's Laws of Model Railroading. (1) Any time you wish to demonstrate something, the number of faults is proportional to the number of viewers. (2) The desire for modeling a prototype is inversely proportional to the decline of the prototype. (*U/S.T.L.*)

Byrd's Last Law of Politics. Potholes know no party. (Senate Majority Leader Robert Byrd, during the 1987 debate on the president's veto of the highway bill.)

Byrne's Law of Concreting. When you pour, it rains. (*U;* Donald Kaul's column in *The Des Moines Register,* December 11, 1978.)

Byron's Tart Caveat to the Voyager. Wives in their husband's absences grow subtler, and daughters sometimes run off with the butler. (Don Widener, in his biography of Jack Lemmon, *Lemmon*; from Barry Hugh Yeakle, North Manchester, Indiana.)

C

C.J.'s Law. Philosophy doesn't get the washing-up done. (The character C.J. in the British television series, *The Rise and Fall of Reginald Perrin;* from Shel Kagan.)

Cabinet Law. A cabinet officer's most efficient activity is foreign travel; his or her most useful activity is domestic travel; time spent in the office is merely the necessary connection between the two. (Jim Kenworthy, Kansas City, Missouri.)

Caen's Law. All American cars are basically Chevrolets. (Herb Caen of the *San Francisco Chronicle; RS.*)

Caffyn's Law. The rosier the news, the higher ranking the official who announces it. (H. R. Caffyn, New York, New York; *AO.*)

Cagle's Law of Interest. The more interesting the activity you are engaged in, the more urgent will be the situation that eventually takes you away from it. (David B. Cagle, Santa Monica, California.)

Caldwell's National Constant. Americans have more time-saving devices and less time than any other group of people in the world. (Duncan Caldwell, quoted in *The Bedside Coronet,* Doubleday, 1952. This of course was decades before the PC, FedEx, fax machine, Internet and Post-It® Notes.)

Calkins's Law of Menu Language. The number of adjectives and verbs that are added to the description of a menu item is in inverse proportion to the quality of the resulting dish. (John Calkins of Washington, D.C., in a letter to the *Washington Post,* May 1977; *JW.*)

Callaghan's Answer to the Balance of Payments Problem. In the 19th century when Britain had defense responsibilities all around the globe, did she have balance of payments problems? No, there were no statistics. (British Prime Minister James Callaghan, in reply to a question at the National Press Club; *TCA.*)

Callahan's Corollary of Smith's Political Dictum. The key to success in politics is absolute honesty. If you can fake that you have it made. (From David M. Callahan, Albuquerque, New Mexico who adds: "This has been variously attributed to Johnson, Nixon, Reagan, and Bush, as well as to Mark Russell and Johnny Carson... I liked it so much I stole it.... It doesn't really matter who said it, it deserves a space in your own book.")

Callen's Correlation. The I.Q. of a group is inversely proportional to the additive total of that of the individuals in the group. (Thomas H. Callen II, Burke, Virginia.)

Callie's Law of Dinner Preparedness. When the smoke alarm goes off, dinner is served. (Caroline Curtis, Falls Church, Virginia.)

Callum's Advice. Find out what you don't do well, then don't do it. (Myles Callum.)

Campbell's Constant. The telephone never rings until you are settled in the bathroom. (Constance E. Campbell, Keokuk, Iowa.)

Campbell's Finding. If you accidentally put the carbon paper in backward, you will type a perfect letter. (Gardner Campbell, Jr., Scarborough, Maine.)

Campbell's Law. Nature abhors a vacuous experimenter. (*U/DRW.*)

Campbell's Law. A sinner can reform, but stupid is forever. (Lt. Col. William P. Campbell III, USAF, Eglin Air Force Base, Florida.)

Campbell's Law of Criticism. When you hear person A criticizing person B, you learn more about person A than about person B. (James G. Campbell, Toorak, Victoria, Australia.)

Camp's Law. A coup that is known in advance is a coup that does not take place. (The law that was reported by *AO* was alluded to by former CIA Director William Colby in a briefing for reporters. It is apparently known throughout the intelligence community and, presumably, was named after a secret operative named Camp.)

Camus's Graffiti. Sisyphus was basically a happy man. (Albert Camus.)

Canada Bill Jones's Motto. It is morally wrong to allow suckers to keep their money. *Canada Bill Jones's Supplement:* A Smith and Wesson beats four aces. (*U/S.T.L.*)

Canfield's Corollary to the "You Can't Win 'em All Rule." You can't even *fight* 'em all. (Monte Canfield, formerly of the General Accounting Office; from Sharon Lynn, Washington, D.C.)

Canine Culinary Warning. Everyone on the Premises is a Vegetarian Except the Dog. (Sign in front of a Loudoun County, Virginia home and reported in Bob Levey's column, *Washington Post,* April 17, 1987.)

Canning's Law. Nothing is as fallacious as facts, except figures. (British Prime Minister George Canning.)

Cannon's Law of Arena Seating. No matter how small the arena, there will always be someone on the top row. (Phil Cannon, Cordova, Tennessee.)

Cannon's Razor. Guys who chew on unlit cigars have a tough time convincing me they're telling the truth. (Sportswriter Jimmy Cannon.)

Capon's Perception. The world looks like it was left in the custody of a pack of trolls. (Robert Farrar Cannon from *The Supper of the Lamb,* Doubleday, 1969. *RS.*)

Captain Airway's Eighth Law. The longer the title, the lousier the movie. (John Carmody, *Washington Post,* February 20, 1980; invoked in discussing *Those Magnificent Men in Their Flying Machines; JCG.*)

Carlin's Law. If you nail together two things that have never been nailed together before, some schmuck will buy it from you. (George Carlin, *Class Clown* album; from Richard Manning.)

Carlisle's Nursing Keystone. If you treat a sick child like an adult and a sick adult like a child, everything works out pretty well. (Ruth Carlisle, quoted in *Reader's Digest,* January 1969.)

Carlisle's Rule. To find the I.Q. of any committee or commission, first determine the I.Q. of the most stupid member and then divide that result by the number of members. *Carlisle's Rule of Acquisition:* The purchase of any product can be rationalized if the desire to own it is strong enough. (Carlisle Madson, Hopkins, Minnesota.)

Carl's Quip. Driveways are always longer in the winter. (Carl Mattson, Winfield, Illinois.)

Carlson's Law. Don't ever try to eat where they don't want to feed you. (Phil Carlson, long-time chief of staff of the Government Operations Committee. It was recited to Jack Sullivan in 1960 when Carlson and Sullivan entered a restaurant in the Canal Zone that refused to serve them. Sullivan suggested they demand to be fed, but Carlson knew better. Sullivan, a former high-ranking state department official, adds, "I have found many subsequent occasions on which Carlson's Law has seemed quite appropriate." In a 2009 e-mail Sullivan reported, "Phil Carlson, who now is deceased, always said that you and I made him famous. He claimed to be in considerable demand as a restaurant guru, even by complete strangers."

Carmel's Construct. When the traffic congestion in a city becomes so serious that getting around the city is difficult, that city will then begin excavating for a subway system, with the result that moving around the city becomes virtually impossible. (Ann Carmel, Phoenix, Arizona, who was in Washington, D.C., when work began on the Metro system.)

Carmichael's Law. For every human reaction there is an over-reaction. (*U/Ra.*)

Carol's Rule. Never run after a bus or a man; if you miss one, there will be another along in a few minutes. (Carol Dennis, Chicago, Illinois.)

Carolyn's Corollary. A penny saved isn't a hell of a lot. (David M. Hebertson, Sandy, Utah, who named this for a former girlfriend "who did not revel in an 'evening out' at Burger World.")

Caron's Suggestions. The pessimist thinks the old days were better; the optimist thinks things will get better. Both are wrong. (Don Caron, Knoxville, Tennessee.)

Carpenter's Rule. Cut to fit—beat into place. (T-shirt from CafePress.com.)

Carrington's Train Laws. (1) The delay of time of your train is directly proportional to the importance of your arriving on time. (2) The size of the crowd in a train is in direct proportion to the amount of work to be done before arrival. (Simon Carrington, Buckinghamshire, England.)

Carroll's Circular Argument. Two wrongs don't make a right. And yet, three lefts do. (Terry Carroll; *TG.*)

Carroll's Law. Never send masking tape to do duct tape's job. (Terry Carroll, status posted on Facebook, Sept. 11, 2010; *TG.*)

Carroll's Law of Black Box Mechanisms. If you leave them alone long enough, they will fix themselves. *Corollary 1:* If they haven't fixed themselves, you haven't left them alone long enough. *Corollary 2:* If you open them up, they will take longer to fix. *Corollary 3:* If you try to fix them, they will be hopelessly beyond repair. *Corollary 4:* If you try to have someone else fix them, it will cost more than a new one. (B. J. Carroll, Lake Forest, Illinois.)

Carson's Comedic Laws. (1) If they buy the premise, they'll buy the bit. (2) Don't do more than three jokes on the same premise. (Johnny Carson, who mentioned these laws on several occasions when he was host of the *Tonight Show; MLS.*)

Carson's Consolation. No experiment is ever a complete failure. It can always be used as a bad example. (From a list entitled "Wisdom from the Giants of Science," found on a wall at National Institutes of Health; *U/MLS.* This has also been reported as Carlson's Consolation.)

Carson's Law of Singularity. There's only one fruitcake in the whole world. (Johnny Carson; *MLS.*)

Carson's Observation on Footwear. If the shoe fits, buy the other one too. (Johnny Carson on the *Tonight Show.*)

Carson's Political Advice. Only lie about the future. (Johnny Carson, on the *Tonight Show.*)

Carson's Travel Law. There is no Gate #1 at any airport. (Johnny Carson, the *Tonight Show,* May 22, 1979.)

Carswell's Law of Productivity. Work smarter, not harder. (Ron Carswell, Texas State Technical Institute, Waco, Texas.)

Carter's Rule. If there is a single puddle in your front yard, the newsboy will hit it, but only on those days when the paper is unwrapped. (Nelson Carter, Aptos, California.)

Carver's Law. The trouble with radicals is that they read only radical literature, and the trouble with conservatives is that they don't read anything. (Professor Thomas Nixon Carver of Harvard; quoted in *The New Republic,* March 28, 1970, and identified as a conservative monument of half a century ago; *JCG.*)

Carville's Challenge. Here's a quarter, call somebody who gives a damn. (Clinton political strategist James Carville, quoted on Whitewater, June 1, 1996.)

Carvlin's Commentaries. (1) In marriage, a warm heart seldom compensates for cold hands. (2) The risk in a business venture should not seriously outweigh the prospective reward, as, for example, in picking a policeman's pocket. (Tom Carvlin, Dolton, Illinois.)

Cason's Laws. (1) *For Plant Operation*: When in doubt, blame the Maintenance Department. (2) *For Economic Analysis*: The assumption you make without realizing you are making it is the one that will do you in. (3) *For Speed Limitation*: They will remember how poorly the job was done long after they have forgotten how quickly it was done. (4) *For Meetings*: Regardless of the length of the meeting, all important decisions will be made in the last five minutes before lunch or quitting time. (Roger L. Cason, Wilmington, Delaware.)

Caudill's Law on Losing. Even Betty Crocker burns a cake now and then. (Bill Caudill, Oakland A's, 1984. Posted on the wall of the Home Plate Diner in Lubbock, Texas and spotted there by Tom Gill.)

Cavalry Journal Discovery. A staff study is a record of the tortuous thought processes between a set of invalid assumptions and a foregone conclusion. (In a mid-1930s issue of that journal; from Jerry Cowan.)

Cavanagh's Laws of Bureaucratic Management. (1) The process is the substance. (2) The staff is the line. (Richard E. Cavanagh, Washington, D.C.)

Cavanaugh's Postulate. All kookies are not in a jar. (*U/DRW.*)

Celine's Laws. (1) National security is the chief cause of national insecurity. (2) Accurate communication is possible only in a nonpunishing situation. (3) An honest politician is a national calamity. (Hagbard Celine in *The Illuminatus!* Trilogy, 1975, by Robert Anton Wilson and Robert Shea; from Neal Wilgus.)

Cerf's Law of Knowledge. You don't have to be in *Who's Who* to know what's what. (Bennett Cerf; from Steve Stine.)

Chadwick's Observation on Book Loaning. The only thing stupider than loaning a book is returning one. (Clifton Chadwick, Santiago, Chile.)

Chafee's Law. Staff expands to fit the space available. (Sen. John Chafee, R., Rhode Island; quoted in *Reader's Digest,* February 1989.)

Chaipis's Conclusion. The majority of people are people. (Tom Chaipis, owner of Magoo's Cafe, New York, New York, quoted in the *The New York Times,* April 4, 1978; *RS.*)

Chamberlain's Laws. (1) The big guys always win. (2) Everything tastes more or less like chicken. (Jeffery F. Chamberlain, Rochester, New York, in a letter to *Verbatim.*)

Chamfort's Unassailable Observation. Bachelor's wives and old maid's children are always perfect. (Don Widener, in his biography of Jack Lemmon, *Lemmon,* MacMillan, 1975; from Barry Hugh Yeakle.)

Chandler's Typification. They are what human beings turn into when they trade life for existence and ambition for security. (Raymond Chandler, *The Little Sister;* from Joseph F. Walsh, Jr.)

Chaplin's Rules. (1) The smaller the democracy, the more complicated its political system. (2) The newer the democracy, the longer its national anthem. (Stephen M. Chaplin, McLean, Virginia.)

Chapman's First Law of Journalism. The amount of attention devoted to a subject is inversely proportional to its substantive content. (Stephen Chapman, in his column, *Chicago Tribune,* July 17, 1985; from Steve Stine.)

Chapman's Theorem of Justice. The courts are the last refuge of the unpersuasive. (Stephen Chapman.)

Character and Appearance, Law of. People don't change; they only become more so. (John Bright-Holmes, editor, George Allen & Unwin, Ltd., London, England.)

Charlemagne's Rule. It's smarter to be lucky than it's lucky to be smart. (Charlemagne, in the musical *Pippin;* from Richard Stone, Stanford, California.)

Charnovitz's Postulate for Elevators. The fewer the floors an elevator has to serve, the more time it takes for the elevator to travel between each floor. (Steve Charnovitz, Falls Church, Virginia.)

Chautauqua Boulevard Law. Just when I finally figure out where it's at... somebody moves it. (Sign in window, Chautauqua Boulevard and Coast Highway, Pacific Palisades, California; *RS.*)

Chavarria-Aguilar's Warning. Beware of learning another man's language: neither of you may really want to know what the other has to say. (O. L. Chavarria-Aguilar, San Jose, Costa Rica.)

Checkbook Balancer's Law. In matters of dispute, the bank's balance is always smaller than yours. (Rozanne Weissman.)

Chensky's Truisms. (1) A carpenter always writes on a board. (2) A fool and his money are soon audited. (Ed Chensky, Riverside, Illinois.)

Cheops's Law. Nothing ever gets built on schedule or within budget. (*S.T.L.*)

Cher's Matrimonial Analogy. Husbands are like fires. They go out when unattended. (Actress Cher; quoted in the *National Enquirer,* August 22, 1983; from Bernard L. Albert.)

Cheshire's Law of Social Climbing. Everything that goes up must come down. (Maxine Cheshire, *Washington Post; MLS.*)

Chess Essay Strategy, The. If you explain it in terms of chess, you get an A. (Explained by its creator Mike Stackpole of Phoenix: "In college I realized that if I could relate any essay question to a chess problem and use that analogy in the essay, I would get an A. The reason was simple: Chess is an intellectual game. If the person correcting the exam understood the example, he would feel smart about himself and I would have made the explanation clear. If the person correcting the exam didn't understand the answer I also won. Either he didn't know chess, which means he'd figure I was smarter than he was because I did, or he did know chess and had to figure I was a better player than he was. In both those cases I have to get an A, or the examiner displays his ignorance of my brilliance. I used the strategy a number of times with smashing results. I mentioned this strategy in an interview with a student at a local community college as an example of something else [probably concerning the universality of games]. I got a call from him two weeks later in which he pronounced the chess strategy a winner. He'd used it on an economics exam, so if it will work there, it must be golden. [I used it in Logic, Education and History classes.]")

Chesterton's Discovery. The only way of catching a train I ever discovered is to miss the train before. (G. K. Chesterton.)

Chesterton's Point. "My country, right or wrong" is a thing that no patriot would think of saying, except in a desperate case. It is like saying, "My mother, drunk or sober." (G. K. Chesterton, in Jonathon Green's *The Cynic's Lexicon*, St. Martin's Press, 1984.)

Chesterton's Warning. Never invoke gods unless you really want them to appear. It annoys them very much. (G. K. Chesterton, from Sarah Risher, Bethesda, Maryland.)

Chi Chi's Conclusion. It's when they call you lucky that you know you're good. (Golfer Chi Chi Rodriguez, 1990.)

Chili Cook's Secret. If your next pot of chili tastes better, it probably is because of something left out rather than added. (The late Hal John Wimberley, editor and publisher, *The Goat Gap Gazette,* Houston, Texas. He says reverently of chili: "I don't know why people screw around with it. It's a marvelous dish if you treat it right, with a few simple ingredients. I mean, look at California cooks—they're likely to throw the whole garden in.")

Chilton's Theological-Clerical Rule. If you work in a church office, you have to keep all your equipment locked up, because nothing is sacred. (Vee Chilton, Easton, Maryland.)

Chinese Fortune Cookie Law. Inappropriate fortunes always find the right person; and you always want more three hours later. (Rozanne Weissman.)

Chisholm Effect—Basic Laws of Frustration, Mishap, and Delay. *1st Law of Human Interaction:* If anything can go wrong, it will. *Corollary:* If anything just can't go wrong, it will anyway. *2nd Law of Human Interaction.* When things are going well, something will go wrong. *Corollary:* When things just can't get any worse, they will. *Corollary 2:* Anytime things appear to be going better, you have overlooked something. *3rd Law of Human Interaction.* Purposes, as understood by the purposer, will be judged otherwise by others. *Corollary:* If you explain so clearly that nobody can misunderstand, somebody will. *Corollary 2:* If you do something which you are sure will meet with everybody's approval, somebody won't like it. *Corollary 3:* Procedures devised to implement the purpose won't quite work. (Francis P. Chisholm was professor of English and chairman of the department at Wisconsin State College in River Falls for many years. His original article, "The Chisholm Effect," was published a number of years ago in a magazine called *Motive.* Because of their resemblance to *Murphy's* and *Finagle's Laws,* his *1st and 2nd Laws* are not well-remembered today, but his *3rd,* complete with *Corollaries,* is one of the most quoted of modern laws. Sometimes the *3rd* is quoted with a *Corollary 4:* "No matter how long or how many times you explain, no one is listening." This may have been written by someone other than Chisholm and added after the original article.)

Chism's Law of Completion. The amount of time required to complete a government project is precisely equal to the amount of time already spent on it. (Shelby Chism, Overland Park, Kansas.)

Christmas Eve, The Primary Myth of. "So simple that a child can assemble it." (Side panel of any toy box that also says, "Some assembly required.")

Christmas Morning, The First Discovery of. Batteries not included. (Small print from the side panel of any toy box.)

Christmas Paradox. If God had wanted us to worship Christ at Christmas, he would never have given us money. (Judie Wayman, Mayfield Heights, Ohio, who heard it from a friend.)

Chuck's Conclusion. No member of society is completely useless—they can always be used as a horrible example. (From a man named Chuck, who sent his finding to the Murphy Center on the stationery of the Alberta Vocational Centre, Lac La Biche, Alberta.)

Chuck's Law of Contract Negotiations. Travesty is a constant—no matter which side of the table you sit on. (Anonymous; from Gerald Lee Steese, Long Beach, California.)

Churchill's Marital Admission. My wife and I tried two or three times in the last forty years to have breakfast together, but it was so disagreeable we had to stop. (Winston Churchill; quoted in *Forbes,* June 30, 1986.)

Ciardi's Poetry Law. Whenever in time, and wherever in the universe, any man speaks or writes in any detail about the technical management of a poem, the resulting irascibility of the reader's response is a constant. (John Ciardi, in his "Manner of Speaking" column in *Saturday Review,* February 13, 1965. He created it in response to the reader outcry over some columns in which he wrote about the technical side of poetry.)

Cicero's Constant. There is no opinion so absurd but that some philosopher will not express it. (Cicero; *ME.*)

City News Motto, The. If your mother says she loves you, check it out. (The long-established motto of Chicago's City News Bureau, that city's legendary journalism "boot camp.")

Civil Service Maxim (a.k.a. The Law of the "New Army"). The pension is mightier than the sword. (Anonymous; unsigned note sent to the Murphy Center.)

Clancy's Observation. The only people who knew anything knew merely that they didn't know very much. (Tom Clancy from his novel *The Sum of All Fears*, Putnam, 1991; submitted by Dallas Brozik.)

Clarke's Law. Improving something is admirable, but inevitably five times zero is still zero. (Dean Travis Clarke, Glen Cove, New York.)

Clarke's Laws. (1) When a distinguished but elderly scientist states that something is possible, he is almost certainly right. When he states that something is impossible, he is very probably wrong. (2) The only way to discover the limits of the possible is to go beyond them to the impossible. (3) Any sufficiently advanced technology is indistinguishable from magic. (Arthur C. Clarke, from his book *Profiles of the Future,* Harper & Row, 1962. In illustrating the first law he uses the example of Lord Rutherford, who "more than any other man laid bare the internal structure of the atom" but who also made fun of those who predicted the harnessing of atomic power. Clarke also elaborates on the meaning of the word "elderly" in the first law. He says that in physics, astronautics, and mathematics, it means over thirty, but that in some fields, "senile decay" is postponed into the forties. He adds, "There are, of course, glorious exceptions; but as every good researcher just out of college knows, scientists over fifty are good for nothing but board meetings and should at all costs be kept out of the laboratory!")

Clarke's Partners Pact Paradox. You, as one partner, will do 90 percent of the research and 99 percent of the actual term paper. While "he," your partner, will contribute 10 percent of the research and 1 percent of the actual term paper. *Corollary 1:* Of course, the 1 percent of the paper is the title page, and your partner will have spelled your name wrong. *Corollary 2:* In typing the title page your partner will give himself top billing. *Corollary 3:* Your teacher, not knowing of the injustice being done, will give your partner a higher grade than the one he gives you. (Milo M. Clarke, Cortland, New York.)

Clark's Clamor. Where are they? How many were they? Which way were they going? I must find them. I am their leader. (From Bob Kerr, Amarillo, Texas, who spotted this sign on the office wall of Hugh Clark. As Bill Young has pointed out this is not a law; but it is an important approach to one's environment which belongs in a book like this.)

Clark's Conclusion. In order not to be boring, generalizations must be slightly risky. (Sir Kenneth Clark.)

Clark's Document Law. Nothing improves proofreading skills like hitting "print". (Steven Clark; from Tom Gill.)

Clark's First Law of Government. When a lot of people are doing something stupid, the reason for it will be found in the tax laws. *Clark's Second Law of Government:* When Congress must decide moral issues while writing a law, that law is beyond Congress' Constitutional authority. (George L. Clark, Sr., Manhattan Beach, California.)

Clark's First Law of Relativity. No matter how often you trade dinner or other invitations with in-laws, you will lose a small fortune in the exchange. *Corollary 1 on Clark's First:* Don't try it: You cannot drink enough of your in-laws' booze to get even before the liver fails. (Jackson Clark, Cuero, Texas; *AO.*)

Clark's Law. It's always darkest just before the lights go out. (Alex Clark, Lyndon B. Johnson School, Texas, at a RAND Graduate Institute meeting; *RS.*)

Clark's Law of Leadership. A leader should not get too far in front of his troops or he will get shot in the ass. (Senator Joseph S. Clark; *MBC.*)

Clark's Rule. Never ask "Mother, may I?" unless you know the answer. (Gen. Wesley K. Clark, when retired as commander of NATO and the U.S. European command, on his approach to battle; quoted in the *Washington Post,* September 28, 2000.)

Clark's Tool-of-the-Trade Law. Th k y always go s out on Saturday night. (This rule was created for failed typewriter keys, but applies as well to sticky keyboards. John Clark, San Francisco, California.)

Claudia's Assurance. When writing a personal letter, as soon as you begin a new sheet of paper, you will run out of things to say. (Claudia Costello, Manassas, Virginia.)

Claudia's Warning. Anything small enough to fit in a pocket will eventually end up in the washing machine. (Claudia H. Sundman, Eaton, New Hampshire, who noted this with the submission of the law: "I first realized the rule while sailing as Purser on the S.S. *Ocean Phoenix,* a factory ship with a crew of 200. The captain asked me why our billet cards [which note duties for emergency and lifeboat drills and are about the size of a credit card] kept ending up in the laundry.")

Clay's Conclusion. Creativity is great, but plagiarism is faster. (Frederick A. Clay, Anaheim, California.)

Clay's Conclusion. If you ever saw a cat and a dog eating out of the same plate, you can bet your ass it was the cat's food. (Representative William Clay, D-Missouri, commenting on the suggestion that public employee unions form a coalition with Jimmy Carter in 1980; from Marshall L. Smith.)

Clements's Premise. Assumption and presumption are the parents of all foul-ups. (E. Staley Clements, Jr., Christiansburg, Virginia.)

Cleveland's Highway Law. Highways in the worst need of repair naturally have low traffic counts, which result in low priority for repair work. (Named for Representative Jim Cleveland of New Hampshire. Its truth was revealed some years ago during Public Works Appropriations hearings as highway aid to New Hampshire was being reduced; *JMcC.*)

Cliffhanger Theorem. Each problem solved introduces a new unsolved problem. (Posted in U.S. Department of Labor; *TO'B.*)

Cliff's Catalog of the Least Credible English Quotations. (1) The check is in the mail. (2) I'm from the government and I'm here to help you. (3) Of course I'll respect you in the morning. (*U/GT.*)

Clifton's Advice. Don't give up high ground until you know you're over the pass. (Kelly H. Clifton, Hiroshima, Japan, who says that it was derived from backpacking but seems to have wider application. *Clifton's Conclusion:* Anything designed to do more than one thing does no thing very well. *Corollary:* Don't buy a car that flies.)

Clinton's Conundrum. When you're starting to have a good time, you're supposed to be someplace else. (Before he was elected president, Bill Clinton told a writer for *USA Today* this was one of the prime rules of being a politician.)

Clinton's Law of Politics. Whenever possible, be introduced by someone you've given a good job to. (President Bill Clinton, after being introduced by Hillary Rodham Clinton in a speech on health care at Johns Hopkins University, October 1993.)

Clinton's Rules of Politics. (1) Most people are for change in general, but against it in particular. (2) Never tell anyone to go to hell unless you can make 'em go. (3) Whenever someone tells you, "It's nothing personal," he's about to stick it to you. (4) Whenever it is possible for a person to shift the heat from himself to the governor, he'll do it. (5) Under enough pressure, most people—but not everybody—will stretch the truth on you. (6) You're most vulnerable in politics when you think you're the least vulnerable. (7) When you start enjoying something, it's probably time to leave. (8) Never look past the next election; it might be your last. (9) There is no such thing as enough money. (10) Don't drink in public. You might act like yourself. (Governor Bill Clinton quoted in *On the Make: The Rise of Bill Clinton*, Regnery, 1994, by Meredith L. Oakley; from the late Charles D. Poe.)

Cloninger's Law. In a country as large as the United States, it is possible to find at least fifty people who will believe/buy/try/or practice anything. (Dale O. Cloninger, Associate Professor of Finance and Public Affairs, University of Houston at Clear Lake City, Texas.)

Clopton's Law. For every credibility gap there is a gullibility fill. (Richard Clopton. *PQ.*)

Close's Clever Cue for Clashing Couples. If I can prove I'm right, I make things worse. (Rev. Henry Close, Fort Lauderdale, Florida, Letters to the Editor, *Time,* March 19, 1979.)

Clovis's Consideration of an Atmospheric Anomaly. The perversity of nature is nowhere better demonstrated than by the fact that, when exposed to the same atmosphere, bread becomes hard while crackers become soft. (E. Robert Clovis; from Stephen Bishop.)

Clyde's Law. If you have something to do and you put it off long enough, chances are someone else will do it for you. (Clyde F. Adams, Auburn, Alabama.)

Coan's Law. If it looks complicated, lose interest. (Nonnee Coan, Houston, Texas.)

Coccia's Barbecue Law. Regardless of where you sit, the wind will always blow the smoke from a barbecue in your face. (James R. Coccia, Glens Falls, New York, Letters to the Editor, *Time,* March 19, 1979.)

Cochran's Definition of Health Insurance. A system of reimbursement that pays many thousands of dollars for treatments that never cure hospital patients but will not pay for a shot of penicillin to cure double pneumonia in the office. (Paul W. Cochran, M.D., Topeka, Kansas.)

Cockrell's Law of Pizza Kinetics. All mushrooms on any given pizza will gravitate to the slice or slices of the one who dislikes them the most, leaving none to those who like them. (Reed Cockrell, Darlington, Wisconsin.)

Coffin's Revision. Some folks say the squeaking wheel gets the grease, but others point out that it is the first one to be replaced. (Harold Coffin, *Associated Press.*)

Cohen Rule of Dealing with Ethnic Groups, The. It's only safe to identify a person ethnically or racially in a positive context. For instance, "Jewish Nobel Prize winner is acceptable. "Jewish stock swindler" is not. "Italian-American auto executive" is okay. "Italian-American mobster" is forbidden. (Richard Cohen, *Washington Post.*)

Cohen's Choice. Everybody's gotta be someplace. (Comedian Myron Cohen; *MLS.*)

Cohen's Law. There is no bottom to worse. (Robert V. Cohen, M.D., Abington, Pennsylvania, who learned the law from his grandfather.)

Cohen's Law of Chronic Illness. The spouse of the chronic patient dies first. (Robert V. Cohen, M.D., Abington, Pennsylvania.)

Cohen's Law of Facts. What really matters is the name you succeed in imposing on the facts—not the facts themselves. (Jerome Cohen, Harvard Law School professor, quoted in *Time,* June 7, 1971.)

Cohen's Laws of Candidates. Many people run for office only because someone they know and don't like is running for the same office. *Of Government Salaries:* Few members of the news media have ever seen a justified pay raise or ever discovered the right time to raise pay or ever learned the right method to raise pay. *Of Political Polling:* Sometimes those who lead in the public opinion polls win the election. *Of Recollections:* Recollections of personal animosities generally last longer than the recollections of the effects of public policies. (Mark B. Cohen, member of the House of Representatives, Commonwealth of Pennsylvania.)

Cohen's Laws of Politics. *Cohen's Law of Alienation:* Nothing can so alienate a voter from the political system as backing a winning candidate. *Cohen's Law of Ambition:* At any one time, thousands of borough councilmen, school board members, attorneys, and businessmen—as well as congressmen, senators, and governors—are dreaming of the White House, but few, if any of them, will make it. *Cohen's Law of Attraction:* Power attracts people but it cannot hold them. *Cohen's Law of Competition:* The more qualified candidates who are available, the more likely the compromise will be on the candidate whose main qualification is a non-threatening incompetence. *Cohen's Law of Inside Dope:* There are many inside dopes in politics and government. *Cohen's Law on Lawmaking:* Those who express random thoughts to legislative committees are often surprised and appalled to find themselves the instigators of law. *Cohen's Law of Permanence:* Political power is as permanent as today's newspaper. Ten years from now, few will know or care who the most powerful man in any state was today. *Cohen's Law of Practicality:* Courses of action which run only to be justified in terms of practicality ultimately prove destructive and impractical. *Cohen's Law of Secrecy:* The best way to publicize a governmental or political action is to attempt to hide it. *Cohen's Law of Wealth:* Victory goes to the candidate with the most accumulated or contributed wealth, who has the financial resources to convince the middle class and poor that he will be on their side. *Cohen's Law of Wisdom:* Wisdom is considered a sign of weakness by the powerful because a wise man can lead without power but only a powerful man can lead without wisdom. (Mark B. Cohen, member of the House of Representatives, Commonwealth of Pennsylvania. Cohen writes his own, as well as collects other people's political laws.)

Cohn's Law. The more time you spend in reporting on what you are doing, the less time you have to do anything. Stability is achieved when you spend all your time doing nothing but reporting on the nothing you are doing. (*U/TO'B.*)

Cohn's Law on the Thickness of a Southern Girl's Southern Accent. The thickness increases by the square of the distance she travels north of the Mason-Dixon line. (Essayist David Cohn; quoted by James J. Kilpatrick; *TG.*)

Cohodas's Law. If it looks too good to be true, it is too good to be true. (Howard L. Cohodas, Marquette, Michigan.)

Colburn's Comment on Professional Meetings. There is more collected stupidity in a professional meeting of educators than in any other gathering of equal size. (John W. Colburn, who adds, "I have been informed that the name of any other profession may be substituted for 'educators' and the comment will still be valid.")

Colby's First Rule. "Never burn an uninteresting letter" is the first rule of the British aristocracy. (Frank M. Colby, editor.)

Cole's Law. Thinly sliced cabbage. (*S.T.L.*)

Collins's Law of Control. Businesses exert the tightest controls over the easiest things to control, rather than the most critical. (Kenneth B. Collins, CBS Publications, New York, New York.)

Collins's Law of Economics. The cost of living will always rise to exceed income. (Roger W. Collins, St. Louis, Missouri; *EV.*)

Collins's Laws of Discontinuity. (1) Objects that start out sequential break sequence by the time you get them. *Corollary:* The volume numbers actually present in a multi-volume work start with the sequence 1, 2, 4, 4, 7. *Corollary:* Any deck of cards contains fifty-one cards at the end of the first hand. (2) Normal distribution isn't. *Corollaries:* The number of television sets required to satisfy the viewing needs of a family on any one night is 0 or 4. The number of passengers on your plane is 7 or 386. The length of warning of the visit of the chief executive is 3.2 minutes or 47 days. The actual amount of food prepared for a party as a percentage of guests' requirements is 86 percent or 192 percent. (D. S. Collins, Harpenden, England.)

Col's Conclusion. Cash in the hand means a bill in the mail. (Colin Hewitt, Gosford, New South Wales, Australia.)

Colson's Law. If you've got them by the balls, their hearts and minds will follow. (From a poster which hung in the office of key Nixon aide Charles Colson; *MLS.* On January 9, 1980, Randal Cornell Teague of Boston, Massachusetts wrote this history of the Law in a letter to the Director: "You are right. Chuck Colson did have this in his office while he was in the Executive Office. In both my positions with Young Americans for Freedom (Executive Director) and the Office of Economic Opportunity within the Executive Office, I had occasion to see it. But it is not Colson's Law, and ego notwithstanding, I am sure Chuck would acknowledge that. As you recall, Colson was a staff aide to Senator Leverett Saltonstall of Massachusetts at the time the Senator was a ranking member of the Senate Armed Services Committee. This is key because the quote is from Rep. L. Mendel Rivers, the late Chairman of the House Committee on Armed Services. I was on the Hill at the time it was first articulated by Rivers in a White House conference of Congressional leaders with President Johnson, during his period of consternation over whether to take the war in Vietnam into North Vietnam. Johnson was hedging for a variety of reasons, not the least of which was likely public and Congressional reaction. Rivers, who in addition to being a hawk, was also convinced that that criticism would be muted by the appearance of leadership, and gave forth with this line. I have always remembered the line as, 'When you grab them by the balls, their hearts and minds will follow,' but I guess that is close enough. Johnson frequently quoted this in defense of his action, i.e., that by stepping up the military action, it would bring the North Vietnamese to the negotiating table faster. It may have, for the Paris peace talks soon began, even though they were fruitless for years.")

Combs's Laws. (1) A lot of people who complain about their boss being stupid would be out of a job if he were any smarter. (2) If you think OSHA is a small town in Wisconsin, you're in trouble. (M. C. "Chuck" Combs, Director, Minnesota Department of Agriculture, Marketing Services. St. Paul, Minnesota.)

Comer's Law. Never mistake asthma for passion and vice versa. (A.J. Comer, Huntington Valley, Pennsylvania.)

Comins's Law. People will accept your idea much more readily if you tell them Benjamin Franklin said it first. (David H. Comins, Manchester, Connecticut; *HW.*)

Committee Rules. (1) Never arrive on time, or you will be stamped a beginner. (2) Don't say anything until the meeting is half over; this stamps you as being wise. (3) Be as vague as possible; this prevents irritating the others. (4) When in doubt, suggest that a subcommittee be appointed. (5) Be the first to move for adjournment; this will make you popular—it's what everyone is waiting for. (Harry Chapman, *Think; FD.*)

Commoner's Three Laws of Ecology. (1) No action is without side effects. (2) Nothing ever goes away. (3) There is no free lunch. (Barry Commoner. See also *Crane's Law.*)

Compensation Corollary. An experiment may be considered successful if no more than half of the data must be discarded to obtain correspondence with your theory. (From list, "Wisdom from the Giants of Science"; *MLS.*)

Computability Applied to Social Sciences, Law of. If at first you don't succeed, transform your data set. (*U/JE.*)

Computer Maxim. To err is human but to really foul things up requires a computer. (*The Farmers' Almanac,* 1978 edition.)

Computer Programming Principles. (1) The computer is never wrong. (2) The programmer is always wrong. (*U/JS.*)

Computer Programming, Laws of. (1) Any given program, when running, is obsolete. (2) Any given program costs more and takes longer. (3) If a program is useful, it will have to be changed. (4) If a program is useless, it will have to be documented. (5) Any given program will expand to fill all available memory. (6) The value of a program is proportional to the weight of its output. (7) Program complexity grows until it exceeds the capability of the programmer who must maintain it. (8) Make it possible for programmers to write programs in English, and you will find that programmers cannot write in English. (SIGPLAN Notices, Vol. 2, No. 2; *JE*.)

Condon's Laws. *Business Eating:* (1) The cost of an expense account lunch is always inversely proportional to the amount of business done. (2) Executive meetings always conclude in time for lunch. (3) Executive lunches never conclude in time to return to the office. *Responsibility:* (1) The Chief Executive is always abroad when the manure hits the fan. (2) The Chief Executive is always available to make an easy decision. (3) The Deputy Chief Executive is always seen to make the lousy decision. (4) The thickness of the Chief Executive's carpet is in direct proportion to the amount of buck-passing carried out. *Return:* The size of the car in which a past pupil arrives for the college reunion is in inverse proportion to the size of the brain of that pupil. (John Condon, Dublin, Ireland.)

Confusion, First Law of. If the boss calls, get his name. (James Warren, Las Cruces, New Mexico.)

Congress, Universal Law of. Neither the House nor the Senate shall pass a law they shall be subject to. (*U;* collected on a radio call-in show. The truth of this law is flawless as Congress has exempted itself from such laws as the Civil Rights Act of 1964, the Equal Pay Act, the Privacy Act of 1974, Americans with Disabilities Act of 1990 and—stand back—the Ethics in Government Act of 1978.)

Connally's Rule. Wage and price controls cause inequities, inefficiencies, distortions, and venality, and therefore should be invoked only when necessary. (John B. Connally; culled from speech by *JMcC*.)

Conner's Food Laws. (1) Whatever the person at the next table orders, it always looks better than yours. (2) All avocados in all stores will always be rock-hard the day you want to make guacamole. (Caryl Conner, Washington, D.C., Letters to the Editor, *The Washingtonian,* December 1978.)

Connolly's Law of Cost Control. The price of any product produced for a government agency will be not less than the square of the initial firm fixed-price contract. *Connolly's Rule for Political Incumbents.* Short-term success with voters on any side of a given issue can be guaranteed by creating a long-term special study commission made up of at least three divergent interest groups. (Ray Connolly, Washington bureau manager and columnist, *Electronics* magazine.)

Connolly's Rules of Travel. (1) Take double the money. (2) Take half the luggage. (3) Make sure you can carry all luggage at least half a mile by yourself. (4) Do your washing. (5) Take a pair of pliers and a screwdriver. (Mike Connolly, New South Wales, Australia.)

Connor's Restaurant Rule. The amount of a waiter's or waitress's tip is inversely proportional to the number of people at a table times the amount of time the party occupies the table. (Kevin Connor, as manager of The Man in The Green Hat restaurant, Washington, D.C. Although Connor admitted that this rule is not immutable, he says that it is true enough to prove true at least once or twice on any given day.)

Conrard's Rules. (1) The person who misses the meeting is generally assigned to the work committee. (2) Conscience is that small, inner voice that tells you someone is watching you. (3) The problem drinker is the one who never buys. (4) One advantage of old age is that there are younger women all the time. (Charles Conrard III, Racine, Wisconsin.)

Conservative/Liberal Razor. A conservative sees a man drowning 50 feet from shore, throws him a 25-foot-long rope, and tells him to swim to it. A liberal throws him a rope 50 feet long, then drops his end and goes off to perform another good deed. (*U/TCA*.)

Considine's Law. Whenever one word or letter can change the entire meaning of a sentence, the probability of an error being made will be in direct proportion to the embarrassment it will cause. (Reporter and author Bob Considine; recalled by Bill Cold in his *Washington Post* column the day after a reader had written in to report that the paper had stated that a woman was "sex weeks pregnant.")

Conway's Law. In any organization, there will always be one person who knows what is going on. That person must be fired. (Letters column, *The New York Times,* May 15, 1980; from Robert W. Sallen.)

Cooch's Law. (See *Joe Cooch's Laws.*)

Cook's Rule. "All politics is local, except when it's not." (Charlie Cook, editor of "The Cook Political Report," which tracks congressional races. It's referring to Tip O'Neill's line that "all politics is local." As quoted by Lou Dubose in *The Washington Spectator,* June 15, 2010.)

Cook's Theorem. If you can't solve a problem forward, it can usually be solved by working it backward. (From Ronald F. Amberger, Staff Chairman, Mechanical Engineering Technology, Rochester Institute of Technology, who says it is named for Professor Cook, his machine-design professor at Rensselaer Polytechnic Institute.)

Cooke's Fundamental Theorem of Political Economics. If you can only cover costs, capitalism is irrelevant. *Cooke's General Business Laws:* (1) Managers with an accounting or legal mentality will take no risk, bend no rules, and the firm will stagnate. (2) The entrepreneur who finds a remarkable new way of financing a company or putting together a conglomerate will be the most surprised when it all falls apart. (3) Just because it works doesn't mean it's right. (4) Just because the industry leader does it that way doesn't mean it's the best way of doing it. (Ernest F. Cooke, Chairman, Marketing Department, University of Baltimore.)

Cooke's Law. In any decision, the amount of relevant information available is inversely proportional to the importance of the decision. (*U.* Michael T. Minerath, West Haven, Connecticut.)

Coolidge Collection. (1) If you don't say anything, you won't be called on to repeat it. (2) Make do, or do without. (3) I've traveled around this country a lot, and I'm convinced that there are so many SOB's in it that they are entitled to some representation in Congress. (In response to an aide's suggestion that Senator so-and-so had gone too far and the president ought to take steps to prevent his renomination.) (President Calvin Coolidge; *TCA, ME,* Louise Curcio.)

Coolidge's Immutable Observation. When more and more people are thrown out of work, unemployment results. (Calvin Coolidge; from Leonard C. Lewin's *Treasury of American Political Humor,* Dial, 1964.)

Coomb's Law. If you can't measure it, I'm not interested. (*U*; from an article in *Human Behavior* called "Peter's People" by Laurence J. Peter, August 1976.)

Cooper's Discovery. Any liquid accidentally spilt automatically doubles in volume. (Lady Curzon Cooper, London, England.)

Cooper's Discovery. Life isn't fair, but neither is death. (Ed Cooper; from Martin Kottmeyer, Carlyle, Illinois.)

Cooper's Law. All machines are amplifiers. (*U/DRW.*)

Cooper's Law for Practicing Politicians. Principles become modified in practice by facts. (Quoted by James J. Kilpatrick in his syndicated column, April 3, 1981; from Steve Woodbury.)

Cooper's Metalaw. A proliferation of new laws creates a proliferation of new loopholes. (*U/DRW.*)

Cooper's Truths. (1) The number of postal clerks is inversely proportional to the number of patrons (this can be proven by visiting any Washington, D.C. post office). (2) The amount of hair removed by a barber is inversely proportional to the cost of the haircut. (The hair stylist at the mall will charge you $15 to rearrange your hair, while the small-town barber on Broad Street will make you look like a Parris Island recruit for $2.) (Bob Cooper, Bethany, Oklahoma.)

Coper's Complaint. We could handle all of life's stress if only we could find the handles. (*U*; Neal Wilgus.)

Corcoran's Law of Packrattery. All files, papers, memos, etc., that you save will never be needed until such time as they are disposed of, when they will become essential and indispensable. (John H. Corcoran, Jr., Washington, D.C. writer and television personality.)

Corcoran's Laws. *Popcorn:* It is impossible to properly salt the lower half of a box of popcorn without oversalting the top half unless you take the saltshaker into the theater with you. *Of Shrinkage:* Everything from your past seems smaller when you see it again, except your old flame. *First Law of Sex Laws:* It is more fun trying to think up sex laws than any other laws. *Of Visiting People Who Own a Poodle:* (1) Never visit people who own a poodle. (2) If you do visit people who own a poodle, never throw a ball or small squeak toy to the poodle if you wish to be left alone during the remainder of the visit. *Of Nonsense:* (1) There is no law of nonsense since laws are logical and nonsense is not. Therefore a logical law of nonsense is nonsense and thus not a law. (2) Since the previous law is nonsense, ignore *Corcoran's First Law of Nonsense.* (3) If you don't like the first two Laws of Nonsense, come up with your own damn Law of Nonsense. (John H. Corcoran, Jr., Washington, D.C. writer and television personality, *Washingtonian* magazine, March 1974. See also *Duffer's Laws.*)

Corcoroni's Laws of Bus Transportation. (1) The bus that left the stop just before you got there is your bus. (2) The amount of time you have to wait for a bus is directly proportional to the inclemency of the weather. (3) All buses heading in the opposite direction drive off the face of the earth and never return. (4) If you anticipate bus delays by leaving your house thirty minutes early, your bus will arrive as soon as you reach the bus stop or when you light up a cigarette, whichever comes first. (5) The last rush-hour express bus to your neighborhood leaves five minutes before you get off work. (6) Bus schedules are arranged so your bus will arrive at the transfer point precisely one minute after the connecting bus has left. (7) Any bus that can be the wrong bus will be the wrong bus. All others are out of service or full. (John H. Corcoran, Jr., aka Corcoroni, *Washingtonian,* March 1974.)

Corey's Law. You can get more with a kind word and a gun than you can with a kind word. (Professor Irwin Corey; *MLS.*)

Corn's Law. At any given potluck you can tell how many lousy or lazy cooks are there by how much the table heaves with hummus. (From: "America's Struggle with Cooking" by Elaine Corn, *Sacramento Bee*, February 12, 2013.)

Cornuelle's Law. Authority tends to assign jobs to those least able to do them. (*U/S.T.L.*)

Corporate Morality, Maxim of. Morality moves down the corporate ladder, but seldom up. (*The 59 Second Employee: How to Stay One Step Ahead of Your One-Minute Manager,* by Rae Andre and Peter Ward, Houghton Mifflin, 1984; from R. Stevan Jonas.)

Corporate Survival, First Law of. Keep your boss's boss off your boss's back. (*U/RA.*)

Corrales's Conclusions. (1) Sophistication is knowing enough to keep out of the crack of the theater seat in front of you. (2) A rut is a grave with both ends kicked out. (3) Toes are what keep your feet from fraying at the ends. (4) A millennium is something like a centennial—only it has more legs. (5) How is it that George Washington slept in so many places and yet never told a lie? (6) Fortunately, the wheel was invented before the car; otherwise the scraping noise would be terrible. (Marsha J. Corrales, San Antonio, Texas.)

Corry's Law. Paper is always strongest at the perforations. (*U/DRW.*)

Corvin's Rule of Rules. If you screw the rules, they will multiply. (G. F. Corvin, Nairobi, Kenya.)

Corwin's Law. If you would succeed in life, you must be as solemn as an ass. All the great monuments on earth have been built to solemn asses. (U.S. Senator Thomas Corwin of Ohio (1794–1865) was known to have a good sense of humor, but he believed the reputation had hurt his political career. "Never make people laugh," he counseled one ambitious young legislator. When former funnyman Senator Al Franken of Minnesota was first elected there were those who reminded him of this law; *FD.*)

Cosgrave's Law. People will often sell their friends down the river in order to impress those they do not like. (Sentiment expressed by former Irish Prime Minister Liam Cosgrave, who noted that the British were noted for selling their friends down the river to appease their enemies; from Peter Robinson, Paris, France.)

Cosnow's Reflection While Attempting to Rodent-Proof a Bird Feeder.

The Guru sat on a mountain high,

above the worldly rush.

His hair had felt no VO5,

his teeth had known no brush.

When I asked him to enlighten me, he spoke these words of truth: "NOTHING IS ALL-PURPOSE AND NOTHING'S SQUIRREL-PROOF." (Allen Cosnow, Glencoe, Illinois.)

Cossey's Advice. Instead of starting at the bottom and working up, people should start at the top and work down. Only when one knows the job above can the one below be done correctly. (Clarence Cossey, Austin, Texas.)

Cost Effectiveness, Three Important Points. (1) The question was raised as to which was the best: (A) a broken watch, or (B) one that ran ten seconds slow per day. A Pentagon cost-effectiveness analysis showed that the broken one was far better. The slow watch will be correct only once every 118 years, whereas the broken one is correct twice per day. (2) The son of a cost-effectiveness specialist bragged to his father that he had saved a quarter by running behind the bus all the way to school. His father complained, "Why didn't you run behind a cab and save $2?" (3) Just before being blasted off into orbit Astronaut Walter Schirra was asked by Dr. E. R. Annis, "What concerns you the most?" Schirra thought and then replied, "Every time I climb up on the couch [in the capsule] I say to myself, 'Just think, Wally, everything that makes this thing go was supplied by the lowest bidder.'" (*FSP.*)

Cotter's Laundromat Mystery. Why is it that when there's an attendant to make change, the change machine works, and when there isn't, it doesn't? (John Cotter, *Washington Post,* December 6, 1987.)

Cotton's Explanation. One can usually tell from the degree of formality with which one senator refers to another what the nature of their personal relations may be. If the reference is made casually as "Senator Jones," they are probably close friends. If someone refers to a colleague as "the Senator from Michigan," one may infer that they have a cordial relationship. If a senator refers to another as "the distinguished Senator from Indiana," one may assume he does not particularly like him. And if he refers to him as the "very able and distinguished Senator from California," it usually indicates that he hates his guts. (Senator Norris Cotton, from his book *In The Senate,* Dodd, Mead, 1978.)

Coucheron-Aamot's Distinction. Foreigners often ask what is the difference between American political parties? It is really very simple: With the Republicans, you worry that they have not found solutions to the nation's problems. With the Democrats, you are afraid that they might think of something. (H. Coucheron-Aamot, Albuquerque, New Mexico.)

Couch's Probabilities. (1) With all the discounts, incentives, and cash-back payments, a new car will cost far more than you had planned. (2) An agenda becomes a list of subjects there wasn't time to discuss. (W. Roy Couch, Saco, Maine.)

Court's Laws. (1) In any country on any given television network or station, the quantity and quality of locally produced programs will vary in an inverse proportion to the quantity and quality of old motion pictures transmitted over the same given network or station. (2) If the media are given the opportunity to get the facts wrong, they probably will. (3) When the media make a mistake, the correction will be inversely related to the size and importance of the error. (Clive Court, Halifax, Nova Scotia.)

Covert Conversation Rule. If you don't want your children to hear what you are saying, pretend you're talking to them. (Anonymous.)

Cowan's Revelation. When a person says, "I'm as good as you are!" it means that he thinks he's better. (Jerry Cowan, St. Croix, Virgin Islands.)

Cox's Conclusion. Self-sealing envelopes don't—except when you have accidentally left the letter out. (Geoff Cox, Harpenden, Hertfordshire, England.)

Cox's Realization. The prediction that will be fulfilled is the one you didn't have the nerve to voice. (Richard Cox, Vandalia, Illinois.)

Cozgriff's First Principle for Dealing with Potentially Life-Threatening Situations. Relax—otherwise you might die all tensed up. (Cadet Ralph Cozgriff; from David Little.)

Cradock's First Law of Diplomacy. It is not the other side you need to worry about but your own. (British diplomat Sir Percy Cradock, *Experiences of China,* John Murray, 1994.)

Craig's Antique Dealer's Rules. (1) Five percent of the collectors account for 95 percent of your sales in 10 percent of your time; 95 percent of the collectors take up the other 90 percent of your time. (2) If I had a nickel for everyone who looked at my merchandise and said "I'll be back," I could retire to the south of France. (3) I am a very wealthy man, but it's all tied up in inventory. (4) The rarity of any item you possess is directly proportional to the number of stupid questions people ask you about it. (Antique dealer John S. Craig, Torrington, Connecticut.)

Craine's Law of Simplicity. For every simple solution there are a number of complex problems. *Corollary:* For every simple problem there are a number of complex problems. (Lloyd Craine, professor and electrical engineer, Pullman, Washington. "This law," he says, "was devised to explain some of the fundamental relationships that escape many laymen and was used during training sessions for persons interested in understanding the energy problem better.")

Cramer's Law of Teaching. When you threaten to send the next kid that talks to the office, the next kid that talks will be the best kid in the class. (Roxanne Cramer, Arlington, Virginia.)

Cramer's Law of the Sea. You're not really seasick when you are afraid you'll die, but when you're afraid you'll live. (Les Cramer, Arlington, Virginia.)

Crane's Law. There ain't no such thing as a free lunch. (Burton Crane, in *The Sophisticated Investor,* Simon and Schuster, 1959. See also *Commoner's Laws, Solis's Amendment to Crane's Law.*)

Crane's Rule. There are three ways to get something done: do it yourself, hire someone, or forbid your kids to do it. (Monta Crane, in *Sunshine Magazine* and requoted in *Reader's Digest,* June 1977.)

Cranford's Communication Law. You can't tell the depth of the well by the length of the handle on the pump. (Bill Cranford, Spartanburg, South Carolina.)

Cranston's Explanation. Inflation is not all bad. After all, it has allowed every

American to live in a more expensive neighborhood without moving. (Senator Alan Cranston, quoted in the *Atlantic Monthly,* January 1981.)

Crenna's Discovery. Futurism is passé. *Crenna's Law of Political Accountability:* If you are the first to know about something bad, you are going to be held responsible for acting on it, regardless of your formal duties. (Policy advisor C. D. Crenna, Ottawa, Ontario.)

Crescimbeni's Rule on Air Travel. Don't be afraid of flying; be afraid of crashing! *Crescimbeni's Rule on Working:* Don't worry about people not working at their jobs in the afternoons. It is in the morning when they don't work. In the afternoons they don't come in. (Joseph Crescimbeni, Lake City, Florida)

Crinklaw's Observation. (1) Nowadays the order of life is reversed: sex is first enjoyed, marriage follows, and after marriage comes virginity. (2) Nice guys may not always finish last, but the bad guys do start with certain advantages. (Don Crinklaw, St. Louis, Missouri.)

Cripps's Law. When traveling with children on one's holidays, at least one child of any number of children will request a restroom stop exactly halfway between any two given rest areas. (Mervyn Cripps, St. Catherines, Ontario, in a letter to *Verbatim.*)

Crisp's Creed. Don't keep up with the Joneses: Drag them down, it's cheaper. (Quentin Crisp; from Richard Isaac, M.D., Toronto, Ontario.)

Critchfield's Certitude. If, while driving and attempting a turn, a driver spots a pedestrian anywhere within the horizon, that pedestrian will be in a position to block said turn for the maximum inconvenience of the driver. *Critchfield's Staple Surmise:* (1) All staplers are empty. (2) Any stapler that isn't empty is broken. (3) Staple supplies may be found only when one is really looking for scissors. (Donald Critchfield, Washington, D.C.)

Crock's Law. No matter how large an area you are in, if a fly is present, it will land on you. (Terry L. Crock, Massillon, Ohio.)

Cronkites' Contrary Views of Death, The. Walter Cronkite: "When I go, I'd like to go like Errol Flynn—on the deck of my 70-foot yacht with a 16-year-old mistress." Betty Cronkite: "You're going to go on a 16-foot boat with your 70-year-old mistress." (In *USA Today's* compilation of 1986's unforgettable quotes.)

Cross's Conclusion. Had the Edsel been an academic department, it would be with us yet. (K. Patricia Cross, quoted in *Change,* June 1974; *RS.*)

Crowell's Undeniable Law of Fate. Whatever will be, will be, whether or not it ever occurs. (Donald K. Crowell, San Bernardino, California.)

Crudup's Law. Mediocrity always succeeds over originality. (Anonymous; from Nigel Stapley.)

Cruickshank's Laws. *Government:* We have met the enemy: in fact we elected him. *Consumerism:* Never buy a used car from a guy who can talk. Never shop in a place that has "bargain" in its name. *Committees:* If a committee is allowed to discuss a bad idea long enough, it will inevitably vote to implement the idea simply because so much work has already been done on it. *Gambling:* My old Scottish grandfather used to say, "The only game that can't be fixed is peek-a-boo." *Gimme Mine:* No matter how bad the idea, or how poor the results, a program will always be considered a howling success at the local level as long as federal funds continue to pay for it. *Sociology:* Never argue with the bouncer. *Corollary 1:* Never argue with a regular customer—the bouncer always decides in his favor. *Corollary 2:* Stay out of joints that need bouncers unless you plan to be a regular customer. (Ken Cruickshank, *The Florida Times-Union,* Jacksonville, Florida; from his June 25, 1978 column.)

Crump's Law. If both Alsops say it's true, it can't be so. (From an undated, unauthenticated paper entitled "Great Days for Crump's Law," by John Kenneth Galbraith. He insists that this law is invaluable in American political forecasting, but adds, "As a man of more than average caution, I have never felt absolutely secure until Evans and Novak have spoken." The paper appears to have been written in 1972. The law alludes to the Alsop Brothers, Joseph and Stewart, who were prominent Washington journalists for about thirty years following the end of World War II. They were at the center of events, both as journalists and as combatants during the war years. They had immense readership as their columns appeared in more than 200 newspapers.)

Culkin's Conclusions. (1) A lot of things have happened in this century, and most of them plug into walls. (2) We don't know who discovered water, but we're pretty sure it wasn't a fish. (Father John Culkin, Fordham University; from *RS* and Stephen J. Chant.)

Culshaw's First Principle of Recorded Sound. Anything, no matter how bad, will sound good if played back at a very high level for a short time. (John Culshaw, in his column for *High Fidelity Magazine,* November 1977.)

Cummings's First Law of Human Behavior. Something not worth doing at all is not worth doing well. (Dr. Nick Cummings, San Francisco, California; from Joseph Zmuda.)

Cummings's Rule. The fish are either shallow, deep, or somewhere in between. (L. L. Cummings, professor and director, Center for the Study of Organizational Performance, University of Wisconsin, Madison.)

Cuomo's Aphorisms. (1) When in doubt, mull. (2) Let them eat polenta. (3) If it's a free press, why do newspapers use coin boxes? (4) In government, a dollar saved is a dollar overlooked. (New York Governor Mario Cuomo, who attributes them to the fictional A. J. Parkinson, according to *The New York Times,* May 22, 1984; from Joseph C. Goulden.)

Cuppy's Evolution of the Species. All modern men are descended from wormlike creatures, but it shows more on some people. (Humorist Will Cuppy.)

Cureton's Advice. Avoid jackrabbit starts. (Stewart Cureton, Jr., Houston, Texas.)

Curley's Law. As long as they spell the name right. (Named for the famous Boston mayor; from Vic Gold's *PR as in President,* Doubleday, 1977.)

Curley's Ratio. Every time you do a favor for a constituent, you make nine enemies and one ingrate. (James Michael Curley, Boston Mayor, Massachusetts Governor, and Congressman.)

Cushman's Law. A fail-safe circuit will destroy others. (*U/S.T.L.*)

Custodiet's Complement. The human hand is made complete by the addition of a baseball. (*U/RA;* first published in *The Official Explanations* (1980). The name which has been attached to this assertion is elusive. *Custodiet* is a Latin verb meaning "to watch" or "to guard" and appears in a well-known quote from Juvenel: "*Quis custodiet ipsos custodes,*" which roughly translated means, "Who will watch the watchmen?," or "Who will guard the guards?," and it was invoked during the "steroid era" in baseball.)

Cutler Webster's Law. There are two sides to every argument, unless a person is personally involved, in which case there is only one. (*U/RS.*)

Cynthia's Verities. (1) The spare has gone flat too. (2) Divorce may be final, but it is not terminal. (Cynthia MacGregor, New York, New York.)

Czecinski's Conclusion. There is only one thing worse than dreaming you are at a conference and waking up to find that you are at a conference; and that is the conference where you can't fall asleep. (Adapted from a translation of a letter from Tadeusz Czecinski to a Warsaw newspaper; *RS.*)

Czusack's Law of Design Changes. Every advantage has a corresponding disadvantage. (Charlie Czusack; from Ronald F. Amberger, Rochester Institute of Technology.)

D

Dabney's Prime Axiom of Washington Thought. All ideas are merely the weapons of political struggle. *Corollaries:* (1) There is no such thing as truth. (2) Anyone who deals in general ideas is merely pushing the interests of his class, or of whoever's paying. (3) There is no such thing as right and wrong. (4) No one is capable of speaking to the general good. (Dick Dabney, *Washington Post,* October 16, 1979.)

Dale's Dictum. People don't make the same mistake twice; they make it three times, four times, or five times. (Michael Dale.)

Dale's Discovery. You can't climb a mountain from inside your tent. (Dale Wilkins, President, DW Explorations, Inc., Larkspur, Colorado.)

Daniel's Delight. If it is ironic, it is probably true. (D. Park Teter, Hazelhurst, Wisconsin.)

Daniels's Discovery. The most delightful advantage of being bald—one can *hear* snowflakes. (R. G. Daniels, from *Quote... Unquote* by Nigel Rees, George Allen and Unwin, 1978.)

Darby's Dicta. (1) If you have to "take it or leave it," leave it! (2) Every time I finally get an iron in the fire, the fire goes out. (*U;* from Mike O'Neill, Citrus Heights, California.)

Darrow's Observation. History repeats itself. That's one of the things wrong with history. (Clarence Darrow.)

Dart's Dictum. Talking to politicians is fine, but with a little money they hear you better. (Justin Dart, Chairman, Dart Industries; quoted by Mark Green in *The New Republic,* December 13, 1982.)

Darwin's Observation. Nature will tell you a direct lie if she can. (Charles Darwin.)

Data Processing Laws (Assorted). (1) On a clear disk you can seek forever. (2) Programs seek to expand themselves beyond available memory. (3) Compatible tapes aren't. (4) The volume of data to be keypunched determines the number of keypunch operators who will call in sick. (5) Profanity is the one language data-processing people know best. (From Virginia Beckwith, Arkansas Social Services, who collected them.)

Dato's Law. Wishes expand in direct proportion to the resources available for their gratification. (Robert Dato, Wynnewood, Pennsylvania.)

Daugherty's Law. Temporary things tend to become permanent. (Richard D. Daugherty, Professor of Anthropology, Washington State University; from Gerald H. Grosso, Port Orchard, Washington.)

Daugherty's List of Seven Things a Person Should Never Say. (1) That's impossible! (2) You can't do that to me! (3) I'll love you forever. (4) And that's my final offer! (5) I'll never hurt you. (6) This hurts me more than it hurts you. (7) It'll be a cold day in hell before I'll ever do that! (William J. Daugherty, Washington, DC.)

Daum's Law of Cuckoo Clocks. At any given party, the cuckoo will always cuckoo at the most embarrassing moment in a conversation. (Michael J. Daum, East Chicago, Indiana.)

Dave's Law of Advice. Those with the best advice offer no advice. *Dave's Rule of Street Survival:* Speak softly and own a big, mean Doberman. (Dave Miliman, Baltimore, Maryland. The law was inspired by Theodore Roosevelt's "Speak softly and carry a big stick; you will go far." Vice President Theodore Roosevelt identified this as an adage when he included it in a speech on September 2, 1901—just twelve days before he became president, following the assassination of President William McKinley. It has been identified variously as being inspired by a proverb from Africa and from Spain.)

Dave's Laws of Ornamentation. (1) The lights at the top of the tree will be the first lights to go out. (2) Just because a string of lights works while it's in the box does not mean it will work when strung on the tree. (David Grimes, "Murphy's Law written for holidays," *Sarasota Herald Tribune,* December 5, 2002.)

David's Law of Habits. Any bad habit is easier than the corresponding good habit. (David McKay, Havertown, Pennsylvania.)

Davidson's Law of Weather Variance. The arrival of spring always trails expectations. The arrival of summer always precedes expectations. Autumn arrives on time. Winter arrives when it wants to. (Jeff Davidson, Falls Church, Virginia.)

Davidson's Maxim. Democracy is that form of government where everybody gets what the majority deserves. (James Dale Davidson, executive director of the National Taxpayer's Union; *JMcC.*)

Davison's Law. One allows to come to rest any sizable object—laundry basket, grocery bag, shoes, etc.—in that exact location to impede as many foot traffic paths as possible. (W. Harper Girvin, Charlottesville, Virginia.)

Davis's Basic Law of Medicine. Pills to be taken in twos always come out of the bottle in threes. (Robert Davis; *AO.*)

Davis's Dictum. Problems that go away by themselves come back by themselves. (Marcy E. Davis, Philadelphia, Pennsylvania.)

Davis's Discovery. If you want to start a bug collection, paint your lawn furniture. (Lee A. Davis, Wilmington, Delaware.)

Davis's Law of Surviving a Hostile Press. If you hear your name mentioned on the radio, turn it off. If you encounter it in the *Congressional Record*, stop reading. Similarly if in a column. (Chester Davis, who held various New Deal positions; quoted by John Kenneth Galbraith in *A Life in Our Times;* Houghton Mifflin, 1981; from Joseph C. Goulden.)

Davis's Law of Traffic Density. The density of rush-hour traffic is directly proportional to 1.5 times the amount of extra time you allow to arrive on time. (Norman M. Davis, Chicago, Illinois.)

Davis's Laws. (1) Writers desire to be paid, authors desire recognition. (2) The further an individual is from the poor-house, the more expert one becomes on the ghetto. (3) In business, price increases as service declines. (4) On soap operas, all whites are in personal touch with (a) a doctor and (b) a lawyer. (James L. Davis, Washington, D.C.)

Davis's Warning. Always be suspicious of a politician who says that something can never happen. (Dr. M. I. M. Davis, Surrey, England.)

Dawes-Bell Law. Whereas in many branches of economic activity employment depends on the number of job openings available, in public service, as also in the advertising business, social science investigation, and university administration, the level of employment regularly depends on the number of men available and devoting their time to the creation of job opportunities. (First reported in *The McLandress Dimension* by Mark Epernay, Houghton Mifflin, 1963.)

Dawn's Judgment. The judgment of any group varies inversely as the square of the number of persons in the group. (If 1 person has x judgment, 2 persons will have ¼x judgment, 10 will have 1/100x judgment, etc.) (Dawn Barry, St. Charles, Illinois.)

De Tocqueville's Law. The lower the calling is and the more removed from learning, the more pompous and erudite is its appellation. (Alexis De Tocqueville, *Democracy in America;* from Kevin C. Long, Quebec.)

Dean-Boyd Law, The. Stupidity is intelligence cleverly disguised. *The Beeton Contradiction to the Dean-Boyd Law:* Maybe it's the other way around. (Kevin A. H. Dean, Don Mills, Ontario, with Jeff Boyd and Carolyn Beeton.)

Dean's Law of the District of Columbia. Washington is a much better place if you are asking questions rather than answering them. (John Dean, former counsel to President Nixon, on the occasion of beginning his syndicated radio interview show.)

DeBleyker's Discovery. Forgetting is a poor excuse for not remembering. (J. R. DeBleyker, Lyndhurst, Ohio.)

Deborkowski's Laundry Law. If you come out of the laundromat with an even number of socks, you have somebody else's laundry. (*U/Ra.*)

DeCaprio's Rule. Everything takes more time and money. (Annie DeCaprio, High Bridge, New Jersey; *HW.* Note similarity to *Cheops's Law.*)

December Constant. During Christmas, all worthwhile social events will occur on the same evening. (Anonymous.)

DeCicco's Law. More policemen die in their autos daydreaming about gunfights than die as a result of gunfights. (Alexander DeCicco, Deputy Sheriff, DuPage County, Illinois.)

De-Evolutionary Observation. God made man, but he used a monkey to do it. (In the song "Jocko Homo" by Devo; from Nigel Stapley.)

Deford's Law. If ain't fixed, don't break it. (This was uttered by Frank Deford on NPR's Morning Edition in March of 1988 and alluded to the plan to put lights in Wrigley Field. This is an important corollary to the *First Rule of Rural Mechanics:* it works, don't fix it.)

Deitz's Law of Ego. The fury engendered by the misspelling of a name in a column is in direct ratio to the obscurity of the mentionee. (Alan Deitz of the American Newspaper Publishers Association to *AO* on the misspelling of his name in *The Wall Street Journal.*)

DeLaney's Laws for Predicting Picnic Weather. (1) If the forecast is 10 percent chance of showers, you'll get the whole 10 percent. (2) The sun will shine brightly at the rejected alternative location. (Robert L. DeLaney, Johnson City, New York.)

Denenberg's Laws. *Of Rhetorical Effectiveness:* I would measure how effective my speech was by how many hours it took the audience to complain to my employer. *Of Inescapable Elements:* You can't escape death, taxes, or life insurance. (Herbert S. Denenberg; *MBC.*)

Denham's Dictum. In a given organization, job performance, whether excellent or incompetent, is overlooked, providing you conform. (Ron Denham, Park Ridge, Illinois.)

Dennis's Principles of Management by Crisis. (1) To get action out of management, it is necessary to create the illusion of a crisis in the hope it will be acted on. (2) Management will select actions or events and convert them to crises. It will then over-react. (3) Management is incapable of recognizing a true crisis. (4) The squeaky hinge gets the oil. (Gene Franklin; from his article in *Computers and Automation; JE.*)

Density Characteristics of Executives Rising in an Organization. Cream rises and sewage floats. (Anonymous.)

Denzel's Law. It's one thing to make money, it's another thing to know how to spend it. (Actor Denzel Washington, interviewed by CNN anchor Tony Harris, September 15, 2010; *TG.*)

Depuy's Dictates. (1) In any magazine, the number of pages lacking pagination numbers is directly proportional to the number of advertisements. (2) Most unnumbered pages occur in those parts of the magazine to which the reader is directed for article continuations. *Penmanship:* The greater one's efforts to write an impressive signature, the more awkward are the results, except when signing insignificant documents such as parcel delivery receipts. *Vision:* When a person who normally wears eyeglasses appears before you without them, you cannot see him as clearly. (Raymond H. Depuy, Chambersburg, Pennsylvania.)

deQuoy's Catalog of Statements People Will Blindly Accept as Proof of Validity. (1) It has been computerized. (2) It has been war-gamed. (Alfred deQuoy, McLean, Virginia.)

deQuoy's Observation. Some of the world's best work has been done by people who didn't feel very well that day. (Glenna deQuoy, New York, New York.)

DeRock's Law of Dullness. Dullness is directly proportional to the number of brown suits in a crowd. (Doug DeRock, Western Springs, Illinois.)

DeRoy's Political Rule. A politician solves every problem before an election but very few after. (Richard H. DeRoy, Hilo, Hawaii.)

Dershowitz's Apologia for Ambulance Chasers. It's not a chase, it's a race. The good ambulance chasers are always in a race against the claims adjusters. (Attorney and professor Alan Dershowitz quoted in the *Boston Globe;* from Bob Skole.)

Desjardins' Discovery. In a puzzle there is always at least one piece missing, and it is usually the last one. (M. Desjardins, Saint-Laurent, Quebec.)

Desk Jockey, Songs of the. (1) The federal government spends enough in one hour to wire the entire population of North Dakota—and the houses, too. (2) Discriminate as little as you can and still comply with federal regulations. (3) Make the new administrator feel welcome in a Saturday afternoon ceremony. As of Monday morning, he will be behind in his commitments to group X. (4) The principle allegiance of modern man is to his group, which differs from a gang chiefly in that gangs rumble in the streets while groups rumble in the courts and on Capitol Hill. (5) A dresser is a kind of bureau that doesn't tell you how to run your life. (6) The fascination of paper clips grows inversely with the appeal of the work at hand. (Ryan Anthony, Tucson, Arizona.)

DeVault's Razor. There are only two laws: (1) Someday you will die. (2) If you are reading this you are not dead yet. (Yvonne G. T. DeVault, Redwood City, California.)

DeViney's Axiom. You should always try to become boss, because otherwise, they'll give it to some other dumbbell. (G. H. DeViney, Palatine, Illinois.)

DeVries's Cosmic Observation. The universe is like a safe to which there is a combination. Unfortunately, the combination is locked up inside the safe. (Peter DeVries, *Let Me Count the Ways;* Little, Brown, 1965; from Arnold Harris.)

Dhawan's Laws for the Non-Smoker. (1) The cigarette smoke always drifts in the direction of the non-smoker regardless of the direction of the breeze. (2) The amount of pleasure derived from a cigarette is directly proportional to the number of non-smokers in the vicinity. (3) A smoker is always attracted to the non-smoking section. (4) The life of a cigarette is directly proportional to the intensity of the protests from the non-smokers. (Raj K. Dhawan, West Covina, California.)

Dial's Discovery. No matter what you do to instant coffee, it always tastes like instant coffee. (Thomas H. Dial, Baltimore, Maryland.)

Diana's Law of Diminishing Enthusiasm. There are more entries in the first half of the alphabet. (Diana VerNooy, Teaneck, New Jersey.)

Diane's Secretary's Axiom. The more you want done, and the faster you want it done, the longer it will take to get it done, and the greater the chance of errors being made because of too much to do in too little time. (Diane K. Stanley, Fremont, Nebraska.)

Dianne's Observation. If a motel advertises itself as "modern," it isn't. (Dianne D. Farrar, Sacramento, California.)

Dibble's First Law of Sociology. Some do, some don't. (Letter to *Verbatim* from Jeffery F. Chamberlain.)

Dickens's Discovery on Justice. If there were no bad people, there would be no good lawyers. (Charles Dickens.)

Dick's Dilemma. If you live in California, your factory authorized sales representative lives in New Jersey. If you live in New Jersey, your factory authorized sales representative lives in White Rock, South Dakota. If you need further assistance, please feel free to contact our home office in Hong Kong. (John A. Mattsen, Finlayson, Minnesota.)

Dickson's Definition. A pessimist is a person who mourns the future. (The late Isabelle C. Dickson, the director's mother, formerly of Hastings-on-Hudson, New York, and Yonkers, New York.)

Dickson's Discoveries. (1) Golf, sex, and child-rearing prove that practice does not make perfect. (2) No two hotel/motel shower faucets work the same way. (3) When weeding, the best way to make sure what you are pulling is a weed and not a valuable plant is to pull on it. If it comes out of the ground easily, it is a valuable plant. (4) Every time you think that you've "paid your dues," you get a renewal notice. (5) You don't know it yet, but your name is on somebody else's list of "things to do today." That person will wait to call you until he or she has plenty of time. Meanwhile, you will put someone else's name on your list of "things to do today." You will wait to call until you have plenty of time to talk. (Paul Dickson, director, Murphy Center.)

Dickson's Rules. (1) *Auto Repair:* If you can see it, it is not serious. If you can hear it, it will set you back some. If you can neither see nor hear it, it will cost you a fortune. (2) *Collecting:* Anything billed as "destined to be a collector's item" (commemorative plates, spoons, Bicentennial kitsch, records sold on late-night TV, etc.) won't be. *Corollary:* Things that aren't, will be. (3) *Telecommunications:* A defective pay phone will find your last dime. (4) *Turnpike Cuisine:* The quality of roadside food decreases in direct proportion to the number of lanes on the road in question. (5) *Insomnia:* Noises, particularly drips and creakings, intensify during the night but abate at dawn. Birds make the most noise at dawn. At *the precise moment* that you *must* get out of bed, there will be absolute quiet. (6) *Transportation:* The bigger the terminal, the worse the public address system. (7) *American Studies:* There is no phenomenon so small that some professor, writer, or politician will not latch on to it and declare that it signifies a turning or tipping point in American history. (8) *Defense Language:* The more innocuous the name of a weapon, the more hideous its impact. (Some of the most horrific weapons of the Vietnam era were named Bambi, Infant, Daisycutter, Grasshopper, and Agent Orange. Nor is the trend new: From the past we have Mustard Gas, Angel Chasers [two cannonballs linked with a chain for added destruction], and the Peacemaker, to name a few.) (9) *Roadside Economics:* Places with the suffix "-tronics" or the word "systems" in their name will charge more for the same goods or service than places with "Mr." or "City" in their name (as in Mr. Carwash or Clean City.) But forced K's (as in Kwick and Klean) aren't as cheap as they look. If you really want to overpay for something, try an antique shop with a crude, hand-lettered sign with the "n" written backward. Stores with first names (John's, Fred's, Maxine's) are generally cheaper than those with last names (Bloomingdale's, Tiffany's, Brooks Brothers, etc.). (10) *Suburban Development:* The more trees a developer cuts down, the woodsier the name of the resulting housing development. (Paul Dickson, director, Murphy Center.)

Dieter's Discoveries, The. (1) The calorie isn't a unit of energy. It's a unit of taste. (2) If it isn't the calories that make it taste good, it's the cholesterol. (Gail White, New Orleans, Louisiana.)

Dieter's Law. Food that tastes the best has the highest number of calories. (Rozanne Weissman.)

Dijkstra's Prescription for Programming Inertia. If you don't know what your program is supposed to do, you'd better not start writing it. (Edsger Wybe Dijkstra, Dutch computer scientist (1930–2002) whose precepts and aphorisms have had great and lasting impact on computer science, for example: "Simplicity is prerequisite for reliability." *JE* carries this with the notation: Stanford Computer Science Colloquium, April 18, 1975.)

Dillon's Rule. The soup de jour is always cream of broccoli. (Janet Dillon, Walnut Creek, California; *TG*.)

Dilwether's Law of Delay. When people have a job to do, particularly a vital but difficult one, they will invariably put it off until the last possible moment, and *most* of them will put it off even longer. (Gordon L. Becker, counsel, Exxon Corp; *AO*.)

Diminishing Appreciation, The Law of. The more secure it is, the less you appreciate it. (Neal Wilgus, Albuquerque, New Mexico.)

Dines's Reminder. If you hear that everybody is buying a certain stock, ask who is selling. (James Dines; quoted in the *Baltimore Sun,* November 9, 1983.)

Diogenes's First Dictum. The more heavily a man is supposed to be taxed, the more power he has to escape being taxed. (*S.T.L.*)

Diogenes's Second Dictum. If a taxpayer thinks he can cheat safely, he probably will. (*S.T.L.*)

Dirksen's Three Laws of Politics. (1) Get elected. (2) Get re-elected. (3) Don't get mad, get even. (Senator Everett Dirksen; recalled by Harry N. D. Fisher for *AO*. See also *Johnson's "Prior" Laws of Politics.*)

Dirksen's Version of an Old Saw. The oil can is mightier than the sword. (Senator Everett Dirksen. This was contained in Donald Rumsfeld's collection of laws.)

Disney World Rule. Children under twelve must be accompanied by money. (James Dent, Charleston [West Virginia] *Gazette.*)

Displaced Hassle, Principle of. To beat the bureaucracy, make your problem their problem. (*MLS,* who is also a law-collector.)

Disraeli's Maxims. (1) A precedent embalms a principle. (2) In politics, nothing is contemptible. (Benjamin Disraeli [1804–1881] who served as British Prime Minister and a founder of the British Conservative Movement.)

Distance, Law of. Happiness is in direct proportion to the distance from the home office. *Contradictory Corollary:* The diner who is farthest from the kitchen is a nervous eater. (Stated by Al Blanchard, *The Detroit News,* in his column for September 16, 1977.)

Distin's Discovery. Cat hair is attracted to and will adhere to anything except the cat. (Mary Distin, Monmouth, Illinois.)

Dixon's Law of Manhattan Movement. Everyone in New York is in a hurry except the person walking in front of you. (Mike Dixon, New York, New York.)

Dmitri's Epigrams. (1) Nobody can ever get too much approval. (2) No matter how much you want or need, *they,* whoever *they* are, don't want to let you get away with it, whatever *it* is. (3) Sometimes you get away with it. (John Leonard's column, who sometimes calls himself Dmitri in his *New York Times* columns.)

Dobbins's Law. When in doubt, use a bigger hammer. (A variation of *Anthony's Law of Force,* probably earlier.)

Dobson's Dilemma. (1) Following the rules won't get the job done. (2) Getting the job done is no excuse for not following the rules. (Bob Vopacke, Sacramento, California.)

Doc Scoggins's Reminder. You're only young once, but you can be immature all your life. (Charles Scoggins, M.D., quoted in the *Internist,* June 1981, in reference to his avocation as a member of a rodeo roping team; from Bernard Albert.)

Dochter's Dictum. Somewhere, right now, there's a committee deciding your future; only you weren't invited. (*U/NDB.*)

Doctor Orbit's Laws. *The Unexpected:* Don't count your chickens before they cross the road. *Discretion:* If one observes shit congregating in the vicinity of a fan, it is prudent to unplug the fan. *Computer Systems:* The relative importance of a computer system is inversely proportional to the contrivedness of its acronym. (Charles A. Belov, West Hartford, Connecticut.)

Documentation, Five Laws of. (1) What is convenient for the documentor will be inconvenient for the user. (2) All manuals are out of date. (3) All distribution lists are inaccurate. (4) Each supplement doubles the number of versions. (5) Clean documentation cannot improve a messy system. (Edmund H. Weiss, *Structured Documentation;* from Steve Stine.)

Doherty's Dictum on Juvenile Work Productivity. One boy, one boy; two boys, half a boy; three boys, no boy. (Indianapolis grocer Patrick Doherty; from Bob Einbinder.)

Dolan's First Law. Bad times make good stories. *First Corollary:* Good times make dull stories. (Michael Dolan, Washington, D.C.)

Dolan's Law. If a person has had any connection with Harvard University or the state of Texas, he will find a way to make that known to you during the first ten minutes of your first conversation. (Marty Dolan; from Joseph M. McCabe. The law might be amended to include the U.S. Marine Corps.)

Dolan's Query. Did your wife ever get a permanent? Where is it now? (Wayne Dolan, Raytown, Missouri.)

Dole's Razor. Public television viewers are "affluent, highly educated, the movers and shakers, the socially conscious and the well informed." What about the rest of us? (Senator Bob Dole, June 3, 1992, citing a description of public television's audience while opposing a bill for public broadcasting.)

Domino Theory II. If you disregard the advice of General Douglas MacArthur and go into the quicksand of an Asian country, like a domino you will fall into the quicksand of another Asian country next to it. (Representative Andrew Jacobs, Jr., D-Indiana, who created it about the time of the U.S. incursion into

Cambodia. The original theory—Domino Theory I—applied to a row of standing dominos and that if the first domino was knocked over then the rest would topple in turn. Applying this to Southeast Asia it was argued that if South Vietnam was taken by communists, then the other countries in the region such as Laos, Cambodia, Thailand, Burma, Malaysia, and Indonesia, would fall as well.)

Don Marquis's Advice to Writers. If you want to get rich from writing, write the sort of thing that is read by persons who move their lips when they are reading to themselves. (Don Marquis; quoted by Franklin P. Adams in his book *Overset,* Doubleday, 1922.)

Donna's Law of Purchase. If you want it, and can afford it, buy it—it won't be there when you go back. (Donna P. H. Day, Rock Hill, Missouri.)

Donohue's Law. What's worth doing is worth doing for money. (Joseph Donohue; *JW.*)

Donsen's Law. The specialist learns more and more about less and less until, finally, he knows everything about nothing; whereas the generalist learns less and less about more and more until, finally, he knows nothing about everything. (Donsen is *U* but can be traced to John Cunningham Lilly's *The Mind of the Dolphin*, Avon, 1967.)

Doolittle's Definition. A bore is a person who monopolizes the conversation, talking about himself when you want to talk about yourself. (In *Doolittle, A Biography,* by Lowell Thomas and Edward Jablonski, Doubleday, 1976; from Stephen J. Chant.)

Doris's Law of Looks. No matter what you wear, you will not look good if you look cold. (Doris Brown, Glen Ellyn, Illinois.)

Dorm Room Living, Laws of. (1) The amount of trash accumulated within the space occupied is exponentially proportional to the number of living bodies that enter and leave within any given amount of time. (2) Since no matter can be created or destroyed (excluding nuclear and cafeteria substances), as one attempts to remove unwanted material (i.e., trash) from one's living space, the remaining material mutates so as to occupy 30 to 50 percent more than its original volume. *Corollary:* Dust breeds. (3) The odds are 6:5 that if one has late classes, one's roommate will have the *earliest* possible classes. *Corollary 1:* One's roommate (who has early classes) has an alarm clock that is louder than God's own. *Corollary 2:* When one has an early class, one's roommate will invariably enter the space late at night and suddenly become hyperactive, ill, violent, or all three. *(U;* Part of a larger collection originating at East Russell Hall, University of Georgia, Athens.)

Dorothea's Comforting Thought for the Day. I've broken so many mirrors in my life, if I live long enough to have all that bad luck, I'll be lucky. (Dorothea Gildar, Washington, D.C.)

Dottie's Law. Any attempt to simplify creates more complications. (Dorothy Turcotte, Grimsby, Ontario.)

Doudna's Given. Whenever you tell someone what you paid for something you bought, you find out either (a) where you could have bought the same thing cheaper, or (b) where you could have bought something better for the same price. (Paul Doudna, Ferguson, Missouri.)

Douglas's Law of Practical Aeronautics. When the weight of the paperwork equals the weight of the plane, the plane will fly. (Airplane builder Donald Douglas, who articulated it for Jerome S. Katzin of La Jolla, California, who passed it along to *AO*.)

Douskey's Rule Concerning the Odds of Capitalizing on Previous Success. Sequels never equal. (Franz Douskey, Mount Carmel, Connecticut.)

Dowd's Rule. Never get involved with women who have 8-by-10 glossies. (Maureen Dowd, *The New York Times,* December 5, 2009 in a column about golfer Tiger Woods and his marital infidelities. She wrote: "Tiger may have been the greatest pro golfer but he was an amateur adulterer. His puffed-up ego led him to leave an electronic trail with a string of buffed and puffed babes. Like so many politicians before him, Tiger ignored the obvious rule: Never get involved with women who have 8-by-10 glossies.")

Dowd's Bath Principle. It takes more hot water to make cold water hot than it takes cold water to make hot water cold. (Larry C. Dowd, Columbia, Missouri.)

Dowling's First Law of Hollywood Moviemaking. No truly bad movie gets that way without consciously attempting to join (or initiate) a trend. (Tom Dowling, *Washington Star,* July 30, 1978.)

Downey's Law for Dressing for Success. When you are on the bottom you can't afford to look like you belong there. (Mike Downey, Houston, Texas.)

Dow's Law. In a hierarchical organization, the higher the level, the greater the confusion. (*U/S.T.L.*)

Dr. Brochu's Professorial Discourse. A "full professor" is not an assistant professor, an associate professor, an adjunct professor, or a part-time professor. He has been a professor for a long time, has filled all of his memory circuits with absolutely essential information; he is full of knowledge. *1st Consequence:* He cannot learn anything new without losing some knowledge essential to his position. *2nd Consequence:* If he does learn something new, the essential information forgotten as a result of consequence #1 will be requested by the Dean the next time they meet. *3rd Consequence:* If he protects essential knowledge by not learning anything new, a student will ask for the unlearned new knowledge the next day. *4th Consequence:* When the students and administration find out how full he is, he will be promoted to Dean. (Frank Brochu, M.D., Professor of Surgery, Salem, Virginia.)

Dr. Futch's Finding. The longer the patient lives, the greater his chances of recovery. (William D. Futch, St. Petersburg, Florida, who points out that it "has been a great comfort to many patients' families.")

Dr. Haslam's Medical Rules. (1) The patients who thank you are the ones for which you have done the least. (2) The nicest people always have the worst illnesses. (3) The patient who begins a consultation with the words "Now you know I don't come to the doctor for every little thing..." is the one who does. (4) When explaining illness to patients, the only way to avoid being misunderstood is never to say anything. (5) Whatever day you tell a patient to start taking the contraceptive pill, her period will be due on her wedding day. (David Haslam, M.D., Cambridgeshire, England, submitted with the full list, which first appeared in *World Medicine,* July 28, 1979.)

Dr. Hayes's Hint. Helpful hints aren't. (Brian E. Hayes, M.D., Rosebud, Oregon.)

Dr. J's Distinction. If they say they love you, trust their behavior. If they say they don't love you, trust their words. (John H. Dickey, Ph.D., Aurora, Colorado.)

Dr. Quoy's Laws of Fishing. (1) The biggest fish always hits the smallest rod. (2) If two lines can get tangled, they will. (3) Whatever bait you're using, the fish are hitting something else. (4) As the hook is bent, so goes the fish. (Herbert C. Quoy, Ph.D.)

Draftee's Discovery. Cleanliness is next to godliness, except in the Army where it is next to impossible. (Martin Russell, Yonkers, New York.)

Drakenberg's Discovery. If you can't seem to find your glasses, it's probably because you don't have them on. (Delores Drakenberg, Willmar, Minnesota.)

Drake's Disaster Dictum. There are two things that don't work when disaster strikes: god and government. (Dorothy Drake, *Birmingham Post-Herald,* September 18, 1992; from Grady Nunn.)

Drasner's First Law of Tax Law. If someone has to go to jail, make sure it's the client. (Washington attorney Fred Drasner in the *Washington Post* August 9, 2001.)

Driscoll's Discovery. The higher one is in a hierarchy, the more befuddled one becomes when one attempts to operate the photocopy machine. (Robert S. Driscoll, Staten Island, New York.)

Drogin's Mealtime Maxim. A balanced meal is whatever gets hot all at the same time. A snack is what doesn't. (Marc Drogin, Roanoke [Virginia] *World-News,* March 23, 1965.)

Dror Law, First. While the difficulties and dangers of problems tend to increase at a geometric rate, the knowledge and manpower qualified to deal with these problems tend to increase at an arithmetic rate. *Dror Law, Second:* While human capacities to shape the environment, society, and human beings are rapidly increasing, policymaking capabilities to use those capacities remain the same. (Yehezkel Dror, Israeli policy analyst at Hebrew University; from "Policy Sciences: Developments and Implications," RAND Corp. Paper P-4321, March 1970.)

Drucker, The Sayings of Chairman Peter. (1) If you have too many problems, maybe you should go out of business. There is no law that says a company must last forever. (2) As to the idea that advertising motivates people, remember the Edsel. (3) The only things that evolve by themselves in an organization are disorder, friction, and malperformance. (4) We know nothing about motivation. All we can do is write books about it. (5) "Marketing" is a fashionable term. The sales manager becomes a marketing vice-president. But a gravedigger is still a gravedigger even when he is called a mortician—only the price of burial goes up. (6) Fast personnel decisions are likely to be wrong. (7) Strong people always have strong weaknesses. (8) Start with what is right rather than with what is acceptable. (9) We always remember best the irrelevant. (10) When a subject becomes totally obsolete, we make it a required course. (11) Medicare and Medicaid are the greatest measures yet devised to make the world safe for clerks. (12) We may now be nearing the end of our hundred-year belief in Free Lunch. (See *Commoner's* and *Crane's Laws.*) (13) Look at governmental programs for the past fifty years. Every single one—except for warfare—achieved the exact opposite of its announced goal. (14) The computer is a moron. (15) The main impact of the computer has been the provision of unlimited jobs for clerks. (Selected by the author from *Drucker: The Man Who Invented the Corporate Society,* by John J. Tarrant, Cahners Books, Inc., 1976.)

Drunk, Rules for Getting. (1) Not too often. (2) In good company. (3) With good wine. (From *In Praise of Drunkenness* by Boniface Oinophilus, published in London, England, in 1812. The author marshals strong proof for each of his rules. For instance, in support of the second rule, he says, "A man in former times would have done very ill to get drunk with Heliogabalus, whose historian reports that, after having made his friends drunk, he used to shut them up in an apartment and at night let loose upon them lions, leopards, and tigers, which always tore to pieces some of them.")

du Pont's Laws. *A Compendium of Helpful Rules Governing the Legislative Process Not to be Found in Jefferson's Manual of Rules and Practices of the House of Representatives.* (1) Vote as an individual; lemmings end up falling off cliffs. Camaraderie is no substitute for common sense, and being your own man will make you sleep better. (2) The speed at which the legislative process seems to work is in inverse proportion to your enthusiasm for the bill. If you want a bill to move quickly, committee hearings, the rules committee, and legislative procedures appear to be roadblocks to democracy. If you do not want the bill to pass, such procedures are essential to furthering representative government, etc., etc. (3) The titles of bills—like those of Marx Brothers movies—often have little to do with the substance of the legislation. Particularly deceptive are bills containing title buzz words such as *emergency, reform, service, relief,* or *special.* Often the *emergency* is of the writer's imagination; the *reform,* a protection of vested interest; the *service,* self-serving; the *relief,* an additional burden on the taxpayer; and the *special,* something that otherwise shouldn't be passed. (4) Sometimes the best law of all is no law at all. Not all the world's ills are susceptible to legislative correction. (5) When voting on appropriations bills, more is not necessarily better. It is as wasteful to have a B-1 bomber in every garage as it is to have a welfare program for every conceivable form of deprivation. (6) The Crusades ended several centuries ago after killing thousands of people. The most important issues arouse intense passions. Earmuffs to block the shouting are inappropriate, but filter the feedback. Joining a cause and leading a constituency are not mutually exclusive, but neither are they necessarily synonymous. Neither welfare nor profits are "obscene." (7) "Beware the [lobbyist], my son, the jaws that bite, the claws that snatch" (with thanks to Lewis Carroll). No matter how noble the cause or well-meaning its professional advocates, lobbyists are still paid to get results. They're subject to errors in judgment, shortcomings in motives, and most of them don't even vote in your district. (8) Mirror, mirror on the wall, who's the fairest one of all? The press is hopelessly biased or genuinely fair, depending upon whose views are being misquoted, misrepresented, or misunderstood. (9) If you are concerned about being criticized—you're in the wrong job. However you vote, and whatever you do, somebody will be out there telling you that you are: (a) wrong, (b) insensitive, (c) a bleeding heart, (d) a pawn of somebody else, (e) too wishy-washy, (f) too unwilling to compromise, (g) all of the above—consistency is not required of critics. (Governor Pierre S. du Pont of Delaware, who wrote them when he was a congressman. The laws were written for incoming members, about whom he said in his introduction to the laws: "A freshman Congressman trying to do his job properly is similar to a quarterback trying to throw a 60-yard pass with a deflated football. The only difference is the quarterback knows there is no air in the ball—the freshman Congressman doesn't even know what game he is playing." See also *Fifth Rule.*)

DuBow's Laws of Attorney Fee Compensation. (1) Never accept a check from a man accused of passing bad ones. (2) Never accept cash from a man accused of counterfeiting. (3) If your client is a good-looking woman and wants a divorce, get your fee in advance. (Myron DuBow, Sherman Oaks, California.)

Dude's Law of Duality. Of two possible events, only the undesired one will occur. This can be expressed mathematically as:

$A \cap B^u = B$ [1]
$A^u \cap B = A$ [2]

where A and B are possible outcomes, where the superscript ^{u} denotes the undesired outcome, and where $\cap$ means either/or. (From Walter Mulé's article, "Beyond

Murphy's Law," in *Northliner.* Mulé says the law was named for Sam Dude, whose genius was cut short by a skydiving accident that occurred just after he was forced to choose between two types of parachute. He was also responsible for the *Third Corollary,* which says: The difficulty of getting anything started increases with the square of the number of people involved. This can be expressed mathematically as: $A \cap B^u = B$ [1], $A^u \cap B = A$ [2] where A and B are possible outcomes, where the superscript ^{u} denotes the undesired outcome, and where $\cap$ means either/or.

Duffer's Laws. (1) No matter how bad a round of golf you play, there will always be at least one stroke so perfect, so on target, and so gratifying that you will come back to play again. (2) The best way for a duffer to go around a tree standing directly in his line is to aim directly at the tree, since you never hit where you're aiming anyway. (3) The only time you'll hit the ball straight is when you're applying *Duffer's Law #2:* (4) Never carry more clubs than you can afford to break. (5) It is a myth that playing an old ball guarantees you will carry the lake. (6) Nobody cares what you shot today, except you. (John H. Corcoran, Jr., Chevy Chase, Maryland.)

Duggan's Law. To every Ph.D. there is an equal and opposite Ph.D. (B. Duggan, quoted from one of Robert Specht's quote-laden calendars, *1970 Expectation of Days.* This law helps explain why it is so easy to find expert witnesses to totally contradict each other.)

Dugger's Law of Texas Politics. Possession is the first nine-tenths of the law, and politics is the tenth. (Ronnie Dugger, *The Politician: The Life and Times of Lyndon Johnson,* Norton, 1982; from Joseph C. Goulden.)

Dukes's Law. The most powerful words in marketing are "Watch this!" (James A. Robertson, El Paso, Texas, who learned it from Carlton Dukes, Dallas, Texas.)

Dull's Advice. If you can use it, pull it. (Joan Dull; from David Finger, Wilmington, Delaware, who points out that it was created by Ms. Dull as a reference to pulling strings to get a job, but that it has broader applications.)

Dumas's Law. Most general statements are false, including this one. (Alexander Dumas; from John C. Armor, Baltimore, Maryland.)

Dunlop's Determination. People complain most about that over which they have the least control—e.g., the weather. (Paul Dunlop, Hamilton, Ontario.)

Dunne's Law. The territory behind rhetoric is too often mined with equivocation. (John Gregory Dunne, "To Die Standing," *The Atlantic,* June 1971.)

Dunning's Law. No more than 50 percent of the blow dryers in men's restrooms will work at any given time. (Bob Dunning, Davis, California *Enterprise,* December 19, 1985; *TG.*)

Dunn's Dally on Doing. Never do now what must be done or you may not find anything to do when you are looking for something to do later. *Dunn's*

Observation. If all the telephone calls from firms claiming that they are in the neighborhood installing siding, solar heat, roofing, carpeting, basement waterproofing, insulation, kitchen cabinets, patios, storm windows, rec rooms, bathroom tile, etc., were true, the city would need massive around-the-clock traffic control on my street so they could get another car in to give me my free estimate "as long as they are in the neighborhood." (Russell J. Dunn, Lakewood, Ohio.)

Dunn's Discovery. The shortest measurable interval of time is the time between the moment I put a little extra aside for a sudden emergency and the arrival of that emergency. (Marvin Dunn; quoted in the *Louisville Courier-Journal.*)

Dunstan's Dilemma. Logic is like cricket: It is admirable as long as you are playing according to the rules. But what happens to your game of cricket when someone suddenly decides to bowl with a football or bat with a hockey stick? That is what is continually happening in life. (Dunstan Ramsay in *The Manticore,* by Robertson Davies, Viking, 1972; from Catherine Pfeifer, Milwaukee, Wisconsin.)

Durant's Discovery. One of the lessons of history is that nothing is often a good thing to do and always a clever thing to say. (Will Durant; from an item in the November 1972 *Reader's Digest* quoting Derek Gill's article on Durant in *Modern Maturity.*)

Durocher's Edict. You don't save a pitcher for tomorrow; tomorrow it may rain. (Leo Durocher; from R. H. Roth, Lamboing, Switzerland.)

Durrell's Parameter. The faster the plane, the narrower the seats. (John H. Durrell of Mason, Ohio, in a letter to the editor, *The Wall Street Journal,* March 15, 1976.)

Duverger's Law. The simple-majority single-ballot system favors the two-party system. (French political scientist Maurice Duverger, *Political Parties: Their Organization and Activity in the Modern State,* John Wiley, 1954; from Charles D. Poe.)

Dwyer's Law of Pins. If you unwrap a new article of clothing that is secured by *n* pins, you will remove *n* -1 pins. And that pin will pierce you in a place that hurts. (Edward J. Dwyer, Cherry Hill, New Jersey.)

Dyer's Discovery. The basic fine print for all insurance policies says, "This policy is void in case of a claim." (Frederick C. Dyer, Somerset, Maryland.)

Dyer's Law. A continuing flow of paper is sufficient to continue the flow of paper. *Dyer's Observation:* It all boils down to two words: "Send money," or "Raise dues," or "Increase taxes." (Professor John M. Dyer, director, International Finance and Marketing Program, University of Miami, Coral Gables, Florida; *FD.*)

Dykema's Laws. *One-on-One Law:* Your house makes strange noises only when you are alone. *Good News for Pencil Rules:* The pen never wears out at the end of a sentence. (Denise Dykema, Morrison, Illinois.)

E

Earle's Law of Relativity. The shortest period of time is that between when the light turns green and when the guy behind you blows his horn. (M. Mack Earle, Baltimore, Maryland.)

Ear's Law. Before a party or a trip, if it can, it will let rip. (From the "Ear" column in the *Washington Star.* It was recalled in print when the Carters' hot water heater burst on their last day in Plains before leaving for the Inauguration.)

Ebert's Box Rule. If a printed ad for a movie features a row of boxes at the bottom, with the stars in those boxes, the movie is not worth watching. (Film critic Roger Ebert, paraphrased from his article, *Chicago Sun-Times,* June 23, 1985; from Steve Stine.)

Economist's First Law of Journalism, The. Never believe anything until it is officially denied. (*The Economist* magazine, May 4, 1991.)

Economists' Laws. (1) What men learn from history is that men do not learn from history. (2) If on an actuarial basis there is a 50/50 chance that something will go wrong, it will actually go wrong nine times in ten.

Eddie's Law of Location. All football is played on the other side of the field. (Euan F. Eddie, Folkestone, Kent, England. This law was presented with a considerable amount of research, including Eddie's observations at one-sided rugby football contests. He reports, "I noticed that in a match in which, for example, team A beat team B by 80 points to 4, when I moved to an observation point behind team B's goal line, which they had been gallantly but ineffectively defending, the time of my arrival coincided exactly with their one and only score of the match at the other end of the field.")

Edington's Theory. Hypotheses multiply so as to fill the gaps in factual knowledge concerning biological phenomena. (Named for C. W. Edington, but first explained by James D. Regan in the April 1963 issue of the *Journal of Irreproducible Results.* Although created for biological phenomena, it was noted in the original article that it applied in other scientific areas as well.)

Edison's Axiom. We don't know one-millionth of one percent about anything. (Thomas Alva Edison, U.S. inventor; *GT.*)

Editorial Correction, Law of. Anyone nit-picking enough to write a letter of correction to an editor doubtless deserves the error that provoked it. (This law was created by Alvin Toffler and published in *The New York Times Magazine* on April 7, 1968. It was written in response to an article by Harold Faber on laws, e.g., "Faber's Law—If there isn't a law, there will be." Toffler said, in part, that a law credited to Anthony Toffler called the *Law of Raspberry Jam* was originated by

Stanley Edgar Hyman. He added, "Not only is my name not Anthony—which I regret—but I heartily disagree with said Law of Raspberry Jam. My book, *The Culture Consumers*, St. Martin's, 1964, mentions it, then spends 14 chapters disputing its contention that 'the wider any culture is spread, the thinner it gets' "; *FD*.)

Editorial Laws. (1) When you proudly publish a significant article and expect a large reader response, you'll get one letter telling you about a typo in the third paragraph. (2) A dangling participle deserves dangling. (3) The poorer the writer, the greater his resistance to editorial changes. (4) The author best qualified to write a special article on a hot topic is always away on a three-month overseas assignment. (5) During an interview with an important official, the point of your pencil will break off at the most quotable quote. (6) If you create a magazine that is so good that subscribers refuse to part with it—that's bad. If, however, you put out a magazine that means so little to each individual that it gets passed from hand to hand, that's good. For advertisers, that is. (7) Never expect a good writer to be a good editor; never expect a former English teacher to be a good writer; or a former typing teacher to be a good manuscript typist. (8) When an article reference and page number are given on your magazine cover, the page number will change before the magazine goes to press. (Selected from *Edpress News,* published by the Educational Press Association of America. Laws 1–6 are by the *Edpress* editor Ben Brodinsky, the next is by "Editorial Experts," Washington, D.C., and the final law is by Walter Craves, *Today's Education.*)

Edwards's Laws. (1) A telephone number is not recorded on the message unless you already know it. (2) Always carry a pen. (3) Go Ivy League? / I sure won't / My shirts taper / But I don't. (Robert V. Edwards, Washington, D.C.)

Edwards's Tautology. Fat men are good-natured because good-natured men are usually fat. (Canadian editor/humorist Bob Edwards.)

Efficiency

An Efficiency Expert Reports on Hearing a Symphony at the Royal Festival Hall in London.

- *For considerable periods, the four oboe players had nothing to do.* The number should be reduced and the work spread more evenly over the whole of the concert, thus eliminating peaks of activity.
- *All twelve violins were playing identical notes; this seems unnecessary duplication.* The staff of this section should be drastically cut. If a larger volume of sound is required, it could be obtained by electronic apparatus.

- *Much effort was absorbed in the playing of demi-semi-quavers; this seems to be an unnecessary refinement.* It is recommended that all notes should be rounded up to the nearest semi-quaver. If this was done it would be possible to use trainees and lower-grade operatives more extensively.
- *There seems to be too much repetition of some musical passages.* Scores should be drastically pruned. No useful purpose is served by repeating on the horns a passage that has already been handled by the strings. It is estimated that if all redundant passages were eliminated, the whole concert time of two hours could be reduced to twenty minutes and there would be no need for an intermission.
- *The conductor agrees generally with these recommendations, but expressed the opinion that there might be some falling off in box-office receipts.* In that unlikely event it should be possible to close sections of the auditorium entirely, with a consequential saving of overhead expenses, lighting, attendance, etc. If the worse came to the worst, the whole thing could be abandoned and the public could go to the Albert Hall instead.

(The Murphy Center has received a number of versions of this report, which was obviously created in England. One fellow says he first saw a copy in London in 1955.)

Ehre's Law of Double Doors. In approaching an entrance that has two doors, you will (1) always enter the locked side; (2) always push when you should have pulled (or vice versa); (3) always, even when the door says to push or pull, do the opposite 90 percent of the time. (Victor T. Ehre, Jr., Edwardsville, Illinois.)

Ehrlich's Rule. The first rule of intelligent tinkering is to save all the parts. (Environmentalist Paul Ehrlich, *The Saturday Review,* June 5, 1971.)

Ehrman's Corollary to Ginsberg's Theorem. (1) Things will get worse before they get better. (2) Who said things would get better? (John Ehrman, Stanford Linear Accelerator Center; *JE.* Of course, you should see *Ginsberg's Theorem.*)

Einstein's Explanation of Relativity. Sit with a pretty girl for an hour and it seems like a minute; sit on a hot stove for a minute and it seems like an hour—that's relativity. (Albert Einstein; *ME.*)

Einstein's Other Formula. If A equals success, then the formula is A = X + Y + Z. X is work. Y is play. Z is keep your mouth shut. (Albert Einstein defining success, news summaries of April 19, 1955; quoted in *Contemporary Quotations,* compiled by J. B. Simpson, Crowell, 1964.)

Einstein's Razor. Things should be made as simple as possible, but no simpler. (Albert Einstein; quoted by Steven R. Woodbury, Springfield, Virginia.)

Einstein's Three Rules of Work. (1) Out of clutter find simplicity. (2) From discord make harmony. (3) In the middle of difficulty lies opportunity. (Albert Einstein; quoted in *Newsweek,* March 12, 1979.)

Eisenhower's Admonition. Never wrestle with a pig, because he has a ball and you wind up washing a heck of a lot of manure out of your hair. (Quoted by General Andrew Goodpaster at a symposium on Eisenhower held at Fort McNair, January 26–28, 2005; sponsored by the Eisenhower Memorial Commission, contained in a proceedings volume, "Forging the Shield," Dennis E. Showalter, editor, Imprint Publications, Chicago, 2005; *JCG.*)

Eisenstein's Laws of Tourism. (1) If you go during the season with the best weather, it will be the worst weather in forty-nine years. (2) No matter where you sit, the view out the other side will be better. (3) If you move from a room into another one because something is wrong, something will be worse in the new room. (4) The best trips are the unplanned ones; this way, you won't worry about fouling up your timetable. Conversely, the tighter the timetable, the more you'll worry and the later you'll be. (Edward L. Eisenstein, University City, Missouri.)

Eisner's Observations. (1) Calories are delicious. (2) Smokers can't read. (3) When you come in late for work, everybody notices; when you work late, nobody notices. (4) Humor is dependent on the truth. (Raymond F. Eisner, Littleton, Colorado.)

Eldridge's Explanation of War. Man is always ready to die for an idea, provided that the idea is not quite clear to him. (Paul Eldridge, American poet, novelist, short story writer and teacher; quoted in *Reader's Digest,* February 1963.)

Electronic Elegy. Beware of buying anything when the manuals are bigger than the equipment. (B.V.D. Smith, Downers Grove, Illinois.)

Eling's Observation. During radio or TV programs, any word you fail to hear will also go unheard by anyone else present. (Stan Eling, Smethwick Warley, West Midlands, England.)

Eliot's Observation. Nothing is so good as it seems beforehand. (English novelist George Eliot, from *Silas Marner,* 1861.)

Ellenson's Miscellaneous Natural Laws. *Interesting Food:* "Interesting" food is that which lies somewhere between palatable and *ptui. Inevitable Boo-boos:* In the course of every endeavor there lurks a mistake not made. *Accountability:* Accountability measures the ability to *account,* not the ability to do the job. *Corollary 1:* If one insists on accountability, that is what one will get. *Corollary 2:* If accountability is paramount, that is *all* one will get. *Reductionist Law of Gottas and Shoulds:* There is only one gotta and one should in life: You *gotta* live with the consequences of your actions, and you *should* remember that. *Causal Loci:* Blame for any given condition or occurrence will automatically shift until it settles on the least influenceable variable (e.g., crime may be blamed on social structure, the failure of a business on national economic conditions, etc.). (Gerald S. Ellenson, Huntington Beach, California.)

Elliot's Law. Ice cream cones always fall scoop-down. (Kandis Edward Elliot, *Journal of Irreproducible Results,* November–December 1985; from Neal Wilgus.)

Elliott's Household Rules. (1) No matter when you start, bedtime happens at 11:30 p.m. (2) There's no such thing as a "long winter evening," since none of the chores saved for a long winter evening ever gets done. (3) All clocks in the house conspire to display totally different readings. (4) The cat never goes out the door the first time you open it. (Owen Elliott, Ridgefield, Connecticut.)

Ellison's Conclusion. The two most common things in the universe are hydrogen and stupidity. (Harlan Ellison, *Omni,* February 1987; from Catherine Pfeifer, who noted that it appeared in the context of comments on censorship: "These would-be censors are monsters. And they will always be with us, because the two most common things in the universe are hydrogen and stupidity.") *Alexander's Corollary:* Not necessarily in that order. (from Michael A. Stackpole, Phoenix, who named it after David Alexander. "David is a magician and faith-healing debunker," wrote Stackpole in September 1989. "I don't imagine he's the first to say it, but he said it to Harlan on Harlan's radio show in California.")

Ellison's Law. In this society... what happens to blacks will eventually happen to whites. (Author Ralph Ellison.)

Ellis's Reciprocal. An unwatched pot boils immediately. *Corollary:* The speed with which boiling milk rises from the bottom of the pan to any point beyond the top is greater than the speed at which the human brain and hand can combine to snatch the wretched thing off the burner. (H. F. Ellis, "Men in Aprons," *Punch;* from Ross Reader.)

Ellis's Rule of the Road. In freeway driving, slow drivers always need left lane exits, fast ones right lane exits. (Andy Ellis, KCBS, San Francisco, California.)

Ellstrand's Law of Dietary Discretion. If it fits on your plate, it fits in your stomach! (Beverly Ellstrand, Park Ridge, Illinois.)

Elway's Response. *Question* (to John Elway during the week before Super Bowl XXI): What's the stupidest question you've been asked this week? *A:* That's it. (*Washington Post,* January 25, 1987.)

Emergency Rule. In Case of Atomic Attack, the Federal Ruling Concerning Prayer in This Building Will Be Temporarily Suspended. (Sign [handwritten] found posted in a federal office building, Washington, D.C.)

Emerson's Insight. That which we call sin in others is experiment for us. (Ralph Waldo Emerson.)

Emerson's Rule. Never read a book that is not a year old. (Ralph Waldo Emerson, who, it is noted by the director of the book-dependent at the Murphy Center, did not say anything about *buying* books before they are a year old.)

Emery's Law. Regulation is the substitution of error for chance. (Fred J. Emery, Director, *The Federal Register*, Washington, D.C.)

Emery's Theory of Relativity. Are you talking fence posts or towns? (Emery Warren; from John A. Staedler, Merced, California, who explains, "Two fence posts a mile apart are quite far, but two towns a mile apart are quite close.")

Emmanuel's Law of Customer Satisfaction. Customer satisfaction is directly proportional to employee satisfaction. (Daniel Emmanuel, Dallas, Texas.)

Energy Matters

1. How You Can Save with a Wood Stove.

Stove, pipe, installation, etc.	$458.00
Chainsaw	149.95
Care and maintenance for chainsaw	44.60
4-wheel-drive pickup, stripped	8,379.04
4-wheel-drive pickup maintenance	438.00
Replace rear window of pickup (twice)	310.00
Fine for cutting unmarked tree in state forest	500.00
Fourteen cases Michelob	126.00
Littering fine	50.00
Towing charge—truck from creek	50.00
Doctor's fee for removing splinter from eye	45.00
Safety glasses	29.50
Emergency room treatment (broken toes—dropped logs)	125.00
Safety shoes	49.95
New living room carpet	800.00
Paint living room walls and ceiling	110.00
Log splitter	150.00
Fifteen-acre woodlot	9,000.00
Taxes on woodlot	310.00
Replace coffee table (chopped up and burned while drunk)	75.00
Divorce settlement	33,678.22
Total first year's cost	54,878.26
Savings in conventional fuel first year	(72.33)
Net cost of first year's woodburning	$54,805.93

(From ME.)

2. Best One-Liner on the Energy Crisis.

If God had meant for us to have enough oil he never would have given us the Department of Energy. (Robert Orben.)

Engineer's Law, The Old. The larger the project or job, the less time there is to do it. (George A. Daher, Philadelphia, Pennsylvania; *AO.*)

Engle's Law. There are only two kinds of things in this world: things you started, and things that are overdue. (Marc Engle, U.S. Geological Survey, from Tom Gill.)

Ensminger's Theory of Multiplicity. Trees always drop more leaves than they bear. (Jim Ensminger; from John Schaefer.)

Enthoven's Discovery. The ideal weapons system is built in 435 congressional districts, and it doesn't matter whether it works or not. (Stanford economist and former Pentagon official Alain C. Enthoven, quoted in the *Washington Post,* January 26, 1992; from Joseph C. Goulden.)

Epperson's Law. When a man says it's a silly, childish game, it's probably something his wife can beat him at. (Don Epperson, quoted in Bill Cold's District Line column in the *Washington Post,* September 11, 1978.)

Epps's Elevator Law. A crowded elevator smells different to a short person. (Buddy Epps; from Don Schofield, Charleston, South Carolina.)

Epstean's Laws. (1) Man always tends to satisfy his needs and desires with the least possible exertion. (2) If self-preservation is the first law of human conduct, exploitation is the second. (Edward Epstean, from Albert Jay Nock's *Memoirs of a Superfluous Man,* Harper, 1943; *JMcC.*)

Epstein's Law. If you think the problem is bad now, just wait until we've solved it. (*U;* from Arthur Kasspe, Ph.D., New York, New York.)

ERDA Law of Materials Procurement, The. Never use lead when gold will do. (ERDA, acronym for the Federal Energy Research and Development Administration *U/CT.*)

Erickson's Law of the Sea. When in doubt, go fast; when in danger, go faster. (L. Bruce Erickson; *MLS.*)

Erkes's Law of Human Incredulity. People will always believe whatever it is that they want to believe and no accumulation of factual evidence will ever be able to dissuade them. "Open minds" are for subjects like the physiognomy of the aphid, that they know nothing about. (Edwin S. Erkes, Glenolden, Pennsylvania.)

Err's Laws. See *Murphy's Law(s).* (Err is basically a synonym for Murphy, but those who quote him over the better-known prophet insist he is as real as Murphy. The basis for their argument: [1] his spirit, like Murphy's, is everywhere and [2] Err is human.)

Ertz's Observation on Immortality. Millions long for immortality who do not know what to do with themselves on a rainy Sunday afternoon. (Author Susan Ertz (1894–1985) from *Anger in the Sky*, Harper, 1943.)

Eternal Questions from Cyberspace. (1) If the #2 pencil is the most popular, why is it still #2? (2) If all the world is a stage, where is the audience sitting? (3) If you try to fail, and succeed, which have you done?

Eternity Rule. Nothing is certain except death and taxes. *Bretagna's Corollary:* If anything else is permanent, it is the fact that, given *any* roadway, somewhere upon it there will be someone going slower than you want to go. (The *Eternity Rule* is one of several names currently being given to various close paraphrases of Benjamin Franklin's line, "In this world, nothing is certain but death and taxes." It first appeared in a letter from Franklin to M. Leroy in 1789. The corollary comes from Nicholas Bretagna II, Orlando, Florida.)

Ettorre's Observation. The other line moves faster. (Barbara Ettorre, New York, New York. This first appeared in *Harper's* in August 1974, and has become a bona fide hit, showing up on many lists of laws produced since it was first published. The original was longer than what is now commonly known as *Ettorre's Observation.* The full version: "The other line moves faster. This applies to all lines—bank, supermarket, tollbooth, customs, and so on. And don't try to change lines. The other line—the one you were in originally—will then move faster"; *HW.*)

Evans On Creation. It is ironic that the most sophisticated eye in all of nature's creations was given to the common housefly—so that it may better sit on your potato salad. (James T. Evans, Houston, Texas.)

Evans's Eternal Question. The Eternal Question is not "What is Truth?" or "What is the Meaning of Life?" The question asked by more people since the beginning of time is "Why do I keep doing this stuff to myself?" (James T. Evans, Houston, Texas.)

Evans's Four Basic Laws. Nothing worth a damn is ever done as a matter of principle. (If it is worth doing, it is done because it is worth doing. If it is not, it's done as a matter of principle). *Evans's Second, Third, and Fourth Laws:* (2) Everyone succeeds 100 percent of the time—at what they're really up to. (3) That man or woman you see who is so beautiful, rich, talented, and charming that you would literally die for them—remember somewhere out there is a person who is sick and tired of them. (4) People and projects, like arrows, tend to hit the ground at the same angle they took off. (James T. Evans, Attorney, Houston, Texas.)

Evans's Law. The car with the dead battery will have all the other vehicles pinned in the garage. (George Evans, Greeley, Colorado.)

Evans's Law of Political Perfidy. When our friends get into power, they aren't our friends anymore. (M. Stanton Evans, who was until recently the head of the American Conservative Union; *JMcC.*)

Evans's Three Simple Laws. (1) Nothing is ever simply black and white; and just as often it's not gray, either. (2) *Everything* is the fault of a repressed Catholic childhood—especially if you didn't have one. (3) I think; but I'm still not convinced I am. (Gareth J. Evans, Loughborough, Leicester, England.)

Evelyn's Determination. Long-range planning works best in the short term. (Doug Evelyn, Washington, D.C.)

Evelyn's Law. A woman is like a tea bag—you never know her strength until she gets into hot water. (Woman named Evelyn, radio call-in show, WRC, Washington, D.C.)

Evelyn's Rules for Bureaucratic Survival. (1) A bureaucrat's castle is his desk...and parking place. Proceed cautiously when changing either. (2) On the theory that one should never take anything for granted, follow up on everything, but especially those items varying from the norm. The greater the divergence from normal routine and/or the greater the number of offices potentially involved, the better the chance a never-to-be-discovered person will file the problem away in a drawer specifically designed for items requiring a decision. (3) Never say without qualification that your activity has sufficient space, money, staff, etc. (4) Always distrust offices not under your jurisdiction which say that they are there to serve you. "Support" offices in a bureaucracy tend to grow in size and make demands on you out of proportion to their service, and in the end require more effort on your part than their service is worth. *Corollary:* Support organizations can always prove success by showing service to someone...not necessarily you. (5) Incompetents often hire able assistants. (Douglas Evelyn, National Portrait Gallery, Washington, D.C.)

Ever Notice "Notice." Ever notice that even the busiest people are never too busy to tell you just how busy they are. (*U;* overheard on Red Line Metro subway, Washington, D.C., 2006.)

Everitt's Form of the Second Law of Thermodynamics. Confusion (entropy) is always increasing in society. Only if someone or something works extremely hard can this confusion be reduced to order in a limited region. Nevertheless, this effort will still result in an increase in the total confusion of society at large. (Dr. W. L. Everitt, Dean Emeritus of the College of Engineering at the University of Illinois.)

Eve's Discovery. At a bargain sale, the only suit or dress that you like best and that fits is the one not on sale. *Adam's Corollary:* It's easy to tell when you've got a bargain—it doesn't fit. (*FD.*)

Evvie Nef's Law. There is a solution to every problem; the only difficulty is finding it. (*Washington Post*, January 1972; *JW.*)

Excuses

We've never done it before.
Nobody else has ever done it.
It has never been tried before.
We tried it before.
Another company (person) tried it before.
We've been doing it this way for 25 years.
It won't work in a small company.
It won't work in a large company.
It won't work in our company.
Why change—it's working okay.
The boss will never buy it.
It needs further investigation.
Our competitors are not doing it.
It's too much trouble to change.
Our company is different.
Marketing says it can't be done.
Sales says it can't be sold.
The service department won't like it.
The janitor says it can't be done.
It can't be done.
We don't have the money.
We don't have the employees.
We don't have the equipment.
The union will scream.
It's too visionary.
You can't teach an old dog new tricks.
It's too radical a change.
It's beyond my responsibility.
It's not my job.
We don't have the time.
It will obsolete other procedures.
Customers won't buy it.

It's contrary to policy.
It will increase overhead.
The employees will never buy it.
It's not our problem.
I don't like it.
You're right, but...
We're not ready for it.
It needs more thought.
Management won't accept it.
We can't take the chance.
We'd lose money on it.
It takes too long to pay out.
We're doing all right as it is.
It needs committee study.
The competition won't like it.
It needs sleeping on.
It won't work in this department.
It's impossible.

Expert Advice, The First Law of. Don't ask the barber whether you need a haircut. (Science writer-columnist Daniel S. Greenberg first revealed this some years ago in the *Saturday Review* and returned to it in late 1977 in his *Washington Post* column. Greenberg attaches the law to "the promotion of a technology by its developers or custodians without any independent check on whether it does what it's supposed to do." He gives several examples, including a chemical shark repellent called Shark Chaser, which the Navy bought in great quantities between World War II and 1974, at which time it was learned that sharks had no aversion to eating Shark Chaser.)

Explanations

A small catalog of previously eluded truths as they appeared in *The Official Explanations*. They are dated—but not irrelevant in 2013:

1. Why America's Bicentennial was not more spectacular.
Because the late Wernher von Braun's suggestion to the Senate Space Committee was not adopted. In September 1969 he proposed putting the President of the United States in orbit to celebrate the two-hundredth anniversary of the Republic.

2. Why one should not be too afraid of the Internal Revenue Service.
Recently the IRS demanded that Elizabeth R. Tunnel of Norfolk, Virginia, pay tax on the many automobiles that the government had determined were in her possession. Ms. Tunnel is the Elizabeth River Tunnel that runs beneath the Elizabeth River. The cars are not hers.

3. Why metric conversion is going to take a lot longer than previously anticipated.
As one radio preacher is reported to have stated, "If God had meant for us to go metric, why did he give Jesus twelve disciples?"

4. Why the United States uses humans in space.
"Man," says a 1965 NASA report on manned space, "is the lowest-cost, 150-pound, nonlinear, all-purpose computer system which can be mass-produced by unskilled labor."

5. Why television is not living up to its promise as an educational medium.
The following was actually edited out of the Nixon-Frost TV interviews:

RN:... We were sitting in the bow of the yacht. I'm an old Navy man. The bow is the rear-end, isn't it?
DF:... I, ah, ... probably.
RN: That's right. No. The stern. We were sitting in the stern.
DF: Let's say end.
RN: All right. We were sitting down at the end of the yacht.

6. Why the government has such a hard time getting out of things it has gotten into.
Here is how the term "exit" has been defined by government experts:

An exit is a means of egress and has three component parts.

First, an exit access: Exit access is that portion of a means of egress which leads to an entrance to an exit.

Second, the exit itself: Exit is that portion of a means of egress which is separated from all other spaces of the building or structure by construction or equipment as required in this subpart to provide a protected way of travel to the exit discharge.

Third, the exit discharge: That portion of a means of egress between the termination of an exit and a public way.

Exploding Water Heater Theory. You should live every day as if tomorrow you were going to be killed by an exploding water heater. (Jeremy Ehrlich, San Francisco, California, who explains, "The background for this theory has to do with the following observations: dentists tend to have clean teeth, for dentists understand the importance of brushing. Chiropractors have good posture, for they understand the importance of a healthy back. Firefighters remember to replace the batteries in their fire alarms, etc, etc. Consider Hypothetical Joe, who tries to do all of this. He brushes his teeth, works out, replaces his batteries, the whole bit. One day he's in his shop in the basement working on some repair around the house when he is killed because he has forgotten to replace his water heater every five to seven years like he was told to do.)

Extended Epstein-Heisenberg Principle. In a research and development orbit, only two of the existing three parameters can be defined simultaneously. The parameters are: task, time, and resources. (1) If one knows what the task is, and there is a time limit allowed for the completion of the task, then one cannot guess how much it will cost. (2) If the time and resources are clearly defined, then it is impossible to know what part of the R&D task will be performed. (3) If you are given a clearly defined R&D goal and a definite amount of money which has been calculated to be necessary for the completion of the task, one cannot predict if and when the goal will be reached. (4) If one is lucky enough and can accurately define all three parameters, then what one deals with is not in the realm of R&D. (From the *JIR* article "Uncertainty Principle in Research and Development," January 1973.)

External Relations. (1) A lobbyist is paid to look like he's telling the truth when he's lying; a department's congressional liaison is paid to look like he's telling the truth when he really has nothing to say. (2) A reporter's brother-in-law who works for the government is known as an "informed source" when he's sober and a "leak" when he's drunk. (Jim Kenworthy, Kansas City, Missouri.)

Exxon's Law of Energy Costs. We've upped ours, now up yours. (*U.*)

Eyberg's Romantic Reminder. Regardless of how good we are in bed, our relationship is entirely dependent on how good we are out of bed. (John E. Eyberg, Columbia, Missouri.)

F

Faber's Laws. (1) If there isn't a law, there will be. (2) The number of errors in any piece of writing rises in proportion to the writer's reliance on secondary sources. (Harold Faber. The first was used as the title of his 1968 *New York Times Magazine* article on laws, and the second, which is also called *The First Law of Historical Research*, was created in response to some errors that appeared in the article—i.e. calling Alvin Toffler, Anthony Toffler. [See *Editorial Correction, Law of.*] At the time the article was written, Faber was editorial director of the Book and Education Division of the *Times*.)

Fadiman's Law of Optimum Improvement. In the realm of objects, as well as in the realm of ethics, there can be an excess of refinement as well as a defect of crudity. It is my further conviction that a proper technological society is not the one capable of endlessly improving its artifacts, but the one able to see at what point it is best, from the point of view of the whole human being (and indeed of the whole human race), to stop the improvement. (Clifton Fadiman, from *This Is My Funniest,* edited by Whit Burnett, Perma Books, 1957. In his essay of the same title as the law, Fadiman gives many examples of "excessive refinement," but one that serves as well as any is book wrapping. He notes that books used to come wrapped in a piece of paper tied with a piece of cord. "In no time you could be reading the book." Now, he points out, they come in "cardboard iron maidens, suitable to the transportation of safes or pianos" or in "thick bags" that are almost impossible to open without ripping. When ripped, "Out flies a bushel of ancient furry shredded gray paper, the perfect stand-in for mouse dirt.")

Falkland's Rule. When it is not necessary to make a decision, it is necessary not to make a decision. (Lord Falkland.)

Family Law. Where there's a sibling, there's quibbling. (Selma Raskin. It originally appeared in *The Wall Street Journal* and is quoted in Charles Preston's *The Light Touch*, Rand McNally, 1965.)

Fannie's Ganif Theory. (1) Most politicians are thieves. (2) Most politicians are slow learners. (3) Therefore, never vote for an incumbent. While the challenger's natural inclinations are equally bad, it will take him time to learn how to achieve his goals. (From Carl T. Bogus, Philadelphia, Pennsylvania, who attributes it to his Aunt Fannie, Mrs. Fagel Kanev.)

Faraday's Lecture Rule. One hour is long enough for anyone. (Scientist Michael Faraday.)

Farber's Laws. (1) Give him an inch and he'll screw you. (2) We're all going down the same road in different directions. (3) Necessity is the mother of strange bedfellows. (Dave Farber, from a Farberism contest list; *S.T.L.*)

Farbinger's Rule. Brown-nosing a professor is best accomplished by asking a pointless question related to his or her own specific academic specialty, and then nodding one's head and uttering "uh-huh" every so often as the professor gives an answer. This will give the appearance of being truly interested and therefore deserving of attention, consideration, and better grades. (Warren Farbinger, Berkeley, California; from Ian Beste.)

Farkas's Law. If you want economy, you have to pay for it. (A current tenet of the aerospace cost analysis community. From Michael Brennan, Pacific Palisades, California, who explains, "The design, fabrication, and assembly of any new (although in theory less expensive) widget will invariably cost more than just turning the crank and building more of an existing (but, in principle, more expensive) widget design.")

Farkus's Law. There will always be a closer parking space than the one you found. *Goodman's Commentary on Farkus's Law:* But if you go looking for it, someone else will already have taken it. (Lee Goodman, Prairie Village, Kansas.)

Farmer's Law. The easiest crops to grow are weeds and pests. (Heard at the University of California, Davis; *TG.*)

Farmer's Law on Junk. What goes in, comes out. *Corollary 1:* He who sees what comes out, and why, gains wisdom. *Corollary 2:* He who sees only half the problem will be buried in the other half. *Corollary 3:* One man's junk is another's income—and sometimes his priceless antique. *Corollary 4:* Ten thousand years from now, the only story this civilization will tell will be in its junk piles—so observe what is important! *Corollary 5:* Seers and soothsayers read crystal balls to find the future. Less lucky men read junk—with more success. *Corollary 6:* A rose is a rose is a rose, but junk is not junk is not junk. It never is quite what you think it is. *Corollary 7:* Happiness at age ten was finding an empty six pack of returnable Coke bottles. The poor kids these days will never know what they missed, which is why we have a generation gap. (Richard N. Farmer, chairperson, International Business School, Indiana University; from his book *Farmer's Law: Junk in a World of Affluence,* Stein & Day Publishers, 1973. One needs to read the whole book to appreciate fully the technique, but the basic law and its corollaries attempt to show you how to read the future, national and international trends, other people's personalities, and competitors' plans—all by reading junk.)

Fashion, Law of. The same dress is indecent 10 years before its time, daring 1 year before its time, chic in its time, dowdy 3 years after its time, hideous 20 years after its time, amusing 30 years after its time, romantic 100 years after its time, and beautiful 150 years after its time. (James Laver; *JW.*)

Fassett's Law. The first elevator to arrive is going in the wrong direction. (Lloyd A. Fassett, M.D.)

Fast Lunch Rule, The. The rich can make you famous, but the poor can make you a hero. (Anonymous; from Dr. Joseph A. Horton.)

Father Damian Randal's Rules for Academic Deans. Rule 1—Hide!!! Rule 2—If they find you, lie!!! (Father Damian C. Randal, former Dean of Academic Affairs, University of Dallas, Texas.)

FCC Policy. Any sufficiently promising technology must be regulated or it will succeed. (R. W. Johnson; from his *Ham Radio Humor,* (Rodney Warren Johnson, from his self-published book, 1977.)

FDA Law. A drug is that substance which when injected into a rat will produce a scientific report. (*U;* originally quoted in Dr. Robert Matz's article "Principles of

Medicine," which appeared in the January 1977 issue of the *New York State Journal of Medicine.*)

Feather's Discovery. Loneliness is something you can't walk away from. (William Feather; *RS.*)

Feazel's Rules. *Travel:* Don't Go Back! It isn't there anymore. *Exception:* Switzerland. *Family Life:* Once you have trained your children to be an efficient team, they go away. (Examples: haying, sailing, fence-building, automotive maintenance, cooking, bridge, firewood procurement.) *Experience:* You never learn anything useful from your mistakes because you never get a chance to make the same one twice. *Jogging:* All hilly courses are uphill both ways. (Betty Feazel, Pagosa Springs, Colorado.)

Federal Emergency Advisory. In case of fire, flee with the same reckless abandon that occurs each day at quitting time. (From Bob Levey's column, *Washington Post,* September 10, 1985, in which he quotes this line from a government bulletin board.)

Feldman's Revisions. (1) For every actor, there's a reactor. (2) As ye sew, so shall ye rip. (3) A snitch in time saves nine. (Monroe Feldman, Silver Spring, Maryland.)

Feliciano's First Rule of Management. As you're charging up San Juan Hill, it's nice to be able to look over your shoulder and see that the troops are following. (Donald V. Feliciano, Herndon, Virginia.)

Feline Frustration, Rule of. When your cat has fallen asleep on your lap and looks utterly content and adorable, you will suddenly have to go to the bathroom. (*U/DRW.*)

Fenster's Law. One man's confusion is another man's Ph.D. thesis. (Bob Fenster, *Sacramento Bee,* February 23, 1986; *TG.*)

Fenster's Movie Food Maxims. (A selection): (1) Never read labels. There is nothing good for you inside a candy bar, so forget it. That's why they keep it dark in movie theaters. (2) Never get serious at a candy counter and order a hot dog because you're hungry. Bad movie hot dogs are a fact of life. Resist the temptation to think you can find nourishment in a theater. (Bob Fenster, quoted in the *Washington Post.*)

Fenwick's Rule. You may never reach a solution, but you're never absolved from the responsibility of trying. (Former Representative Millicent Fenwick, New Jersey; quoted in the *Washington Post,* November 22, 1979.)

Ferguson's Law. You learn more listening than talking. (Wade Ferguson; from Charles H. Meadows, Appomattox, Virginia.)

Ferguson's Office Rules of Thumb. (1) When the boss is out, always answer his line second. He is probably on the other line. (Or, the boss never calls on his own line.) (2) The size and severity of the buck passed is inversely proportional to the size of your paycheck. (3) If all the phone lines ring at once, put them all on hold until they hang up. (4) Never answer a person who says, "May I ask a stupid question?" (5) When callers begin with "I have a problem..." they usually do. When they say, "I have a small problem," it is usually too big for you to handle. (Eve M. Ferguson, Washington, D.C.)

Ferreire's Pentagon Parking Lot Theory of World Affairs. The state of the world can be accurately gauged by the number of cars at the Pentagon parking lot any given midnight. (Larrie Ferreire, Alexandria, Virginia.)

Fertility, First Law of. The less one wants to conceive, the more it is likely to happen, and vice versa. (Hannah Betts in *The Times* [London, England], October 24, 2009, who explained: "Accordingly, where one's offspring-desirous friends may devote months to ovulation charts and temperature readings, all it takes for the lone ranger to conceive is one drunken encounter with someone he wouldn't introduce to his cobbler, let alone his friends.")

Fetridge's Law. Important things that are supposed to happen do not happen, especially when people are looking. (Claude Fetridge, an NBC radio engineer in the 1930s. In 1936 he came up with the idea of broadcasting, live of course, the departure of the swallows from their famous roost at Mission San Juan Capistrano. As was well known in the 1930s, the swallows, which no longer come to Capistrano in large numbers, could always be depended up to depart on October 23, St. John's Day. NBC decided that Fetridge's idea was sound and made all due preparations, including sending a crew to the Mission. The swallows then left a day ahead of schedule. *Fetridge's Law* was all but forgotten until H. Allen Smith recalled it in an essay on laws in his classic work *A Short History of Fingers and Other State Papers* Little Brown, 1963. Smith pointed out that *Fetridge's Law* also has its good points, which are sometimes overlooked. An example from Smith: "In my own case I have often noted that whenever I develop a raging toothache, it is a Sunday and the dentists are all on the golf course. Not long ago, my toothache hung on through the weekend, and Monday morning it was still throbbing and pulsating like a diesel locomotive. I called my dentist and proclaimed an emergency and drove to his office, and going up the stairway, the ache suddenly vanished altogether." Over the years a number of attestations to the veracity of this law have been submitted to the Murphy Center, including this prime example from William G. Downs, Omaha, Nebraska: "I was once privileged to attend an outstanding proof of the absolute truth of *Fetridge's Law.* It was in Sioux City, Iowa; the occasion was the opening of a new channel of the Floyd River, which was being diverted to avoid a repetition of a disastrous flood in the fifties. The corp of engineers had spent millions on levees, bank riprap, etc. The mayor, city council, chief of the engineers, and a representative from the Iowa governor's office gathered to see the great event. The diversion dam had been mined so that a charge would open it and send the water down the new channel. All set, TV cameras ready—telephoto lenses on newspaper pictures. Down the plunger on the charge box—and a little feeble poof—a puff of smoke—dam intact.")

Fiedler's Forecasting Rules. (1) *The First Law of Forecasting:* Forecasting is very difficult, especially if it's about the future. (2) *For this reason:* He who lives by the crystal ball soon learns to eat ground glass. (3) *Similarly:* The moment you forecast you know you're going to be wrong, you just don't know when and in which direction. (4) *Nevertheless, always be precise in your forecasts because:* Economists state their GNP growth projections to the nearest tenth of a percentage point to prove they have a sense of humor. (5) *Another basic law:* If the facts don't conform to the theory, they must be disposed of. (6) *If you've always had doubts about the judgment of forecasters, it's quite understandable because:* An economist is a man who would marry a beautiful young actress for her money. (7) *By the same reasoning, your suspicions about the narrow range of most forecasts are justified:* The herd instinct among forecasters make sheep look like independent thinkers. (8) *Correspondingly:* If a camel is a horse designed by a committee, then a consensus forecast is a camel's behind. (9) *When presenting a forecast:* Give them a number or give them a date, but never both. (10) *When asked to explain your forecast:* Never underestimate the power of a platitude. (11) *And remember Kessel's insight on the value of malarkey:* There must be underinvestment in bulls...just look at the rate of return. (12) *Speaking of profits:* Once economists were asked, "If you're so smart, why ain't you rich?" Today they're asked, "Now that you've proved you ain't so smart, how come you got so rich?" (13) *On the use of survey techniques in forecasting:* When you know absolutely nothing about the topic, make your forecast by asking a carefully selected probability sample of 300 others who don't know the answer either. (14) *In a modern economy everything is related to everything else, so:* Forecasters tend to learn less and less about more and more, until in the end they know nothing about everything... (15) *The oldest saw about the profession:* If all the economists were laid end to end, they still wouldn't reach a conclusion. (16) *Another oldie:* Ask five economists and you'll get five different explanations (six, if one went to Harvard). (17) *How an economist defines "hard times":* A recession is when my neighbor loses his job. A depression is when I lose my job. A panic is when my wife loses her job. (18) *The boss's supplication:* Lord, please find me a one-armed economist so we won't always hear, "On the other hand..." (19) *The forecaster has his own invocation:* Thank God for compensating errors. (20) *Speaking of the Deity:* Most economists think of God as working great multiple regressions in the sky.... [Items (21), (22), and (23) are, respectively, *Murphy's Law, O'Toole's Commentary,* and *Finagle's Constant.*] (24) *A forecaster's best defense is a good offense, so:* If you have to forecast, forecast often. (25) *But:* If you're ever right, never let 'em forget it. (Edgar R. Fiedler, Conference Board economic researcher and vice-president, in the June 1977, issue of the Conference Board's magazine *Across the Board.*)

Fields's Advice. Start off every day with a smile and get it over with. *Fields's Panaceas.* (1) If at first you don't succeed, try, try again. Then quit. There's no use making a fool of yourself. (2) The best cure for insomnia is to get a lot of sleep. (W. C. Fields.)

Fields's Revelation. If you see a man holding a clipboard and looking official, the chances are good that he is supposed to be doing something menial. (Wayne C. Fields, Jr., Newcastle, California.)

Fifth Rule. You have taken yourself too seriously. (This law comes from Governor du Pont, who uses it to sum up his political laws. See *du Pont's Laws.*) He first heard it from NBC's John Chancellor. To quote du Pont: "A veteran British diplomat had a favorite way to put down a pushy or egotistical junior. The diplomat would call the younger man in for a heart-to-heart talk and quite often at the end of the talk would say, 'Young man, you have broken the Fifth Rule: You have taken yourself too seriously.' That would end the meeting—except that invariably, as the younger man got to the door, he would turn and ask, 'What are the other rules?' And the diplomat would smile serenely and answer, 'There *are* no other rules.'"

The Finagle File

People had talked about a mysterious scientist named Finagle for many years before November 1957, when John W. Campbell, Jr., editor of *Astounding Science Fiction,* asked his readers to help him collect and publish Finagle's "famous unwritten laws of science," but after that announcement Finagle became as much a part of scientific lore as Murphy has become to general lore.

The results of Campbell's request were most gratifying. For more than two years the magazine published letters from Finagle's disciples and fans revealing dozens of laws, corollaries, and factors. Here are some of the most important elements of Finaglania:

• ***Four Basic Rules.***

1. If anything can go wrong in an experiment, it will. 2. No matter what result is anticipated, there is always someone willing to fake it. 3. No matter what the result, there is always someone eager to misinterpret it. 4. No matter what occurs, there is always someone who believes it happened according to his pet theory.

• ***The Finagle Factor vs. Other Major Factors.***

The Finagle Factor is characterized by changing the Universe to fit the equation. The Bouguerre Factor changes the equation to fit the Universe.

The Diddle Factor changes things so that the equation and the Universe appear to fit, without requiring any real change in either. This is also known as the "smoothing" or "soothing" factor, mathematically somewhat similar to a damping factor; it has the characteristic of eliminating differences by dropping the subject under discussion to zero importance.

• ***Finagle's Creed.***
Science Is Truth: Don't Be Misled By Facts.

• ***Applied Finaglism. The Law of the Too, Too Solid Point.***
In any collection of data, the figure that is most obviously correct—beyond all need of checking—is the mistake. *Corollary 1:* No one whom you ask for help will see it, either. *Corollary 2:* Everyone who stops by with unsought advice will see it immediately.

• ***Finagle's Very Fundamental Finding.***
If a string has one end, then it has another end.

• ***Finagle's Fifth Rule.***
Whenever a system becomes completely defined, some damn fool discovers something that either abolishes the system or expands it beyond recognition.

• ***Delay Formula.***
After adding two weeks to the schedule for unexpected delays, add two more for the unexpected, unexpected delays.

• ***On Corrections.***
When an error has been detected and corrected, it will be found to have been correct in the first place. *Corollary:* After the correction has been found in error, it will be impossible to fit the original quantity back into the equation.

• ***Travel Axiom.***
He travels fastest who travels alone... but he hasn't anything to do when he gets there.

• ***Law of Social Dynamics.***
If, in the course of several months, only three worthwhile social events take place, they will all fall on the same evening.

• ***Finagle's Contributions to the Field of Measurement.***
1. Dimensions will be expressed in the least convenient terms, e.g.: Furlongs per $(\text{Fortnight})^2$—Measure of Acceleration. 2. Jiffy—the time it takes for light to go one cm in a vacuum. 3. Protozoa are small, and bacteria are small, but viruses are smaller than the both of 'em put together.

• ***Finagle's Proofs, Household Examples.***

Any vacuum cleaner would sooner take the nap off a rug than remove white threads from a dark rug. No dog will knock a vase over unless it has water in it.

• ***Finagle's Rules for Scientific Research.***

1. Do Not Believe in Miracles—Rely on Them.
2. Experiments Must Be Reproducible—They Should Fail the Same Way.
3. Always Verify Your Witchcraft.
4. Draw Your Curves—Then Plot Your Readings.
5. Be Sure to Obtain Meteorological Information Before Leaving on Vacation.
6. A Record of Data is Useful—It Indicates That You've Been Working.
7. Experience Is Directly Proportional to Equipment Ruined.
8. To Study a Subject Best—Understand It Thoroughly Before You Start.
9. In Case of Doubt—Make It Sound Convincing.

• ***Later Findings.***

In the years since the original information on Finagle appeared in *Astounding Science Fiction,* scores of new laws have been discovered and attributed to Finagle. Here is but one example:

Finagles Laws of Information: 1. The information you have is not what you want. 2. The information you want is not what you need. 3. The information you need is not what you can obtain. 4. The information you can obtain costs more than you want to pay!

• ***Friends of Finagle and Examples of Their Laws (from the original ASF letters).***

Sprinkle's Law: Things fall at right angles. *Stockmayer's Theorem:* If it looks easy, it's tough. If it looks tough, it's damn near impossible. *Deadlock's Law:* If the lawmakers make a compromise, the place where it will be felt most is the taxpayer's pocket. *Corollary:* The compromise will always be more expensive than either of the suggestions it is compromising.

• ***Aliases, Pseudonyms, and AKA's for Dr. Finagle.***

Dr. Henri Bouguerre, Dr. Gwen T. Diddle, Bougar T. Factor, Dr. Finnagle, and Dr. von Nagle.

Findsen's First Law. The coffee cup is always emptied just as the waitress goes on break. (Art critic Owen Findsen, *Cincinnati Enquirer.*)

First Sergeant's Response, The. "I'd rather be wrong than look the goddamn thing up." (From Brian M. Foley, Wake Island, Mid-Pacific, who recalled this immortal reply from his "top kick" during his days as a soldier: "I can still remember his voice as it boomed across the company area," writes Foley.)

First Thesis. Everything is nothing. Everything is all. All is one. One is inconceivable, infinite. Therefore it is nothing. Therefore everything is nothing. Everything is matter. Matter is electricity. Electricity is invisible, intangible. Therefore it is nothing. Therefore everything is nothing. Atoms are made up of electrons and protons (protons are also nothing). Fifty billion electrons placed side by side in a straight line would stretch across the diameter of the period at the end of this sentence. Protons are heavier but take up less space. Such an idea is incapable of absorption by the human mind. (From *The Crowning of Technocracy* by Professor John Lardner and Dr. Thomas Sugrue, Laboratory of Robert M. McBride & Co., 1933.)

First Time—Each Time Is Like—Law, The. No matter how many times you have felt miserable because you stayed up too late, drank too much, ate too much, etc., the next time you have the opportunity to stay up late, drink too much, etc., you will be unable to recall and anticipate, as anything more than an abstraction, how miserable you felt/will feel when you did/if you do. Exception: anything that resulted in carsickness. (Hilde Weisert, Teaneck, New Jersey.)

Fischer's Finding. Sex is hereditary. If your parents never had it, chances are you won't either. (Joseph Fischer, W. Melbourne, Florida; *HW.*)

Fischer's First Law of Marine Engineering. On any job requiring the removal of four bolts, three will come easily. (John Fischer; from Bill O'Neill.)

Fishbein's Conclusion. The tire is only flat on the bottom. (*U;* from John L. Shelton, Dallas, Texas.)

Fisherman's Tip. The best day of the week to catch fish is yesterday. (Ione Goodman, Arlington, Texas.)

Fitz-Gibbon's Law. Creativity varies inversely with the number of cooks involved with the broth. (Bernice Fitz-Gibbon in *Macy's, Gimbels and Me,* Simon and Schuster, 1967; *FL.*)

Fitzloff's Fact. Organizational consolidation is invariably followed by a minimum increase in administrators of one third. (John F. Fitzloff, Chicago, Illinois.)

Fitzmaurice's Law. When you come to a stop sign and can't decide whether to turn right or left, any decision will be wrong. (Richard Fitzmaurice, KCBS, San Francisco, California.)

Fitzwater's Prescription for Improving the Clinton White House. A few more fat old bald men wouldn't hurt the place. (Former Bush Administration press secretary Marlin Fitzwater; quoted in *Newsweek,* June 7, 1993.)

Flak Diversion Theorem. A published remark by any congressman that irritates a lobbying association or the White House is automatically labeled by his office as "taken out of context." (*Washington Star* editorial, February 18, 1979.)

Flap's Law of the Perversity of Inanimate Objects. Any inanimate object, regardless of its composition or configuration, may be expected to perform at any time in a totally unexpected manner for reasons that are either totally obscure or completely mysterious. (Dr. Fyodor Flap, encountered in Walter Mulé's "Beyond Murphy's Law." From this Flap builds *Mulé's Law. Flap's Law* is often identified as *Finagle's Law,* but Flap seems more appropriate.)

Flashman's Law of Frontier Diplomacy. There is some natural law that ensures that whenever civilization talks to the heathen, it is through the person of the most obstinate, short-sighted, arrogant, tactless clown available. (The character Sir Harry Flashman in George MacDonald Fraser's *Flashman and the Redskins,* Knopf, 1982; from Bob Einbinder.)

Flip Wilson's Law. You can't expect to hit the jackpot if you don't put a few nickels in the machine. (Wilson on his TV show on October 28, 1971. This was recognized as a universal truth by Thomas Martin.)

Florio's Travel Suggestion. If you will be a traveler, have always the eyes of a falcon, the ears of an ass, the face of an ape, the mouth of a hog, the shoulders of a camel, the legs of a stag, and see that you keep two bags very full: one of patience and another of money. (A man named John Florio, who wrote the above in 1591. Quoted in the Summer 1978, issue of *JD Journal.*)

Flory's Laws. (1) The more crap you put up with, the more crap you are going to get. (2) Whenever you put out a trough full of public money, you are going to find some pigs with all four feet in it. (3) As time goes on, everything gets heavier. *Mrs. Flory's Addition to the Third Law:*... and further. (K. C. Flory, Oconomowoc, Wisconsin.)

Foley's Dicta. (1) People are generally down on things they ain't up on. (2) If the count goes two strikes against you, cancel the meeting. (Joe Foley, Kensington, Maryland; quoted in the *Montgomery Journal,* November 5, 1981.)

Foley's Rules for Politicians. (1) Don't go to spelling bees. (2) Don't shoot muzzle-loading rifles at targets. (3) Don't throw a baseball unless you have a very high box to drop it from... straight down. Do not go out on the mound and try to toss it across the field. (4) Don't wear hats, that sort of thing. (5) Don't ride horses at rodeos. Don't even ride them in parades. (6) Never ride in a Rolls-Royce. (House Speaker Tom Foley to a group of reporters on June 22, 1992, reacting to Dan Quayle's problem spelling "potato[e]" at a spelling bee. Quoted in the *Washington Times,* June 23, 1992.)

Followers' Creed. The lemmings know something we don't. (Alvin W. Quinn, Arlington Heights, Illinois.)

Fonda's Cinematic Distinction. If a man and a woman go into the woods with a picnic basket and a blanket and have a picnic, that's a G. If they go into the woods with a picnic basket and crawl under the blanket, that's a PG. And if they go into the woods without a basket or a blanket and have a picnic anyway, that's an R. (Jane Fonda, 1978 Academy Awards ceremony.)

Forbes's Absolute. There is no exception to the rule that everybody likes to be an exception to the rule. (Malcolm Forbes; quoted by Dale Dauten in the *Albuquerque Journal,* June 15, 2000.)

Forbes's Rule of Parenting. Let your children go if you want to keep them. (Malcolm Forbes, *The Sayings of Chairman Malcolm,* Harper & Row, 1978.)

Formal Attire Rule. Wearing a rented tuxedo causes a flat tire. (Anonymous; *TG.*)

Forthoffer's Cynical Summary of Barzun's Laws. (See *Barzun's Laws.*)

Fortner's Law. It takes less time to avoid it than to explain it. (George A. Fortner, Cincinnati, Ohio.)

Fortune Cookie Message. Don't blame failures on others. You just didn't work hard enough. (Found by James Thorpe, Illinois.)

Fortune-Seeker's Law. Cast your bread upon the water and you get soggy bread. (*U/Ra.*)

Foster's Law. If you cover a congressional committee on a regular basis, they will report the bill on your day off. (Herb Foster. According to Foster it was created some years ago when he was at UPI [then UP] and the Senate Appropriations Committee reported out the biggest civil works appropriations up to that point in history. "I knew nothing of the places or projects involved, but had to cover it." Compounded by many later situations involving Foster and others.)

Foster's Laws. (1) Children will always have to go to the bathroom as soon as you sit down in a restaurant. (2) The person who says, "It is only money," is most likely to want to cheat you. (Marguerite H. Foster, Palo Alto, California.)

Foster's Revelation. For every axiom there is an equal and opposite reaxiom. (Nicholas Foster, Bernardsville, New Jersey.)

Fourth Law of Thermodynamics. If the probability of success is not almost one, then it is damn near zero. (David Ellis, from his classic 1957 paper, "Some Precise Formulations on the Alleged Perversity of Nature"; *RS.*)

Fowler's Constant. No matter where you sit on an airplane, when deplaning, the person in front of you will be unable to locate his/her suit bag in the forward coat closet. (Professor Don D. Fowler, University of Nevada, Reno.)

Fowler's Law. In a bureaucracy, accomplishment is inversely proportional to the volume of paper used. (Foster L. Fowler, Jackson, Mississippi; *AO.*)

Fowler's Note. The only imperfect thing in nature is the human race. (*U/DRW.*)

Fowler's Rule. A book is never finished—it's abandoned. (Gene Fowler, quoted in H. Allen Smith's *The Life and Legend of Gene Fowler,* William Morrow, 1977; from Alan G. Lewis.)

Fox's Epiphenomenon. If you do nothing, nothing will happen. If you do something, something will happen—but not what you intended. (James F. Fox, New York, New York.)

Fraknoi's Lament. Wherever you are, the eclipse is visible somewhere else. (Andrew Fraknoi, Astronomical Society of the Pacific; *TG.*)

France's Law of Law. The law, in its majestic equality, forbids the rich as well as the poor to sleep under bridges, to beg in the streets, and to steal bread. (Anatole France.)

Frand's Eighth and Ninth Laws of Product Development. (8) The amount of time necessary to develop a new product is always one unit of time longer than you think it should be. A one-month project will take one quarter, a two-quarter project will take two years, etc. (9) There is no such thing as a conservative market projection. (Erwin A. Frand, *Industrial Research and Development,* January 1983; from Mack Earle.)

Frankel's Law. Whatever happens in government could have happened differently and it usually would have been better if it had. *Corollary:* Once things have happened, no matter how accidentally, they will be regarded as manifestations of an unchangeable higher reason. (Professor Charles Frankel of Columbia University, from his book *High on Foggy Bottom,* Harper & Row, 1969.)

Frankel's Principle. Always think of something new; this helps you forget your last rotten idea. (Seth Frankel, Hillsdale, New Jersey.)

Frankenfeld's Revised Proverbs. (1) It is better to have loved and had delirious sex than to have loved and lost. (2) All's war in love and fairness. (3) Before having a mid-life crisis, it is usually best to have a life. (4) It is difficult to take any group seriously that actually uses the term "tanning consultant." (5) A watched pot is usually owned by someone without cable. (6) I came. I saw. I refinanced. (7) A bird in the hand usually relieves itself. (8) Too many cooks use lard. (9) Red skies at dawn, sailors be warned. Red skies at dusk, great for photographing Old Forester ads. (Philip J. Frankenfeld, Chicago, Illinois, who has also created an important "Never" rule—"Never date a woman who gets excited by the 'action' music of the *McLaughlin Group.*")

Franklin's Infallible Remedy for Toothache. Wash the root of the aching tooth in vinegar, and let it dry half an hour in the sun. (Benjamin Franklin.)

Franklin's Law. Blessed is he who expects nothing, for he shall not be disappointed. (Gene Franklin; from an article in *Computers and Automation; JE.*)

Franklin's Observation. He that lives upon hope dies fasting. (Attributed to

Benjamin Franklin, 1974 *Expectation of Days*. The original quote ends with the word "fasting" although an error—intentional or typographical—has this in some books as "farting"; *RS*.)

Frank's First Law of Fluid Dynamics. The greatest amount of effort exerted by a homeowner on his plumbing will produce the least amount of results. *Frank's Second Law of Fluid Dynamics:* The least amount of effort exerted by a homeowner on his plumbing will produce the greatest amount of water. (Frank Johnson, Sterling, Virginia.)

Fran's Olfactory Observation. Dirty hands make your nose itch. (From Mary Ann Mrazek, Lombard, Illinois.)

Fraraccio's Law. It's not *what* you know, it's how fast you can find it out. (John C. Fraraccio, Brick Town, New Jersey.)

Fraser's Additions. (1) Almost all emotional wounds are self-inflicted. (2) The longer the cruise, the older the passengers. (3) Life is like chess... all the mistakes are there, waiting to be made. (4) Love is like snow; you don't know when it will come or how long it will last or how much you'll get. (Alex Fraser, Washington, D.C.)

Fred's Forecast. Golf is like children: They're both humbling experiences waiting to happen. (Fred Whistle, North Barrington, Illinois.)

Freeman's Verity No. 9. No good idea is ever accepted and implemented without being carried to extremes. (B. Freer Freeman, Arlington, Virginia, in an October 13, 1994 letter to the *Washington Post* reacting to an editorial commenting on how the educational establishment had embraced low self-esteem to explain a multitude of shortcomings and bad behavior.)

Freemon's Rule. Circumstances can force a generalized incompetent to become competent, at least in a specialized field. (Frank R. Freemon, of the Department of Neurology, Vanderbilt University School of Medicine; from an article of the same title in the *JIR,* March, 1974. *Freemon's Rule* goes beyond the *Peter Principle* to explain such individuals as Ulysses S. Grant, Harry S Truman, and Winston Churchill, who all reached a level of incompetence—Truman and Grant failed in business, and Churchill fared badly in politics in the 1930s—and then went on to become competent.)

Frensham's Maxim of Constructive Apathy. For every reason there is for doing something, there are at least three for not doing it—you just have to find them all. (Ray Frensham, Barkingside, Essex, England, who practices constructive apathy or "the science of life passing you by." He recalls, "It all sprang from the fact that, as a journalist, writer, and TV producer, I was listening to Jeffrey (now Lord) Archer talking about writing. He said, 'Every morning you sit down at that blank page and there are a thousand and more reasons for not writing, but only one for doing it; and every morning you have to find that one reason all over again.' My response was: 'No. Why should we not spend that time pondering on all the reasons for not doing something?'")

Fresco's Discovery. If you knew what you were doing, you'd probably be bored. (Catherine B. Fresco, Winston-Salem, North Carolina.)

Fresco's Query. Why is it when liberals win elections it is called polarization, yet when conservatives are victorious, it is labeled a mandate? (Victor Fresco, letter to the *Los Angeles Times,* June 25, 1981; *RS.*)

Friedman's Comment on Presenting Averages Without Their Components. That is like assuring the nonswimmer that he can safely walk across a river because its average depth is only four feet. (Economist Milton Friedman, *Newsweek,* January 10, 1972; from Don Nilsen.)

Friedman's Law of Elevators. The amount of time an elevator takes in arriving is directly proportional to the lateness of the person waiting for it, and inversely proportional to the amount of weight in that person's arms. *Corollary:* In a crowded elevator, the person getting off first is at the back of the elevator. (Robert J. Friedman, Lansdale, Pennsylvania.)

Fried's 23rd Law. Ideas endure and prosper in inverse proportion to their soundness and validity. (*U/JW.*)

Fried's Third Law of Public Administration. If it's logical, rational, reasonable, and makes good common sense, it's not done. *Corollary:* If it's logical, rational, reasonable, and makes good common sense, don't you do it! (Steve Fried, Ohio Department of Economic and Community Development, Columbus.)

Friendly's Rule. Nobody ever got rich undertipping waiters and stiffing cabdrivers. (Fred Friendly, who ended a distinguished career at CBS as president of CBS News; quoted in Liz Smith, *Natural Blonde,* Hyperion, 2000, p. 433; from Joe Goulden.)

Friendship, The 17th and 18th Rules of. (17) A friend will refrain from telling you he picked up the same amount of life insurance coverage you did for half the price and his is noncancelable. (18) A friend will let you hold the ladder while he goes up on the roof to install your new TV antenna, which is the biggest son of a bitch you ever saw. (From "*Esquire*'s 27 Rules of Friendship," which appears in the May 1977 issue. The items are very clever, but also repetitive. These were picked more or less at random.)

Fri's Laws of Regulatory Agencies. (1) If any agency can regulate, it will. (2) Regulation drives out broad-gauged, long-term thinking. (Robert Fri, former Environmental Protection Administrator; *AO.*)

Frisbee, The 10 Commandments of the. (1) The most powerful force in the world is that of a disc straining to land under a car, just beyond reach. (This force is technically termed "car suck.") (2) The higher the quality of a catch or the comment it receives, the greater the probability of a crummy re-throw. (Good catch = bad throw.) (3) One must never precede any maneuver by a comment more predictive than, "Watch this!" (Keep 'em guessing.) (4) The higher the costs of hitting any object, the greater the certainty it will be struck. (Remember—the disc is positive—both cops and old ladies are clearly negative.) (5) The best catches are never seen. ("Did you see that?"—"See what?") (6) The greatest single aid to distance is for the disc to be going in a direction you did not want. (Goes the wrong way = Goes a long way.) (7) The most powerful hex words in the sport are, "I really have this down—watch." (Know it? Blow it!) (8) In any crowd of spectators at least one will suggest that razor blades could be attached to the disc. ("You could maim and kill with that thing.") (9) The greater your need to make a good catch, the greater the probability your partner will deliver his worst throw. (If you can't touch it, you can't trick it.) (10) The single most difficult move with a disc is to put it down. (Just one more.) (Dan "The Stork" Roddick, editor of *Frisbee World* and director of the International Frisbee Association. Reprinted with permission from the February 1975 issue of *Flying Disc World.*)

Froben's Law of Publishing. Never send a letter requesting information to an editor unless you expect to receive a prolix letter in return. (Froben is the alter ego of Indiana University Press Editor Robert Cook.)

Frost's Working Rule. By working faithfully eight hours a day, you may eventually get to be a boss and work twelve hours a day. (Robert Frost.)

Froud's Law. A transistor protected by a fast-acting fuse will protect the fuse by blowing first. (*U/S.T.L.*)

Fuchs's Fact. If your name can be spelled wrong, it will be. (Monika Fuchs, Stockholm, Sweden.)

Fuchs's Warning. If you actually look like your passport photo, you aren't well enough to travel. (Sir Vivian Fuchs; *MLS.*)

Fudd's First Law of Opposition. If you push something hard enough it will fall over. A note from Nancy Nagler: "I was brought up on *Murphy's Law* and your corollaries have been priceless. I even had the 1982 *Official Rules* desktop calendar. That year, on March 15th, it said, 'If you push something hard enough, it will fall over.' I guess. That evening, we had an F1 tornado go through the entire length of Bartlesville, Oklahoma [total track was 15–20 miles]. It missed the downtown, and the headquarters of Phillips 66 Petroleum by a couple blocks, wiped out a popular restaurant the one day it was closed, and hit a million-dollar supermarket 15 minutes after it closed for the day. And of course it hit a trailer park. Thirty million dollars and only two people hospitalized. Were we lucky or what?" *Fudd's Law of Insertion:* What goes in must come back out (Both laws were created by Sir Sidney Fudd, a creation of the Firesign Theatre, a radio comedy troupe of the late 1960s and early 1970s.)

Fudge Factor. A physical factor occasionally showing up in experiments as a result of stopping a stopwatch a little early to compensate for reflex error.... *Or:* The numerical factor by which experimental results must be multiplied to be in agreement with theory.... *Or:* Any of a number of other statements used to indicate the conscious addition of a bogus factor or figure. (Who was Fudge, you ask? Here is the "Fudge" entry from *The Dictionary of Words, Facts and Phrases* by Eliezer Edwards, Chatto & Windus, London, England, 1901, in its entirety: "*Fudge.* In a 'Collection of some Papers of William Crouch' (8 vo. 1712), Crouch, who was a Quaker, says that one Marshall informed him that 'In the year 1664, we were sentenced for banishment to Jamaica by Judges Hyde and Twysden, and our number was 55. We were put on board the ship "Black Eagle," the master's name was *Fudge,* by some called "Lying Fudge." ' Isaac D'Israeli quotes from a pamphlet entitled "Remarks upon the Navy" (1700), to show that the word originated in a man's name: 'There was, sir, in our time one Captain Fudge, commander of a merchantman, who, upon his return from a voyage, how ill fraught soever his ship was, always brought home his owner a good cargo of lies, so much that now aboard ship the sailors when they hear a great lie told, cry out, 'You *fudge* it!' ")

Fuller's Historical Explanation. In some cases, people were as much a part of the problem as anybody else. (A professor of the same name who uttered this and other statements of this type, thereby causing Steve Cohen, Ithaca, New York, to drop the class.)

Fuller's Law of Cosmic Irreversibility.

1 Pot T = 1 Pot P

1 Pot P ≠ 1 Pot T (R. Buckminster Fuller in a letter to the Director.)

Fullner's Discovery. Perforations are, in reality, reinforcements. (Randall Fullner, Santa Clara, California.)

Fullner's Rules. *Menial Employment:* The more menial a job an individual has, the higher the probability of meeting friends, relatives, and acquaintances while at work. (Discovered working at a filling station.) *Consumerism:* Regardless of who or what is responsible for inflationary increases in the cost of goods and services, the consumer pays. *Social Investment:* A male altering his personal behavior, mannerisms, grooming, etc., to accommodate a female of his attention will, subsequent to the termination of the relationship or acquaintance, meet another receptive female whose preferences concur with his characteristics prior to transformation. *Weekends:* Whenever the only time available to complete a task is on weekends, all suppliers of necessary parts, material, and equipment will be open for business Monday through Friday. *Public Telephones:* A public telephone is never being used except when you want to use it. *Bad Examples:* A bad example is more readily followed than a good one (Randall Fullner, San Jose, California.)

Funkhouser's Law of the Power of the Press. The quality of legislation passed to deal with a problem is inversely proportional to the volume of media clamor that brought it on. (G. Ray Funkhouser, Ph.D., Field Research Corp., San Francisco, California; *AO*.)

Futility Factor. No experiment is ever a complete failure. It can always serve as a bad example, or the exception that proves the rule, but only if it is the first experiment in the series. (Embellished version of *Carson's Consolation*.)

Fyffe's Axiom. The problem-solving process will always break down at the point at which it is possible to determine who caused the problem. (*U/2*.)

G

G Constant (or Godin's Law). Generalizedness of incompetence is directly proportional to highestness in hierarchy. (Guy Godin; from an article with the same title in *JIR,* March 1972. Godin has found an exception to the *Peter Principle,* because he argues that some people are incompetent before they begin to rise. Peter argues that they rise to their level of incompetence. See also *Freemon's Rule*.)

G/B/U Conundrum. When given the choice of being the good, the bad, or the ugly, always take the bad. Let the good and the ugly fight it out. (Kohn D. Runkle, Chapel Hill, North Carolina.)

Gadarene Swine Law. Merely because the group is in formation does not mean that the group is on the right course. (Law derived from the passage in the New Testament in which Christ sent the pigs tumbling into the lake [Mark 5:11–13]. Reported by Robert Cook.)

Gage's Rule. Integrity is like oxygen—the higher you go, the less there is of it. (Pete Gage, Pasadena, Texas.)

Galbraith's First Law. Modesty is a vastly overrated virtue. (John Kenneth Galbraith. This was embroidered on a sampler in Galbraith's elegant sitting room in Cambridge, Massachusetts. The sampler was referred to in his obituary in the *Economist* May 6, 2006 with the comment, "He thoroughly believed it. Save for his humble origins on a farm in Ontario, little about Mr. Galbraith's life was modest.")

Galbraith's Law of Human Nature. Faced with the choice between changing one's mind and proving that there is no need to do so, almost everybody gets busy on the proof. (John Kenneth Galbraith, *Economics, Peace and Laughter,* Houghton Mifflin, 1971.)

Galbraith's Law of Political Wisdom. Anyone who says he isn't going to resign, four times, definitely will. (*AO*)

Galbraith's Law of Prominence. Getting on the cover of *Time* guarantees the existence of opposition in the future. (John Kenneth Galbraith; *MBC.* See also *Crump's Law.*)

Galbraith's Laws. *Junkets:* A junket is any business trip which, if taken by anyone but yourself, would be considered unnecessary. *Congressional Testimony:* A lie at a Congressional hearing gets you by for the moment at the cost of trouble later on. (John Kenneth Galbraith; from Joseph C. Goulden.)

Gallagher's Law. People like crowds. The bigger the crowd, the more people show up. Small crowd, hardly anybody shows up. (Comic Leo Gallagher; from Jim Dawson, Los Angeles, California.)

Gallagher's Rule. Never apologize for your terrible friends. We are all *somebody's* terrible friend. (From the late Jack Gallagher, sometime Dean of Trinity; quoted in Bernard Levin's column, *The Times* [London], July 9, 1980.)

Gallois's Revelation. If you put tomfoolery into a computer, nothing comes out but tomfoolery. But this tomfoolery, having passed through a very expensive machine, is somehow ennobled, and no one dares to criticize it. (Pierre Gallois in *Science et Vie,* Paris, reprinted in the *Reader's Digest.*)

Gall's Principles of Systemantics. (1) *The Primal Scenario or Basic Datum of Experience:* Systems in general work poorly or not at all. (2) *The Fundamental Theorem:* New systems generate new problems. (3) *The Law of Conservation of Anergy:* The total amount of anergy in the universe is constant.[3] (4) *Law of Growth:* Systems tend to grow, and as they grow, they encroach. (5) *The Generalized Uncertainty Principle:* Systems display antics. (Dr. John Gall, from his book *Systemantics: How Systems Work and Especially How They Fail,* Quadrangle/*The New York Times* Book Company, 1977. The laws quoted above are just an abbreviated sampling from a much longer list of axioms and laws revealed and explained in this benchmark book that ranks in importance with *Parkinson's Law* and *The Peter Principle* for anyone trying to understand our modern, technological society. Gall, a professor and practicing physician, has a particular ability to come up with concisely stated truths—e.g., "The dossier is not the person," and "Any large system is going to be operating most of the time in failure mode.")

Gallup's Theological Assertion. I could prove God statistically. (George Gallup; from Don Nilsen.)

Gammon's Theory of Bureaucratic Displacement. In a bureaucratic system, an increase in expenditure will be matched by a fall in production. Such systems

[3] Gall's definition of anergy: "Any state or condition of the Universe, or of any portion of it, that requires the expenditure of human effort or ingenuity to bring it into line with human desires, needs, or pleasures is defined as an ANERGY-STATE."

will act rather like "black holes" in the economic universe, simultaneously sucking in resources and shrinking in terms of "emitted" production. *Or, as restated by Milton Friedman:* In a bureaucratic system, useless work drives out useful work. (British physician Dr. Max Gammon, on the completion of a five-year study of the British health system. Discussed by Milton Friedman in his November 7, 1977, *Newsweek* column. See also *Parkinson's Law,* of which *Gammon's Theory* is an extension.)

Gamson's Geriatric Corollary to Newton's Laws of Gravity. Objects fall to earth at a frequency inversely related to the ability of the dropper to pick them up. (Art Gamson, Chevy Chase, Maryland.)

Ganci's Advice. You can tell a person he's ugly. You can tell a person his feet smell. You can even insult his mother, but never, never, never tell him he's stupid. (Jerome C. Ganci, Brooklyn, New York.)

Gandhi's Observation. There is more to life than increasing its speed. (Mahatma Gandhi.)

Gannon's Theory of Relativity. Grandchildren grow quicker than children. (William P. Gannon, Glenolden, Pennsylvania.)

Gardening, Laws of. (1) Other people's tools work only in other people's yards. (2) Fancy gizmos don't work. (3) If nobody uses it, there's a reason. (4) You get the most of what you need the least. (Jane Bryant Quinn, in her newspaper column syndicated by *Washington Post*, 1975)

Gardner's Discoveries. (1) Pentagon motto: Wait, there's a harder way. (2) How to refute any argument: "That's what you say!" (3) Everybody else's big toe looks funny. (4) The two greatest things in the world are women and cellophane tape. (5) All phallic symbols look like you know what. (6) Better to have body odor than no body at all. (7) The volume of the encyclopedia you want to check in the library is always the one not on the shelf. (8) If we can't fix it, it ain't busted. (9) Half the people in the U.S. have below-average intelligence. (10) Anyone who believes in phrenology should have his head examined. (11) I don't believe in astrology, but I understand it works even if you don't believe it. (12) I don't believe in astrology. I'm a Libra, and we Libras are skeptics. (13) Don't read this. It doesn't say anything. (14) There's no fuel like an oil fuel. (Martin Gardner, Hendersonville, North Carolina. These were contained in a letter to the Center of September 9, 1989. Gardner, who passed away in 2010, was an American mathematics and science writer specializing in recreational mathematics. He was an early and avid supporter of the Murphy Center.)

Gardner's Rule of Society. The society which scorns excellence in plumbing because plumbing is a humble activity and tolerates shoddiness in philosophy because it is an exalted activity will have neither good plumbing nor good philosophy. Neither its pipes nor its theories will hold water. (John W. Gardner, in his book *Excellence.*)

Garland's Law. One man's tax break is another man's tax increase. (Virginia legislator Ray Garland; quoted in the *Washington Post,* February 12, 1979.)

Garreau's Second Law of Publishing. The less the readers know about how a publication is put together by its editors, the happier they are. (Joel R. Garreau, *Washington Post.*)

Gawarecki's Discovery. The wider the tires, the narrower the mind. (Susan Gawarecki, Andersonville, Tennessee.)

Gayer's Amendment to Murphy's Law. Anything that can go wrong will go wrong, except at the repair shop, where it will magically, mysteriously (and temporarily) repair itself. Once outside the repair shop again, see *Murphy's Law.* (Dixon Gayer, quoted in Jack Smith's column, *Los Angeles Times,* June 27, 1985; from Carol T. Stewart, Arlington, Virginia.)

Geanangel's Law. If you want to make an enemy, do someone a favor. (Charles L. Geanangel, teacher, Winter Haven, Florida; *JMcC.*)

Geist's Basic Rule for Travel with Kids. Never in the same direction. (William E. Geist, *The New York Times,* October 10, 1982.)

Gelber's Laws. (1) *Gelber's Law of Universal Learning:* The more you learn about a subject, the more you realize how little you really know. (2) *Gelber's Forecasting Axiom:* The only predictable element about weather is that it will be unpredictable. (3) *Gelber's Law of Universal Forecasting:* Given two forecasting scenarios of equal probability, a meteorologist will choose the wrong option 80 percent of the time to maximize public embarrassment. (TV meteorologist Ben Gelber, Columbus, Ohio.)

Gell-Mann's Dictum. Whatever isn't forbidden is required. *Corollary:* If there's no reason why something shouldn't exist, then it must exist. (Nobel Prize winner Murray Gell-Mann; *JW.)*

General Electric Razor. The next time you're in a meeting, look around and identify the yesbutters, the notnowers, and the whynotters. Whynotters move companies. (From a 1984 General Electric advertisement.)

Generalization. Generally speaking, it is dangerous to generalize. (Michael J. Wagner, St. Albert, Alberta, who says, "I have been told that this truth originated in one of the general organizations, i.e., General Motors, General Electric, General Tire . . .")

Gene's Guidance. Grovel, it works. (Colonel Eugene C. Habisher; from Bob Ackley, Plattsmouth, Nebraska.)

George's Postulate. It is difficult to explain something to someone who has infinite wisdom. (George E. Waggoner, Jr., Dearborn Heights, Michigan.)

Germond's Law. When a group of newsmen go out to dinner together, the bill is to be divided evenly among them, regardless of what each one eats and drinks. (Newsman-columnist Jack Germond. See also *Weaver's Law,* of which *Germond's* is a corollary; *AO.*)

Gerrold's Law of Book Publishing. You always find the one typo in print that you missed in galleys. (David Gerrold, Hollywood, California. See also *Short's Quotations.*)

Gerrold's Laws of Infernal Dynamics. (1) An object in motion will always be headed in the wrong direction. (2) An object at rest will always be in the wrong place. (3) The energy required to change either one of these states will always be more than you wish to expend, but never so much as to make the task totally impossible. (David Gerrold, writer and columnist for *Starlog* magazine. See *Short's Quotations,* which are also his.)

Getty's Lament. In some ways a millionaire just can't win. If he spends too freely, he is criticized for being extravagant and ostentatious. If, on the other hand, he lives quietly and thriftily, the same people who would have criticized him for being profligate will call him a miser. (J. Paul Getty, quoted in *Forbes,* November 13, 1978.)

Getty's Reminder. The meek shall inherit the earth, but not its mineral rights. (J. Paul Getty; quoted by Earl Wilson, among others.)

Getty's Second Law. If you know how much you are worth, you are not worth much. (J. Paul Getty; from Clifton Chadwick, Santiago, Chile.)

Giachini's Law. Every man catches himself in the zipper of his fly once, and only once, during his lifetime. (Walt Giachini, Novato, California.)

Giamatti's Rule of Choice. It is my experience, in planning a course of study or anything else, that the person soonest sad and who laments the longest is the person who has only the courage of other people's convictions. (Angelo Bartlett Giamatti, President, Yale University; quoted in *The Boston Globe,* November 12, 1978.)

Gibson's Bermuda Law. If the grass is greener on the other side of the fence, your neighbor has an elephant for a pet. (Ron Gibson, Germantown, Tennessee.)

Gilbert's Discovery. Any attempts to use any of the new super glues result in the two pieces sticking to your thumb and index finger rather than each other. (Mike Gilbert, Santa Ana, California.)

Gilbert's Observation. The surest sign of a crisis is that when you have a major problem, no one tries to tell you how to do your job. (Anonymous; from Steve Masse, Concord, Massachusetts.)

Gilb's Laws of Reliability. (1) Computers are unreliable, but humans are even more unreliable. *Corollary:* At the source of every error which is blamed on the computer you will find at least two human errors, including the error of blaming it on the computer. (2) Any system which depends on human reliability is unreliable. (3) The only difference between the fool and the criminal who attacks a system is that the fool attacks unpredictably and on a broader front. (4) A system tends to grow in terms of complexity rather than of simplification, until the resulting unreliability becomes intolerable. (5) Self-checking systems tend to have a complexity in proportion to the inherent unreliability of the system in which they are used. (6) The error-detection and correction capabilities of any system will serve as the key to understanding the type of errors which they cannot handle. (7) Undetectable errors are infinite in variety, in contrast to detectable errors, which by definition are limited. (8) All real programs contain errors until proved otherwise—which is impossible. (9) Investment in reliability will increase until it exceeds the probable cost of errors, or somebody insists on getting some useful work done. (Tom Gilb, "The Laws of Unreliability," *Datamation*, March 1975; *JE*.)

Gill's Corollary to Fraknoi's Lament [q.v.]. Don't worry. If you are in the right place to see the eclipse, it will be foggy or overcast anyway. *Gill's Law of Agriculture:* The easiest crops to grow are weeds and bugs. *Gill's Strapping Tape Conundrum:* The package you receive in the mail will be either so insecurely wrapped that the post office has mangled it beyond recognition or wrapped so tightly that King Kong couldn't pry it open. (From Tom Gill, when he lived in Davis, California.)

Gill's Law of Life's Highway. The road to success is always under construction. (Heard by Tom Gill.)

Gillers's Equation. The richer you are, the more justice you get. (Stephen Gillers, New York University law professor, commenting in 1994 on O. J. Simpson's all-star defense team.)

Gillette's Law. Most medical mistakes occur not from ignorance but because a physician fails to do something he or she knows should be done. *Gillette's Principle.* If you want to make people angry, lie. If you want to make them absolutely livid with rage, tell the truth. (Robert D. Gillette, M.D., Director, Riverside Family Practice Center, Toledo, Ohio.)

Gilmer's Law of Political Leadership. Look over your shoulder now and then to be sure someone's following you. (Uttered by Virginia's State Treasurer Henry Gilmer in the 1960s, but recently quoted in a column by James J. Kilpatrick.)

Gilmore's Warning. The worse the society, the more law there will be. In Hell, there will be nothing but law, and due process will be meticulously observed. (Grant Gilmore, *The New York Times,* February 23, 1977; from Don Nilsen.)

Gingras's Distinction. There is a difference between bending over backward and bending over forward. (Armando R. Gingras, Boulder, Colorado.)

Ginsberg's Theorem. (1) You can't win. (2) You can't break even. (3) You can't even quit the game. (*U/S.T.L. See Ehrman's Corollary.*)

Ginsburg's Law. The team you root for will always have a better season the year after you stop rooting for it. (Phil Ginsburg, Concord, New Hampshire.)

Glanville's Observations. The more fragile the product the higher it will be placed in a coin-operated machine. (Bradley Glanville, Chico, California.)

Glasow's Law. There's something wrong if you're always right. (Arnold Glasow, quoted on *Forbes's* "Thought" page, March 15, 1977.)

Glass's Law. Enough money is always $5,000 more than I make. (*U/Ra.*)

Gleason's Advice to Public Administrators. When leaving office, give your successor three sealed envelopes and instructions to open them in order as crises occur in the new administration. The message in the first should read, "blame it on your predecessor"; the second should read, "announce a major reorganization"; and the third should say, "write out three envelopes for your successor." (James Gleason, on leaving the post of County Executive, Montgomery County, Maryland. Quoted in *The Montgomery Journal,* November 24, 1978.)

Gloom of Night Law. Checks are always delayed in the mail; bills arrive on time or sooner. (Donald Kaul's column in *The Des Moines Register,* December 11, 1978.)

Glover-Baxendale Warning. Never step between a young lawyer and a moving ambulance. (Boykin A. Glover, Alexandria, Virginia, and Hadley V. Baxendale, Baltimore, Maryland, who individually came up with this warning in response to a 1979 "National Challenge" contest to come up with a modern maxim. Submitted by J. Baxter Newgate, editor of the "National Challenge.")

Godin's Law of the Sexual Revolution. Sex is here to stay, but it will never be the same. (Guy Godin, Université Laval, Quebec. From his unpublished paper, "The Five or Six Ages of Sex.")

Godsey's Bookselling Laws. (1) You will invariably be sent twenty copies of a particularly bad book and only two copies of a bestseller. (2) If an author has appeared on television promoting his book within the last week, you and the warehouse will be out of stock. (3) The second book in a trilogy will be out of stock. (4) Air conditioning will leak only over books ranging in price from $11.95 and up. (5) No matter how much of an eye you keep on the adult magazines, they will always turn up in the religious section in the back of the store. (6) Two fingers and a typewriter can do a world of damage. (7) The week after you buy a much-wanted book in hardcover, the paperback version will appear; the month after that, the hardcover will go on the bargain table as a remainder. (Joyce Godsey and the staff of Waldenbooks #617, Methuen, Massachusetts.)

Goldberg's Law. If anything can be misconstrued about the Jews, it will be...

and has been. (M. Hirsh Goldberg, author of *Just Because They're Jewish,* Stein & Day, 1978. Quoted in an interview in the *Baltimore News American,* January 31, 1979; *ME.*)

Golden Principle. Nothing will be attempted if all possible objections must first be overcome. (Posted in the Department of Labor; *TO'B.*)

Golden Rule of the Arts and Sciences, The (GRASS). Whoever has the gold makes the rules. (This important and oft-quoted rule was announced in the *Journal of Irreproducible Results* in 1975 by pseudononymous O. W. Knewittoo.)

Golden Rule Revised I. Do unto others . . . then split. (*U/Ra.*)

Golden Rule Revised II. Whatsoever you would laugh at in others, laugh at in yourself. (Harry Emerson Fosdick, from his book *On Being a Real Person,* Harper, 1943.)

Goldman's Law. Opening up a can of worms gives us a chance to understand what's in the can. (Seth Goldman, founder of the Honest Tea Co., quoted in "A Question of Fairness." William Neumann, *The New York Times*, Nov. 23, 2011.)

Gold's Law. A column about errors will contain errors. (Popular *Washington Post* columnist Bill Gold, who announced this law in May 1978, after he had done a column on glitches that get into print—i.e., the "not" which disappears from "not guilty." Before it went into print, Gold was able to find and rid the column of three errors and his copy editor was able to find two more. After all of this (more than 20 careful readings) a just-for-good-measure final reading was made by still another editor and it was put into type. When the first edition of the paper came out, the three segments of the column [or legs] had been pasted up wrong so that the last section was in the middle and the middle at the end.)

Gold's Law. The candidate who is expected to do well because of experience and reputation (Douglas, Nixon) must do *better* than well, while the candidate expected to fare poorly (Lincoln, Kennedy) can put points on the media board simply by surviving. (Vic Gold, in *PR as in President,* Doubleday, 1977.)

Gold's Law. There are two four-letter sources for ninety percent of all human troubles: S-E-X-X and M-U-N-Y. (Herbert Resnicow, *The Gold Solution,* 1983; from Charles D. Poe.)

Goldthwait's Law of Animals. Animals are our friends, but they won't pick you up at the airport. (From the late comedian Bob "Bobcat" Goldthwait; from Steve Stine.)

Goldwynism, Tenets of. (1) Every director bites the hand that lays the golden egg. (2) If you can't give me your word of honor, will you give me your promise? (3) Why only *twelve* disciples? Go out and get thousands! (4) Who wants to go out and see a bad movie when they can stay at home and see a bad one free on TV? (Attributed to Samuel Goldwyn; various sources.)

Goldwyn's Law of Contracts. A verbal contract isn't worth the paper it's written on. (Samuel Goldwyn; *Co.*)

Golfing: Observations, Theories, and Additional Rules. (1) Rail-splitting produced an immortal president in Abraham Lincoln; but golf, with 29,000 courses, hasn't produced even a good A-Number-1 congressman. (2) Man blames fate for other accidents but feels personally responsible for a hole in one. (3) Golf is a form of work made expensive enough for rich men to enjoy. It is physical and mental exertion made attractive by the fact that you have to dress for it in a $200,000 clubhouse. Golf is what letter-carrying, ditch-digging, and carpet-beating would be if those tasks could be performed on the same hot afternoon in short pants and colored socks by gouty looking gentlemen who required a different implement for each mood. (4) In arriving at a judgment on whether or not ground is under repair for purpose of lifting a ball unpleasantly situated without penalty, the player shall toss a coin. If it falls, the ground may be deemed under repair. (5) A ball striking a tree while in flight shall be deemed not to have struck a tree unless the player making the stroke declares that he was deliberately aiming for it. In this case, play shall cease momentarily while his partners congratulate him on his marksmanship. But if the player attests in good faith that it was in no sense his intention to strike the tree, then it is obviously a piece of bad luck that has no place in a scientific game. No penalty shall accrue to the player, who is thereupon permitted to estimate the distance his ball would have traveled, but no more than half the distance to the goal line, or two bases. (Various sources: [1] Will Rogers, [2] *Horizons* magazine, [3] *Essex Golf and Country Club News,* [4 and 5] Mimeographed, unattributed "Rules of Golf"; *ME.*)

Golub's Laws of Computerdom. (1) Fuzzy project objectives are used to avoid the embarrassment of estimating the corresponding costs. (2) A carelessly planned project takes three times longer to complete than expected; a carefully planned project will take only twice as long. (3) The effort required to correct course increases geometrically with time. (4) Project teams detest weekly progress reporting because it so vividly manifests their lack of progress. (*U/JE.*)

Gomez's Law. If you don't throw it, they can't hit it. ("Lefty" Gomez.)

Gomme's Law. A backscratcher will always find new itches. (Andor Gomme, Stoke-on-Trent, England.)

Gonzalez's Laws. (1) The easiest way to change a typewriter ribbon is to go out and buy a new typewriter. (2) If you call and they say "the check is in the mail," be prepared to call them a week later and the week after that. (3) Your enemies always photograph better than you. (Gloria Gonzalez, West New York, New Jersey.)

Goodden's Rule. A woman's opinion of a man's sexual attraction is always in inverse ratio to her own sexual attraction. (B.B.W. Goodden, Twickenham, Middlesex, England.)

Goodfader's Law. Under any system a few sharpies will beat the rest of us. (Al Goodfader, Washington, D.C.; *AO*.)

Goodhardt's Forecasting Rule. Forecasting is never difficult; if it is not easy, it is impossible. (Professor Goodhardt; from James Rothman.)

Goodman's Bookseller's Law. No matter how many authors are published, the same hundred appear in every bookstore. (Ellen Goodman, in her *Boston Globe* column of July 1, 1993.)

Goodman's First Rule for Dining. Never eat anything while it's watching you. (Ellen Goodman, *Boston Globe* columnist, in her February 11, 2001 column about fast foods, which starts off by telling about being served, in a Japanese restaurant, a raw sliced lobster tail, packed back into the shell, with the lobster antennae still twitching, right above the lobster's eyes; from Bob Skole.)

Gooen's Laws of Lost Energy. (1) If it takes one person one hour to do a specific job, it will take two hours for two people to do the same job. (2) If it takes one person an hour to hike two miles on a trail, it will take two people an hour and a half to cover that same distance. (Irwin Gooen, Oneonta, New York.)

Gordon's First Law. If a research project is not worth doing at all, it is not worth doing well. (Robert M. Gordon, who wrote on December 28, 1979 to explain: "When I first made the statement—it was 1967, if I remember correctly; of course, at the time I was also unaware that I was uttering a deathless, universal truth.—It was on the occasion of receiving from the leader of a computer programming project the results of about ten man-years of so-called effort: 'If a thing is not worth doing at all,' I said, 'It is not worth doing well.' It is easy to see how the statement that appears in *The Official Rules* came into being. It is also easy to understand that, at last count, 349 corollaries had been stated and proved; 17 other corollaries are still waiting proof. I am writing in the interest of historical accuracy (not vanity), asking only that you amend the text in subsequent editions of your much-appreciated work.")

Gordon's Law. If you think you have the solution, the question was poorly phrased. (Robert Gordon, East Granby, Connecticut.)

Gordon's Laws of Motion. (1) The fastest way of getting someplace is being there. (2) Go before you leave—this will prevent sudden stops. (3) Don't leave if you have to go. (4) It won't move if you don't fix it. (Dr. Kurtis J. Gordon, Pleasant Grove, Utah.)

Gotwald's Law of Behavior Modification. When a kick in the ass doesn't work, create envy. (Rev. Frederick G. Gotwald, Syracuse, New York.)

Goulden's Axiom of the Bouncing Can (ABC). If you drop a full can of beer, and remember to rap the top sharply with your knuckle prior to opening, the ensuing gush of foam will be between 89 and 94 percent of the volume that would splatter you if you didn't do a damned thing and went ahead and pulled the top immediately. *Goulden's Law of Jury Watching:* If a jury in a criminal trial stays out for more than twenty-four hours, it is certain to vote acquittal, save in those instances where it votes guilty. (Senior Fellow Joseph C. Goulden, writer, developed this law during twenty-seven months of intensive research as a courts reporter for *The Dallas News.*)

Goulden's Rule of Citations. The higher the rank of the author of a military memoir, the lesser the chance of a subordinate officer to be cited in the text, unless he is a batman or the subject of a court-martial (i.e., corps commanders ignore division chiefs of staff, and regimental commanders leave anonymous company and platoon commanders). Conversely, every rifleman in the First Marine Division "fought with General Oliver Smith (or Colonel Chesty Puller) in Korea." (Joseph C. Goulden, Washington, D.C.)

Gould's Two-Shirt Theory of Arctic Exploration. Wear the first shirt until it becomes unbearable; then switch to the second shirt. Wear the second shirt until *it* becomes unbearable, by which time the first shirt will look pretty good again. This process may be repeated indefinitely. (*U/GT.*)

Governor's Rule. Everyone at the executive end of Pennsylvania Avenue considers everyone at the congressional end an SOB and vice versa. The governors consider anyone from Washington an SOB no matter which end of the avenue he comes from. (Discovered by *TCA* when representing the executive branch at the Governors' Conference in Colorado Springs, Colorado, 1949.)

Grabel's Temporary and Freelance Workers' Dilemma. There is always plenty of work when you can't and not enough work when you can. (Steven M. Grabel, San Francisco, California.)

Gracy's Axiom. Don't pay duty. It is such a waste; the government has got more money than is good for it already and would only spend it. (A lady in P. G. Wodehouse's novel *The Luck of the Bodkins* [Little, Brown, 1936], explaining why she wants an expensive necklace smuggled through customs. Used by columnist George Will to explain the passage of Proposition 13 in California.)

Graditor's Laws. (1) If it can break, it will, but only after the warranty expires. (2) A necessary item only goes on sale after you have purchased it at the regular price. (Sherry Graditor, Skokie, Illinois.) *Corollary to Graditor's 2nd Law:* A necessary item only goes into a sale if you have purchased it at the regular price. (Jan Hallowell Jeddah, Saudi Arabia, who adds, "Observation leads me to posit that the amount of time the item takes to go on sale is inversely proportional to the difference between the original price and the sale price.")

Grafton's Law. The computer always knows when you want to show someone something on your screen and immediately slows to a crawl. (John Grafton, Princeton, New Jersey.)

Graham's Laws. (1) *Graham's Law of Dictionaries:* When you are consulting a dictionary, you will always find a more interesting word first. (2) *Graham's Law of Invention:* Whilst man's ability to invent things increases geometrically with time, his ability to maintain things only increases arithmetically. (3) *Graham's Laws of Hotel Elevators:* Your room is always the one farthest from the elevator. On leaving the elevator, your wife will always turn left instead of right, or vice versa. (4) *Graham's Law of Physical Decline:* At sixty you may be a sexagenarian, but by the time you are ninety you will have become a nonagenarian. (5) *Graham's Law of Plumbing:* He who bathes last bathes fastest. (6) *Graham's Comment on Forms Design:* There is never enough space for your full address, but always too much for your name. (Charles Graham, The Mount, Oxford Road, Gerrards Cross, Buckinghamshire, England.)

Grammatical Exclusion Principle. If it can be said clearly, plainly, and in English, it has just as logical and valid a claim for being examined as any other similarly constructed statement. (From an unsigned article of the same name in the July 1963 issue of *Air Force/Space Digest.* The gist of the article is that the author came up with this conclusion after making a tongue-in-cheek but well-worded proposal regarding an Air Force satellite. Later he found the Air Force had adopted his idea—in fact, it had become central to its planning.)

Gramm's Laws. (1) It's crowded at the bottom. (2) The early worm gets the bird. (3) You're always on the wrong end of the train. (Eugene Gramm, New York, New York.)

Grandma Soderquist's Conclusion. A chicken doesn't stop scratching just because the worms are scarce. (Letter from John Peers of Logical Machine Corp., thanking contributors for laws for that company's law collection.)

Granger's Advice. Don't say you've paid your dues until you're at least 40. (Bill Granger, *Chicago Tribune,* May 27, 1984; from Steve Stine.)

Grant's Axiom. If, in any quantity of chicken salad, there exists a single knob of chicken gristle, then it will find its way into the teeth of he who can least stand chicken gristle. *Grant's Idea of Hell:* Hell is where you go after you die, and all the ideas you ever forgot come back to you. (Michael Grant, *San Diego Union*, San Diego, California.)

Grant's Musical Distinction. I know two tunes: one of them is "Yankee Doodle," and the other isn't. (Ulysses S. Grant.)

Gray's Law of Bilateral Asymmetry in Networks. Information flows efficiently through organizations, except that bad news encounters high impedance in flowing upward. (Paul Gray to Robert Machol for his *POR* series. Gray also told Machol, "people at the top make decisions as though times were good when people at the bottom know that the organization is collapsing.")

Gray's Law of Maximum Knowledge. People reach their point of broadest education on the night before they take their Ph.D. prelims. *Gray's Law of the End of Learning:* University faculty learn nothing outside their narrow field of specialization once they have passed the preliminary examination for the Ph.D. (Paul Gray, Claremont, California.)

Gray's Law of Programming. $n + 1$ trivial tasks are expected to be accomplished in the same time as n trivial tasks. (*U/S.T.L.*; See *Logg's Rebuttal to Gray's Law of Programming.*)

Gray's Theorems. *Of $n + 2$:* The number of referred papers required to obtain tenure in an American university is $n + 2$, independent of the number n that have already been published. *Of the Sacrificial Victim:* Nothing gets done in America until somebody dies. (Paul Gray, Professor, School of Business Administration, University of Southern California. He explains, "The first is based on watching tenure review committees for a number of years. The second has some classic examples: drug safety legislation was required by the Thalidomide disaster; exact fare was put in on buses after several drivers were killed; the FAA's R&D budget goes up after each major crash and then declines; pollution became a seriously recognized problem after Donora." Donora, Pennsylvania, was hit with a dense smog in October 1948, which killed twenty and left hundreds ill.)

Graziano's Discoveries. (1) No solution is better than any other solution. (2) Money can't buy happiness. Poverty can't buy happiness. (Cindy Graziano, Chicago, Illinois.)

Great American Axiom. Some is good, more is better. Too much is just right. (*U/Ra.*)

Great, Rule of the. When someone you greatly admire and respect appears to be thinking deep thoughts, he or she is probably thinking about lunch. (*U/DRW.*)

Green's Motto. The will to win is not worth a nickel unless you have the will to practice. (Dallas Green, posted on clubhouse wall when he managed the New York Yankees in 1989. Such mottos were spread throughout various clubhouses ruled by Green. *Another:* A great pleasure in life is doing what people say you cannot do.)

Greenberg's First Law of Influence. Usefulness is inversely proportional to reputation for being useful. (Daniel S. Greenberg, in a column entitled "Debunking the UTK [Useful to Know] Myth," *Washington Post,* October 25, 1977. He attacks the conventional wisdom that says there are people who are useful to know in the sense that they possess inordinate influence. He makes many points in favor of his law, including this one: "What must be noted about the many fallen political celebrities of recent years is that salvation eluded them, though they knew all the people in Washington who are useful to know.")

Greener's Law. Never argue with a man who buys ink by the barrel. (Bill Greener; *AO.*)

Greene's Commentary on Life. The chief enemy of good is better. (Dr. Milton Greene; from Dr. Bradford Walters, Detroit, Michigan.)

Greene's Hotel Razor. The best measure of whether a hotel cares about you or not can be found in your room lamps. If the hotel cares about you, the button to turn the lamp on and off will be found on the base of the lamp, within easy reach. If the hotel does not care, the button will be found somewhere up beneath the shade, or on a little plastic clicker attached to the cord—where you have to search to locate it. (Bob Greene, "Rules of the Road," *Esquire,* August 1983. He adds that the other measure of whether a hotel cares about you is whether or not it has installed a red message light on your telephone.)

Greene's Law. Life is a do-it-yourself project. (Bill Greene; from Joseph M. McCabe, Martinsburg, West Virginia.)

Greenfield's Observation. Too many liberal Democrats have come, over the years, to worship... the state and to see it as the natural agent of the Lord's will, even though you can't reach it by telephone much after 4:30 in the afternoon. (Meg Greenfield, *Newsweek,* December 15, 1980; *RS.*)

Greenfield's Rule of Practical Politics. Everybody is for democracy—in principle. It's only in practice that the thing gives rise to stiff objections. (Meg Greenfield, *Washington Post,* in an article entitled "The People's Revenge," June 14, 1978.)

Greenhaus's Summation. I'd give my right arm to be ambidextrous. (*U/DRW.*)

Green's Dictum. The bottom line is only the tip of the iceberg. (Jay Green, Las Cruces, New Mexico.)

Greenya's Advice. Learn to clip your fingernails with your left hand because you might not always have your right. (Writer John Greenya, Kensington, Maryland, who learned this from his late father.)

Gregory Productivity Axiom, The. Any discussion of increasing productivity refers to that of others. (Walter Gregory, Milford, Connecticut, who explains: "Throughout years of participation in management meetings, a recurring topic was the increasing of productivity. Never once did one of the participants ever submit that his or her own productivity might be increased.")

Grelb's Addition. If it was bad, it will be back. (Loretta Hellrung, Alton, Missouri; *EV.*)

Gren's Law of Public Speaking. It's the hometown audience that expects the most and appreciates you the least. (Jack Gren, Fort Wayne, Indiana.)

Gresham's Law. Bad money drives out good. (Sir Thomas Gresham discovered this law in the sixteenth century. It has been generalized, restated, and redirected to a number of fields, so it appears in many forms, including the currently popular version that says, "Trivial matters are handled promptly; important matters are never solved." An example of a specialized application is "Gresham's TV Law," which appeared in a January 2, 1977 article by Frank Mankiewicz in the *Washington Post:* "In a Medium in which a news piece takes a minute and an 'in-depth' piece takes two minutes, the simple will drive out the complex.")

Gretchen's Defense. They said today that we should stock up on canned goods. So I went out and bought a case of beer. (Galveston carpenter John Gretchen III, preparing for a hurricane, quoted in *Forbes,* October 8, 1984.)

Gretzky's Truism. You miss 100 percent of the shots you never take. (Hockey great Wayne Gretzky, widely quoted.)

Grice's Historical Perspective. We live on the point of the Arrow of Time—and have to look back for the shaft. *Grice's Law of Yellowed Lecture Notes:* Teaching is like prostitution—you got it, you sell it, and you still got it! (John C. Grice, Greensboro, North Carolina.)

Griffith's Maxim. If it makes you nervous, don't watch. (Jean Sharon Griffith, Vice President of Student Services, Richland College, Dallas, Texas.)

Griffitt's Discovery. Pride is no match for dirty diapers. (James J. Griffitts, M.D., Dunnellon, Florida.)

Grissom's Law. The smallest hole will eventually empty the largest container, unless it is made intentionally for drainage, in which case it will clog. (Dave Grissom, Coronado, California.)

Grizzard's Discovery. Regardless of what you might accomplish in life, the size of your funeral is still going to be determined by the weather. (From the late Louis Grizzard.)

Grizzly Pete's Philosophy. (1) Don't do nothin' too much. (2) When a man gives you his reason for an act, just remember the chances are, nine out of ten, the reason is a trail blinder. What does this mean? (3) The most successful liar is the one who lies the least. (4) If there is anything in the theory of the survival of the fittest, a lot of people we know must have been overlooked. (Grizzly Pete of Frozen Dog, alter ego of Col. William C. Hunter, who appears in Hunter's *Brass Tacks,* Reilly and Britton, 1910.)

Grobe's Thought on Memory. If you can't remember it, it couldn't have been important. (*U.*; John L. Shelton, Dallas, Texas.)

Groebe's Law. The more complex the problem, the sooner the deadline. (Larry Groebe, San Antonio, Texas.)

Grold's Law. If you put your head in the sand, you're going to get shot in the butt. (Psychiatrist L. James Grold, widely quoted and applied to those who saw no lessons to be learned from the 1992 Los Angeles riots.)

Grollinger's Axiom on Accountants and Auditors. Old accountants/auditors never die—they just lose their balance. *Grollinger's Intimation on Immortality:* Death is usually incurable, except in Transylvania. *Grollinger's Maxim on Manufacturing:* If it's manufactured in America, it was probably assembled in Mexico or Taiwan. *Corollary:* The converse is also true. *Grollinger's Observation on Opera:* Only in opera can 300-pound sopranos die from consumption. (Stephen J. Grollinger, Westmont, Illinois.)

Grosch's Law. Computing power increases as the square of the cost. If you want to do it twice as cheaply, you have to do it four times as fast. (Herb Grosch, editor, *Computerworld; S.T.L.*)

Grosso's Second Law. Education cannot be substituted for intelligence. (Gerald H. Grosso, Port Orchard, Washington.)

Gross's Law. When two people meet to decide how to spend a third person's money, fraud will result. (Herman Gross, Great Neck, New York; *AO.*)

Gross's Laws. (1) Good work and mediocre work pay about the same. (2) In the search for the guilty, he who gave the warnings will be remembered. (3) There is always money for the task force. (4) It is better to wear out than rust out. (5) Nothing is worse than a nervous boss, especially when you are the one who is making him nervous. (Sidney Gross, Seattle, Washington.)

Groucho's Point. If women dressed for men, the stores wouldn't sell much. Just an occasional sun visor. (Groucho Marx on *You Bet Your Life.*)

Groucho's Razor. Who are you going to believe: me or your own two eyes? (Groucho Marx.)

Gruber's Laws. (1) Common sense and common knowledge are the two most uncommon things in the world. (2) Everybody has to be a somebody. (If not, why get up in the morning?) (3) If you can be intimidated, you will be. (John F. Gruber, Oak Creek, Wisconsin.)

Grubnick's Process for Effecting Action via Paperwork Within the Bureaucracy. (1) Blitz it with paperwork. (2) Say as little as possible, in as many ways as possible, as verbosely as possible. (3) Always try to tell them what they want to hear. (4) And never, never, never let the facts interfere with your story. (David S. Grubnick, Fairbanks, Alaska.)

Gudeman's Paradox. Anyone I know who might qualify for Mensa has brains enough not to. (Al Gudeman, Des Plaines, Illinois.)

Guinther's Law of Problem Solving. It is better to solve problems than crises. (John Guinther, in *The Malpractitioners,* Doubleday, 1978; *MBC.*)

Guinzburg's Warning. If you ever find yourself quixotic enough to lie down with a vampire, don't be surprised if you get a love bite on your neck. (Thomas Guinzburg, former president of Viking Press, after being ousted by its conglomerate owner. Quoted in Hillary Mills's "Publishing Notes," *The Washington Star,* May 13, 1979.)

Guitry's Distinction. You can pretend to be serious; you can't pretend to be witty. (Sacha Guitry, quoted in the *Chicago Tribune,* July 27, 1986; from Steve Stine.)

Gummidge's Law. The amount of expertise varies in inverse proportion to the number of statements understood by the general public. (From an essay in *Time,* December 30, 1966, entitled "Right You Are If You Say You Are—Obscurely." The item opens with a scene at Instant College, where a student is being briefed by key faculty members on the importance of learning jargon on the way to becoming an expert. Dr. Gummidge, professor of sociology, tells the student, "Remember Gummidge's Law and you will never be found out." Gummidge illustrates by telling the student how he would tell the student's mother that he was a lazy, good-for-nothing. He would say the student in question is performing minimally for his peer group and is an emerging underachiever.)

Gumperson's Law. The probability of anything happening is in inverse ratio to its desirability. This very important law first appeared in the November 1957 issue of *Changing Times* and was credited to Dr. R. F. Gumperson (although we have subsequently learned that the real author is John W. Hazard, now the magazine's executive editor). The law was announced in conjunction with a long-forgotten article on firewood, to account for a phenomenon known to anyone who has ever lit fires, to wit: "that you can throw a burnt match out the window of your car and start a forest fire while you can use two boxes of matches and a whole edition of the Sunday paper without being able to start a fire under the dry logs in your fireplace." Gumperson began serious work in 1938 on the *Farmers' Almanac* phenomenon (by which that esteemed annual always does a better job predicting the weather than the official weather bureau) and during World War II went on to develop the procedure for the armed forces "whereby the more a recruit knew about a given subject, the better chance he had of receiving an assignment involving some other subject." It was further reported that Gumperson met with an untimely death in 1947 while walking down the highway. He was obeying the proper rule of walking on the left facing traffic when he was hit from behind by a Hillman-Minx driven by an Englishman hugging the left. Over the years Gumperson has picked up many disciples, including the late H. Allen Smith, who wrote that he felt that the law was written just for him. One of Smith's many examples: "I dislike going to the garage with a rattle in my car, because the moment the mechanic begins his inspection, that rattle will vanish." Some of the many real-life examples he was able to derive from his law and his pioneering work as a divicist:

- That after a raise in salary you will have less money at the end of each month than you had before.
- That children have more energy after a hard day of play than they do after a good night's sleep.
- That the person who buys the most raffle tickets has the least chance of winning.
- That good parking places are always on the other side of the street.

Gumperson's Proof. The most undesirable things are the most certain; e.g., death and taxes. (From Martin S. Kottmeyer, Carlyle, Illinois.)

Gunn's Law. An egalitarian society is one that has only two classes of people—those who are equal and those who keep them that way. (Ben W. Gunn, Hertfordshire, England.)

Gunter's Airborne Discovery. (1) Upon being served a meal aboard an aircraft, the aircraft will encounter turbulence. (2) The strength of the turbulence encountered aboard an aircraft is directly proportional to the temperature of your coffee. (Tony J. Gunter, Fort Jackson, South Carolina.)

Guppy Law. When outrageous expenditures are divided finely enough, the public will not have enough stake in any one expenditure to squelch it. (Fred Reed, columnist for the *Federal Times,* explaining how the bureaucracy minimizes popular resistance to a government program; *AO.*)

Gurney's Album Observation. If you get up to fix a skip on a record, the skip will fix itself just before you get to the turntable. *Corollary:* After you fix a skip on a record, the next skip will not occur until after you are comfortably seated again. (Spencer Gurney, Hanover, New Hampshire.)

Gustafson's Advice. Anything you look for in the Yellow Pages will not be listed in the category you first try to find it under. Start with the second. (John W. Gustafson, San Francisco, California.)

Gustafson's Observation. There is no virtue in consistency if you are consistently wrong. (Art Gustafson; from Lloyd W. Vanderman, Oxon Hill, Maryland.)

Guthery's Observation. In an evolving man-machine system, the man will get dumber faster than the machine will get smarter. (Scott B. Guthery, Austin, Texas.)

Guthman's Law of Media. Thirty seconds on the evening news is worth a front page headline in every newspaper in the world. (Edward Guthman; from *MBC*'s Laws of Politics.)

Guy's Law. If a person puts a "For Sale" sign on the lawn, the water heater blows up. (Caller named Guy, call-in radio show, Grand Rapids, Michigan.)

Gwen's Law. Do not join encounter groups. If you enjoy being made to feel inadequate, call your mother. (Liz Smith, from *The Mother Book,* Doubleday, 1978.)

Gwinn Theory of Necessity. Whenever you need it, it's never there; but if you don't need it, it's everywhere. *Ergo:* It's always in your face except when needed. (Marcel Gwinn, Houston, Texas.)

H

Haas's Rule. Everybody's vacations are a nuisance, except one's own. (Timothy Haas, Woldingham, Surrey, England.)

Haber's Hypothesis. For an employee, the number and length of coffee breaks varies directly with the amount of uncompleted work. (Meryl H. Haber, M.D., Professor and Chairman of the Department of Laboratory Medicine, University of Nevada, Reno. First published in *The Pathologist,* 1970.)

Hacker's Law. The belief that enhanced understanding will necessarily stir a nation or an organization to action is one of mankind's oldest illusions. (*U/RS.*)

Hacker's Law of Personnel. It is never clear just how many hands—or minds—are needed to carry out a particular process. Nevertheless, anyone having supervisory responsibility for the completion of the task will invariably protest that his staff is too small for the assignment. (Andrew Hacker, from *The End of the American Era,* Atheneum, 1970. *The Law of Personnel* has been revised on various lists and is sometimes written as: "Anyone having supervisory responsibility for the completion of a task will invariably protest that more resources are needed.")

Hackett's Rules. (1) Prophets of doom usually find it. (2) Expeditions cause rain. (3) Short-range planning always supersedes long-range planning. (David K. Hackett, Knoxville, Tennessee.)

Hagan's Law of Tool Placement. It's in the other room. (Jim Hagan; from W. E. McKean II.)

Hagemann's Six Principles of the Common Law. (1) People are no damn good. (2) Creditors always win. (3) Avoid litigation. (4) It isn't the principle of the thing, it's the money. (5) The undertaker is always paid first. (6) Those who have all the answers usually don't know what the questions are. (John F. Hagemann, Vermillion, South Dakota.)

Hagerty's Law. If you lose your temper at a newspaper columnist, he'll get rich or famous or both. (James C. Hagerty, President Eisenhower's press secretary, who discovered it after blowing his top over a column by humorist Art Buchwald.

For other press-secretary laws, see *Nessen's Law, Powell's Laws, Ross's Law,* and *Salinger's Law.*)

Hagman's Conclusion. Television is the opium of the last part of the Twentieth Century. (Actor Larry Hagman, on the TV show *Donahue*; from Steve Feinfrock.)

Haig's Law. When you want it bad, you get it bad. (Former U.S. Secretary of State Alexander Haig, September 5, 1990, on the Frank Bough interview, Sky TV, UK; *TG.*)

Hakala's Rule of Survival. Pack your own parachute. (T. L. Hakala, Mesa, Arizona.)

Halberstam's Law of Survival. Always stay in with the outs. (David Halberstam; from *MBC*'s Laws of Politics.)

Haldane's Law. The universe is not only stranger than we imagine, it is stranger than we *can* imagine. (J. B. S. Haldane, British geneticist and Marxist; *JW.*)

Haldane's Rule. Any legislation that does not purport to apply, and is not actually applied (a very different thing), to all social classes alike, will probably be unjustly applied to the poor. (J. B. S. Haldane, quoted in the *New Yorker,* October 22, 1984; from Steven R. Woodbury.)

Hale's Black Hole Rule. Every messy desk contains a black hole, in which papers placed on one side disappear for three months, and then reappear on the other side. *Hale's Company Rule:* The sumptuousness of a company's annual report is in inverse proportion to its profitability that year. *Hale's Mail Rule.* When you are ready to reply to a letter, you will lack at least one of the following: (1) a pen (or pencil or typewriter), (2) stationery, (3) postage stamp, or (4) the letter you are answering. *Hale's Vacation Rule:* More happens in the two weeks you are away from the office on vacation than in the fifty weeks you are there. *Nonvacation Corollary:* More happens in the one hour you are at lunch than in the seven you are in the office. (Irving Hale, Denver, Colorado.)

Hallen's Credo. If you bend like the willow, you will never break your back, but you may find your nose on the ground. (Walter Scott Hallen, Evanston, Illinois.)

Hall's Law. There is a statistical correlation between the number of initials in an Englishman's name and his social class—the upper class have significantly more than three names, while members of the lower class average 2.6. (*U/JW.*)

Hall's Law of Return. The nail that you drive flawlessly into a piece of wood without it buckling will be the same nail that you had previously singled out to show the salesperson how flimsy the nails are that he sold you. (John Hall; from William C. Callis, Falls Church, Virginia.)

Hall's Laws. *Common Sense:* The lower one's intelligence, the more likely one is to believe that intelligence and common sense are inversely related. *Vehicular*

Noise: There is an inverse relationship between the intelligence of the driver and the noise made by the driver's vehicle. *Radio:* The worse the music, the better the reception. *Strapping Things to Cars:* When a group of people finish strapping an unwieldy object to a car, someone in the group will say, "That's not going anywhere!" *Lifeguard:* A whistle on a cord *will* be twirled on the lifeguard's finger. *Teaching:* Nothing is universally obvious. *Markham's Rejoinder:* Everybody knows that. (Paula Markham is the friend to whom I loaned your book) (Donald M. Hall, Radford, Virginia.)

Hall's Laws of Politics. (1) The voters always want less taxes and more spending. (2) Citizens want honest politicians until they want something fixed. (3) Constituency drives out consistency; i.e., liberals defend military spending and conservatives social spending in their own districts. (Robert A. Hall, Minority Whip, Massachusetts Senate.)

Hall's Observations. (1) The word *necessary* seldom is. (2) Most business decisions are based on one critical factor: which method will cause the least paperwork. *Janet's Corollary:* In government, the opposite is true. (Keith W. Hall, Harrisburg, Pennsylvania.)

Halperin's Laundry Rule. All lingerie put in the washer inside out comes out of the washer inside out. All lingerie put in the washer right side out comes out inside out. (Judith Halperin, Chicago, Illinois.)

Halpern's Observation. That tendency to err that programmers have been noticed to share with other human beings has often been treated as if it were an awkwardness attendant upon programming's adolescence, which like acne would disappear with the craft's coming of age. It has proved otherwise. (Mark Halpern; *JE.*)

Hammer's Law. When you can't watch everybody... watch out. (Rapper MC Hammer, explaining the downfall of his financial empire from the VH-1 "Behind the Music" program, September 1996; *TG.*)

Hammer's Rule of Reality. Official and genuine never are. (Ed Hammer; from Don Schaefer, Park Ridge, Illinois.)

Hancock's Law of the Pizza. The one who pays for the pizza gets the last slice. (Jazzman Herbie Hancock, in a Pizza Hut commercial, late 1985; from Steve Stine.)

Hanevy's Rules of Photography. (1) Bad photos are always due to poor processing, and don't reflect on your professional skill as a photographer. (2) If you tell someone not to look at the flash—they will look at the flash. (3) When on vacation, you will take photos similar to those available on postcards—which you won't buy, because your photos are better. (4) If you have to use a flash to get a picture, the use of flash will not be permitted. (5) The best place to take a picture will be closed to the public. (6) The most advanced camera model on the market will be obsolete soon after you buy it. (7) If you are on vacation you will have to buy film at a ridiculously high price. (8) When you get your pictures back there will be at least one that you have no idea what it is of, or why you took it. (9) Batteries only go dead when you have that "once in a lifetime" shot. (10) You always see the "perfect shot" when you are out of film, or when you don't have your camera with you. (John M. Hanevy, Deer Park, New York.)

Hanlon's Classification of Airline Passenger Seats. (1) All window seats are over the wing. (2) All aisle seats are opposite the galley. (3) All "non-smoking" seats are where you can't see the movie. (5) All seats where you can see the movie are next to the window seats whose occupants refuse to pull the shades down. (Alfred Hanlon, Alexandria, Virginia.)

Hansen's Law. If your new car is parked close enough to another car so that its driver can ding you with his door, he will ding you with his door. (Louis S. Hansen, San Francisco, California.)

Hanson's Law of Progress. Any new form is always longer and more complicated than the one it replaces. (Mark D. Hanson.)

Hanson's Observation of Conventions. The most interesting moment at a convention is when you walk in late and everyone watches you. The most irritating moment at a convention is when someone else walks in late and interrupts your thought. (Gary W. Hanson, Sioux Falls, South Dakota.)

Hanson's Treatment of Time. There are never enough hours in a day, but always too many days before Saturday. (Gary W. Hanson, Sioux Falls, South Dakota.)

Harber's Rule of Photography. Open the lens two stops to compensate for the lens cap. (Dick Harber, University of Southern California Department of Cinema, c. 1973; from Richard Manning.)

Harden's Law. Every time you come up with a terrific idea, you find that someone else thought of it first. (Frank Harden, radio personality, Washington, D.C.; *JW.*)

Hardie's Two-Sided Sword. Enthusiasm often masks a great deal of incompetence. *Hardie's License Plate Observation:* Autos with women's names on the plates are usually driven by men. (James Hardie, Phoenix, Arizona.)

Hardin's Law. You can never do merely one thing. (Biologist Garrett Hardin. It applies to any complex system and tells us that even when an action has its intended effect, it also has other, unintended effects. An editorial in the February 1974 *Fortune* said, in part, "If a prize were to be awarded for the most illuminating single sentence authored in the past ten years, one of the candidates would surely be Hardin's Law." *Fortune* said examples were common: e.g., New York City's off-track betting system had its intended effect of weaning waging away from illegal bookies, but it also had the unintended effect of creating a new clientele of horseplayers.)

Hardy's Observation. Though a good deal is too strange to be believed, nothing is too strange to have happened. (Thomas Hardy; from Stephen J. Chant.)

Harkness's Discovery. The harder it is to stay awake on the drive home, the harder it will be to fall asleep when you get there. (R. J. Harkness, Ruth, California.)

Harlan's Advice to Hecklers. Don't start an argument with somebody who has a microphone when you don't; they'll make you look like chopped liver. (Harlan Ellison, in a speech at the University of New Mexico, ca. 1980; as recalled by Steve Stine.)

Harmer's Observation. You spend most of your university career avoiding the people you met during Fresher's Week. (*U;* from Gareth J. Evans. The UK Fresher's Week would be Frosh or Freshman in the US.)

Harrel's Collection of "Worst Questions I Have Been Asked." (1) Where did you lose it? (2) Have I kept you waiting? (3) You asleep? (4) Will you promise not to get mad if I ask you something? (5) You don't remember me, do you? (C. Jack Harrel, Kingfisher, Oklahoma.)

Harrel's Discoveries. (1) When a part of your anatomy is hurting, every friend you meet will hit you in that spot. (2) You can always judge a man's character by his activities when he is away from home. (C. Jack Harrel, Superintendent, Kingfisher Public Schools, Kingfisher, Oklahoma.)

Harriet's Dining Observation. In every restaurant, the hardness of the butter pats increase in direct proportion to the softness of the bread being served. (Harriet Markman; from Steve Markman, Pasadena, California.)

Harrison's Teaching Inequities. Young inexperienced teachers get (1) the worst disciplined classes, (2) the largest classes, (3) the least academic classes, (4) the greatest pupil/teacher contact time, (5) the least financial reward, and (6) the least time for preparation. (R. C. Harrison, teacher, Garden City, England.)

Harris's Discoveries. (1) Candy bars are smaller, but candy-bar wrappers are bigger. (2) A probable event is something good that ought to happen but doesn't. An unlikely event is something bad that should not happen but does. (3) If they catch you playing with a deck with more than four aces, never admit you were cheating. Tell them you thought the game was canasta. (4) No one will ever say no to the question "You know what I mean?" (Roger Harris, Newark *Star-Ledger,* November 15, 1978.)

Harris's Law. Any philosophy that can be put "in a nutshell" belongs there. (Sydney J. Harris, from his book *Leaving the Surface,* Houghton Mifflin, 1968.)

Harris's Restaurant Paradox. One of the greatest unsolved riddles of restaurant eating is that the customer usually gets faster service when the restaurant is crowded than when it is half empty; it seems that the less that the staff has to do, the slower they do it. (Sydney J. Harris, from *On the Contrary,* Houghton Mifflin, 1964.)

Harris's Rule. There is an inverse relationship between front page media coverage and getting things done. (Bill Harris, Cambridge, Massachusetts.)

Harris's Rule of Perennial News. Whatever other news stories may or may not occur from year to year, there will always be (1) a collision or oil spill involving a Liberian freighter; (2) a man, who after slaughtering at least five people with a gun or knife, will be described by his neighbors as a "decent, quiet, family man"; (3) on a monthly basis, at least two substances in common, everyday use that some scientists will claim are cancer-related. (Arnold Harris, Miami, Florida.)

Hartig's "How is Good Old Bill?" "We're Divorced" Law. If there is a wrong thing to say, one will. (Betty Hartig, "The Nantucket Kite Lady.")

Hartig's Sleeve in the Cup, Thumb in the Butter Law. When one is trying to be elegant and sophisticated, one won't. (Betty Hartig.)

Hartka's Theorem. You usually end up eating more cake after deciding to have only one thin piece than if you started with a bigger piece. (Thomas J. Hartka, Severna Park, Maryland. *Johns Hopkins Magazine,* May 1978.)

Hartley's Law. You can lead a horse to water, but if you can get him to float on his back, you've got something. (Let Conrad Schneiker explain how he acquired this law: "Hartley was a University of Arizona student who wandered into my office looking lost, c. 1974"; *S.T.L.*)

Hartman's Automotive Laws. (1) Nothing minor ever happens to a car on the weekend. (2) Nothing minor ever happens to a car on a trip. (3) Nothing minor ever happens to a car. (Charles D. Hartman, Belleair, Florida.)

Hart's Law of Observation. In a country as big as the United States, you can find fifty examples of anything. (*U;* Jeffery F. Chamberlain, letter to *Verbatim.*)

Hart's Thirteenth Law of Political Economics. Financial markets will tolerate a Republican deficit but will run screaming in panic from a Democratic deficit a fraction its size. (Senator Gary Hart, *Houston Chronicle,* July 21,1988; from Charles D. Poe.)

Harum's Theory of Fleas. A moderate amount of fleas is good for a dog; it keeps him from broodin' on bein' a dog. (David Harum, the title character of E. N. Westcott's 1898 novel.)

Harvard Law. Under the most rigorously controlled conditions of pressure, temperature, volume, humidity, and other variables, the organism will do as it damn well pleases. (*U/Co.*)

Harvey's Reminder. In times like these, it is helpful to remember that there have always been times like these. (Paul Harvey; from B. L. Albert.)

Harwitz's Finding. A top-secret government study indicates that we wouldn't be any worse off if we let the economists predict the weather and the meteorologists predict the economy. (Paul Harwitz, *The Wall Street Journal,* March 19, 1980; *RS.*)

Hasselbring's Law. Never remember what you can afford to forget. (Andrew S. Hasselbring, Chillicothe, Ohio.)

Hassell's Modified Maxim. Hard work never hurt anyone, but then neither did a whole lot of good rest. (Richard Arthur Hassell, quoted in the *Journal of Irreproducible Results,* a 1984 issue.)

Hassett's Third Law of Minutiae. The intensity of interest in trivia is in inverse proportion to the magnitude of real-life problems encountered. (W. Gilbert Hassett, Fairport, New York. This law came from his study of a retirement community where he found that the less people had to do, the fewer their real problems, the more they were concerned with little things. Why the *Third Law of Minutiae?* "The first two are inconsequential," says Hassett.)

Hassinger's Rules. (1) Nothing is as simple as you thought it was going to be. (2) Nothing goes as quickly as you expected it to go. (3) Nothing ends up costing what you expected to spend. (Herman Hassinger, Moorestown, New Jersey.)

Hass's Revision of Lord Acton. Power over oneself is a good thing, the more absolute the better. It is power over *others* that corrupts, because the more power one has over others, the less power the others have over themselves. (N. Sally Hass, Sleepy Hollow, Illinois, responding to *Acton's Law:* Power corrupts. Absolute power corrupts absolutely.)

Hastings's Boogie Axiom. The single most requested item in the library is the most likely to grow legs and walk. *Corollary:* As the number of requests for the *Rand McNally Road Atlas* increases, so does the probability of its being stolen. (Carole Marie Hastings, *Reference Librarian,* a 1983 issue.)

Hatton's Law of Conical Probability. The number of orange construction cones preceding a work zone is directly proportional to the likelihood and length of the work crew's coffee break. (Mark Hatton of Ridgewood, New Jersey, from a compilation "Axioms, Rules, And Other Commuting Observations," *The Record* (Bergen County) December 1, 1997.)

Hatton's Law of Digital Reciprocity. Birds that are flipped multiply. (Mark Hatton of Ridgewood, New Jersey, from a compilation "Axioms, Rules, And

Other Commuting Observations." *The Record* (Bergen County) December 1, 1997.)

Haught's Query for Spouses with a Motorcycle. Why don't you get a mistress instead? Nobody ever got killed falling off a mistress. (Jim Haught of the *Charleston (SC) Gazette,* quoting his wife in *Forbes,* February 23, 1987.)

Hauler's Observation of Universal Underestimation. There is no such thing as "five minutes." (Jack Hauler, Malvern, Pennsylvania.)

Hauser's Truths. (1) If you have a garden wedding, the cesspool runs over. (2) The only time you get dealt a royal flush is when you are down to your last five dollars. (Georgia Hauser, Albion, California.)

Havens's Law. Deja vu is only a poor memory—you *have* done it before. (H. Gordon Havens, Kansas City, Missouri.)

Haviland's Discoveries. (1) *Law of Thermodynamics:* Hot air hand driers in public washrooms will shut off just as they reach a sufficient temperature to actually begin the drying process and will always have to be restarted. You will never need the full time on the second cycle. (2) *Observations of False Alarms:* The smoke detector battery will always run out in the night, causing it to start beeping. (3) *Dieter's Despair:* There are more food commercials on TV when you are on a diet. (4) *Time's Truth:* You do not necessarily have to be having fun for time to fly. (5) *Linear Reality:* There is a fine line between pessimism and realism. (6) *Law of Firsts:* The first time you do, you shouldn't have. The first time you don't, you should have; for example, the first time you decide to run that stop sign because "there's never anything coming the other way," there will be, and it will be the police. The first time you don't ask if there is anything you can pick up at the store is the day you come home and find there is no bathroom tissue in the house. (James D. Haviland, Halifax, Nova Scotia.)

Hawkeye's Conclusions. (1) It's not easy to play the clown when you've got to run the whole circus. (2) The tedium here is relieved only by the boredom. (The character Hawkeye Pierce in the television show *M*A*S*H.*)

Hazlitt's Conjecture on Consistency. Never say "never" and always avoid "always." *Hazlitt's Observation:* The right thing to say always comes to mind after you've said the wrong thing and have no opportunity for rebuttal. (John M. Hazlitt, South Bend, Indiana.)

Head's Discovery. "Emotionally disturbed Junior High children" is redundant. (Jacqueline Head, McMinnville, Oregon.)

Health, Three Rules of. One of the ancient natives has just confided to me a pearl of his ripe wisdom. Through 80 years of hard work, hard cider, strong tobacco, and simple food, he has only observed three rules of health: (1) Feet warm. (2) Head cool. (3) Bowels open. (Richardson Wright in *The Gardener's Bed Book,* J. B. Lippincott, 1929.)

Healy's Law of Distance. The promised land always looks better from a distance. (Pat Healy, reporter, *The Boston Globe; MBC.*)

Hearst's Observation. When dining in Washington, Republicans pay more for their food and wine, which makes the owners happy. Democrats tend to tip better, which pleases the wait staff and bartenders. (Joseph Hearst; *TG.*)

Hebert's Best Seven Laws. (1) *Hebert's Hard and Fast Rule for Understanding Women:* There *are* no hard and fast rules. (2) *Hebert's Horizontal Gravity Law:* An injured portion of your anatomy will be attracted to hard, sharp objects during the healing process. (3) *The Law of Natural Compensation:* Any stroke of unexpected good fortune will be compensated for, within 48 hours, by 1.22 strokes of misfortune. *Corollary:* If the checkbook has extra funds, something expensive will go wrong with the car. (4) *First Law of Notification:* Snoring is nature's way of telling you that your spouse is still in the bed. (5) *First and Only Law of Complaints:* Don't complain. The people who will listen can't do anything about it, while the people who can do something about it won't listen. (6) *Hebert's Safe Places Observation:* You are never as clever in locating the thing you put in a "safe place" as you were when putting it there. (7) *First Law of Returns:* If people say, "Oh, here he is" when you get back from wherever, it's not good news. (John M. Hebert, New Baltimore, Michigan.)

Hebert's First Law of Highway Engineering. Freeways aren't. *Hebert's First Law of Nonsuccess:* It's lonely at the bottom too. It's just more crowded. (John M. Hebert, New Baltimore, Michigan.)

Hebertson's Law of Budgets. Don't be overly concerned with the cost of paper clips and other office supplies—fire people, and the paper clips will take care of themselves. (David M. Hebertson, Sandy, Utah.)

Hegel's Heckle. If, as Mies van der Rohe said, "Less is more," then when does nothing become everything? (Gene Hegel, Elgin, Illinois.) *Hegel's Rules of Order:* (1) Before you argue or debate, define the terms. (2) Before that, define "define." (Gene Hegel, Elgin, Illinois.)

Heifetz's Law. No matter what you believe, you always find some people on your side that you wish were on the other side. (Jascha Heifetz; from Earl M. Ryan, Birmingham, Michigan.)

Heilson's Discovery. Time is nature's way of keeping everything from happening at once. (Jeffery W. Heilson, Santa Ana, California.)

Heinemann's Law of Executive Recruitment. The best way to get a good managerial job is to have had a good managerial job, no matter how thoroughly you screwed it up. (George A. Heinemann, Crystal Lake, Illinois.)

Heinlein's Economic Given. People who go broke in a big way never miss any meals. It is the poor jerk who is shy a half slug who must tighten his belt. (Novelist Robert Heinlein, quoted in *Forbes,* April 14, 1980.)

Hein's Law. Problems worthy of attack prove their worth by hitting back. (Piet Hein, from a group of "Quips" in *Journal of Irreproducible Results,* March 1971.)

Heisey's Principle of Reference Librarianship. The only patron on a bad night will spend hours in the mystery section, then come to the desk ten minutes before closing and demand *all* available material on atomic energy for a paper due tomorrow morning. (R. F. Heisey, Arlington, Virginia.)

Helen's Inanimate Object Lessons. (1) The certainty of an object's loss is directly related to the "specialness" of the place you put it. (2) If you buy a new one, the old one will turn up (90 percent probability). *The Cognitive Corollary:* The more confident you are of remembering, the more likely you are to forget. *Helen's Intuitive Rule of Object Placement:* Once you finally find an object, put it in the first place you thought to look for it, particularly if you returned to that place more than once in your search. Do *not* apply any other rule of logic to this choice. Do *not* choose a place that seems in any way "special." *Helen's Model for Predicting the Behavior of Machinery.* All machines are equipped with desperation detectors: The more desperate you are to meet any sort of deadline, the more intractable they become. Operators will note: these detectors are not fooled by superficial acting or the feigned appearance of calm. (Helen Fleisher, Silver Spring, Maryland.)

Helen's Query. If I dialed the wrong number, why did you answer? (Helen E. Jolliffe; from her son.).

Helen's Rule of Two-Year-Olds. (1) They will *never* tell you that they have to go to the bathroom. (2) until after you have dressed them in boots, mittens, coat, snow-pants, scarf, and hat. (3) By the time you undress them, it's too late. (4) If it's not too late, it was a false alarm. (5) If it was a false alarm the first time, it won't be a false alarm once you get them dressed again. (From John A. Mattsen, Finlayson, Minnesota.)

Heller's Myths of Management. The first myth of management is that it exists. The second myth of management is that success equals skill. (Robert Heller, *The Great Executive Dream,* Delacorte, 1972; *JE.* See *Johnson's Corollary to Heller's Law.*)

Hellinger's Law. Today's cheap trick becomes tomorrow's precedent. (The character Nick Hellinger in the TV movie *Hellinger's Law,* which aired on CBS on March 10, 1981. In his review, critic Tom Shales of the *Washington Post* pointed out that it was also the "First Law of Television.")

Hellman's Principle. Keep cool but do not freeze. (From A. Peter Hollis, Wilson, North Carolina. He discovered it one day while looking at the side of a jar of mayonnaise. It is useful for people who have a temper.)

Hellman's Product Development Rule. If you drop something and it doesn't break, mark it heavy duty. (Mitch Hellman, Baltimore, Maryland, learned while in new product development.)

Hellrung's Law. If you wait, it will go away. *Shavelson's Extension to Hellrung's Law:. . . .* after having done its damage. (Loretta Hellrung, Alton, Missouri; *EV.*)

Hell's Angels Axiom. When we do right, you forget. When we do wrong, you remember. (From Hunter S. Thompson's *The Hell's Angels,* Random House, 1967.)

Helmer's Rule of Self-Enlightened Nonresistance. When dealing with fools, do whatever is necessary to make them happy and get them off your back. (John Helmer, *Texas Observer,* September 13, 1985; from Joseph C. Goulden.)

Helms's First Rule for Keeping Secrets. Nothing on paper; paper can be lost or stolen or simply inherited by the wrong people. If you want to keep something secret, don't write it down. (Former CIA Director Richard Helms, quoted in *The Economist,* April 12, 1980; from Joseph C. Goulden.)

Helprin's Discovery. Marxists are people whose insides are torn up day after day because they want to rule the world and no one will even publish their letter to the editor. (Novelist Mark Helprin, *Winter's Tale,* Harcourt, Brace, Javonovich, 1983)

Hembree's Law. Interaction of industrial, scientific, and political entities always selects the course which makes the most profit for the largest corporations. (Hugh Hembree, *Mensa Bulletin,* November 1984.)

Hemingway's Law. The most essential gift for a good writer is a built-in, shock-proof crap detector. (Ernest Hemingway, *Paris Review,* 1958; from James E. Farmer.)

Hempstone's Dictum. When the federal cow wanders into the paddock, somebody's going to milk it. (Syndicated columnist Smith Hempstone; from his column of March 13, 1979.)

Henderson's Absolute. There is nothing crankier than a constipated gorilla. (Dr. J. Y. Henderson, chief veterinarian for Ringling Brothers and Barnum & Bailey Circus. Quoted in the *Los Angeles Times* by David Larsen.)

Henderson's Texas A&M Rule. Once is tacky, twice is tradition. (Lt. Col. Joe C. Henderson, USAF, Texas A&M University.)

Hendrickson's Law. If a problem causes too many meetings, the meetings eventually become more important than the problem. (*U/GT.*)

Henley's Law. Sometimes you get the best light from a burning bridge. (Singer/songwriter Don Henley, from his song "My Thanksgiving"; *TG.*)

Henry J's Rule. When your work speaks for itself, don't interrupt. (Automotive pioneer Henry J. Kaiser.)

Henry's Commentary on Conclusions. Nothing is over when you think it is. (Henry Garcia, Monrovia, California, who sees it in all walks of life from romance to education. He notes that every baseball fan knows at least of one occasion when he or she left the ballpark in the top of the eighth inning, his team losing by seven runs, only to read in the paper the next morning that his team made a great comeback.)

Henry's Law of Annual Reports. The more rewrites a draft of an annual report is put through, the more the final, accepted draft for printing will match the original draft developed prior to administrative review. (C. Henry Depew, Tallahassee, Florida. "Last year," he wrote the Director in 1979, "the annual report I am responsible for producing... thirteen partial and five full rewrites. The final draft... almost matched the initial draft.")

Hensley Proposition, The. The failure of any part on an automobile is impossible if one does not know it exists. (Stephen Allan Hensley, Belton, Texas, who adds, "e.g., the infamous gulp valve on my MGB.")

Hepler's Laws of Business. (1) You never can tell. (2) It all depends. (Professor Hal Hepler, Michigan State University; from Robert Nelson.)

Herblock's Law. If it's good, they'll stop making it. (Conceived by the famous political cartoonist after they stopped making a particular kind of carbon drawing stick that he liked best. Reported on by Sydney J. Harris in his December 28, 1977, syndicated column, "Modern Way: If It's Good, Scrap It"; *FD.*)

Herbst's Laws of Military Survival. (1) Never annoy a finance clerk. Garbage in, garbage out. (2) Have a friend in personnel, finance, supply, the hospital, and the orderly room. It's not what you know but who you know. (3) So conduct yourself so that when your name is mentioned in the orderly room, everyone says "Who?" The invisible man is never on the detail list. (4) There is no way you can get through a day without violating a regulation; therefore, choose the one nobody knows. A mob is the best camouflage. (5) As far as the military is concerned, a person's IQ is in direct ratio to his pay grade. There are more dumb airmen than dumb generals. (6) The detail list is always made the day before you put in for leave, and everyone who could replace you is going on leave the day of your detail. (7) Never assume anything. Thule AB Greenland is manned by the clowns who didn't read the small print. (8) You're never that "short" that someone wouldn't try to get your butt. Wait until you're out the gate before you tell them what you think of them. (9) Never listen to an officer who always says, "I was an enlisted man myself." If he knew what it was all about, he'd still be enlisted. (10) Crap seldom rolls uphill. It rolls down and spreads out. (Anita M. Herbst, T. Sgt., USAF, San Antonio, Texas.)

Herburger's Law of Small-Town Lawyers. Where there is only one lawyer in town, the lawyer can't make a living. But when there are two lawyers in town, both of them will make a good living. (From Calvin E. Deonier, Ritter, Oregon.)

Herman's Law. Put your last change in a coffee machine or soft-drink dispenser, and have it run out of cups. Then watch the machine drink your coffee or soft drink. (Michael P. Herman, Fox Point, Wisconsin.)

Herman's Rule. If it works right the first time, you've obviously done something wrong. (Pat [Mrs. Herman] Jett, Hillsboro, Missouri.)

Hernandez Axiom on Chess. When you got a good man down, kick him. (Ernesto Hernandez, Garland, Texas.)

Herold's Constant. When a politician, particularly on the stump, says that he'll "reconsider," "reevaluate," or "study" something once elected, he's going to kill it. (R. A. Herold, Ottawa, Ontario.)

Herrnstein's Law. The attention paid to an instructor is a constant regardless of the size of the class. Thus, as class size swells, the amount of attention paid per student drops in direct ratio. (Psychologist Richard J. Herrnstein; *AO.*)

Hersh's Law. Biochemistry expands so as to fill the space and time available for its completion and publication. (R. T. Hersh, in a 1962 *American Scientist* article, "Parkinson's Law, the Squid and pU.")

Herth's Law. He who turns the other cheek too far gets it in the neck. (*U/Ra.*)

Hertz's Instructions for the Lost. Having gotten lost while driving, do the following—proceed until you either (1) reach a dead end, or (2) find a more major road. If (1), turn around until you reach (2). Keep this up and you will find yourself on a big enough road that will be recognizable or a big enough town that you can get directions. (Louis D. Hertz, Margate City, New Jersey.)

Hesting's Law of Inspiration. Any brilliant idea conceived after sunset is doomed not to be acted upon; brilliant ideas lose their appeal overnight. (Chad Hesting, Columbia City, Indiana.)

Hewett's Diagnosis. If you are worried about your drinking, you should be. The converse is not true. *Hewett's Observation:* The rudeness of a bureaucrat is inversely proportional to his or her position in the governmental hierarchy and to the number of peers similarly engaged. If there is one window open, it will be staffed by Godzilla's cousin. (Paul C. Hewett, Wilmette, Illinois.)

Hewitt's Laws. (1) If you've got a problem that can be solved with money, you haven't got a problem. (2) When you light a cigarette backward, it will be the last one in the pack. (3) When you think to wind the grandfather clock, one of the hands will be over the keyhole. (4) Babies cry. (5) Old ladies get dizzy. (6) Memos marked "Personal and Confidential" are neither. (7) If it looks like jive, it probably is. (John H. Hewitt, M.D., Rockville, Maryland.)

Hickey's Law. When one is looking at the bank clock for the temperature, the time will always show up. (James K. Hickey, Washington, D.C.)

Hiestand's Law. People who forget to turn off their car headlights almost always remember to lock their doors. (James W. Hiestand, Chattanooga, Tennessee.)

Higgins's Advice to Writers. No one asked you to write. And no one will care if you stop. If you succeed, no one will notice. It's a rough, heartless business. (George Higgins to his students at Boston University, quoted in the *Boston Globe*, December 18, 1990.)

Higgins's Definition of an Optimist. A man treed by a lion who enjoys the view. (The Rev. George Higgins, Briarcliff, New York; from a sign displayed in front of his church.)

Higgins's Razor. This life's hard, but it's harder if you're stupid. (George V. Higgins, titled from *The Friends of Eddie Coyle.*)

Highrise Golden Rule. Do over others as you would have them do over you. Remember one person's floor is another's ceiling. (*U/Ra.*)

Hildebrand's Law. The quality of a department is inversely proportional to the number of courses it lists in its catalogue. (Professor Joel Hildebrand, University of California at Berkeley.)

Hildebrandt's Plotting Principle. If you don't know where you are going, any road will get you there. (John Hildebrandt, Market Research Specialist, Durham, North Carolina; from Gary Russell, New London, Minnesota.)

Hilldrup's Genuine Barbecue Law. Anyone who says he can slice barbecue can't. *Hilldrup's Law of Home Improvement:* There is no such thing as one termite. (Robert P. Hilldrup, Richmond, Virginia.)

Hill's Observations. (1) Circulars are almost invariably rectangular. (2) When I was half this age I didn't get half this tired until twice this late. (David H. Hill, Arlington, Virginia.)

Hill's Pet Law. The life expectancy of tropical fish is in inverse proportion to their purchase price. *Corollary:* Expensive breeds of dogs always run away and get lost; mongrels never do. (Pierre Allen Hill, York, Pennsylvania.)

Hinds's Observation. Man is planned obsolescence. (Alan Hinds, Marion, Ohio, who created this shortly after throwing his back out of joint.)

Hinshaw's Corollary. Gall will get you further than talent. *Hinshaw's Corollary to one of Kenworthy's Laws:* To achieve longevity in an organization, be available but not visible. (Elton Hinshaw, Secretary-Treasurer, American Economic Association, Nashville, Tennessee.)

Hinson's Discoveries. (1) Rarely is anything lost on *top* of something. (2) Anytime that one sets down a loaded trash bag, said bag will slowly fall over in the most undesirable direction. (3) Never, never read the fine print. There ain't no way you're gonna like it. . . . Otherwise, it would be printed in large print. (Archie Edward Hinson, El Cajon, California.)

Hirabayashi's First Law of Housekeeping. There is no convenient time for the cat to throw up on the carpet. (Judy Hirabayashi, Oakland, California.)

Historian's Rule. Any event, once it has occurred, can be made to appear inevitable by a competent historian. (Lee Simonson; from Herbert V. Pronchow's *The Public Speaker's Treasure Chest,* Harper & Row, 1977.)

Hitchcock's Staple Principle. The stapler runs out of staples only while you are trying to staple something. (Wilbur W. Hitchcock, U.S. Consul, Buenos Aires, Argentina.)

Hoadley's Laws: *Decision-making:* People will take tough decisions only when not taking them is tougher. *Inflation:* The roots of inflation are human. Everybody wants more for less work. The political response is axiomatic. It is more blessed to give than to receive, when it is somebody else's money. (Walter Hoadley, executive vice president and chief economist, Bank of America, at a seminar for senior executives, January 9, 1979; *TCA.*)

Hoare's Law of Large Programs. Inside every large program is a small program struggling to get out. (Tony Hoare, computer scientist; *S.T.L.*)

Hoffer's Discovery. The last grand act of a dying institution is to issue a newly revised, enlarged edition of the policies and procedures manual. (Philosopher Eric Hoffer; from W. J. Vogel.)

Hoffman's Law of Hilarity. A true friend will not laugh at your joke until he retells it. (Henry R. Hoffman, Jr., Dallas, Texas.)

Hoffman's Pothole Law. Any public road having waited a minimum of five years for badly needed paving during which time no underground construction has taken place, except by gophers and moles, will within one week of being resurfaced be torn up by at least five public or private entities to make long-scheduled, not emergency, repairs; such entities will always work consecutively and not conjunctively. (Agnes Hoffman, Rio Nido, California; originally published in the *San Francisco Chronicle,* May 20, 1985.)

Hoffman's Rule of the Road. After you have spent $375 to make sure your car is in top shape, invariably three cars will pass you on the turnpike and the drivers will sound their horns and point at your rear wheels. (Jon Hoffman; *MLS.*)

Hoffnagle's Key to Time Management. If you have too much time, procrastination will ensure that you need even more; and if you have too little time, fear will insure that you need even less. (Gene F. Hoffnagle, Clinton Hollow, New York.)

Hoff's Law of Departure. The plane's delayed departure time is directly proportional to the time it took to get to the airport. (E. P. Hoff, Fremont, California.)

Hoff's Rule of Responsibility. Dividing 100 percent responsibility between two persons gives 10 percent for each of them. (Aksel Hoff, Haslev, Denmark.)

Hofstadter's Law. It always takes longer than you think it will take, even if you take into account *Hofstadter's Law.* (Douglas R. Hofstadter, *Scientific American,* January 1982; from Steve Stine.)

Hogg's (Murphy's) Law of Station Wagons. The amount of junk carried is in direct proportion to the amount of space available. *Baggage Corollary:* If you go on a trip taking two bags with you, one containing everything you need for the trip and the other containing absolutely nothing, the second bag will be completely filled with junk acquired on the trip when you return. (Tony Hogg, in an *Esquire* article, "The Right Way to Buy a New Small Car," February 1975.)

Holben's Law. Everything costs at least $100. (Stephen Holben, Denver, Colorado.)

Holberger's Rule. It doesn't matter how hard you work on something; what counts is finishing and having it work. (quoted in Tracy Kidder's *The Soul of a New Machine*, Little, Brown, 1981; from Shel Kagan.)

Holcombe's Law. When everything appears to be going in one direction, take a long, hard look in the opposite direction. (Alfred D. Holcombe, Elmira, New York.)

Holden's Findings. (1) Experience is something you don't get until just after you needed it. (2) When a chamber of commerce brags that its city is halfway between the mountains and the seashore, or equidistant from whatever other attractions, what they're saying is that it's in the middle of nowhere. (William M. Holden, Fair Oaks, California.)

Holistic Revelation. In order to cover up a hole, you've got to dig a new one. (*U/Ra.*)

Hollander's Computing Laws. (1) The most important data will be lost due to parity errors. (2) Two "standard" interfaces are about as similar as two snowflakes. (3) The program that never failed on your last computer will never run on your current computer. (Howard R. Hollander, Roy, Utah.)

Holleran's Recollection. [My father] gave me two pieces of advice: never to save money on shoes, and to treat oneself to a steak dinner now and then. (Andrew Holleran, *Nights in Aruba*, William Morrow, 1983.)

Holliday's Discoveries. (1) People with coughs always have concert tickets. (2) For every member who works for a volunteer organization, there are two others who don't like what he's doing. (3) If lonely, sort laundry, get out the vacuum cleaner, put trash bags inside the door, and company will arrive. (Phillip Holliday, North Webster, Indiana.)

Holloway's Rule. It is impossible to overestimate the unimportance of practically everything. (Clark Holloway, Pittsburgh, Pennsylvania.)

Holloway's Rule. You never know until you find out. (Scott Holloway; from Michael Kehr, York, Pennsylvania.)

Hollywood's Iron Law. Nothing succeeds like failure. (Discussed and reapplied by Sidney Zion in his article "Hollywood's Iron Law Comes to Washington," *New York Magazine,* January 24, 1977. As Zion explains, "If a genius lost a few million on a picture, he was immediately installed in a fancier office with a better title and a bigger budget.... Only after nine straight flops was he eligible to become head of the studio.")

Holmes's Law. Once you have eliminated the impossible, whatever remains, however improbable, must be the truth. (Sherlock Holmes; *MLS.*)

Holmes's Priority Rule. It's better to be a masochist than not kissed at all. (Joseph Holmes, Philadelphia, Pennsylvania.)

Holton's Hypothesis. The length of a presentation is in inverse proportion to its value. (Richard Holton, Western Springs, Illinois.)

Honcho's Law of Wind Chimes. Regardless of the velocity of the wind, your wind chimes chime only when you are trying to go to sleep. ("Honcho" Holland, Encinitas, California.)

Honig's Discovery. Getting your ducks in a row results in a row of duck shit. (Dr. James Honig, Rockledge, Florida.)

Hooligan, Third Law of. The ratio of south ends of northbound horses to the number of horses is always greater than one. (Edward H. Seymour, New York, New York; *AO.*)

Hoover's Benediction. Blessed are the young, for they shall inherit the national debt. (Herbert Hoover, quoted in James Charlton's *The Executive Quotation Book,* St. Martin's, 1993.)

Hoover's Question. If a man tells you that he never tells the truth, can you believe him? (R. Hoover, Worth, Illinois.)

Hopkins's Baby Law. Much of what goes in must come out, but not necessarily by the expected route. (C. M. Hopkins, Berkshire, England. Ms. Hopkins insists that this law does not appear in other collections of laws because either it is too obvious or "it results in so much wearisome work that the human mind has evolved a subconscious automatic repression of it to ensure that too prominent an awareness of it does not endanger the wish to propagate the species.")

Horner's Five-Thumb Postulate. Experience varies directly with the equipment ruined. (Presumably, Little Jack Horner; *AIC.*)

Horomorun Paradox. The more one earns, the smaller becomes the proportion of one's salary one is allowed to spend. (From *The Yam Factor,* by Martin Page, Doubleday, 1972.)

Horowitz Collection. (A selection): (1) Sowing wild oats is no way to break new ground. (2) Live unrepressed. Don't stifle any yawns. (3) Cultivate a green thumb. Hedge your bets. (4) Lane hoppers never achieve the inside track. (5) Nothing succeeds like recess. (6) Send flowers to funerals of people who have [had] no time to smell the roses. (7) Marry a slowpoke and both of you will end up as two peas in a plod. (8) Before getting angry, let off some esteem. (9) Being tied up all day is a poor way to get yourself together. (10) People who make mountains out of molehills suffer from piles. (11) A man of many hats is rarely in top form. (12) Cut your losses. The best bargain is flee-bargaining. (13) Hanging around the water cooler can get you into hot water. (Stanley Horowitz, Flushing, New York; from his unpublished collection of aphorisms, *The Nerd's 500 Peachy-Keen Secrets of Success: An Unlikely Guide to the Top.*)

Horowitz's Laws. (1) It is impossible to be a participant in the march of time and not get a few blisters. (2) There is hope for everything in nature except for the Petrified Forest. (Stanley Horowitz, Flushing, New York.)

Horowitz's Rule. A computer makes as many mistakes in two seconds as twenty men working twenty years. (*U/DRW.*)

Horrigan's Lament. Today, you can get designer pasta, but you can't get your shoes repaired. (Patrick Horrigan, quoted in *Newsweek* on his Manhattan neighborhood, April 20, 1987.)

Horton's Maxims. (1) Nature always wins. (2) Nothing is waterproof. (Scott Horton, San Francisco, California.)

Horton's Observation on Professionalism. It's better to be lucky than good, but slightly less reliable. (Joseph A. Horton, M.D., Morgantown, West Virginia.)

Hoskins's Truth. He, who has not, ain't got. (From George Albrecht.)

Houk's Law. Once is funny, twice is not. (Leslie Houk, Houston, Texas: "I discovered this law when my daughter began to talk. Whenever she heard something that she thought was funny, she would repeat it over and over to anyone who would listen, giggling each time. Later, I discovered that the law also applied to adults, when I would tease my wife about something she said or did in the past. One such teasing would cause her to laugh with me, but repeated teasings were likely to produce the opposite reaction. It has occurred to me that the law could also be phrased as, "It's only funny the first time," but the one I cite above is the one I always repeated to my daughter, so I prefer it.)

Hovancik's Wait-'til-Tomorrow Principle. Today is the last day of the first part of your life. (John Hovancik, South Orange, New Jersey.)

How to Tell the Difference between Democrats and Republicans

Most of these now dated distinctions are from documents published in the *Congressional Record*, and were submitted by Representative Craig Hosmer (R-California) and Andrew Jacobs, Jr. (D-Indiana) in 1974 and 1983 respectively. Both said that the authors chose to remain anonymous. These are, in fact, other embellishments of lists telling of the party differences dating back much earlier. In his autobiography, David Brinkley talks about hundreds of variations on the theme. Brinkley's favorite was a set inserted in the *Congressional Record* in 1956 by Will Stanton that includes some of the same distinctions used by Hosmer and Jacobs. The rest are attributed to various sources but mostly come from a series of 1994 columns by Bob Levey in the *Washington Post* in which readers were asked to send in their pet distinctions.

- Democrats buy most of the books that have been banned somewhere. Republicans form censorship committees and read them as a group.
- Republicans consume three-fourths of all the rutabagas produced in this country. The remainder is thrown out.
- Republicans employ exterminators. Democrats step on the bugs.
- Democrats believe people are basically good but must be saved from themselves by their government. Republicans believe people are basically bad but they'll be okay if they're left alone. (Andy Rooney, from *60 Minutes' "A Few Minutes with Andy Rooney".*)
- Democrats name their children after currently popular sports figures, politicians, and entertainers. Republican children are named after their parents or grandparents, according to where the money is.
- On Saturday, Republicans head for the hunting lodge or the yacht club. Democrats wash the car and get a haircut.
- Republicans smoke cigars on weekdays.
- Republicans eat escargot. Democrats eat snails. (Kevin Mellema of Falls Church, Virginia)
- Republicans have guest rooms. Democrats have spare rooms filled with old baby furniture. Democrats suffer from chapped hands and headaches. Republicans have tennis elbow and gout.
- Democrats leave the dishes in the drying rack on the sink overnight. Republicans put the dishes away every night. (Andy Rooney, from A Few Minutes with Andy Rooney)
- Democrats keep trying to cut down on smoking but are not successful. Neither are Republicans.

- Republicans think Skid Row is a disgrace. Democrats think it merely needs a $530 million grant from HUD. (Martha Watson of Washington, D.C.)
- Republicans tend to keep their shades drawn, although there is seldom any reason why they should. Democrats ought to, but don't.
- Republicans study the financial pages of the newspaper. Democrats put them in the bottom of the birdcage.
- Most of the stuff alongside the road has been thrown out of car windows by Democrats.
- When the attendant brings the car up from an underground parking lot, Republicans walk all the way around it and check for nicks and chips. Democrats don't bother, because they're so relieved that the car wasn't stolen. (Eric Grimm of Washington, D.C.)
- Republicans raise dahlias, Dalmations, and eyebrows. Democrats raise Airedales, kids, and taxes.
- As children, Democrats played Spin the Bottle and Pin the Tail on the Donkey. Republicans played Monopoly. (Nancy L. Peters of Arlington, Virginia)
- Democrats eat the fish they catch. Republicans hang them on the wall.
- Democrats eat soybeans. Republicans' livestock eat soybeans. (Andrew C. Spitzler, Silver Spring, Maryland)
- Republican boys date Democratic girls. They plan to marry Republican girls, but feel they're entitled to a little fun first.
- Large cities such as New York are filled with Republicans up until 5 p.m. At this point people begin pouring out of every exit of the city. These are Republicans going home.
- Democrats make up plans and then do something else. Republicans follow the plans their grandfathers made.
- Republicans are the victims of restructuring. Democrats get laid off. (Roland Williams of Burke, Virginia)
- Republicans sleep in twin beds—some even in separate rooms. That is why there are more Democrats.
- Republicans think that they are holier than thou. Democrats know that they are. (Frank N. Grateau of Charlottesville, Virginia)
- Democrats love television and watch a lot of it. Republicans hate television. They watch a lot of it, too. (Andy Rooney, from *60 Minutes* "A Few Minutes with Andy Rooney")
- Democrats give their worn-out clothes to those less fortunate. Republicans wear theirs. (John E. Fagan of Washington, D.C.)
- Democrats see the water glass as half empty. Republicans want to know who the hell drank their water. (Gordon Thomas of Arlington, Virginia)

- Republicans touch up the paint on their bumpers to maintain the resale value of their cars. Democrats are trying to figure out how to rip Clinton/Gore stickers off theirs (Marshall Goode of Sterling, Virginia)
- Democrats think heavy metal is a kind of rock-and-roll. Republicans think it's an investment opportunity. (Arthur Weitz of Bethesda, Maryland)
- Democrats call "finding their inner self" what Republicans call "a midlife crisis." (Eileen Burke of Washington, D.C., and Christine Basso of Allentown, Pennsylvania)
- Republicans do what's right, Democrats do what's fair; but if either wants a tax reduction, both are doomed. (Joe, a radio call-in guest on WIND, Chicago)
- Finally, there is mega-distinction: Foreigners often ask what the difference is between American political parties. It is really very simple. With the Republicans, you worry that they have not found solutions to the nation's problems. With the Democrats, you are afraid that they might think of something. (H. Coucheron-Aamot of Albuquerque, New Mexico)

Howard's Comparison. Permitting your life to be taken over by another person is like letting the waiter eat your dinner. (Vernon Howard; from Bob Heimberg, Las Vegas, Nevada.)

Howard's First Law of Theater. Use it. (*U/GT.*)

Howe's Law. Every man has a scheme that will not work. *(U/S.T.L.)*

Howe's Verities. (1) When you're in trouble, people who call to sympathize are really looking for the particulars. (2) When in doubt in society, shake hands. (3) Everyone hates a martyr; it's no wonder martyrs were burned at the stake. (4) A good many of your tragedies probably look like comedies to others. (5) Put cream and sugar on a fly; and it tastes very much like a black raspberry. (6) Families with babies, and families without babies, are so sorry for each other. (7) Where the guests at a gathering are well acquainted, they eat 20 percent more than they otherwise would. (E. W. Howe; from his *Country Town Sayings*, Crane and Co., 1911.)

Hoyle's Hoylerism. Good enough isn't. (Betty Hoyle, Orlando, Florida.)

Hubbard's Constant. The fellow that brags about how cheaply he heats his home always sees the first robin. *Hubbard's Credos:* (1) If a man says to you, "It isn't the money; it's the principle of the thing," I'll lay you six-to-one it's the money. (2) The fellow who owns his own home is always just coming out of the hardware store. (3) Everything comes to him who waits, except a loaned book. (4) There is somebody at every dinner party who eats all the celery. (Kin Hubbard, humorist and cartoonist, from various sources.)

Huddleston's Observation. Message importance varies directly with the ignorance of the colleague left in charge of your telephone. (Dr. Jo H. F. Huddleston, Bracknell, Berkshire, England.)

Huffmann's Reminder. Remember, it's everywhere. (William Huffmann; from Martin E. Shotzberger, Arlington, Virginia.)

Huguelet's Law of Systems Design. Frozen specifications are like the abominable snowman—both are myths and both melt with the slightest application of heat. (Thomas V. Huguelet, President, Huguelet Systems Corp., Chicago, Illinois.)

Hull's Warning. Never insult an alligator until after you have crossed the river. (Cordell Hull.)

Human Ecology, The Three Laws of. (1) There is no such thing as an independent individual, no such invention as an isolated technology, no such thing as a single resource, and no such place as an independent nation-state. (2) Humankind is an organized ecosystem of flows and stocks of transformed and reconstructed materials, money, energy, and information. (3) One generation's, community's, or culture's answers, solutions, or opportunities become other people's problems. (From Don C. Miles, the Feeding People Programme Fund, Australia.)

Human Rights Articles, A Sampling of Proposed. *Article I:* All men are born naked. *Article VIII:* All men have the right to wait in line. *Article XV:* Each person has the right to take part in the management of public affairs in his country, provided he has prior experience, a will to succeed, a college degree, influential parents, good looks, a resumé, two 3x4 snapshots, and a good tax record. *Article XVI:* Each person has the right to take the subway. *Article XXI:* Everyone has the right, without exception, to equal pay for equal work. Except women. (Carlos Eduardo Novaes, columnist for *Jornal do Brasil* of Rio de Janeiro, from a much larger collection that appeared in *Atlas*. It was written after the Organization of American States [OAS] was unable to get anywhere in its 1977 debate on human rights. Novaes created a Universal Declaration on Human Rights that he felt that most members of the OAS and United Nations could live with.)

Humpert Unhappy Homily. The older you get, the easier it is to resist temptation, but the harder it is to find. (Joseph H. Humpert, M.D., Ft. Mitchell, Kentucky.)

Humphreys's Rules. (1) Nothing is cheaper than pencils. (2) If they notice the after-shave, you've got too much on. (3) If it needs an exclamation point, it isn't important. (4) It is more helpful to say "no" than to say "I'll think about it." (5) "Why?" is infinitely less important than "What now?" (6) The cost of a fire is never less than the cost of a fire extinguisher. (7) Signatures apart, the more important a person is, the worse his handwriting. (8) Everyone hates the one who cries, "Bingo!" (9) A dog is a dog until he's facing you; then he's Mr. Dog. (10) It is impossible to be famous and private. (David H. Humphreys, English School, Nicosia, Cyprus.)

Humphreys's Second Law of Human Behavior. People will use immediate resources to solve immediate problems. *Corollary:* In 80 percent of cases, you will find the solution to a given problem within your arms' reach, if you are willing to improvise or compromise. (Daniel Humphreys, Cincinnati, Ohio.)

Hungarian Proverb. Life is like a baby's diaper, short and messy. (*U;* uncertain origin. Collected on a radio call-in show, Washington, D.C.)

Hunter's Rule. You see a lot when you haven't got your gun. (*U/Ra.*)

Hunt's Lament. A billion dollars is not what it used to be. (Bunker Hunt, after failing to corner the world's silver market, quoted in *Time,* December 29, 1980.)

Hutber's Law. Improvement means deterioration. (The late Patrick Hutber, city editor of the *London Daily Telegraph,* who created it in the 1960s. It is still invoked when an improvement is announced which results in the curtailment of, say, Saturday deliveries; from Russell Ash.)

Hutzler's Refutation. Desperation, not necessity, is the mother of invention. (Thomas L. Hutzler, T. Sgt., USAF, Fort Fisher, North Carolina.)

Huygen's Theory of Theories. Whenever you explain to a friend a completely new and original theory you have just developed on any political, philosophical, or social subject, you will read your own words the next day in a magazine you know your friend also reads. (Freddy Huygen, Antwerp, Belgium.)

Hynes's Advice. When you have a lot of things to do, get your nap out of the way first. (Jeremiah Hynes; from his daughter Jo Anderson, Deerfield, Illinois.)

Hynes's Discovery. Dilatoriness is a virtue, and is often rewarded—unlike most of the other virtues. (Professor Sam Hynes, Princeton University; from James Thorpe III.)

I

IBM Pollyanna Principle. Machines should work. People should think. (IBM motto, so titled on various computer-oriented lists; *S.T.L., JE,* etc.)

Idea Formula. One man's brain plus one other will produce about one half as many ideas as one man would have produced alone. These two plus two more will produce half again as many ideas. These four plus four more begin to represent a creative meeting, and the ratio changes to one quarter as many. (Anthony Chevins, vice-president of Cunningham and Walsh, in an *Advertising Age* article entitled "The Positive Power of Lonethink," April 27, 1959. James B. Simpson's *Contemporary Quotations,* Crowell, 1964.)

Igbara's Equation. If there are two events of equal importance, they will always conflict, e.g., marriage and career. (Neeka Igbara, Port Harcourt, Nigeria.)

Ike Tautology, The. Things are more like they are now than they have ever been before. (Dwight D. Eisenhower; from Paul Martin to *DRW.*)

Imhoff's Law. The organization of any bureaucracy is very much like a septic tank—the really big chunks always rise to the top. (This first appeared in Thomas L. Martin Jr.'s *Malice in Blunderland,* McGraw-Hill, 1931, with the following footnote: "Professor John Imhoff, Head of Industrial Engineering, University of Arkansas. A distant cousin, Karl Imhoff, invented the Imhoff Septic Tank of international fame.")

Immutability, Three Rules of. (1) If a tarpaulin can flap, it will. (2) If a small boy can get dirty, he will. (3) If a teenager can go out, he/she will. (Anonymous; in the *Robbins Reader,* 1980 issue.)

Immutable Law of Comedy, The. The longer it takes to get to the punch line, the funnier it has to be. (Rob Long in the *National Review,* July 31, 1993.)

Inch, Law of. In designing any type of construction, no overall dimension can be totaled correctly after 4:30 p.m. on Friday. *Corollary 1:* Under the same conditions, if any minor dimensions are given to 1/16 of an inch, they cannot be totaled at all. *Corollary 2:* The correct total will become self-evident at 8:15 a.m. on Monday. (From an unsigned list of laws brought to the Center's attention by Ray Boston.)

Index of Development. The degree of a country's development is measured by the ratio of the price of an automobile to that of the cost of a haircut. The lower the ratio, the higher the degree of development. (Samuel Devons, professor of physics, Columbia University; from Charles P. Issawi's *Issawi's Laws of Social Motion,* Hawthorn Books, 1973.)

Industrial Rules. (1) Interchangeable parts won't. (2) High pressure oil lines will spray visiting dignitaries. (Circulated in the early 1960s at the Raytheon Company in Andover, Massachusetts; from Richard K. Jolliffe, Saskatoon, Saskatchewan.)

Inertia, Law of. Given enough time, what you put off doing today will eventually get done by itself. (C. Gestra, Oregon.)

Inge's Natural Law. The whole of nature is a conjunction of the verb *to eat,* in the active and passive. (Nineteenth-century Clergyman/Writer William Ralph Inge.)

Ingre's Statements of Political Integrity. (1) To proclaim "I am against that" often means "I would not want others to think me in favor of it." (2) The sincerity of one's avowals is usually tempered by a desire to win the approbation of one's fellows. (M. David Ingre, Ottawa, Ontario.)

Inlander's Theory of Relativity. Everybody has relatives. (Charlie Inlander, Philadelphia, Pennsylvania; from Steve Stine. Bill McFadin wrote in response to this "I would add *McFadin's Southern Supplement:* If you live in Florida and have Northern relatives, they will visit. Often. And complain about how far you are from the beach and Walt Disney World. *Commercial Corollary:* If you work in the Florida office of a company headquartered up North, main office bigwigs will visit to inspect the property in January and February. *Commercial Corollary Conundrum:* When they do, the local management must show enough familiarity with the country clubs to get a good tee-off time, but not so much as to indicate too much time is being spent there. (Bill McFadin, Jacksonville, Florida.)

Innuzzi's Universal Law of Justice. Truth is trouble. *(U;* from a column in *Car and Driver* by Patrick Bedard.)

Inskip's Rules. (1) Don't sweat the small stuff. (2) It's all small stuff. (Dr. Richard Inskip, Director of the American Academy of Family Physicians. This set of rules has also been attributed to University of Nebraska cardiologist Robert Eliot.)

Instant Status, Merrill's Rules and Maxims of. (1) The early bird catches the worm as a rule, but the guy who comes along later may be having Lobster Newburg and Crepes Suzette. (2) Genuine status is a rare and precious jewel, and also rather easy to simulate. (3) In a democracy, you can be respected though poor, but don't count on it. (4) Society heaps honors on the unique, creative personality, but not until he has been dead for fifty years. (5) Money is not the measure of a man, but it will do quite nicely if you don't have any other yardstick handy. (6) If at first you don't succeed, you must be doing something wrong. (7) Everybody believes in rugged individualism, but you'll do better by pleasing the boss. (8) To those who doubt the importance of careful mate selection, remember how Adam wrecked a promising career. (9) It is nice to be content in a little house by the side of the road, but a split-level in suburbia is a lot more comfortable. (Charles Merrill Smith, from his book *Instant Status, or How to Become a Pillar of the Upper Middle Class,* Doubleday, 1972. These nine rules and maxims come from a longer list of fifteen. All but one of the remaining items are amplifications of the status theme, save for number fourteen, which states, "When God created two sexes, he may have been overdoing it.")

Institutional Food, Laws of. (1) Everything is cold except what should be. (2) Everything, including the cornflakes, is greasy. *(U;* Part of a collection originating at East Russell Hall, University of Georgia, Athens.)

Institutional Input, Law of. The wider the inter-departmental consultation on a problem, the less will any agency accept responsibility for the final report. *(The Washington Star* editorial, February 18, 1979.)

Institutions, Law of. The opulence of the front-office decor varies inversely with the fundamental solvency of the firm. (*U/DRW.*)

Insurance Catch-22, The. If you want it, you can't get it, but if you'll never use it, and don't need it, you can buy all you want. (Brian McCombie, "My Turn," *Newsweek,* August 11, 1986.)

Intelligence, Laws of. (1) Intelligence is simple; all you have to do is find the needle in the haystack. (2) Don't forget to recognize the needle when you see it. (Gen. William J. Donovan, head of the Office of Strategic Services [OSS] during World War II; *TCA.)*

Inverse Appreciation, Law of. The less there is between you and the environment, the more you appreciate the environment. (U/JW.)

Inverse Peter Principle. Everyone rises to his own level of indispensability, and gets stuck there. (Dr. Barry Boehm, *TRW,* during a speech before the Special Interest Group on Aerospace Computing, March 19, 1979; *RS.*)

Invisible People's Rule of Management. If I tell a man to do what he does not want to do, I am no longer chief. (Words of the chief of the Invisible People in the movie *The Emerald Forest.*)

Iron Law of Consulting. If I make the decision and I am right, you will never remember. If I make the decision and I am wrong, you will never *forget.* (From *Operations Research for Immediate Application: A Quick and Dirty Manual* by Robert E. D. Woolsey and Huntington S. Swanson, Harper & Row, 1975; *RS.*)

Iron Law of Distribution. Them what has, gets. (*Co.*)

Iron's Law of Liquid Assets. Money is the least viscous of all substances. (Andrew Iron, Toronto, Ontario.)

Irregular Verbs

I am firm; you are obstinate; he is a pig-headed fool.
I am an epicure; you are a gourmand; he has both feet in the trough.
I am sparkling; you are unusually talkative; he is drunk.
I am farseeing; you are a visionary; he's a fuzzy-minded dreamer.
I am beautiful; you have quite good features; she isn't bad-looking, if you like that type.
I have reconsidered; you have changed your mind; he has gone back on his word.
I dream; you escape; he needs help.
I am at my prime; you are middle-aged; he's getting old.

I am a liberal; you are a radical; he is a communist.
I am casual; you are informal; he is an unshaven slob.
I am in charge of public relations; you exaggerate; he misleads.
I am a camera; you are a copycat; he is a plagiarist.
I am righteously indignant; you are annoyed; he is making a fuss about nothing.
I am a behavioral researcher; you are curious about people; he is a Peeping Tom.
I am nostalgic; you are old-fashioned; he is living in the past.

(The game of "Irregular Verbs" or "Conjugations" was created quite a few years ago by philosopher Bertrand Russell on the BBC program *Brains Trust* when he declined "I am firm," the first example on our list. Ever since, people have been discovering new examples of how we approach self, present company, and those beyond earshot. The examples used here have come from a number of sources including *The New Statesman, The Nation, Harper's, Time, Isaac Asimov's Treasury of Humor,* Houghton Mifflin, 1971; and Ralph L. Woods's *How to Torture Your Mind,* Funk & Wagnalls, 1969.)

Irreversible Law of the Toe Holes. No matter which side of the toe of a sock the hole is in, you will always put the sock on so that your big toe protrudes through the hole. (Tom Eddins, Harding University, Searcy, Arkansas.)

Irving's Inquiry. Who ever hears of fat men heading a riot? (Washington Irving.)

Irving's Laws. (1) Never judge a book by its cover price. (2) Never get into an argument with a recorded message. (3) Don't let the boss know you're a male chauvinist. She may not like it. ("Irving," quoted in Ed Cooper's column. *Magazine & Bookseller.*)

Isaac's Law of Public Transportation. No matter which direction you are going, the bus/streetcar going in the other direction will come first. *Corollary:* If you are in a hurry, at least three buses/streetcars going in the other direction will come first. (Richard Isaac, M.D., Toronto, Ontario.)

Issawi on Revolution and Revolutionaries. (1) Those who are continually in revolt become revolting. (2) Revolutions are high jumps, not long jumps. One turns right over and seems to reach the sky, but lands very close to where one took off. (3) The Revolution is a sweet, innocent maiden, constantly being seduced and as often betrayed. (Professor of Near Eastern Studies Charles Issawi, *Princeton Alumni Weekly.* He has given us many laws, including what follows.)

Issawi's Laws of Social Motion (A Sampling). *Aggression:* At any given moment, a society contains a certain amount of accumulated stock (3A) and accruing flow (3T), which results in aggressiveness ((A/)T). If more than twenty-one years elapse without this aggressiveness being directed outward in a popular war against other countries, it turns inward, in social unrest, civil disturbances, and political disruption. *Committo-Dynamics, First Law of: Comitas comitatum, omnia comitas. Committo-Dynamics, Second Law of:* The less you enjoy serving on committees, the more likely you are to be pressed to do so. (Explanation: If you do not like committees, you keep quiet, nod your head, and look wise while thinking of something else and thereby acquire the reputation of being a judicious and cooperative colleague; if you enjoy committees, you talk a lot, make many suggestions and are regarded by the other members as a nuisance. *Conservation of Evil, Law of:* The total amount of evil in any system remains constant. Hence any diminution in one direction—for instance a reduction in poverty or unemployment—is accompanied by an increase in another, e.g., crime or air pollution. *Consumption Patterns:* Other people's patterns of expenditure and consumption are highly irrational and slightly immoral. *Cynics:* Cynics are right nine times out of ten; what undoes them is their belief that they are right ten times out of ten. *A Depressing Thought:* One cannot make an omelet without breaking eggs—but it is amazing how many eggs one can break without making a decent omelet. *Dogmatism:* When we call others dogmatic, what we really object to is their holding dogmas that are different from our own. *Factor of Error:* Experts in advanced countries underestimate by a factor of 2 to 4 the ability of people in underdeveloped countries to do anything technical. (Examples: Japanese on warplanes, Russians on the bomb, Iranians on refineries, etc.) *Near and Distant Neighbors:* All countries hate their immediate neighbors and like the next but one. (For example, the Poles hate the Germans, Russians, Czechs, and Lithuanians, and they like the French, Hungarians, Italians, and Latvians.) *Operational Definition of Development:* In an underdeveloped country, when you are absent, your job is taken away from you; in a developed country, a new one is piled on you. *Path of Progress:* A shortcut is the longest distance between two points. *Petroleum, Law of:* (formulated circa 1951) Where there are Muslims, there is oil; the converse is not true. *Social Science Theories:* By the time a social science theory is formulated in such a way that it can be tested, changing circumstances have already made it obsolete. (Professor Charles P. Issawi, Princeton economist and author, from his 1973 book *Issawi's Laws of Social Motion,* Hawthorne Books. Issawi uses the book to attempt to do for social science what Darwin did for biology and Newton did for physics—to state universal laws. He has succeeded, right down to his "Last Words of Advice," which are: "If you pay your taxes and don't get into debt and go to bed early and never answer the telephone, no harm can befall you.")

Issawi's Saws. *On going up and down:* What goes up decelerates; what comes down accelerates. *On sex and money:* Sex and money are like tea and coffee—two delicious ingredients which, when mixed together, produce a foul concoction. *On cutting waste from budgets:* Budget cutters cannot cut waste, because waste is not budgeted. *On letters of recommendation:* A professor knows he has reached the peak of his academic career when the letters of recommendation he writes exceed those he solicits by a ratio of 24 to 1. (Professor Charles P. Issawi.)

Italian Sayings. (1) Every man tries to bring water to his own mill. (2) The world is made of stairs, and there are those who go up and those who go down. (In Ed McBain's *Eight Black Horses,* Arbor House, 1985; from Charles D. Poe.)

J

Jack Frost's Law. If you need statistics to prove it, it probably wasn't true in the first place. (From Dr. Joel A. Tobias, Medford, Oregon, who points out that Frost was his professor of medicine at the University of Pennsylvania.)

Jackson's Basic Truths. (1) Everyone has a photographic memory. Some don't have film. (2) Save the whales. Collect the whole set. (3) A day without sunshine is like night. (4) Change is inevitable, except from a vending machine. (5) I just got lost in thought. It was unfamiliar territory (6) When the chips are down, the buffalo is empty. (7) Seen it all, done it all, can't remember most of it. (8) I feel like I'm diagonally parked in a parallel universe. (6) I wonder how much deeper would the ocean be without sponges. (7) Atheism is a non-prophet organization (Hiram Jackson; *TG.*)

Jackson's Economic Discovery. As Jesse Jackson pointed out in 1978, if a young man or woman goes to any state university in this country for four years, it will cost less than $20,000. But if he or she goes to the state penitentiary for four years, it will cost more than $50,000. (Jesse Jackson, quoted in *Newsweek*, July 10, 1978.)

Jackson's Food Physics Laws. (1) When stale, things innately crisp will become soft and things innately soft will become crisp. (2) The temperature of liquids gravitates toward room temperature, at which those drinks served hot are too cool and those served cold are too warm. (Julie S. Jackson, Laurel, Maryland.)

Jackson's Laws. (1) The next war can't start until the generals from the previous one have had time to write their memoirs. (2) Shopping centers are for people who don't have to go to the bathroom. (3) Baseball players must spit when the TV camera closes in on them. (Michael Jackson, KABC Radio, Los Angeles, California.)

Jackson's Observation on Fame. Fans don't boo nobodies. (Reggie Jackson.)

Jacob's Discovery. If a community's name includes the word "center," it's in the suburbs. If it includes the word "city," it's in the country. If its name is Center City, it's two cottages and a gas station. (Norma Jacob, Kennett Square, Pennsylvania.)

Jacob's Laws of Organization. (1) Never put anything away temporarily. (A dish that is taken in from the dining room and put on the sink, instead of directly into the dishwasher, ends up being put away twice.) (2) Take pity on your poor biographer (organize and date your diaries and albums). (3) Why are people always complaining about being behind when all you have to do to keep up is a little every day? (4) Throwing things away is as great a joy as acquiring things. (5) If it's worth going, there's something worth taking with you. (6) If you are no good at this, give up—and cherish the nearest organized person. (From Judith Martin's article "Organized!" in the Weekend section of the *Washington Post,* December 29, 1978. Jacob [Perlman] was her father.)

Jacobson's Rules and Laws. *Rain:* If you want rain for your new garden, just plan a beach vacation. *Matchmaking:* If you try to sneak your way through a surprise introduction of a co-worker to your best college friend, you will quickly learn they were divorced from one another in 1982. *Law of Promotion, 1967:* Just when you think you've got the promotion in the bag, some new guy will come along and marry the boss's daughter. *Law of Promotion, 1987:* Just when you think you've got the promotion in the bag, some new gal will come along and marry the boss's son. *Money:* If you have no cash in your wallet, you will also have no checks in your checkbook. If you do have a check left in your book, you will not have a suitable I.D. in your wallet. (Roberta B. Jacobson, APO, New York. See also *Linden's Extension of Jacobson's Rule of Money.*)

Jacobson's Sauerkraut Warning. When you read "Made in Germany" on a food product label, keep in mind that "*Die Made*" means "maggot" in German. (Roberta B. Jacobson, Griesheim, Germany.)

Jacobs's First Dictum of Computer Operation. Computers are awfully stupid—they do exactly what you tell them to do. (Lewis G. Jacobs, San Francisco, California.)

Jacoby's Addendum. The rich *are* different from you and me; they have more chutzpah. (Jeff Jacoby, *Boston Globe*, March 3, 1994.)

Jacoby's Law. The more intelligent and competent a woman is in her adult life, the less likely she is to have received an adequate amount of romantic attention in adolescence. (Susan Jacoby in the *The New York Times.* "If a girl was smart," she goes on to explain, "and if she attended an American high school between 1930 and 1965, chances are that no one paid attention to anything but her brains unless she took the utmost care to conceal them.")

Jacoby's Observation on Redskin's Fans Wearing Pig Snouts to Games.

The really scary thing is that some of those people work for the government. (Redskins lineman Joe Jacoby, quoted in *Newsweek*, February 3, 1992.)

Jacquin's Postulate on Democratic Governments. No man's life, liberty, or property are safe while the legislature is in session. *(U/S.T.L.)*

Jake's Law. Anything hit with a big enough hammer will fall apart. (Robert A. "Jake" Jackson, Socorro, New Mexico.)

James's Distinction. "Intelligent" is a term used for someone who agrees with you. "Brilliant" means that you agree with him, but would never have thought of the idea yourself. (Baseball writer and analyst Bill James from his 1983 *Baseball Abstract.*)

James's Lament. The problem with learning to speed read is you run out of funnies too fast. (Alice James, Mesquite, Texas.)

James's Research Rule. The topic you seek is never in the index. (H. L. James, San Jose, California.)

Jane's Gospel. When there are two or more identical articles to be built or repaired, difficulty will be encountered, but only while attempting to build or repair the second (or last) one. *Corollary 1:* When both the hot and cold water faucets are leaking, the knob of the first one will be removed, the washer replaced, and the knob put back on with no complications. While attempting to repair the second, however, one will encounter (a) a permanently welded knob, (b) a screw-head stripped bare, (c) a knob that fit until removed but that cannot possibly be reused, or (d) all of the above. *Corollary 2:* If the first article is dismantled again in order to determine why it went back together so easily, it will not. (Jane L. Hassler, Marina del Rey, California.)

Janitorial Blindness, Law of. Full garbage cans exude a certain substance that causes them to become invisible to the janitors. Empty and nearly empty cans do not have this quality. (David B. Cagle, Santa Monica, California.)

Jan's Law of Sensitivity. If you're not going nuts, you're not paying attention. (Janis Jones, Sunland, California.)

Jan's Measure. There's an ounce of truth in every pound of lie. (Jan Jennier, Bowie, Maryland.)

January's Cruel Lesson. You will not win one of those million dollar magazine sweepstakes that come in the mail. Knowing this, you will spend hours filling them out and in the process will accidentally order a magazine devoted to either subsistence farming, needlepoint, or bow hunting, depending on which of the three you have the least interest in. (The Director.)

Jardine's Constant. In a health club, if there is only one other locker occupied, it will be the one above yours. (Andrew F. Jardine, Philadelphia, Pennsylvania.)

Jaroslovsky's Law. The distance you have to park from your apartment increases in proportion to the weight of packages you are carrying. (*U/AO.*)

Jason's Law. An unbreakable toy is good for breaking other toys. (Bruce W. Van Roy, Vienna, Virginia; from the Style Invitational, *Washington Post*, July 10, 1994.)

Jay's Laws of Leadership. (1) Changing things is central to leadership, and changing them before anyone else is creativeness. (2) To build something that endures, it is of the greatest importance to have a long tenure in office—to rule for many years. You can achieve a quick success in a year or two, but nearly all of the great tycoons have continued their building much longer. (Antony Jay, from *Management and Machiavelli,* Holt, Rinehart and Winston, 1967.)

Jean's Law. Keep your feet close to the ground. (Jean Pike, Modesto, California.)

Jefferson's Ten Commandments. (1) Never put off 'til tomorrow what you can do today. (2) Never trouble another for what you can do yourself. (3) Never spend your money before you have earned it. (4) Never buy what you don't want because it is cheap. (5) Pride costs more than hunger, thirst, and cold. (6) We seldom report of having eaten too little. (7) Nothing is troublesome that we do willingly. (8) How much pain evils cost us that have never happened! (9) Take things always by the smooth handle. (10) When angry, count to ten before you speak; if very angry, count to a hundred. (Thomas Jefferson. Found in B.C. Forbes' [ed.] *Thoughts on the Business of Life*, Forbes, 1937.)

Jeff's Law of the Vanishing Mystique (Male Version). As soon as a ravishing woman actually gets out of a sporty car, she is no longer ravishing. *Jeff's Law of Traffic Lights.* The slowpoke you're stuck behind will always make it through a yellow light, just slow enough so that you can't. (Jeffrey P. Davidson, Falls Church, Virginia.)

Jenkins's Rules for Football Betting. (1) Never take a tip from a guy eating in a luncheonette. (2) Find a team whose players' wives have an abundance of mink coats. Wait until the mink coats are favored by ten or more against a team playing under .500, then load up on the dog. The dog could win the whole game. (3) A team with too many members in the Fellowship of Christian Athletes can draw up to three delay penalties a game. Too much praying in the huddle. (4) Go with a good passing team against defensive backs who collect art. (5) A team with its entire offensive line living within a block of a drugstore could go all the way. (6) Finally, keep an eye out for the Ivy Leaguer in a key position if the Dow takes a sudden dip. (Dan Jenkins, adapted from his article "Getting in on a Zurich," in *Sports Illustrated.*)

Jennifer's Law. The more truth there is in what a woman is saying, the less a man is listening. *Jennifer's Secretarial Law:* Only when the final draft of the document has been typed up and printed will the boss remember a crucial point that must be added to the middle of it. (Jennifer Feenstra, Montreal, Quebec, Canada.)

Jensen's Law. When you're hot, you're hot, and when you're not, everybody is watching. (Lynn Jensen, Littleton, Colorado.)

Jerri's Law. If I have a nickel, I'll spend a dime. (Jerri Locke, Fort Worth, Texas.)

Jesson's Law of Office Supply Dynamics. There is never a paper clip on the floor when you need one. (Dick Jesson, San Francisco, California.)

Jesuit Principle. It is better to ask for forgiveness than permission. (Richard Molony.)

Jewell's Rule of Domestic Horticulture. The probability of grass growing in any given spot is inversely proportional to one's desire to have it there. (History Professor Fred R. Jewell, Harding University, Searcy, Arkansas, who formulated the rule one day "while pulling sizable outcroppings of grass from the cracks in my driveway and simultaneously noting the bare spots in my lawn just a few feet away.")

Jigsaw's Searching Conclusion. You are standing on the piece that has to go in next. (Elizabeth W. Jefferson, Roanoke, Virginia.)

Jim Nasium's Law. In a large locker room, with hundreds of lockers, the few people using the facility at any one time will all be at their lockers and will be next to each other so that everybody is cramped. (Gary Neustadter, San Jose, California.)

Jim's Rule. The rental of any apartment in a major city will guarantee that the building will go condo. (*U;* WIND Radio. Chicago, Illinois.)

Jinny's Law. There is no such thing as a short beer, as in, "I'm going to stop off at Joe's for a short beer before I meet you." *Jinny's Second Law:* At a party, if you run out of ice, the guests stand around and bitch; if you run out of liquor, they go home. (Virginia W. Smith, who is *MLS*'s mother.)

Jinny's Sister's Legacy. Be careful what you give people as gifts; you may get it back when they die. (Margaret W. Carpenter; *MLS.*)

Joachim's Explanation. Nonsmokers create a vacuum and draw the smoke toward themselves. (Gary Joachim, a smoker, who told it to Dianne Coates, a nonsmoker from Reseda, California.)

Joany's Law. The human mind is wonderful thing. It begins working the moment you're born, and doesn't stop until you have to speak in public. (Anonymous; *TG.*)

Jobson's Law of Sailing. If you can't tie good knots, tie plenty of them. (In a Dewar's Scotch ad featuring yacht racer Gary Jobson; from Steve Stine.)

Joe Cooch's Laws. (1) If things are military and make sense, coincidence has entered the picture. (2) To hell with the content, let's get the format straight. (3) Personnel officers exist primarily for the purpose of screwing up other people's careers. (4) The most complicated problems always arise at the most remote locations. (5) Writing a directive and getting people to pay attention to it are two entirely different operations. (6) Staff studies should always be written in support of foregone conclusions; assumptions will be furnished later. (7) The more esoteric the presentation, the thicker the accent of the person presenting it. (8) Generals must be kept busy or their subordinates will be. (9) Greatest consideration in personnel matters is given to those individuals who are the least efficient and the most troublesome; or, if you want top-level support, screw up. (10) It is illegal for any headquarters to admit error. (11) Planners are people who take implausible assumptions, apply these to conditions that could not possibly exist, using resources that will undoubtedly not be available, to produce a plan of action that is inconceivable to be followed out. (12) One thousand guesses added together are not necessarily more accurate than one big guess. (13) The longer you work on a casualty estimate, the less accurate it becomes. (14) If people don't obey a regulation, write another more complicated. (15) Invariably, the least knowledgeable of individuals is the most vocal. (We don't know who Joe Cooch is and wonder if he might be a new incarnation of Murphy—or at least a figure created in Murphy's image. Whatever, his wisdom in the form of the multipart Cooch's Law is starting to show up with Murphy-like frequency. Examples of adaptations of Joe Cooch's code to fields outside the military [scientific research, for one] are beginning to appear. Our guess is that Joe Cooch is on his way to household-name status. Timothy J. Rolfe of the University of Chicago was the first to bring the Cooch contribution to the attention of the Center.)

Joe's Discovery. The reliability of any copier is inversely proportional to the number of copies needed. (*U;* WIND Radio, Chicago, Illinois.)

John Adams's Law of Erosion. Once the erosion of power begins, it has a momentum all its own. (From *MBC*'s Laws of Politics.)

John Cameron's Law. No matter how many times you've had it, if it's offered, take it, because it'll never be quite the same again. *John's Axiom:* When your opponent is down, kick him. *John's Collateral Corollary:* In order to get a loan you must first prove you don't need it. (John Cameron.)

Johns Hopkins Miraculous Secret for the Early Recovery of Patients, The. Inflation. *(U/* Nurse/*Ra.)*

John's Rules. (1) One size fits all means one size fits nobody. (2) Never step in anything soft. (3) A penny saved is a penny. (4) Early to bed, early to rise, and your girl goes out with other guys. (*U;* WRC Radio, Washington, D.C.)

John's Understanding. If you do something really dumb once, it's stupid. If you repeat it often, it's philosophy. (Christopher John, Meadow Valley, California.)

Johnson's Corollary to Heller's Law. Nobody really knows what is going on anywhere within your organization. (*U/S.T.L.*)

Johnson's Creative Caveat. No man but a blockhead ever wrote except for money. (Samuel Johnson.)

Johnson's Culinary Admonitions. Don't spit in the soup. We've all got to eat. (President Lyndon B. Johnson; from Erwin Knoll.)

Johnson's Discoveries. (1) At the end of a talk, an average of three people will shake the speaker's hand. (2) Originality is a vain myth. (3) No matter how many of them you collect, there will always be some more. (Willis Johnson, Jr., Atlanta, Georgia.)

Johnson's Fingernail Corollary. The difficulty of the task requiring longer fingernails increases in direct proportion to the remaining available, usable amount of fingernail. (Frank "Louie" Johnson, Bangor, Maine.)

Johnson's First Law of Auto Repair. Any tool dropped while repairing an automobile will roll under the car to the vehicle's exact geographic center. (*U/S.T.L.* Similar to *Anthony's Law of the Workshop.*)

Johnson's Law of Indices. Any subject, no matter how abstruse or unlikely, will be found in an index, except the subject for which you are searching, no matter how common or likely. (Rita Johnson, Stanley, North Dakota.)

Johnson's Law. The amount of tears produced in a man's eyes while he is cutting onions is directly proportional to the amount of women gathered to watch him. (Carleton E. Johnson, Department of State, Washington, D.C.)

Johnson's "Prior" Laws of Politics. (1) Pay your dues. (2) Attend the meetings. (Lyndon B. Johnson. The "prior" in the title refers to the fact that they precede *Dirksen's Laws of Politics* and must be understood "prior" to understanding *Dirksen's Laws.* Harry N. D. Fisher; *AO.)*

Jolliffe's Rules for Parents. (1) No article of clothing left behind at school will ever be found in the lost and found box. *Exception:* If the lost items were a pair, one of them will. (2) After all have reached agreement, regardless of the bicycle you eventually buy your child, the next-door neighbor's kid will be given the one your child really wanted after all. (3) The amount of time a child plays with a new Christmas toy is always one-fifth of the time it took for the parent to assemble it. (Richard K. Jolliffe, Saskatoon, Saskatchewan. The third rule is also known as the Hawaiian rule. According to the man who discovered the rule, "We bought our daughter a huge Barbie doll house in Hawaii, at a big saving, and lugged it all the way back to Canada. I spent several evenings putting it together and assembling all the furniture. She has played with it for a grand total of one hour and seventeen minutes.")

Jones's Advice on Surviving Thermonuclear War. Just dig a hole, cover it with a couple of doors, then throw three feet of dirt on top. (T. K. Jones, The Pentagon, quoted on the *Washington Post 1982 Calendar.*)

Jones's Anthropological Discovery. There was no profanity in the original languages of the American Indians. But, of course, there was no federal income tax either. (Franklin P. Jones, quoted in the *Wall Street Journal,* August 27, 1983.)

Jones's Law. The man who can smile when things go wrong has thought of someone he can blame it on. (*Co.* This item appears in many collections of laws, yet there is no clue as to who Jones is. See also *Tom Jones's First Law.*)

Jones's Law of Authority. The importance of an authority figure in a field is inversely proportional to the amount that is known about the subject. (Don Jones; from James S. Benton, Los Angeles, California.)

Jones's Law of Inverse Properties. The architectural style of the house is inversely proportional to the personal style of the entertainer. The outré Cher, for example, prefers staid Tudors, while the more reticent Robert Redford lives in a spectacular glass-and-steel aerie perched atop Utah mountains. (Landon Y. Jones, *Great Expectations;* Coward McCann, 1980; from Steve Stine.)

Jones's Laws of Innovation and the Organization. (1) Organizational strength increases with time. (2) Innovative capacity is inversely proportional to organizational strength. *Corollary 1:* The least likely organization to make a significant improvement in a concept is the one that developed it. *Corollary 2:* The first step in developing a new concept is to bypass the existing organization. *Corollary 3:* Organizing for innovation is a contradiction in terms. (Don Jones, from James S. Benton, Los Angeles, California.)

Jones's Mathematical Law. Twice nothing is still nothing. (Cyrano Jones, *Star Trek.* "The Trouble with Tribbles"; *JS.*)

Jones's Maxim. A man on his high horse should be advised to enter his horse into rehabilitation. (Andrew Jones; *TG.*)

Jones's Principle. Needs are a function of what other people have. (*U/JW.*)

Jones's Rule of the Road. The easiest way to refold a road map is differently. (Franklin P. Jones, in the *The Wall Street Journal.*)

Jones's Static Principle. In a static organization, one accedes to his level of comfort. (From J. Thomas Parry, Rockford, Illinois, who attributes it to Hugh Jones, manager of the Minneapolis *TV Guide* office. Parry says, "Mr. Jones, having been in an unchanging job for many years, developed this corollary to the *Peter Principle.*")

Jordan Principle, The. Genius doesn't travel well. (Created by Robert J. Samuelson in the *Washington Post,* March 5, 1997, and named in honor of basketball superstar Michael Jordan's attempt to break into baseball with the AA Birmingham Barons. It has wide application—for example, just because you made a lot of money does not make you an economic philosopher.)

Jordan's Laws. *Of Survival:* You can get over anything but a piece of gravel in your shoe. *Of Technology:* Invention is the mother of necessity. (How long did mankind get along satisfactorily without the telephone?) *Of Psychiatry:* The client already knows all the answers, but he won't tell. The psychiatrist is lucky to guess the right questions. *Jordan's Medical Rules:* (1) Don't make two diagnoses at the same time on the same patient if you can help it; you'll probably be wrong twice. (2) They call it practicing because when you get it right, you can quit.(D. Wylie Jordan, M.D., Austin.)

Journalist's Adage. Never assume anything except a 4¼ percent mortgage. (Dave Kindred, from his "This Morning" column in the *Washington Post,* January 14, 1978.)

Journalist's Ultimate Rule of Skepticism. If your mother says she loves you, check it out. (The longtime motto of Chicago's City News Bureau, that city's legendary journalism "boot camp" It appeared on a gigantic banner at the 100th anniversary party for the Bureau, according to the *Chicago Tribune*, October 7, 1990.)

Joyce's Law of Bathroom Hooks. A bathroom hook will be loaded to capacity immediately upon becoming available. (John Joyce, Waldie and Briggs, Inc., Chicago, Illinois; *AO.* According to Joyce, there is more to this law than immediately meets the eye, as it "applies to freeways, closets, playgrounds, downtown hotels, taxis, parking lots, bookcases, wallets, purses, pockets, pipe racks, basement shelves, and so on. The list is endless." However, he is the first to concede that further research is called for. As he told Alan Otten of *The Wall Street Journal* in a note, "The ultimate test of the law, which I have been postponing, would be to array hooks in a continuous strip around the bathroom to see if the towels, bathrobes, etc., actually meet in the middle of the room, preventing opening of the door and entry of would-be bathers.")

J's Business Maxim. When perplexed, confused, frustrated, and all else has failed, fall back on the truth. (Anonymous.)

J's Density Characteristics of Executives Rising in an Organization. Cream Rises and Sewage Floats. (Anonymous.)

Juall's Law on Losing. You may beat me, but you cannot defeat me. *On Winning:* It doesn't matter if you win or lose, it matters only if you beat the point spread. *Juall's Law on Nice Guys:* Nice guys don't always finish last: (a) Sometimes they don't finish. (b) Sometimes they don't get a chance to start. (Wally Juall, East Lansing, Michigan.)

Judy's Observation. You can't taste the onion in your salad until the last bit—then the taste stays with you for the rest of the day. (Judy Barkman, Hamburg, Pennsylvania.)

Juhani's Law. The compromise will always be more expensive than either of the suggestions it's compromising. (*U/DRW.*)

Juliet's Advice. (1) Never start before you are ready. (2) People will do to you what you let them. (Juliet Awon-Uibopuu, River Edge, New Jersey.)

Jump's Query. One of the great mysteries of life is how the idiot your daughter married can be the father of the smartest grandchildren in the world. *Jump's Rule of Monthly Meetings:* Monthly meetings always last two hours, regardless of the number and importance of the items on the agenda. This is because if there is little to be discussed, the participants will spend more time discussing each point because there is no pressure to move things along... [T]he time available... is controlled by the same factor which limits meetings to two hours when there is much to discuss, which is that when you have reached two hours there are always a few people who are being called by nature, and usually the chairperson is one of them. (Gary Jump, Bensenville, Illinois.)

Just's Seventh Law of Traffic Behavior. The more decrepit the vehicle, the more maniacal the driver. (The Rev. Christian F. Just, Euclid, Ohio.)

K

K Rule. Words with a *k* in them are funny. If it doesn't have a *k,* it's not funny. (Willie Clark, explaining to his nephew why certain things are funny, in Neil Simon's *The Sunshine Boys.* Clark goes on to explain that "chicken" and "pickle" are funny, but "tomato" and "roast beef" are not. This rule is discussed in some detail in Thomas H. Middleton's "Light Refractions" column in *Saturday Review,* November 13, 1976. Middleton, incidentally, finds some exceptions to the *K Rule,* for example, that "pike" is not a terribly funny word but that "herring" is.)

Kachur's Elementary School Teacher Laws. (1) The loudest human voice cannot compete with a pencil sharpener. (2) Parents who show up for conferences or open house are the ones who don't need to. The parents of the problem kids never show up. (3) The students with the worst behavior have the best attendance. (4) If Easter recess comes early, it'll snow; if late, it'll rain. If you decide to vacation in Florida, after you arrive, you'll hear on the radio weather news that it's sunny and mild back home. (Miriam Kachur, Pennsauken, New Jersey.)

Kae's Law. Changing the baby's diaper causes the phone to ring. (Kae Evensen Marty, Sacramento, California.) *Gill's Corollary to Kae's Law:* Cooking something that tells you to stir constantly for five minutes also causes the phone to ring. (*TG.*)

Kafka's Law. In the fight between you and the world, back the world. (Franz Kafka. *RS*'s 1974 *Expectation of Days.*)

Kagan's Principle of Operational Verisimilitude. You don't test something to see if it will work if you think it won't work. (Susan Kagan; from Shel Kagan, New York, New York.)

Kagan's Theorem of the Hidden Agenda. There is always more going on than you think. *Corollary:* And it's always worse than you imagine. (Shel Kagan, Canoga Park, California.)

Kagle's Rule for Winning Stock Car Races. Keep to the left, and get back here as soon as you can. (Reds Kagle, late-model sportsman champion, Old Dominion Speedway, 1976–77, Manassas, Virginia; *JCG.*)

Kahn's Laws. (1) Vice presidents never call back. (2) Entrepreneurs always call back. (Steve Kahn, *The Wall Street Journal,* March 21, 1984.)

Kamin's Seventh Law. Politicians will always inflate when given the opportunity. (Identified by Conrad Schneiker as an economist from Ventura, California.)

Kami's Law of Telephones. The cessation of ringing of a phone is *not* a function of the responder's distance, velocity, or time of access. It will stop ringing just when you reach for it, no matter how far you have to come, how fast—or slowly—you have traveled to cover the distance between you and said phone. (S. Kami, Professor, University of New Mexico, Department of Electrical Engineering and Computer Science. Kami supports his discovery with this statement: "[It] is truly empirical, having been tested in the field for over twenty years—a total of some 40,000 experiments. No theoretical proof is known to exist at this time, although some of the best brains are involved in its pursuit.")

Kamoose Taylor's Hotel Rules and Regulations. (A selection): A deposit must be made before towels, soap, or candles can be carried to rooms. When boarders are leaving, a rebate will be made on all candles or parts of candles not burned or eaten. Not more than one dog allowed to be kept in each single room. Quarrelsome or boisterous persons, also those who shoot off without provocation guns or other explosive weapons on the premises, and all boarders who get killed, will not be allowed to remain in the House. When guests find themselves or their baggage thrown over the fence, they may consider that they have received notice to quit. The proprietor will not be accountable for anything. Only regularly registered guests will be allowed the special privilege of sleeping on the Bar Room floor. Meals served in own rooms will not be guaranteed in any way. Our waiters are hungry and not above temptation. All guests are requested to rise at 6:00 a.m. This is imperative as the sheets are needed for tablecloths. To attract attention of waiters or bellboys, shoot a hole through the door panel. Two for ice water, three shots for a deck of cards, and so on. (Rules posted September 1, 1882, at the MacLeod Hotel in Alberta by Henry "Kamoose" Taylor, proprietor. This important piece of Canadian lore appears in *Columbo's Little Book of Canadian Proverbs, Graffiti, Limericks and Other Vital Matters* by John Robert Columbo, Hurtig Publishing, 1975.)

Kaplan's Dictum. If you are unable to decide between two things, do whichever is cheaper. (*U;* Fred Bondy, Wilmette, Illinois.)

Kaplan's Law of the Instrument. Give a small boy a hammer and he will find that everything he encounters needs pounding. (Abraham Kaplan; *S.T.L.*)

Karen's Constant. If a small object is dropped in the bathroom, it will go down the drain. A large object falls into the toilet. (Karen Statzel, Kirkwood, Missouri.)

Karl's Laws of Bureaucratic Paperflow. (1) Every bureaucracy generates paperwork in a logarithmic fashion. A one-page directive will inevitably lead to a five-page guideline, a ten-page procedure, and a twenty-five-page report. (2) Any attempt to clarify the information contained in a directive, guideline, or procedure will increase the amount of paperwork in each of the subsequent steps. (Ed Karl, Urbana, Illinois.)

Kass's Plagiarism. Those who can—do. Those who cannot—teach. Those who can do neither—inspect. (Lt. Col. Nicholas E. Kass [Retired], USAF, Fort Walton Beach, Florida.)

Kass's Truth. If you plan a pot luck for a club of thirty-seven members, you will end up with a meal of thirty-seven jars of dill pickles. (Connie Kass, St. Paul, Minnesota.)

Kastor's Rule Number One for Speech-Givers. Before lobbing a joke at anyone else, aim one at yourself. (Elizabeth Kastor, *Washington Post,* February 4, 1985. She followed the rule with this: "'All my life I've wanted to run for president in the worst possible way,' Walter Mondale told a National Press Club audience Saturday night. 'And I did.'")

Kathleen's Hypothesis of Earth-Water Kinesis. The lighter the color, the higher the heel, and the more the cost of the shoes, the deeper the mud in the puddle just outside the car door. (Kathleen, told to Michael L. Lazare, Armonk, New York.)

Katz's Aphorisms. (1) That which cannot be explained in a brief article is never explained in a big book. (2) Few things inhibit the undertaking of a new venture more than the fear of ridicule. (3) The scientist who claims that your research is not in the mainstream really means that only his is. (4) The mathematician who insists there can be no such thing as non-Newtonian calculus is more often than not the fellow who specializes in non-Euclidean geometry. *Katz's Laws:* (1) No new theory is recognized until some expert claims it was plagiarized.

(2) Never send your new theorem to a specialist in counterexamples. (Robert Katz, Rockport, Massachusetts.)

Katz's Maxims. (1) Where are the calculations that go with the calculated risk? (2) Inventing is easy for staff outfits. Stating a problem is much harder. Instead of stating problems, people like to pass out half-accurate statements together with half-available solutions which they can't finish and which they want you to finish. (3) Every organization is self-perpetuating. Don't ever ask an outfit to justify itself, or you'll be covered with facts, figures, and fancy. The criterion should rather be, "What will happen if the outfit stops doing what it's doing?" The value of an organization is easier determined this way. (4) Try to find out who's doing the work, not who's writing about it, controlling it, or summarizing it. (5) Watch out for formal briefings; they often produce an avalanche—a high-level snow job of massive and overwhelming proportions. (6) The difficulty of the coordination task often blinds one to the fact that a fully coordinated piece of paper is not supposed to be either the major or the final product of the organization, but it often turns out that way. (7) Most organizations can't hold more than one idea at a time... Thus complementary ideas are always regarded as competitive. Further, like a quantized pendulum, an organization can jump from one extreme to the other, without ever going through the middle. (8) Try to find the real tense of the report you are reading: Was it done, is it being done, or is it something to be done? Reports are now written in four tenses: past tense, present tense, future tense, and pretense. Watch for novel uses of *congram* (*con*tractor *gram*mar), defined by the imperfect past, the insufficient present, and the absolutely perfect future. *Katz's Other Observations:* (1) Brevity and superficiality are often concomitants. (2) Statements by respected authorities which tend to agree with a writer's viewpoint are always handy. (3) When you are about to do an objective and scientific piece of investigation of a topic, it is well to have the answer firmly in hand, so that you can proceed forthrightly, without being deflected or swayed, directly to the goal. (All of these, as well as the maxims, were written by Amrom Katz, senior RAND Corp. staff member and former assistant director of the Arms Control and Disarmament Agency. The Maxims first appeared in the November 1967, *Air Force/Space Digest* as part of a much longer article entitled "A Guide for the Perplexed, or a Minimal/Maximal Handbook for Tourists in a Classified Bureaucracy." Katz compiled the first five in the 1950s and added six through eight in the 1960s. The sampling of "Other Observations" came from three Katz articles: respectively, "Good Disarmament and Bad," *Air Force/Space Digest,* May 1963; "On Style in R&D," *Air Force/Space Digest,* February 1962; and "A Tribute to George W. Goddard," *Airpower Historian,* October 1963; *RS.*)

Kauffmann's Law. Authors (and perhaps columnists) eventually rise to the top of whatever depths they were once able to plumb. (Critic Stanley Kauffman; *JMcC* to *AO.)*

Kaufman's Laws. (1) A policy is a restrictive document to prevent a recurrence of a single incident, in which that incident is never mentioned. (2) A roadblock is a negative reaction, based on an irrelevant assumption. (J. Jerry Kaufman, Dallas, Texas.)

Kaul's Collection. (1) It does not rain on water-resistant materials. (2) The only thing alike in all cultures is the police. (3) A sinking ship gathers no moss. (4) Abstinence makes the heart grow fonder. (5) Do not try to solve all life's problems at once—learn to dread each day as it comes. (6) Crime doesn't pay unless you write a book about it. (7) A fool and his money are welcomed everywhere. (8) Don't bake cookies; the children will only eat them. (9) A man can have more money than brains, but not for long. (10) Suicide is the sincerest form of self-criticism. (11) A coward dies a thousand deaths, a hero dies but one—but which one? (Donald Kaul, *The Des Moines Register.* These are laws and observations sent to Kaul by readers of his "Over the Coffee" column.)

Kautzmann's Law of Negativism. Whatever you propose to do can't be done. *Corollary:* If they do what you propose, it won't work. (Gary E. Kautzmann, Allentown, Pennsylvania.)

Kaye's Duplicate Bridge Players' Rule of Thumb. The laws of chance positively ensure that you will always play the most difficult contracts against the most competent opponents, and the "laydowns" against the beginners. *Corollary:* Whenever a partnership has lost a match by a very few points, each partner will invariably remember (and be willing to discuss *ad nauseam*) his own brilliant plays and his partner's errors. (Joan C. Kaye, Los Gatos, California.)

Kazurinsky's Discovery. It is impossible to know if the refrigerator light really goes out when you close the door because you eat the only witnesses. (Tim Kazurinsky, on the television show *Saturday Night Live.*)

Keating's Reminder. The real world is only a Special Case, albeit an Important One. (Barry Keating, Assistant Professor of Business Economics, Notre Dame University, South Bend, Indiana.)

Keeleric's Law. Persecution of deviants (for a doctrine) is inversely proportional to the deviation. (George Keeleric, Galway, Ireland.)

Keil's Warning. In becoming sly as a fox, you will catch fleas. (Peter A. Keil, St. Louis, Missouri.)

Kelleher's Explanation. The Congress is constitutionally empowered to launch programs, the scope, impact, consequences and workability of which are largely unknown, at least to the Congress, at the time of enactment; the federal bureaucracy is legally permitted to execute the congressional mandate with a high degree of befuddlement as long as it acts no more befuddled than the Congress must reasonably have anticipated. (U.S. District Court Judge Robert Kelleher,

Central District, California, *American Petroleum Institute* v. *Knecht,* August 31, 1978; from Steven R. Woodbury.)

Keller's Law of the Theater. A whisper backstage will be heard with greater intensity than a line spoken in a normal voice onstage. (William S. Keller, Streamwood, Illinois.)

Kelley's Law. Last guys don't finish nice. (Princeton professor Stanley Kelley, Jr., occasioned by the increasing bitterness of political campaigns; *AO.*)

Kelley's Law of Bladder Capacity. The bladder capacity of a spectator at a public event (football game, concert, etc.) is inversely proportional to his or her distance from the aisle. (John R. Kelley, Jr., Alexandria, Virginia.)

Kellough's Laws of Waiting. (1) The amount of time you must wait is directly proportional to the uncomfortableness of the settings you must wait in. (2) The magazines in a doctor's, dentist's, or barber's place of business are always at least three months old. The boringness of those magazines is directly proportional to the length of time you have to wait. (David Kellough, Chillicothe, Ohio.)

Kelly's Counsel on Hiring Counsel. On any given day, 50 percent of the lawyers in American courtrooms are losers. (Thomas W. Kelly, Washington, D.C.)

Kelly's Credos. (1) The older you get, the greater the difference between the age you look and the age you think you look. (2) The ability to take off a pair of tight jeans while standing up without holding onto anything correlates positively with your ability to enjoy whatever activity follows their removal. (3) If at any gathering of 12 or more persons you say something nasty about an absent person, a friend or relative of that person will be present. (Mary Evalyn Owen Kelly, Kansas City, Missouri, who sent these in a 1995 note with this P.S.: "My birth certificate says that I am 77, but I'm pretty sure there's some mistake.")

Kelly's Law. An executive will always return to work from lunch early if no one takes him. (*U;* "Laws to Live By," *The Farmers' Almanac.*)

Kelly's Run-Around Theorem. (1) To get published, one should get a literary agent. (2) To get a literary agent, one should be published. (William W. Kelly, Hollywood, Florida.)

Kempley's Equine Cinematic Rule. When a horse is on the screen (unless of course it's the famous Mr. Ed), the Kleenexes on the floor should outnumber the Milk Dud boxes. (Film critic Rita Kempley, *Washington Post,* October 12, 1984.)

Kener's Law. Tape doesn't stick where (or when) you want it. Tape only sticks to itself. (Reed Kener; from Larry Groebe, San Antonio, Texas.)

Kennedy Law, The. If you have a sore toe, care should be exercised in removing your trousers. Do not drop them or your belt buckle will invariably fall on the sore toe. (Wallace Kennedy, Chesterfield, Missouri.)

Kennedy's Judgment. Generally speaking, a lawyer who becomes a judge believes the explanation is that God noticed his work, saw that it was good, and rewarded him. This is almost never true, but if you are a trial lawyer, it is a bad idea to suggest to a judge that it is false.(The character Jeremiah Kennedy in George V. Higgins' 1992 work *Defending Ryan;* spotted by Bob Skole.)

Kennedy's Law. Excessive official restraints on information are inevitably self-defeating and productive of headaches for the officials concerned. (Edward Kennedy, AP correspondent best known for his work during World War II; *JW.)*

Kennedy's Market Theorem. Given enough inside information and unlimited credit, you've got to go broke. (Joseph P. Kennedy; from Lawrence Gutter.)

Kennevan's Conundrum. Why is it that when a professor says, "That's a good question," he never has a good answer? (Walter J. Kennevan, Professor Emeritus, American University, Bethesda, Maryland.)

Kenny's Law. There is a critical mass of lawyers in any transaction (the number being different for every transaction) which, if exceeded, means the deal will become undoable. (Attorney Robert Kenny, Lawrenceville, New Jersey, who adds, "The manifest truth of this theorem is borne out by many years of practice in corporate and tax law.")

Kent's Law. The only way a reporter should look at a politician is down. (From Vic Gold's *PR as in President,* Doubleday, 1977; attributed to the *Baltimore Sun*'s Frank Kent.)

Kenworthy's Laws of the Bureaucracy. (A selection): *Competency:* The competency of any executive level official of government is inversely proportional to the number of his or her "special" or "executive" assistants. *Assistants:* The arrogance of any "special" or "executive" assistant to a secretarial level official is inversely proportional to the age and experience thereof. *Career Bureaucrats:* The influence of any Government Service career bureaucrat is inversely proportional to the age of the furnishings of his or her office. *The inflexible reality of a bureaucracy:* The deeper the carpet you are called upon, the deeper the trouble you're in. (Jim Kenworthy, Washington D.C. Some of these were published as "Rules of the Bureaucracy" in the *Washington Post,* March 20, 1999.)

Keokuk, First Law of. The ability and adeptness of the towboat captain varies inversely with the rapidity of the approach of 8:30 a.m. and 4:30 p.m. (Constance E. Campbell, Keokuk, Iowa. She explains: "Keokuk...is a river town on the Mississippi River. There is a swing-span toll bridge connecting Keokuk and Hamilton, Illinois, at the foot of Main Street. A new, inexperienced towboat captain seems always to be trying unsuccessfully to maneuver his towboat into our lock invariably at the times people are trying to get to work or to get home from work.")

Kerber's Law on the Inverse Half-Life of Kid's Cars. Give a kid under 21 a first car of any make, model, age, etc. The expected life of that car will be between three weeks and three months. You can double the expected life of any subsequent cars. It keeps doubling. (Robert L. Kerber, Oceanside, California.)

Kernan's Correlation. Every time you lend money to a friend, you damage his memory. (F. G. Kernan.)

Kernan's Fine Principles of Travel. (1) Whatever your friends told you, they are wrong. (2) You can't read at the beach. (3) Beware of smiling cabbies. (4) Avoid jolly groups, unless you are in one. (Michael Kernan, *Washington Post,* April 14, 1985.)

Kerouac's Admonition. Walking on water wasn't built in a day. (Jack Kerouac; collected by Beat poet Allen Ginsberg who put this in context: "Once when Kerouac was high on psychedelics with Timothy Leary, he looked out the window and said, 'Walking on water wasn't built in a day.' Ginsberg added: "Our goal was to save the planet and alter human consciousness. That will take a long time, if it happens at all.")

Kerr-Martin Law. In dealing with their own problems, faculty members are the most extreme conservatives. In dealing with other people's problems, they are the world's most extreme liberals. (Clark Kerr.)

Kerr's General Rules of Life, Plus Culpability Clause. (1) Always run a yellow light. (2) Never say no. (3) The younger, the better. *Culpability Clause:* Never admit anything. Never regret anything. Whatever it is, you're not responsible. (Kerr works with Sharon Mathews of Arlington, Virginia.)

Kerr's Rules. (1) The day the letter jackets or letter sweaters are given to an athletic team, it will be barely cold enough to wear them. (2) In most instances, there must be onions in fast foods and peanuts in candy. (3) Surplus toothpaste on the toothbrush results in a liquid that drops from the mouth but is solid enough to stick to the sink. (4) If you don't desire an elected office in a club or organization, you will probably be elected to it. *Corollary:* One sure way to be elected to an undesired office in a club is to be out of town the day of the election. *Corollary:* To prevent being elected to an unwanted office, chair the nominating committee. (Bob Kerr, Amarillo, Texas.)

Kerr's Three Rules for Trying New Foods. (1) Never try anything with tomatoes in it. (2) Never try anything bigger than your head. (3) Never, *never* try anything that looks like vomit. (Then, as he says, he broke all three rules by discovering pizza. Kerr works with Sharon Mathews of Arlington, Virginia.)

Kerr's Three Rules for a Successful College. Have plenty of football for the alumni, sex for the students, and parking for the faculty. (Clark Kerr, as the 12th President of the University of California; *MLS.*)

Kesulab's Laws. *Dictionaries:* Never look up a word you cannot spell. Never spell a word you cannot look up. *Western Movie First Aid:* No matter where the good guy is wounded, bandage the arm and shoulder. *Band-Aids:* Band-Aids stick to children only when the children are in traction. (Gary O. Balusek, Xenia, Ohio.)

Kettering's Laws. (1) If you want to kill any idea in the world today, get a committee working on it. (2) If you have always done it that way, it is probably wrong. (Charles F. Kettering, probably the nation's most quotable inventor; *Co.*)

Key to Happiness. You may speak of love and tenderness and passion, but real ecstasy is discovering you haven't lost your keys after all. (*U/Ra.*)

Key to Status. S = D/K. S is the status of a person in an organization, D is the number of doors he must open to perform his job, and K is the number of keys he carries. A higher number denotes a higher status. Examples: The janitor needs to open 20 doors and has 20 keys (S = 1), a secretary has to open two doors with one key (S = 2), but the president never has to carry any keys since there is always someone around to open doors for him; with K = 0 and a high D, his S reaches infinity. (Psychologist Robert Sommer, from his paper "Keys, Kings and Kompanies." See also his *No. 3 Pencil Principle.*)

Kharasch's Institutional Imperative. Every action or decision of an institution must be intended to keep the institution machinery working. (Washington lawyer Robert N. Kharasch, from his book *The Institutional Imperative,* Charterhouse Books, 1973. From the basic principle others follow, such as the *Law of Institutional Expertise,* which says, "The expert judgment of an institution, when the matters involve continuation of the institution's operations, is totally predictable, and hence the finding is totally worthless." See also *Security Office, Special Law of.; AO.*)

Khomeini Corollary. Take the revolution to where the reporters want to be and you'll get worldwide coverage. (Charles Peters, in *The Washington Monthly.* Peters says that this discovery is owed to the Shah of Iran, who drove the Ayatollah Khomeini to Paris. "Now reporters who would never dream of going to Mashhad, Tabriz, or Zahidan could cover the main issues of the Iranian revolution from Paris.")

Kibble's Law. Miles per gallon are no problem if you occasionally forget to record a fill-up. (G. V. Kibblewhite, Goldhurst, Kent, England.)

Kidd's Enlightenment. Things aren't like they used to be, and they never were. (Ted Kidd, Traverse City, Michigan.)

Kiesel's Railroading Analogy. You often find that one track minds are narrow gauge as well. (George F. Kiesel, St. Louis, Missouri.)

Kime's Law for the Reward of Meekness. Turning the other cheek merely ensures two bruised cheeks. (Jack Kime, Las Cruces, New Mexico.)

King's Law of Swimming Pools. When you build a swimming pool, hire a state highway engineer. They always build highways that hold water. (John J. King, Pitts, Georgia.)

King's Religious Observation. The shorter the gospel, the longer the sermon. (Donald King, Philadelphia, Pennsylvania.)

Kingfield's Constant. Nothing can be taken back. Everything is in the "record" . . . *always!!* (Professor Kingfield in the television series *The Paper Chase;* from Steve Feinfrock.)

Kington's Law of Perforation. If a straight line is made in a piece of paper, such as a sheet of stamps or a check, that line becomes the strongest part of the paper. The most obvious example is a roll of lavatory paper. There is a subsidiary law which states that a sharp tug at a perforated lavatory roll pulls the whole roll on the floor (the only real life example of perpetual motion). The roll can never be rolled back. (Miles Kington, *Punch.*)

Kinsley's Law. Insincere flattery is even more flattering than sincere flattery. *Corollary:* All flattery is flattering. *Kinsley's Law of Magazines:* New owners always replace the editor, especially if they begin by expressing complete confidence. (Michael E. Kinsley, *The New Republic,* January 2, 1985; from Joseph C. Goulden.)

Kipling's Comparison. There's worser things than marchin' from Umballa to Cawnpore. (From Rudyard Kipling's "Route Marchin'!")

Kirkland's Law. The usefulness of any meeting is in inverse proportion to the attendance. (AFL-CIO Secretary-Treasurer Lane Kirkland; *AO.*)

Kirkup's Law. The sun goes down just when you need it the most. (Jon Kirkup; *RS.*)

Kirshbaum's First Axiom of Publishing. There is always a shortage of the books that sell and an overabundance of the books that don't. (Laurence J. Kirshbaum, President, Warner Books, quoted in *The New York Times,* January 18, 1988; from Joseph C. Goulden.)

Kissel's Cat Cause. Cats have an instinctive ability to detect those people who have severe allergies to them. Once a cat has found such an individual, it will first rub on the person's leg (to ensure the embedding of plenty of cat hair on the poor fellow's slacks), then proceed to jump on the person's lap and cling until it is removed with a crowbar or another prying device. (Margo-Rita Andrea Kissell, Toledo, Ohio.)

Kissinger's Discovery. The nice thing about being a celebrity is that when you bore people, they think it's their fault. (Henry Kissinger, quoted by Bob Swift in the *Miami Herald,* January 3, 1987.)

Kitchen Law. If you're not at the table, then you're on the menu. (Attributed to any number of people, including economist Julius Hobson, and Oscar Wilde.)

Kitman's Canons of TV Law. (1) The man on trial is never guilty. (2) The guilty person is in the court. (3) A lawyer whose name is in the title of the show never loses a case. (Marvin Kitman, who studied for the TV bar by watching *Perry Mason*, *Newsday,* May 25, 1986; also the following, which appeared in his column of September 16, 1984.)

Kitman's First Law of Television. Each season is worse than the one preceding it. (Marvin Kitman, from his book *You Can't Judge a Book by Its Cover,* Weybright and Talley, 1970. He discovered the law during the 1969–1970 season.)

Kitman's Second Law of Television. Pure drivel drives out absolute drivel. (Marvin Kitman, from his book *You Can't Judge a Book by Its Cover,* Weybright and Talley, 1970. This law was created at the beginning of the 1967 season in which *The Flying Nun* began its two-year run. In explaining the law, Kitman wrote, "It is inconceivable that three competing networks, working independently in complete secrecy, could produce by accident twenty-six new series so similar in quality.")

Klawans-Rinsley Law. Large projects require more time, small projects require less time. (Alan J. Klawans and Donald B. Rinsley, M.D.)

Klein's Conclusions. (1) The two most common elements in the universe are hydrogen and stupidity. (2) If at first you don't succeed, skydiving is not for you. (3) Money can't buy happiness, but it sure makes misery easier to live with. (4) Nothing in the known universe travels faster than a bad check. (5) The trouble with doing something right the first time is that nobody appreciates how difficult it was. (6) Vital papers will demonstrate their vitality by moving from where you left them to where you can't find them. (Ken Klein.)

Klein's Law of Social Causation. The explanation for something being done that shouldn't be—or something not being done that should be—can usually be found by investigating who is or isn't making a buck on it. (Larry Klein, *Stereo Review,* November 1976.)

Klein's Law of Utilitarian Discipline. You always have to keep a few screw-ups in the organization; otherwise, what would we use as a yardstick to judge our flawless performance? (William S. Klein, Springfield, Illinois.)

Klein's Theory of Neglected Composers and Compositions. There's a reason. (From Lee Goodman, Prairie View, Kansas, who writes, "Conceived after Michael Klein and I attended a recital of obscure works...")

Klutz Factor, The. Philosophic argument always is imperfectly translated into public policy. (Anonymous; quoted in George Will's column, December 3, 1978.)

Kneass's Law. If you are a writer, editor, publisher, or affiliated with an advertising agency, everyone knows more about your business than you do. (Jack Kneass, Huntington Beach, California.)

Knight's Rules of Business. (1) Do business only with people whose word you consider to be as good as their written contract. (2) Then get it in writing anyway. (Gary Knight, Baton Rouge, Louisiana.)

Knoll's Law of Media Accuracy. Everything you read in the newspapers is absolutely true except for that rare story of which you happen to have firsthand knowledge. (Erwin Knoll, editor, *The Progressive.*)

Knopf's Rule of Best-Selling Books. A historical novel has a woman on the jacket but no jacket on the woman. (Alfred Knopf, quoted by Stefan Kanfer in *The New Republic,* August 11, 1986.)

Knopfler's Law. Sometimes you're the windshield, sometimes you're the bug. (Mark Knopfler, from his song "The Bug" on the album *On Every Street* by Dire Straits, released in 1991.)

Knowles's Debate Law. The length of debate is in inverse proportion to the importance of the subject. (Robert P. Knowles, New Richmond, Wisconsin, a twenty-two-year veteran of the state legislature. He writes, "At one point, the Wisconsin senate spent an entire day debating the proper construction of a doghouse. The bill finally failed to pass. The next day, a highly complex bill having to do with a three-phase formula for corporate taxation passed without a word of debate or a dissenting vote.")

Knowles's Law. The bumper sticker always stays on longer when the candidate wins. (Robert P. Knowles, New Richmond, Wisconsin. Consider please this corollary from *McFadin's Rule of Political Intelligence*: The smart man puts his bumper stickers on the morning *after* the election. (Bill McFadin, Jacksonville, Florida.)

Knowles's Law of Legislative Deliberation. The length of debate varies inversely with the complexity of the issue. *Corollary:* When the issue is simple and everyone understands it, debate is almost interminable. (Robert Knowles; *AO.*)

Knowlton's Law. One's belief in astrology is in inverse proportion to one's knowledge of astronomy. (Mary Alice Knowlton, San Francisco, California.)

Knowlton's Law of Involvement. Fight to the death for anything in which you truly believe—but keep those kinds of commitments to a bare minimum. (Gary Knowlton, Portland, Oregon.)

Koelle's Rule of the Self-Employed. There is no such thing as vacation—it's all just deferred work. (Jack Hauler, Malvern, Pennsylvania.)

Kohn's Discovery. The intellectual tone of a paper is improved when it has at least one word in it that is unfamiliar to the readers. *Kohn's Second Law:* An experiment is reproducible until another laboratory tries to repeat it. (Dr. Alexander Kohn, editor in chief, *JIR,* and Department of Biophysics, Israel Institute for Biological Research, Ness Ziona, Israel. *JIR,* December 1968.)

Kondracke's Rule. If literally anything goes, it's entirely possible that at some point, everything goes wrong. (Morton Kondracke's syndicated column May 12 1998; *TG.*)

Koolman's Laws of Physics. (1) If it gives you trouble, get rid of it. If you can't get rid of it, ignore it. (2) If you can't understand it, it is intuitively obvious. *Corollary:* If it works, use it. (3) Occam's Razor is invalid (and dull). *Corollary:* If you think it's confusing now, wait until you find out what it's really about. *Corollary:* Logical constructs are only used to make the picture of the universe more confusing than before. *Corollary:* Use generalities wherever possible, as it makes things more difficult to understand. *Corollary:* Always introduce an arbitrary constant to confuse the issue. (4) All fundamental particles (constants, rules, etc.) of the same kind are identical, except those that are different. *Corollary:* Anything that breaks a general rule is either totally correct and the rule wrong, or is to be ignored. (5) A meaningful concept is one that violates every rule possible. *Corollary:* A meaningful concept is usually meaningless and confusing, unless your instructor or boss formulated it, in which case you'd best learn it anyway. (6) A physicist cannot relate to his environment. *Corollary:* If you want to prove something, remake the universe so that it is true. (7) All inconsistencies are consistent with recognized theories. (8) Contradiction is the essence of all physical theorems. (9) In any calculation, a constant of "pi," "e," or "-1" is always lost. (10) Always use ideal constructs with no real analogues to explain them. *Corollary:* Everything is useless. *Corollary:* Reality doesn't work. *Corollary:* If you prove it can't exist, it does, and vice versa. *Corollary: See* Law 6. (Ron Koolman, Cincinnati, Ohio. These laws were expounded to an unfortunate student over several years by many professors, based on the original premise learned in high school: Physics is an Exact Science.)

Koolman's Truths. *Clerical:* Everything can be filed under "miscellaneous." *Dog's Life:* Life's a bitch, but even a bitch wags her tail when you scratch behind her ears. *Cats:* Anything you do to stop a cat from yowling outside your window at 3:00 a.m. will cause a neighbor to call the police. (Ron Koolman, Golf Manor, Ohio.)

Kopcha's Commercial Reality. Often the smartest thing to do is the most obvious thing to do; it is also often the hardest thing to sell. (Stephen C. Kopcha, Bloomfield Hills, Michigan, in the University of Missouri alumni magazine; from Bob Skole.)

Koppel's Credo with Definition. The optimist believes in the triumph of hope over expectations, my favorite definition of which is an accordion player with a beeper. (Ted Koppel, in a commencement address at Tufts University, 1994.)

Koppett's Law. Whatever creates the greatest inconvenience for the largest number must happen. (*U;* from a 1977 Red Smith column, "World Series Rhetoric." Smith says it was first promulgated when "baseball teams began flying around like rice at a wedding in pursuit of the championship of North America.")

Koppett's Rule. Baseball will inconvenience the largest number of people as often as possible. (Leonard Koppett, quoted widely at the time of his death at age 79 [June 22, 2003] by Hal Bodley in *USA Today*. Bodley stated that for many years the first thing that a rookie baseball writer learned was this rule: "During long rain delays, inconvenient schedule changes, day-long waits for owners' meetings to end, tired reporters would grouse 'Remember Koppett's Rule,'" *USA Today*, June 24, 2003. Though fashioned for baseball, the Rule can be applied to other human activities including the Armed Forces.) *Koppett's Other Rule:* Poor fielding will lose many more games than good hitting will win games.

Korbus's Warning. Never bet the other fellow's trick. (Bill Korbus, Austin, Texas.)

Korologos's Kollection of 95 Percent Odds. (1) The odds are 95 percent that when you press the HOLD button on an elevator for one more passenger, he will press a button for a floor below yours. The odds immediately go to 100 percent when you are in a hurry, at which time he will always hit a button on a floor below yours by mistake before punching the correct floor—which also is below yours. (2) The odds are 95 percent that every time you go into an underpass, the radio announcer will immediately start saying something you want to hear. The odds immediately go to 100 percent when it is a newscast affecting you, a friend, or your business. (3) The odds are 95 percent that when your plane pulls into a gate at the airport, the gate will be the farthest possible one from the terminal. The odds immediately go to 100 percent if there are no other planes at any gate. The reverse also is true: the odds are 95 percent that your boarding gate is the last gate in the terminal. The odds immediately go to 100 percent if you are carrying your own luggage. (Tom C. Korologos, Great Falls, Virginia.)

Korologos's Laws. (1) The length of an answer in a public hearing is inversely related to its truth. (2) The closer you get to Congressional recesses, the better good government you get. (3) Congresses do two things best—nothing and overreact. (4) When fifty-one senators tell you they'll be with you if needed, you've got a problem. (5) "Thank God! They killed the prayer amendment." (Tom C. Korologos, Great Falls, Virginia.)

Korzybski's Warning. God may forgive you your sins, but your nervous system won't. (Alfred Korzybski, scientist and writer; *ME.*)

Kostal's Observation. Select theaters aren't. (Mark Kostal, Downers Grove, Illinois.)

Kottmeyer's Ring-Around-the-Tub Principle. Telephones displace bodies immersed in water. (Martin S. Kottmeyer, Carlyle, Illinois.)

Kozub's Laws. (1) Home-grown ice—in your freezer—is never clear. (2) Super glue isn't. (3) Tab A rarely fits Slot A. (4) Absence makes the heart go wander. (4) Fishing teaches you that instinct can outwit intelligence. (5) When you're thirsty, all glasses are too small. (6) Body wash that is labeled energizing, rejuvenating, etc., ain't. (7) No one ever admits to not getting "a good deal" when buying a car. (8) You always need just one more power tool. (9) The magazine article you wanted to save is always in last week's trash. (10) Commercially produced art prints are never sized to fit commercially produced frames. (11) Stick-proof muffin pans aren't. (12) Bathwater is never the right temperature. (Fred Kozub, Richmond, Virginia.)

Kraft's Admonition. Do it now—otherwise, by the time you get around to it, it will be too late. (Barbara S. Kraft, Washington, D.C.)

Kramer's Law of Polygraphy. Whenever someone says he is being perfectly frank, he is being less than perfectly frank. (Victor H. Kramer; from Andrew Jay Schwartzman, Washington, D.C.)

Kramer's Rules. (1) Monday is a depressing way to spend one seventh of your life. (2) If you're at the top of the ladder, cover your ass; if you're at the bottom, cover your face. (3) Whatever is dreaded arrives promptly. (Professor Mary Kramer, Lowell, Massachusetts.)

Krantz's Rule. If you ever pose for a magazine in an unlikely position—that's the shot they're going to use. (Author Judith Krantz, quoted in the *New Yorker,* October 13, 1980; from Mike Feinsilber.)

Krause's Discovery. In the jungle, a press card is just another piece of paper. (Charles Krause, *Washington Post.*)

Kraus's Correlation. The I.Q. of the power boat operator is inversely proportional to the cubic inch displacement of the engine. (Paul A. Kraus, M.D., Waterbury, Connecticut.)

Krauthammer's Law of Conservation of Indignation. Even in Washington, the capacity for waxing indignant is not infinite. (Charles Krauthammer, *Washington Post,* December 26, 1986.)

Kraver's Law. Their defective shopping cart will find Ruth Kraver. (Ruth Kraver, on a Washington, D.C. radio call-in show.)

Kriedt's Law. Sanity and insanity overlap a fine gray line. (Charles van Kriedt, who, according to Laurence J. Peter, reported on a conversation about a politician in which one participant said, "I don't think they could put him in a mental hospital. On the other hand, if he were already in, I don't believe they'd let him out." From the article "Peter's People" in *Human Behavior*, August 1976.)

Kristol's Law. Being frustrated is disagreeable, but the real disasters in life begin when you get what you want. (Irving Kristol, quoted in George F. Will's *Newsweek* column for November 28, 1977, "Pharaoh in the Promised Land"; *JW*.)

Krobusek's Law. As soon as you precisely figure out the wickets of any approval cycle, some bureaucrat will change one of the wickets. *Corollary 1:* You always have the obsolete form (or you never have the correct form.). *Corollary 2:* As soon as a procedure or checklist is developed, someone will change the physical hardware so that the procedure must be changed. (Richard D. Krobusek, Plano, Texas.)

Kroeger's Laws. *Car Repair:* After repair, your car will have more things wrong with it than it did before the mechanic worked on it. If you are lucky, it will still get you home. It will usually stop functioning as soon as the check clears. *File Storage Management:* The old files/records needed are requested in inverse proportion to the number of days since you discarded them. *Public Relations Account Management:* The client on the smallest budget is the one that requires the most attention and account service time. (Judi Kroeger, Allentown, Pennsylvania.)

Krotky's Truism. You can't get an omelet and a chicken out of the same egg. (Emil Krotky; from Larry Bryant.)

Krukow's Explanation. Even a blind dog finds a bone once in a while. (San Francisco Giants pitcher Mike Krukow, on driving in a winning RBI.)

Krukow's Observation on Public Life. You haven't lived until some ten-year-old kid calls you a hemorrhoid. (Mike Krukow, collected by John Rush, Austin, Texas.)

Krupka's Observation. When you see an individual wearing a white lab coat, you can be sure he thinks he is a scientist. (*U;* from an unpublished paper, "Famous Laws and Principles of Science," by Ray S. Hansen, Corvallis, Oregon, and Robert A. Sweeney, Buffalo, New York.)

Kruse's Observation on Cultural Enlightenment. The more you try to cultivate people, the more you turn up clods. (Stephanie Kruse, Chicago, Illinois, who got it from her father.)

Kruszelnicki's Law. Anything, no matter how boring, looks interesting under the electron microscope. (Australian physicist Karl S. Kruszelnicki, winner of the 2002 Ig Nobel Prize, commenting on his analysis of belly button lint with an electron microscope, in "Navel Lint Studies, Continued," *Annals of Improbable Research*, Vol. 15, no. 2, p.7, March–April 2009.)

Krutch's Indictment. The most serious charge that can be brought against New England is not Puritanism but February. (Naturalist Joseph Wood Krutch.)

Kudzu's Law of the Land. The smaller the town the higher the hair. (From Doug Marlette's *Kudzu* comic strip, November 24, 1994.)

Kuiper's Law of Baseball. As soon as a substitute player enters the game, the next player is guaranteed to hit a line drive straight at him. (Duane Kuiper, San Francisco Giants, July 1984.)

Kusche's Catch. Any event can be made to look mysterious, if relevant details are omitted. (Paraphrased from Larry D. Kusche's *The Bermuda Triangle Mystery—Solved,* Harper, 1975; from Steve Stine.)

Kyger's Laws. 1) Getting caught is the mother of invention. 2) When you play with fire, there is a 50/50 chance something will go wrong, and nine out of ten times it does. (Nicole Kyger from Tom Gill.)

L

La Rochefoucauld's Law. It is more shameful to distrust one's friends than to be deceived by them. (François VI, duc de La Rochefoucauld, Prince de Marcillac; *S.T.L.*)

Lada's Commuter Corollary. As soon as construction is complete on the fastest, most convenient expressway route from your home to your place of work, you will be transferred to another place of work. *Lada's Important Definitions for the Bureaucratic Environment Committee:* A work group created with the main purpose of finding and articulating reasons why a new idea will not work, or, failing that, why adoption of the new idea will cause more anguish within the institution than the idea's benefits are worth. *Policy:* A written statement, ordinarily using as many words as possible, to articulate an institutional position on a subject in a manner vague enough to permit multiple contradictory interpretations. *Task Force:* A group organized to present the illusion of progress without the inconvenience of actually moving the institution forward. (Stephen C. Lada, Wayne, Michigan.)

Ladof's Laws of Legal Services. (1) A client with a bagful of papers is trouble. Ditto for briefcases or any other containers. (2) Never take a case more seriously than your client does. (3) Most parents, when they demand custody, never seem to remember that it means they get the kids. (Attorney Anne Ladof, Emigsville, Pennsylvania.)

Ladwig's Laws for Travel. (1) A light-year is defined as the time it takes to emerge from the middle of the plane upon landing when you have five minutes to make a connecting flight. (2) The speed of light is defined as how fast your connecting flight backs away from the gate as you come running down the concourse. (Alan Ladwig, Office of Exploration, NASA, Washington, D.C.)

Laithwaite's Rules. (1) Experiment is always right, the theory never! Experiment rules. (2) Never mind if you don't understand the theory; just have a go at using it. (Professor Eric Laithwaite, Imperial College, London, quoted in *Felix,* October 9, 1981; from Tony Lang, London, England.)

LaLanne's Conclusion. I can't die. It would wreck my image. (From the late Jack LaLanne, *Los Angeles Times,* December 24, 1980; *RS.* LaLanne, who was born September 26, 1914, was an American fitness, exercise, nutritional expert, and motivational speaker who has been called "the godfather of fitness.")

Lamb's Law. The world meets nobody halfway. (Charles Lamb.)

Lament for Public Defenders. It's harder when they're really innocent. (Anonymous.)

Lament of the Parched. You get the most thirsty when traveling through areas where they tell you "don't drink the water!" (In a *New York Times* travel column, November 1983.)

Landers's Law of Mind Over Matter. If nobody minds, it doesn't matter. (Ann Landers column, February 10, 1986; *TG.*)

Landers's Law of the Pinch. Usually when the shoe fits, it's out of style. (Ann Landers, in her column for February 6, 1977.)

Landers's Revision. The best things in life aren't things. (Ann Landers in *Forbes* magazine FYI column.)

Landon's Law of Politics. It's a sin in politics to land a soft punch. (Alf Landon, in an interview with David S. Broder, *Washington Post,* December 14, 1977.)

Langin's Law. If things were left to chance, they'd be better. (*U;* Unsigned letter to *Playboy.*)

Langley's Laws. (1) The bigger the bore, the greater the knowledge of computers. (2) The fancier the restaurant, the smaller the piece of pie. (3) Whenever a newspaper headline asks a question, the answer is "We don't know." (4) Paper won't refuse ink. (Roger Langley, "Dean of Comedy College," Rockville, Maryland.)

Lang's Law of Bureaucratic Entropy. The total amount of bureaucracy in an organization can never decrease. It can only increase—and usually does. (Tony Lang, Imperial College, London, England.)

Lani's Principles of Economics. (1) Taxes are not levied for the benefit of the taxed. (2) $100 placed at 7 percent interest compounded quarterly for 200 years will increase to more than $100,000,000, by which time it will be worth nothing. (3) In God we trust, all others pay cash. (*U/S.T.L.*)

Lansburgh's Observation. There's no column on the scorecard headed "remarks." (Sidney Lansburgh, Jr., quoted in Julius M. Westheimer's column in *The Baltimore Evening Sun,* March 22, 1979.)

Larson's Conclusion. Shunning women, liquor, gambling, smoking, and eating will not make one live longer. It will only seem like it. (M. Sgt. Robert V. Larson, USAF [retired], Golden Valley, Minnesota.)

Larson's Law of Social Interaction. For every action, there is an opposite but *more than* equal reaction. (Curtis W. Larson, Chattanooga, Tennessee.)

Last Law of the Performing Arts. When thy opus becomes thy onus, thou art out on thy anus. (Quoted in concert by Steve Goodman; from Steve Stine.)

Latecomer's Rule. If you are impatiently waiting for someone to arrive who is late, go to the bathroom and that person will arrive instantly in your absence. (A. S. Boccuti, Baltimore, Maryland.)

Latecomers, Law of. Those who have the shortest distance to travel to a meeting invariably arrive the latest. (Carl Thompson, executive vice-president, Hill and Knowlton; *AO.*)

Laub's Third Rule of Economics in Romance. Two cannot live as cheaply as one. Two cannot even live as cheaply as three. (James A. Laub, Los Angeles, California. This rule was later amplified by Bill McFadin of Jacksonville, Florida: "While true, it deserves *McFadin's Addition:* 'Two *can* live as cheaply as one... so long as one doesn't eat.'" This, of course, also leads to *McFadin's End-of-Marriage Economic Truth:* Divorce is defined as two people making a mistake and one continuing to pay for it.

Lauder's Law. When a person with experience meets a person with money, the person with experience will get the money. And the person with the money will get the experience. (Leonard Lauder, President, Estee Lauder, Inc.; from Mel Loftus, Alexandria, Virginia.)

Laura's Law. No child throws up in the bathroom. (*U/DRW.*)

Laurel's Law. Honest people and stupid people have a common characteristic; they take it in the shorts a lot. (Laurel Siemans Moore; from D. F. Siemans, Jr.)

Laur's Advice to Negotiators and Traders. You've got to let the monkey *have* the banana every once in a while. (Ed Laur, Amarillo, Texas.)

Laver's Example of Murphy's Law. There are more *j*'s and *z*'s on my typewriter keyboard tjan the Englizj languzgue requires. (Murray Laver, Sidmouth, Devon, England.)

Law Laws. (1) Aphorism is better than none. (2) In the beginning, Murphy condensed the human condition into twelve laws. The rest of us want to get into somebody's book. (Ryan Anthony, Tucson, Arizona.)

Lawrence's Laws. (1) Paperwork is inversely proportional to useful work. (2) In any bureaucracy, the triviality of any position can be derived by counting the number of administrative assistants. (Bob Ackley, T. Sgt., USAF, Plattsmouth, Nebraska.)

Lawson's Law of Analysis. Everything can be assessed rationally—from a distance. (John Lawson, Burlington, Ontario.)

Lawson's Laws of Travel. (1) If you get to the station early, the train will be late. (2) Postcards sent on a short vacation will arrive after you get home. (3) Any witty observations made on postcards will be obliterated by the postal cancellation. (4) Punctures in bicycle tires are more likely to occur in the rain than on a dry day. (5) If you exchange your money for a foreign currency, the likelihood of that currency then being devalued varies in proportion to the amount you have exchanged. (6) If someone giving you directions says, "You can't miss it," you will. (7) The discovery that you have forgotten the corkscrew will occur at the farthest point from which a corkscrew may be obtained. (8) If you are driving through several foreign countries and the fan belt breaks, it will break in a country in the language of which no one in your party knows the word for "fan belt." (Sarah Lawson, London, England.)

Lawton's Conclusion. The creation of random numbers is too important to be left to chance. (M. H. Lawton, Oakland, California.)

Lawton's Vision of Armageddon. When the last bug hits the last windshield, it will be in the driver's direct line of sight. (Tom Lawton, Indialantic, Florida.)

Lawyer's Law. The phone will not ring until you leave your desk and walk to the other end of the building. (Linda A. Lawyer, Pittsburgh, Pennsylvania.)

Lawyer's Paradox. If it were not for lawyers, we wouldn't need them. (A. K. Giffin, Dorval, Quebec.)

Lawyer's Rule. When the law is against you, argue the facts, When the facts are against you, argue the law. When both are against you, call the other lawyer names. (*U/JW*)

Lawyers' Language

Toward a better understanding of the law . . .

- ***"As Your Honor Well Recalls."***

Tip-off by a lawyer that he is about to refer to a long-forgotten or imaginary case. (Adapted from a similar definition by Miles Kington, *Punch*, November 12, 1975.)

• ***Basic Concept.***

Murder—don't do it; Theft—don't do it; Fraud—don't do it; etc. (G. Guy Smith, Media, Pennsylvania.)

• ***Brief.***

Long and windy document. Should be at least 10,000 words long to qualify.

• ***Costs.***

Amount required to bankrupt the acquitted. (Miles Kington.)

• ***Duty of the Lawyer.***

When there is a rift in the lute, the business of the lawyer is to widen the rift and gather the loot. (Arthur Garfield Hays.)

• ***"Equality Under the Law."***

. . . forbids the rich as well as the poor to sleep under bridges, to beg in the streets, and to steal bread. (Anatole France.)

• ***Incongruous.***

Where our laws are made. (Bennett Cerf.)

• ***"It has been long known that . . ."***

"I haven't been able to find the original reference."

• ***"It might be argued that . . ."***

"I have such a good answer for this argument that I want to make sure it is raised."

• ***Lex Clio Volente.***

The client is always right—particularly when he has further causes to entrust. (Del Goldsmith, *American Bar Association Journal.*)

• ***Nine Points of the Law, The.***

(1) A good deal of money. (2) A good deal of patience. (3) A good case. (4) A good lawyer. (5) A good counsel. (6) Good witnesses. (7) A good jury. (8) A good judge. (9) Good luck.

• ***Proper Pronoun.***

Louis Nizer has pointed out that most lawyers on winning a case will say, "We have won," but when justice frowns on the case the lawyer customarily remarks, "You have lost."

• ***Plea Bargaining.***

Ending a sentence with a proposition.

• ***Res Ipsa Loquitur.***

Latin for "the thing speaks for itself." Anything that speaks for itself is an abomination to the law and reason enough for a lawyer to be paid to speak for something that speaks for itself. (Adapted from Miles Kington.)

- ***Will.***
  Where there's a will, there's a lawsuit. (Oliver Herford.)
- ***"With All Due Respect."***
  Introductory phrase for a disrespectful statement.
- ***"Yes, Your Honor."***
  Witty rejoinder by lawyer to judge. (Miles Kington.)

LAX Law. Flying is not in itself dangerous, but the air is like the sea—very unforgiving of those who make mistakes. (Sign seen in a hangar at the Los Angeles International Airport. William C. Young, Ballston Lake, New York.)

Le Bon's Mot. Science has promised us truth. It has never promised us either peace or happiness. (Gustave Le Bon.)

Le Carré's Assumption. When in doubt about something like this, assume a screw-up. (John Le Carré, quoted in the *Los Angeles Times,* April 8, 1974; *RS.*)

Le Chatellier's Law. If some stress is brought to bear on a system in equilibrium, the equilibrium is displaced in the direction which tends to undo the effect of the stress. (Traditional law in the physical sciences that tends to get wide application or, as *Esquire* put it when it listed "Scientific Principles for English Majors," "This may not be one of the all-time essential scientific principles, but it has a certain ring to it.")

Le Pelley's Law. The bigger the man, the less likely he is to object to caricature. (Guernsey Le Pelley, editorial cartoonist for the *Christian Science Monitor,* quoted in the Lewiston, Maine *Daily Sun,* July 18, 1977.)

League Principle, The. Enjoying the game is almost entirely a matter of having chosen the appropriate league to play in. (Stu Goldstein, M.D., Danville, California.)

Leahy's Law. If a thing is done wrong often enough, it becomes right. *Corollary:* Volume is a defense to error. (Richard A. Leahy, Boston, Massachusetts; *AO.*)

Leavitt's Law of Pizza and Other Delicacies. There are two kinds of people in the world—the quick and the hungry. (Jane Leavitt, East Peoria, Illinois, who adds that her law is "to be uttered when someone in the group complains he didn't get his share.")

Lec's Immutables. (1) The first requisite for immortality is death. (2) All gods were immortal. (3) Even a flounder takes sides. (Stanislaw J. Lec, from *Unkempt Thoughts,* St. Martin's Press, 1962.)

Lederer's Law of Ferris Wheel Roulette. The more acrophobic the passenger, the greater the chance the Ferris wheel will come to a stop with that person parked at the top of the circle, the farthest point from terra firma. (Richard Lederer, Concord, New Hampshire.)

Ledge's Law of Fans. (Or, why you can't run when there's trouble in the office.) No matter where you stand, no matter how far or fast you flee, when it hits the fan, as much as possible will be propelled in your direction, and almost none will be returned to the source. (*U;* John L Shelton, Dallas, Texas.)

Lee's Law. Mother said there would be days like this, but she never said there'd be so many. (Jack Lee, WLAK Radio, Chicago, Illinois.)

Lee's Law of Business Competition. Always remember to keep your swash buckled. (Gerald Lee Steese, Long Branch, California.)

Legal Proverbs from Around the World. (1) Lawyers and painters can soon change black to white. (Danish) (2) If the laws could speak, they would first complain of lawyers. (American) (3) A lean compromise is better than a fat lawsuit. (English) (4) Fear not the law but the judge. (American) (5) Laws, like the spider's web, catch the fly and let the hawk go free. (Spanish) (6) He that goes to law holds a wolf by the tail. (English) (7) A countryman between two lawyers is like a fish between two cats. (Spanish) (8) Three Philadelphia lawyers are a match for the devil. (American) (9) Going to law is losing a cow for the sake of a cat. (Chinese) (10) He that is his own lawyer has a fool for a client. (American) (11) Lawyers and soldiers are the devil's playmates. (German) (12) A lawyer's opinion is worth nothing unless paid for. (American) (13) A good lawyer is a bad neighbor. (American) (14) The houses of lawyers are roofed with the skins of litigants. (Welsh)

Le Guin's Strategy. When action grows unprofitable, gather information; when information grows unprofitable, sleep. (Ursula K. Le Guin, in her science-fiction novel *The Left Hand of Darkness*, Harper, 1969; from Kenneth W. Davis.)

Lehrer's Explanation. When Henry Kissinger can get the Nobel Peace Prize, what is there left for satire? (Songwriter Tom Lehrer, explaining his retirement, *Los Angeles Times,* July 8, 1980; *RS.*)

Lehrer's Theory of Music. The reason most folk songs are so atrocious is that they were written by the people. (Tom Lehrer, on the album *An Evening Wasted With Tom Lehrer* [1959], quoting his friend Hen3ry [the 3 is Silent, Lehrer explains]; from Neal Wilgus.)

Leigh's Camping Discovery. Familiarity breeds in tents. (Richard Leigh, Cheshire, England.)

Lender's Law. The law of lending is to break the borrowed article. (*U/Ra.*)

Lenin's Law. Whenever the cause of the people is entrusted to professors, it is lost. (Nikolai Lenin; *RS.*)

Lennie's Law of the Library. No matter what you want, it's always on the bottom shelf. (Lennie Bemiss, Assistant Librarian, Estes Park Public Library, Estes Park, Colorado.)

Leonard's Constant. There are many changes in one's life, but there is one rule that remains constant: In a men's room, incoming traffic has the right of way. (Hugh Leonard, from his 1975 play *Da*.)

Leonard's Warning. Never eat any product on which the listed ingredients cover more than one-third of the package. (Joseph Leonard, quoted by Herb Caen in his column, March 3, 1986; from Janerik Larsson, Sweden.)

Leo's Law. The harder it is to find, the easier it is to fix. And vice versa. (Widely attributed to "Ask Leo!" by the popular technology columnist Leo Notenboom. However, it was earlier posted online by "Hank Hill" in a HVAC discussion board in 2007; *TG*.)

Leo's Laws. (1) Small talk drives out meaningful talk. (2) If a song sounds like a commercial, it will become a hit. (3) The less the product, the bigger the ad. (Doug "Leo" Hanbury, Des Moines, Iowa.)

Leo's Wiper Law. Even a new windshield wiper will leave one smudged arc. *Corollary:* The smudged arc will always be at the eye level of the driver. (Leo Kosowski, South Saint Paul, Minnesota.)

Leslie's Law of Great Expectations. The richer the relative, the easier it is to remember his or her birthday. (*U;* from Arlen Wilson.)

Leterman's Laws. (1) No rule for success will work if you don't. (2) A man should work eight hours and sleep eight hours, but not the same eight hours. (Elmer G. Leterman, quoted in *Forbes,* June 21, 1982.)

Leveut's Cause for Rejoicing. There is always more hell that needs raising. (Lauren Leveut; *RA*.)

Levey's Law of Thermogumular Dynamics. If you toss your gum around, you will sooner or later step in someone else's. (Bob Levey, in his *Washington Post* column, November 25, 1987.)

Levien's Lament. The fault lies not with our technologies, but with our systems. (Roger Levien, the RAND Corp.; *RS*.)

Levine's Declaration. Long delays on crowded expressways are due to rubbernecking by passersby observing insignificant events. However, when I finally reach this particular point, I feel that I deserve to take time to participate in the distraction. (Kenneth C. Levine, Doraville, Georgia.)

Levin's Law. Any attempt to adjust the air conditioner will make it worse. (Bernard Levin, *The Times* (London), July 9, 1980.)

Levinson's Law No. 16. If you check your coat at the theatre, there will be ten empty seats around you when you sit down. (Leonard Louis Levinson, from his book *Webster's Unafraid Dictionary,* Macmillan, 1967.)

Levinson's Lesson. Many people have come to expect too much of work. Work is work, no matter how you slice it. (Dr. Harry Levinson, of "The Levinson Letter," quoted in *Behavioral Sciences Newsletter,* July 25, 1983.)

Levy's Newtonian Corollary. Deadlines have gravity: the closer you get to them, the more pull they exert on you. (D. Levy; from Richard Lederer.)

Levy's Ten Laws of the Disillusionment of the True Liberal. (1) Large numbers of things are determined, and therefore not subject to change. (2) Anticipated events never live up to expectations. (3) That segment of the community with which one has the greatest sympathy as a liberal inevitably turns out to be one of the most narrow-minded and bigoted segments of the community.[4] (4) Always pray that your opposition be wicked. In wickedness there is a strong strain toward rationality. Therefore, there is always the possibility, in theory, of handling the wicked by outthinking them. *Corollary 1:* Good intentions randomize behavior. *Subcorollary 1:* Good intentions are far more difficult to cope with than malicious behavior. *Corollary 2:* If good intentions are combined with stupidity, it is impossible to outthink them. *Corollary 3:* Any discovery is more likely to be exploited by the wicked than applied by the virtuous. (5) In unanimity there is cowardice and uncritical thinking. (6) To have a sense of humor is to be a tragic figure. (7) To know thyself is the ultimate form of aggression. (8) No amount of genius can overcome a preoccupation with detail. (9) Only God can make a random selection. (10) Eternal boredom is the price of constant vigilance. (Marion J. Levy, Jr., who at the time of his death in 2002 was the Musgrave Professor of Sociology and International Affairs, emeritus, at Princeton University. These oft-quoted laws were only nine until recently, and Dr. Levy said, "I have been toying with an 11th. The 11th, if I decide to add it to the 10th, will read as follows, 'Default is more revolutionary than ideals.'")

Lewandowski's Air Turbulence Principle. An airline flight will remain smooth until beverage and/or meal service begins. A smooth flight will resume when beverage and/or meal service ends. (J. A. Lewandowski, Parma, Ohio.)

Lewin's Deduction. The age of our universe is a function of time. (Walter Lewin, Professor, MIT. Richard Stone, Stanford, California.)

Lewis's Law. People will buy anything that's one to a customer. (Sinclair Lewis, quoted by Leo Rosten in his "Diversions" column in *Saturday Review,* May 15, 1976.)

Lewis's Law of Travel. The first piece of luggage out of the chute doesn't belong to anyone, ever. (Dave Lewis, Columbus, Georgia.)

---

[4] At this point, Levy refers to *Kelly's Law* ("Last guys don't finish nice") as a reformation of number 3.

Libbrecht's Law. With politicians, no answer you get from them is straight. With scientists, no answer you get from them is short. (Ken Libbrecht, professor of physics at Caltech, quoted on National Public Radio's "Morning Edition" January 21, 2008; *TG.*)

Lichtenberg's Conclusions. (A few of many): (1) Philosophy cannot fly in the face of facts without coming out with a bloody nose. (2) Man has climbed so far on the tree of knowledge that he finds himself out on a limb. (3) Talk is cheap, conversations dear. (4) Many atheists would believe in God if they were the ones being worshiped. (5) It is rootlessness that distinguishes man from vegetables. (6) Man is the problem-solving animal, thus also the problem-making one. (7) Life is an experiment in which you are the experiment. (8) Before you climb the ladder of success, find out who is holding it. (9) Friends often desert you in time of need. Enemies can be found anytime you need them. (10) People can prove anything they want to prove as long as they control the meaning of the word *proof.* (11) The best way to be completely flexible is to have no backbone. (12) To the adolescent, adult is spelled a-d-o-l-t. (13) You usually get fleeced before you get your sheepskin. (14) Self-expression is fine, but only if you have something worth expressing; every fart would prefer to be heard at a party rather than wasting itself in the solitude of the bathroom. *Lichtenberg's Insights.* (1) If life were "just a bowl of cherries"... we would soon die of a deficiency disease. (2) We can never get to the Promised Land, for if we did, it would no longer be the Promised Land. (3) We say that the plow made civilization, but for that matter, so did manure. (4) The zoning laws in most American neighborhoods would not *permit* the construction of a Parthenon. (5) There is no occupation as practical as love; theories are useless in bed. (Benjamin Lichtenberg, Verona, New Jersey; from his book *Insights of an Outsider,* Jaico Publishing, 1972.)

Liddy's Revision. Obviously, crime pays or there'd be no crime. (G. Gordon Liddy, quoted in *Newsweek,* November 10, 1986.)

Liebermann's Law. Everybody lies, but it doesn't matter since no one listens. (Anonymous; from Richard Leigh, Cheshire, England.)

Liebling's Law. If you just try long enough and hard enough, you can always manage to boot yourself in the posterior. (A. J. Liebling, in *The Press,* Ballantine Books, 1975. There are a number of versions of this line. Humorist Robert H. Yoakum of Lakeville, Connecticut reported in 1981, "I had occasion to use it in an article a few years ago, and, to confirm my memory of the thing, asked a friend/editor on the *New Yorker* to get the official version from the magazine's fabled checking department. They came up with 'If you are smart enough you can kick yourself in the seat of the pants, grab yourself by the back of the collar, and throw yourself out on the sidewalk.' I still prefer the version I recalled [and my friend said that there may be several, printed at different times], which went like this: 'If you are smart enough, but *just* smart enough, you can grab yourself by the collar and the seat of the pants and throw yourself out on the sidewalk.' ")

Liebling's News Constant. The people who have something to say don't talk—the others insist on talking. (A. J. Liebling, *Holiday* magazine, February 1950.)

Liebling's Revision. Freedom of the press is limited to those who own one. (A. J. Liebling, quoted in *Business Week,* June 15, 1981.)

Liebman's Laws of Auto-motion. (1) If you get a great parking spot, you've probably shown up on the wrong day. (2) The later you are, the heavier the traffic conspiracy. (Sam Liebman, Montreal.)

Lief's Law #28. There's always plenty of free cheese in the mousetrap. (Greg Lief, Arlington Virginia.)

Liggett's Law of Archaeology. (1) Dirt takes up to five times as much space outside the hole as it does inside. (2) No matter where you put the dirt, you're going to have to move it. (3) The hole will eventually be deeper than your arm is long, and you will end up at the bottom of it, throwing dirt over your head. (Archaeologist Barbara Liggett, quoted in the *Philadelphia Inquirer,* August 3, 1981; from Edward J. O'Neill.)

Lightfoot's Lament for Collectors of (fill in the blank). The one time you *don't* visit a dealer, flea market, auction, or whatever, is the one time that there is an abundance of rare, fine-quality (fill in the blanks). *Lightfoot's Rules:* (1) Great minds run around in the same circles. (2) Women aren't as stupid as men think they are. Men aren't as stupid as women think they are. (Fred Lightfoot, Greenport, New York.)

Lilla's Distinction. The difference today between an old pair of suede shoes and a professor is that the former is given to Goodwill when it has served its purpose; the latter is given tenure. (Mark Lilla, in *The New Republic;* from Bernard Albert.)

Lincoln, Ten Points He Did Not Make. (1) You cannot bring about prosperity by discouraging thrift. (2) You cannot strengthen the weak by weakening the strong. (3) You cannot help small men up by tearing big men down. (4) You cannot help the poor by destroying the rich. (5) You cannot lift the wage-earner up by pulling the wage-payer down. (6). You cannot keep out of trouble by spending more than your income. (7) You cannot further the brotherhood of man by inciting class hatred. (8) You cannot establish sound social security on borrowed money. (9) You cannot build character and courage by taking away a man's initiative and independence. (10) You cannot help men permanently by doing for them what they could and should do for themselves. (*Not* Abraham Lincoln. This list of admonitions has been published far and wide—almost always attributed to Lincoln. It has shown up in newspapers, Christmas cards, official documents, the *Congressional Record,* and magazines, with one of the more recent appearances being in the October 1975 issue of the *Saturday Evening Post.* A May 19, 1950, report from the Library of Congress definitely determined that the ten points were not Lincoln's, but concluded, "there seems to be no way of overtaking the rapid pace with which the mistaken identity has been spreading.")

Lincoln's Rule of Return. When you ask from a stranger that which is of interest only to yourself, always enclose a stamp. (Abraham Lincoln.)

Linda's Law. The best two hours of sleep start exactly one hour before the alarm clock goes off. (Linda Welsch from "Life Au Naturel" by Roger Welsch in the March 1992 issue of *Natural History.*)

Linden's Extension of Jacobson's Rule of Money. If you have only one check left in your checkbook and a suitable I.D. in your wallet, you will make a mistake when writing the check which will necessitate the check being voided. *Linden's Law:* Any letter that opens with "Gentlemen" is certain to be read first by an oversensitive feminist. (Carol Schuette Linden, Wilmette, Illinois.)

Lindsay's Law. When your draft exceeds the water's depth, you are most assuredly aground. (*U/ME.*)

Lindsey's Law. The more complex a problem is, the simpler it is to resolve, in that more assumptions are available. (Ron Lindsey, Media, Pennsylvania.)

Lindsey's Law of Youth. The youth are always worse than the preceding generation were, in the opinion of the latter. (In Judge Ben B. Lindsey's *The Revolt of Modern Youth,* Boni and Liveright, 1925; from Leon M. Louw.)

Lindvig's Law. If it's there, you'll step in it. If it's not, (1) it's already on your shoe, (2) it's on your car's floor mat, (3) it's on your new carpet. (Larry Lindvig, Chicago, Illinois.)

Lindy's Law. The life expectancy of a television comedian is proportional to the total amount of his exposure on the medium. (Reported on by Albert Goodman in an article, "Lindy's Law," in *The New Republic,* June 13, 1964. Lindy's, of course, refers to the restaurant where comedians traditionally hung out in New York.)

Linenger's Law. Specialization is for insects. Man should be able to change a diaper, run a marathon, build a house, write a book, appreciate good music, and fly in space. (Jerry M. Linenger, Astronaut, from *Off The Planet*, McGraw-Hill, 2000.)

Linklater's Immutable Laws of Recession. (1) The really useful jobs go first, the really useless ones are protected. (2) You cannot rebuild an economy on a workforce of compliance officers and diversity consultants. (Magnus Linklater, in "Here In Quangoland The Silly Jobs Are Safe; The Bloated And Self-Spawning Public Sector Is Neatly Protected From The Downturn—For Now." *The Times,* [London], January 28, 2009.)

Lin's Maxim. Happiness is a state of minimum regret. (Wallace E. Lin, Hartford, Connecticut.)

Linus's Law. There is no heavier burden than a great potential. (From Linus, *Peanuts;* Gerald M. Fava, Lake Hiawatha, New Jersey.)

Lippmann's Law of Conformity. When all think alike, no one thinks very much. (Walter Lippmann; *MBC.*)

Lippmann's Political Rule. A democratic politician had better not be right too soon. Very often the penalty is political death. It is much safer to keep in step with the parade of opinion than to try to keep up with the swifter movement of events. (Walter Lippmann, in *The Public Philosophy,* Little, Brown, 1955.)

Lipsett to Kelly to Lipsett Law, The. You don't know someone until you live with him, but you don't know him well until you divorce him. (Donna Lipsett, El Paso, Texas.)

Lipsitt's Law. In matters of adversity, whatever you have the most of, you are going to get more of. (Lewis P. Lipsitt, Professor of Psychology and Medical Science, Brown University. Lipsitt points out that this law is a more sophisticated version of his original discovery, which is that "One goddamned thing leads to another goddamned thing." Of his law, Lipsitt says, "I have found that living by this expectation not only helps to explain for me what to others is inexplicable, but that I can proceed in my life with the clear and soothing expectation that nothing surprisingly terrible or terribly surprising is likely to happen.")

Liston's Dictum. Everything eventually becomes too high priced. (Robert A. Liston, Shelby, Ohio.)

Liston's Law of Gift Wrapping. No matter how many boxes you save, you will never have one the right size. (Jean Liston, Shelby, Ohio.)

Little Doc's Animal Laws. (1) There is no such thing as a free cat. (2) The less a person knows about a breed, the more he will pay for a specimen. (3) The less a person knows about a species (e,g. skunk, ocelot), the more he wants one. (Dr. E.S. [Little Doc] Lundgren, Spring Hills, Kansas.)

Litt's Paradox of Deadlines. The reason for the rush is the delay, and, conversely, the reason for the delay is the rush. (Lawrence Litt, Executive Editor, *The Fugue,* Miami, Florida.)

Livingston's Adjuration. You can't win. Shoot for a tie. (E. A. Livingston, Richmond Hill, New York.)

Llarena's Law of the Bungle. If you are in a hurry, don't take shortcuts. Take the old beaten path—you will save more time that way. (A. Francisco L. Llarena, Jr.)

Lloyd George's Razor. A politician is a person with whose politics you don't agree; if you agree with him, he is a statesman. (David Lloyd George.)

Lloyd-Jones's Advice to the Lazies. If you are always at the top of your class, you're in the wrong class. *Lloyd-Jones's Law of High Fidelity:* A good system is one sensitive enough to let you hear its own faults. *Lloyd-Jones's Law of Leftovers:* The amount of litter on the street is proportional to the local rate of unemployment. (David Lloyd-Jones, Tokyo, Japan; *AO.*)

Lloyd's Laws of Autopsy. (1) Always make sure you're doing the autopsy on the right body. (2) Always make sure the patient is dead. (Pathologist Humphrey Lloyd of Beverly, Massachusetts; collected by Bob Skole on an April 1997 flight from New York to Chicago on which he sat next to Dr. Lloyd.)

Lobenhofer's Law. Any emergency sufficiently well-planned for will not happen. (R. W. Lobenhofer, *Modern Casting* magazine, January 1979.)

Local Anesthesia, Law of. Never say "oops" in the operating room. (Dr. Leo Troy.)

Lockhart's Law. He who laughs last...thinks slowest. (Bob Lockhart, Middlebury, Connecticut.)

Lockwood's Longshot. The chances of getting eaten by a lion on Main Street aren't one in a million, but once would be enough. (John Lockwood, Washington, D.C.)

Loderstedt's Rule. Measure twice because you can only cut once. (Bob Loderstedt, Mendham, New Jersey.)

Lodge's Law. The good old days are neither as good nor as bad as we remember them. (From Tom Gill, who heard it from someone named Lodge.)

Loeb's Laws of Medicine. (1) If what you're doing is working, keep doing it. (2) If what you're doing is not working, stop doing it. (3) If you don't know what to do, don't do anything. (4) Above all, never let a surgeon get your patient. (*U;* originally quoted in Dr. Robert Matz's article "Principles of Medicine," which appeared in the January 1977 issue of the *New York State Journal of Medicine.*)

Loevinger's Law. Bad news drives good news out of the media. (Lee Loevinger, partner, Hogen and Hartson, and former Federal Communications Commission member. An analogue of *Gresham's Law; AO.*)

Loewe's Rules of Governance. (1) If the government hasn't taxed, licensed, or regulated it, it probably isn't worth anything. (2) The ability of the government to create money is likened to a child's desire to change the rules of a game he is losing. (Donald C. Loewe, Chicago, Illinois.)

Loftus's Latest Collection. (1) *Loftus's Law of Great Expectorations:* Don't spit into the wind. (2) *Hooker's Observation:* All the prostitutes ain't on the street. (3)

McDonald's Dilemma: Fast food is neither. (4) *John Henry's Rule:* It is a lot more fun to sing about hard work than to actually perform hard work. (5) *Loftus's Sixth Rule of Government:* When it comes to government programs, no matter how noble the purpose or grand the design, implementation is everything. (6) *Loftus's Seventh Rule of Government:* Government programs never go away; they only change their titles. (7) *Loftus's Observation on Meetings:* Meetings that you chair are infinitely better than those that you merely attend. (8) *Life Magazine's Dilemma:* Pictures lie. (9) *Physical Fitness Razor:* Richard Burton outlasted Jim Fixx. (10) *Loftus's Advice for the Work Place:* Research has repeatedly shown that the best response to the supervisor's query, "Got a minute?" is "No." (Mel Loftus, Alexandria, Virginia.)

Logan's Beatitude. Blessed is he who has nothing to say, and cannot be persuaded to say it. (C. Sumpter Logan, Sr., Lexington, Kentucky.)

Logg's Rebuttal to Gray's Law of Programming. n +1 trivial tasks take twice as long as n trivial tasks for n sufficiently large. (Ed Logg of *S.T.L.*)

Lois's Law. What is logic to one is chaos to another. (Lois Smith, Palo Alto, California.)

Lomasney's Law. Never write if you can speak; never speak if you can nod; never nod if you can wink. (Martin M. Lomasney, known as "The Boston Mahatma" (1859–1933). Lomasney was a legendary Boston political boss, serving variously as an alderman, state representative, and state senator for nearly forty years, starting in 1892; from Bob Skole.)

Lone Eagle Law. Before you fly, make sure you're on board. (Sign in the Lone Eagle Saloon, Minneapolis-St. Paul Airport.)

Lone Star Cafe Motto. Too much ain't enough. (New York City restaurant motto; from Judy Tillinger.)

Longfellow's Elevator Rules. (1) Face forward. (2) Fold hands in front. (3) Do not make eye contact. (4) Watch the numbers. (5) Don't talk to anyone you don't know. (6) Stop talking with anyone you do know when anyone you don't know enters the elevator. (7) Avoid brushing bodies. (Psychologist Layne Longfellow, quoted in *New York,* November 21, 1977, in the article "What New Yorkers Do in Elevators." Longfellow says we observe these rules "to protect against the possibility of intimate contact.")

Long-Range Planning, The (F)law of. The longer ahead you plan a special event, and the more special it is, the more likely it is to go wrong. (David and Jayne Evelyn, Arlington, Virginia.)

Long's Law of Hyphens. In any paragraph, the number of hyphenated words is inversely proportional to the author's understanding of the relationship between the words thus hyphenated; for example: Indo-European, Hindu-Arabic, politico-theological, socio-economic, mathematical-physical, Judeo-Christian, and Anglo-Saxon. (Kevin G. Long, Quebec.)

Long's Law of Johns. Successful people never have to go to the bathroom. *Corollary:* All committee chairmen have infinitely large bladders. (Eugene A. Long, Boston, Massachusetts.)

Long's Notes. (A handful): (1) Always store beer in a dark place. (6) Small change can often be found under seat cushions. (7) It's amazing how much "mature wisdom" resembles being too tired. (8) Secrecy is the beginning of tyranny. (11) An elephant: a mouse built to government specifications. (14) Waking a person unnecessarily should not be considered a capital crime. For a first offense, that is. (17) Rub her feet... (21) Never try to outstubborn a cat. (22) Natural laws have no pity. (23) You can go wrong by being too skeptical as readily as by being too trusting. (28) A skunk is better company than a person who prides himself on being "frank." (The main character of *Time Enough for Love: the Further Adventures of Lazarus Long* by Robert A. Heinlein, Putnam, 1973. Long was the oldest human being in the galaxy, and his "Notes" were his collected observations and opinions. The "Notes" section of the book has become widely read, quoted, and imitated, especially among science fiction readers. *Also see* Short's Quotations.)

Long's Rules of Hospital Care. (A selection): (1) All conveniences such as radio, TV, telephone, and call button will in all cases be located on the same side of your incision. *Corollary:* If your incision is in front, all conveniences will not function at all or function poorly. (2) There are very good nurses and very bad nurses. There is no such thing as a mediocre or average nurse. This rule does not apply to doctors for reasons of their omnipotence. (3) Although there are one hundred ways of getting in and out of bed, each one will result in the same amount of pain. (4) The length of stay will vary proportionately with the degree of pain. (5) The intensity of nursing care will vary inversely with the length of stay. (6) The nicest and most admired of all flower bouquets will come from the least expected person, usually your worst enemy or ex-wife. (Eugene A. Long, Natick, Massachusetts.)

Longworth's Philosophy. Fill what's empty. Empty what's full. And scratch where it itches. (Alice Roosevelt Longworth.)

Loomis Fortune Modification, The. Any fortune cookie fortune can be improved by appending the words "in bed" to it. (Named for Rick Loomis, who explained it to Michael Stackpole, Phoenix.)

Looney's Rule of Potato Chips. You don't eat potato chips before noon. (Douglas S. Looney, from an article on potato chips in *The American Way* magazine, December 1978.)

Lopez, The Axiom on Art and Crosswords. Just as some art exists only for its own sake, some words exist only for the sake of crossword puzzles. *The Lopez*

Dictum on Dining: Waiters and waitresses generally wait until your mouth is full before asking how you like the food. Otherwise, how can they be sure you are really eating it? *The Lopez Law of Life:* Never be without a book. The day you forget to bring a book is the day you will get stuck in an elevator (traffic jam, etc.) for two hours and forty-five minutes. *Third Lopez Law of Life:* Never help your kids with their homework. Getting help with the homework defeats the purpose of education, which is to teach humility. (Marsha Lopez, Westmont, Illinois.)

Lopez's Grade Point Principle. In American schools, your popularity is inversely proportional to your grade point average. *Lopez's Law of Lunches:* No matter what the school menu claims, it's really horsemeat. (Manfred Lopez [age 13], Westmont, Illinois.)

Lord Cohen's Aphorism. The feasibility of an operation is not the best indication for its performance. (Originally quoted in Dr. Robert Matz's article "Principles of Medicine," which appeared in the January 1977 issue of the *New York State Journal of Medicine*; *U.*)

Loren's Basic Principle for Bureaucratic Survival. The appearance of a bureaucracy is infinitely more important than its function. (John A. Mattsen.)

Los Angeles Dodgers Law. Wait 'til last year. (Johnny Carson, the *Tonight Show,* August 2, 1979.)

Loughrige's Lesson. The middle of the road is the best place to get run over. (Alan Craig Loughrige, Springfield, Missouri.)

Louis's Lament. Has God forgotten all I have done for him? (Louis XIV, after the French defeat at Malplaquet.)

Louw's Collected Laws. (1) If you think you may have forgotten something, you have. If you think you haven't forgotten something, you have. (2) The main trouble with self-evident truths is that they aren't self-evident. (3) The busiest day of the year is the worst day for the post office and the best day for the supermarket. (Leon M. Louw, Melrose, South Africa.)

Lovell's Law. The closer to the bottom of the job scale, the higher the level of incorruptibility. (Marc Lovell, in his novel *The Spy Game*, Doubleday, 1980; from William F. Deeck, College Park, Maryland.)

Lovett's Observation on Gift-Giving. If you give a bald man a comb, he will never part with it. (Aaron Lovett; from Raymond E. Lovett, Garrett Park, Maryland.)

Lowell's Constant. Whatever you may be sure of, be sure of this: that you are dreadfully like other people. (James Russell Lowell, quoted in *Catchwords of Worldly Wisdom,* 1909.)

Lowell's Formula. Universities are full of knowledge; the freshmen bring a little in and the seniors take none away, and knowledge accumulates. (Educator Abbott Lawrence Lowell.)

Lowell's Law. You will always find the easiest, fastest, most economical way to do any project around the time you are finishing it. (Jeffrey Lowell, Cleveland Heights, Ohio.)

Lowell's Law of Life. Life is a hypothesis. (Poet Robert Lowell; *MBC.*)

Lowe's Law. If two pills are required, three pills will come out of the bottle. *Corollary:* When attempting to put the third pill back in the bottle, two pills will go in. (Judith Lowe, Hertfordshire, England.)

Lowrey's Law. If it jams, force it. If it breaks, it needed replacing anyway. (*U; Scientific Collections.*)

Lowry's Law of Expertise. Just when you get really good at something, you don't need to do it anymore. (William P. Lowry, Sidney Ill. *HW.*)

Lubarsky's Law of Cybernetic Entomology. There's always one more bug. (*U/DRW.*)

Lubbock Distinction. In reference to the person who complained about men wearing baseball caps in nice restaurants, they should be aware that this could be due to religious preference. There are two types of people who wear their hats while eating—Orthodox Jews and Texans. (Editorial in the *Lubbock Avalanche Journal*, March 11, 2000; *TG.*)

Lubin's Law. If another scientist thought your research was more important than his, he would drop what he is doing and do what you are doing. (From the law collection of William K. Wright, administrative officer, Naval Health Research Center, San Diego, California.)

Luce's Law. No good deed goes unpunished. (Clare Boothe Luce.)

Lucht's Observation. The single most common mistake young achievers make in their bid for career advancement is to attempt to prove their competence. (Anonymous; from John A. Mattsen. See *Zimmerman's Corollary to Lucht's Observation.*)

Lucy's Law. The alternative to getting old is depressing. (*U/DRW.*)

Lucy's Law of Horizontal Gravity. . . . causes any object she drops to disappear under the bed or under the dresser. (Paul S. Humphries, created by his wife, Mishawahn, Indiana.)

Lucy's Truism. Once a thing goes wrong on a job, things keep going wrong. (Lucy Kline, Cocoa, Florida.)

Luke's Law. When competence collides with custom, custom often wins at the expense of competence. (Robert A. Luke, Jr., Garrett Park, Maryland.)

Lunt's Advice to Young Actors. Say the words so they can be heard, and don't bump into the stage furniture. (Alfred Lunt; from Joseph C. Goulden.)

Luten's Laws. (1) When properly administered, vacations do not diminish productivity: for every week you're away and get nothing done, there's another when your boss is away and you get twice as much done. (2) It's not so hard to lift yourself by your bootstraps once you're off the ground! (Daniel B. Luten, Berkeley, California; *AO.)*

Lykken's Lament. In most controversies, whether scientific, ethical, or political, about 25 percent of the population tend to be right most of the time, another 25 percent tend always to be wrong, while the remaining 50 percent are the swing votes that will get it right eventually if one can induce them to pay attention. *Lykken's Law:* In decision making, the objective dominates the subjective, the simple squeezes out the complicated, the quantitative gets more weight than the nonmetrical, and dichotomous (yes/no, pass/fail) evidence supersedes the many-valued. (David T. Lykken, *A Tremor in the Blood: Uses and Abuses of the Lie Detector,* New ed., Plenum, 1998; from Roger Knights.)

Lynch's Instruction on How to Buy Smart. Spend at least as much time researching a stock as you would choosing a refrigerator. (Investment guru Peter Lynch.)

Lynes's Law. No author dislikes to be edited as much as he dislikes not to be published. (Russel Lynes; from Adrian Janes, Urban, Illinois.)

Lynn's Law. There are no part-time jobs. *Corollary:* Anyone with a part-time job works full-time for half salary. (Denise D. Lynn, Woodstock, Connecticut.)

Lynott's Law of the Reverse Learning Curve. Wisdom and knowledge decrease in inverse proportion to age. (William J. Lynott, Abington, Pennsylvania; *AO.* The proof of this law, according to its author, comes when you engage in conversation with someone younger than yourself and find that person knows far more about any subject than you do.)

Lytle's Third Law. Eat fat, be fat. Eat thin, be thin. (The late Dr. Ivan Lytle, University of Arizona; from "an appreciative student," Meribeth Meixner Reed, Claremont, Oklahoma.)

M

Ma Bell's Public Relations Principle. We don't care. We don't have to. (Bumper sticker cited by John Stephen Smith, Lincoln, Nebraska. This law has been transferred to later monopolies, namely cable television companies.)

Macdonald's Moral. You have to be sincere to sell out; it's like making money—if your heart's not in it, the customer...sees through the imposture. (Dwight Macdonald, quoted in *The New York Times Book Review,* November 21, 1982. It was invoked in the context of a story about Delmore Schwartz trying to write a "piece of junk" to win a $1,000 prize in a contest.)

MacEwan Principle, The. All benefits conferred on humanity by new inventions and discoveries will be applied in such a way as eventually to achieve (by other means) the same standard of misery as before. (Douglas M. C. MacEwan, Kent, England.)

Macfarlane's Law. When a number of conflicting theories coexist, any point at which they all agree is the one most likely to be wrong. (G. Macfarlane, *Howard Florey, the Making of a Great Scientist*, Oxford, 1979; from David L. Cowen, Jamesburg, New Jersey.)

MacLeish's Literary Law. If you write a novel about fruitcakes, you will hear from fruitcakes. (Rod MacLeish, quoted in the *Washington Post,* May 24, 1979. The discovery was occasioned by his novel *The Man Who Wasn't There,* Random House, 1976, about a man being driven insane. He got a call from a man in Idaho, who claimed MacLeish had stolen his life story and demanded a check for $9 million.)

MacPherson's Law. No matter how good a bargain you have purchased, the first person you show it to could have got it cheaper if you had only told them. *Corollary:* If you ask the same people before you purchase, their supply has just run out, and they "can't get them for love or money." (Ian MacPherson, London, England.)

MacPherson's Working Formula. The number of interruptions received during a work period is proportionate to the square of the number of employees occupying an office—thus, one person in an office = one interruption per hour; two in an office = four interruptions per hour; three people = nine per hour, etc. (Ian MacPherson, Regina, Saskatchewan.)

Macrae's Law. In modern conditions of high elasticity of both production and substitution, we will generally create a temporary but large surplus of whatever the majority of decision-influencing people five or ten years earlier believed was going to be in most desperately short supply. This is because the well-advertised views of the decision-influencers tend to be believed by both profit-seeking private producers and consensus-following governments, and these two then combine to cause excessive production of precisely the things that the decision-influencers had been saying would be the most obviously needed. (Walter Macrae, *The Economist,* October 26, 1975; from Joseph C. Goulden.)

Maddocks's Law of Thermopolitical Dynamics. If a less powerful person or group makes things hot for a more powerful person or group, that person or group is likely to make things an awful lot hotter for junior. (Melvin Maddocks, in a *Christian Science Monitor* article on whistle-blowers, February 20, 1981; from Steven R. Woodbury.)

Madison's Question. If you have to travel on the *Titanic,* why not go first class? (*U/DRW.*)

Magary's Principle. When there is a public outcry to cut the deadwood and fat from any government bureaucracy, it is the deadwood and fat that does the cutting. *Magary's Summation of Climatological Evolution:* Weather Man, Weather Girl, Weather Person, Meteorologist. (John T. Magary, Royal Oak, Michigan.)

Magnasco's Laws. (1) If, when calling an 800 number, you do not like the answer you get, call back and speak to a different person. Repeat until you get the answer you wanted to hear. (2) No matter which floor you enter or exit a mall's anchor store from, you will always go by the perfume counter. (3) The most annoying, schlockish songs are the ones that the radio stations will play the most. (4) Anything that is logical to normal human beings is illogical to a bureacracy and vice versa. (Source unknown to the Murphy Center.)

Mahon's Silicon Valley Rule. Don't let your employees do to you what you did to your former boss. (Tom Mahon, in *Charged Bodies: People, Power and Paradox in Silicon Valley*; from Jack Limpert.)

Mahr's Law of Restrained Involvement. Don't get any on you. (*U;* Norton Mockridge's syndicated column, February 14, 1979; *ME.*)

Maier's Law. If facts do not conform to the theory, they must be disposed of. (N. R. F. Maier first announced this oft-quoted law in the March 1960 issue of *American Psychologist.* At that time he also revealed that psychologists commonly obey the law by failing to report the facts or giving them a new name.)

Mailer's Organizational Observation. The person who answers the phone in an organization knows the least of anyone. *Corollary:* The person you want to speak with is always in a meeting or away from the desk. (Mark Mailer, Chicago, Illinois.)

Maine Haircut, How to Get One. If the name of the place where you go to get your haircut does not contain the name of the guy who is going to cut your hair, go somewhere else. (In *The Wicked Good Book*, Tapley, 1985; by Steve Bither.)

Maines's Music Maxim. You can't write a country song if you haven't been divorced. (Natalie Maines of the Dixie Chicks on why their album had only one original song, quoted in *The University Daily*, Texas Tech University, April 20, 1999; *TG.*)

Main's Points. (1) Phillips screwdrivers always have lead tips. (2) Bars of hand-soap are molded around a thin, sharp plastic sliver. (3) If you overtip a waitress for good service, the busboy will pick it up. (4) Concrete never hardens until somebody has initialed it. (John A. Main, Yorba Linda, California.)

Major's Rule. When the curtain falls, it is time to get off the stage. (John Major, acknowledging the sweeping victory of Tony Blair and the Labour Party, ending 18 years of conservative rule. *Newsweek,* January 5, 1998.)

Makower's Immutable Laws of Computing. (1) No matter how much you know about computers, you can find an expert who can render everything incomprehensible. (2) You will never run out of disks or printer ribbons during business hours. (3) The price of a software package is in inverse proportion to the readability of its manual. (4) The size of a computer error is in direct proportion to the importance of the data lost. (5) For every computer error, there are at least two human errors, one of which is blaming it on the computer. (6) No matter how long you delay your purchase of a computer product, a faster, cheaper, and more powerful version will be introduced within forty-eight hours. (7) The power never goes out at the beginning of a computing session. (8) If you back up a disk, the original is guaranteed not to fail. (9) Printers are not intended to work the first time you set them up. If they do, it is because you didn't follow instructions. (10) You never lose data you don't need. (Joel Makower, in his book *Personal Computers, A to Z,* Doubleday, 1984.)

Malek's Law. Any simple idea will be worded in the most complicated way. (*U/S.T.L.*)

Malik's Observations. (1) Living on earth may be expensive, but it includes a free trip around the sun. (2) The same piece of tape that would not hold up your child's drawing will not come off the refrigerator. (3) When it comes time to sink or swim, procrastinators float. (Julia Malik, Richboro, Pennsylvania.)

Malone's Caution. Never hire a workman who spends his first 15 minutes criticizing his predecessor's work. (Mary Malone, Trenton, New Jersey.)

Mame's Lament. Life is a banquet, and most damned fools are starving to death. (The character Auntie Mame in the play *Auntie Mame.*)

Manchester's Skeleton Theory. A man with nothing in the closet may have nothing in the attic, either. (Author William Manchester, discussing John F. Kennedy on the CBS Evening News, November 8, 1983.)

Mankiewicz's Laws. *Law of Crowds:* The more enthusiastic, unruly, and large the candidate's crowds in the week before the election, the less likely he is to carry the area; e.g., JFK in Ohio. *Environmental Law:* People who are excessively concerned about the environment invariably turn out to own a great deal of land. There are damn few unemployed and renters in the ecology movement. *Law of Provincial Hotels:* The amount of quaint, authentic, rustic charm varies inversely with the pounds per square inch of water pressure in the shower. High charm, low pressure. *School Law:* The higher the tuition, the fewer days they spend in school. *Second Law of Politics:* A politician will always tip off his true belief by stating the opposite at the beginning of the sentence. For maximum comprehension, do not start listening until the first clause is concluded. Begin instead at the word "but," which begins the second—or active—clause. This is the way to tell a liberal from a conservative—before they tell you. Thus: "I have always believed in a strong national defense, second to none, but..." will be said by a liberal, about to propose a $20 billion cut in the defense budget. (Frank Mankiewicz, president of National Public Radio and formerly press secretary to the 1972 McGovern campaign. The *Second Law of Politics* originally appeared in the *Washingtonian,* July 1975. As for his *First Law of Politics,* he explains, "All of my laws of politics are 'second' on the theory that I will find a better one.")

Mann's Proposition. Any politician who perceives a problem insists upon full credit for its solution. (Robert T. Mann, Chairman, Florida Public Service Commission; from D. Franklin Skinner, Miami, Florida.)

Mann's Rules. In a corporate takeover of a well-liked cleaning product: (1) It *must* be "improved" by adding an obnoxious odor, and (2) It *must* be wrapped in a slick foil-like wrapper, to more readily slip from a wet hand. (Mrs. Henry Mann, Holliston, Massachusetts; *AO*.)

Manning's Law of Inflation. What goes up doesn't always come down. (Gerald Manning, Cork, Ireland.)

Manning's Maxim. Getting from one point to another known point is called navigation. Getting from one unknown point to another unknown point is called "being lost." (Harvey Manning, *Backpacking One Step at a Time;* Vintage, 1973; from Harvey O. Hays.)

Man's Law. No matter what happens, there is always somebody who knew that it would. (*U/LSP.*)

Manske's Maxim. It doesn't matter what you do. It only matters what you say you've done and what you say you're gonna do. (Nancy Manske, Winter Park, Florida.)

Mantel's First Great Law of Economics. If two lines on a graph cross, it must be important. (*U;* Ernest F. Cooke, Chairman, Marketing Department, University of Baltimore.)

Marcotte's Disaster Law. The first persons to arrive at the scene of any disaster are generally those least able to offer any type of aid or assistance. (J. T. Marcotte, USCG, Opa Locka, Florida.)

Marcus's Law. Never divorce the boss's daughter (or son). (Stanley Marcus, Dallas, Texas, *Quest for the Best*, Viking, 1979.)

Marcus's Law. The number of letters written to the editor is inversely proportional to the importance of the article. (Robert L. Marcus, Scarsdale, New York, in a letter published in *The New York Times* on April 7, 1968. It was in response to the *Faber's Law* article, which had occasioned a number of letters; *FD.*)

Margolis's Marcos Maxim. A dictator who doesn't even know how to steal elections is a total incompetent. (Jon Margolis, *Chicago Tribune,* May 21, 1984; from Steve Stine.)

Margo-Rita's Hyphenated Name Law. People tend to ignore the second part of a hyphenated name. *Corollary:* When they don't eliminate the second name, they just eliminate the hyphen and mush the whole name together. (Margo-Rita Kissell, Toledo, Ohio.)

Marguccio's Absolute. Never buy the last item on the shelf. (Thomas Marguccio, New York, New York.)

Maria's Law. Never argue probability with a nine-foot-tall canary. (Valerie Shubert, Langston, Oklahoma, who offers this explanation: "Named after the character on *Sesame Street*, who persisted in ignoring it despite common sense and experience, but I think it has more general applications. The canary is, I think, a little less than nine feet tall, but the stricture still applies.")

Mark's Dental Chair Discovery. Dentists are incapable of asking questions that require a simple yes or no answer. (Norman Mark, Chicago, Illinois.)

Mark's Washington Journalism Rule. In this town don't believe anything you hear and half of what you see. (Ross Mark, former Washington correspondent for the *London Daily Express*, recalled at his memorial service at the National Press Club, 2006.)

Markgraf's Observation. Upon switching on a TV set, one will first see a commercial. (Richard Markgraf, Granville, Ohio.)

Marks's Law. Stand on any street corner in any city in the world. Close your eyes. Stick out your arms. You will touch a schmuck. (William Marks, Chicago, Illinois.)

Marlin-Jones's Conclusion. Most of us don't sell out because nobody wants to buy. (Critic Davy Marlin-Jones; from Marshall L. Smith.)

Marquis's Revised Maxim. Every cloud has its silver lining, but it is sometimes a little difficult to get it to the mint. (Humorist Don Marquis, who also gave us the item below.)

Marquis's Understanding. Middle age is the time when a man is always thinking that in a week or two he will feel as good as ever.

Marshall Cook Theory, The. Jurors will give up the casual clothing they've been wearing for coats, ties, and formal dresses on the day their verdict is ready.

(Named for a U.S. Marshal in the court of Judge Aubrey E. Robinson, Jr., and reported in the *Washington Times* by Jay Mallin, July 11, 1986; from Joseph C. Goulden.)

Marshall's Distinction. A government could print a good edition of Shakespeare's works, but it could not get them written. (Economist Alfred Marshall; *RS.*)

Marshall's Generalized Iceberg Theorem. Seven-eighths of everything can't be seen. (*U/S.T.L.*)

Marshall's Memorandum to Vice-Presidential Aspirants. There were two brothers: One ran away to sea, and the other was elected to vice president—and nothing was ever heard from either of them again. (Vice President Thomas R. Marshall.)

Marshall's Universal Laws of Perpetual Perceptual Obfuscation. (1) Nobody perceives anything with total accuracy. (2) No two people perceive the same thing identically. (3) Few perceive what difference it makes... or care. (Jack A. Marshall, Arlington, Massachusetts. *AO.*)

Marsh's Law. Pain is always worse at night (after office hours). (Wallace S. Marsh, M.D., Lompoc, California.)

Marsolais's Law of Diminishing Credibility. Your trusty dependable lawn mower starts every time on the second pull, the only exception being when you're trying to sell it to your neighbor. At that time twenty-seven pulls are required to start it. *Marsolais's Law of Unfittingness:* No matter which utility company sends you a bill, the envelope they provide for its return to themselves is always one-quarter inch shorter than the bill. *Marsolais's Law of Worst Possible Timing:* During the course of a meal, the waitress will drop by no fewer than ten times to inquire whether everything is all right; nine of those ten times, your mouth will be full. (Maurice Marsolais, Fairfax, Virginia.)

Martin-Berthelot Principle, The. Of all possible committee reactions to any given agenda item, the reaction that will occur is the one which will liberate the greatest amount of hot air. *Martin's Laws of Academia:* (1) The faculty expands its activity to fit whatever space is available, so that more space is always required. (2) Faculty purchases of equipment and supplies always increase to match the funds available, so these funds are never adequate. (3) The professional quality of the faculty tends to be inversely proportional to the importance it attaches to space and equipment. *Martin's Law of Committees:* All committee reports conclude that "it is not prudent to change the policy [or procedure, or organization, or whatever] at this time." *Martin's Exclusion:* Committee reports dealing with wages, salaries, fringe benefits, facilities, computers, employee parking, libraries, coffee breaks, secretarial support, etc., always call for dramatic expenditure increases.

Martin's Law of Communication: The inevitable result of improved and enlarged communication between different levels in a hierarchy is a vastly increased area of misunderstanding. *Martin's Laws of Hierarchical Function:* (1) All hierarchies contain administrators and managers, and they tend to appear at alternating levels in the hierarchy. (2) Administration maintains the status quo. (3) Management directs and controls change. *Martin's Minimax Maxim:* Everyone knows that the name of the game is to let the other guy have all of the little tats and to keep all of the big tits for yourself. *Martin's Plagiarism of H. L. Mencken:* Those who can—do. Those who cannot—teach. Those who cannot teach become deans. (Thomas L. Martin, Jr., from *Malice in Blunderland,* McGraw-Hill, 1971.)

Martindale's Proverbial Logic. (1) If you can lead him to water, and force him to drink, he isn't a horse. (2) The worst part of valor is indiscretion. (3) If it boils and is watched, it can't be a pot. (4) The second best policy is dishonesty. (5) If you refuse to eat the pudding, what proof have you? (6) If you are marketing a five-cent cigar of high quality, you are serving admirably this country's needs. (Canadian writer Herb Martindale, in his book *The Caledonia Eye Opener,* Alive Press, 1975. These items were developed from a premise stated by Dereck Williamson in *Saturday Review:* Since one picture is worth a thousand words, one word must be worth .001 of a picture.)

Martinez's Key. The key to effective verbal communication is to never state what the key to anything is. *Martinez's Observation:* In exactly 91.37 percent of all cases in which a percentage figure is cited, the percentage figure is incorrect. (Daniel G. Martinez, University Park, New Mexico.)

Martin's Basic Laws of Instant Analysis. (1) *The Law of Nondefinition:* If it is generally known what one is supposed to be doing, then someone will expect him to do it. (2) *The Law of Minimum Effort:* In any given group, the most will do the least and the least the most. (3) *The Law of Augmented Complexity:* There is nothing so simple that it cannot be made difficult. (4) *The Law of Nonresponsibility:* In any given miscalculation, the fault will never be placed if more than one person is involved. (5) *The Law of Prior Menace:* People see what they have been conditioned to see; they refuse to see what they don't expect to see. (6) *The Law of Randomness:* Consistency is the product of small minds. (Paraphrasing Emerson on the "hobgoblin of little minds.") (7) *The Law of Instant Response:* A quick response is worth a thousand logical responses. (Merle P. Martin, Anchorage, Alaska, in his 1975 *Journal of Systems Management* article entitled "The Instant Analyst." Martin, a systems analyst, uses the article to reveal the secrets of that profession—or, at least, the instant version. One of the highlights of the piece is the collection of "instant phrases" Martin suggests to use when applying the *Law of Instant Response.* Among others, he sanctions the use of: "Don't stop to stomp ants when the elephants are stampeding," "That's only true because it's true," "That is utterly preposterous," and "Trust me!" *RS.*)

Martin's Definition of Drunkenness. You're not drunk if you can lie on the floor without holding on. (Dean Martin; *S.T.L.*)

Martin's Discovery. Saying everything that is on your mind is one of the greatest sources of bad manners. (Judith Martin, a.k.a. Miss Manners, quoted in *U.S. News & World Report,* December 6, 1982.)

Martin's Rule. By the time you run into the house, get the binoculars, and run back outside, the strange bird will have left its perch. (Lynn Martin, Mount Laurel, New Jersey.)

Martin's Theory of Scientific Research. Nothing is too much trouble if somebody else does it. (Archer Martin, Nobel laureate, quoted at the time of his death in the *Albuquerque Journal,* August 9, 2002; *TG*)

Marxist Law of the Distribution of Wealth. Shortages will be divided equally among the peasants. (John W. Gustafson, Chicago, Illinois.)

Mary Louise's Law. You can't tell from where you sit when the man in the balcony will drop his program. (Mary Louise Gabauer; *MLS.*)

Mary Principle, The. If many individuals remain too long at their level of incompetence, they will destroy the organization, because their presence demonstrates to others that competence is not a prerequisite for success. *(U/J;* Thomas Parry, Rockford, Illinois.)

Mary's Rule. All men/women have ten faults. Pick ten faults you can live with. (Mary Williams; from her son Jon, South Melbourne, Australia, who adds that the rule can also apply to such things as cards, houses, and jobs.)

Ma's Rule. No matter how many pencils or pens there are in the house, none will ever be within fifteen feet of a telephone. (*U/Ra.*)

Masefield's R&D Rule. The principle function of an advanced design department nowadays is to keep up with the public relations department. (Peter Masefield, British Aircraft managing director, quoted in Leonard Louis Levinson's *Webster's Unafraid Dictionary,* Macmillan, 1967.)

Maslow's Maxim. If the only tool you have is a hammer, you treat everything like a nail. (Abraham H. Maslow, the noted psychiatrist, obtained from Sydney J. Harris, the noted columnist. Harris told me that it was his "favorite modern saying." Originally published in Maslow's *The Psychology of Science*, Harper & Row, 1966.)

Mason's Law of Heat Transfer. Light bulbs are always too hot to touch when they need replacement. *Corollary:* Flashlights, matches, and candles disappear when light bulbs burn out. *Mason's Law of Probability.* Due to Brownian Movement, given enough time, everything will either disperse or turn into coal. (H. Lawrence Mason III, D.M.D., Louisville, Kentucky.)

Masson's Admonition. "Be yourself!" is about the worst advice you can give some people. (Tom Masson, American humorist and editor.)

Masterson's Law (or "The Iron Law of Wagers"). If a guy wants to bet you that he can make the jack of diamonds jump out of a deck of cards and spit apple cider in your ear, *don't* take that bet. Sure as shootin', you're gonna wind up with an earful of cider. (Sky Masterson to Nathan Detroit in Frank Loesser's 1950 musical *Guys and Dolls; MLS.*)

Matheson's Law. Structure commands function. If you could breed an oyster the size of a horse, it wouldn't take first place in the Kentucky Derby no matter who rode it. (Joan Matheson, from Robert F. Tatman, Wynnewood, Pennsylvania.)

Matsch's Maxim. A fool in high station is like a man on the top of a high mountain: everything appears small to him and he appears small to everybody. (Professor Leader W. Matsch.)

Matthews-Butler Principles of Plagiarism. In the case of the first person to use an anecdote, there is originality; in the case of the second, there is plagiarism; with the third, it is lack of originality; with the fourth, it is drawing from a common stock; and in the case of the fifth, it is research. (Professors Brander Matthews and Nicholas Murray Butler, both of Columbia University, from *Man in the Street,* J. S. Ogilvie, publisher.)

Matthews' Maxim. Don't get so far ahead of the parade that you can't hear the music. (Chris Matthews on the MSNBC "Hardball" program, first used May 30, 2006, and again on May 8, 2012; from Tom Gill.)

Mattsen's Corollary to the Bureaucratic Oath. Go ahead and rock the boat. The only people who will care are the ones who can't swim. (John A. Mattsen, Finlayson, Minnesota.)

Mattuck's Law. In any given problem, difficulty is conserved; i.e., there are no true "shortcuts." (Professor Arthur Mattuck, MIT; from Richard Stone, Stanford, California.)

Matz's General Laws. (1) No amount of genius can overcome a preoccupation with detail. (2) Textbooks of a previous generation were as large as the textbooks of today, but contained a different body of misinformation. (Originally quoted in Dr. Robert Matz's article "Principles of Medicine," which appeared in the January 1977 issue of the *New York State Journal of Medicine.*) (3) New equipment and new procedures may improve medical care, but seldom decrease the cost. (4) Every psychoneurotic ultimately dies of organic disease. (From Dr. Matz's "Principles of Medicine.")

Maugham's Advice. Death is a very dull, dreary affair, and my advice to you is to have nothing whatsoever to do with it. (Somerset Maugham.)

Maverick's Observations. (1) You can fool some of the people all of the time and all of the people some of the time—and them's pretty good odds. (2) A coward dies a thousand times; a hero only once. A thousand to one is pretty good odds. (3) Work is all right for killing time, son, but it's no way to make a living. (The old television show *Maverick;* from Don Coles of St. Louis, Steve Stine, and Bernard L. Albert.)

Maxims. People living in stone houses shouldn't throw glasses. People in glass houses might as well answer the doorbell. A closed mouth gathers no foot. (*U/Ra.*)

Mayes's Law of Instant Retaliation. When forced to accept the dirty end of the stick, always shake hands with the guy who gives it to you. Regrettably, this is effective only for right-handed people. (Colin D. Mayes, Hitchin, Hertfordshire, England.)

May's Law. The quality of the correlation is inversely proportional to the density of the control—the fewer the facts, the smoother the curves. (*U/DRW.*)

May's Maxim on Meetings. The only meeting that will ever start on time is the one for which you are late. (Bruce M. May, O.D., Reading, Pennsylvania.)

May's Mordant Maxim. A university is a place where men of principle outnumber men of honor. (Historian Ernest May; *AO.*)

May's Observations on Meetings. (1) Well-planned and organized meetings do not run well. (2) Poorly planned and organized meetings run even worse, or not at all. (Bruce M. May, O.D., Reading, Pennsylvania.)

MBA Maxims. (1) Never try to teach a pig to sing; it wastes your time and it annoys the pig. (2) Sometimes the crowd is right. (3) Customers want ¼ inch holes—not ¼ inch drills. (4) Dollars become what you label them. (These maxims were inspired by a collection of business maxims that appeared in *MBA Magazine.* The maxims were solicited for *The Official Rules.* For reasons unclear, the maxim about teaching a pig to sing has been widely attributed to the author of this work. If you enter the words of the maxim and "Paul Dickson" in Google you will get more than 44,000 hits.)

McAdoo's Rule of Political Self-Interest. Whenever a beneficial measure is opposed by powerful financial interests, the real reason for the opposition is never given. *McAdoo's Rules of Political Mendacity:* The first principle of political lying is to make the lie highly personal, for lies about a party or a class are too cold and abstract to arouse more than a faint public interest. The second principle of the art is to create and disseminate a vague story, rather than one which hangs on precise data. The more vague and foggy it is the better, as it is likely to live longer than a detailed lie, which can be disputed by facts. Its vagueness is a sort of protective coloration; in the first place, it cannot be pinned onto its originator, for if it comes back to him and is slapped in his face, he will either deny it outright or declare that he was misunderstood. Vagueness leaves a great deal to the imagination, and people are likely to imagine the worst. The great lie-masters have learned by experience that much dependence can be placed on the widely diffused capacity for invention. All you have to do is to launch the lie in general terms, and the public will supply the details so that the story grows by much retelling. (William G. McAdoo, Secretary of the Treasury under Woodrow Wilson, in *The Crowded Years*, Houghton Mifflin, 1931; from Joseph C. Goulden.)

McAfee's Law of Physical Material Balance. Matter can be neither created nor destroyed. However, it can be lost. (E. Ray McAfee.)

McAfee's Theorem. A word to the wise is insipid. (Professor R. Preston McAfee, Purdue University.)

McAlister's Principle. The rate of cooling of coffee in a cup is inversely proportional to the amount of time you have to drink it. (R. G. McAlister, Ukiah, California.)

McBain's Constant. All ticket sellers always seem to be counting something no matter when you approach their windows. They are either counting money, or new tickets, or cancelled tickets, or stamps, or schedules, or sometimes they are counting their big toes, but they are always counting something, and they are always too busy with what they are counting to look up at you. (Ed McBain, *The Heckler*, Simon and Schuster, 1960; from Bob Skole.)

McCabe's Law. Nobody *has* to do anything. (Charles McCabe, *San Francisco Chronicle; RS.*)

McCabe's Law of Relativity. The older you get, the faster time seems to pass. *McCabe's Law of Ultimate Uncertainty:* Even if it already worked once, that could have been a fluke. *McCabe's Notation:* Ninety percent of the people in any group think that they are in the top 10 percent. *McCabe's Observation:* Sometimes you're the dog, sometimes the hydrant. *McCabe's Romantic Opera Rules:* (1) The tenor always gets the girl. (2) They never get to live happily ever after. *McCabe's Rules of Financial Planning:* (1) You must have a set of rules. (2) You must obey all the rules. (3) Never invest money with anyone who telephones from another state. (4) Do not pay retail prices for your investments. *McCabe's Rules of the Road:* When driving in the District of Columbia, you are in the greatest danger when (1) stopping for a red light or (2) going through a green light. (Joseph M. McCabe, Washington, D.C.)

McCaffery's Law. They—whoever they may be—can do whatever they want. *McCaffery's Reality:* When you finally join "them," you find out that McCaffery didn't know what he was talking about. (James Manus McCaffery, New Orleans, Louisiana.)

McCarthy's Adage. The only thing that saves us from the bureaucracy is inefficiency. An efficient bureaucracy is the greatest threat to liberty. (Eugene McCarthy, quoted in *Time,* February 12, 1979.)

McCarthy's Law of Intelligence. Being in politics is like being a football coach. You have to be smart enough to understand the game and dumb enough to think it's important. (Eugene McCarthy; *MBC's* Laws of Politics.)

McCarthy's Realization. If I had my life to live over, I'd probably make the same mistakes—only I'd make them sooner. (Charlie McCarthy, ventriloquist Edgar Bergen's star dummy, on their radio show.)

McCarthy's Warnings. (1) It is dangerous for a national candidate to say things that people might remember. (2) Remember that the worst accidents occur in the middle of the road. (3) (To new members of Congress) Vote against anything introduced with a "re" in it, especially reforms, reorganizations, and recodifications. This usually means going back to something that failed once and is likely to do so again. (Eugene McCarthy, quoted in the *Washington Post,* September 4, 1984, and his article, "Ten Commandments for New Hill Members," *Washington Post,* January 4, 1981.)

McClaughry's Iron Law of Zoning. When it's not needed, zoning works fine; when it is essential, it always breaks down. (John McClaughry, Concord, Vermont. The law was born when McClaughry was studying the effects of zoning in the course of the 1974 debate on the Vermont Land Use Plan. As he explains, "A speaker had urged state zoning to 'keep Vermont from turning into Los Angeles.' When it was pointed out that Los Angeles had had zoning in force since 1923, *McClaughry's Iron Law* rapidly emerged. I was at the time chairman of the Planning Commission of Kirby, Vermont, population 230, which had zoning but absolutely no need for it since there was no development pressure.")

McClaughry's Law of Public Policy. Politicians who vote huge expenditures to alleviate problems get reelected; those who propose structural changes to prevent problems get early retirement. *McClaughry's Second Law:* Liberals, but not conservatives, can get attention and acclaim for denouncing liberal policies that failed; and liberals will inevitably capture the ensuing agenda for "reform." (John McClaughry.)

McConnell's Observation. The only thing that works in an old house is the owner. (Spero McConnell; from his brother Ray, Miami, Florida.)

McConnell's Organizational Observation. The purpose of organizations is to stop things from happening. (Richard McConnell, San Francisco, California.)

McCormick's Conclusion. You're either too young or old enough to know better, but you're never the right age. (Peggy McCormick, San Mateo, California.)

McCormick's Laments. (1) My problem is that my passport photos look like me. (2) When I finally get to the head of the line, I usually have forgotten what I was supposed to get or do when I got there. (Ernest J. McCormick, West Lafayette, Indiana.)

McCullough's Laws of Inertial Reality. (1) When the situation starts to go down the tubes, it will complete the trip. A rolling stone gathers great momentum. (2) If you're getting nowhere in a hurry, you still won't get there any sooner. (3) If the inertia of reality heads downward, it will slow geometrically as it nears to bottom. Or, as apprehension increases with the certainty of a worst possible outcome, reality takes its own sweet time getting there and even longer leaving. (D. Lee McCullough, Stonewall, Texas.)

McDonough's New Age Maxim. If you have to buy something, it's business. If you have to do something, it's enlightenment. (Lisa McDonough, Palm Beach Gardens, Florida.)

McDougal's Law. Planning never beat dumb luck. (From Howard Hamer, Long Branch, New Jersey.)

McEwen's Rule of Relative Importance. When traveling with a herd of elephants, don't be the first to lie down and rest. (Robert A. McEwen, Maumee, Ohio.)

McGarr's First Law. Whatever government does, it does more or less badly. (Judge Frank J. McGarr, U.S. District Court of Northern Illinois, from his commencement address at Loyola University Law School, June 13, 1976.)

McGarry's Gynecological Givens. (1) When running an artificial-insemination-by-donor clinic, it is soon discovered that four-sevenths of women ovulate on the weekend. (2) The first and last people to take up any operation or technique are good doctors; the other ninety-eight are mediocre. (3) If, whilst on holiday in a strange town, a doctor enters a news agent to peruse a few girly magazines, he will be recognized and spoken to by an ex-patient (female) from his hometown, whose name he has forgotten. (John McGarry, consulting gynecologist, Barnstaple, Devon, England.)

McGee's Law of Football. When you pass the ball, six possible things can happen, and five of them are bad. (The character Travis McGee, in John D. MacDonald's *The Scarlet Ruse*, Lippincott, 1973; from Charles D. Poe.)

McGee's Sad Fact. All you need to become ill in our modern world is to follow ordinary patterns of diet and lifestyle. (Dr. Charles T. McGee, in his *How to Survive Modern Technology*, Ecology Press, 1979; quoted in *Time,* December 24, 1979.)

McGlinchey's Law of Trust. Never trust a world leader. (Herbert J. McGlinchey, former U.S. Congressman, Pennsylvania state senator, and Philadelphia ward leader; *MBC.*)

McGoorty's Warning. One of the worst things that can happen in life is to win a bet on a horse at an early age. (Danny McGoorty, quoted in Robert Byrne's *The 637 Best Things Anyone Ever Said,* Atheneum, 1892.)

McGovern's Law. The longer the title, the less important the job. (Robert

Shrum, who was one of George McGovern's speechwriters, recalled this law for *AO*. McGovern discovered the law in 1960, when President Kennedy tried to persuade him that being director of the Food for Peace Program was a more influential job than secretary of agriculture.)

McGregor's Revised Maxim. The shortest distance between two points is under construction. (Scott D. McGregor, Moscow, Idaho.)

McGuire's Distinction. When a guy takes off his coat, he's not going to fight. When a guy takes off his wristwatch, watch out! (Sportscaster Al McGuire, quoted by Norman Chad in the *Washington Post,* April 21, 1986. Also see the McGuireism below, which first appeared in *Playboy.*)

McGuire's Rule of the Table. The person who reaches for the check and gets it never wanted it in the first place. (John Kessel.)

McGurk's Law. Any improbable event which would create maximum confusion if it did occur will occur. (H. S. Kindler, from *Organizing the Technical Conference,* Reinhold Publishing Co., 1960. McGurk, no doubt, is Murphy's first cousin.)

McKay's Dental Translations. (1) "It's deep." = "I think you're going to need a root canal." (2) "This won't hurt." = It will. (3) "Don't worry." = Worry. (4) "Extensive." = Expensive. (Michael S. McKay, D.M.D., Uncasville, California.)

McKean's Law. Any correction of the speech or writing of others will contain at least one grammatical, spelling, or typographical error. (Erin McKean, *VERBATIM*, 2001.)

McKean's Law of Automotive 20/20 Hindsight. The sports car you really craved twenty years ago but your father counseled was too frivolous and a bad investment because of low resale value now has become a classic and sells for three to ten times the original purchase price... and you still can't afford one. (W. E. McKean II, Sioux Falls, South Dakota.)

McKenna's Law. When you are right, be logical; when you are wrong, be-fuddle. (Gerard E. McKenna, president, Gerard E. McKenna & Associates, Middle Grove, New York.)

McKenna's Observations. (1) Legibility of handwriting declined proportionately with the proliferation of the ballpoint pen. (2) One who manufactures assumptions then doles them out as facts generally owns his own business. (3) Pessimism means never having to be disappointed. (Thomas A. McKenna, Ardmore, Pennsylvania.)

McKeon's Law of the College Catalog. The university catalog is much like the campus—it lies about the university. (Thomas J. McKeon, Assistant Dean, Case Institute of Technology, Cleveland, Ohio.)

McKinley's Memorial Dictum. The worst time to ignore possible future events of high negative impact is when you are successfully building an empire and you are loved by the people. (In honor of William McKinley; from Wayne Boucher in his article "Finding the Future," *MBA Magazine,* August/September 1978.)

McKinney's Law. The probability of your knee hitting the leg of the table increases geometrically in direct relation to the amount of coffee in your cup. (Bruce C. McKinney, State College, Pennsylvania.)

McKinney's Discoveries. (1) If dogs could talk they likely wouldn't be man's best friend. (2) All the ingredients for a healthy human diet are conveniently packaged in a jar of mayonnaise. (3) The discovery that you are wearing a mismatched pair of socks grows exponentially with the distance you find yourself from your dresser. (4) Burial of a loved one in a rented tuxedo can, over the years, become expensive. (Arlen McKinney, New Richmond, Wisconsin.)

McKinnon's Realization. In real life, there is no background music. (Leila A. McKinnon, St. Louis, Missouri.)

McLandress's Theorems of Business Confidence. (1) The confidence of the business executive in a president is inversely related to the state of business. (2) Government action and inaction both gravely impair business confidence. (3) Reassurance of business by a president has an unfavorable effect on confidence. (4) Unkind words do not enhance business confidence. (5) That politics has a bearing on business confidence is unproven. (Mark Epernay, in *The McLandress Dimension,* Houghton Mifflin, 1963. By way of explanation, if one thinks of Herbert Hoover, the theorems come into better focus. For example, no modern president enjoyed the level of business confidence that Hoover did [Theorem (1)], and the only time that he did not enjoy that confidence was in 1930 and 1931, after he tried to reassure them [Theorem (3)]. Epernay's book reveals and discusses many other theories first offered by the legendary but mythical Dr. Herschel McLandress. For instance the "Dimension" mentioned in the book title is a measure of human behavior determined by finding "the arithmetic mean or average of the intervals of time during which a subject's thoughts remained centered on some substantive phenomenon other than his own personality." Art Buchwald, for instance, had a high score of two hours; Norman Cousins, three minutes; and Richard Nixon one of the lowest, at three seconds. In case you have not heard of Epernay, the author of this book, some light was shed on the matter when a Christmas card was found tucked in a used edition of the book.)

Dear______, *Dec 16*

We hope that you both enjoy this "spoof," we have. There is a strong rumor around Cambridge that "Mark Epernay" is a pen name for John Kenneth Galbraith. That seems plausible. This is not what I hoped to be able to send.

McLaren's Motto. Sic Transit Gloria Tuesday! (Jack McLaren, from *Colombo's*

Little Book of Canadian Proverbs, Graffiti, Limericks, and Other Vital Matters, by John Robert Columbo, Hurtig, 1975.)

McLaughlin's Law. The length of any meeting is inversely proportional to the length of the agenda for that meeting. (G. Robert McLaughlin, John Hancock Mutual Life Insurance Co., Boston, Massachusetts; *AO*.)

McLaughlin's Law of Walking on Railroad Ties. They're too far for one step, but too close for two. (Brian McLaughlin, recorded by John Hall [c. 1953] and submitted by Hilde Weisert, Teaneck, New Jersey. Ms. Weisert insists that it has wide application.)

McLaughlin's Query. What is it called when you spend 25 minutes looking for a restaurant, 20 minutes finding a place to park, 15 minutes standing in line to place your order, 10 minutes waiting for your food, and 5 minutes trying to locate an empty table? Fast food. (Scott McLaughlin, quoted in Bob Levey's column, the *Washington Post*.)

McMullin's Law of Excessive Acquisitiveness. Greed is its own reward. (Roland McMullin, North Kansas City, Missouri.)

McNaughton's Rule. Any argument worth making within the bureaucracy must be capable of being expressed in a single declarative sentence that is obviously true once stated. (John McNaughton, a government national security expert. It was sent to *AO* by Harvard political scientist Graham Allison.)

McNulty's Law. Never dive in a bikini. (Jeffrey Chamberlain, Nassau County, New York.)

McPherson's Reassurance. Three trees make a row. (Professor of English David McPherson, University of New Mexico; from Sandra Adams, who says it is used to reassure students who want to make a point with a few examples.)

McQuarrie's Observations. (1) When running, cycling or walking along a two-lane highway, vehicles will approach from both directions, and the drivers of both vehicles will adjust their speed so that they pass each other precisely at the same time that they pass the runner, cyclist, or walker. (2) On unmarked intersections, he who has the most to lose goes last. This also holds true for 4-way stop intersections. (Keith McQuarrie, Carbondale, Illinois.)

McSpiritt's Discovery for Garage Sale Shopping. To ensure finding the perfect item you've been looking for, at a good price, be certain the vehicle you're in is totally inappropriate. (For example: finding a magnificent solid oak dining room table with eight chairs and you're in your old VW, or finally locating one hundred pounds of good-quality horse manure, unbagged, for your garden, and you're driving your Rolls Royce. (F. D. McSpiritt, Flint, Michigan.)

Mead's Diplomatic Rule. Vows of eternal friendship and cooperation are the oldest tradition in diplomacy; the second oldest is breaking them. (Walter Russell Mead, *Houston Chronicle,* June 10, 1988; from Charles D. Poe.)

Mead's Distinction. You are totally unique, just like everyone else. (Margaret Mead; from Catherine Pfeifer.)

Mead's Law of Human Migration. At least 50 percent of the human race doesn't want their mother-in-law within walking distance. (Margaret Mead, explaining rural migration to a symposium on the phenomenon. Submitted by Paul Martin to *DRW.*)

Mead's Law of Problem Solving. All major problems will be worked upon diligently until they are split into two minor problems. These will be worked on, less enthusiastically, until they are divided into four less important problems. Whereupon the 32, 64, 128, or whatever quantity now very minor problems that remain, are superseded by the new "major" problem. Thus problems are never really solved; they are just broken down into minor and rather ignorable problems until such time as a new one appears. (R. H. Mead, Ithaca, New York, who developed it "after some twenty-seven years in the engineering profession.")

Means's Law of Restaurant Illumination. The harder it is to read the menu, the higher the prices on it. (John Means, quoted in Bob Levey's column, the *Washington Post,* November 12, 1985.)

Medes and Persians, Law of. One man's Mede is another man's Persian. (George S. Kaufman.)

Meditz Subway Phenomenon. No matter which train you are waiting for, the wrong one comes first. (J. R. Meditz, New York, New York.)

Meier's Law. People are like electricity—they take the path of least resistance. (Leroy W. Meier, Mt. Healthy, Ohio.)

Melbourne's Razor. If it were easy, everyone would be doing it. (Marian Melbourne, Newport Beach, California.)

Melcher's Law. In a bureaucracy, every routing slip will expand until it contains the maximum number of names that can be typed in a single vertical column, namely, twenty-seven. (Daniel Melcher; *JW.*)

Meller's Six Sociological Laws. (1) Anyone who can be exploited will be. (2) If you understand the direction of the flow of money, you can predict human conduct. From this it follows that if you can control the direction of the flow of money, you can control human conduct. Man is like a sailboat and the flow of money is the wind. (3) Anything based on greed and avarice is on a firm foundation and will prevail. (4) Everyone feels that he is underpaid and overcharged. (5) For every human act, there are two reasons—the stated one and the real one. These two have a correlation coefficient that varies from one to zero. (6) We have more to fear from the bungling of the incompetent than from the machinations of the wicked. (R. L. Meller, M.D., Minneapolis, Minnesota; from J. Thomas Parry, who states: "Dr. Meller is a psychiatrist who after many, many years of practice developed these laws. Dr. Meller states with conviction that these are the only laws necessary to understand human behavior.")

Mel's Law. If it wasn't for the last minute, nothing would get done. (*U;* Radio call-in show, New York, New York.)

Mencken's Law. Whenever A annoys or injures B on the pretense of saving or improving X, A is a scoundrel. (H. L. Mencken. Joe Goulden, writer and student of Mencken, reports that this appeared in Mencken's *Newspaper Days* as Mencken's Law, but that it was derived from The Law of the Forgotten Man, found in "The Absurd Effort to Make the World Over," *The Forum,* XVII, 1894, by the Social Darwinist William Graham Sumner, to wit: "When A and B join to make a law to help X, their law always proposes to decide what C shall do for X, and C is the Forgotten Man." Mencken acknowledged his debt to Sumner, but still called his version Mencken's Law. Goulden adds that Mencken had another version that concludes, "A is a scoundrel, and should be briskly clubbed." Still another variation appeared in a recent column by James J. Kilpatrick where it was termed Mencken's Working Hypothesis of the Legislative Process and stated as: "Whenever A attempts by law to impose his moral standards on B, A is most likely a scoundrel.")

Mencken's Meta-law. For every human problem, there is a neat, plain solution—and it is always wrong. (H. L. Mencken; *AO.*)

Mencken's Rule of Unanimity. When everyone begins to believe anything, it ceases to be true; for example, the notion that the homeliest girl at the party is the safest. (H. L. Mencken.)

Mendenhall's Axiom for Bailing Out. Never practice that which must be perfect the first time. (Mo Mendenhall, former Marine fighter pilot, Camarillo, California.)

Mendonca's Discovery. If a man wears one light brown sock and one dark blue sock to work, it is more than likely that he will have a similar pair at home. (Jovit Mendonca, London, Ontario.)

Mendoza's Laws of Purchasing. (1) When shopping, never look for something specific—you won't find it. (2) Always shop for nothing—you'll always come back with something. (3) After a heavy day's shopping, the perfect purchase is in either the first or the last place you've looked. (Liz Mendoza, Fargo, North Dakota.)

Menkus's Principles of the Organizational Ecosystem. (1) Small failures are punished; big ones are rewarded—sometimes lavishly. (2) The value of an idea is more likely to be perceived in terms of the status/rank of its proponent rather than its inherent qualities. 3) Risk-taking furthers personal advancement; risk avoidance furthers personal survival. (Belden Menkus, Middleville, New Jersey; from a longer list. *Journal of Systems Management,* August 1981.)

Merrill's First Corollary. There are no winners in life; only survivors. (*U/S.T.L.*)

Merrow's Law. Optimism tends to expand to fill the scope available for its exercise. (Edward Merrow, RAND Corp. economist, who uses his law to describe synthetic fuel enthusiasts; *RS.*)

Meskimen's Laws of Bureaucracies. (1) When they want it bad (in a rush), they get it bad. (2) There's never time to do it right, but always time to do it over. (John K. Meskimen, Falls Church, Virginia; *AO.*)

Mesmerisms of Review and Control, The Twelve. (1) In order to keep engineers and scientists cognizant of the importance of progress, load them down with forms, multiple reports, and frequent meetings. (2) Remember, the more engineering projects there are, the more products there will be. (3) The less management demands of engineers and scientists, the greater their productivity. (4) Computer-based management information systems will cure most review and control problems. (5) The greater the number of professionals (advanced degrees preferred) assigned to a project, the greater the progress. (6) Cost consciousness and sophisticated design are basically incompatible. (7) If enough reports are prepared and technical reviews are held, negative information will always filter its way to senior management. (8) High salaries equals happiness equals project progress. (9) The expenditure of funds is critical—engineers and scientists should not be permitted to authorize any purchase. (10) Scientists and engineers set high performance standards for themselves; therefore, performance appraisal and career planning are perfunctory. (11) Since blue-sky projects are targeted for major breakthroughs, they are relatively immune from effective planning and control. (12) Vastly improved review and control will result by promoting the most productive engineers and scientists to management positions. (Richard F. Moore, the National Cash Register Co., Dayton, Ohio; *JIR*, January 1973.)

Metropolitan Edison's Variation on Murphy's Law. Anything that man makes will not operate perfectly. (Walter M. Creitz, president of Metropolitan Edison, the company that operated the Three Mile Island nuclear plant at the time of the 1979 accidental partial core meltdown. At the time Metropolitan Edison was a subsidiary of GPU, Inc., which subsequently merged with FirstEnergy Corporation. Quoted in *The New York Times,* March 30, 1979.)

Metzger's Maxim. You're only as old as you feel—the next day. (Daniel J. Metzger, Belleville, Illinois.)

Metz's Rules of Golf for Good Players (Whose Scores Would Reflect

Their True Ability if Only They Got an Even Break Once in a While). (1) On beginning play, as many balls as may be required to obtain a satisfactory result may be played from the first tee. Everyone recognizes a good player needs to "loosen up" but does not have time for the practice tee. (2) A ball sliced or hooked into the rough shall be lifted and placed in the fairway at a point equal to the distance it carried or rolled in the rough. Such veering right or left frequently results from friction between the face of the club and the cover of the ball, and the player should not be penalized for erratic behavior of the ball resulting from such uncontrollable mechanical phenomena. (3) A ball hitting a tree shall be deemed not to have hit the tree. Hitting a tree is simply bad luck and has no place in a scientific game. The player should estimate the distance the ball would have traveled if it had not hit the tree and play the ball from there, preferably from atop a nice firm tuft of grass. (4) There shall be no such thing as a lost ball. The missing ball is on or near the course somewhere and eventually will be found and pocketed by someone else. It thus becomes a stolen ball, and the player should not compound the felony by charging himself with a penalty stroke. (5) When played from a sand trap, a ball which does not clear the trap on being struck may be hit again on the roll without counting an extra stroke. In no case will more than two strokes be counted in playing from a trap, since it is only reasonable to assume that if the player had time to concentrate on his shot, instead of hurrying it so as not to delay his playing partners, he would be out in two. (6) If a putt passes over the hole without dropping, it is deemed to have dropped. The law of gravity holds that any object attempting to maintain a position in the atmosphere without something to support it must drop. The law of gravity supersedes the law of golf. (7) Same thing goes for a ball that stops at the brink of the hole and hangs there, defying gravity. You cannot defy the law. (8) Same thing goes for a ball that rims the cup. A ball should not go sideways. This violates the laws of physics. (9) A putt that stops close enough to the cup to inspire such comments as "you could blow it in" may be blown in. This rule does not apply if the ball is more than three inches from the hole, because no one wants to make a travesty of the game. (Donald A. Metz, Devon, Pennsylvania.)

Meuse's Law. Anything with teeth sooner or later bites. (Jim Meuse, Huntington Beach, California.)

Meyer Meyer's Rule. You never get a generous and delicious cocktail in a proper glass in a restaurant where the food is bad. (The character Meyer Meyer in *Cinnamon Skin,* Harper, 1982; by John D. McDonald; from Joseph C. Goulden.)

Meyer's Law of Human Relations. In all emotional conflicts, the thing you find hardest to do is the one thing you should do. (Travis McGee's friend Meyer in John D. McDonald's *Pale Gray for Guilt*, Lippincott, 1968; from Stephen M. Lonsdale, Abington, Massachusetts.)

Miazga's Discovery. Death is nature's way of telling you the FDA was right. (Robert Miazga, Danbury, Connecticut.)

Micah's Musing. Relationships are like wine. Really expensive ones get better with age, but most turn to vinegar after six months. (Micah Charles, June 17, 2012; from Tom Gill.)

Michehl's Theorem. Less is more. (*U/S.T.L.* See *Pastore's Comment on Michehl's Theorem.*)

Michel's Iron Law of Oligarchy. The larger an organization grows in size, the more it oppresses its members. (Robert Michel; from Walter Shearer, Tokyo, Japan.)

Michener's Rules for Writers. If you have written a successful novel, everyone invites you to write short stories. If you have written some good short stories, everyone wants you to write a novel. But nobody wants anything until you have already proved yourself by being published somewhere else. (James Michener, quoted in Barbara Rowes's *The Book of Quotes,* Dutton, 1979.)

Midas's Law. Possession diminishes perception of value, immediately. (John Updike, *New Yorker,* November 3, 1975.)

Mikadet's Cardinal Rule for Parents of Adult Children. An eighteen-year-old can: (a) vote, (b) rebuild an automobile engine, (c) swallow a guitar pick. (T. K. Mikadet, Lompoc, California.)

Mike's Mailbox Maxim. No matter how slow the Post Office becomes, bills and junk mail will arrive as quickly as before. (Mike Mikolosko, Great Falls, Virginia.)

Miles's Law. Where you stand depends on where you sit. (Rufus Miles, former career administrator at the Department of Health, Education and Welfare, to express the fact that your opinion depends on your job. Appeared in *AO's* column and elsewhere. Has become one of Robert Machol's *POR.*)

Miles's Political Prayer. Yea, even though I graze in pastures with jackasses, I pray that I will not bray like one. (William Miles, Anna Marie, Florida.)

Miller's Axioms for Football Betting with Tucker's Corollaries. (1) Place your largest bets on the game you win; never, never place a large bet on a game you lose. *Corollary:* You can't place your bets after the game. (2) The greatest team will have one terrible game each season; likewise, the most pathetic dogs will have one great game. *Corollary:* You never know when those games will be. (Chris Tucker, *D Magazine,* Dallas, Texas.)

Miller's Axioms of Outdoor Grilling. (1) The fire is always at its peak fifteen minutes after dinner. (2) If you overhear the cook saying, "No problem, I'll just dust it off," it's time to visit the salad bowl. (Bryan Miller, *The New York Times,* June 27, 1984; *TG.*)

Miller's Corollary. Objects are lost because people look where they are not instead of where they are. (Henry L. Miller, London, England.)

Miller's Distinction. There is a thin line of distinction between the avant-garde and the *Gong Show.* (*U/Ra.*)

Miller's Law. The corruption in a country is in inverse proportion to its state of development. (Nathan Miller, Chevy Chase, Maryland. *AO.*)

Miller's Law. The yoo-hoo you yoo-hoo into the forest is the yoo-hoo you get back. (Merle Miller; *RS.*)

Miller's Law. Unless you put your money to work for you—you work for your money. (Joe Miller, Fort Myers, Florida.)

Miller's Law. You can't tell how deep a puddle is until you step into it. (*U/S.T.L.*)

Miller's Principle. Abstinence makes the heart grow fonder. (Mark R. Miller; from Andrea Miller.)

Miller's Slogan. Lose a few, lose a few. (Don Miller, Livermore, California.)

Milligan's Formula. Middle age is halfway between your age and one hundred. (R. D. Milligan, Rolling Meadows, Illinois.)

Mills's Law. The bigger the problem, the fewer the facts. (Harlan D. Mills, *Mathematics and the Managerial Imagination;* from Mel Loftus.)

Mills's Law. The ease by which a man can be convinced, by artful manipulation of language, of something contrary to common sense, is directly proportional to his advance in philosophy. (J. S. Mills, *A System of Logic,* Harper, 1848; from Kevin C. Long, Quebec.)

Mills's Law. There is no task so great that it cannot be done in one night. (This law, created by Patty Mills, Mount Holyoke College, 1964, and submitted by Hilde Weisert, points out that it seems to work better in college than in "life after college.")

Mills's Law of Transportation Logistics. The distance to the gate from which your flight departs is inversely proportionate to the time remaining before the scheduled departure of the flight. (Edward S. Mills, National Association of Blue Shield Plans; *AO.*)

Milner's Distinction. A difference to be a difference must make a difference. (T. H. Milner, San Francisco, California.)

Milroy's Law. All machines have an innate sense of irresponsibility. *Mary Milroy's Corollary:* Machines are misogynists. (Ian Milroy, Avon, England.)

Ming's Warning. Science will overcome all things—even the human emotions. (The character Ming the Merciless in "Flash Gordon," 1936.)

Mintzlaff's Law of Social Tolerance. Do not judge other people; just snicker at them. (Charles Mintzlaff, Milwaukee, Wisconsin.)

Mintz's Law. The best things in life are messy. (Ann Emmons Mintz, Philadelphia, Pennsylvania.)

Mirsky's Law of Auditioning. If they say "Thank you," you've got a shot.... If they say "Thank you very much," forget it. (Steven D. Mirsky, Ithaca, New York.)

Miseries of 1806

In the early days of the 19th century, a cluster of half a dozen or so books appeared in England with the key word "miseries" in their titles. Each small volume was written pseudonymously and contained a series of "groans" attesting to the conspiracy of events, objects, and other humans that kept the authors in, as one put it, "a frenzy of vexation."

These books are desperately hard to find today, but through the Library of Congress two classics of the genre—both published in 1806—have been found. The importance of rediscovering these miseries is simply that the books give us clear proof that the so-called curses of modernism predate the Modern Era and knowledge of the inherent perversity of things has been a constant for longer than we commonly realize.

Enough preamble. Let us move on to some of the specific miseries cited in two early Murphylogical classics, *The Miseries of Human Life or the Groans of Samuel Sensitive and Timothy Testy* by Samuel Sensitive and Timothy Testy (Wm. Miller, London, 1806) and *More Miseries!! Addressed to the Morbid, the Melancholy and the Irritable* by Sir Fretful Murmur (H.D. Symonds, London, 1806).[5]

- All your acquaintance telling you that a portrait which you are aware is rather flattering, is not at all like you.
- Being requested by a foreigner who understands very little of the English language, to hear him read Milton.
- Calling on a sultry day upon a friend who has the mania for planting upon him; who marches and countermarches you three or four miles to see his plantations, after which he irresistibly presses you to ascend a considerable eminence of ground, about half a mile off, to see a couple of pines which he planted on the day his first child was born.
- Attempting, at a strange house, to take down a book from a high, crowded shelf, bringing the library upon your nose.

[5] Some scholarly scratching leads to the conclusion that Sensitive and Testy were one man, James Beresford of Merton College, Oxford, and that Murmur was a writer named Robert Heron.

- As an author—those moments during which you are relieved from the fatigues of composition by finding that your memory, your intellects, your imagination, your spirits, and even your love of the subject, have all, as if with one consent, left you in the lurch.
- Writing with ink of about the consistency of pitch, which leaves alternatively a blot and a blank.
- Writing upon a thin sheet of paper, very small crumbs of bread under it.
- Looking for a good pen (which is your personal destiny never to find, except when you are indifferent about it), and having a free choice among the following varieties: 
- Having a pimple on your chin, covering it with sticking plaster, and just as you enter the drawing room, discovering that it curls on all sides.
- Being bored by a man whom you don't like, having to dine with him, and being nailed by his begging you to fix your own day.
- Living in chambers under a man who takes private lessons in dancing.
- Sitting at dinner next to a man of consequence with whom you wish to ingratiate yourself, being told that he has superstitious horror of the salt being spilt, and from excess of caution sending the contents of the salt cellar into his plate.
- Whilst you are making a sketch, having a number of impertinent persons staring behind you, until the crowd increases to that degree that you are obliged to abandon your subject.
- Asking a lady to permit you to look at a beautiful string of very small pearls, breaking it in two, scattering them over the floor, and crushing several under your feet in endeavouring to collect them.
- Toasting a bit of bread at the end of a short dessert fork, before a good brisk fire, and burning the ends of your fingers without being able to toast it to your liking.
- Having succeeded in fixing yourself in a most seducing, and graceful attitude, letting your cocked hat fall.
- Knocking at a door, and by a horrible and unaccountable lapse of memory, forgetting the name of the master or mistress of the house.
- Upon paying the first visit after the funeral of a relation, a distant cousin for instance, to the immediate friends of the deceased, finding them all in tears from some unaccountable counteraction of nature, and not being able to look grave upon the occasion.

- Upon returning from a Tour to the Continent, being asked by everyone you meet for your private opinion of things in general.
- Trying to pass a man who waddles.
- Being requested to say something to entertain the party.
- Sitting for your portrait to a subordinate painter who renders the likeness with such exasperating exactness, that every pimple, blotch and blemish in the face are faithfully represented.
- Striking your foot against another step after you had concluded that you had reached the top of the stairs.
- Being seized with a violent bowel complaint, whilst you are riding on horseback with two young ladies, to one of whom you are paying your addresses; being obliged to alight in great confusion, telling your fair companions that there is an exquisite bit of scenery round a hedge, and which you should like very much to sketch, assuring them that you will return in five minutes, and remembering afterwards that it was well known that you never drew in your life.

(These are but a few of hundreds of miseries catalogued by these pioneers. It boggles the mind to consider what they could have come up with if they had been alive for the coming of the telephone, IRS Form 1040, computer, television, automobile, superhighway, Twitter, Facebook, and other elements of human progress.)

Miss Manners's Travel Distinction. There are two classes of travel in America: steerage and steerage with free drinks. You pay a great deal extra for the free drinks, of course. (Judith Martin, in her syndicated column, September 1, 1985.)

Missinne's Observations. (1) The most vocal opponents of water fluoridation are always people with false teeth. (2) It is one thing not to ask much of life, but it is another not to get anything. (Jeff Missinne, Superior, Wisconsin.)

MIST Law—Man in the Street. The number of people watching you is directly proportional to the stupidity of your action. (*U.*)

Mitchell's Explanation. People are confused about the weather in Washington. I shall explain the basics: Winter is cold. Summer is hot. Every year these truths get the populace with the force of a thunderbolt. (Henry Mitchell, *Washington Post*, 1982.)

Mitchell's Reminder. All anybody needs to know about prizes is that Mozart never won one. (Henry Mitchell in the *Washington Post.*)

Mitchell's Rustic Rule. Changing barnyards will not transform a turkey into a golden goose. (Kevin Mitchell, Eden Prairie, Minnesota.)

Mix's Law. There is nothing more permanent than a temporary building. There is nothing more permanent than a temporary tax. (Averill Q. Mix, Los Gatos, California.)

Miz Beaver's Summation of Walt Kelly's Philosophy. "He allus said, don't take life too serious . . . it ain't nohow permament." (Miz Beaver, in the *Pogo* comic strip, the Christmas following Walt Kelly's death.)

Mockridge's Major Maxim. If an idea is successful, the first person to claim credit for it will be the person who contended all along that it wouldn't work. (Syndicated columnist Norton Mockridge.)

Modell's Laws. (1) Nothing is so serious that it can't be teased until it is ragged at the edges. (2) Nothing is so simple that it cannot be made too complex to work. (*U/GT.*)

Momma's Rule. If you can't stand to eat, get out of my kitchen. (From the comic strip *Momma* by Mell Lazarus.)

Mom's Law. Children only agree with you when they're on their way to something worse. (The comic strip *Cathy,* July 1986; *TG.*)

Mom's Law II. When they finally do have to take you to the hospital, your underwear won't be new or clean. (Dennis Rogers.)

Money Maxim. Money isn't everything—for instance, it isn't plentiful. (Bill Woods, *DRW*'s father.)

Money, The Natural Law of. Anything left over today will be needed tomorrow to pay an unexpected bill. (Betty Canary, in her *Surviving as a Woman,* Henry Regnery Publishing, 1970.)

Montagu's Maxim. The idea is to die young as late as possible. (Anthropologist Ashley Montagu; *MLS.*)

Montero's Principle. An attorney who informs the judge that he has "just one more question" will, invariably, keep the witness on the stand an additional half-hour to forty-five minutes. However, if he informed the judge that he has "just several more questions," then the witness will be on the stand for several days. (Wilson M. Montero, Jr., New Orleans, Louisiana.)

Montgomery's Explanation of the Facts of Life. All normal young people want to do this thing. It is natural, like fighting. (Attributed to Lord Montgomery.)

Montore's Maxims. (1) A true environmentalist will use both sides of a piece of paper in presenting a position paper. (2) Every journey, great and small, begins with unrealistic expectations. (3) Love expands to fill the available hearts. (4) Man's superiority to the rest of the animal kingdom is due primarily to his imagination. He imagines he is superior. (5) No balls, no blue chips. (R. J. Montore, Henderson, Kentucky.)

Moore's Law. The computing power of silicon chips will double every 18 to 24 months. (Gordon Moore, co-founder of Intel, in his famous 1965 article in *Electronics Magazine* entitled "Cramming More Components into Integrated Circuits".)

Moore's Airline Constant. Departing connecting flights always leave on time. (Bob Moore, Atherton, California.)

Moore's Constant. Everybody sets out to do something, and everybody does something, but no one does what he sets out to do. (Irish novelist George Moore.)

Moore's Definition of Insect Repellant, The. One of a number of gag items available in bait and tackle shops. (Dick and Rick Moore, in their "Fishing Forecast," Anderson Valley *Advertiser,* April 17, 1985.)

Moore's Economic Discovery. Now I know why you rarely see a thin economist. It's because of all those words they have to eat. (Mary Tyler Moore; from Bernard L. Albert.)

Moore's Law. The degree to which a topic is understood is inversely proportional to the amount of literature available on it. *Corollary:* That which seems vague is frequently meaningless. (Terry C. Moore, Indianapolis, Indiana. Moore finds widespread application of this law and corollary in fields as diverse as child rearing, business management, macroeconomic theory, and transactional analysis.)

Moore's Observation on Irresistible Forces. Trailer parks attract tornadoes. (David E. Moore, Wakefield, Rhode Island.)

Moore's Stages in the Development of a Movie Star. (1) Who's Dudley Moore? (2) Get me Dudley Moore. (3) Get me a Dudley Moore type. (4) Get me a young Dudley Moore. (5) Who's Dudley Moore? (Dudley Moore; from Chad Hesting. A similar set of stages was attributed to Herschel Bernardi.)

Moos's Law. When it is necessary to choose between ignorance and stupidity, choose ignorance. It is curable. (Phil Moos, D.D.S., St. Cloud, Minnesota.)

Moran's Theorem for the Self-Employed. You spend the first half of your career wondering if people will buy your services and the second half wondering when they'll ever get around to paying for them. (Frank J. Moran, Los Angeles, California.)

Morford's Rule. Nothing fails like success. (Ida B. Morford, Glassboro State College, Glassboro, New Jersey. Submitted by Rose Primack, one of Dr. Morford's colleagues, who says it came out of a postmortem on a "highly successful environmental education program that was almost universally applauded" when it was discontinued.)

Morgan's Correlation. The longer the vacuum cleaner cord, the sooner it gets caught on something. (Karen Sorensen Morgan, New York, New York.)

Morgan's Discovery. The average man is a little below average. (Satirist Henry Morgan, who delivered the discovery to the author after appearing on his radio show, 1979.)

Morgan's Law of Air Travel. The occurrence of air turbulence will always coincide with the serving of the meal. (Elizabeth S. Morgan, Gaithersburg, Maryland.)

Moriarity's Secret for Financial Success. BLASH. (Named for a highly successful investment broker named Morton P. Moriarity, who was once one of the biggest failures on Wall Street. When destitute and reduced to sleeping on park benches, he had a dream in which a bearded holy man handed him a piece of paper with the word "BLASH" on it. Moriarity ran all around New York in search of a bearded holy man who could tell him what BLASH meant. Finally, after a year-long search, he found his man, who told him it stood for "Buy Low And Sell High." This, from Carl Winston's book, *How to Run* a *Million into a Shoestring and Other Shortcuts to Success,* G.P. Putnam's Sons, 1960.)

Morley's Advice to Travelers. Avoid plays acted in a foreign language and buildings entirely rebuilt since the war. Beware of government-sponsored stores and light operas. Limit yourself to one cathedral, one picture gallery, and one giant Buddha a week. (Actor Robert Morley, from *A Musing Morley,* Robson Books,1974.)

Morley's Conclusion. No man is lonely while eating spaghetti. (Christopher Morley. The full quip "No man is lonely while eating spaghetti, for it requires so much attention" first appeared in a story published in *Harper's Magazine* in 1926 and was later reprinted in his book, *The Arrow,* Doubleday, 1927. The quotation is often attributed—incorrectly—to rotund British screen actor Robert Morley.)

Morley's Credo. My theology, briefly, is that the universe was dictated, but not signed. (Christopher Morley; from John Ohliger.)

Morrison's Last Theorem. If you hang in there long enough and grit your teeth hard enough, your orthodontist bill will go up. (Stan Morrison, retired basketball coach, University of the Pacific, quoted in *Sports Illustrated;* from Michael L. Lazare, Armonk, New York.)

Morrison's Second-Sheet Law. When you are doing two copies of anything, the carbon always turns out better than the original. (Vivian M. Morrison, Shreveport, Louisiana.)

Morris's Law. When writing in ink, you never make a mistake until you are at least three-fourths of the way through. (John C. Morris III, Riverside, Connecticut. Morris, who when this law was submitted was believed to be the youngest of all Murphy Center Fellows, was a fifth-grade student in the Greenwich public schools. The law was forwarded by Annie C. Harvey, one of his teachers.)

Morris's Laws of Animal Appeal. (1) The popularity of an animal is directly correlated with the number of anthropomorphic features it possesses. (2) The age of a child is inversely correlated with the size of the animals it prefers. (Desmond Morris from *The Naked Ape,* McGraw-Hill, 1967.)

Morris's Query. Isn't "behind my back" and "behind my front" the same thing? (Vernon Morris, Professor of Chemistry, Howard University.)

Morris's Tips for Beginning Writers. (1) Although most magazines maintain that they pay so much a word, virtually none of them will buy words submitted individually. Keep this in mind, and your mailing costs will nose-dive. (2) To sell inspirational pieces and "cute" poems, you *must* have a three-part name, preferably Elyse McBride Sensenbrenner. (3) The placing of Happy Face stickers on or about your manuscript does not measurably enhance its appeal. (Edward Morris, in his article "Keeping the Crayons Sharp," *Writer's Digest,* December 1977.)

Morton's Assurance. Bleeding always stops. *Morton's Law:* For difficult yes/no decisions, especially regarding the opposite sex, you'll always wish you did if you didn't, but you'll rarely wish you didn't if you did. (Joseph A. Morton, M.D., Philadelphia, Pennsylvania, who adds that this is also known as the "Ah Posteriori Law.")

Moseley's Truism. You may not always get what you pay for but you always pay for what you get. (Albert G. Moseley, West Melbourne, Florida.)

Mosher's Law. It's better to retire too soon than too late. (Representative Charles A. Mosher, R-Ohio, on retiring at seventy after sixteen years in Congress; *JW.*)

Mother Sigafoos's Observation. A man should be greater than some of his parts. (Uttered by a character of the same name in Peter De Vries's *I Hear America Swinging,* Little, Brown, 1976; *RS.*)

Motley's Hospital Questions. (1) When you're on a restricted diet, why do they always give you a roommate who isn't? (2) Do nurses give baths only during visiting hours? (3) If we can put a man on the moon, why can't we warm up a stethoscope? (4) Why do I get all the rookies? (5) Why do they always give your roommate the remote control that works? (6) Why do they always give you the bill when you're standing up? (*Motley's Crew* comic strip, March 1, 1992.)

Moulton's Law. The ease with which the toilet paper holder turns is directly proportional to the thickness of the toilet paper. (D. N. Moulton, Argyle, New York.)

Moutsatson's Law. If you don't do anything, you can't do anything wrong. (Pete Moutsatson, Chairman, Business Studies Department, Montcalm Community College, Sidney, Michigan.)

Moyers's Discovery. The worst thing you can do to the liberals is to deprive them of their grievances. (Commentator Bill Moyers, at the Democratic National Convention, August 13, 1980; *RS.*)

Moynihan's Architectural Solution. Whereas in the fall of 1980 the frame of the New Senate Office Building was covered with plastic sheathing in order that construction might continue during the winter months; and Whereas the plastic cover has now been removed revealing, as feared, a building whose banality is exceeded only by its expense; and Whereas even in a democracy there are things it is as well the people do not know about their government: Now, therefore, be it *Resolved,* that it is the sense of the Senate that the plastic cover be put back. (New York Senator Daniel P. Moynihan, text of Senate Resolution #140, May 19, 1981.)

Moynihan's Law. If the newspapers of a country are filled with good news, the jails will be filled with good people. (Senator Daniel P. Moynihan; *JW.*)

Moynihan's Maxim. Whenever any branch of the government acquires a new technique which enhances its power in relation to the other branches, that technique will soon be adopted by those other branches as well. (Senator Daniel P. Moynihan; *AO.*)

Moynihan's Revelation. Statistics will prove anything, even the truth. (Sir Berkeley Moynihan; from Bernard L. Albert.)

Mrs. Albert's Law. If the house is neat, it doesn't have to be clean. (Forwarded by Dr. Bernard L. Albert, Scarsdale, New York.)

Mudgeeraba Creek Emu-Riding and Boomerang-Throwing Association, Rule of the. Decisions of the judges will be final unless shouted down by a really overwhelming majority of the crowd present. Abusive and obscene language may not be used by contestants when addressing members of the judging panel, or, conversely, by members of the judging panel when addressing contestants, unless struck by a boomerang. (From Benjamin Ruhe's *Many Happy Returns: The Art and Sport of Boomeranging,* Viking, 1977. The rule was created to underscore the informality and casualness of boomerang competition.)

Mueth's Law. Use the last key in the bunch because that's the only one that will unlock the door. (Charles J. Mueth, Belleville, Illinois.)

Muir's (Latest) Observations. (1) There is no such thing as "a little dull." (2) Always buy thermometers in the summer because they come with more mercury. (Frank Muir, on the BBC's "My Word.")

Muir's Golden Rule of Menus. If you can't pronounce it, you can't afford it. (Frank Muir, in the *English Digest.*)

Muir's Law. If it's right and you've checked that it's right, you can be sure that someone will come along and correct you. (Georgette Muir, New York, New York.)

Muldoon-Becker Rules. (1) Software, when left unattended, rots! (2) Thank God it's Friday—only two more working days this week. (Ed Muldoon and Nick Becker, Des Plaines, Illinois.)

Mulfinger's Laws. (1) Anything will conduct electricity if the voltage is high enough. (2) Anything can be welded if the current is high enough. (George Mulfinger, Greenville, South Carolina.)

Munnecke's Law. If you don't say it, they can't repeat it. (Wilbur C. Munnecke, quoted in a letter to Ann Landers from one "Benton Harbor Ben.")

Munning's Favorite Saying. Life's short. Art's long. (Dick Francis's character Alfred Munning, *In the Frame*, Harper, 1976; from Charles D. Poe.)

Munro's Rediscovery of Defoe's Law. Only Robinson Crusoe had everything done by Friday. (C. A. Munro, London, England.)

Murchison's Law of Money. Money is like manure. If you spread it around, it does a lot of good. But if you pile it up in one place, it stinks like hell. (Clint Murchison, Jr., Texas financier, repeating his father's advice; *Time,* June 16, 1971.)

Murphy's Law(s). (1) If anything can go wrong, it will. (2) Nothing is ever as simple as it seems. (3) Everything takes longer than you expect. (4) If there is a possibility of several things going wrong, the one that will go wrong first will be the one that will do the most damage. (5) Left to themselves, all things go from bad to worse. (6) If you play with something long enough, you will surely break it. (7) If everything seems to be going well, you have obviously overlooked something. (8) If you see that there are four possible ways in which a procedure can go wrong, and circumvent these, then a fifth way, unprepared for, will promptly develop. (9) Nature always sides with the hidden flaw. (10) Mother Nature is a bitch. (11) It is impossible to make anything foolproof, because fools are so ingenious. (12) If a great deal of time has been expended seeking the answer to a problem with the only result being failure, the answer will be immediately obvious to the first unqualified person. (Having examined dozens of printed, typewritten, and photocopied listings of *Murphy's Laws,* we can report that no two are exactly alike. Even those which at first appear to have been copied by hand from one another tend to show discrepancies in order, phrasing, or both. (This is, of course, a direct confirmation of Murphian theory.) If there is any semblance of consistency, it is with the first and ninth laws, which are the same on a number of lists but not all. This confusion is so pervasive and in the spirit of Murphy that it seems to have mystic overtones—one expects that if you photocopied enough copies of a given list, eventually one would emerge with a glitch in it.

Murphylogical Research—1976 Findings

Who was Murphy Anyhow?

Good question. The Murphy Center has devoted considerable time and expense to this question. Various approaches were taken, including, for instance, contacting a fair sampling of Murphys, such as Patrick V. Murphy, former New York City police commissioner and present director of the Police Foundation in Washington. He, along with the other Murphys contacted, had no idea who the original lawmaker was. Nor, for that matter, were any meaningful clues unearthed through a study of famous Murphys, including possibilities as promising as William Lawrence Murphy (1876–1959), the inventor and man who gave his name to the fabled folding bed. However, some interesting theories and clues emerged from the quest, including the following:

- ***The Kilroy Theory.***

  Like those kingpins of World War II folklore, Kilroy and Murgatroyd the Kluge Maker, one body of thought concludes that somewhere along the line there *may or may not* have been a real Murphy, but that this is beside the point.[6] The point is that Murphy has come to represent a spirit and presence that transcends one human being. If one accepts this, then virtually any accounting works, whether it be the Edsel Murphy of the engineering magazines or the Finn Cool O'Murphy who allegedly recorded his rules on a runic scroll in the first century A.D.

- ***The Knoll Shut Theory.***

  To quote, "I'm afraid I can only offer you a conjecture about the original Murphy. Thirty years ago, when I lived in the Crown Heights section of Brooklyn, the neighborhood synagogue was widely known (at least among the young hoodlums with whom I consorted) as Murphy's Shul. I have no idea who that Murphy was, or how he happened to lend his name to an orthodox synagogue, but I have always assumed—since first I encountered Murphy's Law—that it must be the same Murphy. Somehow it figures." (Erwin Knoll, editor of *The Progressive,* in a letter to the author.)

[6] Kilroy was a household name during the war, and the line "Kilroy was here" appeared everywhere, from the hulls of battleships to the tattooed chests of sailors. There were many theories as to who he was, but none stuck. He was represented by this: Murgatroyd was a young man who finagled himself a nice billet on a ship as a "Kluge maker." He got away without doing anything for a long time, but finally, on the occasion of an admiral's visit, he was told to make a Kluge to impress the VIP. He worked all night, and just as the admiral arrived he ran up on deck, started to present it, tripped, and it fell overboard. As it sank it went, "Kluge."

• ***The Great Teacher Theory.***

To quote, "One day a teacher named Murphy wanted to demonstrate the laws of probability to his math class. He had thirty of his students spread peanut butter on slices of bread, then toss the bread into the air to see if half would fall on the dry side and half on the buttered side. As it turned out, twenty-nine of the slices landed peanut-butter side on the floor, while the thirtieth stuck to the ceiling."[7, 8]

• ***The Yulish Blur Hypothesis.***

An exhaustive search by a New York consulting firm concluded that Murphy (a) had no first name, (b) could not hold a job, (c) never prepared a resumé. Little else was known about him.

While all of these theories are worth considering, the real story may have recently come to light without great fanfare. On January 13, 1977, Jack Smith, a columnist for the *Los Angeles Times,* revealed that he had gotten a letter from George E. Nichols of the Jet Propulsion Laboratory in Pasadena stating that he not only knew the origin of the law but the true identity of Murphy. According to the Nichols letter, "The event [that led to the naming of the law] occurred in 1949 at Edwards Air Force Base . . . during Air Force Project MX981 . . . The law [was named after] Capt. Ed Murphy, a development engineer from Wright Field [Ohio] Aircraft Lab. Frustration with a strap transducer that was malfunctioning due to an error in wiring the strain gauge bridges caused him to remark [of the technician who had wired the bridges at the lab], 'If there is any way to do it wrong, he will.' I assigned the name Murphy's Law to that statement and the associated variations."

Nichols went on to point out that the law was off and running after it was alluded to in a press conference a few weeks later. A similar letter appeared in late 1977 in Arthur Bloch's book *Murphy's Law.* Further detail on Project MX981 and Murphy were supplied to the author when he contacted Robert J. Smith, Chief of the History Office at Wright-Patterson Air Force Base. Smith was unable to confirm the actual naming but was able to supply information. Murphy—graduated from West Point in 1940—was a pilot as well as an engineer, worked on a number of research projects and would be sixty years old today. The mysterious-sounding MX981 was intended "to study the factors in human tolerance to high decelerative forces of short duration in

[7] Letter to William and Mary Morris from Gary M. Klauber of Silver Spring, Md. It appears in their *Dictionary of Word and Phrase Origins,* Vol. III, Harper & Row, 1971. The Morrises solicited theories on Murphy through their newspaper column.

[8] Press release from the firm of Charles Yulish Associates in New York.

order to determine criteria for design of aircraft and protective equipment." As Smith adds, "If this project gave birth to Murphy's Law, hopefully, the consequences were minor."

Do You Believe This?

Yes, as a matter of fact, but there is still much to be said for the Kilroy theory, which says that if Ed Murphy had not discovered *Murphy's Law,* someone else would have. Then again, one of the many corollaries to *Murphy's Law* states that on the rare occasion on which something is successful, the wrong person gets the credit.

Are There Other Names for Murphy's Law?

Certainly. Other names include "Thermodamnics," "Snafu Theory," and "Klugemanship." One should also be aware of the name D. L. Klipstein, who has worked out several score corollaries for engineers. Also see the entries in this book for Finagle, O'Toole, and Sod.

Murphylogical Research—1980 Findings

An Interview with the Director of the Murphy Center

[Q] The Center's interest in the prophet Murphy and the many laws attributed to him and named in his honor is, of course, keen. Yet there still seems to be some question as to who Murphy actually was or is. Do you have any new discoveries to report?

[A] Yes. As you may recall from the Center's last report (*The Official Rules,* Delacorte, 1978) it was tentatively concluded that the great Murphy was a military man, Capt. Ed Murphy, who first announced the basic law of "If anything can go wrong it will" in 1949. Other Murphylogical scholars came to the same conclusion. But now new evidence has come to the Center's attention, posing some intriguing new possibilities.

[Q] The suspense is too much. What are they?

[A] The first comes from Theodore C. Achilles. I shall quote directly from his letter to the Center:

> Many people believe that the real author was the late Ambassador Robert Murphy. During his career of more than forty years in the

> Foreign Service during which he served, in addition to many other trouble spots, in Hitler's Germany, Laval's France, immediate post-war Germany, he accumulated monumental evidence of its validity. I suspect he formulated it definitively at the end of the 1930s. In the late 1920s as a young vice consul in Munich, he and his friend Msgr. Pacelli, apostolic delegate to Bavaria, spent an evening in a *bierstube* listening to the ranting of a young man named Adolf Hitler. After the speech and a few steins, they agreed to report to their respective authorities that the young man was merely a blowhard who was unlikely to have any significant effect on events in Germany or anywhere else. Some years later, after Pacelli had become Pope Pius XII, Bob gently reminded him of their consensus. "Ah yes," replied His Holiness, "that was before I became infallible."

Another body of evidence has reached the Center to the effect that the basic law and Murphy's name were well known during the early days of World War II. Charlie Boone, of the incomparable Boone-Ericson radio show in Minneapolis, testifies to this point: "The inspiration may go back to the training camps of World War II or earlier. At the Infantry Training School at Fort Benning, Georgia, in 1942, almost every demonstration included a Private Murphy. In the serious business of training officers, Private Murphy provided comic relief, for he never failed to take the wrong action, make the wrong decision. His negative action often reinforced the instructor's teaching better than any school solutions or field manuals could."

Still another batch of suggestions come from those who insist that, regardless of who Murphy was, the basic principle dates back centuries to a number of sources including Julius Ceasar, who once said, "*Quod malum posset futurum,*" which turns out to be Murphy's Law roughly translated. Others suggest that Murphy lies within our collective ages-old consciousness and that variations and corollaries of Murphy's Law can be found in the proverbs of many cultures: "The spot always falls on the best cloth" (Spanish), "The hidden stone finds the plow" (Estonian), and "One always knocks oneself on the sore place" (English).

[Q] Fascinating. Are there more?

[A] Just one I think is the best explanation to date. James V. Stewart of St. Petersburg, Florida, is the person who uncovered it. Let me quote from his letter:

> *Murphy's Law* was first formulated by Samuel Beckett in his novel named, of course, *Murphy*, which was first published in 1938.

As I'm sure you are aware, there is no way I would be able to know if Beckett's book is, in fact, the origin of *Murphy's Law;* nevertheless, Beckett's reference to "If anything can go wrong, it will" is earlier than any other that you cite as possible origins, so I thought you might appreciate being placed on notice.

For this wonderful bit of scholarship, the Center is bestowing on Mr. Stewart the coveted title of Fellow.

[Q] Now that we've settled that issue . . .

[A] Hold on. No research center worth its salt ever truly settles an issue, because if it did, it would soon run out of issues and put itself out of business. As befits a modern American think tank, the only true conclusion we have reached is that the need for further research is indicated.

[Q] Pardon me. On to other matters. Has the Center discovered variations and corollaries to *Murphy's Law?*

[A] Scores of them—some universal and some that have been adapted to the realities of a certain profession or pursuit. Here are some of our acquisitions:

Barton's Amendment to Murphy's Law. . . . and even if it can't, it might. (A. J. Barton, The National Science Foundation.)

Crowell's Law. *Murphy's Law* never fails. (Walter J. Crowell, Bethpage, N.Y.)

Murphy Validity Proof, The. If it's funny, it must be true. (Sidney I. Riskin, Tarrytown, New York.)

Royster's Refinement of Murphy's Law. When things go wrong somewhere, they are apt to go wrong everywhere. (Vermont Royster, in *The Wall Street Journal.*)

The Yulish Additions. • Persons disagreeing with your facts are always emotional and employ faulty reasoning. • Enough research will tend to confirm your conclusions. • The more urgent the need for decision, the less apparent becomes the identity of the decision-maker. • The more complex the idea or technology, the more simpleminded is the opposition. • Each profession talks to itself in its own unique language. Apparently there is no Rosetta Stone. (From a collection of "Murphy's Fundamental Laws" published by Charles Yulish Associates, Inc., of New York, 1975.)

Warren's Law. The likelihood of anything happening is in direct proportion to the amount of trouble it will cause if it does happen. (Sam W. Warren, editor and publisher, *The Northside Sun,* Jackson, Miss.)

Mrs. Murphy's Law. Anything that can go wrong will go wrong *while he is out of town.* (Mrs. Murphy, Valrico, Fla., quoted in Ann Landers's column of May 9, 1978.)

NBC's Addendum to Murphy's Law. You never run out of things that can go wrong. (Associated Press Television writer Peter Boyer, in his column for August 3, 1979, on NBC's problems.)

One of the most comprehensive codifications we have ever seen has to do with Murphy and marketing, which appeared in *Mainly Marketing: The Schoonmaker Report to the Electronics Industry* published by Schoonmaker Associates of Coram, N.Y., and which contains approximately sixty-five Murphylogical dictums. A small sampling:

• ***Advertising:***

The longer management delays in approving a radically new campaign, the greater the odds that a competitor will preempt the basic concept. The larger the group and the higher the rank of agency members pitching a prospect, the lower the rank and the smaller the team serving the account after the contract has been signed.

• ***Market Planning:***

In planning a related product family, the least amount of attention will be paid to the model that will prove most popular. It will prove to be impossible to meet the demand by modifying other members of the family. The more smoothly a complicated plan runs from the start, the deeper and more intricate the problems will be once the point of no return has been passed.

• ***Market Research:***

The most academically sound survey design will yield findings in terms that are least usable (such as sales in dollars when units are needed).

• ***Sales:***

Psychological testing that is 80 percent accurate will assign members of the 20 percent group to the most sensitive territories and accounts. The more cordial the buyer's secretary, the greater the odds that competition already has the order.

[Q] Is there any evidence to show that the force of *Murphy's Law* is growing?

[A] You jest. How else can one find any suitable explanation for the recent past—Watergate, the Department of Energy, the swine flu vaccine, OPEC, the "vast promise" of nuclear energy, metric conversion, tax reform, the WIN program, the gas line, the Ayatollah, and so much more. On a more workaday level it is the only way that one can explain the fact that if you left here and went to a supermarket, you would immediately gravitate to a shopping cart with either a square wheel or a wheel that is pointed in a direction that is precisely 90 degrees from the other three.

One of the things that the Center is working on right now is a collection of incidents that perfectly illustrate the law in action. Frank S. Preston of the University of North Carolina has discovered an example that fits this category of "perfect." As he reports, "One of the best cases I know of involves a World War II German airplane that was hung from the ceiling of the Smithsonian Institution for exhibit. Although this airplane survived World War II unscratched, it has crashed twice inside the Smithsonian."

Now, one of my pet instances is contained in this little clipping I carry around in my wallet. Listen to this: "Brian Chellender, twenty-nine, a bricklayer, was bending down to pick up a pin for good luck, whereupon he was knocked unconscious by a falling brick."

[Q] Hold on a second. This strikes me as somewhat depressing—downright depressing, actually—all of this dwelling on things that backfire.

[A] Not so. You have missed the point of the Law and the Center. The very fact that there is a Center that sorts, studies, and helps formalize all of this is as uplifting as—and I hate to admit this—a Jaycee Awards dinner or—more painful to admit—those silly smile faces that some people stick on their letters. You see that laying off all of these gaffs, flubs, and miscues on universal law is ultimately reassuring and comforting.

In all of our lives, there is the raw material to prove *Murphy's Law* or one of its corollaries, an amazing example of shared humanity. Rather than deny all of this, the Center celebrates the universal and unlimited imperfectability of people, organizations, and objects.

[Q] Is the Center doing research on this?

[A] Of course. One of the things we're working on right now is the "Theory of the Perverse Wind." Specifically, we have evidence that we think will eventually prove there is a particular wind that dies the minute you try to launch a kite, starts up when you drop a $20 bill, and gives off a tiny puff when you are taping something, thereby forcing the tape to stick to itself.

[Q] Very interesting. Anything else?

[A] Much more. Just to give you an idea of some of the things under investigation here, I'll quickly list some of the specific elements of the Center's research agenda:

- Zipper behavior.
- Telehydrotropism (or, in lay language, the ability of wrong numbers to ring when one is taking a bath).
- The reproductive ability of wire coat hangers.
- The aerodynamics and camouflage of the contact lens.
- Child-proof aspirin bottles that have the ability to incense adults with hangovers and refuse to open for them.
- Calculators that only go out during final exams and the day before taxes are due.
- Pocket genetics—trying to unlock the secret that will explain why your grandfather's fountain pen leaked in his pocket, why your father's ball-point pen leaked in his pocket, and why your marker pen leaks in your pocket.
- Key telekinesis—the supernatural process by which everyone gets a mystery key on his or her key ring that doesn't fit anything.
- The origin of that wonderful, universal hospital custom whereby patients are wakened from a sound sleep to take a sleeping pill.
- Finally, I should mention that we have one large-scale research project which just started. Called "Project Hercules," it is a worldwide effort enlisting all of the Center's Fellows. We are trying to see if anyone, anywhere, has actually performed certain fabled superhuman feats. For instance, we're combing the globe to find someone who has actually opened a detergent box by following the instructions, "Press flap gently, lift and pull back." Tests at our secret lab have required a minimum of one chisel, a heavy rock, and an electric saber saw to manage this. Another top priority is finding someone who has completed one of those "easy weekend" projects in the home-oriented magazines in less than a month of Sundays.

Murphy's Constant. All constants are variables. (*U/Ra.*)

Murphy's Discovery. Do you know presidents talk to the country the way men talk to women? They say, "Trust me, go all the way with me, and everything will be all right." And what happens? Nine months later you're in trouble! (Maureen Murphy, on TV's *Tonight Show; RS.*)

Murphy's Hope. Today's "hopefully" is tomorrow's "It had been hoped." (Sal Rosa, New York City.)

Murphy's Law and Correlative Collegiate Cabalae. (1) During an exam, the pocket calculator battery will fail. (2) If only one parking space is available it will have a blue curb.[9] (3) Exams will always contain questions not discussed in class. (4) All students who obtain a B will feel cheated out of an A. (5) Campus sidewalks never exist as the straightest line between two points. (6) When a pencil point breaks, the nearest sharpener is exactly 1,000 feet away. (7) At five minutes before the hour, a student will ask a question requiring a ten-minute answer. (8) If a course requires a prerequisite, a student will not have had it. (9) The office space and salaries of college administrators are in inverse proportion to those of the instructors. (10) Slightly deaf students will have instructors who mumble. (11) The next class is always three buildings away on a rainy day. (12) He who can will. He who can't, will teach. (13) When a student actually does a homework problem, the instructor will not ask for it. (14) All math classes begin at 8 a.m.; also, movies on Federal Government. (15) Students who obtain an A for a course will claim that the instructor is a great teacher. (16) If an instructor says, "It is obvious," it won't be. (17) When wool sweaters are worn, classroom temperatures are 95 degrees Fahrenheit. (18) If a student has to study, he will claim that the course is unfair. (19) Ambidextrous instructors will erase with one hand while writing with the other. (20) An A is easily obtained if a student calls the instructor "Professor." (21) When slides are shown in a darkened room, the instructor will require students to take notes. (22) When... then... (You fill in the blanks.) (M. M. "Johnny" Johnston, Ormond Beach, Fla.)

Murphy's Law Number 51. If a plank doesn't warp, it will split. (Ad for the Trus Joist Corp. in *Engineering News Record.*)

Murphy's Law of Copiers. The legibility of a copy is inversely proportional to its importance. (Letter to *AO* from C. H. Brandenburger, Butte, Montana, containing illegible photocopy of *Murphy's Laws.*)

Murphy's Law of Priorities. Whatever you want to do, you have to do something else first. (Art Kosatka, a staff assistant to Rep. John M. Murphy [!] of New York, quoted in Bill Gold's column in the *Washington Post,* March 7, 1978.)

Murphy's Law of Product Geography. The extent of problems with any new product varies directly as the distance between buyer and seller. (*ME.*)

Murphy's Law of the Open Road. When there is a very long road upon which there is a one-way bridge placed at random and there are two cars only on that road, it follows that: (1) the two cars are going in opposite directions and (2) they will always meet at the bridge. (B. D. Firstbrook, Westmount, Quebec; *AO.)*

Murphy's Law of Thermodynamics. Things get worse under pressure. (*S.T.L.*)

Murphy's Laws for Grunts. (1) Suppressive fire—won't. (2) Friendly fire—isn't. (3) When in doubt empty your magazine. (4) Never forget that your weapon

[9] Not prohibitions against X-rated movies, but curbs painted blue and reserved for "STAFF."

was made by the lowest bidder. (5) If your attack is going *really* well, it's an ambush. (6) The enemy diversion you are ignoring is the main attack. (7) If the enemy is in range, so are you. (8) Tracers work both ways. (9) If you take more than your fair share of objectives, you will have more than your fair share to take. (10) All five-second grenade fuses will burn down in three seconds. (11) Anything you do can get you shot, including doing nothing. (12) The important things are always simple. (13) The simple things are always hard. (14) The easy way is always mined. (15) Professional soldiers are always predictable, but the world is full of amateurs. (16) Murphy was a grunt. (17) If it's stupid but works, it ain't stupid. (18) Don't look conspicuous—it draws fire. (19) Never share a foxhole with anyone braver than you are. (20) Try to look unimportant. They may be low on ammo. (21) If you are short of everything except enemy, you are in combat. (22) When you have secured an area, don't forget to tell the enemy. (23) Make it too tough for the enemy to get in, and you can't get out. (24) Never draw fire—it irritates those around you. (25) The enemy invariably attacks on two occasions: (a) when you're ready for them. (b) when you're not ready for them. (26) Both sides are convinced they are about to lose; they are both right. (27) Teamwork is essential; it gives them other people to shoot at. (28) Incoming fire has right of way. (29) No inspection ready unit has ever passed combat. (30) If at first they don't succeed, they will make you try again. (This particular set of anonymously created rules and laws, which were circulated everywhere among NATO troops in the Gulf in late 1990 and early 1991, thanks to copy machines, faxes and computer modems, took their cue from the original *Murphy's Law* which holds that "If anything can go wrong, it will" and were sired by collections of laws created for the Vietnam War; e.g., "Body count math is 2 VC + 1 NVA + 1 water buffalo = 37 KIA." There were many versions of this one which came from several originals including a photocopy of a photocopy, mailed from one infantryman to another.)

Murphy's Laws of Analysis. (1) In any collection of data, the figures that are obviously correct will contain errors. (2) It is customary for a decimal to be misplaced. (3) An error that can creep into a calculation, will. Also, it will always be in the direction that will cause the most damage to the calculation. (Three of twenty-nine laws that appear in C. C. Beakly's and Ernest C. Chilton's *Introduction to Engineering Design and Graphics,* Macmillan, 1973.)

Murphy's Laws of College Publishing. (1) Availability of manuscripts in a given subject area is inversely proportional to the need for books in that area. (2) A manuscript for a market in which no textbooks currently exist will be followed two weeks after contracting by an announcement of an identical book by your closest competitor. (*Computer Science News,* December 1972.)

Murphy's Observation on Organizations and Management. Amazing! How things so wrong can last so long. (Buz Murphy, Haddonfield, New Jersey.)

Murphy's Posological Principle. For a particular ailment, the more remedies available, the less the chance of any of them working. (Peter A. Murphy, Toronto, Ontario.)

Murray's Analogy. Law sufficiently complex is indistinguishable from no law at all. (Charles Murray, *National Review,* June 10, 1988; from Charles D. Poe.)

Murray's Law (Another). The quality of restaurant food is in inverse ratio to the number of hanging plants. (David Murray, in a letter to *The New York Times,* July 26, 1983.) *Corollary:* The quality of a restaurant's food is inverse to the level of the illumination within it. (Belden Menkus of Hillsboro, Tennessee, who added, "If the place is as dark as a tomb when you enter it, the food will be terrible.")

Murray's Law. The worst whistlers whistle the most. (Robert E. Murray, San Francisco, California.)

Murray's Law (Yet One More). There are only twenty people in the whole world. (Jim Murray, GM of the Philadelphia Eagles. This law has been explored in several newspaper columns, including Tom Fox's in the *Philadelphia Inquirer,* January 9, 1983. Fox writes of Murray: "Just talk to twenty people, anywhere, anytime, and," he says with total certitude, "during the course of conversation with those twenty people you will find that you have some remarkable coincidence in common with at least one of them"; from Mack Earle.)

Murray's Laws. (1) Cars with the lucky pieces hanging off the rearview mirror will always seem to star in bad accidents. (2) You can fool all of the people all of the time—if you own the network. (3) If everything else fails, throw it away. (Jim Murray of the *Los Angeles Times,* from his column of November 23, 1978.)

Murray's Observation. Golf is the most over-taught and least-learned human endeavor. If they taught sex the way they teach golf, the race would have died out years ago. (Columnist Jim Murray in *Golf Magazine*, 1989.)

Murray's Probability. If you have a 50 percent chance of being right, 90 percent of the time you are wrong. *Proofs:* (1) When trying to decide if the word is spelled "ie" or "ei," I'm wrong 90 percent of the time. (2) There are two lines at the post office window, the bank teller's windows, or the toll gates, and you pick the slow one 90 percent of the time. (Robert H. Murray, Wescosville, Pennsylvania.)

Murray's Rule. Any country with "democratic" in the title isn't. (Columnist Jim Murray, *Los Angeles Times,* August 3, 1980; *RS.*)

Murstein's Law. The amount of research devoted to a topic in human behavior is inversely proportional to its importance and interest. (Bernard I. Murstein; *JW.)*

Muster's Law. Software "bugs" are always infectious. (Dwight A. Muster, State College, Pennsylvania.)

Muzik's Tenet. To be a research scientist, you must have a high tolerance for ambiguity. (Tom Muzik, Jubail, Saudi Arabia.)

Myers's Observation. A parent who sends a child to school with the understanding that the child is to call if he is not feeling better should expect a call. (Elementary school principal G. E. Myers, Sumpter, South Carolina.)

Mykia's Law. Has anyone, since the birth of the nation, on dropping the bathroom soap, retrieved it without discovering its need for depilation? (Mykia Taylor, Glenside, Pennsylvania.)

N

N-1 / N-minus-1 Law. If you need four screws for a job, the first three will be easy to find. (*U;* WRC Radio, Washington, D.C.)

Naden's Law. Any idea held by a person that was not put in by reason cannot be taken out by reason. (Kenneth D. Naden, Bethesda, Maryland.)

Nader's Law. The speed of exit of a civil servant is directly proportional to the quality of his service. (Ralph Nader, from *The Spoiled System,* Charterhouse, 1975, a study of the Civil Service Commission by a Nader task force; *AO.*)

Nanna's Observations. (1) Saturday's newspapers are always smaller. (2) There is always a line for the ladies' room. (R. A. Nanna, Toms River, New Jersey.)

Napa Flood Rule. Trying to stop a flood with sandbags is like trying to shove a noodle up a tiger. (Observation by a Napa, California, man flooded out by torrential rains; spotted in the Sacramento *Bee* by *TG.*)

Napier's Completeness Law. The absolute conviction that a task has been completed is a good indication that part of it remains to be done. (Thomas M. Napier, West Lothian, Scotland, who discovered the law "as a consequence of throwing out the washing-up water before finding more dishes to wash.")

Napier's Discovery. In the past 200 years, America has manufactured close to 100 billion pencils—and we still can't keep one by the phone. (Arch Napier, from *The Wall Street Journal.*)

NASA Skylab Rule. Don't do it if you can't keep it up. (Johnny Carson, the *Tonight Show,* August 2, 1979.)

NASA Truisms. (1) Research is reading two books that have never been read in order to write a third that will never be read. (2) A consultant is an ordinary person a long way from home. (3) Statistics are a highly logical and precise method for saying a half-truth inaccurately. (From a file in the NASA archives on "Humor and Satire.")

Nash's Exception. Certainly there are things in life that money can't buy, but it's very funny—Did you ever try buying them without money? (Ogden Nash.)

Natalie's Law. Aging is tough, but the alternative is worse. (Natalie Davis, Sept. 9, 2010; *TG*.)

Nathan-Dommel Law of Federal Grants. Given the chance, governments will spread benefits so as to provide something for everybody. (Richard Nathan and Paul Dommel, "Understanding the Urban Predicament," *The Brookings Bulletin,* 14:1–2, 1977.)

Nathan's Knowledge. There is never a day so bad that tomorrow couldn't be worse. (Harriet Nathan, Chicago, Illinois.)

Nations, Law of. In an underdeveloped country, don't drink the water; in a developed country, don't breathe the air. (An item that originally appeared in *Changing Times* and was quoted in the *Reader's Digest* of June 1976.)

Navy Law. If you can keep your head when all about you others are losing theirs, maybe you just don't understand the situation. (Traditional sign that has been showing up on ships and offices of the U.S. Navy for years. It is found elsewhere, too, but is primarily associated with the Navy.)

Navy Maxim. A sailor never thinks that his ship is as good as the one that he was on before, or as nice as the one he wants to be transferred to. (From Vincent A. Orbish, LCDR USN (Retired), San Diego, California.)

Nelson's Explanation. Life is nothing but a series of comebacks.(Singer Rick (Ricky) Nelson, as explained by his sons Gunnar and Matthew, interviewed by George Noory on "Coast To Coast AM," on Feb. 7, 2010.)

Nelson's Law. Negative thinking never got nobody nothing. (Bert Nelson, Los Altos, California.)

Nelson's Political Postulates. (1) A real problem exists when there is no apparent solution to the condition being evaluated by any political or legislative body.(2) When one or more political solutions exist there is no longer a real problem, only undesirable political solutions. (3) The political solution to a problem is the undesirable political solution that is disliked the least by the most. (4) The political solution to a problem is mutually exclusive of any and all real solutions that work. (Errol Nelson, Issaquah, Washington.)

Nelson's Theory of the Dead End. Everybody at a party will sift into the room that has only one door, no matter how small or cramped. (Designer George Nelson, quoted in the *Washington Post,* July 2, 1978; *JCG*.)

Nesman's Reassurance. Bomb threats are almost always false. (Les Nesman, played by Richard Sanders, on the TV show *WKRP in Cincinnati*; from Steve Stine.)

Nessen's Law. Secret sources are more credible. (Ron Nessen, President Ford's press secretary, who was quoted in *Newsweek,* January 31, 1977: "Some statements you make in public... are reported as... an unnamed source.... Nobody believes the official spokesman... but everybody trusts an unidentified source." From the latest version of Martin Krakowski's paper "Anthropogenic Ills.")

Nestor's Law. Anything worth doing makes a mess. (Sibyl W. Nestor; from Bonnie Nestor Johnson, Oak Ridge, Tennessee.)

Neudel's Laws. (1) Any organization created to unite a proliferation of splinter groups inevitably becomes another splinter group. (2) Any person hired by a bureaucracy to respond to public complaints has no power to remedy them. *Corollary:* The only people worth talking to in a bureaucracy are the ones who never deal with the public. (3) The spouse who snores always falls asleep first. (Marian Henriquez Neudel, Chicago, Illinois.)

Neuhaus' Rule. If you like a girl, her boyfriend is always a jerk. (Robert Neuhaus, Chicago, Illinois.)

Nevers. (*An assortment*): (1) Never buy a portable TV set on the sidewalk from a man who's out of breath. (From Joseph C. Goulden.) (2) Never trust a man with a tattoo on his face. (3) Never go to a dentist who has teeth painted on his lips. (From the *B.C.* comic strip.) (4) Never start a project until you've picked out someone to blame. (5) Never buy real estate from a man who works out of a tent. (From *The Wizard of Id* comic strip.) (6) Never eat prunes if you're famished. (*U.*) (7) Never play poker with a man whose nickname is a city. (Attributed to Stewart Wolpin in the November 1991 issue of *Vital Speeches.* (8) Never, ever mess with the Ladies' Auxiliary. (The Andy Griffith Show.) (9) Never wear your best pants when you go to fight for freedom. (Fortune found in an Annandale, Virginia Chinese restaurant, August 1989.)

Nevin's Nemesis. If reality won't fit the plan, then force it. (John A. Mattsen.)

Nevitsky's Observation. If a tedious job requires a certain rhythm so that it can be performed quickly and efficiently, that rhythm will be broken immediately upon psychological realization of the rhythm. (William C. Callis, Falls Church, Virginia.)

New Laws of Marriage. (1) Loose change on the bureau is community property. (2) Twice is always; i.e., if you forget to take out the garbage twice, you *always* forget to take out the garbage. (Anonymous.)

Newchy's Law of Observation. The probability of being observed is in direct proportion to the stupidity of your actions. (Newchy Mignone, Las Vegas, Nevada.)

Newell's Truisms. (1) Whenever possible, analyze planned performance—

actuals are too elusive. (2) A cumulative impact never equals the sum of its increments. (Roger Newell, Webster, New York.)

Newlan's Truism. An *acceptable* level of unemployment means that the government economist to whom it is acceptable still has a job. (Anonymous; from John W. Gustafson.)

Newman's Discovery. Your best dreams may not come true; fortunately, neither will your worst dreams. (R. A. Newman, Cherry Hill, New Jersey.)

Newman's Law. Hypocrisy is the Vaseline® of social intercourse. (*U/DRW.*)

Newman's Law. It is useless to put on your brakes when you're upside down. (Actor Paul Newman, quoted in *Playboy*; from Shel Kagan.)

Newton's Little-Known Seventh Law. A bird in the hand is safer than two overhead. (*U/S.T.L.*)

NICAR's Law. The longer you spend typing out your explanation of a problem, the faster the solution will come to you after you mail it to an entire list. (Teresa Nazario, as found on the NICAR [National Institute of Computer-Aided Reporting] e-mail list, by Bob Skole.)

Nichols's Rule of Success. Success is when your mother reads about you in the newspaper. (Mike Nichols, quoted by Henry Hanson in the *Chicago Magazine,* September 1982; from Joseph C. Goulden.)

Niebuhr's Law of the Jungle. Everyone out there is someone else's lunch. (Mike Niebuhr, Dallas, Texas.)

Nienberg's Law. Progress is made on alternate Fridays. (*U/S.T.L.*)

Nierenberg's Rule. There are times when you can't finesse any more. (William Nierenberg, quoted in *Discover,* January 1984.)

Nies's Law. The effort expended by the bureaucracy in defending any error is in direct proportion to the size of the error. (John Nies, Washington patent lawyer and *AO*'s neighbor.)

Nineteenth Hole Observation. The older I get, the better I used to be. (Overheard by reader and reported in Bob Levey's column, *Washington Post,* April 16, 1986.)

Ninety-Nine Rule of Project Schedules. The first 90 percent of the task takes 90 percent of the time, the last 10 percent takes the other 90 percent. (*Co.*)

Nixon's Principle. If two wrongs don't make a right, try three. (Laurence J. Peter. *MLS.*)

No. 3 Pencil Principle. Make it sufficiently difficult for people to do something and most people will stop doing it. *Corollary:* If no one uses something, it isn't needed. (Another important discovery from psychologist Robert Sommer. He discovered the principle when he worked for a government agency and his office manager decided to ban soft, comfortable-to-use No. 2 pencils and ordered No. 3s, which are scratchy and write light. Pencil consumption in the office went down and the office manager was able to prove that No. 3s "last longer." Sommer revealed his finding in the December 1973 issue of *Worm Runner's Digest.*)

Nobel Effect. There is no proposition, no matter how foolish, for which a dozen Nobel signatures cannot be collected. Furthermore, any such petition is guaranteed page-one treatment in *The New York Times.* (Daniel S. Greenberg, from his *Science and Government Report,* December 1976; *RS.*)

Nobel's Law of the Conversion of Trouble. Trouble is incompressible. (Joel J. Nobel, M.D., Plymouth Meeting, Pennsylvania.)

Noble's Law of Political Imagery. All other things being equal, a bald man cannot be elected President of the United States. *Corollary:* Given a choice between two bald political candidates, the American people will vote for the less bald of the two. (Bald writer Vic Gold in his *Washingtonian* article "Can a Bald Man Be Elected President?" Noble is C. Vance Noble, author of *The Hirsute Tradition in American Politics,* widely believed to be one of Gold's alter egos.)

Nock's Grim Truth. In proportion as you give the State power to do things for you, you give it power to do things *to* you; and the State invariably makes as little as it can of the one power, and as much as it can of the other. (Albert Jay Nock from his *Memoirs of a Superfluous Man,* Harper, 1943; *JMcC.*)

Nock's Sad Reminder. The hope for any significant improvement of society must be postponed, if not forever, at any rate to a future so far distant that consideration of it at the present time would be sheer idleness. (Albert Jay Nock.)

Nofziger's Law of Details. The American people aren't interested in details. (Lyn Nofziger of Ronald Reagan's campaign staff, on such matters as Senator Barry Goldwater analyzing the comparative defense capabilities of a General Dynamics prototype aircraft *vs.* Boeing's model. From Vic Gold's *PR as in President. See* Spencer's [Contradictory] Corollary.)

Nolan's Comment on Midlife Crisis. Sex takes up an infinitesimal amount of one's time, and to have to live with somebody who is listening to this crazy music while you want to listen to the Benny Goodman Quartet is a hell of a price to pay for a little sexual pleasure. (Dr. William Nolan, quoted by Bob Swift in the *Miami Herald,* January 3, 1987.)

Nolan's Law. If you outsmart your lawyer, you've got the wrong lawyer. (Attorney John T. Nolan, Iowa City, Iowa.)

Nonreciprocal Law of Expectation and Results. Positive expectations yield negative results. Negative expectations yield negative results. (*U;* Richard B. Bernstein.)

Norris's Advice. Always err on the side of truth. (Ken S. Norris, marine-mammal authority and founder of the University of California Natural Reserve System.)

Norris's Caution. Actions which invite a reaction often get an over-reaction. *Norris's Distinction:* Garlic breath is only a problem for other people. *Norris's Realization.* Getting up early to go jogging when living alone is unlikely. An audience is required when you return, soaked in sweat. (Bob Norris, Palma de Majorca, Spain.)

North Carolina Equine Paradox. VYARZERZOMANIMORORSEZASSEZANZERAREORSES? (Sign seen on the walls of print shops in North Carolina; reported to *AO* by Carl Thompson of Hill and Knowlton.)

North's Law of Investment Advisors. There are some extremely sharp investment advisors who can get you in at the bottom of the market. There are some extremely sharp ones who can get you out at the top. They are never the same people. *Corollary:* You will act on the advice of the wrong one at least 50 percent of the time. (Gary North, executive director, American Bureau of Economic Research, Durham, North Carolina.)

Norton's Laws. (1) The washer at the laundromat will turn most of your shorts inside out. But if they were inside out when you put them there, they will stay that way. Similar to *Halperin's Lingerie Law.* (2) On a cold winter morning, your car will have more snow or frost on it than anyone else's. (George Norton, Logan, West Virginia.)

Norvell's Reminder. If you would be remembered, do *one* thing superbly well. (Saunders Norvell; *ME.)*

Notes from a Life in Progress. (*A selection*): (1) Science has proven that within the breast of every organism of field-mouse rank or higher there beats the desire someday to shout "Stop the presses!" (2) Money in a wallet tends to be spent. (3) The best and the worst make history. The mediocre breed. (4) Saints always muck up the demographics. (Ryan Anthony, Tucson, Arizona.)

Notturno's Law. Stepping on the gas to get through a green light activates the red light. (Peter W., Canton, Ohio.)

Novinson's Revolutionary Discovery. When comes the revolution, things will be different—not better, just different. (Ronald M. Novinson, Alexandria, Virginia.)

Novlan's Law. If you add a lot of ice cream to humble pie, it doesn't taste too bad. (Dave Novlan, meteorologist, El Paso, Texas, July, 2010; *TG.*)

Novotney's Law of Correctives. Whenever a practice or procedure is finally seen to be irrational and intolerable, the practice or procedure instituted to correct the situation will be equally irrational. *Corollary:* Every practice or procedure is actually irrational; it is only a matter of time until it is seen to be so. (Andrew J. Novotney, S.J., Rockhurst College, Kansas City, Missouri.)

Nursing Mother Principle. Do not nurse a kid who wears braces. (Johnny Carson, the *Tonight Show,* August 2, 1979.)

Nusbaum's Rule. The more pretentious the corporate name, the smaller the organization; for instance, the Murphy Center for the Codification of Human and Organizational Law, contrasted to IBM, AT&T, etc. (Harvey Nusbaum, Rochelle Park, New York.)

Nutter's Dictum. Good judgment comes from experience, and experience comes from bad judgment. (Economist G. Warren Nutter, quoted by Walter B. Wriston in *The New York Times,* November 4, 1983.)

Nye's Maxim. Kind words will never die—neither will they buy groceries. (Bill Nye, nineteenth-century American humorist.)

Nyhan's Law. You never have more friends than the day before you announce a run for president. (David Nyhan in his *Boston Globe* column of November 3, 1995.)

Nyquist's Theory of Equilibrium. Equality is not when a female Einstein gets promoted to assistant professor; equality is when a female schlemiel moves ahead as fast as a male schlemiel. (Ewald Nyquist; *RS.*)

O

Oakland School Bulletin Board Item Notice. This Dept. Requires No Physical Fitness Program: Everyone Gets Enough Exercise Jumping to Conclusions, Flying Off the Handle, Running Down the Boss, Knifing Friends in the Back, Dodging Responsibility & Pushing Their Luck. (Found posted in an Oakland, Calif., school by Charles F. Dery, San Francisco, California.)

Oaks's Unruly Laws for Lawmakers. (1) Law expands in proportion to the resources available for its enforcement. (2) Bad law is more likely to be supplemented than repealed. (3) Social legislation cannot repeal physical laws. (Dallin B. Oaks, formerly president of Brigham Young University and president of the American Association of Presidents of Independent Colleges and Universities. The laws appeared in the essay, "Unruly Laws for Lawmakers," by Oaks, which appeared in *The Congressional Record* March 17, 1978. Oaks, who makes no effort to hide his bias against lawmaking as the solution to all problems, also uses the essay to list three hypotheses which have come out of his research on the first law: (1) The public is easily fooled by government claims of economizing. (2) An uninformed lawmaker is more likely to produce a complicated law than a simple one. (3) Bad or complicated law tends to drive out good judgment.

Obis's Law. Someone else probably has the same idea—so (a) get started, (b) plan to do it better. (Paul Obis, Jr., Milford, Connecticut.)

O'Brien's First Law of Politics. The more campaigning, the better. (Larry O'Brien, who stated it when he ran John F. Kennedy's campaign in 1960; *FL.*)

O'Brien's Law. If an editor can reject your paper, he will. *Corollary:* If you submit the paper to a second editor, his journal invariably demands an entirely different reference system. (Maeve O'Connor of *The British Medical Journal* on discovering at least 2,632 possible ways of setting out references in scientific articles. Named for O'Brien, who is first cousin to Murphy.)

O'Brien's Law of Take-out Food. No matter what or how much you order, it always takes twenty minutes. (Edward L. O'Brien, Washington, D.C.)

O'Brien's Principle (aka The $357.63 Theory). Auditors always reject any newsman's expense account with a bottom line divisible by 5 or 10. (Named for Emmet N. O'Brien and passed along to *AO* by Jake Underbill of the New York Life Insurance Company. Underbill worked for O'Brien, as did Germond of *Germond's Law. O'Brien's, Germond's,* and *Weaver's Laws* form a set that came of research conducted around Albany, New York in the early 1950s. Underbill terms the experience the "Albany Reportorial School of Economics." See also *O'Doyle's Corollary.*)

O'Brien's Rule. Nothing is ever done for the right reasons. (*U/LSP.*)

Obvious Law. Actually, it only *seems* as though you mustn't be deceived by appearances. (Donald R. Woods, Stanford, California.)

Occam's Electric Razor. The most difficult light bulb to replace burns out first and most frequently. (Writer Joe Anderson.)

Occam's Razor. Entities ought not to be multiplied except from necessity. (William of Occam, a fourteenth-century scholar, whose call to keep things simple has many modern incarnations, including the following:

- The explanation requiring the fewest assumptions is the most likely to be correct. (*JW.*)
- Whenever two hypotheses cover the facts, use the simpler of the two. (*Forbes.*)
- Cut the crap. (*Esquire.*)

O'Connor's Dicta. (1) In any classroom, the question is always more important than the answer. *Corollary:* The necessity of providing an answer varies inversely with the amount of time the question can be evaded. (2) In any piece of electronic equipment, it is foolhardy to assume that jiggling "X" will not diddle "Y," however unlikely. (Vincent D. O'Connor, Winona, Minnesota.)

O'Connor's Opinion. Everywhere I go, I'm asked if I think the universities stifle writers. My opinion is that they don't stifle enough of them. (Flannery O'Connor, collected by the late Bob Snider.)

Oddo's Axiom. *Never* say you don't know—nod wisely, leave calmly, then run like hell to find an expert. (S.M. Oddo, San Diego, California.)

Ode (Poem) to a Washer (non-human type). Oh, what is so rare, these days of machines/And soap that comes in a box/As a washer and dryer which always return/An even number of sox? (Richard M. McBride, La Jolla, California.)

O'Doyle's Corollary. No matter how many reporters share a cab, and no matter who pays, each puts the full fare on his own expense account. (Edward P. O'Doyle of Melrose Park, Illinois, to *AO*. This is a corollary to *Weaver's Law*. It is sometimes referred to as *Doyle's Corollary*.)

Oeser's Law. There is a tendency for the person in the most powerful position in an organization to spend all his time serving on committees and signing letters. (*U/Co.*)

Office Holders, First Law of. Get re-elected. (U/Co.)

Official Explanations, Law of. When the word "official" is used in conjunction with an explanation, it can only follow that the explanation is unwittingly wrong, a half-truth, or an outright lie. (This law is rediscovered with each major crisis in history, but seldom has it returned with such ferocity as it did during the 1979 Three Mile Island nuclear incident. Within forty-eight hours of the initial problem, there were seven different official explanations.)

Offut's Unnamed Law on the Development of Statistics. Garbage in; Gospel out. (Craig Offut, Fairfax, Virginia.)

Ogden's Law. The sooner you fall behind, the more time you have to catch up. (Sam Ogden, Amherst, Massachusetts; from the Letters section, *Time,* March 19, 1979.)

O'Harro's Law. Modesty is the opiate of the mediocre. (Michael O'Harro, Washington, D.C.)

O'Houlihan's Law. Don't waste your time worrying about rich people, because they sure as heck don't worry about you. (Cited in an editorial in the *Alexandria Journal* of August 27, 1991, reacting to the fact that *Regardie's* magazine had pared its list of the area's 100 richest families to 75.)

O.J.'s Revision. It doesn't matter if you win or lose... until you lose. (O. J. Simpson, on ABC's *Wide World of Sports*; from J. P. O'Shee.)

Olbers's Paradox. The contradictory fact is that the sky is dark at night, although by all calculations involving star radiance it should be as bright as the surface of the sun. (German astronomer Wilhelm Olbers. This is a useful bit of information to employ when calculated reality and reality don't jibe.)

Old Boy's Law. You don't learn anything the second time you're kicked by a mule. (*U/Ra.*)

Old Childrens' Law. If it tastes good, you can't have it. If it tastes awful, you'd better clean your plate. ("The Wizard," FM 101, Youngstown, Ohio.)

Old Doc Moos's Law. When it is necessary to choose between ignorance and stupidity, choose ignorance. It is curable. (Phil Moos, D.D.S., St. Cloud, Minnesota.)

Old Economist's Razor. If you owe your bank a hundred pounds, you have a problem; but if you owe a million, it has. (This has been attributed to John Maynard Keynes; e.g., in *The Economist,* February 13, 1982, and *Time,* September 6, 1982. However, a letter from Theodor Schuchat of Washington, D.C., points out, "No one has found it in his writings, and Lady Keynes assured me, in writing several years ago, that to the best of her knowledge he never said it.")

Old Fisherman's Rules. (1) Be there when the fish are biting. (2) He catches the most fish who does the most fishing. (Essay titled "Roccus Lineatus" [Latin name for Striped Bass]—about fishing for striped bass at Cape Cod—in *The House on Nauset Marsh* by Wyman Richardson, Norton, 1955.)

Old Fraternity Meeting Rule. The time spent at a fraternity meeting discussing any matter is inversely proportional to the significance of the matter discussed. For example, the theme for the next house party will be discussed for hours; whereas whether the fraternity should abandon its charter will occupy only a few minutes of discussion. (A. S. Boccuti, Baltimore, Maryland.)

Old Pilot's Maxim. Better to be on the ground and wish you were in the air than to be in the air and wish you were on the ground. (Quoted in Diana Griego Erwin's column in the *Sacramento Bee*, October 27, 1994.)

Old Saws Resharpened

Many of the proverbs and bits of cautionary advice we have grown up with make about as much sense today as a hearty, cholesterol-heavy breakfast to "keep you running and on top of the world" or taking up cigarette smoking to "calm the nerves." These are not ancient notions, but passed for sensible not too long ago. Lines like "Handsome is as handsome does" and "Starve a cold, feed a fever" (or is it "Feed a cold, starve a fever"?) make no sense whatsoever. Does "haste makes waste" when trying to put out a fire? Or, for that matter, don't we demand a little haste in a hospital emergency room?

We seem to be awash in inherited but wrongheaded "wisdom," flawed common sense and bad assumptions, and the fact is that a lot of the commonest aphorisms and bits of conventional wisdom are in need of scrapping or serious revision.

The realization that the proverbs and platitudes embroidered on the cushions at our grandparent's homes are no longer relevant—or in some cases, all wet from the start—is the reason why many people are creating and borrowing their own sets of rules that make sense for them. It has been said that life is a do-it-yourself project without a set of instructions. These then become the instructions. Some of them help us cope; others actually instruct.

The time is ripe for a recasting of traditional proverbs. Many of the old ones are simply worn out. Here are some proposed revisions from the files of the Murphy Center created by a number of people but with several from Philip J. Frankenfeld of Washington, D.C., who is master at the art of the revised proverb.

- A bird in the hand is superfluous.
- A fool and his money are some party.
- A penny saved is a penny.
- A penny saved is ridiculous.
- A rolling stone angers his boss.
- A rolling stone leaves broken objects in its wake.
- A watched pot is usually owned by someone without cable.
- A word to the wise is superfluous.
- As you sew, so shall you rip.
- Don't look a gift horse in the mouth . . . unless you're an equine dentist. (Heard on "All Things Considered" on NPR, April 30, 2010.)
- Don't put off until tomorrow what you can get done sometime next week.
- Early to bed gets the worm.
- Early to bed, early to rise and your girl goes out with other guys. (From a guy named John who seemed to have learned this one the hard way.)
- Exceptions disprove rules—a single exception to the law of gravity would be enough.
- He who hesitates is bossed.
- If at first you don't succeed, give up. No use being a damn fool.
- If at first you don't succeed, redefine success.
- If at first you don't succeed, you're running about average.

- If wishes were horses, you could horse upon a star.
- Many hands want light work.
- Money is the root of all evil, and man needs roots.
- Never judge a book by its cover price.
- People who live in glass houses aren't very smart.
- Practice does not make perfect (Golf, sex and child-rearing all prove this. No matter how many times we have done it, it is no easier to get up in the morning)
- The early bird catches the worm but, on the other hand, the early worm gets eaten by the bird.
- Too many cooks use lard.
- Why put off 'til tomorrow what you'll never do anyway?

Old Teacher's Law, The. Minds at rest rust. (*U;* from radio station WRC, Washington, D.C.)

Oldfield's Explanation. Hey, I just want a condo, a Mercedes—be like the other amateurs. (Shot putter Brian Oldfield, on why he tried to regain Olympic eligibility, quoted in the Anderson Valley *Advertiser.*)

Old's Conclusion. The peaking of the output of a committee versus the number of committee members [is] seven-tenths of a person. Obviously one must conclude that either further research is required or that people are no damned good. (Bruce S. Old, in his 1946 *Scientific Monthly* article "On the Mathematics of Committees, Boards and Panels.")

Olly's Observations. (1) The tap water is always coldest after you have finished your drink. (2) When you remove a bread and butter plate, your thumb always goes where the butter was. (W. A. "Olly" Herold, Islington, Ontario.)

Olmstead's Law. After all is said and done, a hell of a lot more is said than done. (Clark Olmstead, Hanau, West Germany.)

Olsen's Necktie Law. The only way to prevent getting food on your necktie is to put it in the refrigerator. (*U/Ra.*)

Olsen's Realization. Once you have pulled his pin, Mr. Grenade is no longer your friend. (Mark Olsen)

Omar's Maxim. The smaller the country, the greater the passport formalities. (Margaret K. Omar, U.S. Embassy, Tunisia.)

O'Neill's First Law of the Sea for Yachtsmen. If everything works, it's not a boat. (Bill O'Neill, Annapolis, Maryland.)

O'Neill's Law of Time Saturation. The news of the day, no matter how trivial or unimportant, always takes up more time than a married man has. *Corollary:* News stories expand and time contracts, meeting inexorably each day precisely twenty minutes after a man is supposed to be home for dinner. (Named for Ray O'Neill, who was national affairs editor of *The New York Times.* It was explained in detail in an April 22, 1956, column by James Reston, entitled "A Note to Miss Truman." Reston quotes Clifton Daniel as having told reporters that his hours at the *Times* were from 9:30 to 5:30. Countered Reston, "It is not a reporter's working hours that count, but the hours he works." He added, "These are regulated by the news, and the news is regulated by a very simple mathematical rule." The rule, of course: *O'Neill's Law.*)

O'Neill's Observation. Nobody is too old to learn—but a lot of people keep putting it off. (William O'Neill, Diamond Bar, California.)

Oppenheimer's Observation. The optimist thinks this is the best of all possible worlds; and the pessimist knows it. (J. Robert Oppenheimer, in *The Bulletin of the Atomic Scientists,* February, 1951; *RS.*)

Optimum Optimorum Principle. There comes a time when one must stop suggesting and evaluating new solutions and get on with the job of analyzing and finally implementing one pretty good solution. (Robert Machol, in his *POR* series. To illustrate the point of this principle, he points out that some years ago, an ABM expert said that for optimal protection, the entire continental United States could be covered with a mile-thick layer of peanut butter—it would be impenetrable and have the support of the peanut industry. Says Machol, "The point of this anecdote is that the solutions which may be suggested for a problem are inexhaustible.")

Orben's Ornithological Statistic. There are 40 million pigeons in the United States—30 million are birds, and the rest are people who pay $40 for designer blue jeans. (Bob Orben, Arlington, Virginia.)

Orben's Packaging Discovery. For the first time in history, one bag of groceries produces two bags of trash. (Humorist Robert Orben. See also his *Travel, First Law of.*)

Orben's Query. If sex is such good medicine, how come everybody always needs a refill? (Bob Orben, Falls Church, Virginia.)

Organizational Inaction, The Four Theorems of. (1) *The Time Theorem:* The present is too soon (or too late) to discuss any important issue. (2) *The Subject Matter Theorem:* The topic is too narrow (or too broad) to be considered. (3) *The Group Size Theorem:* The group is too small (or too large) for effective action. (4) *The Excitement Theorem:* The topic is too controversial (or too dull) to deal with. (In "The Principles of Organizational Inaction," by J. Barnstep Clagg and Norma Mealstom, in *The Bureaucrat,* Summer 1979.)

Organizational Parable. Once upon a time there was a handsome young lion. He was captured in the African jungle and brought to America, where he was put on display in a zoo. This made the lion very unhappy because he preferred the freedom of his wild native land and the companionship of other jungle beasts. But after a time he became resigned to his fate and made up his mind that if he had to live behind bars, he would be the best zoo lion around. In an adjoining cage there was another lion, an old and lazy one with a negative responsibility and no signs of ambition or capability of any kind. He lay all day in the sun, arousing no interest from visitors. In sharp contrast, the young lion paced for hours back and forth in his cage. He acted the true King of Beasts, rolling his maned head, snarling and baring his teeth. The crowds loved him. They paid no attention to the indolent old lion asleep in the next cage. The young lion appreciated the attention he was getting, but he was annoyed by his failure to win adequate reward. Each afternoon the zookeeper came through the cages to feed the animals. The lazy old lion, who made no effort to please the spectators, was given a big bowl of red horsemeat. The young lion, now a star attraction, was given a bowl of chopped-up oranges, bananas, and nuts. This made him very unhappy. "Perhaps," he mused, "I am not trying hard enough. I will improve the act." So he strutted longer and more spectacularly. To the snarls and gnashing of teeth he added frequent roars that shook the bars of his cage. The crowds got bigger. Thousands of citizens came to see his performance, and he was pictured on page one in the local newspaper. But the diet did not change. Still the lazy lion got the red meat, and the young lion stayed on a vegetarian diet. Finally he could endure it no longer. He stopped the keeper with a challenge. "I'm getting sick and tired of this," he complained. "Each day you give that no-good lazy type next door a big bowl of meat, and you feed me oranges, bananas, and nuts. It is grossly unfair. Why do you think all these people come to the zoo? They come to see me. I'm the star attraction, the lion that's doing all the work, and the one that gets the results. Why am I not entitled to meat for dinner?" The keeper did not hesitate with his reply. "Young man," he said, "you don't know how lucky you are." "Our Table of Organization in this zoo calls for one lion. You are being carried as a monkey." (*FSP.*)

Oristano's Laws of Personal Service Contract Negotiations. If you want to play the game, you have to play the game. When negotiating salary, let your conscience be your guide, plus 20 percent. (Mark Oristano, Arlington, Texas.)

Ormerod's Rule. Don't try to think like the top until you are the top. (David Ormerod, Middletown, Ohio.)

Orwell's Bridge Law. All bridge hands are equally likely, but some are more equally likely than others. (After George Orwell by Alan Truscott, in his *New York Times* bridge column for December 23, 1974.)

Osborn's Law. Variables won't, constants aren't. (Don Osborn, associate director, State of Arizona Solar Energy Commission; *S.T.L.*)

OSHA's Discovery. Wet manure is slippery. (The Occupational Safety and Health Administration [OSHA], in a finding reported in *Washington Post* of June 18, 1976. This replaces an earlier U.S. Navy finding: "Classified material is considered lost when it cannot be found.")

O'Shee's Observation. It always works better in the commercial. (J. P. O'Shee, Ville Platte, Louisiana.)

Oshry's Laws. (1) It only snows on sale days. (2) Memorandums say less than memos. Memos say less than picking up a phone. (3) No name, no matter how simple, can be understood correctly over the phone. (James B. Oshry, Elizabeth, New Jersey.)

Osman's Law. If the plug will only fit into the socket one way, you will always put it in the wrong way first. (Charles I. Osman, Hampton, Virginia.)

O'Steen's Rules of Illness. (1) The germ will keep the child home from work (i.e., school) but not play (i.e., ball game). (2) The opposite is true for adults. (Joan O'Steen Hill, Oak Ridge, Tennessee.)

Ostmark's Rules. (1) *Taxis:* Taxis have two speeds: 20 and 80 miles per hour. (2) *The Road:* On a narrow road when you come up to a stalled car, bicycle rider, or pile of gravel, you will invariably meet another vehicle coming from the opposite direction at that precise moment even if you don't meet another for your entire trip. (3) *Deciphering Tourist Brochures:* The words "magical" and "enchanting" in travel ads mean your drinks will cost four times more than they're worth, plus you get sandflies. (H. Eugene Ostmark, San Pedro, Honduras.)

O'Sullivan's Law. An organization that is not explicitly right-wing will become left-wing over time. (John O'Sullivan, *National Review*, July 31, 1995.)

O'Toole's Commentary on Murphy's Law. Murphy was an optimist. (Perhaps the most quoted of all the laws and corollaries to come in as a result of the *AO* columns, yet the name of the author or discoverer of the commentary is illegible. This unreadable signature could quickly lead to a situation in which O'Toole could raise as many questions as Murphy. Rumor has it that O'Toole was [a] a policeman in Newark during the 1967 riots and [b] a White House clerk during the last months of the Nixon Administration.)

O'Toole's Observation. Nothing is done so ineptly that the federal government cannot make it worse. (John E. O'Toole, Chairman, Foote, Cone and Belding.)

O'Toole's Rule. It is far better to play Hamlet in Denver than to play Laertes in New York. (Actor Peter O'Toole; *MLS.*)

Otten's Law of Testimony. When a person says that in the interest of saving time, he will summarize his prepared statement, he will talk only three times as long as if he had read the statement in the first place. (*AO.*)

Otten's Law of Typesetting. Typesetters always correct intentional errors, but fail to correct unintentional ones. (*AO.*)

Otten's Revision. The wages of sin are royalties. (Jane Otten, in *Washington Post,* February 12, 1978; Richard Nixon, Wilbur Mills, Margaret Trudeau, etc.)

Ottinger's Analogy. Remember that a politician is like a contraceptive: he gives you a reasonable feeling of security while you are being screwed. *Ottinger's Law of the Executive Task:* When faced with a situation you "wouldn't touch with a ten-foot pole," your duty is to seek out a store selling eleven-foot poles. (Charles Ottinger, Mercerville, New Jersey.)

Owens's Law. All humans will defend, on moral grounds, that which fattens their pocketbooks. (Gwinn Owens, in the *Baltimore Evening Sun*, May 9, 1979; *ME.*)

Oxford Rule. Isn't is is not, it isn't ain't, and it's it's, not its, if you mean it is. If you don't, it's its. Then too, it's hers. It isn't her's. It isn't our's either. It's ours, and likewise yours and theirs. (A very useful rule from Oxford University Press that appeared in *Edpress News,* April 1979.)

Ozard's Rain Rule. The amount of rain is directly proportional to the length of time your raincoat is at the dry cleaner. (Bill Ozard, Calgary, Alberta.)

Ozark's Blessing. His limitations are limitless. (Baseball manager Danny Ozark, on infielder Mike Andrews.)

Ozian Deception. Pay no attention to that man behind the curtain. (The Wizard of Oz to Dorothy and friends, from the 1939 film; from Larry Groebe, San Antonio, Texas.)

Ozian Option. I can't give you brains, but I can give you a diploma. (The Wizard of Oz to the Scarecrow; *RS.*)

Ozmon's Laws. (1) If someone says he will do something without fail, he won't. (2) The more people talk on the phone, the less money they make. (3) People that go to conferences are the ones who shouldn't. (4) Pizza always burns the roof of your mouth. (Howard Ozmon, Richmond, Virginia.)

P

Pachter's First Law of Packing. The only way to avoid packing too little is by packing too much. *Pachter's Second Law of Packing: The First Law* doesn't work. You're going to forget something important anyway. (Josh Pachter.)

Paige's Six Rules for Life (Guaranteed to Bring Anyone to a Happy Old Age). (1) Avoid fried foods which angry up the blood. (2) If your stomach disputes you, pacify it with cool thoughts. (3) Keep the juices flowing by jangling around gently as you move. (4) Go very lightly on the vices, such as carrying on in society, as the social ramble ain't restful. (5) Avoid running at all times. (6) Don't look back, something might be gaining on you. (Baseball immortal Satchel Paige. These first appeared in *Collier's* magazine, June 13, 1953, as a sidebar to an article about Paige. It is one of the most famous sets of life rules ever set in print. Despite this, they are often mangled in the re-quoting—"Don't look behind something might be catching up with you," is how it appears in one non-baseball book (*The Rivals: America and Russia Since World War II*, Viking, 1971 by Adam B. Ulam). For many years after they appeared, Paige gave out business cards with his rules on the back. When Frank Deford left *Sports Illustrated* after 29 years in 1987, he was asked to write some words of advice and listed Paige's rules, adding one of his own: (7) Choose your friends in inverse proportion to how seriously they pay attention to the NFL draft. (*Sports Illustrated* May 8, 1989). *Paige's Addenda to the Six Rules:* (1) Work like you don't need the money. (2) Love like you've never been hurt. (3) Dance like nobody's watching. (*Satchel Sez,* Three Rivers Press, 2001.)

Pajari's Postulate Study. (Of particular interest to those developing proofs of hypotheses posed in math textbooks). If it couldn't be proved, it wouldn't be in the book. (George Pajari, Vancouver, British Columbia.)

Paliwoda's Premise. The best way to make money is not to lose it. (Steve Paliwoda, Anchorage, Alaska.)

Palmer's Comment on Retirement. It really bothers me to think I may never throw a home-run pitch again. (Jim Palmer, reflecting on his forced retirement from the Baltimore Orioles, quoted in *Sports Illustrated.*)

Palmer's Law. The only thing better than a lie is a true story that nobody will believe. (Joe Palmer.)

Pancake House Rule, The. If anything is sticky, everything is sticky. (KMOX call-in September 24, 1989.)

Pancoast's Periodical Discovery. The part of a magazine cover that you especially want to see has been covered with the address label. (Charles Pancoast, Akron, Ohio.)

Pandora's Rule. Never open a box you didn't close. (Mike Berman, Killeen, Texas.)

Pangraze's Secret. Plan Backward! (Joe Pangraze, Lynn, Massachusetts.)

Panic Instruction for Industrial Engineers. When you don't know what to do, walk fast and look worried. (Bob Duckies, now with the Department of Commerce, picked this up from a plant engineer who had learned it at the Ford Motor Company.)

Paper's General Law. Printing a text in any writing system other than Roman, Greek, or Cyrillic most likely results in text appearing either upside down or backwards. (Herbert H. Paper, Hebrew Union College, Jewish Institute of Religion, Cincinnati, Ohio.)

Paper's Other Laws. (1) The older you get, the more like yourself you got. (2) If a museum owns one cuneiform tablet, the likelihood is very high that it will be displayed upside down. (Herbert H. Paper, Dean, School of Graduate Studies, Hebrew Union College, Cincinnati, Ohio; from his letter in *The Biblical Archaeology Review,* May/June 1979. Paper adds in a letter to the Center that the law is applicable to any unfamiliar script—for instance, a recent U.S. government poster in which Korean script is displayed is upside down.)

Paradox of Selective Equality. All things being equal, all things are never equal. (Marshall L. Smith.)

Pardee's Law. There is an inverse relationship between the uniqueness of an observation and the number of investigators who report it simultaneously. (A. B. Pardee, in his 1962 *American Scientist* article "pU, a New Quantity in Biochemistry"; *FD.*)

Pardieck's Laws of Commencement. (1) The amount of ceremony, pomp, and circumstance involved in a commencement program is in inverse proportion to the level of education. (2) The value of the graduation gift received is in inverse proportion to class rank. (Robert L. Pardieck, Director of Placement, Bradley University, Peoria, Illinois.)

Pardo's Postulates. (1) Anything good is either illegal, immoral, or fattening. (2) The three faithful things in life are money, a dog, and an old woman. (3) Don't care if you're rich or not, as long as you can live comfortably and have everything you want. (*U/S.T.L.*)

Parent's Law. By the time you're right, you're dead. (Sally Winter, Spring Valley, New York.)

Pareto's Law. (The 20/80 Law, The 80/20 Law.) The significant items in any group make up a relatively small portion of that group. Twenty percent of the customers account for 80 percent of the turnover, 20 percent of the components account for 80 percent of the cost, and so forth. Conversely, 80 percent of what you learn will come from 20 percent of what you read, etc. (After Vilfredo Pareto, the Italian economist/sociologist; *S.T.L.*)

The Parkinson Contribution

On November 19, 1955, an unsigned article appeared in *The Economist* simply entitled, *Parkinson's Law.* As it was put in the first sentences:

It is a commonplace observation that work expands so as to fill the time available for its completion. Thus, an elderly lady of leisure can spend the entire day in writing and dispatching a postcard to her niece at Bognor Regis. An hour will be spent in finding the postcard, another in hunting for spectacles, half an hour in search of the address.

The article went on to point out that the law came with two axiomatic additions that helped relate it to organizations:

Factor I—An official wants to multiply subordinates, not rivals; and
Factor 2—Officials make work for each other.

In proving his contentions, the mysterious Parkinson showed, for example, that between 1914 and 1928 the number of ships in the Royal Navy went down by 67.74 percent, while the number of dockyard officials and clerks went up by 40.28 percent, and Admiralty officials by a stunning 78.45 percent.

At first many thought that Parkinson was a fanciful name created by the magazine's editors. He was, in fact, C. Northcote Parkinson, a little-known history professor at the University of Malaya. Within a few years Parkinson became an international celebrity. His book was a bestseller on both sides of the Atlantic and found its way into fourteen languages. He became an immensely popular lecturer, visiting professor, and essayist who occasionally added another law to his collection. As *Dun's Review* summed it up in a 1975 article on him, "Parkinson has made a lucrative twenty-seven-year career out of [a few] seemingly simple words." Parkinson, who lived on the island of Guernsey during his final years, was asked many times why he thought his law had such an impact and seemed to be as well used and widely quoted today as it was when it was newly coined. He always responded by saying that the main reason is that the law is true. He told *Dun's Review,* "[It] is as valid today as it was twenty years ago, because as a rule of nature it is immutable."

Here is a documented collection of Parkinson's laws:

- ***Parkinson's First Law.***
  Work expands so as to fill the time available for its completion.
- ***Parkinson's Second Law.***
  Expenditure rises to meet income.
- ***Parkinson's Third Law.***
  Expansion means complexity and complexity, decay; or to put it even more plainly—the more complex, the sooner dead.

- ***Parkinson's Law of Delay.***
  Delay is the deadliest form of denial.
- ***Parkinson's Law of Medical Research.***
  Successful research attracts the bigger grant, which makes further research impossible.
- ***Mrs. Parkinson's Law.***
  Heat produced by pressure expands to fill the mind available, from which it can pass only to a cooler mind.
- ***Parkinson's New Law.***
  The printed word expands to fill the space available for it.
- ***Parkinson's Principle of Non-Origination.***
  It is the essence of grantsmanship to persuade the Foundation executives that it was they who suggested the research project and that you were a belated convert, agreeing reluctantly to all they had proposed.
- ***Parkinson's Finding on Journals.***
  The progress of science varies inversely with the number of journals published.
- ***Parkinson's Telephone Law.***
  The effectiveness of a telephone conversation is in inverse proportion to the time spent on it.
- ***Parkinson's Law of 1,000.***
  An enterprise employing more than 1,000 people becomes a self-perpetuating empire, creating so much internal work that it no longer needs any contact with the outside world.[10]

The Parkinson contribution is twofold. First, his law is not only noteworthy when an institution shows that it is an exception to it rather than an example of it. Many years ago the late Anthony Lewis wrote in *The New York Times* that the Supreme Court "alone" among the great

---

[10] 1. Book of the same title, Houghton Mifflin, Boston, 1957. 2. Essay of same title from *The Law and the Profits,* Houghton Mifflin, 1960. 3. Essay of same title from *In-Laws and Outlaws,* Houghton Mifflin, 1962. 4. Book of the same title, Houghton Mifflin, 1971. 5. Article of same title, *New Scientist,* 13:193 (1962.) 6. Book of the same title, Houghton Mifflin, 1968. 7. Article of same title, *Reader's Digest,* February 1963. 8. Same source as number 5. 9. *JIR,* Vol. 11/2.10. Article of same title, *The New York Times Magazine,* April 12, 1974. 11. This appears in various locations, including direct quotes from Parkinson that appear in F. P. Adler's "Relationship between Organization Size and Efficiency," *Management Science Journal,* October 1960. Parkinson also told Adler, "With a research establishment the same point is reached but only after the staff is double that size" (i.e. 2,000).

institutions did not conform to the law. At the end of 1976, *Newsweek* asked if Jimmy Carter could repeal the law during his administration; evidence suggests he did not. Second, Parkinson, more than anyone else, helped break the stranglehold of the pure sciences and mathematics on immutable laws, principles, and named effects. He paved the way for others and created an atmosphere in which an explanation like this could appear in *The Manchester Guardian*: "...much blame must attach itself to the [U.N.] administrative system, which has not only set out to prove *Parkinson's Law,* but which religiously follows the *Peter Principle* of promoting mediocrities."[11]

In addition to the basic set of laws there are these which Parkinson added:

Parkinson's Architectural Law. When an organization commissioned an architectural masterpiece for itself, it was almost always done at precisely the moment when that organization was on its last legs. (C. Northcote Parkinson, 1958. "During a period of exciting discovery or progress, there is no time to plan the perfect headquarters," he wrote. "The time for that comes later, when all the important work has been done. Perfection, we know, is finality; and finality is death." Writing in *Facades* magazine, Witold Rybczynski presented a 1998 corollary to *Parkinson's Law:* "Just as perfect buildings mask decaying institutions, a new institution that starts life by building a perfect building risks choking itself." The magazine added: "There is a recent tragi-comic example. The American Center in Paris set out to make its mark by hiring the celebrated architect Frank Gehry to design its new building. Gehry delivered a characteristically striking design. It was perfect: it won awards, the architectural critics loved it, it made the American Center an overnight sensation. The problem was that the construction was expensive, indeed, so expensive that the building stood empty for months after it was finished. The American Center for Paris is now up for sale. Only ailing organizations need apply." *Facades*, Summer, 1998.)

Parkinson's Eighth or *Tenth* (who's counting?) *Law.* The chief product of a highly automated society is a widespread and deepening sense of boredom. (C. Northcote Parkinson, in an interview that appeared in *The New York Times,* September 25, 1987.)

[11] Hella Pick, *The Manchester Guardian Weekly,* July 25, 1970.

Parkinson's Postulate for Elevators. The fewer the floors an elevator has to serve, the more time it takes for the elevator to travel between each floor. (Steve Charnovitz, Falls Church, Virginia, who has dedicated his postulate to C. Northcote Parkinson.)

Parkins's Deduction. If a system is too complex for one person to understand, it is too complex for any finite number of people to understand it. (Richard P. Parkins, Hampshire, England.)

Parliament, Simple Rules for Interpreting Acts of. Always avoid reading the preamble, which is likely to confuse rather than to enlighten. It sets forth not what the act is to do, but what it undoes, and confuses you with what the law was instead of telling you what it is to be. When you come to a very long clause, skip it altogether, for it is sure to be unintelligible. If you try to attach one meaning to it, the lawyers are sure to attach another; and, therefore, if you are desirous of obeying an act of Parliament, it will be safer not to look at it, but wait until a few contrary decisions have been come to, and then act upon the latest. When any clause says either one thing or the other shall be right, you may be sure that both will be wrong. (This comes from an old British Comic Almanac and appears in the anthology *Comic Almanac,* edited by Thomas Yoseloff, published by A. S. Barnes and Co., New York, 1963.)

Parry's Law of Weather Forecasting. When the weatherman predicts 30 percent chance of rain, rain is twice as likely as when 60 percent chance is predicted. (J. Thomas Parry, Rockford, Illinois.)

Parson Weems's Law. Historical fancy is more persistent than historical fact. (*American Heritage,* April 1971. A law that explains Washington and the cherry tree, Pilgrims leaping onto Plymouth Rock, Lincoln courting Ann Rutledge, and more.)

Parsons's Honesty Rule. If someone shouts a reply to your questions, "Well, to be honest," you are entitled to assume that up to that moment, he has been telling the most appalling lies. (Denys Parsons, London, England.)

Parsons's Laws. (1) If you break a cup or plate, it will not be the one that was already chipped or cracked. (2) A place you want to get to is always just off the edge of the map you happen to have handy. (3) A meeting lasts at least 1½ hours, however short the agenda. (4) A piece of electronic equipment is housed in a beautifully designed cabinet, and at the side or on top is a little box containing the components which the designer forgot to make room for. *Parsons's Rule:* At whatever stage you apologize to your spouse, the reply is constant—"It's too late now." *Parsons's Rules for Collectors:* An essential factor in collecting anything at all is to start twenty years ago. (Denys Parsons, London, England.)

Passman's Paradox of Flexible Mortality. There are plenty of things you can do to help you live longer; there is nothing that you can do to help you live forever. (David L. Passman, Chicago, Illinois.)

Pastore's Comment on Michehls's Theorem. Nothing is ultimate. *Pastore's Truths:* (1) Even paranoids have enemies. (2) This job is marginally better than daytime TV. (3) On alcohol: four is one more than more than enough. (Jim Pastore, former Control Data Corp. manager; *S.T.L.*)

Patient's Rule. (*Concerning his symptoms*): It is not a matter of life and death—it's much more important than that. (*U;* originally quoted in Dr. Robert Matz's article "Principles of Medicine," which appeared in the January 1977 issue of the *New York State Journal of Medicine.*)

Patinkin's Admonition. Never buy a used car if the radio buttons are all on hard-rock stations. (Mark Patinkin, *Providence Journal;* from Ben Willis, Jr.)

Patrick's Theorem. If the experiment works, you must be using the wrong equipment. (*U; Scientific Collections.*) Same as *Bowie's Theorem.*

Pat's Subscription Law. If I want to know when my magazine subscription expires, the date on the sticker on the cover of the magazine is in a computer code that I can't decipher. (Ralph C. "Pat" Wolfe, Walnut, Illinois.)

Patton's Law of Sacrifice. You don't win wars by dying for your country; you win wars by making the other poor bastard die for his country. (General George Patton; from Joseph A. Morton, M.D., Philadelphia, Pennsylvania.)

Patton's Laws of Immortality. No one is considered immortal until he is dead. (Rick Patton, LaHabra, California.)

Paturi Principle. Success is the result of behavior that completely contradicts the usual expectations about the behavior of a successful person. *Reciprocity Theorem:* The amount of success is in inverse proportion to the effort in attaining success. (Felix R. Paturi, pseudonym for a successful management engineer, who explains his principle and other theories in *The Escalator Effect,* Peter H. Weyden, 1973. The book contains many examples of the principle in operation. Here is just one: a small child who needs to get home quickly begins walking slower. He eventually stops and makes the "inaccurate and therefore inverse statement, 'I just can't anymore.' So then daddy carries him home.")

Paul Principle. People become progressively less competent for jobs they once were well equipped to handle. (Paul Armer, director of Stanford University's Computation Center, who first described it for a large audience in the June 1970 issue of *The Futurist.* Armer is very concerned with the occupational hazard of "technological obsolescence" and argues for educational sabbaticals and other forms of continuing education. It was written, in part, in response to the *Peter Principle.*)

Paula Principle. In a hierarchy, women are not allowed to rise to their level of incompetence. (This discovery was announced in a paper "The Paula Principle and Women's Liberation," by Benjamin Mittman, Evanston, Illinois. Mittman examined the *Peter Principle* ["In a hierarchy, every employee tends to rise to his level of incompetence"] and asked the following: "[If] the *Peter Principle* were universally true, why has not society crashed into the chasm of incompetence? How can institutions, governments, and business survive? What has prevented the *Peter Principle* from destroying civilization? What mitigating influence has saved us?" The answer is the *Paula Principle,* which has "sustained society"; *RS.*)

Paulg's Law. Remember: In America it's not how much the item costs, it's how much you save. (Sale ad for Kroch's & Brentano's Bookstores, the *Chicago Tribune,* December 7, 1978.)

Paul's Commentary. There is so much apathy in the world today...but who cares? (Steven J. Paul, Rapid City, South Dakota.)

Paulson's Solution for a Stagnant Career. Sex discrimination need not stifle your opportunities for career advancement if you are flexible enough to consider a sex change. (Pat Paulson; from John A. Mattsen.)

Payack's Update. One hologram is worth 1,000,000,000 words. (Peter Payack, *The New York Times,* October 1, 1980.)

Payne's Observation. There is no man so low some woman does not want him. (Mabel Payne, Indianapolis, Indiana.)

Pea Soup Anderson's Law. We do pea soup well and we make the most out of that. (Ray Beitez, of Pea Soup Anderson's Restaurant, Buellton, California, quoted by Jim Sullivan in *Service That Sells Newsletter.*)

Peachum's Principle. The road to good intentions is paved with hell. (Ted Peachum, in Peter DeVries's *Consenting Adults,* Penguin, 1981; *RS.*)

Peacock's Laws of Teaching. (1) You never teach an easy class. Neither does anyone else. (2) Any lesson consists of 60 percent instruction, 40 percent discipline, and 5 percent embarrassing mistakes. (Norman Peacock, Bedford, England.)

Pearson's Principle of Organizational Complexity. The difficulty in running an organization is equal to the square of the number of people divided by the sum of their true applied mentalities. For example:

Normal Individual:

$$\frac{1^2}{1} = 1.$$

Family of four (one teen, one child):

$$\frac{4^2}{1+1+.5+.3} = 5.71$$

Government:

$$\frac{\text{Many}^2}{13.2} = \infty$$

(Carl M. Pearson, Dallas.)

Peary's Preachment. Many are cold, but few are frozen. (Attributed to the Arctic explorer by Col. William C. Hunter in his *Brass Tacks,* Reilly & Britton, 1910.)

Peck's Laws. (1) Experience is the ability to recognize the same mistake when you make it again. (2) "That won't hold water" is probably what everyone said to the man who invented the sieve. (3) The tremendous advantage of being paranoid is that everything fits. (4) Creative cynicism is the only mortar which can bind rock-headed optimism into the cement of civilization. (Edward L. Peck, Chevy Chase, Maryland.)

Pecor's Health Food Principle. Never eat rutabagas on any day of the week that has a "y" in it. (Charles J. Pecor, Macon, Georgia.)

Peer's Theorem. The person you're leaving a note for always appears just as you finish writing it. (Mrs. Clifford R. Peer, Palos Verdes Estates, California.)

Peers's Law. The solution to a problem changes the nature of the problem. (John Peers, president, Logical Machine Corp.)

Pendleton's Law of Background Music. The inappropriateness of the "background" music in the restaurant will be exceeded only by its volume. *First Corollary:* The more inappropriate the music, and the greater the volume, the more likely it is that you will be seated directly beneath a cracked speaker. *Second Corollary:* The more inappropriate the music, the greater the chance that it was selected by the bus boy. *Third Corollary:* The louder the music, the greater the chance that the volume was set by the dish washer so he could hear it in the kitchen. *Fourth Corollary:* If the music is so bad and so loud that you feel it necessary to complain, the hostess/manager will be at least two generations removed, and no doubt convinced there is nothing wrong. *Fifth Corollary:* Even if your spouse agrees that the music is bad and loud and your complaint was ignored, said spouse will veto any notion of changing restaurants. *Sixth Corollary:* The more offensive the music, the greater the chance that you funded the composer through the National Endowment for the Arts. *Seventh Corollary:* If Congress passes a law to address this problem, it will require restaurants to play more music funded by the National Endowment for the Arts. (Ken Pendleton, Indianapolis, Indiana.)

Penner's Principle. When the math starts to get messy—QUIT! (*U;* From an unsigned, typewritten paper entitled "Handbuch Für Uplousen das Laboratorywerke und Ubercovern das Grosse Goofups"; *TJR.*)

Pennsylvania Dutch Saying (paraphrased). Blondness don't last; brains do.

(In *The Gold Solution,* St. Martin's, 1983; by Herbert Resnicow; from Charles D. Poe.)

Penny-Pincher's Rule. On the day your bill comes to $10.04, you won't be carrying any pennies. On the day you want to get rid of your pennies, it'll come to $10.00 exactly. (Tom Gill, Davis, California.)

People's Action Rules. (1) Some people who can, shouldn't. (2) Some people who should, won't. (3) Some people who shouldn't, will. (4) Some people who can't, will try, regardless. (5) Some people who shouldn't, but try, will then blame others. (Bob Kerr, who says these rules apply to a host of activities, including driving, gambling, and drinking.)

Pepperoni Principle of Conflict Resolution. When facing a fight that cannot be won or that might prove too costly, order a pizza. (From an August 14, 1987, *Christian Science Monitor* editorial in which it was pointed out that White House lobbyist Tom Loeffler had dropped by House Speaker Jim Wright's house with a pizza on the way to an agreement between the two.)

Pepys's Prediction. If we give women equal rights, the next thing you know, they'll want to send their children to the same schools as our children. (Roy West, Philadelphia, Pennsylvania.)

Perelman's Point. There is nothing like a good painstaking survey full of decimal points and guarded generalizations to put a glaze like a Sung vase on your eyeball. (S. J. Perelman, quoted in *RS*'s *Expectation of Days,* 1974.)

Perfection Unmasked. If your own performance of a job looks perfect to you, it isn't because you've done a perfect job. It's only because you have imperfect standards. (*U/ME.*)

Perlsweig's Law. People who can least afford to pay rent, pay rent. People who can most afford to pay rent, build up equity. (*U/DRW.*)

Perot's Political Polemic. What most politicians stand for is re-election. If you can organize the grass roots, you could probably get a law passed saying the world's square. (H. Ross Perot; from Nick Kass.)

Persius's Point. How sweet it is to have people point and say, "There he is." (Roman poet and satirist Persius.)

Perversity of Nature, Law of the (aka Mrs. Murphy's Corollary). You cannot successfully determine beforehand which side of the bread to butter. (*Co.*)

Perversity of Production Precept. If it works well, they'll stop making it. (*AO* credits Jane Otten and Russell Baker for this law. See also *Herblock's Law,* which it is close to.)

Peter Principle, Corollaries, Inversion, etc. *Peter Principle:* In every hierarchy, whether it be government or business, each employee tends to rise to his level of incompetence; every post tends to be filled by an employee incompetent to execute its duties. *Corollaries:* (1) Incompetence knows no barriers of time or place. (2) Work is accomplished by those employees who have not yet reached their level of incompetence. (3) If at first you don't succeed, try something else. *Peter's Inversion:* Internal consistency is valued more highly than efficiency. *Peter's Law:* The unexpected always happens. *Peter's Paradox:* Employees in a hierarchy do not really object to incompetence in their colleagues. *Peter's Placebo:* An ounce of image is worth a pound of performance. *Peter's Theorem:* Incompetence plus incompetence equals incompetence. (Dr. Laurence J. Peter and Peter Hull, from their book *The Peter Principle,* William Morrow and Co., 1969, with the exception of *Peter's Law,* which is from *PQ.* The *Peter Principle* ranks with *Parkinson's Law* and *Murphy's Law* as one of the most famous and widely applied laws of modern life. The *Peter Principle* is not without its critics, as others have attempted to revise or amend it [see, for instance, the *Paul Principle*], and no less an authority than Parkinson has remarked that it does not always work out in real life. Parkinson says that we get on an airplane with a fairly high level of confidence that the pilot and navigator will be able to find their destination. He concluded, however, that Peter had a right to make the conclusion that he did since he had spent his life in an area where the principle is literally true—institutions of higher education. In 2010, twenty years after Peter's death, a Google search for "The Peter Principle" yields 3,260,000 hits.)

Peter's Paradoxical Paradox. Man is complex—he makes deserts bloom and lakes die. (Dr. Laurence J. Peter, *Los Angeles Times,* March 8, 1983.)

Petersen's Law of Business Reports. The length of a report has an inverse relationship to the author's status in the organization. (Dean M. Petersen, Memphis, Tennessee.)

Petersen's Postulate. Any sentence beginning "Ironically" will not contain an irony. (Clarance Petersen, *The Chicago Tribune.* See *White's Certainties No. 4* for a Corollary to *Petersen's Postulate.*)

Peterson's Admonition. When you think you're going down for the third time, just remember you may have counted wrong. (Rolfe Peterson, quoted by Bennett Cerf in *The Laugh's on Me,* Doubleday, 1959.)

Peterson's Law. History shows that money will multiply in volume and divide in value over the long run. Or expressed differently, the purchasing power of currency will vary inversely with the magnitude of the public debt. (Economist William H. Peterson, from his article in the November 1959 issue of *Challenge.*)

Peterson's Rules. (1) Trucks that overturn on freeways are filled with something sticky. (2) No cute baby in a carriage is ever a girl when called one. (3) Things that tick are not always clocks. (4) Suicide works only when you're bluffing. (Donna Peterson, San Gabriel, California.)

Peters's Principle of Success. Get up one time more than you're knocked down. (Country singer Jimmie Peters, quoted in the *San Antonio Express News,* January 19, 1979.)

Peters's Secret. The secret of life is that there is no secret of life. (Kurt M. Peters, San Francisco, California.)

Peters's Third Law of Politics. The number of parking tickets issued declines in direct proportion to the number of days remaining before the next municipal election. (Charles Peters, *Washington Monthly.*)

Petroff's 27th Law of Hierarchical Behavior. Humility decreases with every promotion, and disappears completely at the vice-presidential level. *Corollary:* Arbitrariness increases with every promotion, and becomes absolute at the vice-presidential level. (John N. Petroff, Dhahran, Saudi Arabia.)

Petty's Pronouncement on Personal Pacing. In order to finish first, you must first finish. (Race car driver Richard Petty; from David Little.)

Pfeifer's Philosophy. All of life is rejection. Make sure you are thrown out by the best. *Pfeifer's Test for a Great Truth:* The opposite of one great truth is another great truth. (Catherine Pfeifer, Milwaukee, Wisconsin.)

Pfister's Law of Teaching. Overteach, because students underlearn and overforget. (Fred R. Pfister, Point Lookout, Missouri.)

Phases of a Project. (1) Exultation. (2) Disenchantment. (3) Confusion. (4) Search for the Guilty. (5) Punishment of the Innocent. (6) Distinction for the Uninvolved. (Project manager's wall poster, Battelle Memorial Institute, Columbus, Ohio.)

Phelps's Law of Retributive Statistics. An unexpectedly easy-to-handle sequence of events will be immediately followed by an equally long sequence of trouble. (Charles Phelps, RAND Corp. economist; *AO.*)

Phelps's Laws of Renovation. (1) Any renovation project on an old house will cost twice as much and take three times as long as originally estimated. (2) Any plumbing pipes you choose to replace during renovation will prove to be in excellent condition; those you decide to leave in place will be rotten. (Lew Phelps, Chicago, Illinois; *AO.*)

Philanthropy, First Law of. It is more blessed to give than to receive, and it's deductible. (*The Wall Street Journal; TCA.*)

Phillips' Investment Rule #1. Every time you have a 50–50 chance of being right, you're wrong about 90 percent of the time. (Douglas E. Phillips, Senior Partner & CEO, Oxford Capital Group, Nashville, Tennessee, who appends his law with this note: "After 21 years in the business, it still stands true.")

Phillips's Academic Laws. (1) *Practicality:* Anything that works is not scholarly.

(2) *Clarity:* The best way to confuse people is to make something perfectly clear. (3) *Writing:* You can prove you have been a writer by producing what you have written. You can never prove you are going to be a writer. (4) *Competency:* To the extent a student is competent, he offends the teacher who is not. (5) *Promptness:* If you can't do it correctly, do it by the deadline. (6) *Plagiarism:* If you footnote every seventh line, you will never be accused of plagiarism. (Gerald M. Phillips, University Park, Pennsylvania; from a larger collection.)

Phillips's Rule of Planning. Remember the future is written in sand—the past in concrete. (Sherry A. Phillips, Wichita, Kansas.)

Phister's Law. Sometimes, it turns out you plan ahead. (Monte Phister, who explained in an e-mail of December 5, 2000. "I'm a computer engineer, and in the '50s I worked for a company that made stock market quotation systems. We were improving our keyboard by adding a display. The keyboard console had an insert at the top which was used for several display lights, and we found out that four digits of a commercially available numerical display fit perfectly into that insert—though of course, we designed a console with no idea we would later add a display. I made the remark, 'it turns out we planned ahead' and it became something of a slogan for us engineers at Quotron Systems.")

Pi R Rule.

πr^2

πr^2—Pie are square.
$\pi r^{\not 2}$—Pie are not square!
πr°—Pie are round.
Cr^2—Cornbread are square.
(From Wayne C. Fields, Jr., Newcastle, Cal., who found it on the wall of the library men's room at the California State University, Sacramento.)

Pickle's Law (Jake). If Congress must do a painful thing, the thing must be done in an odd-numbered year. (Representative Jake Pickle, quoted by James J. Kilpatrick.)

Pickle's Law (Micah). Numbers are rational, people aren't. (Micah "Mike the Pickle" Kenfield, Houston, Texas; *TG*, April 2010.)

Pidduck's Principle. A pessimist only receives *pleasant* surprises. (Ruth Piddick, Lachine, Quebec.)

Pierson's Law. If you're coasting, you're going downhill. (L. R. Pierson; from *Rumsfeld's Rules.*)

Pietropinto's Peter Pan Principle. Marriages peter out or pan out. (Anthony Pietropinto, M.D., in *Husbands and Wives,* Times Books, 1979.)

Pike's Law of Punditry. Success provides more opportunities to say things than the number of things the pundit has worth saying. (Douglas Pike, Washington, D.C.)

Pilot's Report. I am lost, but I'm making record time. (Anonymous pilot somewhere over the Pacific, World War II; Andrew Weissman, New York, New York.)

Pipe, Axiom of the (aka Trischmann's Paradox). A pipe gives a wise man time to think and a fool something to stick in his mouth. (From *S.T.L.* collection; According to Conrad Schneiker, Trischmann worked in system design at CDC in Sunnvale, California and "yes, he did have a pipe.")

Piper's Givens. (1) Fat people use more soap than thin people. (2) There is always plenty of good free cheese in a rat trap. (3) Today's gifts are tomorrow's yard sales. (4) Fifty percent of all doctors graduated in the bottom half of their class. (James W. Piper, Concord, New Hampshire.)

Pirus Law of Cumulative Clutter. Accumulation of old magazines is directly proportional to the cost of the publications and their relationship to special interests, and inversely proportional to the number of persons in the household. (Douglas I. Pirus, *The Journal of Irreproducible Results,* 1988; from Norman D. Stevens.)

Pitsinger's Law of Negative Motivation. The ability of anyone to do anything is reduced proportionately to the strength of the thought that one can't, until a point is reached where the individual believes they cannot and they truly can't. (Roger Pitsinger, Lake Oswego, Oregon.)

Pittelko's Distinction. Getting unstuck is not the same as coming unglued. (Mike Pittelko.)

Pitt's Hypothesis. When things go wrong, there are always two faults, the second of which becomes apparent only after the first has been rectified. (*U; Adhesives Age* magazine, March 1979; *ME.*)

Plato's Distinction. Man is a two-legged animal without feathers. (Plato.)

Plato's Observation. People who campaign for the other party are called ward heelers. People who campaign for your party are said to be interested in ensuring the survival of the democratic system. (Ed Karl, whose dog is named Plato.)

Player's Razor. They say Sam Sneed is a natural golfer. But if he didn't practice, he'd be a natural bad golfer. (Gary Player on the importance of practice.)

Plimpton's Correlation. There exists an inverse correlation between the size of a ball and the quality of writing about the sport in which the ball is used. (The correlation was suggested by the late George Plimpton, who explained, "I have a theory: The larger the ball, the less the writing about the sport. There are superb books about golf, very good books about baseball, not many good books about football, and very few good books about basketball. There are no books about beach balls." It may have first appeared in *Sports Illustrated*, May 10, 1982. Plimpton may be the exception to his own rule as his book about his moment of glory with the Detroit Lions, *Paper Lion*, Harper, 1966, may be one of the best books ever about football, which overshadows Plimpton's "small ball" books.)

Plotnick's Lament. My pot of gold lies at the end of a circle. (Bernard Plotnick, Pompano Beach, Florida.)

Plotnick's Third Law. The time of departure will be delayed by the square of the number of people involved. Simply stated, if I wish to leave the city at 5 p.m., I will most likely depart at 5:01. If I am to meet a friend, the time of departure becomes 5:04. If we were to meet another couple, we won't be on our way before 5:16, and so on. (Paul D. Plotnick, Stamford, Connecticut, in a letter to *The New York Times,* April 7, 1968; *FD.*)

Plugge's Barb. The day Microsoft makes something that doesn't suck is probably the day they start making vacuum cleaners. (Ernst Jan Plugge. This first appeared on Usenet on April 27, 1988.)

Plunkitt's Principles of Practical Politics. (1) I seen my opportunities and I took 'em. (2) There's only one way to hold a district: you must study human nature and act accordin'. (3) The politicians who make a lastin' success in politics are men who are always loyal to their friends, even up to the gate of state prison, if necessary. (4) We've got hookworms, too, in the organization. But we don't make them district leaders. We keep them for ornaments on parade days. (5) Above all things, avoid a dress suit. (6) You see, there's degrees of patriotism just as there's degrees in everything else. (7) A political organization has to have money for its business as well as a church, and who has more right to put up than the men who get the good things that are goin'? (8) I'm one of the best friends the saloon men have—but I don't drink their whiskey. (9) Tammany don't care to get in the papers. It goes right along at tendin' to business quietly and only wants to be let alone. (10) I see a vision. I see the civil service monster lyin' flat on the ground. I see the Democratic party standin' over it with a foot on its neck and wearin' the crown of victory. I see Thomas Jefferson lookin' out from a cloud and sayin': "Give him another sockdologer; finish him." And I see millions of men wavin' their hats and singin' "Glory Hallelujah!" (George Washington Plunkitt, quoted from *Plunkitt Of Tammany Hall: A Series Of Very Plain Talks On Very Practical Politics,* by William L. Riordon, first published in 1905 (Dutton paperback, 1963). Full subtitle: *A Series of Very Plain Talks on Very Practical Politics, Delivered by Ex-Senator George Washington Plunkitt, the Tammany Philosopher, from his Rostrum—the New York County Court House Bootblack Stand;* from Neal Wilgus.)

Poer's Laws. *Los Angeles Driving:* You can't go around the block. *Motion Picture Production:* It's not the time it takes to take the take that takes the time; it's the time between the takes that takes the time. (John M. Poer, Canoga Park, California.)

Poe's Observations. (1) Sylvester Stallone is the thinking man's Chuck Norris. (2) Any accountant who has joined a band of anti-government guerrillas is a revolutionary fiduciary. (Charles D. Poe, Houston, Texas.)

Pogo's Dictum. A long run of good luck is a sure sign of bad luck. (Pogo; from Michael L. Lazare, Armonk, New York.)

Poker, Iron Law of. The winners tell funny stories; the losers cry "Deal!" (*U/MLS.*)

Pole's Law. Every American president makes his predecessor look good. (J. R. Pole, *The New Republic,* May 16, 1983.)

Political Law of Nature. To err is human; to blame it on the other party is politics. (From *The Light Touch,* edited by Charles Preston, Rand McNally and Co., 1965.)

Political Leadership, The First Law of. Find out where the people want to go, then hustle yourself around in front of them. (James J. Kilpatrick, in *Nation's Business,* January 1979.)

Politicians' Rules. (1) When the polls are in your favor, flaunt them. (2) When the polls are overwhelmingly unfavorable, (a) ridicule and dismiss them, or (b) stress the volatility of public opinion. (3) When the polls are slightly unfavorable, play for sympathy as a struggling underdog. (4) When too close to call, be surprised at your own strength. (*U/JW.*)

Politico's Law. No one ever lost an election for a speech he didn't make. (*MLS.*)

Pollock's Discovery. Whichever way you stand, when you empty the Hoover bag, the dust always blows in your face. (H. M. Pollock, Sevenoaks, Kent, England.)

Pollyanna's Educational Constants. The hyperactive child is never absent. The student who hit the teacher is the one with the lawyer. Just because the specialists find a label for a child doesn't mean they know what's wrong with him. (Susan Ohanian, Troy, New York.)

Polsby's Law of Families. The children of your parents' friends are always nerds. (Presidential scholar Nelson Polsby; *AO.*)

Pompey's Law of Harassment. If you are getting run out of town, get in front of the crowd and make it look like a parade. (Sherman Lee Pompey, Florence, Oregon.)

Poole's Rule of Flattery. Always address recipients of typed correspondence as "Dr." You will be either correct or flattering. (Charles Poole, Washington, D.C.)

Poorman Flaw, The. In any home improvement project, there will be one mistake so gross that the only solution is to incorporate it into the design. (Paul A. Poorman, Ohio.)

Poorman's Rule. (1) When you pull a plastic garbage bag from its handy dispenser package, you always get hold of the closed end and try to pull it open. (2) The defroster on the passenger side of your car always works better than the one on the driver side. (3) It is always the up escalator that is being repaired. (Paul A. Poorman, Ohio.)

Pope's Garage Sale Law. You will get your own junk back in three years. It will cost twice as much. You didn't need it until you sold it. You won't need it after you buy it back. (William G. Pope, Somers, New York.)

Popplewell's Law of Retirement. Eat 'til you're sleepy. Sleep 'til you're hungry. (W. Popplewell, Wills Point, Texas.)

Pop's Law. Watched boils never pop. (Paul Seabury, who submitted this law on his stationery from the Hoover Institution on War, Revolution, and Peace, Stanford, California.)

Porter-Givens's Perception. The delay and expense involved in any action soar in perpendicular proportion to the number of approvals essential to take that action. (Columnist Sylvia Porter and Attorney Richard A. Givens, from Porter's column, August 11, 1978.)

Porter's Home Rule. Home is where your garbage is. (David Porter; from Ian MacPherson, Regina, Saskatchewan.)

Posner's Distinction. Only tax-supported institutions are closed on a minor holiday. (George E. Posner, Berkeley, California.)

Potter's Law. The amount of flak received on any subject is inversely proportional to the subject's true value. (*U/S.T.L.*)

Poulsen's Law. When anything is used to its full potential, it will break. (*U/DRW.*)

Pournelle's Pronouncement. Sometimes it may be better to have it Wednesday than perfect. (Jerry Pournelle, *Byte,* December 1983; from Shel Kagan.)

Povich's Rule on Dollars and Forgiveness. Forgiveness is directly proportional to dollars. Where there is big money, there is big forgiveness. (Adapted from the *Washington Post's* late sportswriter Shirley Povich, quoting the "Fight Doctor" Ferdie Pacheco on July 3, 1997, referring to the second Tyson/Holyfield fight.)

Powell's Law. Never tell them what you wouldn't do. (Adam Clayton Powell, cited by Julian Bond in a radio interview.)

Powell's Laws. (1) Bad news does not improve with age. *Corollary:* When in doubt, get it out. (2) (For handling professional baiters at daily briefings and other appropriate problems of life.) Indifference is the only sure defense. (Jody Powell, President Carter's press secretary.)

Powell's Variation on Murphy's Law. We have found over and over that if any statement can be screwed up and reported in a way that is disquieting to the public and the economy, it will be screwed up. (Jody Powell, quoted in the *Washington Post,* June 6, 1979.)

Powell's Warning. Avoid having your ego so close to your position that when your position fails, your ego goes with it. (Colin Powell, quoted in *USA Weekend,* September 3, 1993.)

Pratley's Prophecy. The fixing of one malfunction results in damage or malfunction to another part of the thing being fixed. (James R. Pratley, Rancho Bernardo, California, quoted in Jack Smith's column, *Los Angeles Times,* sometime in 1985.)

Pratt, The Rules of. (1) If an apparently severe problem manifests itself, no solution is acceptable unless it is involved, expensive, and time-consuming. (2) (a) Completion of any task within the allocated time and budget does not bring credit upon the performing personnel—it merely proves the task was easier than expected. (b) failure to complete any task within the allocated time and budget proves the task was more difficult than expected and requires promotion for those in charge. (3) Sufficient monies to do the job correctly the first time are usually not available; however, ample funds are much more easily obtained for repeated major redesigns. (From an undated clipping from *IEEE Spectrum.*)

Pratt's Rules. (1) A travel clock must be wound at least every twelve hours or it will stop, unless it is in the suitcase at home—then it will run for three days without winding. (2) When the regulated want to make a change, it is a laborious process; however, when the regulatory agency wants to make a change, a simple clarification of the regulations is all that is required. (Harvey A. Pratt, Catonsville, Maryland.)

Prentice's Congressional Constant. There are two periods when Congress does no business: one is before the holidays, and the other after. (American journalist and humorist George D. Prentice.)

Preudhomme's Law of Window Cleaning. It's on the other side. (*U/DRW.*)

Pribram's Laws Of Subjective Behaviorism. (1) A train of thought once set in motion tends to remain in motion. A mind at rest tends to remain at rest. (2) For every truth there is an equal and opposite half-truth. (3) The force of attraction between a speaker and his ideas is inversely proportional to the mass of the evidence and directly proportional to the square of the distance to the truth. (Karl Pribram, Radford University; from Donald Hall, Radford, Virginia. Submitted with an unsigned handout entitled "The Story of Pribram's Laws": In San Francisco during the early 1960s there was a time when the Beatniks had faded from view but the Flower Children had not yet blossomed. In such a time enterprising academicians needed a new theme around which to organize their public gatherings [a "hook," as it were, by which paying customers and foundation grants could be attracted]. They hit upon the idea of interdisciplinating and induced their colleagues to actually do it collectively in public view. It was at such a gathering under the title of "Control of the Mind" that Karl Pribram was one of the invited interdisciplinators. After his presentation a member of the audience approached him and asked, "But where *is* the mind?" "That's like asking, '*Where* is gravity?'—gravity isn't down there someplace," he replied, pointing toward the center of the earth. That incident has passed into the oral tradition of conference groupies and gradually extended in the brilliance of its Newtonian spirit to the form in which it appears above. As far as is known, however, this is its first expression in written form. At the same conference a psychiatrist friend of Dr. Pribram's was taking criticism from a radical behaviorist who objected to the very use of the word mind. "All right," he said, "I don't have to use the word 'mind.' Let's talk about subjective behaviorism." So to honor the insights of interdisciplinators in that historic moment, we now speak of *Pribram's Laws of Subjective Behaviorism.* But then we also recall the famous statement of that great American intellect, benefactor, and industrialist Henry Ford when he said, "History? History is bunk!")

Price's Advice. It's all a game—play it to have fun. (C. Kevin Price, Plymouth, Minnesota.)

Price's First Law. If everybody doesn't want it, nobody gets it. (Roger Price from his book *The Great Roob Revolution*; from Roger Knights.)

Price's Rule. A fool and his money get a lot of attention from headwaiters. (Roger Price, from *In One Head and Out the Other,* Simon and Schuster, 1951.)

Price's Law of Politics. It's easier to be a liberal a long way from home. (Don Price, dean of Harvard's Graduate School of Government, who discovered this when working with foundations that were more willing to undertake controversial projects overseas than in the United States; *AO.*)

Price's Law of Science. Scientists who dislike the restraints of highly organized research like to remark that a truly great research worker needs only three pieces of equipment: a pencil, a piece of paper, and a brain. But they quote this maxim more often at academic banquets than at budget hearings. (Don Price; *RS*'s *Expectation of Days,* 1978.)

Prince Philip's Rule. Never pass a bathroom. (The Duke of Edinburgh; from Robert J. T. Joy, M.D., Bethesda, Maryland.)

Prince's Actuarial Axiom. Destiny is statistics by another name. (J. M. Prince, University of Tennessee, Knoxville.)

Principal's Principle. Star quarterbacks always take classes from teachers who give passing grades. (Principal Murdo I. MacLeod, Santa Ana, California.)

Priorities, Two Laws About. (1) Nobody dies wishing they'd spent more time with their business. (2) Better to be a king for a night than schmuck for a lifetime. (From Steve Stine, who heard the second from the character Rupert Pupkin [Robert De Niro] in the movie *King of Comedy*.)

Probable Dispersal, Law of. (Sometimes called *The How Come It All Landed on Me Law*.) Whatever hits the fan will not be evenly distributed. (Logical Machine Corporation ad, the *New Yorker,* 1976.)

Procrastination, Laws of. (1) Procrastination shortens the job and places the responsibility for its termination on someone else (the authority who imposed the deadline). (2) It reduces anxiety by reducing the expected quality of the project from the best of all possible efforts to the best that can be expected given the limited time. (3) Status is gained in the eyes of others, and in one's own eyes, because it is assumed that the importance of the work justifies the stress. (4) Avoidance of interruptions, including the assignment of other duties, can be achieved, so that the obviously stressed worker can concentrate on the single effort. (5) Procrastination avoids boredom; one never has the feeling that there is nothing important to do. (6) It may eliminate the job if the need passes before the job can be done. (*U/DRW.*)

Proctor's Discovery. Virtue is its own revenge. (Mert Proctor, *Stars and Stripes*.)

Professional's Law. Doctors, dentists, and lawyers are only on time for appointments when you're not. (Rozanne Weissman, Washington, D.C.)

Professor Gordon's Rule of Evolving Bryographic Systems. While bryographic plants are typically encountered in substrata of earthly or mineral matter in concreted state, discrete substrata elements occasionally display a roughly spherical configuration which, in the presence of suitable gravitational and other effects, lends itself to combined translatory and rotational motion. One notices in such cases an absence of the otherwise typical accretion of bryophyta. We therefore conclude that a rolling stone gathers no moss. (*U/S.T.L.*)

Proposal-Writing Rules. (1) Never mention money. "Resources" is the prime substitute, although "allocations" and "appropriations" are also popular. (2) Fluff up a proposal with the sort of euphemisms that bestow an aura of importance without revealing anything specific. (Louis Kaplan, planner, quoted in *Newsweek,* May 6, 1968.)

Propriis's Bottom Line. A man should be intelligent enough to wish he were more so. (*U/RA.*)

Proverbial Law. For every proverb that so confidently asserts its little bit of wisdom, there is usually an equal and opposite proverb that contradicts it. (Writer Richard Boston in a review of *The Oxford Dictionary of English Proverbs* which appeared in *The New Statesman* for October 9, 1970. "Though many hands make light work, too many cooks spoil the broth," is just one example of Boston's discovery.)

Proverbs in Need of Revival. (1) An emperor may have the measles. (2) The man who breaks his eggs in the center is a fool. (3) Shave with a file if you like, but don't blame the razor. (4) The hasty man drinks his tea with a fork. (5) New milk is not got from a statue. (From an old British almanac, quoted in *Comic Almanac*, edited by Thomas Yoseloff, A.S. Barnes and Co., 1963.)

Proverbs Revised. (1) Early to bed gets the worm. (2) Two in the bush is the root of all evil. (3) People who live in glass houses are not too smart. (4) All's fair when you settle out of court. (5) A rolling stone gathers smashed objects in its path. (The first two from James O. Stevenson, Bethesda, Maryland; the second two written by schoolchildren and quoted by Johnny Carson on the *Tonight Show;* number 5 from Margie Mereen, Burnsville, Minnesota, who got it from her husband.)

Pryor's Observation. How long you live has nothing to do with how long you are going to be dead. (Richard Pryor, on the *Tonight Show.*)

Public Relations Client Turnover Law. The minute you sign a client is the minute you start to lose him. (James L. Blankenship, senior vice-president, the public relations firm of R. C. Auletta and Co. Inc., New York, New York.)

Public Relations Priority. Incoming fire has the right of way. (Anonymous. As explained by a leading crisis public relations firm: "When your product and/ or company is under enemy fire, resist the impulse to respond in kamikaze fashion. Think and respond strategically. Step out of harm's way, assess the situation, identify your attackers' weaknesses and then execute your response." From Joe Goulden. This rule also appears as Rule 2 in the collection known as *Murphy's Laws of Combat.*)

Public Relations Truism. There's nothing either good nor bad that can't be made more so. (Earle Ferris, public relations counsel, quoted in *The Care and Feeding of Executives*, by Millard C. Foeght and Lawrence Hammond, Wormwood Press, 1945.)

Public Relations, Prime Rules of Political. (1) Experts do not like surprises. It makes them look bad at the home office (e.g., JFK picking LBJ, Nixon picking Agnew, Reagan picking Schweiker). (2) Never say maybe in the same circulation area where you just said never. (Vic Gold; from his *PR as in President.* The second was written relative to candidate Jimmy Carter saying no embargoes on grain shipments at the Iowa State Fair and then telling newspaper editors in Des Moines that he would make exceptions in times of national emergency.)

Public Speaking, First Rule of. Nice guys finish fast. (*Reader's Digest,* June 1976.)

Pugh's Theory of the Individual Quotient of Vice. When abandoning a vice or vices, one will, sooner or later, substitute a new vice or vices which offset the vice or vices abandoned. (Restated from an article on this topic by Jodie T. Allen, *Washington Post*, January 1, 1988. It is named for Robert Pugh of George Mason University. The principle also applies to cultural behavior. The author of the article asks, "What can so simply and satisfactorily explain the rise of pornography in this country as the concomitant disappearance of spitoons?")

Pugsley's Revision. Nobody's human. (M.E. Pugsley, Salt Lake City, Utah.)

Purina Paradox. You don't need to fly to have more fun with wings. (Writer Joe Anderson discovered this law when he covered a story for *The Daily Oklahoman* in 1949. Let him explain: "In the late forties, a Midwestern university and a manufacturer of chicken feed collaborated in breeding a wingless chicken which would prove meatier and more tender because it didn't flop around as much. It has never reached the market, however, because a rooster uses his wings to balance himself while in the process of impregnating a hen.")

Putney's Law. If the people of a democracy are allowed to do so, they will vote away the freedoms which are essential to that democracy. (Snell Putney in *The Conquest of Society,* Wadsworth Publishing, 1972; *JW.*)

Putt's Law. Technology is dominated by two types of people: those who understand what they do not manage and those who manage what they do not understand. (Archibald Putt [pseudonym], in *Research/Development* magazine, January 1976; *ME.* It was later expanded into the book *Putt's Law and the Successful Technocrat: How to Win in the Information Age*, Wiley-Interscience, 2006.)

Putt's Laws of Survival. (1) To get along, go along. (2) To protect your position, fire the fastest-rising employees first. (Archibald Putt, in *Research/Development* magazine; from Paul J. Lambeck. Belden Menkus of Hillsboro, Tennessee notes that the first of these was used by Sam Rayburn, the long-time speaker of the U.S. House of Representatives, in the 1930s and 1940s in a lecture that he gave every two years to incoming members of that body. He also used to advise them: "Don't get mad; get even.")

Q

Q's Law. No matter what stage of completion one reaches in a North Sea (oil) field, the cost of the remainder of the project remains the same. (*U/GT.*)

Qaddafi's Dietary Qualifier. We plant roses, we breed chickens, and we eat candy—but before we eat candy, we must eat the kidneys of our enemies. (Libyan dictator Muammar Qaddafi, quoted in *US News and World Report*, 1986.)

Quality of Life Constant. Each time in your life when you think you are about to be able to make both ends meet, somebody moves the ends. (*U/Ra.*)

Quick's Law of Women's Panties and Men's Briefs. When one puts one's foot through the wrong hole, the undergarment must be completely removed before the situation can be corrected. (David J. Quick, Brentwood, California.)

Quigley's Law. Whoever has any authority over you, no matter how small, will attempt to use it. (Anonymous; received in an unmarked envelope.)

Quigley's Laws. (1) If you take off your right-hand glove in very cold weather, the key will be in your left-hand pocket. (2) Any system that works perfectly will be revised. (3) Backfire hurts only those who get behind things. (4) Courage of conviction results in the conviction of courage. (Martin Quigley, editor of the *Midwest Motorist; EV.*)

Quinn's Creed of the Follower. Lemmings know something we don't. (A. W. Quinn, Arlington Heights, Illinois.)

Quinn's Law. Whenever a golfer messes up a hole with a series of unfortunate shots and unaccountable tragedies before reaching the green, said golfer will invariably three putt. (Eleanor and Floyd Taylor, Los Angeles, California.)

Quinn's Rule on Staying Alive as a Financial Forecaster. Give 'em a number or give 'em a date, but never give 'em both at once. (Jane Bryant Quinn, quoted in Bob Levey's *Washington Post* column of February 5, 1988.)

Quinn's Rules to Eat By. (1) Never eat in a restaurant that calls itself a nightclub. (2) Never eat in any restaurant recommended by anybody who teaches in a college. (3) Never eat in an empty restaurant. Everybody who's not there must know something. (4) Never eat in any restaurant with a souvenir shop attached. (5) Never order bratwurst in a Chinese restaurant. (From a much longer list that appears in *But Never Eat Out on a Saturday Night,* Doubleday, 1983; by Jim Quinn.)

Quinn's Sporting Proposition. The only thing on the level is mountain climbing. (Eddie Quinn from Bill Gerk.)

Quinn's Understanding. Economists carry their projections out to two decimal points only to prove they have a marvelous sense of humor. (Jane Bryant Quinn, quoted by *RS* in *An Expectation of Days,* 1986.) Similar to one of Fiedler's forecasting rules.

Quin's Postulate. A man must sometimes rise above principle. (Representative Percy Edwards Quin, Mississippi, 1921.)

Quirk's Zipper Discovery. Zippers tend to fail at crucial moments simply because they are treacherous, back-stabbing little fiends. (Dr. Emory Quirk, the Cleveland Institute of Inanimate Hostilities, quoted in a column by Dan Myers, the *San Francisco Chronicle,* June 3, 1979.)

Quisenberry's Theory of Relativity. I have seen the future, and it's a lot like the present, but much longer. (The late Kansas City Royals pitcher Dan Quisenberry, quoted in the *St. Petersburg Times* by Roger Angell, April 8, 1985.)

Quixote's Conclusion. Facts are the enemy of truth. (Don Quixote, in *Man of La Mancha;* from William C. Young, Ballston Lake, New York; quoted by Bob Levey in the *Washington Post*, September 3, 1979.)

R

Rabbe's Revision. The check's in the fax machine. (Don Rabbe, Lincoln, Nebraska.)

Rabinowitz's Rule. Let a smile be your umbrella, and you'll get a lot of rain in your face. (The character Gary Rabinowitz on the television show *Archie Bunker's Place; TG.*)

Rabinow's Law. If the top man is no good, all the people below him will be no good in the same way. (Jacob Rabinow, National Bureau of Standards; *FSP.*)

Racker's Remark. Scientific discoveries pass through three stages: first, they are disbelieved; second, they are believed but rejected as trivial; finally, they are accepted as correct and significant but dismissed as old hat. (Efraim Racker; from David Welford, Birmingham, England.)

Radcliffe's Rule. There's no such thing as a single call to a federal agency. (Charles W. Radcliffe, Minority Counsel, House Committee on Education and Labor, quoted in the *National Report for Training and Development,* Sept. 24, 1982; from Mollie N. Orth.)

Radović's Rule. In any organization, the potential is much greater for the subordinate to manage his superior than for the superior to manage his subordinate. (Igor Radovic, in *How to Manage the Boss; or, The Radović Rule*, M. Evans, 1973.)

Rae's Dilemma. When you move something to a better place for safekeeping, you can never remember the location of the better place. (Mrs. Rae P. Jensen, San Francisco, California.)

Rafferty's Laws of Education. (1) Educational research that flies in the teeth of common sense is for the birds. (2) In any election, the candidate supported by the teachers' union is always the one to vote against. (3) Every educational problem is caused by (a) stupidity or (b) unwillingness to work. (4) Fifty percent of all school administrators are superfluous. (5) Sixty percent of the things schools do have nothing to do with education. (6) Any educational area supported by federal funds deteriorates in quality and output in exact proportion to the amount of said federal aid. (Conservative educator/columnist Max Rafferty; *ME*.)

Ragucci's Collected Wisdom. *The Purple Magnet Theory:* In any given crowd, the weirdo will automatically and immediately seek you out. *First Truth of Love:* Love is exhausting. *Hospital Law of Room Assignments:* Whenever possible, patients with similar sounding names will be put on the same floor in the same room. (John J. Ragucci, Everett, Massachusetts.)

Rahlin's Rule. Not to have a credit rating is the best credit rating anyone can have. (Rahlin J. Quast.)

Rainbow Ice Cream Co.'s Point. A person who doesn't like ice cream doesn't like a good laugh, goes to the beach and complains about the sand, sleeps in pajamas, and kisses with his mouth closed. (Paraphrased from the aforementioned San Francisco institution by Bill Shea.)

Rajneesh's Razor. Experts consult; never wise men. (Shree Rajneesh; from Shel Kagan.)

Rakove's Laws of Politics. (1) The amount of effort put into a campaign by a worker expands in proportion to the personal benefits that he will derive from his party's victory. (2) The citizen is influenced by principle in direct proportion to his distance from the political situation. (Milton Rakove of the University of Illinois, who first spelled them out in *The Virginia Quarterly Review,* Summer 1965; *FL*.)

Ralph's Rule. If you can't get somebody else to do it for you, it's not worth doing at all. (From Dave Pawson, Dallas.)

Rambam's Law. Whatever purpose a piece of information may have been created and shared for, it will eventually be used for something else. (Steven Rambam, *The Economist,* January 1, 2009.)

Randall's Observation. The first person to spot and chastise a phony is either as big a phony as or a bigger phony than the one he's passed judgment on. (Randall L. Koch, Kenosha, Wisconsin.)

Randall's Reminder. The closest to perfection a person ever comes is when he fills out a job application form. (Stanley Randall, quoted by Patrick Ryan in *Smithsonian*.)

Randall's Rule of Economic Indicators. Increased productivity occurs when the number of unemployed not working is greater than the number of employed who are not working. (Warren Randall, Stony Brook, New York.)

Randolph's Cardinal Principle of Statecraft. Never needlessly disturb a thing at rest. (Early American statesman John Randolph of Richmond, Virginia. Cited in a column by James J. Kilpatrick.)

Ranger's Rule. We have done so much with so little for so long that now we can do anything with nothing. (This came from U.S. troops in Vietnam and has been applied widely since.)

Rangnekar's Modified Rules Concerning Decisions. (1) If you must make a decision, delay it. (2) If you can authorize someone else to avoid a decision, do so. (3) If you can form a committee, have them avoid the decision. (4) If you can otherwise avoid a decision, avoid it immediately. (*U/GT.*)

Ranthony's College Notebook. (1) A liberal education teaches what is possible. Experience teaches what is not. (2) Songs of the tenured immovable object: (a) I teach to have something to test. I test to have something to grade. (b) Publish the thought or perish the thought. (3) Remember that one advantage of a very good college is that you leave behind the sort of person who functions best in chaos. You will not be at his mercy again unless you are drafted, sent to jail, or teach school. (4) Motto over every university's main gate: *Ici e Collegium in mundus bunchum juvenalia de primer stratum passum, et alumni cum cupiditas becommen, Dei Gratia.* (5) Just as starlight seen from Earth shows the stars as they were in the past, so does a university's reputation in the lay community reflect the accomplishments of an earlier time—and for the same reason: distance. (6) The college fraternity is dedicated to the study and celebration of the various liquids and solids that—either naturally or by force—go in and come out of the human body. (7) Two rules of housekeeping: (a) Treat bedsheets like litmus paper: leave them alone until they change color. (b) That part of the room which is within one inch of the floor (three inches beneath the bed) is the province of dust, and the rest is yours. Dust, in return for being granted sanctuary, will stay where it is, not rolling in a big ball out to the middle of the room to beg for pennies and paper clips, embarrassing you in front of guests. (Ryan Anthony, Tucson, Arizona.)

Ranthony's Observation on Cussing. The English language has so few cuss words that, much like the flag, they should not be displayed day after day, but kept inside, lovingly rolled up and stored away, to bring forth proudly, unfazed, and effective on special occasions. (Ryan Anthony, Tucson, Arizona.)

Raper's Rules. (1) Hit the ball over the fence and you can take your time going around the bases. (2) Don't claim too much. The manufacturer of hair restorer never advertises that it will grow hair on the back of the neck. (3) The proof of the pudding is in the demand for it. (4) Patience is fine, but it never helped a rooster lay an egg. (John W. Raper, in *What This World Needs,* World, 1945.)

Rapoport's Rule of the Roller-Skate Key. Certain items which are crucial to a given activity will show up with uncommon regularity until the day when that activity is planned, at which point the item in question will disappear from the face of the earth. *Rapoport's Rule on Eating at Cocktail Parties:* You will eat just enough hors d'oeuvres to ruin your appetite for dinner but not enough to satisfy it. (Dan Rapoport, Washington, D.C.)

Rappo's Laws of Pediatrics. (*A selection*): (1) Children are not small adults, although adults frequently act like large children. (2) Not all short physicians are pediatricians; some short physicians are anesthesiologists. (3) Children rarely outgrow things they like. (4) Mother's Day is not in May; it's the first day of school. (Peter D. Rappo, M.D., Brockton, Massachusetts.)

Raskin's Zero Law. The more zeros found in the price tag for a government program, the less Congressional scrutiny it will receive. (Marcus Raskin, the Institute for Policy Studies, Washington, D.C.; collected by the late Barbara Raskin, novelist.)

Raspberry Jam, Law of. The wider any culture is spread, the thinner it gets. (Stanley Edgar Hyman. This was incorrectly attributed to Alvin Toffler in a *New York Times* article, which, in turn, gave birth to *Toffler's Law of Editorial Correction* [See *Editorial Correction, Law of.*] Toffler had reason to dispute it, as he had spent fourteen chapters of his book *The Culture Consumers*, St. Martin's, 1964, arguing that the *Law of Raspberry Jam* was wrong.)

Rathbun's Generalization. Generalizations and value judgments are all bad. *Rathbun's Rule:* There is no harder nor more thankless taskmaster than the self-employed. (J. M. Rathbun, M.D., Cumberland, Wisconsin.)

Rather's Rule. In dealing with the press, do yourself a favor. Stick with one of three responses: (a) I know and I can tell you; (b) I know and I can't tell you; or (c) I don't know. (Dan Rather, CBS. These were originally stated some years ago and appear in a collection of rules put together by Donald Rumsfeld.)

Raub's Law. The more expensive the toy, the greater the tendency for the child to play with the box. (I. Raub Love, Dayton, Ohio.)

Raufar's Observations. Earthquake preparedness is a contradiction in terms. (Dhyan Raufa, San Francisco, California.)

Ravage's Rule of Foot. Excursions on foot will be approximately 58 percent uphill in both directions. This percentage will increase as the temperature rises. (John M. Ravage, Philadelphia, Pennsylvania.)

Rayburn's Law. When you get too big a majority you are immediately in trouble. (House Speaker Sam Rayburn after Franklin D. Roosevelt's 1936 landslide. Quoted by William Safire in his column of November 4, 2004.)

Rayburn's Rule. If you want to get along, go along. (House Speaker Sam Rayburn; *Co.*)

Raymie's Rule of Repair. No job is done until you bleed on it. (Suzie Radus, Pittsburgh, Pennsylvania.)

Raymond's Rule on Junk Mail. If it doesn't look as if there is a check or a personal letter in it, there's nothing in it—so throw it out. (Columnist John Raymond, *The Atlanta Constitution,* March 13, 1979.)

Reach's Rule. The secret of happiness is to let the other fellow do the worrying. (A.J. Reach, of baseball and sporting goods fame, quoted in *Sporting News,* July 28, 1906.)

Reagan's Razor. Anything we do is in the national interest. (Ronald Reagan, quoted in Lou Cannon's column, *Washington Post,* January 19, 1986. The president had uttered the line the previous July when asked whether sending helicopters to Bolivia for drug enforcement was in the national interest.)

Reasons Why Not (50 Handy-Dandy Excuses). (1) We've never done it before. (2) Nobody else has ever done it. (3) It has never been tried before. (4) We tried it before. (5) Another company (person) tried it before. (6) We've been doing it this way for 25 years. (7) It won't work in a small company. (8) It won't work in a large company. (9) It won't work in our company. (10) Why change?—It's working OK. (11) The boss will never buy it. (12) It needs further investigation. (13) Our competitors are not doing it. (14) It's too much trouble to change. (15) Our company is different. (16) The ad department says it can't be done. (17) The sales department says it can't be sold. (18) The service department won't like it. (19) The janitor says it can't be done. (20) It can't be done. (21) We don't have the money. (22) We don't have the personnel. (23) We don't have the equipment. (24) The union will scream. (25) It's too visionary. (26) You can't teach an old dog new tricks. (27) It's too radical a change. (28) It's beyond my responsibility. (29) It's not my job. (30) We don't have the time. (31) It will obsolete other procedures. (32) Customers won't buy it. (33) It's contrary to policy. (34) It will increase overhead. (35) The employees will never buy it. (36) It's not our problem. (37) I don't like it. (38) You're right, but... (39) We're not ready for it. (40) It needs more thought. (41) Management won't accept it. (42) We can't take the chance. (43) We'd lose money on it. (44) It takes too long to pay out. (45) We're doing all right as it is. (46) It needs committee study. (47) Competition won't like it. (48) It needs sleeping on. (49) It won't work in this department. (50) It's impossible. (This list has been popular in engineering circles for years. The earliest published appearance was in *Product Engineering,* July 20, 1959. It was supplied to the magazine by E.F. Borisch of the Milwaukee Gear Co.)

Rebecca's House Rules. (At Least One Fits Any Occasion):

(1) Throw it on the bed.
(2) Fry onions.
(3) Call Jenny's mother.
(4) No one's got the corner on suffering.
(5) Run it under the cold tap.

(6) Everything takes practice, except being born. (Sharon Mathews, Arlington, Virginia.)

Recording Engineer, Ultimate Threat of. Don't tell me how to do my job, or I might do exactly what you say. (From Steve Stine, who learned it at a recording engineer seminar in 1976 at Columbia College/Sonart Studios.)

Rees' First Law Of Quotations. When in doubt, ascribe all quotations to George Bernard Shaw, except when they obviously derive from Shakespeare, the Bible, or Kipling. *Corollary:* In time, all humorous remarks will be ascribed to Shaw whether he said them or not. (Nigel Rees from his *The Quote... Unquote Newsletter.* He added: "The names Oscar Wilde, Winston Churchill, Mark Twain, Abraham Lincoln... may be substituted for Shaw's but the form remains the same.")

Reform, Fundamental Tenet of. Reforms come from below. No man with four aces howls for a new deal. (John F. Parker, *If Elected, I Promise,* Doubleday, 1960.)

Reidling's Rule for High School Football Broadcasts. The defensive end who falls on a fumble in his opponent's end zone is wearing a number that isn't on your program. (From Paul Biler, who says that this is named for Jerry Reidling, Sports Director, WFRO, Fremont, Ohio. During a game, no one in the pressbox could identify a running back who ran for 175 yards and two touchdowns.)

Reid's Reminder. If you are looking for one thing in a stack of stuff, if it is a horizontal stack, it will be at the back; if it is a vertical stack, it will be at the bottom. (Rosemary Reid, San Francisco, California.)

Reik's Razor. If you see a snake coming toward you in a jungle, you have a right to be anxious; if you see it coming down Park Avenue, you're in trouble. (Theodore Reik.)

Reilly's Insurance Realization. With my luck, nothing will ever happen to me. (From the old radio show, "The Life of Reilly." Chester Reilly was played by William Bendix.)

Reinstedt's Reminder. Just because you have an irrational fear of flying doesn't mean you're not going to crash. (Bob Reinstedt; from Robert D. Specht.)

Reisman's Rule of Hustling Table Tennis. First you need a good racquet, then you need a lot of balls. (Marty Reisman; from J. M. McCabe.)

Reisner's Rule of Conceptual Inertia. If you think big enough, you'll never have to do it. (John H. Reisner III.)

Reis's Law of Airplane Travel. Whatever airline you fly and whatever airport you fly to, you always land at Gate 102. (Harold Reis; *AO.*)

Reiss's Rule of Restaurant Ruination. No restaurant, diner, or other eating establishment has ever been improved by a change of ownership. (Edward B. Reiss, Scottsdale, Arizona.)

Remusat's Reconciliation. (1) You must pay for your sins. (2) If you've already paid, please disregard this notice. (Jeanne Remusat, Forest Hills, New York. This appeared originally in a *New York* magazine competition, November 28, 1977.)

Renning's Maxim. Man is the highest animal. Man does the classifying. (Anonymous; from T. J. Nelson.)

Repartee, First Rule of. Better never than late. (*U/Ra.*)

Restaurant Acoustics, Law of. In a restaurant with seats which are close to each other, one will always find the decibel level of the nearest conversation to be inversely proportionate to the quality of the thought going into it. (Stuart A. Cohn; *AO.*)

Reston's Lesson to Journalists. You should always look around for the guys who are unhappy. (James Reston, who got a number of scoops from the Nationalist Chinese during the Dumbarton Oaks conference of 1944 when the United Nations was created; from Joseph C. Goulden, who spotted it in Gay Talese's *Kingdom and the Power*, World, 1969.)

Retsof's Rush Hour Blizzard Law. If there is a suitable morning snowstorm, an employee will leave after the storm to go to work. Given an equivalent afternoon snowstorm, the employee will leave before the storm to go home. (John C. Foster, Columbus, Ohio. For reasons unclear, Foster spells his name backward when composing laws.)

Revised Proverbs

Nothing hangs on quite like an old proverb, which is one reason they require occasional scrapping and updating. The list of those that should be abandoned is long—starting with such inanities as:

- A picture is worth a thousand words. (Leo Rosten has rebutted this with, "Okay. Draw me a picture of the Gettysburg Address.")
- Handsome is as handsome does. (A notion that is wrong-headed beyond belief.)
- You can't make a silk purse out of a sow's ear. (First of all, who would want to? Second, some years ago a Boston research firm actually made such a purse distilling a silky substance from a pot of sow's ears.)

As for revisions, the possibilities are limitless. For instance, all of these collected updates of one old saw are more to the point than the original (First six from *MLS.*):

- A fool and his money are some party.
- A fool and his money are soon spotted.
- A fool and his money are soon mated.
- A fool and his money are invited everywhere.
- A fool and his money are the prime-time television target audience.
- A Pool. And your money is soon parted.

In no special order, here are some other relevant revisions:

- Many hands want light work.
- The early worm, on the other hand, gets eaten by the bird.
- If you give a man enough rope, he'll hang you.
- Perversity makes for strange bedfellows.
- The wages of sin vary considerably.
- A word to the wise is superfluous.
- Counting your chickens before they've hatched is sensible long-range planning.
- Familiarity breeds.
- People who live in stone houses shouldn't throw glasses.
- Early to bed and early to rise and you'll be groggy when everyone else is alert.
- Out of the mouths of babes comes Gerber's strained apricots.
- Every silver lining has its cloud.
- If at first you don't succeed, you've got one strike against you.
- A bird in the hand is inconvenient.
- Lots of Jack makes all work play.
- A milligram of prevention is worth a kilogram of cure.
- A rolling stone angers his boss.
- Poets are born not paid.
- Some are born great, some achieve greatness, and some have a great thirst upon them.
- He who hesitates is bossed.

Revisionist's Rule. The easiest way to change history is to become a historian. (Unattributed quote, NASA file.)

Revisited. A 1969 District of Columbia Court of Appeals decision on Breathalyzer tests rules that for the test to be valid, the drunk-driving defendant must be sober enough to give voluntary, informed consent to letting the test be administered. (Reported in *The Washington Star,* April 16, 1979.)

Reyna McGlone's Discovery. Lint, dog and cat hair, dirt, dust, etc., are most strongly attracted to objects of opposite color. *Corollary:* There is no such thing as a carpet that doesn't show dirt. (Augustin Reyna McGlone; from Don Hall.)

Reynolds's First Law of Politics. Politicians will act rationally only when all other alternatives are exhausted. (John Reynolds, Jr., Sandy, Utah.)

Reynolds's Law. It's just as easy to make a *big* mistake as a small one. (Joan A. Reynolds, Hyattsville, Maryland.)

Reynolds's Table Rules. (1) If you order your coffee without sugar, the waiter will bring it without cream. (2) You never make the right number of pancakes. (C. Reynolds, M.D., Vancouver, British Columbia.)

Rhodes's Law. When any principle, law, tenet, probability, happening, circumstance, or result can in no way be directly, indirectly, empirically, or circuitously proven, or derived, implied, inferred, induced, deducted, estimated, or scientifically guessed, it will always, for the purpose of convenience, expediency, political advantage, material gain, or personal comfort, or any combination of the above, or none of the above, be unilaterally and unequivocally assumed, proclaimed, and adhered to as absolute truth to be undeniably, universally, immutably, and infinitely so, until such time as it becomes advantageous to assume otherwise, maybe. The full impact of this fundamental law may be invoked by use of the following symbolic logical operator, commonly referred to as *Charlie's Loop.* (Charles E. Rhodes, Allison Park, Pennsylvania. Rhodes, who has been working on his law for some time, states that the original discovery was made c. 1971 in its original, less scientific form: When in doubt, fake it.)

Rhy's Rule. If it feels good, do it. If it doesn't feel good, do it anyway. It will feel good when it is over with. (From James D. Haviland, Halifax, Nova Scotia, who got it from a co-worker. He points out: "This one has gotten me through a number of unpleasant tasks, including university.")

Riberdy's Observations. (1) Dirty dishes attract surprise visitors. (2) Most swimmers will run for shelter at the first signs of rain. (3) If a picture hangs straight on the first attempt, expect it to fall. (4) Junk mail multiplies if left in the box. (J. Riberdy, Windsor, Ontario.)

Rice's Rule. No matter when you turn on the TV, there is *always* an ad showing. (Edith K. Rice, East Boothbay, Maine.) See also *Markgraf's Observation.*

Rich Richard's Almanacation. When driving, don't look at anything lying on the road. If you look, chances are very good you'll see something you'll wish you hadn't. *Rich Richard's Truism:* God has given man the seemingly infinite capacity to remember telephone numbers and *one* zip code. (V. Richard Smith, Willow Springs, Ohio.)

Richman's Inevitables of Parenthood. (1) Never enough. (2) The sun always rises in the baby's bedroom window. (3) Birthday parties always end in tears. (4) Whenever you decide to take the kids home, it is always five minutes until that when they break into fights, tears, and hysteria. (Phyllis C. Richman, as writer and restaurant critic for the *Washington Post.*)

Rickey's Axiom. Luck is the residue of design. (The most famous and oft-quoted aphorism created by baseball executive Branch Rickey, it was embedded in a longer sentiment: "Things worthwhile generally just don't happen. Luck is a fact, but should not be a factor. Good luck is what is leftover after intelligence and effort have combined at their best. Negligence or indifference or inattention are usually reviewed from an unlucky seat. The law of cause and effect and causality both work the same with inexorable exactitudes. Luck is the residue of design." The words were recorded by Arthur Daley in *The New York Times,* November 17, 1965.)

Rickover's Reminder. At any moment during a twenty-four hour day, only one-third of the people in the world are asleep. The other two-thirds are awake and creating problems. (Adm. Hyman Rickover; from Jack Kime.)

Rickover's Rule. If you have a choice of sinning against God or the bureaucracy, sin against God, because he will forgive you; the bureaucracy will not. (Advice from the Admiral, cited in *Nuclear Fuel,* May 10, 1993.)

Riesman's Law. An inexorable upward movement leads administrators to higher salaries and narrower spans of control. (David Riesman; *JW.*)

Riggs's Hypothesis. Incompetence tends to increase with the level of work performed. And, naturally, the individual staff needs will increase as this level of incompetence increases. (Arthur J. Riggs, in his article "Parkinson's Law, the Id Principle, and the Riggs Hypothesis—A Synthesis," from the *Michigan Business Review,* March 1971. Riggs gives much detail on how his hypothesis fits in with the other principles in the title of his article. He also suggests a typical Riggs progression: "from competent line worker to slightly incompetent foreman to incompetent supervisor"; *FD.*)

Rigsbee's Law of Priorities. Given the choice between doing something for which one is well-prepared and paid, or doing something for which one is ill-prepared and not paid, most individuals will choose the latter. (Ken Rigsbee, Bartlesville, Oklahoma. His proof for this law: "I have just written you this letter on company time.")

Rigsbee's Principle of Management. Your brightest, sharpest new employees are the first to leave your organization—as the cream rises to the top it will be skimmed off. (Ken Rigsbee, Bartlesville, Oklahoma.)

Rimmer's Law of Human Superiority. The thing that sets us (human beings) apart from other animals is the fact that we do not clean our genitals with our own tongues. (From D. Reynolds, Golden Valley, Minnesota, quoting Arnold J. Rimmer, a character on the British comedy space-opera *Red Dwarf.*)

Rinzler's Theory of Relativity. Traffic is never a problem when you're trying to kill time; it builds up in direct proportion to the urgency of your schedule. (Carol E. Rinzler in *Woman's Day.*)

Rippetoe's Certification Rule. Customer satisfaction at auto repair shops is inversely proportional to the number of mechanics on the staff who have passed written exams testing their mechanical skills. *Corollary:* No amount of practical evidence will convince college-educated liberals that written tests are worthless in judging mechanical skill. *Rippetoe's Motherly Musing:* Parenthood is the only job with a reverse apprenticeship. You start the job with no experience or practical knowledge and total responsibility for a helpless child; as you gain experience and knowledge, your responsibility is gradually reduced to practically nothing. (Rita Rippetoe, Citrus Heights, California.)

Rist's Junk Drawer Discoveries. (1) All houses have a junk drawer. (2) Anything wanted from the junk drawer will be found at the bottom. (3) Once any item is removed from the junk drawer—no matter how large or small—the junk drawer will not close. (Philip Rist, Cleveland, Ohio.)

Ritchie's Rules. (1) Everything has some value—if you use the right currency. (2) Paint splashes last longer than the paint job. (3) Search and ye shall find—but make sure it was lost. (Peter Ritchie, Jr., Bowling Green, Virginia.)

Ritter's Law of Philosophical Redundancy. Doctoral graduates in philosophy will create clones. (Dan Ritter, Coudersport, Pennsylvania, who explains, "The only practical use for a terminal degree in philosophy is as a qualification to teach philosophy to others who will go on to do the same.")

Ritters' Rule. Well-documented junk is still junk. (K. Ritters, "Creativity abhors Prescription." *Landscape Ecology,* 2011, vol. 26, p. 1359.)

Rives's Discovery. Everything falls apart on the same day. (Rives calls this Efaots Day, and he pronounces it *E fouts.*) (John Rives, Lafayette, Colorado.)

Rizzo Rule, The. If you are telling the truth, never take a lie-detector test. If you're not telling the truth, never take a lie-detector test. (Daniel Rapoport, Washington, D.C., *Los Angeles Times,* November 6, 1981; *RS.*)

Rizzo's Reassurance. The streets are safe in Philadelphia; it's only the people who make them unsafe. (Philadelphia Mayor Frank Rizzo.)

RJ's 1st Corollary to Murphy's Law. The amount of time airport security spends inspecting your luggage will vary in inverse proportion to the time remaining until your flight departs. (R.J. Tillotson, Flower Mound, Texas, who reports on how he made his discovery: "After four years of carrying my toolbox on flights with me [if you want to see *Murphy's Law* really kick in, try showing up for a service call without tools!], it seemed that if I was an hour early for a flight, nobody in security even looked inside. But if there were only five minutes to catch the flight, there would be some self-important clown asking, 'Hey Herb, does this look like a bomb to you?' ")

Road Construction, Law of. After large expenditures of federal, state, and county funds; after much confusion generated by detours and road blocks; after greatly annoying the surrounding population with noise, dust, and fumes; the previously existing traffic jam is relocated by one-half mile. (Alan Deitz, American Newspaper Publishers Association; *AO*.)

Robbins's Law of Student Enrollment. In required courses, failures create their own demand. (Stephen P. Robbins, Professor, Department of Management, Concordia University, Montreal, Quebec.)

Robert's Paradox. My teacher says strangers are people we don't know. But that can't be true, because there are people who don't know us and we're not strangers. (Robert, son of Arnold R. Isaacs, cited in Arnold's "The Rules of the Game" in *The Baltimore Sun,* December 31, 1978.)

Robert's Rules of Home and Garden. (1) If at first you don't succeed, hire a contractor. (2) Two plus two equals four—unless you're talking about inches in a two-by-four. (3) Mulch is ado about nothing. (4) An idle mind should not mess around in a power workshop. (5) We must all hang together or assuredly the pictures will be crooked. (6) Somebody said it couldn't be done. I'll go along with that. (Bob Herguth, the *Chicago Sun-Times; RS.*)

Robertson's Law. Everything happens at the same time with nothing in between. (*U;* From Paul Hebig, Chicago, Illinois, who adds, "It usually refers to social engagements and business meetings.")

Robertson's Rules of Lunch. (1) If it isn't deductible, don't. (2) There are no free lunches, but usually the IRS will pay for a part. (3) Everyone has to eat. (4) When there are no other ways to minimize the cost of the meal, most diners try to stiff the waiter. (James A. Robertson, El Paso, Texas.)

Roberts's Restaurant Realization. If you don't like water, you don't like much. (Dave Roberts; from Michael Sawhill, Buffalo, Wyoming.)

Robinson's Law of Restaurant Keeping. (1) When you are busy, it does not matter for what time they book—they will all arrive together. (2) No restaurant is ever as good as your best notice. *Corollary:* Neither is it as bad as your worst. (3) A client who is convinced that he is about to have a terrible meal is seldom disappointed. The reverse doesn't hold, but at least you have a better chance. (4) The one time the president wants to eat with you is midway during your annual holidays. (5) The clients in the biggest hurry are those who are still there after all the others have left. (6) If you run out of one item during service, you will soon run out of others, each item in each course being the only thing on the menu the one customer really wanted. (7) All restaurants thrive on chaos—the successful ones are those which hide this fact from their clients, at least most of the time. (Peter Robinson, who submitted these truths when he ran *La Ferme Irlandaise,* Paris, France.)

Robinson's Rationale for Grade Inflation. A student never complains about getting an A. (Associate Professor Judith Robinson, State University of New York, Buffalo.)

Robotics, The Three Laws of. (1) A robot may not injure a human being or, through inaction, allow a human being to come to harm. (2) A robot must obey the orders given it by human beings except where such orders would conflict with the *First Law.* (3) A robot must protect its own existence as long as such protection does not conflict with the *First* or *Second Laws.* (Isaac Asimov, from "The Handbook of Robotics, 56th Edition, 2058 a.d.," which appears in his *I, Robot,* Gnome Press, 1950.)

Robson's Rule. Learning always occurs after the job is finished. (Thayne Robson, University of Utah; from William D. Hickman.)

Rochester's Theorem. Before I got married, I had six theories about bringing up children; now I have six children and no theories. (Lord Rochester.)

Rock-and-Roll Rules of the Road. (*A selection*): (1) No one will request a song you know how to play. (2) Never challenge a heckler to come up and play it better than you just did. He or she will. (3) If necessary, a guitar is an excellent medium-range weapon. (T. C. Acres, Calgary, Alberta.)

Rockne's Rule. One loss is good for the soul. Too many losses are not good for the coach. (Knute Rockne, *Sports Illustrated*, February 12, 2001; *JCG*.)

Roddenberry's Realization. They say that 90 percent of TV is junk. But 90 percent of *everything* is junk. (TV Producer Gene Roddenberry, quoted in *TV Guide,* April 27, 1974; from Don Nilsen.)

Roemer's Law. The rate of hospital admissions responds to bed availability. Or, if we insist on installing more beds, they will tend to get filled. (Dr. Milton Roemer of UCLA, first suggested it in 1959. It is an entirely serious statement, which, according to Victor R. Fuchs in his book *Who Shall Live?,* Basic Books, 1974, "has received considerable support in recent econometric studies"; *RS*.)

Roeper's Rules of the Universe. (*A selection*): (1) Gas station attendants are hired based on their lack of knowledge regarding directions. (2) All men look like geeks for seventy-two hours after a haircut. (3) You will not get the hiccups when you are alone. You will get the hiccups in the middle of your bar exam, or at a funeral, or on a first visit to your future in-laws' house. (4) If you think your pants have split, they have. (5) If you think your nylon has a run in it, it does. (6) The question you will be asked most often in you life is "Do you want fries with that?" (Richard Roeper, *Milwaukee Journal,* February 18, 1987; from Catherine Pfeifer.)

Rogawski's Laws of Medical Science. (1) A paper supporting any claim can be found somewhere in medical literature. (2) For any published paper, there is a paper giving opposite conclusions. (Michael A. Rogawski, Department of Pharmacology, Yale University, originally quoted in Dr. Robert Matz's article "Principles of Medicine," which appeared in the January 1977 issue of the *New York State Journal of Medicine*, Yale University.)

Roger Jones's Laws of Life. (1) Not everybody loves you. (2) Knowing that not everybody loves you means that you cannot please everybody. (Roger B. Jones, Savannah, Georgia; from Neal Wilgus.)

Rogers's Advice. Think like a hare, but act like a turtle. (Kenneth J. Rogers, Pontiac, Michigan.)

Rogers's Boss Law. There will always be beer cans rolling on the floor of your car when the boss asks for a lift home from the office. (Dennis Rogers.)

Rogers's Collected Thoughts. (1) Don't gamble; take all your savings and buy some good stock and hold it till it goes up, then sell it. If it don't go up, don't buy it. (2) There is only two sure ways to lose a friend. One is to go camping with him, the other is to loan him money. (3) Politics ain't worrying this country one-tenth as much as parking spaces. (4) Things will get better despite our efforts to improve them. (Will Rogers; from various sources.)

Rogers's Ratio. One-third of the people in the United States promote, while the other two-thirds provide. (Will Rogers, quoted in Leonard C. Lewin's *Treasury of American Political Humor,* Dial, 1964.)

Rogers's Sure-fire Formula. The best way to make a fire with two sticks is to make sure one of them is a match. (Will Rogers.)

Rolark's Reminder for Radicals and Revolutionaries. You never destroy the "establishment"; you simply replace it. If you do take over, *you* become the establishment. (Bruno Rolark.)

Rollins's Rule on Speech Duration. Any speaker who begins by saying "This shouldn't take long" will speak twice as long as the time allocated. *Rollins's Rule on Speech Quality:* The people who speak the loudest usually have the least to say. (Kyle Rollins, Provo, Utah.)

Rooke's Reminder. Nothing is as simple as it seems. (William Rooke, Anaheim, California. He uses this law when people call him to suggest a project that they insist is a "no-brainer.")

Rooney's Law. A picture tells a thousand words, nine hundred ninety-nine of which you didn't mean to say. (Tyrone Rooney, Assistant Professor of Geology, Michigan State University, at an invited lecture at the University of Texas, El Paso, on January 28, 2010; *TG.*)

Rooney's Laws. (1) You're much more likely to lock a member of your family out of your own house than a burglar. (2) You could be wrong. (3) When people say to me, "You're the boss," they don't mean it. (Andy Rooney, respectively, from *60 Minutes*, the book *And More By Andy Rooney,* Atheneum, 1982, and his Tribune Media Service column of August 31, 1986.)

Roosevelt's Resolution. Do what you can, with what you have, where you are. (Theodore Roosevelt.)

Rosalynn's Rule. Don't worry about polls—but if you do, don't admit it. (Rosalynn Carter, quoted by Donnie Radcliffe in the *Washington Post,* October 5, 1978.)

Rosa's Buzz-off Theory. After completing that memo or report, substitute each buzzword with an everyday word. All on distribution will feel self-congratulatory at having for once understood a piece of writing in total. You will make friends. (Sal Rosa, New York, New York.)

Rosa's Good Lord Willing Law. If all causes of mishaps are insured against except "Acts of God," the good Lord will invariably oblige. (Sal Rosa, New York, New York.)

Rosato's Revelation. The world is full of sane people taking medicine to enable them to cope with all the insane ones who should be using medication but refuse to do so. (Donald J. Rosato, M.D., Devon, Pennsylvania.)

Rosenau's Law of Revolting Developments. There will be at least one. (Milton D. Rosenau, Jr., Santa Monica, California.)

Rosenbaum's Rule. The easiest way to find something lost around the house is to buy a replacement. (Jack Rosenbaum, in the *San Francisco Examiner and Chronicle.*)

Rosenblatt's Laws. (1) The duration of a modern marriage is in direct proportion to the distance from one's relatives. (2) A basic law of modern education states that the farther east one's university, the more honored one is the farther west he or she travels. (3) A politician who doesn't swear at all is either an imposter or under indictment. (Roger Rosenblatt, from his columns for the *Washington Post.*)

Rosendahl's Corollaries. (1) All bad things happen at night, especially if the weather is up. (2) There is always one too few backup systems. (3) The manual left on shore is the one needed now. When you get the manual, the fine print will explain why you can't fix the problem. (4) There are no pleasant surprises. If you doubt it's right, then it's not; if you doubt it will work, then it won't; and when you think the repair is temporary, it is. (Bruce Rosendahl, quoted in an article by Bob Wilson in the Duke University magazine on his scientific work in East Africa; from Steve Woodbury.)

Rosengren's Theorem. That which has already achieved the highest degree of perfection can be made even more perfect as long as it pays off. (Bjorn Rosengren, head of the Swedish Municipal Workers; from Bob Skole.)

Rosen's Immutable Factory Outlet Law. Regardless of your actual summer destination, you will inevitably end up at a factory outlet. (R. D. Rosen, *New England Monthly,* May 1985.)

Rosenstock-Huessy's Law of Technology. All technology expands the space, contracts the time, and destroys the working group. (Eugen Rosenstock-Huessy, the German-American philosopher and historian.)

Rose's First Law of Investments. One should never invest in anything that must be painted or fed. (Showman Billy Rose; from William M. Mills, Hutchinson, Kansas.)

Rosoff's Rugrat Rule. A baby learns to say "Grandma" within an hour after she has left on the 2,000-mile trip home. (Denise Rosoff, APO, New York.)

Rosoff's Rule of Thermodynamics. A scalding hot cup of coffee will be too cool one instant after it has been adjudged to be at a drinkable temperature. (Henry Rosoff, APO, New York.)

Ross's Law. Bare feet magnetize sharp metal objects so they always point upward from the floor—especially in the dark. (Al Ross; *JW.*)

Ross's Law. Never characterize the importance of a statement in advance. (Charles G. Ross, President Truman's press secretary. This, along with *Hagerty's* and *Salinger's Laws,* was collected by Robert Donovan of the *Los Angeles Times* a number of years ago. They have appeared in a number of places, including *FL* and *S.T.L.*)

Ross's Law of Public Transportation. Scheduled changes always mean cutbacks. *Corollary:* Minor schedule adjustments always affect your bus (train, whatever). (Steve Ross, editor, *New Engineer.*)

Rothman's Lemma. The accuracy of a forecast varies inversely with the extent of its publication. (James Rothman, London, England.)

Roubin's Law. Why is it that no matter where you live or how many times you move, your neighbor's taste in music is always in inverse proportion to the volume it's played at? (M. B. Roubin, Estes Park, Colorado; *Stereo Review,* March 1988.)

Rough Rider's Dictum. Get action. Do things. Be sane. Don't fritter away your time. Create. Act. Take a place wherever you are and be somebody. (Quoted by Thomas Boswell, *Washington Post,* August 2, 1983, and applied to Baltimore Oriole catcher Rick Dempsey.)

Rover's Law. A dog always wants to be on the other side of the door. (*U /Ra.*)

Rowan's Immutable Law of The Digital Age. Data collected for one purpose may be used for purposes never originally intended. (David Rowan, editor of the UK edition of *Wired Magazine*, from his article on Google's car-mounted Street View cameras: "Stuck In The Web; The Company That Launched A Nifty Search Engine Has Become A Huge, Unregulated And Profit-Driven Keeper Of Details About Every Aspect Of Our Daily Lives," *The Times* [London], March 28, 2009.)

Rowe's Law. Nobody's in a hurry when you are. (Lynton S. Rowe, Epping, New South Wales, Australia.)

Rowe's Rule. The odds are 6 to 5 that the light at the end of the tunnel is a headlight of an oncoming express train. (*U/LSP.*)

Royal's Rule. Think lucky. If you fall in a pond, check your hip pockets for fish. (University of Texas football coach Darrell Royal.)

Royko's Law. Young people will always eat anything that is convenient, then wait until you buy some more convenient foods, and they will eat them too. (Mike Royko, *Like I Was Saying*, Dutton, 1984; from Steve Stine.)

Royko's Rule. In a strange bar, never use the phone more than once or they will think you are planning a stickup. (Mike Royko.)

Royko's Rule of Public Broadcasting. No matter when I look, all I ever see on PBS is one of four shows: (1) insects making love; (2) a lion walking along with a dead antelope in its jaws; (3) some spiffily dressed, elderly Englishman sitting in a tall-backed chair in a room that is paneled in dark wood; (4) a station announcer talking about what great shows they have and urging us to send more money. (Mike Royko, abridged from his column, June 4, 1986.)

Rubenstein's Rumination. If you're one in a million, there are 5,000 people like you. (Hal Rubinstein from *Paisley Goes With Nothing*, Doubleday, 1995; quoted by Michael Kesterton in his "Social Studies" column in the *Toronto Globe and Mail*, October 16, 1995.)

Rubin's Rules. (1) The easiest way to make money is to stop losing it. (2) Auditors are the people who go in after the war is lost and bayonet the wounded. (3) Criticize behavior, not people. *Rubin's Reminder:* Never confuse brilliance with a bull market. (Paul Rubin, Toledo, Ohio.)

Rubman's Law. You always find something the first place you look the second time. (Barbara Solonche, who named it for a relative who has proven the law.)

Ruby's Principles on Close Encounters. The probability of meeting someone you know increases when you're with someone you don't want to be seen with. (Walter Busch, St. Louis, Missouri; *EV.*)

Ruby's Remedy. The best bridge between despair and hope is a good night's sleep. (Harry Ruby, quoted in the *Reader's Digest*, July 1952.)

Ruckelshaus's First Law of Garbage. Everybody wants you to pick it up, and nobody wants you to put it down. (Former Environmental Protection Agency Chief William Ruckelshaus, quoted in *American Demographics* 11.7, 1989. "Americans have come to expect the effortless disappearance of trash, just as they expect water out of their faucets. But the national trash can is finally full. Consumers will soon have to pay to buy a product and pay again to throw it away.")

Rucker's Law. If one asks the wrong question, the odds are very high that one will receive the wrong answer. (Professor T. Donald Rucker, Ohio State University.)

Rudder's Law. Anything that begins well ends badly. Anything that begins badly ends worse. (*U/S.T.L.*)

Rudd's Discovery. You know that any senator or congressman could go home and make $300,000 to $400,000, but they don't. Why? Because they can stay in Washington and make it there. (Hughes Rudd, *Los Angeles Times,* August 15, 1980; *RS.*)

Rudd's Universal Explanation. Things like this happen. (*U;* from Ronald W. Tucker, Veracruz, Mexico.)

Rudin's Law. In a crisis that forces a choice to be made among alternative courses of action, most people will choose the worst one possible. (S. A. Rudin of Atlanta, Georgia; from a 1961 letter to the *New Republic; FL.*)

Ruination, Three Rules of. There are three ways to be ruined in this world: the first is by sex, the second is by gambling, and the third is by engineers. Sex is the most fun, gambling is the most exciting, and engineers are the surest. (*U;* commonly found printed on cards passed out at engineering conferences.)

Rumsfeld's Rules *(A sampling). On Serving the President:* Don't play President—you're not. The Constitution provides for only one President. Don't forget it and don't be seen by others as not understanding that fact. Where possible, preserve the President's options—he will very likely need them. Never say "The White House wants"—buildings don't "want." Don't speak ill of your predecessors (or successors)—you did not walk in their shoes. *On Keeping Your Bearings in the White House:* Keep your sense of humor about your position. Remember the observation (attributed to General Joe Stilwell) that "the higher a monkey climbs, the more you see of his behind"—you will find that it has more than a touch of truth. Don't begin to believe you are indispensable or infallible, and don't let the President, or others, think you are—you're not. It's that simple. Don't forget that the fifty or so invitations you receive a week are sent not because those people are just dying to see you, but because of the position you hold. If you don't believe me, ask one of your predecessors how fast they stop. If you are lost—"Climb, conserve, and confess." (From the *SNJ Flight Manual,* as I recall from my days as a student naval aviator.) *On Doing the Job in the White House:* Read and listen for what is missing. Many advisors—in and out of government—are quite capable of telling the President how to improve what has been proposed, or what's gone wrong. Few seem capable of sensing what isn't there. *On Serving in Government:* When an idea is being pushed because it is "exciting," "new," or "innovative"—beware. An exciting, new, innovative idea can also be foolish. If in doubt, don't. If in doubt, do what is right. Your best question is often, "Why? *On Politics, the Congress, and the Press: The First Rule of Politics:* You can't win unless you are on the ballot. Politics is human beings. Politics is addition, not subtraction. When someone with a rural accent says, "I don't know anything about politics," zip up your pockets. If you try to please everybody, somebody is not going to like it. With the press, it is safest to assume that there is no "off the record." *On Life (and other things):* It takes everyone to make a happy day. (Marcy Kay Rumsfeld, age seven.) In unanimity there may well be either cowardice or uncritical thinking. *On Rules:* If you develop rules, never have more than ten. (Donald Rumsfeld, from the rules and observations he created and collected while at the Pentagon and White House. The rules here were excerpted from an article in the February 1977 *Washingtonian,* entitled "Rumsfeld Rules." The article, in turn, was excerpted from Rumsfeld's original eighteen-page memo on rules.)

Runyon's Law. The race is not always to the swift, and the battle to the strong, but that's the way to bet. (Damon Runyon; *PQ*.)

Runyon's Rules for Newspaper Columnists. (1) Never let them give you a desk, because they'll always know where they can find you. (2) Get mad as you want, but never get off the payroll. (3) Keep your byline in there every day. Otherwise, your readers might miss it—or worse yet, they might not. (In *The Gossip Wars,* by Milt Machlin, 1981; from Joseph C. Goulden.)

Rupp's Rule. If you demonstrate competence, it becomes part of your job description. (Sandra K. Rupp, RN, Monticello, Florida.)

Rural Mechanics, First Rule of. If it works, don't fix it. (From William O'Neill, the National Geographic Society News Service. This was one of the first laws collected by the Murphy Center. An important corollary appeared in 1988 as *Deford's Law.*)

Rush's Reminder. People who work the hardest, get paid the least. (John Rush, Austin, Texas.)

Ruskin's Realization. The most beautiful things in the world are the most useless—peacocks and lilies, for example. (John Ruskin; from Gene Hegel.)

Russell's Classroom Rules. (1) No working not permitted. (2) The tardy student will always want to leave early. (3) The size of the grade marked on a paper will be inverse to its importance (small A's and large F's). (Gene H. Russell, Director, The Emperor Norton Society, Orland, California.)

Russell's Observation. In America, everybody is of the opinion that he has no social superiors, since all men are equal, but he does not admit that he has no social inferiors, for, from the time of Jefferson onward, the doctrine that all men are equal applies only upwards, not downwards. (Bertrand Russell, *Unpopular Essays*, Simon and Schuster, 1951; *RS*.)

Russell's Right. If it succeeds, it is right; if it fails, it is wrong. (Martin Russell, Yonkers, New York.)

Russell's Seismological Discovery. Everything east of the San Andreas Fault will eventually plunge into the Atlantic Ocean. (Jim Russell, from his book *Murphy's Law,* Celestial Arts, 1978.)

Russert's Commandment. Thou Shalt Not Whine. (Large wooden sign in the office of newsman Tim Russert, featured in a 2009 re-creation of Russert's office at the Newseum in Washington.)

Rutherford's Rule. The more you don't know how to do, the less you have to do. (Larry Rutherford, Virginia Military Institute.)

Ruth's Law. When you have washed all the dishes, there is always one more piece of cutlery in the bottom of the dishpan. (Mykia Taylor, Glenside, California.)

Ryan's Gap. The interval between the election of your best friend and his hiring of your worst enemy to be his administrative assistant. On average, *Ryan's Gap* is thirty-seven hours and twelve minutes. (John L. Ryan, quoted in *Conservative Digest,* April 1981; from Joseph C. Goulden.)

Ryan's Law. Make three correct guesses consecutively and you will establish yourself as an expert. (*U/RS,* Santa Monica, California.)

Ryder's Reminders. (1) The person who has all the answers understands none of the problems. (2) Never mistake activity for progress. (Bruce A. Ryder, Richmond, Virginia.)

S

Sachar's Observation. Some people grow with responsibility—others merely swell. (Abram Sachar, Chancellor of Brandeis University; from Richard S. Luskin, Needham, Massachusetts.)

Sacramento Manifesto. When you're out to make your mark in the world, watch out for guys with erasers. (Spotted by *TG* on a T-shirt in the California capital.)

Sadat's Reminder. Those who invented the law of supply and demand have no right to complain when this law works against their interest. (Anwar Sadat, quoted in the 1975 book *Expectation of Days; RS.*)

Sadat's Rule. Never review the troops until you *know* whose troops they are. (D. H. Lee, University of Louisville, Kentucky.)

Safire's New Law of Who/Whom in Headlines. When "whom" is correct, use some other formulation. (William Safire, *The New York Times Magazine,* March 25, 1979; from Rabbi Wayne Allen, Staten Island, New York.)

Sagan's Paradox. We live in a society exquisitely dependent on science and technology, in which hardly anyone knows anything about science and technology. (Carl Sagan.)

Sailor's Dictum. If you don't make waves, you're not underway. (Leonard P. Gollobin, Fairfax, Virginia.)

Saint Murphy's Rule of Researching Religiously. Read enough theological books and you will find someone who supports your beliefs. *Corollary:* Have enough Bible translations in your library and you will find one that agrees with what you think a particular passage says. (Ron Birk, San Marcos, Texas; from his longer list of *Saint Murphy's Commandments.*)

Saint Silicon's Gospel. (1) Left-brain people use PCs, right-brain people don't use computers, and no-brain people use Macs. (2) If a hard disc crashes when no one's in the office, is any data really lost? (3) They call it Windows because it's a pain to use. (Jeffrey Armstrong, computer comic, Santa Cruz, California, quoted in the *Orange County Register.*)

Saki's Advice to Travelers. Never be flippantly rude to elderly strangers in foreign hotels. They always turn out to be the King of Sweden. (Saki [British author Hector Hugh Monro], quoted in *A Dictionary of Catch Phrases,* Stein and Day, 1986; by Eric Partridge and Paul Beale.)

Salak's Observations. (1) Nothing makes you more tolerant of a neighbor's midnight party than being there. (2) Don't try to step into a revolving door behind someone and expect to come out ahead. (Joseph C. Salak, Deland, Florida.)

Saliers's Law. Whenever two of anything are tossed to the same person, they will arrive at the same time. He will catch neither. *Tennis Corollary:* People enjoy tossing balls so they arrive at the same time. (Richard R. Saliers, Grandville, Michigan.)

Salinger's Law. Quit when you're still behind. (Pierre Salinger, President Kennedy's press secretary. He discovered it when he protested news reports that a lavish reception the President had held was "expensive"; *FL.*)

Sally's Collected Conclusions. (1) *Witch Doctor's Fail-Safe:* If the spell works, the witch doctor takes the credit. If it fails, the patient gets the blame. This fail-safe also works well for diet doctors, psychotherapists, and self-improvement gurus of every stripe. (2) *Mail:* Junk mail never goes astray. (3) *Child Expert's Chide:* Whatever children really like is bad for them. (4) *Animal Acquisition Axiom:* Free kittens eat expensive lunch. *Cat-Lover's Corollary:* They are worth it. (N. Sally Hass, Sleepy Hollow, Illinois.)

Sally's First Law. Ten minutes of eating equals one week of dieting. (From the *Sally Forth* comic strip of January 9, 1993.)

Sally's Law of Beauty. In any given beauty salon, the total beauty of the operators exceeds that of the customers by a factor of 4:1. The sex of the operators and customers is immaterial. (N. Sally Hass, Sleepy Hollow, Illinois.)

Sally's Rule of Aquatic Relativity. The neatest thing that can happen to a girl at the pool is to have two guys take her hands and feet and throw her into the water, unless the two guys are her brothers, in which case it is the worst thing that can happen to a girl. (Sally, a teenager known to Michael L. Lazare, Armonk, New York.)

Sam Goldwyn's Rule. Never name a movie character "Joe." (*The Takers,* by William Flanagan, Bantam, 1984; from Joe Goulden.)

Sam's Axioms. (1) Any line, however short, is still too long. (2) Work is the crabgrass of life, but money is the water that keeps it green. (*U/S.T.L.*)

Sam's Law. Only fools can be certain; it takes wisdom to be confused. (The character Sam in the television show *Quincy;* from Steve Feinfrock.)

Samuels' Rules. (1) Whosoever believes whatsoever is said by whomsoever is howsoever a fool. (2) If everyone were suddenly to become as nice, sensitive and thoughtful as we want everyone to be, we'd have a hell of a garbage-disposal problem on our hands. (3) Inevitability can usually be avoided by changing the outcome. (4) Most telephone call-forwarding recordings offer you a number of push-button options, the ultimate usefulness of which may be indicated by pressing "0." (5) The frequency with which you are interrupted while reading usually corresponds closely to the number of times you have asked not to be. (6) The fastest and surest way to lose pounds is to spend an hour in a British gambling casino. (Arthur Samuels, Montreal, Quebec, Canada.)

Samuelson's Corollary. Public bureaucracy breeds private bureaucracy. (Robert J. Samuelson, *Washington Post,* June 6, 1978. As he explains, "The more government expands, the more it stimulates a vast supporting apparatus of trade associations, lawyers, lobbyists, research groups, economists, and consultants—all trying to shape the direction of new federal regulations and spending programs.")

Sandburg's Law of Presidential Policy. If he [the President] opens any door of policy, he is sure to hear it should be opened wider, it should be closed entirely, or there should be a new door; or return to the door that was there before; or the original intention of the Founding Fathers was that a window would be better than a door anyhow. (Carl Sandburg; from James E. Farmer, Indianapolis, Indiana.)

Sanders's Counterpunch. Mayor Jimmy Walker once said that no girl was ever ruined by reading a book. If I believed that, I'd throw away my typewriter. (Novelist Lawrence Sanders, quoted in *The New York Times Book Review*, June 8, 1982.)

Sanders's Law. You never get walked on unless you throw yourself on the floor. (Chicago radio personality Betty Sanders.)

Sandia Rules. (1) I don't know what I want to hear until I hear what I don't want to hear. (2) The more important a thing is, the less time you are given to do it. (3) There are more ways to do something wrong than there are to do it right. (James D. Plimpton, Albuquerque, New Mexico, who reports that these rules have been "floating around" Sandia National Labs for a while.)

Sandy's Theory. Depression and lack of inspiration are in equal proportion to the lack of involvement and motivation. (Ellie Saraquese, Carmichael, California.)

Sans Souci Rule. You are where you eat. (Named for the Washington, D.C. restaurant of the same name. The rule was given to Art Buchwald by Pierre Salinger when Buchwald first arrived in Washington.)

Santayana's Philosophical Reminder. It is a great advantage for a system of philosophy to be substantially true. (George Santayana.)

Santulis's Personal Computer Corollary. Personal computers will always remain inexplicable to the layman. *Proof:* The person frustrated with these conditions sets out to rectify this information gap by learning about computers and then explaining them to others without the use of jargon that makes the layman's eyes glaze over. The problem is that when a certain amount of knowledge on computers is attained, the former novice immediately loses the detail of his or her former ignorance and becomes just as unintelligible to a layman as any other "winky-blink." Thus computers will always remain complicated and mysterious to the general public, and people who use them will always seem slightly odd to those that don't. (Kevin Santulis, Oregon, Wisconsin.)

Sartorial Homogeneity, The Law of. If you are called on to speak at a gathering of your superiors and you are wearing brown, everyone else is wearing blue. If you are wearing blue, everyone else is wearing gray. (Michael L. Lazare, Armonk, New York; from his own empirical studies.)

Sattinger's Law. It works better if you plug it in. (Irvin J. Sattinger, Ann Arbor, Michigan.)

Sattinger's Laws of Politics. (1) The individual American voter has an extraordinary ability to simultaneously hold mutually contradictory political opinions. (2) Every politician knows how to balance the federal budget in such a way as to do the least damage to his prospects for re-election. (3) Whenever an event of political or economic significance occurs, it is immediately interpreted by each citizen in such a manner as to reinforce all previously held prejudices. (Irvin J. Sattinger, Ann Arbor, Michigan, who submitted these to the Murphy Center in 1980.)

Sattler's Law. There are 32 points to the compass, meaning that there are 32 directions in which a spoon can squirt grapefruit; yet the juice almost invariably flies straight into the human eye. (Professor Louis Sattler, whose discovery appears in the important essay "Fetridge's Law Explained," in M. Allen Smith's *A Short History of Fingers,* Little, Brown, 1963.)

Sauget's Law of Education. Sit at the feet of the masters long enough and they'll start to smell. (John Sauget, Urbana, Illinois.)

Saul's Screwing Saw. When fastening down something held by several screws, don't tighten any of the screws until all of them are in place. (M. Saul Newman; from Steve Stine.)

Saunders's Discovery. Laziness is the mother of nine inventions out of ten. (Millionaire inventor Philip K. Saunders, quoted by Bennett Cerf in his *Laugh Day,* Doubleday, 1965.)

Savage's Law of Expediency. You want it bad, you'll get it bad. (Richard C. Savage.)

Sawhill's Rule. Potential is finite. (Michael Sawhill, Buffalo, Wyoming.)

Sayers's Observation. It is always pleasant to see a fellow creature toiling still harder than one's self. (Dorothy L. Sayers, *Busman's Honeymoon*, Harcourt, Brace, 1937; from David F. Siemens, Jr.)

Sayre's Third Law of Politics. Academic politics is the most vicious and bitter form of politics, because the stakes are so low. (Wallace Sayre of Columbia University has been given credit for this. A later corollary states: "They're the most vicious form of politics because the fighting is over issues decided five years earlier"; *AO.*)

Scanlan's Law. Wedding presents always come in pairs: two toasters, two blenders, two umbrella stands. (Phyllis Scanlan, Ellyn, Illinois.)

Schaefer's Rule of Distance. The floor moves farther away when you bend over. (Don Schaefer, Park Ridge, Illinois.)

Schapiro's Logical Explanation. The grass is always greener on the other side, but that is only because they use more manure. (Ken Schapiro, Montclair, New Jersey.)

Scharringhausen's Conclusion. Self-praise stinks. (William L. Scharringhausen, Park Ridge, Illinois.)

Schenk's First Principle of Industrial Market Economics. Good salesmen and good repairmen will never go hungry. (Economist Robert E. Schenk, St. Joseph's College, Rensselaer, Indiana; *AO*.)

Scheussler's Rule of Four. In a group of four people, one will always be honest, one will always be crooked, and the other two must be watched. (R. W. Scheussler, Pittsburgh, Pennsylvania.)

Schinto-Bacal's Four Steps to Becoming a Legend in Your Own Time. (1) Start a fad or religion. (2) Charm birds off trees. (3) Build an empire. (4) Never volunteer. (Gene Schinto and Jules Bacal; from their book *How to Become a Legend in Your Own Lifetime,* Abelard-Schuman, 1966.)

Schlegel's Two-Student Theory. Of two students, one will begin immediately working on a difficult problem set (or other homework) while the other fools around. The night before the homework is due, the "fooler" will seek out the "worker" and will want to find out how to do the problems. The "fooler" will then: (1) Gleefully point out all the errors in the "worker's" solution, and (2) Get a better grade on the homework. (Eric M. Schlegel, Bloomington, Indiana.)

Schmidt's Theory of Highway Velocities. You will always feel safer from the law if you are speeding in the right lane of the highway. If you go the same speed in the left lane, it's a whole different feeling. (Marty Schmidt, Glen Ellyn, Illinois.)

Schmitz's Law of Television Viewing. If you watch a show twice during the year, the second time will be a rerun of the first. (Edward J. Schmitz, Vienna, Virginia.)

Schnepper's Secret. You can fool some of the people all of the time, and all of the people some of the time, but if you work it right, that's all you need to make a comfortable living. (Jeff Schnepper, American College, Bryn Mawr, Pennsylvania.)

Schonfeld's Law of Cameras. The best shots occur: (1) when you are out of film; (2) when you don't have your camera; (3) when you are looking the other way. (Jerry Schonfeld, Portsmouth, Virginia.)

Schorr's Laws of Economics. (1) If there are imperfections in the structure of the marketplace, entrepreneurs will make lots of money. (2) If there are no imperfections in the structure of the marketplace, entrepreneurs will make imperfections in the structure of the marketplace. (Kenneth L. Schorr, Little Rock, Arkansas.)

Schorr's Theological Comment on Investigative Reporting. Apparently they will not forgive us our presspasses. (Daniel Schorr, on National Public Radio, March 12, 1985; from James E. Farmer.)

Schroeder's Admonition. Don't ask questions you don't want answers to. (Capt. Schroeder, USCG; from W. R. Jurgens, Bowie, Maryland.)

Schrumpf's Law. The most benefit is derived from money spent on items used between you and the ground. For example, shoes, mattresses, and tires. (Lee Schrumpf, Bridgeton, Missouri.)

Schuckit's Law. All interference in human conduct has the potential for causing harm, no matter how innocuous the procedure may be. (Schuckit would appear to be a pseudonym. Collected by William K. Wright, San Diego, California.)

Schulman's First Law. Books will exceed bookshelving. (J. Neil Schulman, *The Rainbow Cadenza*, Simon and Schuster, 1983; from Neal Wilgus.)

Schultze's Law. If you can't measure output, then you measure input. (Charles Schultze as Chairman, Council of Economic Advisors; *JW.*)

Schulze's Restatement. Always stop along the way to smell the roses—your competitors will be happy to get you out of their way. (Paul Schulze III, Chicago, Illinois.)

Schumacher's Conclusion. It is amazing how much theory we can do without when work actually begins. (E. F. Schumacher; from Steven Woodbury.)

Schumer's Law of Traffic. You can never catch a red light when you really need to. (Bob Schumer, Jenkintown, Pennsylvania.)

Schumpeter's Observation of Scientific and Non-scientific Theories. Any theory can be made to fit any facts by means of appropriate additional assumptions. (Submitted by Schenk, of *Schenk's First Principle* above; *AO.*)

Schwartz's Observation on Check-Out Lines. If the law is true that the other check-out line always moves faster, this does not mean that the people in the other line are exempt from the law. It means one of three things: (1) there is a line in the store moving even faster than theirs, (2) they are purchasing the wrong items at a faster rate than you are, or (3) they had a lot of time to kill and now they have even more. (Steve Schwartz, Burnsville, Minnesota.)

Schwartz's True View of Life. Don't look for your real success until you're past fifty. It takes that long to get over the distractions of sex. (Eddie Schwartz of Minneapolis, Minnesota, quoted in *A Couple of Cards* by Alfred McVay and Ed Hickey, Associated Marketing Enterprises, 1973.)

Schwemer's Pontification. The number of variables required to define completely a system or process will always exceed by one the number of experiments performed, regardless of the number of experiments performed. (Warren Schwemer, Ashland, Kentucky.)

Science, Basic Definitions. (1) If it's green or wiggles, it's biology. (2) If it stinks, it's chemistry. (3) If it doesn't work, it's physics. (*U/TJR.*)

Science, Two Important Observations from the Collection of Robert D. Specht. (1) Science is a wonderful thing, but it has not succeeded in maximizing pleasure and minimizing pain, and that's all we asked of it. (2) A stagnant science is at a standstill. (The first comes from an unsigned "Notes and Comment" item in the June 13, 1970, issue of the *New Yorker.* The second is from *JIR*, December 1973.)

Scott's Do-It-Yourself Code. (1) Any tool left on top of a ladder will fall off and hit you in the head. (2) Any rope left dragging from any object in any location will catch on something. (3) For the successful completion of any task requiring tools, it is necessary to bleed at least once. (Bill Scott, Tujunga, California.)

Scott's Hypothesis. If it doesn't play in Peoria—it probably will in Dubuque. (Sid Scott, former Peoria resident, now living in Dubuque.)

Scott's Theory. Younger men aren't better until they get older. (Jenna Scott; from Robert L. Stakes, El Paso, Texas.)

Scoville's Law. The most complicated rules, regulations, and procedures are created by people who don't have to make them work. *Corollary:* Complex rules, regulations, and procedures are created by people who need to appear busy to keep their job. (Wilber E. Scoville, Oshkosh, Wisconsin.)

Screwdriver Syndrome. Sometimes, where a complex problem can be illuminated by many tools, one can be forgiven for applying the one he knows best. (Robert Machol, from his *POR.* It is illuminated by an anecdote in which an operations researcher is at home for the weekend with nothing to do and decides to tighten all the loose screws in the house. When he runs out of screws to tighten, he gets a file and begins filing slots in the heads of nails, which he dutifully begins tightening.)

Seckel's Explanation for Such Things as People Who Invoke the Healing Power of Quartz Crystals to Fix Their Cars. There are a lot of people with their umbilical cords out looking to stick it into something, to remove responsibility. (Physicist Al Seckel, quoted in *The New York Times,* April 8, 1988; from Joseph C. Goulden.)

Second-Ratedness, Unfailing Law of. Never be first to do anything. (Ken S. Wayland, Massachusetts; in Ann Landers's column, 1978.)

Security Office, Special Law of. Threats to security will be found. *Or, as an*

Axiom: The finding of threats to security by a security office is totally predictable, and hence the finding is totally worthless. (Robert N. Kharasch, in *The Institutional Imperative,* Charterhouse Books, 1973; *AO.*)

Seeberg's Law. Whenever you approach a car in a parking lot with its lights left on, the doors will be locked. (Marge Seeberg, Northbrook, Illinois.)

Seersucker Principle. For every seer, there is a sucker. (From Steven Stine, who heard it in an old *Alfred Hitchcock Presents* rerun. A character played by Jack Klugman says it to a character played by E. G. Marshall.)

Segal's Law. A man with one watch knows what time it is; a man with two watches is never sure. (*U/S.T.L.*)

Selective Gravity, Law of. An object will fall so as to do the most damage. *Jennings's Corollary:* The chance of the bread falling buttered side down is directly proportional to the cost of the carpet. (The law is common on scientific lists. The corollary was first spotted in a list by Arthur Bloch, "18 Unnatural Laws," which appears in the best-selling *Book of Lists*, Bantam, 1979; by David Wallechinsky, Irving Wallace, and Amy Wallace.)

Seleznick's Theory of Holistic Medicine. Ice cream cures all ills. Temporarily. (Mitchel J. Seleznick, M.D.; from Sol G. Brotman.)

Seligson-Gerberg-Corman Rule of Sexual Sameness. Having bad sex with someone you care about is the same as having bad sex with someone you don't care about. (Marcia Seligson, Mort Gerberg, and Avery Gorman, from their book, *The Everything in the World That's the Same as Something Else Book,* Simon and Schuster, 1969.)

Sellen's Observation. It doesn't take all kinds; we just have all kinds. (Robert W. Sellen, Georgia State University, Atlanta, Georgia.)

Sells's Law. The first sample is always the best. (*U;* from William K. Wright.)

Selzer's Scalpel. A minor operation is one that is done on someone else. (Dr. Richard Selzer.)

Sendak's Lament for the Rich. There must be more to life than having everything. (Writer Maurice Sendak.)

Serendipity, Laws of. (1) In order to discover anything, you must be looking for something. (2) If you wish to make an improved product, you must already be engaged in making an inferior one. (From William K. Wright's collection. He attributes the first to Harvey Neville and the second to Jacob A. Varela.)

Serjak's Law. If you wait long enough, you'll be there all day. (Jacob Serjak; from Gordon Serjak, North Miami, Florida.)

Servan-Schreiber's Law. Democracy is completely dependent on oil. (Jean-

Louis Servan-Schreiber, *The World Challenge*, Simon and Schuster, 1981; from Charles D. Poe.)

Sevareid's Law. The chief cause of problems is solutions. (Eric Sevareid, on *CBS News,* December 29, 1970.)

Seymour's Beatitude of the Bureaucracy—on the treatment of employee complaints. The first time you're a disgruntled employee. The second time you're a pain in the ass. The third time you're a nut. (John Seymour, Bayonne, New Jersey.)

Sgt. Preston's Law of the Wild. The scenery only changes for the lead dog. (Curt Heinfelden, Baltimore, Maryland.)

Shadoan's Law. If it's not one thing, it's ten. (Dan Shadoan, University of California, Davis; *TG.*)

Shaffer's Law. The effectiveness of a politician varies in inverse proportion to his commitment to principle. (*Newsweek* reporter Sam Shaffer; *JW.*)

Shales's TV Testimonial. Well, of course, you can't avoid watching television, I mean, what would life be but an endless series of real experiences? (Critic Tom Shales, *On the Air!*, Summit, 1982.)

Shalit's Law. The intensity of movie publicity is in inverse ratio to the quality of the movie. (Gene Shalit, the *Today* show; *S.T.L.*)

Shanahan's Law. The length of a meeting rises with the square of the number of people present. (Eileen Shanahan, former economics reporter for *The New York Times; FL.*)

Shanebrook's Law. If you do a job twice, it's yours. (J. Richard Shanebrook, Chairman, Mechanical Engineering Department, Union College, Schenectady, New York.)

Shannon's Law. Nothing is simple. (Stan Shannon, Dallas, Texas.)

Shannon's Observation. Nothing is so frustrating as a bad situation that is beginning to improve. (William V. Shannon; *ME.*)

Shapiro/Kaufman Law. The lag in American productivity is directly related to the steady increase in the number of business conferences and conventions. (Walter Shapiro and Aleta Kaufman in their article "Conferences and Conventions: the $20-Billion Industry That Keeps America from Working"; *Washington Monthly,* February 1977.)

Sharkey's 4th Law of Motion. Passengers on elevators constantly rearrange their positions as people get on and off so there is at all times an equal distance between all bodies. (John Sharkey of the *Washington Post.*)

Sharples's Philosophy. (1) A rolling stone gathers momentum. (2) Progress is nondirectional. (3) Don't be taken by the vitamin itself. (Virginia M. Sharples, Houston, Texas.)

Shawn's Observation. Twitter makes you like people you don't know, and Facebook makes you hate people you do. (Shawn Holland, posted on Facebook, July 18, 2012.)

Shaw's Axiom. For every problem science solves, it creates ten new ones. (George Bernard Shaw, from Sydney J. Harris.)

Shaw's Golden Rule. Do not do unto others as you would that they should do unto you; their tastes may be different. (George Bernard Shaw, from *The Revolutionist's Handbook,* at the end of *Man and Superman*, Constable, 1903; *RS*.)

Shaw's Principle. Build a system that even a fool can use and only a fool will want to use it. (Christopher J. Shaw; *JE*.)

Shaw's Solution. If you can't get rid of the family skeleton, you may as well make it dance. (George Bernard Shaw; from Catherine Pfeifer.)

Shaw's Syllogism. If a statement, either written or spoken, begins with, "As a matter of fact," whatever follows is likely to be a downright lie. (George Bernard Shaw; from Francis J. Hennessy.)

Shea's Discovery. Unlimited warranties are usually neither. (Bill Shea, Daly City, California.)

Sheehan's Law of Rational Government. Using logic to deal with government is illogical; using illogic to deal with government is logical. (Raymond J. Sheehan, Springfield, Massachusetts.)

Sheehan's Law. As the quality of government goes down, the number of meetings increases. (Anonymous; WRC radio, Washington, D.C.)

Shelton's Law of Bill Paying. The bill was due before you got it. (John Shelton.)

Shem's Laws of the House of God. (*A selection*): (1) At a cardiac arrest, the first procedure is to take your own pulse. (2) The patient is the one with the disease. (3) If you don't take a temperature, you can't find a fever.(From the novel *The House of God*, by Samuel Shem, M.D.; Richard Marek, 1978. Shem is the pseudonym of a young physician.)

Shephard's Law of Flubdubbery. Problems are simple. It's just that people are simpler. (W. W. Shepherd; from G. B. Shepherd, Santa Ynez, California.)

Shephard's Query. Dirt is a universal constant; why push it around? (Anonymous; WRC radio, Washington, D.C.)

Sheppard's Laws of Organization. (1) If a surface is flat, pile things on it. (2) If a pile grows to more than one foot tall, start a new pile. (Jeffrey Sheppard, in the *Washington Post,* January 5, 1979.)

Sherekis's Rules of the Road (abbreviated). (1) Gas is always five cents cheaper at the station two miles down the road from wherever you fill your tank. (2) Everything is farther than you think. (3) The windshield washers, wipers, and defrosters on the passenger side of all automobiles, domestic or foreign, will work with the force and efficiency of a car wash, while those same accessories on the driver's side will leave a three-inch wide band of mud, moth intestines, and steam at the exact eye level of the driver, whatever size he or she may be. (4) Five individuals make all the calls into all the all-night talk shows in the country. One is a 52-year-old male who belongs to the National Rifle Association, the American Legion, the Baptist Church, and the Posse Comitatus, who believes that Ronald Reagan is good on the economy but soft on communism. Two are hopeless alcoholics past middle age, one of each sex, who are known by their first names to all the talk-show hosts and who feel that everything would be okay if people would be nicer to each other. (5) If a motel advertises that a "single" is anywhere from $12.50 to $22.95 per night, the same room will be available for a party of two or more for $52.80, including tax. (6) The pungent, earthy smell of manure in the countryside will generate more tasteless jokes and gross accusations among people under eighteen than any other single phenomenon. (Rich Sherekis, from a larger collection he published in the *Illinois Times,* September 1984.)

Shick's Problematic Laws. (1) Small problems have deep roots: a zero variance normally indicates that errors of +1000 and –1000 have occurred simultaneously and canceled one another. (2) Large problems are the cause of small problems; an error in judgment in the beginning brings on an awful lot of judgment for error in the end. (3) There is no problem a good miracle can't solve. (Harry R. Shick, San Bernardino, California.)

Shields's Laws of New Parenthood. *The First Outing with the New Baby Rule:* The more obvious a person's flu symptoms are, the greater the likelihood that they will insist on grabbing your baby's hands and cooing breathlessly in your baby's face. *The Rule of Unsolicited Parenting Suggestions:* The closer the relative, the more annoying the advice. *The Baby Spit-up Discovery:* The more expensive the blouse, the more copious the spit-up. *Corollary A to the Baby Spit-up Discovery:* The more times you change your blouse, the greater the likelihood that your baby will repeat the above performance. *Corollary B to the Baby Spit-up Discovery:* After your baby finishes spitting up on you, your husband will be next. *The New Parents' Amorous Desire Rule:* The more you want to make love, the greater the likelihood that the baby will wake up crying. (Sandra Stark Shields, LaCrescenta, California, created in January 1995 when her daughter was eight months old.)

Shively's Rule. Your favorite song always comes on the car radio when you reach your destination. (Cynthia Shively, Lawrence, Kansas.)

Shoe's Instructions for Rest Room Hand Dryer Machines. (1) Push button. (2) Rub hands gently under nozzle. (3) Wipe hands on pants. (Jeff MacNelly's *Shoe* comic strip, June 19, 1980.)

Shoe-Shopper's Rule. If it feels good, it's ugly. If it looks good, it hurts. (N. Sally Hass, Sleepy Hollow, Illinois.)

Shopping Mall Collision Law #1. There will be no witnesses when someone backs into your car in the mall parking lot. However, there will be one witness when you back into a car—the attorney sitting in the car you hit. *Corollary to Shopping Mall Collision Law #1:* Bigger cars back into smaller ones, except when it is your fault. You will back your large car into a small and expensive foreign import. (John Culver, San Luis Obispo, California.)

Shore's Absolute Law. Any unexpected and undesirable negative quantities or results may be rectified by the judicious insertion of absolute-value signs and prayerful interjections; e.g. "Dammit!" (*U;* from Warren Schwemer, Ashland, Kentucky.)

Shorris's Assumption. Assumptions keep us awake nights. (Earl Shorris, quoted in *Forbes,* February 9, 1987.)

Short's Quotations. (*A new selection*): (1) The hardest lesson to learn is that learning is a continual process. (2) The only thing worse than learning the truth is not learning the truth. (3) The human brain is the only computer in the world made out of meat. (4) A human being is a computer's way of building another computer: usually a better one. That's why computers will never decide to replace human beings. We are their sex organs. (5) One fact can change your whole point of view. For instance, did you know King Kong was a Vegan? (6) If the opposite of *pro* is *con,* then what is the opposite of progress? (7) The more you treasure the object, the more noticeable the flaw. (8) Even *Murphy's Law* goes wrong sometimes. (David Gerrold, a.k.a. Solomon Short, from his work in progress *Quotebook of Solomon Short.* See also *Gerrold's Laws.*)

Short's Quotations (Some of many). (1) Any great truth can—and eventually will—be expressed as a cliché—a cliché is a sure and certain way to dilute an idea. For instance, my grandmother used to say, "The black cat is always the last one off the fence." I have no idea what she meant, but at one time, it was undoubtedly true. (2) Half of being smart is knowing what you're dumb at. (3) Malpractice makes malperfect. (4) Neurosis is a communicable disease. (5) The only winner in the War of 1812 was Tchaikovsky. (6) Nature abhors a hero. For one thing, he violates the law of conservation of energy. For another, how can it be the survival of the fittest when the fittest keeps putting himself in situations where he is most likely to be creamed? (7) A little ignorance can go a long way. (8) Learn to be sincere. Even if you have to fake it. (9) There is no such thing as an absolute truth—that is absolutely true. (10) Understanding the laws of nature does not mean we are free from obeying them. (11) Entropy has us outnumbered. (12) The human race never solves any of its problems—it only outlives them. (13) TINSTAFL!—There is no such thing as free love. (14) Hell hath no fury like a pacifist. (David Gerrold, from two of his 1978 columns in *Starlog.* They come from his *Quote-book of Solomon Short,* Short being a first-cousin to Robert A. Heinlein's Lazarus Long. [See *Long's Notes.*] He is also the author of Gerrold's Three Laws of Infernal Dynamics.)

Shouse's Rule. A Ph.D. is a person to whom you must explain the perfectly obvious, in great detail, several times. (Walter L. Shouse, *Knoxville News Sentinel,* Gatlinburg, Tennessee.)

Showbiz Thermodynamics, The First Law of. No celebrity energy can be created or destroyed. (This law was authored by Josh Wolk in *Entertainment Weekly,* December 30, 2005. Wolk explained that all celebrity gossip is a zero-sum game. As for 2005 he explained: "Bennifer II get married and have a baby.... Nick and Jessica's marriage breaks up....Martha gets out of jail....Lil' Kim goes in....Mariah rebounds from rumors of strange behavior....Dave Chappelle vanishes amid rumors of strange behavior....Pat O'Brien uses his phone a little too much....Russell Crowe throws his phone a little too hard. Though scientifically it may have been a zero-sum game, to us 2005 added up to one crazy year in entertainment.")

Shula's Computer Age Razor. If it can't fit in a few filing cabinets, is it really that important? (Columnist Jeff Shula, Waldo [County, Maine] *Independent,* on a local high-school principal's request for a $29,000 computer to store school records.)

Siegel's Law of Knife Sharpening. The first thing a freshly sharpened knife cuts is the sharpener's thumb or one of his fingers. (Peter V. Siegel, Jr., APO, San Francisco, California.)

Sieger's Law. You will have the same amount of money left at the end of the month, no matter how many raises, bonuses, or windfalls occur during the month. (*U/Ra.*)

Silverman's Sagacities. (1) What man can think of, man can do!—I think. (2) Man gets irritated and winds up with ulcers; oysters get irritated and wind up with pearls. (Isador Silverman, University Heights, Ohio.)

Simmons's Law. The desire for racial integration increases with the square of the distance from the actual event. (*U/JW*)

Simon's Law. Everything put together sooner or later falls apart. (Singer Paul Simon. *S.T.L.*)

Simon's Translation. In my country we have a name for sushi...bait. (Comedian Jose Simon, quoted in Bob Swift's column, *Miami Herald,* January 3, 1987.)

Simonson's Laws. (1) When all other reasons fail, local government officials who want to undertake large public projects will justify such expenditures by saying, "This is needed for our economic development." (2) If a public project is undertaken to stimulate economic development, there is a better than even chance it will do just the opposite. (Lee Simonson, Lewiston, New York.)

Sinner's Law of Retaliation. Do whatever your enemies don't want you to do. (Gary Novak, Highmore, South Dakota.)

Sisley's Second Law. We exist in a state of overcorrection. (John R. Sisley, Jr., Utica, New York, who notes, "Sisley has no first law. It is very much more impressive to begin with a second law.") *Sisley's Third Law:* Life is a soap opera, only a little slower. *Sisley's Fourth Law:* The misdeeds of a member of any minority are attributed to all the persons in that minority, while the misdeeds of a member of the majority are attributed to that individual alone. (John R. Sisley, Jr., Utica, New York.)

Sissman's First of Twenty Rules of Reviewing. Never review the work of a friend. (Critic L. E. Sissman, quoted by Jonathan Yardley in the *Washington Star,* March 11, 1979; *JCG.*)

Sister Cheyney's Universal Mother's Response. All right! Share! (F. D. McSpiritt, Flint, Michigan, who adds that it applies to all situations save those involving razor blades or matches.)

Sit, Whittle, and Spit Club Rules. (1) Don't sit in the sun. (2) Don't whittle toward yourself. (3) Don't spit against the wind. (Reported by Clyde W. Wilkinson, in his article "Backwoods Humor" in the *Southwest Review,* January 1939.)

Skinnell's Rule. You don't start traditions—traditions start. (K. W. Skinnell, Bethel Park, Pennsylvania.)

Skinner's Constant. That quantity which, when multiplied by, divided by, added to, or subtracted from the answer you get, gives you the answer you should have gotten. (*U/AIC;* Sometimes known as *Flannegan's Finagling Factor. FD* says this was called *DeBunk's Universal Variable Constant* in the 1930s.)

Skinner's Law. Anyone who owns a telephone is at the mercy of any damn fool who knows how to dial. (Jean Skinner Ostlund, Willmar, Minnesota, who learned it from her father, the late Arthur Z. Skinner.)

Sklenar's Second Rule. No time is a convenient time for a meeting. (Leslie James Sklenar, Chicago, Illinois.)

Skole's Hotel Law. When, through hard work, chance, position, or other fortuitous circumstances, you finally can stay in a hotel you could only dream of in your youth, it has deteriorated into a dump. *Skole's Perfection Principle:* Anything named perfect should be suspect. *Skole's Restatement of the Old Boston Election Guideline:* Vote for a rich guy. He doesn't have to steal as much. *Skole's Rule* *of Antique Dealers:* Never simply say, "Sorry, we don't have what you are looking for." Always say, "Too bad, I just sold one the other day." *Skole's Statistical Law:* The statistic you want is hard to find; the statistic you need is impossible to find. (Robert Skole, Boston and Stockholm.)

Skye's Rules. (1) Never make friends with a person whose nickname is "Gator," "Moose," or "Flower." (2) You can't throw away a trash can. (3) A watched pot never boils over. (J. Skye, San Antonio, Texas.)

Slate's Law. Growing old may be mandatory, but growing up is strictly optional. (Claudia Slate, Dallas, Texas.)

Slavens's Discoveries. (1) The toilet paper never runs out on the other guy. (2) Never let a drunk friend drive—especially if the party was at *his* place. (3) People with strong minds have weak eyes. (4) A good newspaper column cannot be written unless there is a can of beer on one side of the typewriter and a bag of Doritos on the other. (Larry M. Slavens, publisher, *The Fontanelle Observer,* Fontanelle, Iowa.)

Slay's Rule. Don't do anything dumb. *Slay's Corollary:* I'll decide what's dumb. (General Alton D. Slay; from Lt. Col. William P. Campbell.)

Slevin's Rule. The more a person is confused by what you say sincerely, the more likely he or she is to agree with you in principle. (Martin Slevin, Whitmore Park, Coventry, England.)

Slick's Distinction. There are two types of dirt: the dark kind, attracted to light objects; and the light kind, attracted to dark objects. (Ely Slick from Tom Gill.)

Slide Presentation, Law of. In any slide presentation, at least one slide will be upside down or backwards, or both. (John Corcoran, whose entry in the *Directory of Washington Independent Writers* reads, in part, "Send for clips to see how I write. If you don't, frogs will sneak into your house and eat your fingers.")

Slim's Law. Any significant military action will occur at the junction of two or more map sheets. (Field Marshal Viscount Slim of Burma; from Richard J. Keogh, Honolulu, Hawaii.)

Slous's Contention. If you do a job too well, you'll get stuck with it. (Roy Slous; from T. S. Durham.)

Slug's Constant. No matter how fast a computer is, inefficient programs will evolve so that the machine will appear to run at the same speed as always. (John Dvorak, *PC Magazine,* May 12, 1987; from Shel Kagan.)

Smith-Johannsen's Secret of Longevity. Stay busy, get plenty of exercise, and don't drink too much. Then again, don't drink too little. (Herman "Jackrabbit" Smith-Johannsen, 103-year-old Canadian cross-country skier, quoted in *Sports Illustrated,* August 21, 1978.)

Smith's Commuter Observations. (1) If your lane moves faster than all the others, it's time to change lanes. (2) There is always room to merge behind a diesel bus. (Dan Smith, Walnut Creek, California.)

Smith's Cosellian Confession. I have tried hard to like that man, and I have failed miserably. (The late Red Smith, on Howard Cosell, quoted by Shirley Povich, *Washington Post.*)

Smith's Final Reflections. (1) No man is an SOB to himself. (2) A straight line is not the shortest distance between persons. (3) Only he who tickles himself may laugh as he pleases. (4) The spiritual overshadows and purifies the religions. (5) Rules of life are plural, willy-nilly. (From a longer list by T. V. Smith, in his autobiography *A Non-Existent Man,* 1962. Smith was a philosopher who became a congressman. From Wayne I. Boucher.)

Smith's Fourth Law of Inertia. A body at rest tends to watch television. (C. Guy Smith, Media, Pennsylvania.)

Smith's Glue Givens and Adhesive Axioms. (1) Regardless of its intended purpose, an adhesive will always stick to your fingers best. (2) When the sophisticated two-part adhesive systems are measured accurately and mixed and timed precisely, they can be expected to work every bit as well as model airplane cement. (3) If you break the handle on a coffee cup, consider the new space age adhesives and then buy a new cup. (V. Richard Smith, LaGrange, Illinois.)

Smith's Hypotheses. (1) Wear white pants; no one will ask you to do dirty work. (2) When you are young, you think that everyone is watching you. After twenty, you try to get people to notice you, and it is only when you get old that you realize that no one was *ever* looking. (3) The best seat on a commercial airplane is the one behind the one with its back stuck in its upright position. (4) The sales receipt that you are most likely to lose is the one that you need to return with a rebate; *and* I would like to be able to buy the special glue that they use on the bottle labels that must be removed to accompany a rebate; *and* might we be able to make a nice dent in the "National Debt" with all the money that is not redeemed on rebates? (V. Richard Smith, LaGrange, Illinois.)

Smith's Law. The two worst things that can be made public about a person are (1) being guilty of a heinous crime, and (2) being a recipient of a large sum of money. (V. Richard Smith, LaGrange, Illinois.)

Smith's Law of Dietary Certainty. People who eat natural foods will die of natural causes. (Robert H. Smith, Oceanside, California.)

Smith's Law of Municipal Location. When in a strange city, the first person that you ask directions of will also be from out of town. (V. Richard Smith, LaGrange, Illinois.)

Smith's Laws. *Small Appliance Axiom:* If it doesn't break immediately, it can never be fixed. *2nd Small Appliance Axiom:* If it breaks immediately, by the time it's fixed it will be too late to fix it if it breaks again. *Marketing:* You can never buy the new improved version because a new improved version is already replacing it. (Jerry Smith, Florissant, Missouri.)

Smith's Laws of Politics and Other Things. (1) A politician always abuses his own constituency and placates the opponent's. (2) The main beneficiaries of federal aid are those states that most oppose the principle. (3) A baseball player who makes a spectacular defensive play always leads off the next inning. (4) A person over age 65 who drinks says that his doctor recommends it. (Bob Smith, Washington, D.C., founder, editor, and publisher of the *Privacy Journal.*)

Smith's Conclusion. There is nothing so trivial, so esoteric, so unique, or so commonplace, that someone will not spend time and effort in an attempt to codify it. (John Stephen Smith, Lincoln, Nebraska.)

Smith's Observation. At a sit-down dinner at the family reunion, the probability of the cuckoo clock striking during the pre-meal prayer varies directly with the number of children seated at the table. (Dr. Terry B. Smith, Kirksville, Missouri.)

Smith's Political Dictum. When caught with your hand in the cookie jar, it's easy to explain to your enemies, but try to explain it to your friends. (James R. Smith, Petoskey, Michigan.)

Smith's Principles of Bureaucratic Tinkertoys. (1) Never use one word when a dozen will suffice. (2) If it can be understood, it's not finished yet. (3) Never do anything for the first time. (*U;* from Paul Herbig, Chicago, Illinois.)

Smith's Rule of Bar Decorum. Never take a punch at a man named Sullivan. (The late H. Allen Smith, *Life in a Putty Knife Factory*, Doubleday, 1943; from Joseph C. Goulden.)

Smith's Rule. When ironing a piece of clothing, the unremovable spot or unrepairable damage will be found on the last area to be ironed. (Suzy Smith, Tampa, Florida.)

Smith's Rules. (1) Discount by at least 90 percent the truth of any statement preceded by the phrase "Of course." (2) In a civil war, "cease fire" means "before bombing military targets, bomb the historic church and the children's hospital." (3) The success or failure of diplomatic negotiations is determined by whatever is in those bottles that are always on the table. (4) You always pull the wrong shoelace first. (5) A Band-Aid string always pulls free before opening the wrapper. Once opened, the adhesive strips always stick together before the Band-Aid is applied. (Dr. Terry Smith, Northeast Missouri State University, Kirksville, Missouri.)

Smith's Suggestions to New Graduates. (1) Dirty laundry never goes away. (2) There's no such thing as a "friendly" divorce. (3) A few years after graduation, everyone becomes a high-school letterman. (Wes Smith, "Welcome to the Real World," *Modern Maturity,* June-July 1985.)

Smith's Writing Rule. In composing, as a general rule, run your pen through every other word you have written; you have no idea what vigor it will give your style. (English clergyman and essayist Sydney Smith.)

Smock's Travel Observations. (1) Every country is a "land of contrast." (2) Wherever you travel, the weather is "unusual for this time of year." (Ruth J. Smock, Silver Spring, Maryland.)

Smokler's Razor. The secret is not to learn something you don't want to practice. (This law stems from an item in the *Dallas Morning News* in an article August 16, 1998, about a Mrs. Smokler, whose job was to keep the books on a dairy farm, but who had never once milked a cow because she was too smart to learn how.)

Smolik's Law. (1) A politician will always be there when he needs you. (2) Anything highly publicized needs to be. (Richard C. Smolik, St. Louis, Missouri.)

Smythe's Laws. (1) If you want to hide a needle, don't put it in a haystack; put it in a box of needles. (2) You get screwed to the extent that you prostitute yourself. (3) You can catch more flies with honey than with vinegar, but if you really want to catch flies, use putrid hamburger. (Anonymous; from Marshall L. Smith.)

SNAFU Principle. Communication is only possible between equals. (In *The Illuminatus! Trilogy,* Dell, 1975; by Robert Shea and Robert Anson Wilson; from John W. Gustafson, Chicago, Illinois.)

Snaper's Last Law. The obvious isn't. (Alvin A. Snaper, Las Vegas, Nevada.)

Snead's Advice. Keep close to your nickels and dimes; stay away from whiskey and never concede a putt. (Quoted in golfer Sam Snead's obituary in *The New York Times,* May 24, 2002; *JCG.)*

Snow's Rules For New Inhabitants Of The White House. (1) Don't get a big head. If you lose your humility, someone will return it to you with compound interest. (2) In Washington, you can't take friendship personally. (3) In Washington the urgent overwhelms important. (4) Make friends in low places. Get to know the people who have worked forever in the White House. (Tony Snow in the *Washington Times,* January 21, 2001. *JCG*)

Snyder's Data Processing Rule of Thumb. The usefulness of a computer printout is inversely proportional to its weight. (Timothy H. Snyder, letter to *Business Week,* November 23, 1987.)

Snyder's Law. In any situation involving more than one person doing similar jobs, the important information will be given to the person not involved in the project, and he will forget to pass it along as it does not involve him. (Daniel K. Snyder, Pearl City, Hawaii, who offered this example: "While researching material for the completion of a job, my cohort was informed that the job was cancelled, a fact that I was informed of two days later, upon completion of the job.")

Socio-Genetics, First Law of. Celibacy is not hereditary. (Proposed by Guy Godin in *JIR* in 1975 and quickly questioned. Wrote one reader, "If your parents didn't have any children, the odds are that you won't have any.")

Socio-Genetics, Second Law of. The law of heredity is that all undesirable traits come from the other parent. ("Morning Smile" column, *The Toronto Globe and Mail,* February 21, 1979; from Richard Isaac, M.D., Toronto, Ontario.)

Sod's Law. The degree of failure is in direct proportion to the effort expended and to the need for success. (Generally speaking, "Sod" is the British incarnation of Finagle, Gumperson, Murphy, *et al.* One authority on *Sod's Law* is Richard Boston of London, who has written of it in such periodicals as *The New Statesman* and *The Times Literary Supplement.* Boston does not claim to be its author: on the contrary, he has traced a version of it back to a Lancashire proverb dating from 1871: "The bread never falls but on its buttered side." He also reports that in France, it is called *La loi d'emmerdement maximum.* However, Boston's greatest contribution may be in telling the story of the man whose bread fell and landed buttered side up. He ran straight away to his rabbi to report this deviance from one of the basic rules of the universe. At first, the rabbi would not believe him but finally became convinced that it had happened. However, he didn't feel qualified to deal with the question and passed it along to one of world's leading Talmudic scholars. After months of waiting, the scholar finally came up with an answer: "The bread must have been buttered on the wrong side.")

Sod's Law of Change. The more you want something to change, the more it stays the same. The more we want things to stay the same, the more they change. (John Emsley in the *New Scientist,* April 2, 1987.)

Softball's Ten Commandments. (1) Do unto others as they do unto you, but do it in the early innings. (2) If you don't know the score, you can be pretty sure that you're behind. (Francis O. Walsh, whose rule has been quoted for years in women's softball publications.) (3) If you don't know what kind of softball you're playing, ask the coach. (4). In true amateur softball there is no such thing as a "routine play." (5). Don't Take It Too Seriously ("It" being anything but softball—work, one's reputation, one's capacity for humility, and virtually any issue of life and death.). (6) A ball will travel farther in the early innings of a game. A ball will travel farther on some days than on others, depending on the weather conditions. (True. It will travel 15 to 30 feet farther on a hot, dry, sunny day than it will on cold or cool damp days, or very humid days.) (7) Always beware of a team with a hard industrial/patriotic name. "American Rivet" or "Eagle Masonry" has a built-in two-run edge over your "Ed's Lounge" or your "Beerhunters." (8) Whomsoever shows the greatest bravado in a victory celebration is almost certainly the person who did the least to ensure that victory. (9) In any given game, at almost any given level of play a dog or a crying child will appear on the field to temporarily stop play.(In *Softball! So What?,* Frederick Stokes, 1940, Lowell Thomas and Ted Shane point out that back in the 1930s the extra rule they played with was "A dog on the field means a drink on the house, if you can find the house.") (10). If someone yells to a teammate that "A walk is as good as a hit" this means that there is a terrible fear that the batter might actually try to take a poke at the ball. (Composed from multiple sources by the author for his *Worth Book of Softball Facts on File,* 1994.)

Soika's Law. Wherever you park your car in the summertime, when you get back, the sun will be shining on the driver's seat. (George R. Soika, Oshkosh, Wisconsin.)

Solberg's Saw. All progress isn't forward. (E. W. Solberg, Calimesa, California.)

Solis's Amendment. There is no such thing as a free lunch—the lunch gets more expensive each year. (L. L. Solis, Columbus, Ohio. Letter to the *Wall Street Journal,* November 11, 1974.)

Solomon's Explanation. The only function of economic forecasting is to make astrology look respectable. (Stanford economist Ezra Solomon, *USA Today,* June 26, 1984.)

Somary's Fifteenth Law. The less protection the State provides for its citizens, the more it charges for the job. (Swiss banker Felix Somary; one of his twenty social laws from *Crisis and the Future of Democracy.* Quoted by Brian Crozier in *The National Review,* March, 1979; *JCG.*)

Sommers's Official Explanation of Why a Cold Makes One Miserable. There's no point in having a cold if it doesn't make you miserable. (Jeffrey Sommers, Cincinnati, Ohio.)

Soudriette's Pickle. You can never tell which way a pickle will squirt until you bite it. (William C. Soudriette, New York, New York.)

Spaatz's Three Rules for the Conduct of Air Force Officers Before Congressional Committees. (1) Don't try to be funny. (2) Don't lie. (3) Don't blurt out the truth. (Gen. Carl Andrew "Tooey" Spaatz, Chief of Staff, USAF; from Brig. Gen. William J. Becker, USAF.)

Spano's Law of Nutrition. The tastiness of any food is directly proportional to the amount of cholesterol contained within. *Corollary:* If it tastes good, spit it out. (Franco J. Spano, M.D., and Gregory G. Spano, M.D., Chicago, Illinois.)

Spare Parts Principle. The accessibility, during recovery of small parts which fall from the workbench, varies directly with the size of the part and inversely with its importance to the completion of the work underway. (*AIC.*)

Spats's Restatement. Every silver lining has a cloud. (The character "Spats" Baxter in *Movie Movie.*)

Specht's Discovery. A condominium is just an apartment with a down payment. (*RS,* Santa Monica, California.)

Specht's Meta-law. Under any conditions, anywhere, whatever you are doing, there is some ordinance under which you can be booked. (Robert D. Specht of the RAND Corp., who is also collector *RS.*)

Specialist's Law of Hole-Digging, The. It's a mighty sight better to have a little privy over a big hole than a big privy over a little hole. (Charles (Chic) Sales in his best-selling book about outhouses, T*he Specialist*, 1929; *TG,* Lubbock, Texas.)

Speculating on Margin, Three Good Rules for. (1) Don't! (2) Do not! (3) If, after careful perusal of the two aforementioned rules, you are still resolved upon folly, go to your bank, cracked teapot, old stocking, or other financial depository where your hard-earned cash is kept, and, having therefrom taken one thousand dollars... roll them carefully in strong, brown wrapping-paper and seal the ends. You are now ready for the next step. Placing the roll in your inside vest pocket, proceed briskly to the nearest ferry slip and take the first boat which leaves. When midway between the termini, walk to the stern of the boat, take out the roll, and heave it far into the troubled waters. Your money will have then arrived at its terminus, and you should calmly proceed to yours. By following this method of deposit for your margin, you not only save brokers' commission and interest, but many anxious days and sleepless nights, besides having anticipated by a few hours the sinking of your money. (Gideon Wurdz [Charles Wayland Towne] in *Foolish Finance,* J.W. Luce, 1905.)

Spencer's (Contradictory) Corollary (to Nofziger's Law of Detail). If a political candidate chooses to go into specifics on a program that affects a voter's self-interest, the voter *gets* interested. If the proposal involves money, he gets very interested. (Stuart Spencer of President Ford's PR staff, about Reagan's proposed $90 billion cut in the federal budget. From Vic Gold's *PR as in President,* Doubleday, 1977.)

Spence's Admonition. Never stow away on a kamakazi plane. (T. R. M. Spence, Sydney, Australia.)

Spindel's Motivator. Aim at nothing and you will hit it. (Donald T. Spindel, St. Louis, Missouri.)

Sprague's Law. Satisfaction derived from a trip goes down as expectation goes up *if* reality is unchanged: $S = R/E$. As reality becomes more favorable, the chance for satisfaction goes up *if* expectation is unchanged. (Hall T. Sprague, *The New York Times,* Travel section, January 16, 1977; *JW.*)

Sprehe's Discovery. How to locate the slow-moving traffic lane or check-out line: Get in it. (J. Christopher Sprehe, Shawnee Mission, Kansas.)

Springer's Law. Whenever someone you know, or someone you do business with, moves to a new location, it's always farther away. (Sherwood Springer, Hawthorne, California.)

Springer's Observation. There are no failures at a class reunion. (Jerry Springer; from Anthony McMullin.)

Spring's Olfactory Axiom. It doesn't smell until you step in it. (Bernard Spring, D.D.S., Windsor, Ontario.)

Stabler's Law of Moving. If you pack up and move, when you look for something you will not find it, but when you are looking for something else you will. (Laurence Stabler, Gainesville, Florida.)

Staedler's Reaction. Television is like throwing a diamond in an outhouse. There is something good in there, you just have to dig through so much crap to find it. (John A. Staedler, Mercer, California.)

Stamp's Statistical Probability. The government [is] extremely fond of amassing great quantities of statistics. These are raised to the *n*th degree, the cube roots are extracted, and the results are arranged into elaborate and impressive displays. What must be kept ever in mind, however, is that in every case, the figures are first put down by a village watchman, and he puts down anything he damn well pleases. (Attributed to Sir Josiah Stamp, H.M. collector of inland revenue; from rules collected by Donald Rumsfeld.)

Stanley's Rules of the Road. (1) The later you are, the greater the length of the red light. (2) The least-traveled roads have the longest green lights. (Randall L. Stanley, St. Charles, Missouri; *EV.*)

Stanton's Law of Minimum Requirements. Bad breath is better than no breath at all. (Marsha Stanton, Dhahran, Saudi Arabia.)

Stapley's Laws. *Interviewers:* Never ask a politician for a short answer, as the politician will then give a longer answer than if one had not been so specific about its length. *Young People:* Marry an ugly girl/boy; in thirty years' time, you won't notice the difference as much. *Denial:* The louder or bigger or more frequent the denial, the more likely it is that the original accusation was correct. (Nigel Stapley, Dyfed, Wales.)

Stark Theorem on Lobbyists, The. The more boring and incomprehensible a piece of legislation is and the fewer taxpayers it affects, the more lobbyists it will attract. Or, L(3) = P/I [AF^2 X D] - 93(AFDC + SSI + food stamps) or, (L(3), the Length of a Line of Lobbyists, equals the Population of the Nation (P) divided by the Number of Individuals Impacted (I). This figure is then multiplied by the square of Arcaneness Factor (AF) times the Dullness Factor (D) minus 93, times the number of references to poor people. (Pete Stark, California, whose findings were reported in the *Washington Weekly*, October 22, 1984. The inspiration for this theorem was the scant number of lobbyists who show up for Medicare hearings (affecting millions and millions of people) contrasted with the hordes who lobby for lower corporate taxes.)

Stasny's Elevator Strategy. If you're in the front of a packed car and hear footsteps down the hall followed by the words, "Hold the elevator!" here's a way to mollify everybody: Lunge for the control panel, but deliberately miss the "Door Open" button. The person staring at you from the outside will think you tried, and the restless mob behind you will be glad you didn't. (Jim Stasny, "Surviving the Shaft," *Washington Post,* November 12, 1987.)

State Service Syndrome. Never ask a business question during lunch hour. (James Brown, former state employee; from Gary Knowlton, Portland, Oregon.)

Steckel's Rule to Success. Good enough isn't good enough. (Paul W. Steckel, Gainesville, Florida.)

Steele's Fifth Law of Water Beds. Bodies tend to oscillate at the same rate that they accelerate. (Ashley H. Steele, Toledo, Ohio.)

Steele's Law of Excellence. Only 10 percent of anything can be in the top 10 percent. (Guy L. Steele, Jr., Cambridge, Massachusetts.)

Steele's Plagiarism of Somebody's Philosophy. Everyone should believe in something. I believe I'll have another drink. (Mary Steele; *S.T.L.*)

Steese's Law of the Body Politic. It is much more difficult to discern the forest when you're one of the trees. (Gerald Lee Steese, Long Beach, California.)

Steger's Law of Sound Stewardship. Ten saved dimes total the dollar with which, by careful shopping, you may be able to buy a dime's worth. (Shelby Steger, Berkeley, California.)

Steinbeck's Law. When you need towns, they are very far apart. (John Steinbeck, on the occasion of coming down with car trouble on a lonely road in Oregon while researching *Travels with Charley*, Viking, 1962; recalled by H. Allen Smith in *A Short History of Fingers*, Little, Brown, 1963.)

Steiner's Observation. The Stone Age didn't end because we ran out of rocks. (Christopher Steiner, author of *$20 Per Gallon, How the Inevitable Rise in the Price of Gasoline Will Change Our Lives for the Better*; from Tom Gill.)

Steinert's Rule. Whenever you need somebody, you can never find him, but when you don't need him, you can't get rid of him. (Terrell W. Steinert, FPO, San Francisco, California.)

Stein's Simplified Economic Theory. The money stays the same, the pockets just keep changing. (Gertrude Stein; from William Lurie.)

Stengel's Law. Good pitching will always stop good hitting, and vice versa. (Casey Stengel; from Steven D. Mirsky, Ithaca, New York.)

Stephen's Law of Averages. Based on the summation of parts, divided by the number of samples, the *average* human has one breast and one testicle. (Stephen J. Grollman, Hartsdale, New York.)

Stern's Constant. When you have a bad back, anything that can fall—does! (Rhoda Stern, Skokie, Illinois.)

Stevens' First Law of Outdoor Recreation. Never go water skiing alone. (Doug Stevens, Colony, Texas.)

Stevenson's Presidential Paradox. By the time a man is nominated for the Presidency of the United States, he is no longer worthy to hold the office. (Adlai Stevenson, 1956; from Sydney J. Harris.)

Stewart's Observation. Believing is seeing. (John O. Stewart, Denver, Colorado, who explains, "The above was first appreciated as a result of interviewing many witnesses during the conduct of criminal investigations, but since then it has been found to account for much of what people perceive in any activity.")

Stimson's Lesson. The chief lesson I have learned in a long life is that the only way you can make a man trustworthy is to trust him; and the surest way to make him untrustworthy is to distrust him and show your distrust. (Henry L. Stimpson, then Secretary of War and perhaps the most experienced and thoughtful of advisors to President Roosevelt in WWII, offered the lesson in an exceptionally important Memorandum to the President, written on September 11, 1945, in which he proposed a national action plan on the control of atomic weapons. The entire text of this memorandum can be found in H. L. Stimpson and McGeorge Bundy, *On Active Service in Peace and War* (New York, 1947), pp. 642–646; from Wayne I. Boucher.)

Stine's Laws and Rules. *Communication:* Communication is 90 percent reception. *Relative Beauty:* If you make something yourself, all you see in it is the mistakes. *Bedtime Stories:* You cannot underestimate a child's capacity for repetition. You cannot underestimate a child's capacity for repetition. *Finding Restaurants and Gas Stations While Driving on Limited Access Highways:* If you can't see it from the road, it doesn't exist. *Mumblers:* If somebody mumbles something and you ask them to repeat it, you will understand it all, except the part you didn't get the first time.

Techno-Logic: In any technical subject, the more basic information is, the harder it is to find out. *Thinking:* When people get lost in thought, it is usually because they are in unfamiliar territory. *Troubleshooting:* Just because you've fixed a problem doesn't mean you've fixed the problem. *Dialogue for Marital Bliss:* My wife, Diane, says there are two things that are essential to a successful marriage: communication and simple politeness. I replied, "That's stupid, and I don't want to talk about it."(Steve Stine, Skokie, Illinois.)

Stock Market Axiom. The public is always wrong. (Steve Stine, Skokie, Illinois; *U/Co.*)

Stockbroker's Declaration. The market will rally from this or lower levels. (Larry W. Sisson, Seattle, Washington; *AO.*)

Stockmeyer's Stock Quotations. (1) Closet space is like money—you will use up as much as you have. (2) The more expensive the dress, the smaller the size you will be able to fit into. (Claire Stockmeyer, Washington, D.C.)

Stock's Observation. You no sooner get your head above water than someone pulls your flippers off. (*U/DRW.*)

Stoebner's Law. Do not pour any more milk for the child than you want to wipe up. (Ben E. Stoebner, Tehachapi, California.)

Stoll's Laws. (1) People who try to make things better usually make them worse. (2) The more expensive the suit, the greater the size of the waist in proportion to the size of the jacket. (Austin Stoll, Chicago, Illinois.)

Stones's Track and Field Maxim. Never turn your back on the javelin competition. (Olympic high-jumper Dwight Stones; from Sally G. Pecor, Washington, D.C.)

Story's Laws. (1) Even failures aren't perfect. (2) Accordion players always wear a ring. (3) An apple a day keeps the doctor away, but why stop there? An onion a day keeps everyone away. (Thomas W. Story, Antioch, California.)

Storz's Revision. Early to bed and early to rise makes a man tired in mid afternoon. (Rudolf Storz, Huntingdon, Tennessee.)

Straus's Axioms. (1) Everything the government touches turns to solid waste. (2) After the government turns something to solid waste, it deregulates it and turns it into natural gas. (V. Michael Straus, Washington, D.C.)

Strout's Law. There is a major scandal in American political life every 50 years: Grant's in 1873, Teapot Dome in 1923, Watergate in 1973. Nail down your seats for 2023. (Richard Strout, quoted in *Time,* March 27, 1978.)

Stults's Situation Report. Our problems are mostly behind us—what we have to do now is fight the solutions. (Banker Alan P. Stults, quoted in the *Chicago Tribune,* July 11, 1975.)

Stump's Flu Shot Law. If everyone else has a flu shot, you don't need one. (Richard B. Stump.)

Sturgeon's Law. Ninety percent of everything is crud. (Science fiction writer Theodore Sturgeon. This law is widely quoted—from the *Washington Post* to *Harper's*—with the percentages varying from 90 to 99 percent and the last word variously "crud" or "crap." The law first appeared in the S.T.L. list, and according to a note from Conrad Schneiker "resulted from a reply to a question about his writing of sci-fi TV material.")

Suhor's Law. A little ambiguity never hurt anyone. (Charles Suhor, deputy executive director, National Council of Teachers of English. He formulated the law when he discovered "the universe is intractably squiggly.")

Sukhomlinov Effect, The. In war, victory goes to those armies whose leaders' uniforms are least impressive. (Roger A. Beaumont and Bernard J. James, *Horizon* magazine, Winter 1971.)

Sullivan's Law. All great organizations were built on the backs of blind mules on treadmills. *Corollary:* No great organization was ever built with one-eyed mules. (J. M. Sullivan, Creve Coeur, Missouri.)

Sullivan's Proverbial Discovery. Proverbs usually read just as well backwards, or jumbled up. Fine words do not a parsnip make nor iron bars a summer. (Humorist Frank Sullivan, from his essay "It's Easy to Quote a Proper Proverb.")

Summer Help. And some are not. (R. F. Heisey, Arlington, Virginia.)

Suplee's "Self-Help Book" Conclusion. There's a succor born every minute. (Curt Suplee, *Washington Post,* October 17, 1982.)

Surprenant's Law of Gardening. The easiest vegetables to raise in a garden are those you like least, and vice versa. Tastes of insects and animal pests are directly proportional to your own. (Donald T. Surprenant, Barrington, Illinois.)

Survival Formula for Public Office. (1) Exploit the inevitable, which means, take credit for anything good which happens whether you had anything to do with it or not. (2) Don't disturb the perimeter, meaning don't stir a mess unless you can be sure of the result. (3) Stay in with the Outs—the Ins will make so many mistakes you can't afford to alienate the Outs. (4) Don't permit yourself to get between a dog and a lamppost. (*AO.*)

Susan's Law. Before you ask, don't. (*U;* WRC Radio, Washington, D.C.)

Sutton's Law. Go where the money is. (Named after bank robber Willie Sutton who, when asked why he robbed banks, replied, "Because that's where the money is." It is used regularly in a number of fields today where, when the question of which direction to take is asked, it is common to simply say, "Let *Sutton's*

Law apply." Machol uses it as one of his Principles of Operations Research, but it is also applied in fields as diverse as medical research and broadcasting.)

Sutton's Laws. (1) If at first you don't succeed, don't try again until you have successfully identified the bastards who are against you. (2) Extreme desirability never survives acquiral. (3) The emergence of a good business opportunity always occurs at a period of peak load. (Francis W. A. Sutton, St. Austell, Cornwall, England, who also offers the observation below.)

Sutton's Second Observation on Mental Health. When you have searched your pockets five times over and looked high and low for your car keys, and no possible explanation for their loss or whereabouts is forthcoming, don't lose heart. Things could be much worse. Think of those poor people who do not have cars—but, nevertheless, are looking for their car keys.

Svaglic's Rule. The ability of a professional person is inversely proportional to the number of credentials he displays on his office wall. (James M. Svaglic, Webster Groves, Missouri.)

Svensson's Law. If spring arrives on Monday, that's the day you have to work. (Translated from the original by Valfried Skapenhuggare, in *Dagens Nyheter,* February 5, 1988; from Bob Skole.)

Swanson's Lament. I'm still big. It's the pictures that got small. (Gloria Swanson, in *Sunset Boulevard.*)

Swanson's Law. When the water reaches the upper deck, follow the rats. (Claude Swanson, Secretary of the Navy under Franklin D. Roosevelt.)

Swanson's Law of Poverty. Everyone thinks everyone else has money. (Eugene D. Swanson, Waco, Texas.)

Swartz's Maxim. Live every day as if it were your last... and some day you'll be right. (*U/Ra.*)

Sweeney's Laws. (1) The joy that is felt at the sight of a new fallen snow is inversely proportional to the age of the beholder. (2) Today's society will ignore almost any form of public behavior except getting in the express line with two extra items. (3) Never trust a skinny cook. (Paul Sweeney, in the *Quarterly,* which he writes for the Defense Mapping Federal Credit Union.)

Swinehart's Definition. The lecture is that procedure whereby the material in the notes of the professor is transferred to the notes of the students without passing through the mind of either. (Donald F. Swinehart, Department of Chemistry, University of Oregon; *TJR.*)

Swipple Rule of Order. He who shouts loudest has the floor. (*U/S.T.L.*)

Switzer's Embellishment. You might remember that Mies van der Rohe said "Less is More" which is true, more or less. (John E. Switzer, Bethesda, Maryland.)

Sybert's Law. Ignorance is blissful only to the intelligent. (Christopher Sybert, Lutherville, Maryland.)

Sybert's Law of the Workshop. Whenever a project is undertaken, the least expensive but most important item for its completion will be forgotten; e.g., sandpaper, paintbrushes, etc. (Christopher Sybert, Lutherville, Maryland.)

Sykes' Message on Life to High-School Graduates. (1) Life is not fair; get used to it. (2) The world won't care about your self-esteem. The world will expect you to accomplish something *before* you feel good about yourself. (3)You will *not* make 40 thousand dollars a year right out of high school. You won't be a vice president with a car phone, until you earn both. (4) If you think your teacher is tough, wait until you get a boss. He doesn't have tenure. (5) Flipping burgers is not beneath your dignity. Your grandparents had a different word for burger flipping; they called it opportunity. (6) If you mess up, it's not your parents' fault, so don't whine about your mistakes, learn from them. (7) Before you were born, your parents weren't as boring as they are now. They got that way from paying your bills, cleaning your clothes, and listening to you talk about how cool you are. So before you save the rain forest from the parasites of your parents' generation, try "delousing" the closet in your own room. (8) Your school may have done away with winners and losers, but life has not. In some schools they have abolished failing grades; they'll give you as many times as you want to get the right answer. This doesn't bear the slightest resemblance to *anything* in real life. (9) Life is not divided into semesters. You don't get summer off and very few employers are interested in helping you find yourself. Do that on your own time. (10) Television is *not* real life. In real life people actually have to leave the coffee shop and go to jobs. (11) Be nice to nerds. (Charles J. Sykes, best known as the author of *Dumbing Down Our Kids: Why American Children Feel Good about Themselves, but Can't Read, Write, or Add,* St. Martin's, 1995; from an op-ed piece that appeared in the *San Diego Union-Tribune* on September 19, 1996. It began making the e-mail rounds under Bill Gates's name in February 2000 and is still far more often attributed to Gates than to Sykes—which is unfortunate, but, like the man said: Life isn't fair; get used to it.)

Symington's Law. For every credibility gap there is a gullibility gap. (Senator Stuart Symington, quoted in an Ann Landers column. *See Clopton's Law.*)

Symons's Law of Flirting. When a girl appears not to know you exist, it means she is definitely interested in you. Or that she is definitely uninterested in you. Or that she does not know you exist. (Don Symons, Santa Barbara, California.)

Szadokierski's Law of the Street. When the sign says walk, it means run. (Mark Szadokierski, Charlottesville, Virginia.)

Szasz's Observation. Why is it that when you are between 7 and 12, the children of your parents' friends are always of the opposite sex; but when you're between 15 and 20, they never are. (Ferenc M. Szasz, Albuquerque, New Mexico.)

Szymanski's Law. Having been a physics major at the University of Notre Dame, having studied under one of Einstein's students, having worked on the Manhattan Project in WWII developing the atom bomb, and having been a physics teacher at the University of San Francisco, I thought I understood the Theory of Relativity. However, it wasn't until I became a probate judge that I really understood the Theory. It is that, at death, you have a number of relatives directly proportionate to the amount of money you leave behind. (The late Judge Frank S. Szymanski; from his son Judge David J. Szymanski, Detroit, Michigan.)

Szymcik's Universal Law of Experts. An expert is not someone who is often right, as opposed to a non-expert; each is wrong about the same percent of the time. But the expert can always tell you why he was wrong; so you can always tell the difference. (Rev. Mark Szymcik, Leominster, Massachusetts.)

T

T. Camille's Axioms. (1) You are always doing something marginal when your boss drops by your desk. (2) You've made a decision whether or not you decided. (3) Title distinctions are functions of everything they shouldn't be. (4) It is easier to do it the hard way. (5) You'd always rather be doing something else when you are doing what you thought you wanted to do. (6) The least important and the most important information gets passed on at the office copying machine. (7) If you haven't asked yourself "Why the hell did I go to college anyway?" you must be teaching. (8) You haven't not worked until you've worked for the government. (9) He's not smarter than you—he's just more convincing. (10) If you feel incompetent, you probably are. (11) If someone else's clout depends on your productivity, she/he'll be on your back. (12) I'll do it Monday. (13) May the odds be with you! (14) Nobody likes a smart-ass; nobody likes a dumb-ass, either. (T. Camille Flowers, Cincinnati, Ohio.)

Tammeus/Case Scientific Theory, The. All otherwise inexplicable phenomena of science can be explained by magic. (Bill Tammeus, in his column, *Kansas City Star,* June 5, 1988. This is a law he learned in eighth grade from David Case.)

Tammeus's Rake Rule. The last 50 leaves take as long to rake as the first 5,050.

Tansik's Law of Bureaucratic Success. Success in a bureaucracy depends not so much on whom you please, but on whom you avoid making angry. *Corollary:* To succeed, concentrate not on doing great things but on the avoidance of making mistakes. (David A. Tansik, Associate Professor, University of Arizona.)

Taranto's Theorem. The amount of intelligence on Earth is finite; the population increases exponentially. (Harry V. Taranto, New York, New York.)

Tatman's Assumption. Always assume that your assumption is invalid. (Robert F. Tatman, Wynnewood, Pennsylvania.)

Taxi Principle. Find out the cost before you get in. (Posted in U.S. Department of Labor. *TO'B.*)

Taylor's Discovery. In any organization there are only two people to contact if you want results—the person at the very top and the person at the very bottom. (Warren E. Taylor, Burlington, North Carolina.)

Taylor's Law of Axis. Taxis are soluble—they dissolve in rain. (Rod Taylor, in the movie *Sunday in New York;* from Dick J. Hessing.)

Teacher's Truism, The. The only time parents are willing to accept their child as "average" is at the moment of birth. (*U;* from Richard E. Fisher, Homestead, Florida.)

Teaford's Observations on Sewing Machine Personality/Functioning. (1) One "damn it" restores machine's functioning. (2) Two "damn its!" are self-canceling. (3) One "son-of-a-bitch" will cause a full bobbin to immediately run out of thread. (4) Crying helps a lot. (Robert M. Teaford, Napa, California.)

Technology, Law of. The very technology that makes our living simpler makes society more complex. The more efficient we get, the more specialized we become and the more dependent. (Thomas Griffith, *The Waist-High Culture,* Harper & Row, 1959.)

Television Truisms. (1) If a television character coughs, that character has an incurable disease and/or is going to die. (2). If a television character drops something, the character has the same disease Gary Cooper had in *Pride of the Yankees.* (Kevin Whitmore, Fairmount, Indiana.)

Teller's Truism. Fail-safe prescription bottle caps are always filled by the pharmacist, for whatever ailment, to those people who have arthritis in their hands. (Herbert J. Teller, Spruce Pine, North Carolina.)

Temps's Discovery. You can't lead a cavalry charge if you think you don't look good on a horse. (Mable L. Temps, Fremont, California.)

Tennis Players' Ten Commandments. *I.* Thou shalt have no sport other than tennis. *II.* Thou shalt remember thine appointed court time and put nothing before it. *III.* Thou shalt honor thy backhand as instructed by thy pro. *IV.* Thou shalt not bear false witness as to when thou wast last the provider of new tennis balls. *V.* Thou shalt not take the name of the Lord in vain when thy shot hitteth the tape and faileth to roll over. *VI.* Thou shalt not destroy thy racquet after having lobbed directly to thine opponent at the net. *VII.* Thou shalt not commit a double fault at set point. *VIII.* Thou shalt not steal thy partner's overhead smash. *IX.* Thou shalt not covet they neighbor's court time, nor his or her partner. *X.* Thou shalt not use four-letter expletives when thou hast caused an easy volley to be ensnared in the net. (*U/NDB.*)

Terkel's First Law of Interviewing. Listen, don't talk. (From an article on Studs Terkel, shortly after his death, in the *Independent* [London, England] November 4, 2008: "His technique of prodding people's views and recollections with a few canny questions, but essentially just letting them talk, and transcribing their words more or less verbatim, was the ultimate expression of the interviewer as facilitator.")

Terman's Law of Innovation. If you want a track team to win the high jump, you find one person who can jump seven feet, not seven people who can jump one foot. (Frederick E. Terman, Provost Emeritus, Stanford University. See also *Bowker's Law.*)

Tests and Examinations

(1) M.I.T. Graduate Qualifying Examination. (U/ME.)

• ***Instructions.***

Read each question thoroughly. Answer all questions. Time limit—four hours. Begin immediately.

• ***History.***

Describe the history of the papacy from its origins to the present day; concentrate specially but not exclusively on the social, political, economic, religious, and philosophical impact on Europe, Asia, America, and Africa. Be brief, concise, and specific.

• ***Medicine.***

You have been provided with a razor blade, a piece of gauze, and a bottle of Scotch. Remove your own appendix. Do not suture until your work has been inspected. You have fifteen minutes.

• ***Public Speaking.***

2,500 riot-crazed aborigines are storming the classroom. Calm them. You may use any ancient language except Latin or Greek.

• ***Biology.***

Create life. Estimate the differences in subsequent human culture if this form of life had developed 500 million years earlier, with special attention to the probable effects on the English parliamentary system. Prove your thesis.

• ***Music.***

Write a piano concerto. Orchestrate it and perform it with flute and drum. You will find a piano under your seat.

• ***Psychology.***

Based on your knowledge of their works, evaluate the emotional stability, degree of adjustment, and repressed frustrations of each of the following: Alexander of Aphrodisias, Ramses II, Hammurabi. Support your evaluation with quotations from each man's work, making appropriate references. It is not necessary to translate.

• ***Sociology.***

Estimate the sociological problems that might accompany the end of the world. Construct an experiment to test your theory.

• ***Management Science.***

Define management. Define science. How do they relate? Why? Create a generalized algorithm to optimize all managerial decisions. Assuming an 1130 CPU supporting 50 terminals, each terminal to activate your algorithm, design the communications interface and all the necessary control programs.

• ***Economics.***

Develop a realistic plan for refinancing the national debt. Trace the possible effects of your plan in the following areas: Cubism, the Donatist controversy, the wave theory of light. Outline a method from all points of view. Point out the deficiencies in your point of view, as demonstrated in your answer to the last question.

• ***Political Science.***

There is a red telephone on the desk beside you. Start World War III. Report at length on its socio-political effects, if any.

• ***Epistemology.***

Take a position for or against the truth. Prove the validity of your position.

• ***Physics.***

Explain the nature of matter. Include in your answer an evaluation of the impact of the development of mathematics on science.

• ***Philosophy.***
Sketch the development of human thought; estimate its significance. Compare with the development of any other kind of thought.

• ***General Knowledge.***
Describe in detail. Be objective and specific.

(2) North Dakota Null-Hypothesis Inventory (NDNI).

Instructions. Respond to each statement with one of these three answers: (1) Sometimes, (2) Always, (3) Never.

- I salivate at the sight of mittens.
- At times I am afraid my toes will fall off.
- Chopped liver makes me laugh.
- As an infant, I had very few hobbies.
- Some people never look at me.
- I sometimes feel that my earlobes are longer than those of other people.
- Spinach makes me feel alone.
- My sex life is A-okay.
- I often fart in crowds.
- Dirty stories make me think about sex.
- I am anxious in rooms that have hairy walls.
- Cousins are not to be trusted.
- Sometimes I think someone is trying to take over my stomach.
- I have never eaten a fly.
- I cannot read or write.
- As an infant I hated chopped liver.
- I have killed mosquitoes.
- My teeth sometimes leave my body.
- I am never startled by a fish.
- I have never gone to pieces over the weekend.
- My parents always faced catastrophe with a song.
- Recently, I have been getting shorter.
- I have taken shoe polish to excess.
- I have always been disturbed by the size of Lincoln's ears.
- Chicken liver gives me a rash.
- I like mannish children.
- Most of the time I go to sleep without saying good-bye.
- I am not afraid of picking up doorknobs.
- Chiclets make me sweat.
- I stay in the bathtub until I look like a raisin.

- Frantic screams make me nervous.
- It makes me angry to have people bury me.
- I hate orgies, if nobody else is there.
- I am afraid of Vikings.

(Shortened version of a longer NDNI. The NDNI is another classic of unknown origin that the author first encountered in 1964 in New York. It is, of course, a replacement for the ubiquitous Minnesota Multiphasic Personality Inventory [MMPI], which is used to create data for everyone ranging from college administrators to prison wardens. There is now an even newer test called the "No-Nonsense Personality Inventory," published for the first time in the November 1978 issue of *The Journal of Irreproducible Results,* which asks for responses to such statements as: "I am often bothered by thoughts of sex while having intercourse," "God rarely answers my questions," "Weeping brings tears to my eyes," and "I often bite other people's nails.")

(3) Test Entitled "Can you follow directions?" (Three-minute time test).

- Read everything before doing anything.
- Put your name in the upper right-hand corner of this paper.
- Circle the word "Name" in sentence two.
- Draw five small squares in the upper left-hand corner of this paper.
- Put an X in each square.
- Sign your name under the title of this paper.
- After the title, write "Yes, yes, yes."
- Put a circle around sentence seven.
- Put an X in the lower left-hand corner of this paper.
- Draw a triangle around the X you just put down.
- On the back of this paper, multiply 703 by 66.
- Draw a rectangle around the word "paper" in sentence four.
- Loudly call out your first name when you get to this point in the test.
- If you think you have followed directions carefully to this point, call out "I have."
- On the reverse side of this paper, add 8950 and 9850.
- Put a circle around your answer and put a square around the circle.
- Count out in your normal speaking voice, from ten to one backward.
- Punch three small holes in the top of this paper with your pencil.
- If you are the first person to get this far, call out loudly, "I am the first person to this point, and I am the leader in following directions."
- Underline all even numbers on the side of this page.

- Put a square around every number written out on this test.
- Say out loud, "I am nearly finished, I have followed directions."
- Now that you have finished reading carefully, do only sentence two.

(Variations on this test show up from time to time on college campuses and military installations, where it is given to underscore the true meaning of following directions. This particular version appears in *Urban Folklore from the Paperwork Empire* by Alan Dundes and Carl R. Pagter, American Folklore Society, 1975.)

Thanksgiving Thought from Ann Landers. Some of us should be thankful that we don't get what we deserve. (Ann Landers from her syndicated column of November 25, 1993.)

Thatcher's Law of Politics. The unexpected happens. (Revealed by former British Prime Minister Margaret Thatcher at the National Press Club, June 26, 1995.)

Thermodynamics of Political Gossip. When affection for a sitting President cools down, the chatter about the senior available Kennedy heats up. (*Newsweek,* May 8, 1978.)

Thermodynamics, First and Second Laws in Layman's Terms. (1) When you put a spoonful of fine wine into a vat of sewage, you get sewage. (2) When you put a spoonful of sewage into a vat of fine wine, you get sewage. (From "Cleve" Bishop, who heard it elsewhere.)

Thermopolitical Rhetoric, Laws of. (1) Cant produces countercant. *Corollary:* The quantity of rhetoric has been directly proportional to the lack of action. (2) Social groups are generally in disarray. To protect themselves from other groups, especially the groups just below them, groups will attempt to convey an appearance of interior order and purpose they do not possess. (3) Social institutions will change only at the speed required to protect them from attack—slowly or fast to the degree required, but usually slowly. They will put off change as long as possible.(Arthur Herzog, from his book *The B. S. Factor: The Theory and Technique of Faking It in America,* Simon and Schuster, 1973.)

Thidias's Law of Ironic Fate. When you go down in history, they'll spell your name wrong. (N. Sally Hass, Sleepy Hollow, Illinois. Also known as *Thyrsus's Law, Thyreus's Law, Thydeus's Law, Thidius's Law,* and *Agrippa's Law.*)

Thien's Distinction. You can always tell a home that has a 5-year-old in it. You have to wash the soap before using it yourself. (Alex Thien, in the *Milwaukee Sentinel.*)

Thomas's Observation. No child-proof bottle is absolutely "childproof." (John and Joyce Thomas, Grissom AFB, Indiana.)

Thomas's Reality Check. If the Super Bowl is the ultimate game, why is there another one next year? (Former Dallas Cowboy Duane Thomas, quoted in *Time,* January 24, 1983.)

Thomas's Rules of School Life. (1) Ink smudges, however long it is left to dry. (2) Pens always run out of ink during dictation. (3) Five-hundred-word essays always lose 100 words between writing and handing in to be marked. (4) Pencil sharpeners do no such thing. (5) Homework is always for this Thursday, not next Thursday. (6) The amount of homework given on Fridays is directly proportional to the number of parties, etc. that you had planned to go to. (7) Excuses have always been heard before. (8) Teachers expect miracles. (9) Miracles never happen. (Schoolboy Matthew Thomas, Mid Glamorgan, South Wales.)

Thomas's Rules of the Game. (1) No matter how well you do something, someone won't like it. (2) No matter how trivial the assignment, it is always possible to build it up to a major issue. (3) A good, illegible signature is a key to success. (Robert H. Thomas, Farmington, Michigan.)

Thompson's Corollary. With an expense account, anything is possible. (Writer Hunter S. Thompson, who was oft-quoted on this tenet of his self-styled brand of "gonzo" journalism.)

Thompson's Publication Premise. The probability of anyone reviewing a document in full diminishes with the number of pages. (Charles I. Thompson III, Port Jefferson Station, New York.)

Thompson's Rule. If you can't do anything about it, don't. (William I. Thompson, West Hempstead, New York.)

Thomson's Law. Ten percent of your subcontractors will give you 90 percent of your aggravation. (Kenneth D. Thomson, San Francisco, California.)

Thoreau's Law. If you see a man approaching you with the obvious intent of doing you good, you should run for your life. (Attributed to Henry David Thoreau by William H. Whyte, Jr., in *The Organization Man,* Simon and Schuster, 1956 and quoted in *MB, S.T.L.,* etc.)

Thoreau's Query. It is an interesting question how far men would retain their relative rank if they were divested of their clothes. (Henry David Thoreau; from Bernard L. Albert.)

Thoreau's Rule. Any fool can make a rule, and every fool will mind it. (Henry David Thoreau; *JW.*)

Thorn's First Law of Return. The closer the alumni live to the old hometown, the less likely they are to show up at the twentieth anniversary reunion.

(Bill Thorn; quoted in Clarence Page's *Chicago Tribune* article on reunions, July 24, 1985.)

Thorpe's Parents' Rule for Rock Concerts. It might be okay to go to a rock concert if your friend's parents will let her go, and her parents may let her go to the concert if your parents say it is okay for you to go. (The late James Thorpe III.)

Thurber's Amplification. Love is blind, but desire just doesn't give a good goddamn. (James Thurber, in his *Further Fables for Our Time,* Simon and Schuster, 1956.)

Thurber's Conclusion. There is no safety in numbers, or in anything else. (James Thurber, *Fables for Our Time,* Harper & Row, 1940. *RS.*)

Thurston's Law. The higher the drifts, the harder to find a boy with a shovel. ("Thirsty" Thurston, in the *Hi and Lois* comic strip.)

Thwartz's Theorem of Low Profile. Negative expectation thwarts realization, and self-congratulation guarantees disaster; or, simply put, if you think of it, it won't happen quite that way. (Michael Donner, editor of *Games* magazine; from the Editor's Message in the September/October 1979 issue; *DRW.*)

Tiberius's Law of Politicians. Caesar doesn't want Caesar's. Caesar wants God's. (N. Sally Hass, Sleepy Hollow, Illinois.)

Tiedemann's Conclusion. Procrastination is the root of all boredom. (JoAnn Tiedemann, Tomahawk, Wisconsin.)

Tiger's Rule. The bigger and more abstract the activities an organization has to perform, and the less real human contact is necessary to maintain a steady state, the more its form of written communication will depart from vernacular speech. (Anthropologist Lionel Tiger, *The Manufacture of Evil,* Harper, 1987; from George L. Whally.)

Tigner's "You Can't Take It With You" Truism. You never see a Brinks truck following a hearse. (Dr. Steven S. Tigner, University of Toledo; from Margo-Rita Andrea Kissell.)

Tiller's Theory. Car washing precipitates precipitation. (George Tiller, Memphis, Tennessee; quoted in *Johns Hopkins Magazine,* May 1978.)

Tillinger's Rule. Moderation in all things, including moderation. (Judy Tillinger, New York, New York.)

Tilp's Equation. Progress plus people produces pollution, or people plus pollution produce progress. (Frederick Tilp, Alexandria, Virginia.)

Timerman's Rules. (1) If the president or prime minister wears a uniform, the citizens of this country can expect to salute, be treated by the numbers and lose their rights as individuals. (2) If a president or prime minister has a lot of titles after his name, it means that he considers himself everybody and the rest, as government officials, are nobodies. (3) The length of the president or prime minister's speeches is in inverse proportion to the degree of democratization and diversity communications tolerated in a country. (Herbert Mitgang in his *New York Times* review of Jacobo Timerman's *Cuba—A Journey*, November 10, 1990.)

Timothy's Principle of Crawling Infants. Any infant who can crawl tends toward the most expensive accessible object. *Corollary 1:* Nothing is inaccessible to a crawling infant. *Corollary 2:* All babies crawl, especially when you are not looking. (Peter H. Dolan, M.D., Anchorage, Alaska.)

Tim's Admonition. They can't chase you if you don't run. (Pat Jett, Hillsboro, Missouri, to her fourth-grade son Tim, who was being chased at school by sixth graders.)

Tipper's Law. Those who expect the biggest tips provide the worst service. (Rozanne Weissman.)

Tishbein's Law. There are more horses' backsides in the military service of the United States than there are horses. (*U;* Robert J. Clark of Southampton, New York learned this as a plebe at West Point and passed it along to *AO.*)

Titanic Coincidence. Most accidents in well-designed systems involve two or more events of low probability occurring in the worst possible combination. (Robert Machol, in *POR.*)

Titanic Law. If you worry about missing the boat—remember the *Titanic.* (From John Kessel, Boulder, Colorado.)

Tobias's Law. The most sensible investments are mundane. (Financial writer Andrew Tobias, who insists that it is easier, less risky, and a "better investment" to save $1,000 a year through special sales and discounts on everyday household items than it is to try to clear $1,000 in the stock market. Quoted in an interview in *The Baltimore Sun,* March 7, 1979; *ME.*)

Tobin's Pearls of Wisdom. *First Pearl:* Nobody can do everything at the same moment—you have to do one thing after another. *Further Pearl:* In traffic, as elsewhere, just because it's permissible doesn't mean it's a good idea. *Splendid Pearl:* A mistake is not a failure. *Ultimate Pearl:* Nothing ever happens by itself. *Exuberant:* This is the day to be happy—there is no other. *Empirical:* Things always seem to come in bunches. *Travel:* When in Rome, do what you feel like. *Psychological:* A fault is when somebody does things in a way you don't like. (Art Tobin, Longueuil, Quebec.)

Todd's Law. In an area where the degree of confusion approaches infinite proportions—major disasters pass unnoticed. (J. K. Todd, M.D., Calgary, Alberta.)

Todd's Laws. (1) Facts are not judgments, and judgments are not facts. (2) Emotion is a rotten base for politics. (3) Envy is the root of all evil. (4) The most damaging lies are told by those who believe they're true. (Dick Francis, *In the Frame*, Harper, 1976; from Charles D. Poe.)

Todd's Rules. (1) *The Barcode Malfunction Predictability Rule:* The bar code in the checkout line won't work on items you're embarrassed to be buying. (2) *12 Items or Less Rule:* Cashiers may not count your items in the express lane—but the other customers will. (Todd Hermetz, Decatur, Alabama.)

Tolkien's Reminder. It does not do to leave a live dragon out of your calculations, if you live near him. (J. R. R. Tolkien, quoted in *Reader's Digest,* September 1978.)

Tom Jones's Law. Friends may come and go, but enemies accumulate. (Dr. Thomas Jones, president of the University of South Carolina.)

Tom Sawyer's Great Laws of Human Action. (1) In order to make [a person] covet a thing, it is only necessary to make the thing difficult to attain. (2) Work consists of whatever a body is *obliged* to do, and play consists of whatever a body is not obliged to do. (Samuel Clemens, *Tom Sawyer.*)

Tomlin's Request. If love is the answer, could you rephrase the question? (Lily Tomlin, quoted in *Time,* March 28, 1977.)

Tom's Catechism. *On Investing:* You will get in too late and get out too soon. *On Becoming a Millionaire:* You will not win the lottery. *On Sudden Business Lunches:* Blue socks and brown socks match in a dark restaurant. *On Movie-Going:* Meryl Streep will have an accent. *The Corollary to "All Important Phone Calls Are Missed":* If you buy an answering machine, you will forget to turn it on. If you turn it on, you will forget to rewind the tape. If you do everything right, the only people who will call are those you don't want to talk to—you are now obligated to call them back. *On Hosting:* There is not enough ice. You will run out of brie before you run out of bread. You will have made too much onion dip. *Maxim:* News travels fast. Bad news travels faster. *On Cracker Jack Prizes:* It's Sticker Fun. It's Jokes No. 2. It's not a whistle. *On the Classification of Insects:* It's big. It's ugly. It will fly at your face. *Tom's Reminder:* You will need a No. 2 pencil. (Tom Cipullo, Hialeah, Florida.)

Tom's Kaka and the Fan Theory. Some of us dance because we like the music. The rest of us are just dodging the falling debris. (Tom English.)

Toner's Theory of Parenthood. Parents never live up their children's expectations. (Mike Toner, Parkville, Maryland; from Christopher Sybert.)

Toni's Solution to a Guilt-Free Life. If you have to lie to someone, it's his or her fault. (Toni Schmitt; from Mary Lou Waddell, Oak Ridge, Tennessee.)

Toomey's Rule. It is easy to make decisions on matters for which you have no responsibility. (Jim Toomey, the St. Louis Cardinals, St. Louis, Missouri.)

Torch's Laws. (1) The more important the meeting, the more likely one is to make an embarrassing noise sliding into a restaurant booth. (2) Thin envelopes seldom contain good news. (3) Most people get well by themselves; in fact, most people get well by morning. (4) People who call you Doc do not pay bills. (5) The essence of discretion is silence. (Evan M. Torch, M.D., Medical College of Georgia, Augusta.)

Torquemada's Law. When you are sure you're right, you have a moral duty to impose your will upon anyone who disagrees with you. (Robert W. Mayer, Champaign, Illinois; *AO*.)

Townsend's Aphorisms. (1) Anybody who can still do at 60 what he was doing at 20 wasn't doing much at 20. (2) Marriage teaches you loyalty, forbearance, self-restraint, meekness and a great many other things you wouldn't need if you had stayed single. (Jimmy Townsend, Georgia mountain philosopher, quoted in *Everything to Gain*, Random House, 1987; by Jimmy and Rosalynn Carter.)

Townsend's Law of Life. Everybody wants to go heaven, but nobody wants to die. (O. J. Bud Townsend, Canoga Park, California.)

Towson State College Rule. If you are smart enough to fill out the application, you don't need to be here. (Towson State student; *Ra*.)

Trace's Law. Whenever a political body passes legislation on behalf of the consumer, the consumer will wait longer and pay more for the same product or service. (Richard W. Trace, Kingston, Michigan.)

Transcription Square Law. The number of errors made is equal to the sum of the "squares" involved. (*AIC*.)

Trauring's Discovery. Technical reports are expanded from outlines so that aides can recondense them for executive use. (Mitchell Trauring, Los Angeles, California.)

Travel, First Law of. No matter how many rooms there are in the motel, the fellow who starts up his car at five o'clock in the morning is always parked under your window. (Comedy writer Bob Orben.)

Travelers, Advice to. It is wise to travel in pairs so there is always someone to blame for leaving the insect repellent at home. (From *Far Eastern Economic Review,* Hong Kong; quoted in *Reader's Digest*.)

TRB's Law of Scandals. When wrongdoing is exposed, the real scandal is what's legal. (Timothy Noah, the *New Republic,* July 11, 1988.)

Treaty Ruling. Treaties should be interpreted as to make sense, if possible. (U.S. Supreme Court; *TCA.)*

Tribune Tower, Law of. Elevators traveling in the desired direction are always delayed, and on arrival tend to run in pairs, threes of a kind, full houses, etc. (Pete Maiken, *The Chicago Tribune.*)

Trillin's Conclusion. Immigration laws have been traditionally based on bland food. *Trillin's Rule for Finding Good Food in a Strange City:* Stick with the cooking of ethnic groups large enough to have at least two aldermen on the city council. (Calvin Trillin, quoted by Phyllis C. Richman in the *Washington Post,* May 18, 1983.)

Tristan's Law of Disappearances in the Bermuda Triangle and Other "Dangerous" Sea Areas. The more people there are in any given sea area, the more novices, fools, and incompetents there will be, and therefore the more inexplicable disappearances. (Tristan Jones, *Adrift*, Macmillan, 1980.)

Tromberg's Laws. (1) Oil is thicker than blood. (2) Just because you can do it doesn't mean you can make a living at it. (3) You ain't got it till you got it and even when you got it you may not. (4) When you see the word "net" in a contract, it means "nothing." (Sheldon Tromberg, writer/radio personality, Washington, D.C.)

Tromberg's Truisms. (1) The future isn't even here yet. (2) Aging simply means the present is shorter than the past and longer than the future. (Shelly Tromberg, Washington, D.C.)

Tropf's Discovery. If any car you own develops a major problem, any other car you own will develop a major mechanical problem within one week. (David Tropf. Ph.D., Oviedo, Florida.)

Trudeau's Discovery. This is the only country in the world where failing to promote yourself is widely regarded as being arrogant. (Cartoonist Garry Trudeau, commenting on his reluctance to grant interviews, *Newsweek,* October 6, 1986.)

True Theorem. Thodium pentathol. (Charles Poole, Washington, D.C.)

Truman's Law of Qualifications. Always vote for the better man. He is a Democrat. Anyone who votes for a Republican gets what he deserves. (Harry S Truman; *MBC.*)

Truman's Law. If you can't convince them, confuse them. (Harry S Truman; *Co.*)

Truman's Parental Instruction. I have found that the best way to give advice to your children is to find out what they want, and then advise them to do it. (Harry S Truman; *MBC.*)

Truman's Triple Tenet. Three things can ruin a man—money, power, and women. I never had any money. I never wanted power, and the only woman in my life is up at the house right now. (Harry S Truman, quoted in *Scandals in the Highest Office*, Random House, 1973; by Hope Ridings Miller. Also, this forwarded by Nick Kass: *Truman's Truism*: When the "amens" get too loud in the back of the church, that's the time to go home and lock the smoke house.)

Trumm's Law. You can't make a fact out of an opinion by raising your voice. (Bruce Trumm; from Robert D. Gillette, M.D., Cincinnati, Ohio.)

Truths of Management. (1) Think before you act; it's not your money. (2) All good management is the expression of one great idea. (3) No executive devotes effort to proving himself wrong. (4) Cash in must exceed cash out. (5) Management capability is always less than the organization actually needs. (6) Either an executive can do his job or he can't. (7) If sophisticated calculations are needed to justify an action, don't do it. (8) If you are doing something wrong, you will do it badly. (9) If you are attempting the impossible, you will fail. (10) The easiest way of making money is to stop losing it. (Robert Heller, *The Great Executive Dream,* Delacorte, 1972; *JE*.)

Truth-Seeker's Discovery. (1) Time goes faster as we grow older because we need less time. (2) Time goes slower when we are young because we need more time for things such as education, finding a mate, learning a job, and raising children. (Linda Cearbaugh, Raleigh, North Carolina.)

Tuchman's Axiom. When something is perfect the way it is, someone will come along to improve it—and screw it up. (Stephan A. Tuchman, Rockville Centre, New York, quoted in a letter to *Money* magazine on the magazine's new look. The letter appears in the February 1979 issue.)

Tufte's First Law of Political Economy. The politicians who make economic policy operate under conditions of political competition. (Edward R. Tufte, professor of political science, Yale University, from his *Political Control of the Economy*, Princeton, 1978; *TCA*.)

Tuppeny's Truism. (1) We are all in this alone. (2) Put the burden on the other guy—where it belongs. (3) Good news never comes before 9:00 a.m. Good news never comes registered mail. (4) Always means "more than once." (5) It's impossible to "drown your trouble" in cottage cheese. (6) The fancier the car, the uglier the driver. (Peg Tuppeny, Chicago, Illinois.)

Turcotte's Law. If we weren't all a little crazy, we'd go nuts. (Dorothy Turcotte, Grimsby, Ontario, who learned it from her son Paul.)

Turk's Laws of Traffic. (1) It is always rush hour. (2) "Fast lanes" do not exist. (3) An accident in one lane will slow all lanes, regardless of their number and direction. (Brian Turk, Phoenix, Arizona.)

Turner's Law of Modesty. The nurse never inquires about a patient's bodily functions unless there is a roomful of visitors. The nurse inquires by shouting from the doorway. (Ms. Sidney P. Turner, Baltimore, Maryland.)

Turner's Law. Nearly all prophecies made in public are wrong. (Malcolm Turner, Scottish journalist; passed along to *AO* by his son Arthur Campbell Turner, a California political scientist.)

Turtle Principle, The. If you go slow enough long enough, you'll be in the lead again. (Wayne Hoy, Rutgers University, Graduate School of Education; from Gerald Fava, Lake Hiawatha, New Jersey. Fava lists a few of the many areas in which the *Turtle Principle* applies: *Criminal Justice:* victim's rights vs. criminal's rights. *Political Science:* centralization vs. decentralization. *Physics:* wave theory vs. particle theory of subatomic entities.)

Tussman's Law. Nothing is as inevitable as a mistake whose time has come. (Anonymous; quoted by John Petrella in a letter to the journal *Integra;* from Neal Wilgus.)

Twain's Addendum. Familiarity breeds contempt—and children. (Samuel Clemens.)

Twain's Rule. Only kings, editors, and people with tapeworm have the right to use the editorial "we." (Samuel Clemens; *Co.*)

Twain's Warning. Be careful about reading health books. You may die of a misprint. (Samuel Clemens quoted in Richard Lederer's column, *Concord Monitor,* November 18, 1985.)

Twenty-Third Qualm, The.

The professor is my quizmaster, I shall not flunk.
He maketh me to enter the examination room;
He leadeth me to an alternative seat;
He restoreth my fears.
Yea, though I know not the answers to those questions, the class average comforts me.
I prepare my answers before me in the sight of my proctors.
I anoint my exam papers with figures.
My time runneth out.
Surely grades and examinations will follow all the days of my life,
And I will dwell in this class forever. (*U/TJR.*)

Twyman's Law. Any statistic that appears interesting is almost certainly a mistake. (From Iwan Williams, London, who got it from A.S.C. Ehrneberg, Professor of Marketing, who got it from a colleague.)

Tylk's Law. Assumption is the mother of all foul-ups. (*U/LSP;* A corollary to Tylk's Law is an old U.S. Army Law: To assume something is the preparatory command for an ass chewing. (C.G. Meyer, San Antonio, Texas.)

Typesetter's Punctuation Rules. Set type as long as you can hold your breath without getting blue in the face, then put in a comma. When you yawn, put in a semicolon. And when you want to sneeze, that's time for a paragraph. (*U/Ra.*)

U

Ubell's Law of Press Luncheons. At any public relations luncheon, the quality of the food is inversely related to the quality of the information. (Earl Ubell, who created it when he was the New York *Herald Tribune*'s science writer; recalled by Ben Bagdikian.)

Udall's Admonition. Don't shear the sheep that laid the golden egg that is going to cause the well to run dry. *Udall's Fourth Law:* Any change or reform you make is going to have consequences you don't like. (Representative Morris Udall, quoted in the *Congressional Record,* October 31, 1985, and the *Washington Post,* June 14, 1981; from Joseph C. Goulden.)

Udall's Fourth Law of Politics. If you can find something everyone agrees on, it's wrong. (Morris Udall, quoted in *The New York Times,* April 4, 1975.)

Udall's Observation on Discourse. Everything that can be said about a subject has been said—just not everyone has said it. (Morris K. Udall.)

Uhlmann's Razor. When stupidity is a sufficient explanation, there is no need to have recourse to any other. *Corollary:* (Also, the *Law of Historical Causation.*) "It seemed like the thing to do at the time." (Michael M. Uhlmann, who was assistant attorney general in the Ford Administration; *AO* and *JMcC.*)

Ultimate Advice to Graduation Speakers. Think of yourself as the body at an Irish wake. They need you in order to have the party, but nobody expects you to say that much. (Attributed to an unnamed university president by National Security Adviser Anthony Lake in a 1995 graduation speech at the University of Massachusetts.)

Ultimate Law. All general statements are false. (R. H. Grenier, Davenport, Iowa; *AO.*)

Ultimate Principle. By definition, when you are investigating the unknown, you do not know what you will find. (*Scientific Collections.*)

Umbrella Justice.

The rain it raineth on the just
And also on the unjust fella;
But chiefly on the just because
The unjust stole the just's umbrella.

(Sir George Bowen, quoted by Senator William Proxmire, U.S. Senate, March 26, 1979.)

Umbrella Law. You will need three umbrellas: one to leave at the office, one to leave at home, and one to leave on the train. (James L. Blankenship, R. C. Auletta and Co., New York, New York.)

Umhoefer's Rule. Articles on writing are themselves badly written. (Joseph A. Umhoefer, editor and writer; from Frederick C. Dyer, who notes that Umhoefer "was probably the first to phrase it so publicly; however, many others must have thought of it long ago.")

Uncle Ed's Rule of Managerial Perception. You always think the boss is a son of a bitch until you're the boss. *Uncle Ed's Rule of Thumb:* Never use your thumb for a rule. You'll either hit it with a hammer or get a splinter in it. (Edward Karl, Urbana, Illinois.)

Uncle Irving's Three Phases of Life. First, youth. Then, middle age. Then "Gee, you look wonderful." (Quoted by Bob Levey in the *Washington Post,* September 3, 1979.)

Underwood's Banking Maxim. The greenest and/or slowest tellers are invariably assigned to the drive-up windows, especially Friday afternoons. (Dale M. Underwood, Santa Rosa, California.)

Underwood's Distinction. The extent to which a service organization has become a bureaucracy is measured by the degree to which useless work has driven out useful work. In pure bureaucracy, all work is useless and tends only to perpetuate the bureaucracy. In pure service, all work is useful, altruistic, and of greater ultimate value than the organization itself. (The Rev. John F. Underwood, King of Prussia, Pennsylvania.)

Unintended Consequences, Law of. Government regulations always have unintended consequences and their importance outweighs the intended consequences. (Created in the mid-1930s by Columbia University sociologist Robert K. Merton. It is commonly cited, for instance, when trying to explain why the movement to create rights for the mentally ill through deinstitutionalization created so many homeless people.)

Unitas's Law. If you hang around long enough, you'll end up somewhere.

(Quarterback Johnny Unitas, on being notified of his election to the Football Hall of Fame, January 29, 1979.)

United Law. If an organization carries the word "united" in its name, it means it isn't, e.g., United Nations, United Arab Republic, United Kingdom, United States. (Professor Charles I. Issawi, quoting Warner Schilling, professor of political science, who is quoting Professor Harry Rudin; from *Issawi's Laws of Social Motion*, Hawthorn, 1973.)

United States Army Engineer General Orders. (1) Measure it with a micrometer; mark it with a grease pencil; cut it with an ax. (2) If it doesn't fit, get a bigger hammer. (3) Pound to fit and paint to match. (U.S. Army Engineer Training Brigade, Fort Leonard Wood, Missouri; *MLS*.)

Universal Field Theory of Perversity (or Mulé's Law). The probability of an event's occurring varies directly with the perversity of the inanimate object involved and inversely with the product of its desirability and the effort expended to produce it. (Walter Mulé, from his article "Beyond Murphy's Law" in *Northliner.* Mulé uses his article as proof of the law, whereas if it had not appeared in print, it would have been an example of *Murphy's Law*.)

Universality of the So-Called "Rebel Yell." Ain't nobody doesn't know to commence hollering "Yee-haw!" when circumstances dictate. (*U/RA*.)

Unnamed Law. If it happens, it must be possible. (*RS*.)

Unruh's Understanding of Political Alliances. If I had slain all my enemies yesterday, I wouldn't have any friends today. (Jesse Unruh, California State Treasurer; *TG*. Unruh also uttered one of most quoted lines of his time: "Money is the mother's milk of politics.")

Unspeakable Law. As soon as you mention something if it's good, it goes away. If it's bad, it happens. (From Bloch's list in *The Book of Lists*.)

Upward-Mobility Rule. Don't be irreplaceable. If you can't be replaced, you can't be promoted. (Desk sign/*Ra*.)

Useful Refrain. When you're down and out, lift up your voice and shout, "I'M DOWN AND OUT!" (Unknown origin; sung to the compiler on a radio call-in show.)

V

Vacation Rule No. 1. Thou shalt never answer a telephone before 8:00 a.m. (Armen Keteyian, *Sports Illustrated,* March 31, 1986.)

Vail's First Axiom. In any human enterprise, work seeks the lowest hierarchical level. (Charles R. Vail, vice president, Southern Methodist University.)

Valenti's Rule for a Successful Political Career. Do your own Xeroxing. (Attributed to Jack Valenti when an advisor to Lyndon B. Johnson, but more recently expanded to also include paper shredding.)

Values in the Bureaucracy. (1) In government, influence is most admired; longevity is most respected; but anonymity is most prized. (2) Respect is what is earned from one's supervisors instead of a promotion or raise. (3) The deeper the carpet you're called upon, the deeper the trouble you're in.)

Van der Byl's Law of Progress. It is far better to get nowhere fast than to get nowhere slowly. (A. R. van der Byl, Transvaal, South Africa.)

Van Der Velde's Laws of News Coverage. (1) The closer you are to a news story, the more inaccurate the coverage appears to be. (2) Law #1 makes you wonder about all the other stories. (Robert J. Van Der Velde, Kirtland, Ohio.)

Van Dongen's Law of Heredity. Twits beget twits. (Van Dongen, Saskatoon, Saskatchewan.)

Van Herik's Discovery. Any combination of commercially mixed vegetables will invariably be made up of an oversupply of inedible broccoli stalks. (Doris E. Van Herik, West Chicago, Illinois.)

Van Leuvan Storm Theory, The. If it is raining now and wasn't a little while ago, it is moving this way. (Jeff Van Leuvan; from his old college roommate Earl Allen, Manhattan, Kansas.)

Van Roy's Laws. *Van Roy's Basic Law:* Honesty is the best policy—there's less competition. *Rule of Empowerment at Work:* Never agree with your boss until he says something. *Limitations Rule of Work Complexity:* Anything that is simple to do is never easy to accomplish. *Self Evident Marriage Motto:* Marriage is like a bra—it's not really necessary but provides useful support. *Bruce's Wildest Dream Come True Law:* I dreamed I invented sex and everyone had to pay me royalties. *Bruce's Sports Point:* A rolling football gathers no score. *Bruce's Rule of Intelligent Manners:* Never talk with your mouth full or your head empty. *Humanity's Self Realization Rule from the Supreme Being:* God gave us two ears and one mouth—maybe he was trying to tell us something. *Van Roy's Postulate:* Love is like a pair of socks—you have to have two, and they gotta match. (Bruce W. Van Roy, Vienna, Virginia.)

Van Tassel's Computer Graffiti. (1) They say it's automatic, but you really have to push the button. (2) It is easier to change a program than to change a bureaucracy. (3) Some of the best programs owe their greatness to the fact that all the work was lost halfway through the project. (4) If computers are so fast, why do we spend so much time waiting around the computer center? (Dennie Van Tassel, Santa Cruz, California, in *Introductory Cobol*, Holden Day, 1980.)

Vance's Rule of 2½. Any military project will take twice as long as planned, cost twice as much, and produce only half of what is wanted. (Attributed to Cyrus Vance when he was Deputy Secretary of Defense; *AO*.)

Vancini's Discovery. In a bureaucracy, good ideas go too far. (John Vancini, Brooklyn Center, Minnesota.)

Van der Rohe's Explanation. God is in the details. (Mie van der Rohe; from Anthony M. Cresswell, Evanston, Illinois.)

Vargas's Varied Laws. *Of Contrary Geography:* If the directions for finding a place include the words "you can't miss it," you will. *Of Free Booze:* People who hardly drink at all will imbibe stingers at 8:00 a.m. if the drinks are served on an airplane and free. *Of Paucity:* There is no such thing as a little garlic... or a mild heart attack... or a few children. *Of Jars:* A jar that cannot be opened through any combination of force, household tools, and determination will open instantly if picked up by the lid. *Of Human Statistics:* Figures don't lie, they lay. (Joie Vargas of Reno, Nevada, discovered all of these save for the last, which is from her husband, George L. Vargas.)

Vaughan's Rule of Corporate Life. The less important you are on the table of an organization, the more you'll be missed if you don't show up for work. (Bill Vaughan of *The Kansas City Star*.)

Veeck's Law of Enforced Humility. When you've run as fast as you can up the highest mountain you can find, you will find something or somebody waiting at the top to deflate you. (Bill Veeck in his 1962 book *Veeck—as in Wreck*, Putnam's.)

Veeck's 12 Commandments. (1) Take your work very seriously. Go for broke and give it your all. (2) Never ever take yourself seriously. (3) Find yourself an alter ego and bond with him for the rest of your professional life. (4) Surround yourself with similarly dedicated soul mates, free spirits of whom you can ask why and why not. And who can ask the same thing of you. (5) In your hiring, be color-blind, gender-blind, age- and experience-blind. You never work for Bill Veeck. You work with him. (6) If you're a president, owner or operator, attend every home game and you never leave until the last out. (7) Answer all your mail; you might learn something. (8) Listen and be available to your fans. (9) Enjoy and respect the members of the media, the stimulation and the challenge. The "them against us" mentality should exist only between the two teams on the field. (10) Create an aura in your city. Make people understand that unless they come to the ballpark, they will miss something. (11) If you don't think a promotion is fun, don't do it. Never insult your fans. (12) Don't miss the essence of what is happening at the moment. Let it happen. Cherish the moment and commit it to your memory. (For most of his lifetime, baseball owner

Bill Veeck lived by a set of 12 commandments to which he felt anyone in the business of baseball should adhere. In making the Hall of Fame acceptance speech in her late husband's behalf, Mary Frances Veeck recalled them in the hope that future baseball ownership will feel the same about the game as her late husband did.)

Verbov's Explanation. A police officer directing the traffic is the usual explanation for the long traffic delays. (Julian Verbov, M.D., Liverpool, England.)

Velarde's Law. You can't shine if you don't polish. (Roberto Velarde, El Paso, Texas from Tom Gill.)

Vernooy's Law of Psychopharmacology. The antidepressant medication that makes you feel like having sex again will cause anorgasmia (or impotence). (Diana Vernooy, Teaneck, New Jersey, *American Journal of Psychiatry,* September 1987.)

Verplanke's Discovery about Snobs. I have never known a superior person who was a snob. (Hans Verplancke, Leiderdorp, The Netherlands.)

Vest's Laws of Air Travel. (1) No matter where you sit in an airplane, the person in the seat in front of you will recline the seat into your lap. (2) No matter where you sit in an airplane, the person in back of you will stick his feet against your elbow or stick knees against the back of your seat. (3) No matter where you sit in an airplane, there will be, no further than three seats away, a woman with a hyper three-year-old child who will alternatively scream or throw food. (C. R. Vest, Washington, D.C.)

Vielmetti's Letter-into-Envelope Law. If you think you have folded it enough, you haven't. (Ed Vielmetti, Michigan.)

Vietinghoff's Precept. He who controls the forms controls the program. (William F. Vietinghoff, Space Shuttle Main Engine Systems, Rockwell International, Canoga Park, California.)

Vijlee's Cosmic Principle. In most cases, real life performance will not match laboratory test results. (A. Vijlee, McKees Rocks, Pennsylvania, from his article in *Machine Design,* April 23, 1987; from Lee A. Webber, Huntington Beach, California.)

Viking Reminder, The. Always remember to pillage *before* you burn. (*U;* from Bob Skole, Boston and Stockholm, Sweden.)

Vincent's First and Fourth Laws. (1) As the intelligence of the participants at conferences increases, so disagreement among them increases by geometric progression. (4) Authors expand; editors abridge; publishers cut. (Ben Vincent, Radlett, Hertfordshire, England.)

Vique's Law. A man without religion is like a fish without a bicycle. (Semi-*U;* Conrad Schneiker identifies Vique as a friend of Edith Folta's in Urbana, Ill. It became a popular law that soon began to show up in variant forms, such as at a

NOW conference, where several delegates were reported to have said, "A woman without a man..." etc.)

Visco on How to Write Good. My several years in the word game have learnt me several rules: (1) Avoid alliteration. Always. (2) Prepositions are not words to end sentences with. (3) Avoid clichés like the plague. (They're old hat.) (4) Employ the vernacular. (5) Eschew ampersands & abbreviations, etc. (6) Parenthetical remarks (however revelant) are unnecessary. (7) It is wrong to ever split an infinitive. (8) Contractions aren't necessary. (9) Foreign words and phrases are not apropos. (10) One should never generalize. (11) Eliminate quotations. Ralph Waldo Emerson once said: "I hate quotations. Tell me what you know." (12) Comparisons are as bad as clichés. (13) Don't be redundant; don't use more words than necessary; It's highly superfluous. (14) Profanity sucks. (15) Be more or less specific. (16) Understatement is always best. (17) Exaggeration is a billion times worse than understatement. (18) One-word sentences? Eliminate. (19) Analogies in writing are like feathers on a snake. (20) The passive voice is to be avoided. (21) Go around the barn at high noon to avoid colloquialisms. (22) Even if a mixed metaphor sings, it should be derailed. (23) Who needs rhetorical questions? (Frank L. Visco from an undated clipping where he is identified as a vice president and senior copywriter at US Advertising; *MLS*.)

Vito's Rule of Nonviolent Encounters. Never get into a battle of wits without ammunition. (Unknown; WRC radio, Washington, D.C.)

Vlachos Law. There is always one more squeeze in the toothpaste or the lemon. (Unknown; from Mykia Taylor.)

Voell's Three Laws. (1) They never put the executive suite in the basement. (2) Living in the king's house does not make one the king. (3) An illusion is a conviction waiting for a place to fail. (James W. Voell, M.D., Silver Spring, Maryland.)

Vogel's Nevers. Never attempt levity while filling out your insurance forms. Never think you can lose both gloves. Never get in a gun fight with seven men when you only have a six-shooter. (W. J. Vogel, Toppenish, Washington.)

Vogel's Observation of Office Behavior. When an executive on vacation picks up pebbles and small shells from the beach and flippantly tosses them into the air, it is merely a continuation of his career-long habit of zipping rubber bands at the back of the head of his busy secretary. (Arthur R. Vogel, Evanston, Illinois.)

Vogel's Rules. (1) Nothing gives more satisfaction than telling a hypochondriac how well he is looking. (2) The length of a minute depends on which side of the bathroom door you're on. (3) The simplest incentive program: One mistake and you're through. (4) To shorten the winter, borrow some money due in the spring. (5) The wrong number on a telephone is never busy. (6) You will never lock your keys in the car at home. (W. J. Vogel, Toppenish, Washington.)

Volunteer's Law. If you dance with a grizzly bear, you had better let him lead. (From Stu Beck, Orleans, Massachusetts.)

Von Braun's Law of Gravity. We can lick gravity, but sometimes the paperwork is overwhelming. (Wernher von Braun, during the early months of the U.S. space program.)

Vonnegut's Venting. Another flaw in the human character is that everybody wants to build and nobody wants to do maintenance. (Kurt Vonnegut in *Hocus Pocus*, Putnam's, 1990; from Neal Wilgus.)

W

Waddell's Law of Equipment Failure. A component's degree of reliability is directly proportional to its ease of accessibility; i.e., the harder it is to get to, the more often it breaks down. (Jonathan Waddell, crew member, *Exxon New Orleans* oil tanker.)

Wade's Law of Performance Appreciation. The likelihood of a standing ovation is directly proportional to (1) (for professional performances) the fame of the performer(s); (2) (for amateur performances) the number of relatives and close friends of the performer in the audience. *Corollary:* There is no relationship whatsoever between the likelihood of a standing ovation and the quality of the performance. (Luther I. Wade, Hammond, Louisiana.)

Waffle's Law. A professor's enthusiasm for teaching the introductory course varies inversely with the likelihood of his having to do it. (*U;* Quoted in "The Geologic Column" in *Geotimes* for July-August 1968. The author of the column is Robert L. Bates; *FD.)*

Wain's Conclusion. The only people making money these days are the ones who sell computer paper. (*U/DRW.*)

Wakefield's Refutation of the Iron Law of Distribution. Them what gets—has. (Dexter B. Wakefield of Coral Gables, Florida, in a letter to *The Wall Street Journal,* November 11, 1974.)

Waldo's Observation. One man's red tape is another man's system. (Dwight Waldo, from his essay "Government by Procedure," which appeared in Fritz Morstein Marx's *Elements of Public Administration,* Prentice-Hall, 1946.)

Walinsky's Laws. (1) The intelligence of any discussion diminishes with the square of the number of participants. (2) *His First Law of Political Campaigns:* If there are twelve clowns in a ring, you can jump in the middle and start reciting

Shakespeare, but to the audience, you'll just be the thirteenth clown. (Adam Walinsky; *AO.*)

Walker's Law. Associate with well-mannered persons and your manners will improve. Run with decent folk and your own decent instincts will be strengthened. Keep the company of bums and you will become a bum. Hang around with rich people and you will end by picking up the check and dying broke. (Stanley Walker, city editor of the New York *Herald Tribune* during the 1930s. It was rediscovered by Alan Deitz of the American Newspaper Publishers Association, who passed it along to *AO* with this comment: "Although there are no facts to substantiate this, it was probably enunciated by Walker after spending an evening with Lucius Beebe and Ogden Reid in Jack Bleek's.")

Walker's Rule. If you're there before it's over, you're on time. (Politician James J. Walker.)

Wall Street Journal Rule. In order to learn from mistakes, you have to first recognize you are making mistakes. (*Wall Street Journal* editorial, January 9, 1982.)

Wallace's Two-out-of-Three Theory.
SPEED
QUALITY
PRICE
Pick any two. (James M. Wallace, Minneapolis, Minnesota. Wallace says that the dictum applies particularly to advertising, print shops, etc. He adds, "This is, of course, theoretical. In real life, one is usually hard-pressed to get any *one*.")

Wallner's Rule. If a thing is worth doing, hire it out. (Marilyn Wallner, Carmichael, California.)

Wall's Aphorism. Survival is the ability to adapt to change. (Gregory C. Wall, Carmel, Indiana.)

Walter's Rule. All airline flights depart from the gates most distant from the center of the terminal. Nobody ever had a reservation on a plane that left from a close-in terminal. (Robert Walters, Washington, D.C.)

Walters's Law of Management. If you're already in a hole, there's no use to continue digging. (Roy W. Walters, Roy Walters Associates, Glen Rock, New Jersey.)

Ward's Conversational Dictum. No meaningful verbal exchange ever takes place anywhere except the exact narrowest portion of a doorway. (C. F. Ward, San Diego, California.)

Ward's PC Law. Don't buy now. In six months it will be better and cheaper. Six months later you will have to wait again for the same reason. (Chuck Ward, Oviedo, Florida.)

Wareham's Rule. Nobody says anything by accident. (John Wareham, in his 1980 book *Secrets of a Corporate Headhunter,* Atheneum.)

Warner Swayze Axiom. When small men begin to cast large shadows, it is a sure sign that the sun is setting. (In a Warner Swayze ad; from Robert E. Blay.)

Warning-of-the-Century. Do not place this Wine Brick in a one-gallon crock, add sugar and water, cover and let stand for seven days, or else an illegal alcoholic beverage will result. (Label from a Prohibition-era product made of compressed grapes.)

Warren's Dilemma. Life ain't worth living, but what else can you do with it? (Grace A. Warren, Sacramento, California.)

Warren's Law. Nobody does anything for one reason. (Bill Warren, Hollywood, California. "Except perhaps," writes Warren, "throw up, but you want laws that are in good taste.")

Warren's Word of Wisdom. There's a lot to be said for brevity. (Russell Warren; from Terry B. Smith, Kirksville, Missouri.)

Warson's Truths. (1) If you can't join them, beat them. (2) Sometimes it is too late to win. But it's never too late to lose. (3) Every action is imperfect. (4) If a picture is worth a thousand words, one act is worth a thousand pictures. (5) It is "expensive" only if it can't get the job done. (Tom Warson, Santa Fe, New Mexico.)

Washington Post Rules of Washington. (1) If it's worth fighting for, it's worth fighting dirty for. (2) Don't lie, cheat or steal unnecessarily. (3) There is always one more son of a bitch than you counted on. (4) An honest answer can get you into a lot of trouble. (5) The facts, although interesting, are irrelevant. (6) Chicken Little only has to be right once. (7) "No" is only an interim response. (8) You can't kill a bad idea. (9) If at first you don't succeed, destroy all evidence that you ever tried. (10) The truth is a variable. (11) A porcupine with his quills down is just another fat rodent. (12) You can agree with any concept or notional future option in principle, but fight implementation every step of the way. (13) If you can't counter the argument, leave the meeting. (*Washington Post,* May 19, 1997.)

Washington Rule, The. No one is ever to be held accountable for anything done in the course of business. *Corollary:* In official Washington, you can try to murder a foreign leader by day and make small talk with his ambassador that evening. (Columnist Richard Cohen, *Washington Post,* January 14, 1986.)

Washington's First Law of Summer Survival. Because so little of consequence happens here in August, whatever does occur is embellished, embroidered, and otherwise exaggerated far beyond reality. (Political writer Robert Walters, who used the law to explain *l'affaire* Andrew Young during the summer of 1979.

Young, in the position of American Ambassador to the United Nations, met secretly for meetings, in violation of American law, with representatives of the Palestine Liberation Organization, which culminated in President Carter asking for Young's resignation.)

Washington's Law. Space expands to house the people to perform the work that Congress creates. (Haynes Johnson, *Washington Post,* August 14, 1977.)

Washington's Seven Cardinal Rules. (1) Don't make enemies you don't need to make. (2) Don't start believing you're indispensable. (3) Don't confuse what's good for you with what's good for the President. (4) Don't forget that you are not the elected official. (5) Don't start blaming the boss if you get into trouble. (6) Don't unilaterally announce you are going to run things, rather than letting the President announce who will run things. (7) Someone must pay the price when the polls plummet, and anyone who has maintained a high profile will be a prime target. (Maureen Dowd, in an article entitled, "Sununu Downfall: He Broke 7 Cardinal Rules," *The New York Times,* December 5, 1991.)

Wattenberg's Law. There is nothing so powerful as an old idea whose time has come again. (Ben Wattenberg, quoted by Hugh Sidey in the *Washington Star,* May 6, 1979.)

Wearing Hats, Law of. Never wear a hat that has more character than you do. (Hatmaker Michael Harris; from Bill Spivey, San Francisco, California.)

Weaver's Law. When several reporters share a cab on assignment, the reporter in the front seat pays for all. (Named for Warren Weaver of *The New York Times.* See also *Doyle's Corollary* and *Germond's Law; AO.*)

Weaver's Wall Motto. It's what you learn after you know it all that counts. (Baltimore Orioles Manager Earl Weaver's Office Wall Statement, as quoted by Thomas Boswell in the *Washington Post,* November 25, 1992.)

Weber's Law. If you have no trouble finding a place to park, you won't be able to find your car. (Philip Weber, Sacramento, California.)

Webster's Law. The damage rarely exceeds the deductible. (Doug Webster, Hartford, Connecticut.)

Weed's Axiom. Never ask two questions in a business letter. The reply will discuss the one in which you are least interested, and say nothing about the other. (Brian J. Weed, Carmel, California.)

Weidner's Queries. (1) The tide comes in and the tide goes out, and what have you got? (2) They say an elephant never forgets, but what's he got to remember? (*U;* from Dave Miliman, Baltimore, Maryland.)

Weight-Lifters' Law. If you can't place it down easy, don't pick it up. (Sign seen at a Chicago Health Club; from Steve Stine.)

Weight-Watcher's Law. Better to throw it out than throw it in. (Attributed to one Skinny Mitchell in a letter from "Benton Harbor Ben"; from an Ann Landers column.)

Weiler's Law. Nothing is impossible for the man who doesn't have to do it himself. (A. H. Weiler of *The New York Times; FL.*)

Weinberg's Law. If builders built buildings the way programmers wrote programs, then the first woodpecker that came along would destroy civilization. *Corollary:* An expert is a person who avoids the small errors while sweeping on to the grand fallacy. (Gerald Weinberg, computer scientist, University of Nebraska; *S.T.L.*)

Weiner's Wisdom. Indecision is the key to flexibility. (Lt. T. F. Weiner, USN; from R. J. Montore, Henderson, Kentucky.)

Weisert's Law. If somebody will fund it, somebody will. (Hilde Weisert, Teaneck, New Jersey.)

Weisman's College Exam Law. If you're confident after you've just finished an exam, it's because you don't know enough to know better. (Jay Weisman, Easton, Pennsylvania.)

Weissman's Discovery. When a man says he's "separated," it means he hasn't seen his wife since breakfast. (Rozanne Weissman, Washington, D.C.)

Weiss's Nine "Nevers" of Organizational Nuance. (1) Never blame on malice what can be explained by stupidity. (2) Never assume a letter of complaint is sincere if it also implies the virtue of the writer. (3) Never stop beating a dead horse until the boss administers the burial. (4) Never confuse agency policy with agency intentions; nor expect either to be necessarily reflected in agency actions. (5) Never assume priorities transcend an organizational change, even if it is a minor one. (6) Never regard as accurate a policy decision flow chart with more than one feedback loop. (7) Never claim a particular piece of data was necessary to support a policy, since it might turn out to be wrong. (8) Never use all your data in supporting a decision if you expect someone to question it later on. (9) Never believe a sentence that uses the phrase (a) comprehensive review, (b) cooperative process, (c) total systems analysis, (d) final decision, (e) final budget projections, or (f) long-term policy. (Martin H. Weiss, Springfield, Illinois.)

Welby's Law. No problem is so deep or intractable that it can't be successfully overcome in the allotted time-slot. (Named for television's Dr. Marcus Welby; from a column by Alan M. Kriegsman in the *Washington Post,* January 19, 1979.)

Welch's Potluck Principle. At any gathering, there will never be enough meat, vegetables, etc., but there is always enough Jell-O. (Patrick Welch, Clearwater, Florida.)

Welch's Rule. An apple every eight hours keeps three doctors away. (David P. Welch, Bloomington, Indiana.)

Welford's Dilemma. It is the students who least require assistance that are most forthcoming in asking for it. (David Welford, Birmingham, England.)

Wells's Law. A parade should have bands *or* horses, not both. (Nancy M. Wells, San Pedro [California] High School teacher and representative-at-large to the National Council of Teachers of English.)

Wells's Law. When in doubt, use clout. (Stephen Wells, North Tarrytown, New York.)

Welton's Clock-Radio Law. Any machine tends to fix itself, if you wait long enough. (From Michael Grant of the *San Diego Union,* who got it from a colleague on the paper. Grant reports that a friend had the EGR warning light on his car go on only to go out again eight years later.)

Wemhoff's Law of Trade-offs. Every advantage of any given course of action has a correspondingly equal and opposite disadvantage that, over the long run, fully offsets the advantage. *Corollary 1*: Over the short run, a specific advantage or disadvantage may predominate in any course of action. *Corollary 2:* Success in business consists in judging the short-run ascendancy of any specific advantage or disadvantage. (Joseph A. Wemhoff, Chicago, Illinois.)

Westheimer's Discovery. A couple of months in the laboratory can frequently save a couple of hours in the library. (Frank Westheimer, Harvard chemist; from Joseph A. Morton, M.D., Philadelphia, Pennsylvania.)

Westheimer's Rule. To estimate the time it takes to do a task, estimate the time you think it should take, multiply by two, and change the unit of measure to the next highest unit. Thus we allocate two days for a one-hour task. (*U/S.T.L.*)

Westmeyer's Collegiate Constant. No matter where you build the sidewalks, students will find a shortcut across the grass. If you build a sidewalk on the shortcut path, students will construct another shortcut between it and the original sidewalk. (Paul Westmeyer, San Antonio, Texas.)

West's Latest Discoveries. (1) Artificial hearts are no big deal; they've been around since the first banker. (2) When generals and admirals finally grow up, they go into retirement. (3) Social sobriquet: The cream rises to the top; unfortunately, so does the scum. (Roy W. West, Philadelphia, Pennsylvania.)

West's Laws. *West's Basic Law:* The difficulty in arranging a meeting varies as the square of the number of people involved. *The Law of Professionalism:* The value of the service or product you buy increases as the cube of its quality and professionalism and rarity; e.g., the baseball player who bats .360 is worth more than twice as much as the player who bats .180. In fact, the .360 hitter is in Hall-of-Fame territory, while the .180 hitter is on the verge of flunking out of the business altogether. (Richard E. West, Rye, New Hampshire.)

West's Proven Facts. (1) Man has yet to invent any substance that a Ping-Pong ball cannot get over, under, around, or through on its way to the most inaccessible spot in the playroom. (2) Electronically timed tests show that it takes a brand new tennis ball less than ten seconds to find, and stop dead-center in, the *only* puddle of water on any given tennis court. A ball that has been used until it barely bounces won't find such a puddle if you play all summer. (Robert T. West, Minneapolis, Minnesota.)

West's Rules. *Lex Logica:* The logical man has a shorter life expectancy than the practical man, because he refuses to look both ways on a one-way street. *Efficiency:* A well-fed wastebasket will serve you better than the best computer. *Publishing:* Go ahead and print it—the readers will proof it anyway. *Academia:* There is nothing so funny that a professor of folklore can't flatten it with an academic paper. *Legislation:* The more pork in the barrel, the faster it rolls. *Cash Flow:* If he can shut off your water, pay him first. *Boat Ownership:* The next best thing to having a friend with a boat is having a boat. *West's Mushroom Cloud Theory of Barbecuing.* Use enough fluid and you can start cinderblocks. (Roy W. West, Philadelphia, Pennsylvania.)

West's Time Constant. A split second is the time that elapses between the moment you step into a perfectly adjusted shower and someone turns on the washing machine and the dishwasher and flushes every toilet in the house. (Robert Tree West, Minneapolis, Minnesota.)

Wexford's Law. In a two-car family, the wife always has the smaller car. (In Ruth Rendell's *The Best Man to Die*, Doubleday, 1978; from D. J. Camp, Plymouth, England.)

Whatley's Axioms. (1) No auto clock ever worked right, if at all. (2) No Hudson was ever recalled. (3) Money usually ruins a good idea. *Whatley's Plerophories.* (1) Practical jokes aren't. (2) Money doesn't talk—it just never shuts up. (3) Religion is the last refuge of the religious. (4) Still water runs deep, but the fishing stinks. (5) They don't even make plastic like they used to. (6) Forgive thine enemies, then kiss them off. (7) Fat is hereditary—you get it from your government. *Whatley's Truths:* (1) There's more than one way to skin a knee. (2) Four out of five doctors recommend another doctor. (3) Anything is impossible. (4) Build a better mousetrap and the world will beat a path across your face. (5) Everything sounds romantic in French. Everything sounds like an order in German. Everything sounds like an argument in Italian. (6) What's right or wrong depends on which end of the food chain you're on. (Craig Whatley, San Rafael, California.)

Wheel Wisdom. (1) Before the squeaky wheel gets the grease, check first to see if it isn't just spinning. (2) If you insist on telling everyone you are a big wheel, in due time "little" wheels will let you carry the load. (3) The inventor of the wheel must have decided that life did *not* have to be a drag. (Chuck Werle, Chicago, Illinois.)

Whipple's Law of Organizations. In any pecking order, the ratio of peckers to peckees is always greater than one. (Donald G. Whipple, Torrance, California.)

Whispered Rule. People will believe anything if you whisper it. (*The Farmers' Almanac,* 1978 edition.)

White Flag Principle. A military disaster may produce a better postwar situation than victory. (Shimon Tzabar, in a book of the same title, Simon and Schuster, 1972. He says that if you can accept the principle, then there can be a science of military disasters as there is a science of military victories. He adds, "Such a science must comprise a theory and a practice. The practice should provide the armies with handbooks and textbooks for the accomplishment of defeats and surrenders. The fact that the big powers of today are powerful enough to make absurd any effort by lesser powers to overcome them in the traditional way, makes an alternative to victory the more urgent.")

White House, First Law of Life in the. Don't do anything you're not prepared to see in the papers the next morning. (Stated by a former White House staffer at the time of the Dr. Peter Bourne resignation; quoted in *Newsweek,* July 31, 1978.)

Whitehead's Injunction. Seek simplicity—and distrust it. (Alfred North Whitehead to his students; from Sydney J. Harris.)

Whiteman's Findings. *Wind Law for Pilots:* A head wind will reverse directions on the return flight. *First Corollary to Parkinson's Law:* Eight people will do ten people's work better than twelve people. *Measure of Success*: The measure of success is not how much money you have in the bank, but rather how much money the bank will lend you. (Jack W. Whiteman, Phoenix, Arizona.)

White's Certainties. (1) Anybody who tells you he is shy isn't. (2) People who use your first name in every other sentence cannot be trusted. (3) Anybody who refers to himself in the third person is overpaid. (4) When somebody says "ironically," she means "coincidentally." (5) Despite advertising claims, there is no such thing as an odor-free litter box. (Diane White, *The Boston Globe.*)

White's Corollary of Taxation. Taxes are not designed to be fair; they are designed to raise money. (Gordon White, Alexandria, Virginia, letter to the *Washington Post,* September 15, 1980.)

White's Dilemma. Old age is a special problem for me because I've never been able to shed the mental image I have of myself—a lad of about 19. (Essayist E. B. White.)

White's Discovery. He from whom you first ask the way will be a stranger too. (Leonard White, Camberley, Surrey, England.)

White's Law. Things are never as bad as they turn out to be. (Richard N. White, Director, School of Civil and Environmental Engineering, Cornell University.)

White's Laws. (1) If you are paid to make a decision, then bloody well make a decision, even if it is a wrong one. (2) If it is the wrong one, you can always change it tomorrow. (Reg White; from Alan Kilburn, England.)

White's Medical Rule. The less we know about a disease, the more medicines are available to treat it. (Robert I. White, M.D., Johns Hopkins University School of Medicine, Baltimore, Maryland.)

White's Medical Rule II. In the practice of medicine (and I suspect other fields of endeavor, too), gratitude received bears no relation to effort expended. (Benjamin V. White, M.D., West Hartford, Connecticut.)

White's National Security Rule. Security declines as security machinery expands. (E. B. White, quoted in *Federal Times,* October 29, 1979; from Joseph C. Goulden.)

White's Observations of Committee Operation. (1) People very rarely think in groups; they talk together, they exchange information, they adjudicate, they make compromises. But they do not think; they do not create. (2) A really new idea affronts current agreement. (3) A meeting cannot be productive unless certain premises are so shared that they do not need to be discussed, and the argument can be confined to areas of disagreement. But while this kind of consensus makes a group more effective in its legitimate functions, it does not make the group a creative vehicle—it would not be a new idea if it didn't, and the group, impelled as it is to agree, is instinctively hostile to that which is divisive. (*U/GT.*)

White's Political Rule of Thumb. Political campaigns do not truly start until the guys in bars stop arguing about the World Series. (Teddy White, quoted in *National Review,* July 8, 1988; from Charles D. Poe.)

White's Rule. The effectiveness of a therapy for a disease is inversely proportional to the number of therapies available to treat the disease. (Robert I. White, Jr., M.D., Johns Hopkins University School of Medicine. Dr. White amplifies, "Instead of therapy, one might substitute drugs, etc. Good examples of this would be the wide variety of non-narcotic pain medicines or common cold remedies. The reverse, of course, is that if a patient has appendicitis, there is only one therapy, namely, appendectomy, which is extremely effective.")

White's Statement. Don't lose heart.... *Owen's Comment on White's Statement:*... they might want to cut it out. *Byrd's Addition to Owen's Comment on White's Statement:*... and they want to avoid a lengthy search. (*U/S.T.L.*)

Whitmore's Rule for Public Speakers. If you haven't struck oil in twenty minutes, quit boring. (Kevin Whitmore, Fairmount, Indiana.)

Whitney's Distinction. A diamond ain't nothing but a lump of coal with a migraine. (L. P. Whitney, Blue Hill, Maine.)

Whitney's Second Law of the Democratic Process. In a democracy, having been born, death ensues. Everything else is negotiable. (Peter Whitney, Tucson, Arizona.)

Whittet's Observations. (1) Enemies are more likely to activate you than friends. (2) It is easier to fool the eye than any of the other senses. (3) In any improbable situation, the only solution is another improbability. (4) It is not winning I enjoy so much as defeating you. (George Sorley Whittet, Carshalton, Surrey, England.)

Whole Picture Principle. Research scientists are so wrapped up in their own narrow endeavors that they cannot possibly see the whole picture of anything, including their own research. *Corollary:* The director of research should know as little as possible about the specific subject of research he is administrating. (*U/DRW.*)

Why This Book Will Bring You Luck

This book will bring you good luck. The luck is in your hands. Don't ruin it. You are to receive good luck within 14 days of buying this book if you follow instructions.

This is no joke.

To ensure your luck, buy 20 additional copies and send them to people you think need good luck. Please do not send them money or any other book. All 20 books must be mailed within 96 hours.

Place the names and addresses of three of the 20 people at the top of the next page along with your own name and address. Each subsequent recipient is to remove the top name when adding new names.

See what happens. It works. Accept no other chain letters. Dan G. of Denver has, at last count, 4,311 copies, and the estate of Harriet P. of Toledo has 1,406 copies (accumulated before she broke the chain and died).

Don't break the chain, and don't tell the spoilsport postal authorities about it.

Wicker's Law. Government expands to absorb revenue—and then some. (Tom Wicker, *The New York Times*. Florida.)

Wickre's Law. On a quiet night, there will always be two good movies on TV, or none at all. (*U/NDB*.)

Wiio's Laws of Communications. (1) Communication usually fails—except by chance. *Corollary:* If you are satisfied that your communication is bound to succeed, then the communication is bound to fail. (2) If a message can be understood in different ways, it will be understood in just the way that does the most harm. (3) There is always somebody who knows better than you what you meant by your message. (4) The more communication there is, the more difficult it is for communication to succeed. *Corollary:* The more communication there is, the more misunderstanding will occur. (5) In mass communication, it is not important how things are; the important thing is how things seem to be. (6) The importance of a news item is inversely correlated with the square of the distance. (Professor Osmo Wiio, Director of the Institute for Communications Research at the University of Helsinki.)

Wilcox's Axiom. Everything has an eventual use if you plan to live forever. (The character, Carl Wilcox, created by writer Harold Adams.)

Wilcox's Law. A pat on the back is only a few centimeters from a kick in the pants. (*U/RS*.)

Wilde's Maxim. Nothing succeeds like excess. (Oscar Wilde.)

Wilgus' Warning. Always slow down for Dead Man's Curve. (Neil Wilgus, Lubbock, Texas. *Personal Note from the Director:* When this came in I immediately added it to my ever-growing list of personal rules to live by. For this American male, then in his late 50s, this new warning was a much wittier and trenchant reminder to diet, exercise, and observe general mid-life in moderation than, say, a long list of traditional do's and don'ts. I posted *Wilgus' Warning* next to the closet where I keep my walking shoes.)

Wilgus's Principles of Cultural Inflation. (1) Everything once a subject is now a field. (2) With the knowledge explosion, new fields are constantly being created. (3) Everyone who once had an interest in a subject is now an expert in a field. (4) Everything you need to know about a field can be covered in a five-minute TV interview with an expert. (Neal Wilgus, Albuquerque, New Mexico.)

Wilkes' College Guide for Students. When in doubt, cut. When confused, drop. (Anonymous; Wilkes-Barre, Pennsylvania.)

Willets on Aging. There is an engaging legend abroad in the land that advancing years mellow one and somehow bring out the kindliest impulses of one's nature; that the countryside swarms with repentant Scrooges. My own observation has been that when a bastard grows old, he simply becomes an old bastard. (Isabel M. Willetts, LeClaire, Iowa.)

Willey's Discoveries. (1) The length of stay of out-of-town guests is inversely proportional to their desirability. (2) There are three absolute maxims for the handyman—your garden hose, extension cord, and ladder are always too short. (Boots Willey, Lehigh Acres, Florida.)

William Lyon Phelp's Second Law. The value of an earned doctorate varies in inverse proportion to the extent of its use by the recipient. (In *Context,* March 15, 1980; from Jeffrey Chamberlain.)

Williams' Discovery. You get to go on a guy's front lawn and kick him in the shorts every night. (NBC's Brian Williams on why being a White House correspondent is a fun job; quoted in the *Hill,* August 16, 1995.)

Williams's Critical Key. Any critic can establish a wonderful batting average by just rejecting every new idea. (J. D. Williams, quoted in Bennett Cerf's *The Sound of Laughter,* Doubleday, 1970.)

Williams's Diet Advisory. Throw out all women's magazines; they'll drive you schizo. Page 1 is a diet. Page 2 is a chocolate cake. It's a no-win situation. (Kim Williams, in her *Book of Uncommon Sense*, HP Books, 1981; from Joseph C. Goulden.)

Williams's Law of Political Rhetoric. Never underestimate the ability of a politician to (a) say something and tell you not very much, (b) do it with style, and (c) touch all the bases. (Robert H. Williams, in the *Washington Post.* His proof was a statement made by Senator Henry M. "Scoop" Jackson to Israel's Prime Minister Menachem Begin: "As we Christians approach the Christmas season, we can all be thankful to a Moslem and a Jew.")

Willis Catch-88. (1) When the speed limit is raised from 55 to 65 mph, it actually becomes 75 because motorists think they won't be ticketed unless they exceed the limit by more than 10 mph. (2) No matter who he is, the next president of the United States will be perceived to be a failure, because his duties have been multiplied dramatically, while his hands will be tied by a crippling national debt and deficit, and by a Congress which is oversensitive to the "wish lists" of single-issue pressure groups, including ex-congressmen turned professional lobbyists. (Jane B. Willis, letter to the *Sarasota Herald-Tribune,* April 15, 1988; from Ben Willis, Jr.)

Willis Reminder, The. "All natural ingredients" sounds super wholesome, but arsenic, cyanide, coal dust, and manure are all natural, too. (Ben Willis, Jr., McLean, Virginia.)

Willis's Law of Public Administration. In any federal management report, the recommendations that would result in actual savings will be rejected, but the rejection will be "balanced" by the enthusiastic acceptance of those which increase costs. (Bennett Moser Willis, McLean, Virginia, former Chief of Management, U.S. Department of Justice.)

Willis's Observation. Except for courtship and travel, everything seems to take longer and cost more than: (a) it used to, (b) the estimate. (Bennett Moser Willis, McLean, Virginia, former Chief of Management, U.S. Department of Justice.)

Willis's Rule of Golf. You can't lose an old golf ball. (John Willis, WCVB-TV, Boston, Massachusetts.)

Will's Law. All economic news is bad, and all news is economic news. (George F. Will, *Newsweek,* April 23, 1984.)

Will's Paradox of Popular Government. People are happiest when they are in a position to complain about government; and they can complain with minimum confusion and maximum righteousness when they acknowledge, indeed insist, that government is not "by the people." (Columnist George Will, in his *Washington Post* column for June 8, 1978.)

Will's Rule of Informed Citizenship. If you want to understand your government, don't begin by reading the Constitution. It conveys precious little of the flavor of today's statecraft. Instead read selected portions of the Washington telephone directory containing listings for all the organizations with titles beginning with the word "National." (George Will; *JW.*)

Wilson's Definition (for economics and political science professors). The difference between communism and capitalism is this: in capitalism, man exploits man; in communism, it's the other way around. *Corollary:* By the time you learn this, you've probably been teaching it backwards for years. (Professor John R. M. Wilson, Mid-America Nazarene College, Olathe, Kansas, who developed it with Gary Moore and Steve Cole.)

Wilson's Dietary Discovery. It is impossible to lose weight lastingly, and all diets are atrocious. (Sloan Wilson, from *What Shall We Wear to This Party? The Man in the Gray Flannel Suit Twenty Years Before and After,* Arbor House, 1976.)

Wilson's First Three Life Lessons. (1) Liquid shoe polish doesn't work. (2) A man who wants time to read and write must let the grass grow long. (3) Beware of people who are always well-dressed. (Author Sloan Wilson, in *What Shall We Wear to the Party? The Man in the Gray Flannel Suit Twenty Years Before and After,* 1976; from Daniel Humphreys, Cincinnati, Ohio.)

Wilson's Law of Demographics. The public is not made up of people who get their names in the newspapers. (Woodrow Wilson; *MBC.*)

Wilson's Laws for Academic Administrators. (*A selection*): *Wilson's Second Law:* Stimulate self-doubt only in those who are confident that they know it all. *Wilson's Ninth Law:* Listen patiently always, but also know when to talk fast. *Wilson's Seventeenth Law:* Take everybody seriously but yourself. *Wilson's Twentieth Law:* Make no rule which you cannot or will not enforce. *Wilson's Twenty-first Law:* Make as few rules as possible. *Wilson's Twenty-fifth Law:* Never answer hypothetical questions. (Kenneth G. Wilson, Storrs, Connecticut. The full list appeared in the *Journal of Personnel Evaluation in Education* in 1992.)

Wilson's Laws of Flight. (1) You want a drink and the smallest bill you have is a twenty. (2) Offering a flight attendant a $20 bill for a $2 drink is like spitting on an Alabama state trooper. (3) On arrival, passengers without time constraints are the first to fill the aisle. (Louis D. Wilson, from a much longer list of flight laws published in *The Wall Street Journal,* June 30, 1986.)

Wilson's Laws. (1) All policy interventions in social problems produce the intended effect—*if* the research is carried out by those implementing the policy or their friends. (2) No policy intervention in social problems produces the intended effect—*if* the research is carried out by independent third parties, especially those skeptical of the policy. (James Q. Wilson, Harvard political scientist, in his article "On Pettigrew and Armor" in *Public Interest,* Winter 1973.)

Wilson's Rule of Annoyance. A caller who dials the wrong number will call a second time as soon as you have comfortably returned to your living room chair and will act as if he or she is the one being inconvenienced. (Mike Wilson, Jackson, Michigan.)

Wilson's Third Law of Poker. Whoever provides the chips gets first crack at the dip. (Hank Wilson.)

Wing-Walking, First Law of. Never leave hold of what you've got until you've got hold of something else. (Donald Herzberg, dean of Georgetown University's graduate school, reported to *AO.* It came from the days of the barnstorming pilots and is now applied in situations such as when one quits a job before having another lined up.)

Winkler's Rule. Assumptions are the termites of relationships. (Actor Henry Winkler in his Emerson College graduation speech, June 1995.)

Winners' Law. It isn't whether you win or lose, but how much you win by. (Paul J. Spreitzer, age fifteen, Chicago, Illinois.)

Winston's Second Rule of Success. Your greatest assets are other people's money and other people's patience. (Carl Winston, in *How to Run a Million into a Shoestring and Other Shortcuts to Success,* G. P. Putnam's Sons, 1960.)

Winterhalder's Wisdom. Cop-outs aren't necessarily lies; in fact, the best cop-outs are absolutely true. (*U.*)

Winter's Law of the Stranded. The shortest distance to aid is in the opposite direction. (Robert F. Winter, M.D., Spring Valley, New York.)

Winters' Rule. In a crowded place, the person directly behind you always has the loudest voice. *Corollary:* People with loud voices never have anything interesting to say. (Christine Winters, *Chicago Tribune.*)

Witzenburg's Law of Airplane Travel. The distance between the ticket counter and your plane is directly proportional to the weight of what you are carrying and inversely proportional to the time remaining before takeoff. (Gary Witzenburg, Troy, Michigan.)

Wober's SNIDE Rule. Ideal goals grow faster than the means of attaining new goals allow. (Mallory Wober, *JIR,* March 1971. The acronym SNIDE stands for Satisfied Needs Incite Demand Excesses.)

Woehlke's Law. Nothing is done until nothing is done. To cite a few examples: (1) Middle managers can never get the people they need for a job as long as they continue to muddle through by means of overtime, ulcers, and superhuman effort. But when enough people quit in frustration so that the job is not finished, upper management will approve the hiring of the necessary people. (2) Ditto for salaries. (3) The energy crisis (substitute your favorite crisis) will worsen until the whole house of cards collapses. Then and only then will effective measures be taken. (Richard A. Woehlke, Sutton, Massachusetts.)

Wohlford's Baseball Formula. Ninety percent of this game is half mental. (Outfielder Jim Wohlford, quoted in *Sports Illustrated,* October 24, 1977. In an article entitled "Baseball's Mental Game," which appeared in the 2002 edition of the journal *Nine*, anthropologist and former minor leaguer George Gmelch wrote: "In keeping with the sports mania for quantifying everything, baseball players and coaches often put a number on the mental dimension as a way of stressing its importance. 'Succeeding in pro ball is 90 percent mental. It's big,' said Diamondbacks infielder Andy Fox. 'Baseball is 80 percent mental,' said one manager, 'you have got to make players believe in themselves to perform well.' Or, in the words of former Kansas City outfielder Jim Wohlford, 'Baseball is 90 percent mental half the time.' Actually, Wohlford's Yogi-ism is probably the most accurate of the three in that some aspects of baseball are more mentally demanding than others.")

Wolfe's Law. Satire diminishes in direct ratio to the size of your audience. That is, as your audience base grows greater, your satire grows less. (Digby Wolfe quoted by Cecil Smith, *Chicago Tribune,* January 15, 1969. Wolfe worked with George Schlatter in developing that exercise in television insanity, *Laugh In.* "Obviously, the only thing you can satirize is something people know about," said Wolfe. "For instance, you can't do a satire on grand opera for people who've never seen an opera.")

Wolfe's Rule. There is nothing that can make one look younger than being younger. (Doris Wolfe, Springfield, Missouri.)

Wolf's Law. You never get a second chance to make a first impression. (*U;* from N.D. Butler.)

Wolf's Law (An Optimistic View of a Pessimistic World). It isn't that things will necessarily go wrong (*Murphy's Law*), but rather that they will take so much more time and effort than you think, if they are not to. *Tactics:* If you can't beat them, have them join you. (Charles Wolf, Jr., head, economics department, the RAND Corp., and director, RAND Graduate Institute; *RS.* See also *Baldy's Law,* which is also *Wolf's.*)

Wolf's Laws. *Historical Lessons:* Those who don't study the past will repeat its errors. Those who do study it, will find other ways to err. *Decision-making:* Major actions are rarely decided by more than four people. If you think a larger meeting you're attending is really "hammering out" a decision, you're probably wrong. Either the decision was agreed to by a smaller group before the meeting began, or the outcome of the larger meeting will be modified later when three or four people get together. *Briefings:* In briefings to busy people, summarize at the beginning what you're *going to tell* them, then *tell* them, then summarize at the end what you *have told* them. *Good Management:* The tasks to do immediately are the minor ones; otherwise, you'll forget them. The major ones are often better to defer. They usually need more time for reflection. Besides, if you forget them, they'll remind you. *Meetings:* The only important result of a meeting is agreement about next steps. *Planning:* A good place to start from is where you are.

Wolf's Laws of Cookery. *Liquid Sugar:* A drop of honey, molasses, or other liquid sugar will spread itself in a layer one molecule deep over every available surface. *Corollary:* Double this area if small children are present. *The Absolutely Necessary Ingredient:* You don't have it. *Corollary 1:* You can't get it at any shop within a fifty-mile radius. *Corollary 2:* It's gone bad. *Measurements:* The most fabulously fascinating recipe available will be expressed in terms of grams (if you have no scales) or firkins (if you do). *Company:* Your soufflé falls when, and only when, there are guests. *Double-boilers:* (a) If you turn your back on it, it will boil dry. Or burn. (b) If you watch it like a hawk, it will boil dry or burn when the phone rings. *Bread-and-telephone Law:* The telephone will ring only at the messiest stage of kneading. *Drop-ins:* If you have the reputation of being a good cook, your mother-in-law will drop in when, and only when, you are serving canned beans. *Leftovers:* It turned green. *Corollary:* The probability of fur-bearing leftovers increases logarithmically on days when you have (a) morning sickness, (b) flu, (c) a hangover. (Molly Wolf, cook and biochemistry student, Halifax, Nova Scotia; from a longer list.)

Wolpe's Law of Mortality. If you live long enough, something will kill you. (Bruce C. Wolpe, North Sydney, Australia.)

Woman's Equation. Whatever women do, they must do twice as well as men to be thought half as good. Luckily, this is not difficult. (Charlotte Whitton from Robert Specht, who explained in a letter dated April 15, 1979: "I have an unreliable impression that she was Mayor of Ottawa . . . I have a note scribbled from somewhere that 'Whatever women do' was quoted in *Canada Month,* June 1963. "The statement was first made by the late Charlotte Whitton, for many years the Mayor of Ottawa. Miss Whitton was a tiny bulldog of woman, and a fierce fighter for women's rights. John Duffie, Victoria, British Columbia.)

Woodruff's Work Rule. *Everybody* works for the sales department. (Jeff Woodruff, ABC; *MLS.*)

Wood's Incomplete Maxims. (1) All's well that ends. (2) A penny saved is a penny. (3) Don't leave things unfinishe (Donald R. Woods, Stanford, California.)

Wood's Law. The more unworkable the urban plan, the greater the probability of implementation. (Robert Wood, *Ekistics,* October 1969; *JW.*)

Woods's Rule for Drinking. I always drink standing up because it is much easier to sit down when I get drunk standing up than it is to stand up when I get drunk sitting down. (Ralph L. Woods, *How to Torture Your Mind,* Funk & Wagnalls, 1969.)

Woodward's Law. A theory is better than its explanation (H. P. Woodward, in a letter to Robert L. Bates, who published it in his "Geologic Column" in the July–August 1968 *Geotimes.*)

Woolridge's Razor. It's one thing to hear about it from your coach, but when your wife tells you it stinks, you tend to work on it. (Orlando Woolridge of the Chicago Bulls on why he raised his free-throw percentage.)

Woolsey-Swanson Rule of Problems. People would rather live with a problem they cannot solve than accept a solution they cannot understand. (Robert E. D. Woolsey and Huntington S. Swanson, from their book *Operations Research for Immediate Application: A Quick and Dirty Manual,* Harper & Row, 1975; *R.*)

Work Rules

Found posted in various locations about the working world during the 1970s and '80s.

RULES:

1. The Boss is Always Right.
2. When the Boss is Wrong, Refer to *Rule 1.*

THE WORKER'S DILEMMA:

1. No matter how much you do, you'll never do enough.
2. What you don't do is always more important than what you do do.

NEW WORK RULES:

• ***Sickness.***

No excuses will be acceptable. We will no longer accept your doctor's statement as proof of illness, as we believe that if you are able to go to the doctor, you are able to come to work.

• ***Leave of Absence (for an Operation.)***

We are no longer allowing this practice. We wish to discourage any thoughts that you may not need all of whatever you have, and you should not consider having something removed. We hired you as you are, and to have anything removed would certainly make you less than we bargained for.

• ***Death (Other Than Your Own).***

This is no excuse. If you can arrange for funeral services to be held late in the afternoon, however, we can let you off an hour early, provided all your work is up to date.

• ***Death (Your Own).***

This will be accepted as an excuse, but we would like at least two weeks' notice, as we feel it is your duty to teach someone else your job.

Also, entirely too much time is being spent in the washrooms. In the future, you will follow the practice of going in alphabetical order. For instance, those whose surnames begin with "A" will be allowed to go from 9 to 9:05 a.m., and so on. If you are unable to go at your appointed time, it will be necessary to wait until the next day when your time comes around again.

THE TWO KINDS OF WORK:

Work is of two kinds: (1) Altering the position of matter at or near the earth's surface relative to other such matter; (2) Telling other people to do so.

The first is unpleasant and ill paid; the second is pleasant and highly paid.

—*The Rotarian*

Eat a live toad the first thing in the morning and nothing worse will happen to you the rest of the day.

Our troops advanced today without losing a foot of ground.

—*Spanish Civil War Communiqué*

Anyone can do any amount of work provided it isn't the work he is supposed to be doing at that moment. —*Robert Benchley.*

ANNOUNCEMENT:

(These rules were printed in the *Boston Globe* some years ago and were reported to be the rules posted by the owner of a New England carriage works in 1872, as a guide to his office workers.)

- Office employees will daily sweep the floors, dust the furniture, shelves, and showcases.
- Each day fill lamps, clean chimneys, and trim wicks. Wash the windows once a week.
- Each clerk will bring in a bucket of water and scuttle of coal for the day's business.
- Make your pens carefully. You may whittle nibs to your individual taste.
- This office will open at 7 a.m. and close at 8 p.m. except on the Sabbath, on which day we will remain closed. Each employee is expected to spend the Sabbath by attending church and contributing liberally to the cause of the Lord.
- Men employees will be given off each week for courting purposes, or two evenings a week if they go regularly to church.
- After an employee has spent his 13 hours of labor in the office, he should spend the remaining time reading the Bible and other good books.
- Every employee should lay aside from each pay a goodly sum of his earnings for his benefit during his declining years, so that he will not become a burden on society or his betters.
- Any employee who smokes Spanish cigars, uses liquor in any form, or frequents pool and public halls, or gets shaved in a barber shop, will give me good reason to suspect his worth, intentions, integrity and honesty.
- The employee who has performed his labors faithfully and without a fault for five years, will be given an increase of five cents per day in his pay, providing profits from the business permit it.

Wright's Perspective. Give me the luxuries of life and I will willingly do without the necessities. (Frank Lloyd Wright; from Bernard L. Albert.)

Wynne's Law. Negative slack tends to increase. (*U/S.T.L.*)

Xerces Englebraun's Big Man Syndrome. The importance of the man and his job, in that relative order, rises in direct proportion to the distance separating his audience from his home office. (This Shanghai psychiatrist appears in *For Men With Yen*, by Alan Rosenberg and William J. O'Neill, Wayward Press, Tokyo, Japan, 1962.)

X's Boss Discoveries. (1) The boss does not sleep—he/she rests. (2) The boss is never late—he/she is delayed. (3) The boss never leaves work early—his/her presence is required elsewhere. (4) The boss is never sarcastic—he/she is witty. (5) The boss is not hard to work for—he/she is a stern taskmaster. (*U.*)

XXcellent Mxssagx from thx Coach. Who makxs a txam a succxss? Evxn though my typxwritxr isn't a nxw modxl, it works quitx wxll xxcxpt for onx kxy. I had wishxd sxvxral timxs that it workxd pxrfxctly. It is trux that thxrx arx 41 othxr kxys opxrating wxll xnough, howxvxr just onx not making thx xffort makxs all thx diffxrxncx. Somxtimxs it sxxms to mx a txam can bx somxwhat likx my typxwritxr... not all of thx mxmbxrs arx xxpxnding xnough xffort. Pxrhaps you txll yoursxlf "Wxll, I'm only onx pxrson. I won't makx or brxak our txam." But it doxs makx a diffxrxncx bxcausx a txam, to bx xffxctivx, nxxds activx participation from xvxry singlx pxrson, xvxn thosx on thx bxnch. So thx nxxt timx you think you arx only onx playxr, and your xfforts arx not nxxdxd, rxmxmbxr my old typxwritxr and txll yoursxlf, "I am a kxy pxrson on thx txam and I am nxxded vxry much." (John Kessel, "Thoughts and Quotes for Volleyball Coaches," 1986.)

Y

Yakolev's Rule of Diplomacy. Everyone is entitled to say "no"—except diplomats. (Aleksandr Yakovlev, Soviet Politburo member and chief architect of Mikhail Gorbachev's *glasnost* policy; from an interview in the *Washington Times*, December 9, 1988; from Joseph C. Goulden.)

Yapp's Basic Fact. If a thing cannot be fitted into something smaller than itself, some dope will do it. (Eric Frank Russell, in a November 1959 letter to *ASF.* Yapp discovered this fact at an early age when he got his head stuck in a fence and had to be freed by the fire department; *FD.*)

Yardley's Restaurant Law. No matter how many good tables are free, you will always be given the worst available. (Jonathan Yardley, *Washington Post* book critic, quoted in *A Writer's Companion,* LSU Press, Louis D. Rubin, Jr. with Jerry Leath Mills, 1995.)

Yauger's Law of Backstabbing. When you talk about someone behind their backs, their backs will be right behind you. (David Yauger, Leesburg, Virginia.)

Yearwood's Admonition. To err is human, so do not use up the eraser before the pencil. (R.L. Yearwood, Hereford, Texas.)

Yearwood's Emmylou Factor. You know you've recorded a good country album if you run into Emmylou Harris on a Nashville street and can hold your head up and look her in the eye. (Trisha Yearwood, quoted by *Country Music* editor Chet Flippo; *TG.*)

Yhprum's Law. Just sometimes, every damn thing goes right. (Quoted from *The River,* Knopf, 1997; by Colin Fletcher and forwarded by Helen Grinstead.)

Yoakum's Rule. Don't put off until tomorrow what you can get done sometime next week. (Robert Yoakum, Yoakum Features, Lakeville, Connecticut.)

Yolen's Law of Self-Praise. Proclaim yourself "world champ" of something—tiddly-winks, rope-jumping, whatever—Send this notice to newspapers, radio, TV, and wait for challengers to confront you. Avoid challenges as long as possible, but continue to send news of your achievements to all media. Also, develop a newsletter and letterhead for communications. (Will Yolen, former PR man and kite VIP, who by now probably owns a suitcase filled with clippings of articles that talk about him and his world championships.)

Young's Law. Nothing is illegal if one hundred businessmen decide to do it. (Andrew Young, author, civil rights activist, U.S. congressman, mayor, and UN ambassador.)

Young's Law of Conservation of Fat. Within any random population of adults numbering 100 or more, weight can be neither gained nor lost—it can only be redistributed. (David R. Young, McKinleyville, California.)

Young's Research Law. All great discoveries are made by mistake. *Corollary:* The greater the funding, the longer it takes to make the mistakes. (*U/DRW.*)

Young's Rule. When using humor in a speech, the laughter at the end of the joke should be directly proportional to the time invested to obtain the laughter. (Jeff C. Young, Phoenix, Arizona.)

Z

Zais's First Postulate. As long as you retain the capacity to blush, your immortal soul is in no particular danger. (Elliot Zais, Corvallis, Oregon.)

Zawada's Conundrum. The easier it is to correct mistakes, the more often mistakes will be made. (Donald F. Zawada, Lisle, Illinois, who adds, "First discovered ten years ago while watching computer programmers at interactive terminals: rediscovered more recently while watching our secretary at a word processor.")

Zeek's Discovery. The key to flexibility is indecision. (Valentino J. Zeek, Maitland, Florida.)

Zellar's Law. Every newspaper, no matter how tight the news hole, has room for a story on another newspaper increasing its newsstand price. (Ed Zellar, Park Ridge, Illinois; *AO*.)

Zimmerman's Corollary to Lucht's Observation. Looking competent is just as ineffective as being competent. (John A. Mattsen.)

Zimmerman's Law. Regardless of whether a mission expands or contracts, administrative overhead continues to grow at a steady rate. (*LSP;* list, which identifies him as Charles J. Zimmerman.)

Zimmerman's Law of Complaints. Nobody notices when things go right. (M. Zimmerman; *AO*.)

Zipf's Principle of Least Effort. Learning favors methods that require the least writing, the least new learning, and the least memorizing. (*U;* U.S. Department of Agriculture Press Release.)

Zisla's Discoveries. (1) A good administrator tries to do as little as possible; a bad administrator tries to do as much as possible. (2) Don't concern yourself too much with the "bottom line." There will be a new one tomorrow or even before. (3) It doesn't matter how many catastrophes you survive; living will still kill you. (4) It is possible to paint zebra stripes on an elephant—though it won't do much good as a disguise. The zebras will know it is still an elephant and even though they will be puzzled, maybe even confused, so will the other elephants. (Harold Zisla, South Bend, Indiana.)

Zisla's Law. If you're asked to join a parade, don't march behind the elephants. (Harold Zisla, South Bend, Indiana.)

Zmuda's Principle. It's a lot easier to work on a nonexistent problem because there are fewer—if any—obstacles to overcome. (Joseph Zmuda, San Francisco, California.)

Zuckerman's Explanation. Women prefer tabloids because their arms are shorter. (Mortimer Zuckerman explaining, in early 1993, why he felt his acquisition of the *New York Daily News* would be a success.)

Zusmann's Rule. A successful symposium depends on the ratio of meeting to eating. (*U;* from a group of "Quips" in the *JIR*, March 1971.)

Zymurgy's First Law of Evolving System Dynamics. Once you open a can of worms, the only way to recan them is to use a larger can. Old worms never die, they just worm their way into larger cans. (The truth can now be told: The oft-quoted Zymurgy is actually Conrad Schneiker, who was the source of the next item. Schneiker commented in a letter to the author that "the name originated from the name of a "phantom" file used by CDC operating systems. Also, the name of an important branch of chemistry; the science of fermentation, often the last word in small dictionaries.) *Zymurgy's Law on the Availability of Volunteer Labor:* People are always available for work in the past tense.

Disclaimer

Notice to the Readers of *The Official Rules:*

This text may contain explicit material some readers may find objectionable; parental guidance is advised. Keep away from sunlight, no money down, slippery when wet.

A consumer credit report may be requested in connection with this application or in connection with updates, renewals, or extensions of any credit granted as a result of this application. Member FDIC. Keep away from pets.

This offer is void where prohibited, taxed or otherwise restricted, and no purchase is necessary; however, entries must be postmarked by October 11. Some assembly required.

Action figures sold separately, no preservatives added, and there is a substantial penalty for early withdrawal. Use only with proper ventilation, keep away from open flame, and do not inhale fumes. At participating stores. Slightly higher west of the Rockies and you must be 18 to enter, licensed drivers only. If ingested, do not induce vomiting, and if symptoms persist, consult a physician. Dealer prep extra; batteries not included. Sold for industrial use only.

If any defects are discovered, do not attempt to fix them yourself; return to an authorized service center or send pre-paid to manufacturer. You need not be present to win.

Please allow four to six weeks for delivery; no salt added. Taxes are not included and the price is plus tax and your old tires. This offer expires at midnight, December 31, member FSLIC. All sales final, all rights reserved, and prices subject to change without notice. Keep out of the reach of children, limit one-per-family please. Call before you dig.

Quantities are limited while supplies last; not street legal in some states. Offer good only in U.S.A. Prices and mileage may vary; hardware and instructions are included and wattages stated are maximum recommended. Sorry, no CODs. This product is guaranteed to be free of any physical defects, design flaws, and poor workmanship. Misuse or abuse invalidates the guarantee. Product must be used only for its intended purpose and in accordance with manufacturer's specific warning. Read and follow label instructions. Any amount paid is not refundable without proof of purchase (UPC) and cashier's receipt showing date and place of purchase with the amount paid for this product encircled.

This message is intended for the private use of our readers and any reproduction, rebroadcast, or any other accounts of this message without the prior written consent of the National Football League is strictly prohibited. Check local zoning laws before ordering; slightly enlarged to show detail. We make no warranty, either expressed or implied, including, but not limited to, any implied warranties of merchantability or fitness for a particular purpose, regarding these materials, and make such materials available solely on an "as is" basis. Close cover before striking.

For external use only and occupancy by over ten persons is prohibited by the Fire Marshall and the laws of this state. If a rash, irritation, redness, or swelling develops, discontinue use. Pat. pending, Reg. U.S. Pat. Off. Copyrighted, trademark on file with the Federal Trade Commission, and failure to reduce speed so as to avoid collision with any vehicle on, near, or entering the highway is in violation of I.C.C. 9-4-1-57(a). Tumble dry only.

The sole and exclusive liability, regardless of the form of action, shall not exceed the purchase price of the materials described herein. Do not exceed recommended dosage and those who brought you this message are solely responsible for its content. Which, by the way, contains *no* sodium, carbohydrates, or polyunsaturated fats; it is *low* sugar and is caffeine free. Before using consult your doctor.

Tested and rated by Underwriters Laboratories; avoid extreme temperatures and store in cool, dry place. No artificial colors or flavoring has been added; hard hat and safety goggles are required. We are not responsible for lost articles or personal property, public or private. You break it, you bought it! Do not place near a magnetic source. Recommended for adults over 21 only and in no event shall we be liable to anyone for specific, collateral, incidental, or consequential damages in connection with or arising out of purchase or use of these materials. Some restrictions apply. Do not use if safety seal is broken.

Any resemblance to actual persons, living or dead, is unintentional and purely coincidental. This warranty gives you specific legal rights which vary from state to state. Sorry, we cannot be responsible for errors in typing, typography, or photography. The possibility of electrical shock does exist if you remove the cover and leave any of the devices plugged in and/or turned on. Be sure to unplug the device from the power outlet and clean only with a soft, dry cloth. Keep away from moisture, rain, snow, gloom of night, and so forth. User assumes full responsibility.

The Surgeon General of the United States has warned that smoking this product could be hazardous to your health and that the best safeguard, second only to abstinence, is the use of a condom. Except as provided herein, no employee, agent, franchisee, dealer, or other person is authorized to give any warranties of any nature. Some states do not allow the limitation or exclusion of incidental or consequential damages, so the above may not apply to you.

We make no warranty as to the design, capability, capacity, or suitability for use except as provided in this paragraph. Do not fold, mutilate, or spindle. Money orders or cashier's check only. Terms and specifications may change without notice. All returns must be accompanied with a Credit Return Authorization number on shipping carton.

To avoid accidental erasure, remove appropriate tab or cover write-protect notch with tape. No part of this message covered by the copyright herein may be reproduced or copied in any form or by any means—graphic, electronic, or mechanical, including photo copying, recording, taping, or information storage and retrieval systems—without written permission of the author and publisher. No admittance by anyone under 17 unless accompanied by an adult. Shut off engine. Do not puncture, incinerate, or store above 120 degrees Fahrenheit. Avoid contact with eyes and skin and avoid inhaling vapors. Do not clean with abrasives and do not use on suede, leather, vinyl, or plastic or allow to come in contact with paint finish or chrome. Information in this message is subject to change; see your representative for the latest information. An equal housing lender. Do not leave unattended. Live, except on the West Coast.

Connect ground wire to avoid shock. Do not remove protective covering. Price and availability subject to change. Four-week clearance on personal checks. Compatibility not guaranteed. Add 3 percent for Visa and MasterCard, 5 percent for American Express. Texas residents add 8.25 percent sales tax. Color monitor not included. Do not remove this tag under penalty of law. Return shipments are subject to a restocking fee. Add 3 percent for shipping and handling. We reserve the right to substitute equivalent items. Bridge freezes before highway.

Payment in U.S. currency only. Warranty does not cover accidental damage, misuse, misapplication, or damage resulting from modification or service other than by an authorized service center. Minimum order $10.00; some shipments subject to additional freight. Watch for fallen rock. An equal opportunity employer. No shoes, no shirt, no service.

The purpose of this warning is to advise service personnel that using anything but factory-specified components may affect the approval or safety of the unit. It is recommended that only direct replacement parts be used, and that extreme care be taken in servicing items in hazardous or potentially hazardous locations.

UL approval requires that only the specified battery for which the unit was designed is used. Use of any other battery may invalidate the UL listing. Substitution of components may impair intrinsic safety. Do not recharge mercury batteries and do not dispose of batteries in fire as an explosion may occur.

Furthermore, the purchase or use of this product or service shall not be deemed to grant either directly or by implication, estoppel, or otherwise, any license under the normal nonexclusive royalty free license to use that arises by operation of law in the sale of a product.

Caution: Federal law prohibits the transfer of this product to any person other than the patient for whom it was prescribed and the law further prohibits dispensing without a prescription. (Harmful if swallowed and minor allergic skin reaction may occur whether swallowed or administered to any portion of the body.) Take with food or milk.

Note: This warning label may self-destruct and/or the paper on which it is printed can burn if placed in an environment capable of combustion (i.e., where oxygen and an ignition source are available). If this document/label should ignite, place in a nonflammable container, remove to a safe area, preferably out-of-doors, and either extinguish using methods approved by fire safety codes in your area and the State Fire Marshall's Office or cover container with a fireproof material to eliminate oxygen supply to burning substance.

Offer limited to one coupon per specified product. Any other application constitutes fraud. Reproductions will not be honored.

If this document is burning, do not inhale fumes or permit smoke to get in your eyes nor should you touch the material at any time.

We offer no extensions or exceptions to the manufacturer's warranty policies. All defective products shipped by us will be handled in accordance with the manufacturer's stated warranty terms in the owner's manual of the defective product.

We reserve the right to correct any shipping error. Any customer receiving an incorrect product, which is not the product ordered, must contact us within five working days after receiving the incorrect product to obtain return authorization. The product must be returned within twenty-one days. After receipt, the product will be promptly inspected to ensure it is in "new condition." After inspection, we will promptly reship the product at our expense.

Products shipped but not accepted will be refunded less a restocking fee of 10 percent of the original purchase price but not less than ten (10) dollars. Second, shipping costs will also be deducted from the refund. We ship only *new* products; therefore, once a customer orders and accepts an order it cannot be returned for a refund or credit, as it is then considered *used* merchandise.

To avoid danger of suffocation, do not use in cribs, beds, carriages, or playpens. This warranty does not cover misuse, accident, lightning, flood, tornado, tsunami, volcano eruption, earthquake and other Acts of God, neglect, damage caused by improper installation, incorrect line voltage, improper or unauthorized repair, broken antenna or marred cabinet, missing or altered serial numbers, blasting by mine crews, jack-hammering, or sonic boom vibrations and customer adjustments that are not covered in the instruction book. Warranty valid only on products purchased and used in the United States. Warranty is *not* valid if incident occurs owing to an airplane crash, ship sinking or taking on water, motor vehicle crashing, or because of dropping item. This warranty does not cover fallen rock, leaky roof, broken glass, or mud slide, forest fire, or projectile (which can include, but not be limited to, arrows, bullets, shot, BB's, shrapnel, lasers, napalm, torpedoes or emissions of X-rays, Alpha, Beta 6- or Gamma rays, darts, knives, stones, etc.).

Liability for loss, delay, or damage to baggage is limited, unless a higher value is declared in advance and additional charges are paid. A coat, umbrella, pocketbook, camera, binoculars, infant food, and reading material for the trip are carried free and not included in the free baggage allowance. Baggage is subject to tariffs, including limitations of liability therein contained.

Passenger shall comply with government travel requirements, present exit and entry and other required documents, and arrive at airport by the time fixed by carrier or, if time is not fixed, early enough to complete departure procedures.

No agent, servant, or representative of carrier has authority to alter, modify, or waive any provision of this contract.

No merchandise will be accepted without a current return authorization number clearly shown on the outside of the package. Return authorizations are obtained through our Customer Relations Department.

"Lovely to look at, delightful to hold; but if you break it, consider it sold."

The user takes full responsibility for everything and anything that could and/or does go wrong resulting in any kind or type of problem, difficulty, embarrassment, loss of money or goods or services or sleep or anything else whatsoever. We are not responsible for lost articles.

The preceding was a paid political announcement.

(The preceding Universal Disclaimer [UD] was assembled by Joseph E. Badger of Santa Claus, Indiana in 1989, who proposed that it appear on all new products. He was kind enough to allow the Murphy Center, which assumes no responsibility for its use, to pioneer its use as a book disclaimer. A year later Badger wrote to say that he had neglected an important addition: Some of the contents may have settled during transit.)

The Murphy Center Newsletter—Vol. 1, No. 1

CENTER DENIED FOUNDATION GRANT WHICH IT DIDN'T ASK FOR IN THE FIRST PLACE: DIRECTOR HONORED

A letter from a top official of an important philanthropic foundation who was applying for a Center Fellowship ended his letter with the request that the Murphy Center *not* attempt to get a grant from his foundation. *"Our foundation,"* he explained, *"contributes only to frivolous programs, not serious ones like yours."*

The Director of the Center issued an immediate statement that said in part, "We think we are honored by this philanthropic first. As far as we can tell, we are the only research institute in the nation that not only does not have any foundation or government grants but has been peremptorily turned down for one. And for good reason."

Professor Puts Center Research to Good Use

A professor in the natural sciences, who shall remain nameless to protect his ruse, has found that the Center is a boon to his hobby of terrorizing graduate students. What this resourceful scientist does is to use oral examinations as a chance to ask hapless Ph.D. candidates to recite and explain one or two of the Center's laws, principles, or hypotheses. Invariably, the students conclude that the law in question is a key biological concept that they somehow missed during years of relentless study.

"Whatevers" Collection Growing

For reasons unclear, people have increasingly taken to sending the Center their pet "whatevers"—odds and ends that are hard to define save by example. Our file contains such gems as:

- A copy of the text that the late Rube Goldberg allegedly asked to have put on his tombstone: "Dear God, Enclosed please find Rube Goldberg. Now that you've got him, what are you going to do with him?"
- A sign found in a Japanese hotel room: "Please to bathe inside the tub."

- A yellowed clipping—undated, unsigned, unattributed—in which the writer suggests that there is deep satisfaction to be had from going out and intentionally violating conventional, proverbial wisdom. For instance, visiting a farm and putting all your eggs in one basket and then counting all your chickens before they're hatched.
- A small item from *The Wall Street Journal* reporting that Princeton University has installed a 3 x 5 card-file system to replace a computer that kept breaking down. (Two Fellows brought this to the attention of the Center.)
- More. Cartoons, religious tracts, "simple assembly instructions" that make no sense, chain letters, etc.

The Center is proud of this collection and thanks those who have helped start what may become one of the best whatever collections around.

New Research Suggested

From time to time, Fellows suggest new areas for Center investigation. Here is the best we have ever received:

I might also mention that I have a very large collection of instances where persons' names and either their occupations or preoccupations are in synchrony. This is an area of human lawfulness which has not been sufficiently or seriously organized. I knew that there was orderliness here when I noted that on the Brown University campus a Mrs. Record was in charge of alumni files, Mr. Banks was the Controller, and Mr. Price was in charge of purchasing. Looking a bit beyond my own campus, I found that Dr. Fish was indeed the head of the University of Rhode Island Oceanographic Institute, and he had hired one staff member named Saila and another named Seaman. I won't belabor the situation further, beyond mentioning simply that my own research area is that of sucking behavior in infants.

Sincerely Yours,
Lewis P. Lipsitt
Professor of Psychology and Medical Science
Director, Child Study Center

Center Takes Up Arms . . . Motto

Resourceful friends of the Center have been most helpful in giving it a stronger institutional identity. Robert N. Brodie of New York City has suggested a slogan: "Ain't it the truth!" and Marshall L. Smith of Washington, D.C., has researched and presented us with the "Arms of the Edsel Murphy Family with Family Motto." The slogan, arms, and motto have all been officially adopted by the Center. Here are the arms with Smith's explanation.

Arms: Gules three mismatched cogwheels, or two monkey wrenches salient, *or* three tack caltraps rampant.

Crest: An arm dressed, holding a broken pencil proper; spilt milk and India ink mantling.

Motto: Calamitas Necessaria Esɟ (Disaster Is Inevitable).

Note from Murphy Center's Director for Life

This is the definitive work in a series of books which strove to describe elements of the real world through laws, rules, principles and maxims. It will over time be further refined through additions and corrections.

Needless to say, the director is ever eager to collect new laws and hear from readers, either by e-mail or snail mail:

Director for Life, The Murphy Center
Box 280
Garrett Park, MD 20896–0280
e-mail: newdefiner@aol.com

Shortly after the [original] *Official Rules* was published in 1978, the author received a letter from a woman from Pagosa Springs, Colorado who said: "Once discovered, *The Official Rules* is like sex, indispensable."

Ever since then the Director has relished the task of going to the mailbox for the Center's mail.

One of the benefits that accrue to those who help the Murphy Center with its research is their appointment as a Fellow of the Murphy Center. The value of such a title should be reckoned by the fact that it can be given only by the director and cannot be bought (at least not cheaply) and cannot be taken away by anyone but the Director (who has yet to decommission a Fellow). There are now so many Fellows that it would be impossible to list all of them at the end of the book—as was the practice in earlier Center publications.

Senior Fellowships

In addition to the army of regular Fellows there is a select group of people who have contributed so much to the work of the Center over the last thirty-five years that they have achieved the rank of Senior Fellow. They cannot be thanked enough; but I will do it one more time:

They are: the late Theodore C. Achilles, Joseph E. Badger, Charles Boyle, Nancy Dickson, the late Russell Dunn Sr., Fred Dyer, M. Mack Earle, John Ehrman, Monika Fuchs, Tom Gill, Joseph C. Goulden, John Hagemann, Shel Kagan, Edward Logg, Martin Kottmeyer, Herbert H. Paper, the late Charles D. Poe, Frank S. Preston, Conrad Schneiker, Bob Skole, Marshall L. Smith, Robert D. Specht, Steve Stine, Gregg Townsend, the late Robert T. West, Neal Wilgus, Bennett Willis, Jr., Jack Womeldorf, Steve Woodbury, and Donald R. Woods.

Acknowledgments

Three Laws of Robotics, by Isaac Asimov: Used by permission of the author.

Berkeley's Laws, reprinted with permission from *The Notebook on Common Sense, Elementary and Advanced,* copyright © 1978 and published by Berkeley Enterprises, Inc., 815 Washington Street, Newtonville, Massachusetts 02160.

From "At Wit's End" by Erma Bombeck: Copyright © 1978 by Field Enterprises, Inc. Courtesy of Field Newspaper Syndicate.

From "Farmer's Law" by Richard N. Farmer: Copyright © 1973 by Richard N. Farmer. Reprinted with permission of Stein and Day Publishers.

Fiedler's Laws: Copyright © 1977 by Edgar R. Fiedler. First published in *Across the Board.*

Gilb's Laws: Reprinted with permission of DATAMATION® magazine, Copyright © by Technical Publishing Company, a Division of Dun-Donnelley Publishing Corporation, A Dun & Bradstreet Company, 1978—all rights reserved.

"Gerrold's Law" and "Short's Quotation": Copyright © 1978 by David Gerrold. Used by permission.

From "WrapAround": Copyright © 1974 by *Harper's Magazine.* All rights reserved. Excerpted from the August 1974 issue by special permission.

From *The Journal of Irreproducible Results:* Used by permission of the publisher.

Levy's Laws: Used by special permission of the copyright owner, Marion J. Levy, Jr.

From *Malice in Blunderland* by Thomas Martin: Used by permission of McGraw-Hill Book Company.

Excerpts from "Faber's Law: If There Isn't a Law, There Will Be" *(The New York Times Magazine,* March 17, 1968) and *The New York Times Magazine,* April 7, 1968: Copyright © 1968 by The New York Times Company. Reprinted by permission.

Parkinson's 1st, 2nd, and 3rd Laws; Law of Delay; Law of Medical Research; Principle of Non-Origination; Finding on Journals; and Mrs. Parkinson's Law, by C. Northcote Parkinson: From *Parkinson's Law* copyright © 1957 by C. Northcote

Parkinson. *The Law and the Profits* copyright © 1960 by C. Northcote Parkinson, *Mrs. Parkinson's Law* copyright © 1968 by C. Northcote Parkinson, *The Law of Delay* copyright © 1970 by C. Northcote Parkinson and *Inlaws and Outlaws* copyright © 1959, 1960, 1961, 1962 by Roturman, S. A. Used by permission of Houghton Mifflin Co.

The Peter Principle, Peter's Corollary, Peter's Paradox, Peter's Placebo, and five words from entry under "imcompetance": From *The Peter Principle* by Dr. Lawrence J. Peter, and Raymond Hull. Copyright © 1969 by William Morrow and Company, Inc. Used by permission of William Morrow & Company, Inc.

Peter's Law: from *Peter's Quotations* by Dr. Lawrence J. Peter. Copyright © by Lawrence J. Peter. Used by permission of William Morrow & Company, Inc.

Rumfeld's Rules: Reprinted with permission. Copyright © 1976 Donald H. Rumsfeld. All rights reserved.

Excerpts from "This Way to the Exit" by Dr. Ross K. Baker: Copyright © 1978 by The New York Times Company. Reprinted by permission.

Children's Birthday Parties and Adults at Parties from *My War With the 20th Century* by Pierre Berton: Copyright © 1965 by Pierre Berton. Reprinted by permission of Doubleday & Company, Inc., and Curtis Brown, Ltd.

Excerpt from "Getting In On A Zurich" by Dan Jenkins: reprinted courtesy of *Sports Illustrated,* September 4, 1978. Copyright © 1978 Time Inc.

Murphy's Marketing Maxims: Copyright © 1971 by Schoonmaker Associates, P.O. Drawer M, Goram, NY 11727.

Murray's Laws: Copyright © 1978, *Los Angeles Times.* Reprinted with permission.

Robert's Rules of Home and Garden: Reprinted with permission from the *Chicago Sun Times.* Excerpts from the column "Poor Robert's Almanac for Home Handymen and Gardeners" by Bob Herguth.

Rosenblatt's Rules: Copyright © 1979 *Washington Post.*

Boettcher's Attribution, Close's Law, Coccia's Law, and Ogden's Law: *Time,* "Letters" column, March 19, 1979, copyright © 1979 Time Inc. All rights reserved.

From *Instant Status or How to Become a Pillar of the Upper Middle Class* by Charles Merrill Smith: Copyright © 1972 by Charles Merrill Smith. Reprinted by permission of Doubleday & Company, Inc.

From *Drucker: The Man Who Invented the Corporate Society* by John J. Tarrant: Reprinted by permission of CBI Publishing Company, Inc., 51 Sleeper Street, Boston, MA 02210.

Index

The rules with the text are listed in alphabetical order. Index entries are thematic, with relevant rules listed within each.